Lecture Notes in Computer Sc

Edited by G. Goos and J. Hartmanis

Advisory Board: W. Brauer   D. Gries   J. Stoer

Witold Litwin   Tore Risch (Eds.)

Applications of Databases

First International Conference, ADB-94
Vadstena, Sweden, June 21-23, 1994
Proceedings

Springer-Verlag
Berlin Heidelberg New York
London Paris Tokyo
Hong Kong Barcelona
Budapest

Series Editors

Gerhard Goos
Universität Karlsruhe
Postfach 69 80
Vincenz-Priessnitz-Straße 1
D-76131 Karlsruhe, Germany

Juris Hartmanis
Cornell University
Department of Computer Science
4130 Upson Hall
Ithaca, NY 14853, USA

Volume Editors

Witold Litwin
University of Paris-Dauphine
Place de Marechal De Lattre de Tassigny, F-75016 Paris, France

Tore Risch
Department of Computer and Information Science, Linköping University
S-58183 Linköping, Sweden

CR Subject Classification (1991): H.4, H.2, H.3, I.2.4, J.1, J.2, J.6, J.7

ISBN 3-540-58183-9 Springer-Verlag Berlin Heidelberg New York
ISBN 0-387-58183-9 Springer-Verlag New York Berlin Heidelberg

CIP data applied for

© Springer-Verlag Berlin Heidelberg 1994
Printed in Germany

Typesetting: Camera-ready by author
SPIN: 10128062   45/3140-543210 - Printed on acid-free paper

Foreword

The first International Conference on Applications of Databases (ADB-94) was held on June 21-23, 1994, in Vadstena, Sweden. ADB-94 was organized in cooperation with and sponsored by major professional organizations. This new conference aimed at developing a synergy between database researchers, developers and application designers. It was intended as a forum to explore innovative applications of databases and innovative database services for specific applications. New applications are the driving force for the evolution of database technology. Applicability is the ultimate test for the numerous proposals debated at database technology conferences.

One hundred papers from 26 countries were submitted to ADB-94. Each paper was evaluated by at least three referees. The program committee selected twenty-eight papers for presentation at the conference. The committee also invited three distinguished speakers to present one keynote talk and two invited papers. The keynote talk, 'Database Applications in Telecom Systems' was given by Bernt Ericson, Director of Applied Research at Ericsson AB. The conference included three tutorials, selected out of ten submissions. Finally there were three panels debating selected database application domains.

These proceedings contain the material presented at the conference. The tutorials are listed by abstract. A variety of database applications are discussed: Air Traffic, Product Modelling, Trademark Registration, Maps, Environment, Finance, Medicine, Engineering, Electronic Publishing & Digital Libraries, Biology, and Chemistry. The discussion evaluates the numerous innovative database services these applications need: Application Modelling, Image Text & Multimedia Management, Fuzzy Set Based Querying, Knowledge Management, Active Database Management, Heterogeneous Multidatabase Management, Object Brokers, Portable DBMSs, and Intelligent Networks. The material shows the large potential for applications of database technology. We hope that this outcome from ADB-94 will stimulate further research and development in this field.

ADB-94 could not have been organized without the help of many people and organizations. Our thanks go to the members of the International Program Committee and the Regional, Panel and Tutorial Chairmen. We also thank the external referees and the members of the Organizing Committee. Finally, we would like to thank the cooperating professional organizations and our industrial sponsors for their financial support.

Linköping, April 26th, 1994

Witold Litwin	Program Committee Chair
Tore Risch	General Chair
Anders Törne	Organizing Committee Chair

Sponsorship

Sponsored by:

The Swedish Board for Technical Development (NUTEK), Hewlett-Packard,
CelsiusTech AB, GMD, Softlab AB, Ellemtel AB.

In Cooperation with:

ACM, AFCET, AICA, ERCIM, GI, IFIP TC-2, INRIA, ODMG,
VLDB Endowment Inc., Dataföreningen i Sverige

Swedish National Board for Industrial and
Technical Development

Organization

General Chair

Tore Risch, Linköping University, Sweden

Organizing Committee

Chair: Anders Törne, Linköping University, Sweden

Ingrid Nyman, Linköping University, Sweden

Anne Eskilsson, Linköping University, Sweden

ERCIM Liaison: Keith Jeffrey, RAL, Great Britain

Program Committee

Program Chair

Witold Litwin, University of Paris 9, visiting HPLabs & University of Berkeley

Tutorial Program

Umesh Dayal, Hewlett-Packard Laboratories, USA

Panel Program

Ming-Chien Shan, Hewlett-Packard Laboratories, USA

American V-Chair

Dan Fishman, Hewlett-Packard Laboratories, USA

European V-Chair

Erich Neuhold, GMD-IPSI, Germany

Far East V-Chair

Ron Sacks-Davis, RMIT, Australia

Contents

Invited Papers

Tutorials (Abstracts)

Database Application Modelling

Image Database Applications

Database Applications in Geography & Environment

Financial, Medical, and Engineering Database Applications

Text Retrieval Database Applications

Database Applications in Biology and Chemistry

Legacy Databases

New Database Services

Developing the Singapore National Information Infrastructure

Michael Yap

National Computer Board, Singapore

(Extended Abstract)

Singapore has embarked on an extensive effort to examine how IT can be effectively exploited to create national competitive advantages and enhance the quality of life. The goal of the IT2000 Project is to transform Singapore into the Intelligent Island where an advanced information infrastructure interconnects every home, office, school and factory.

The vision of an Intelligent Island presupposes the unobstructed flow of information across and within all sectors in Singapore. It assumes a nation-wide infrastructure that promote, capture, integrate and exploit information and service flows. We call this information superhighway the National Information Infrastructure (NII).

The role of the NII in the Intelligent Island is akin to what the highway system is to a good road system. A good road system is better realized if a nation-wide highway system exists. NII is deemed as the super infrastructure needed to realize SingaporeUs vision as the first Intelligent Island.

The building of the NII is not just about constructing an efficient digital distribution system, although it would be the prerequisite. The goal of the NII is to provide a more efficient and effective alternative to doing business and conducting our daily life. To achieve the goal, the NII must strive to bring about as many of commonly available Rreal worldS services or their equivalent into cyber world. For example, the NII need to provide the necessary business infrastructures such as charging and payment by having electronic fund transfer and digital signatures in place. Support for day-to-day operations can be realized with the general availability of services including electronic mail, video conferencing and word processor. The need to have in-house computer systems to support standard business practices can be met with the provision of customizable software components such as electronic ledger, personnel system and procurement applications.

To realize its goals, the NII must provide for a software environment that can help transform application development from "cottage industry" into "production line" efficiency. To achieve this, the NII must focus on making transparent hardware and software differences, provide for a rich set of common computing services and, support the reuse of large components, over and above providing a physical information highway. In addition, the NII must actively support the migration and integration of 3rd party software and existing systems that are currently available.

The talk will briefly discussed the IT2000 project and then zoom into the details of the NII. We will discuss the architecture and progress to date. A closer look at one of its components, the Database and Transaction Services, leads to the discussion on how support for database interoperability and legacy access in the context of a national infrastructure can be realised.

An Architecture for a Cooperative Database System

Parke Godfrey[2], Jack Minker[1,2], Lev Novik[2]

[1] University of Maryland Institute for Advanced Computer Studies
[2] Dept. of Computer Science, Univ. of Maryland, College Park, MD 20742, U.S.A.

Abstract. Database systems can be difficult to use. Part of the problem is that systems do not, for the most part, help a user when a query *fails* or fails to evaluate as the user expects. Schema and semantics of databases are often complex, and are rarely understood in entirety by the lay user. As a consequence, queries a lay user casts may not make sense with respect to a database's semantics. A system which returns informative responses beyond a query's answer set itself can elucidate the schema and semantics of the database, which can greatly help the user to cast the queries intended. Such a database system is to be called a *cooperative database system* (CDBS).

A number of cooperative behaviors and methods have been introduced to be incorporated into information systems to make them more informative and, hence, easier to use. We have identified a fundamental set of such cooperative techniques that we believe relational and deductive systems should be extended to include. We present an architecture for such a CDBS which supports these, and which uses existing relational technologies. We have built the Carmin system based on the proposed architecture. Carmin is intended both as a research platform for cooperative answering and as a practical, efficient CDBS.

The paper presents the architecture of Carmin, and, by example, a general architectural approach for CDBSs. The architectural components of Carmin are outlined and discussed in turn. The implementation issues and cost overhead of Carmin are discussed, and the architectural choices are argued.

1 Introduction

The general paradigm of database systems for query answering is as follows:

1. a database system accepts a query written in a formal query language (SQL and Datalog are two such languages);
2. evaluates the query against a database (in the relational case, a collection of relational tables); and
3. returns the complete set of tuples *satisfying* the query, the *answer set*.

---

* This work was supported by the Air Force Office of Scientific Research under grant AFOSR-91-0350 and by the National Science Foundation under grant IRI-9300691.

Most everything else a database system does goes towards supporting this simple paradigm.[1] Systems do some further things that can be viewed as cooperative features, that are *user friendly* and make the system easier to use. For instance, they identify when a query is not legal, when it does not parse with respect to the query language. They identify when a relation name non-existent in a database is used in a query. However, these are simple syntactic checks that must be done before the system can evaluate the query. Database systems do little else to help users trouble-shoot queries or to interpret better the results.

Research has been done in how this simple paradigm could be extended to make database systems easier to use by making them more informative. (Another approach is to adopt a different paradigm, but that is not a topic explored here.) Much of this research comes from a field that can be called *cooperative answering*. The basic query/answer paradigm is augmented to allow the system to return *meta-answers*, or *responses* besides just the answer set itself, in response to a query. These responses might be corrections to a *semantically impaired* query, a rewriting of the query into a simpler form, a useful characterization of the query or answer set, and so forth. The paradigm may also be augmented so the system assists in formulating queries and offers the user possible subsequent queries to cast. We will call such a system a *cooperative database system* (CDBS).

We are engaged in a project to build such a cooperative database system. We call our system Carmin. There are two primary goals of the Carmin project and system. The first is to create a research platform to be used to test cooperative answering techniques, and to explore how these cooperative behaviors can be implemented efficiently in a database environment. The second is to create a realistic CDBS that can be used to evaluate its effectiveness and to generate feedback to design better systems.

There are a number issues involved in the design of the Carmin system, and in the design of any CDBS. These include deciding which cooperative behaviors ought to be supported. We have selected a set of what we believe to be fundamental cooperative behaviors for Carmin to support. They are introduced and discussed in the following sections. Just as important is how these behaviors and the system are to be organized, Carmin's architecture. This is the topic of this paper. By illustrating Carmin's architecture, a pragmatic approach to building a CDBS is presented which reuses existing relational database management systems (RDBMSs) and their technologies.

In Sec. 2, background is given on work on cooperative answering, the cooperative answering work at Maryland, and other cooperative database systems. Section 3 introduces the architecture of the Carmin system. Section 4 discusses the costs of Carmin stage by stage, and argues why the proposed architecture is appropriate. Section 5 concludes with the current status of the system and future work planned. An appendix shows some initial timing results for Carmin's performance.

---

[1] In fact, database systems do much more. They support transactions, concurrency, and many other vital utilities. However, our focus is the query/answer aspect of database systems.

2 Background

2.1 Cooperative Answering

Central to a CDBS is what information it can provide about a query above and beyond the answer set itself. Many researchers have been interested in this question (for information systems at large), and many different *cooperative answering techniques* have been suggested and explored. In this background section, several such techniques are presented. See the survey [15] (or [17] in which it reappears) for a comprehensive overview of cooperative answering work.

One question people have considered is what to do when a query *fails*. A query is said to *fail* when its evaluation produces the empty answer set. An empty answer set is uninformative to the user. It is presumed that the user expects there to be answers to the query asked.[2] So when a query fails, it often surprises the user. A system could be cooperative by helping to trace the *reason* for the query's failure, or at least help to pinpoint the failure.

The type of queries considered in this paper are conjunctive query formulas.[3] Let Q be such a query.

$$Q \equiv A_1 \wedge \ldots \wedge A_k$$

Each of the A_i's are literals. Call Q' a *subquery* of Q iff

$$Q' \equiv A_{s_1} \wedge \ldots \wedge A_{s_j}, \text{ and } \{s_1, \ldots, s_j\} \subset \{1, \ldots, k\}$$

If a subquery fails, then the query itself must fail. Therefore, it is a stronger statement to report the failure of the subquery than to report the failure of the query itself. Such a failing subquery is called a *false presupposition* to the query. The best possible response is to report a *minimal* failing subquery (MFS).[4]

Consider that the following query fails:

$$\leftarrow \textbf{ward}\,(P,\ maternity),\ \textbf{has\_infection}\,(P,\ I), \qquad (1)$$
$$\textbf{contagious}\,(I),\ \textbf{staff}\,(I).$$

This query asks if there are any patients on the maternity ward with a contagious staff infection. The answer is no, but the answer that the subquery

$$\leftarrow \textbf{has\_infection}\,(P,\ I),\ \textbf{staff}\,(I).$$

fails is much more informative. Coupled with the knowledge that this is a minimal failing subquery, it is even more informative; for instance, it states implicitly that there are patients with infections.

---

[2] Otherwise, why ask it? Of course, there are cases when a user is attempting to ascertain that a given query fails, but this is not the majority case.

[3] This is without loss of generality.

[4] A failing subquery is *minimal iff* no subquery of it fails.

Let **DB** ≡ **RB** ∪ State, where **RB**, the *rulebase*, represents the rules (views) and integrity constraints (ICs) associated with the database (written in Datalog), and State is the current state of the database, the extensions of the base predicates (or, in other words, the instantiation of the base relations). Let **q** be the variables in the query formula $\mathcal{Q}$. (This is the tuple template for the answer set.) A query fails when

$$\textbf{DB} \not\vdash \exists\textbf{q}.\mathcal{Q} \qquad (2)$$

When a query has a false presupposition, there may be no *reason* for the query to fail. The current state of the database simply has no data that satisfies the query. Future states of the database may. However, sometimes when a query fails, it must always fail for all possible states of the database. If it did not, it would contradict the semantics of the database. In such cases, it is said that the query contains a *misconception*. When a query has a misconception, there is a *reason* for the query to fail. This reason can be returned to the user in the form of an explanation. The explanation is based on a *proof* that the query fails over the rules and integrity constraints of the database (the rulebase). In other words, a query contains a *pure misconception iff*

$$\textbf{RB} \vdash \not\exists\textbf{q}.\mathcal{Q} \qquad (3)$$

This is strictly stronger in a logical sense than *false presuppositions*, and is epistemologically worth more, because misconceptions have explanations and they are guaranteed to hold until the *schema* of the database changes. A false presupposition is guaranteed to hold only until the *state* of the database changes.

For instance, consider the query[5]

$$\leftarrow \textbf{ship\_type}\,(shipid:\ ID_1,\ ship:\ SH_1,\ type:\ T_1,\ surface:\ subsurface), \qquad (4)$$
$$\textbf{ship\_type}\,(shipid:\ ID_2,\ ship:\ SH_2,\ type:\ T_2,\ surface:\ surface),$$
$$\textbf{radar}\,(type:\ T_1,\ radar:\ 'SPS\text{-}37'),\ \textbf{radar}\,(type:\ T_2,\ radar:\ 'SPS\text{-}37').$$

It asks to find pairs of ships, one surface and one subsurface, both equipped with SPS-37 radar. In the Navy database for which this query is intended, it must fail. There are no radar which are both for surface and subsurface ships.

A logical proof of this can be used to generate an explanation, as the following demonstrates. Using the definition of *ship_type* :

ship_type *(ship: SH, shipid: ID, type: T, surface: subsurface)* ←
     ship *(num: ID, name: SH, type: T)*, **type** *(type: T, ss: subsurface)*.

The query is unfolded into:

$$\leftarrow \textbf{ship}\,(num:\ ID_1,\ name:\ SH_1,\ type:\ T_1),\ \textbf{type}\,(type:\ T_1,\ ss:\ subsurface),$$

---

[5] This is query $\mathcal{Q}_5$ from the test suite used to evaluate Carmin as shown in the appendix. The explanation is lifted from that Carmin generated for the query.

ship_type *(ship: SH_2, shipid: ID_2, type: T_2, surface: surface)*,
radar *(type: T_1, radar: 'SPS-37')*, **radar** *(type: T_2, radar: 'SPS-37')*.

Using the definition of *ship_type* a second time, the query is further unfolded into:

    ← **ship** *(num: ID_1, ship: SH_1, type: T_1)*, **type** *(type: T_1, ss: subsurface)*,
      ship *(num: ID_2, ship: SH_2, type: T_2)*, **type** *(type: T_2, ss: surface)*,
      radar *(type: T_1, radar: 'SPS-37')*, **radar** *(type: T_2, radar: 'SPS-37')*.

This unfolding must fail, for if it were to have an answer, a contradiction would result. From the rule

    subsurface_radar *(radar: R)* ←
      radar *(type: T, radar: R)*, **type** *(type: T, ss: subsurface)*.

subsurface_radar *('SPS-37')* would hold. From the rule

    surface_radar *(radar: R)* ←
      radar *(type: T, radar: R)*, **type** *(type: T, ss: surface)*.

surface_radar *('SPS-37')* would hold. Then the integrity constraint

    false ← **subsurface_radar** *(radar: R)*, **surface_radar** *(radar: R)*.

would be violated.

2.2 Cooperative Answering at Maryland

Research in cooperative answering at the University of Maryland, College Park has a long tradition. More recently, work has commenced in CDBSs. Our interest in cooperative answering arose from work in *semantic query opitimization* (SQO). SQO endeavors to rewrite a query into a semantically equivalent query which is easier to evaluate. RDBMSs perform query optimizations already, but these operations are syntactic; they do not exploit the semantic information of the database.[6] Chakravarthy, Grant, and Minker [1, 2, 3, 4] introduced techniques to analyze and rewrite queries based on the available ICs to achieve optimizations.

The work in SQO offered tools that could be used for computing various kinds of cooperative information, primarily misconceptions.[7] Gal and Minker [21, 22, 23] showed how queries could be evaluated for misconceptions, and how these misconceptions could be presented to the user. They constructed a prototype system, the *Cooperative Answering System at Maryland*, to demonstrate this. The system is based on the SQO analysis techniques mentioned above.

---

[6] This semantic information comes primarily in the form of integrity constraints.
[7] Finding a misconception in a query is the ultimate optimization; in such a case, the query does not have to be evaluated at all.

As work proceeded with cooperative answering, new cooperative techniques were found that should be supported. In [16], Gaasterland, Godfrey, and Minker present a mechanism to *relax* a given query into a set of more general, "related" queries. Evaluating one of these queries results in new answers with respect to the original query, and may be of interest to the user. In [14, 19, 20], Gaasterland, Minker, and Rajasekar introduced the notion of *user constraints* as a means to tailor the answer set with respect to the original query to include only information in which the given user is interested. Gaasterland, Godfrey, and Minker in the survey [15] review a number of other cooperative answering techniques that warrant consideration.

With the Carmin–I prototype, Gaasterland, Godfrey, Minker, and Novik aimed to combine a number of fundamental cooperative techniques uniformly into one cooperative system [16, 18]. Carmin–I is written in QUINTUS Prolog and exists entirely in the Prolog session. The system was meant as a testbed for cooperative techniques, to explore how they could be combined effectively and how they could be implemented.

Work on the Carmin–II prototype commenced in spring of 1993, and represents a departure from the previous prototype in two ways.[8] First, the system needed to be coupled with a real database system to be realistic. Considering the query evaluation (via the RDBMS) as a distinct stage has major ramifications for the organization of the system. (Carmin–I does not have to make a distinction between the query analysis and evaluation.) While Carmin–I is, at most, a cooperative answering system, Carmin–II is a cooperative database system.

Carmin–II differs in a second way also. It was originally assumed that each cooperative behavior could be implemented somewhat independently of the others. Furthermore, each would be realised as a *meta-interpreter* in the Prolog shell. In retrospect, this reasoning is flawed. Many of the cooperative answering techniques require the same type of analysis of the query. Implementing them independently incurs redundant work. Worse yet, a number of the techniques are computationally complex, and are not amenable to the meta-interpreter approach. The issue of efficiency has become a most important one, and has necessitated that particular mechanisms and algorithms be implemented to provide these behaviors efficiently.

2.3   Other Systems and Work

There are other systems designed with the specific intent to provide certain cooperative behaviors to database systems. One of the first was CO-OP (A Cooperative Query System) by Kaplan [29, 30]. The system combined a natural language query front-end over the CODASYL database management system SEED. The system was tested over a real database from the National Center for Atmospheric Research on both users and programmers.

Motro [33, 34, 35] has considered modifications to the relational model that are easily incorporated into a relational database system to allow for certain

---

[8] References to the Carmin system in this paper refer to Carmin–II.

cooperative behaviors. In [35] he introduces a system (a user interface) FLEX for relational database systems that can correct queries which have apparent mistakes, and yield to the user *corrected* queries with which to proceed. Motro introduces the notion of returning to a user related queries that may more closely match the user's intended question. FLEX also incorporates false presupposition analysis for queries which have empty answer sets.

Motro's earlier system SEAVE [34] is designed to find false presuppositions in queries. He extends the notion of false presupposition to that of weakening the query. So instead of throwing literals away to obtain subqueries, they are replaced with weaker literals.[9] This unifies a notion of query generalization with false presupposition search.

A major CDBS project has been underway at UCLA and has produced the CoBase system [5, 9]. Chu et al.'s CoBase is complementary in many ways to the Carmin system. It covers a different set of cooperative techniques.[10] The focus of CoBase is to find *related* answers to users' queries. The system consists of three parts: 1) approximate and conceptual query answering [8]; 2) associative query answering [6, 7]; and 3) explanation systems.

CoBase is written in LISP and interfaces with Oracle. A simpler version of CoBase is written in SmallTalk and interfaces with the object-oriented database system Gemstone. The CoBase system is currently being rewritten in C++.

The system is being used in the transportation initiative (ARPA) by ISI and ISX. It is being used also by the Hughes Research Laboratory. CoBase is being tested over a knowledge-based medical image system called KMeD (in Gemstone), a medical project at UCLA.

There are many other systems relating to cooperative answering work (again, see [15]), and many more for natural language dialog systems. Only those that are explicit extensions of database system technology, CDBSs, have been discussed in this section.

3 Architecture of Carmin

3.1 The Carmin Shell

To the user, Carmin appears to be a deductive database system. One commences a Carmin session, specifies the database to used, and proceeds to ask queries in Datalog. Carmin is a CDBS in that it returns more information to the user than just the query's answer set.

To a database administrator, Carmin is a front-end user interface for IN-GRES. The databases belong to, and are maintained via, the RDBMS. The administrator need not be concerned with Carmin.

Carmin is, in fact, a simple deductive database system. It is a *shell*, a program, which acts as a front-end and back-end to an RDBMS. (See Fig. 1.) It can

---

[9] For example, $S > 30$ can be replaced by $S > 29$, since $(S > 30) \Rightarrow (S > 29)$.

[10] For instance, CoBase does not analyze the query for misconceptions, and does not find MFSs, as do Carmin and FLEX.

be used either by an applications program or by a user for an interactive query session. Input are queries in Datalog. Carmin analyses the query, and then may translate it into SQL and ship it to the RDBMS for evaluation. Carmin intercepts the answer set the RDBMS returns and may analyze the query further, depending on the results. The answer set, along with other possible information, is presented to the user.

The current Carmin system interfaces with INGRES-89, a public domain version of the INGRES database system.[11] Queries are translated into QUEL, INGRES's query language, a near variant of SQL. However, the system would be easily adapted to operate with other RDBMSs.

The Carmin shell is written in QUINTUS Prolog. It communicates through a C code interface to INGRES. The shell is not inherently tied to Prolog. A different implementation language could have been chosen. Prolog was chosen for convenience (our previous prototypes are Prolog based), and for its flexibility— Carmin is meant as a research platform.

There are a number of advantages to using an existing RDBMS. The system inherits the RDBMS's performance and optimizations. It is not necessary to reinvent database management—indexing, relational operators and query evaluation, syntactic query optimizations, and concurrency to name a few. Perhaps more importantly, Carmin can be used with existing databases and RDBMSs.

The Carmin system requires a *rulebase* to perform with a given database. The rulebase is to the database as knowledge is to data. It is the explicit representation of the database's schema, views, and integrity constraints (ICs). For Carmin, rulebases are kept in Datalog form. A rulebase is easily distilled from an INGRES database, and can be automatically extracted. Of course this needs to be redone whenever the database's schema changes.

A database administrator may define additional rules and ICs directly in the rulebase. This may be beneficial, especially if there are ICs that hold in the database, but are not explicitly stated there. They need to be explicitly represented in the rulebase if Carmin is to use them.

As Datalog is more expressive than SQL, there are rules that can be added to the rulebase which are not expressible in SQL, or are not supported in the view facility of the RDBMS. For instance, Datalog allows recursive rules.[12] Also, RDBMSs do not allow the full SQL to be used in defining views. INGRES does not allow **union** (called append in QUEL). So a view may only be a single **select** (called retrieve in QUEL) statement. This is equivalent to a rule predicate in Datalog which has only a single clause in its definition. However, rule predicates with *multiple* clauses may be defined in the rulebase.

The rulebase may be used to store other semantic information as well. This may include knowledge that characterizes users, or classes of users. In [14, 19, 20], *user constraints* are introduced and developed. User constraints have the form of ICs (and, hence, are representable in Datalog in the rulebase), but have a different semantic value. They are used to *shield* answers to a query for which it

---

[11] It is also called University INGRES.

[12] The current Carmin system does not handle recursion, but may in future versions.

is known that the user has no interest. Such techniques and knowledge can be used to tailor the system's response and behavior to given users.[13]

It is expected that a rulebase will be small, with respect to the size of the database itself. Carmin loads into memory the corresponding rulebase whenever a database is requested. The rules and ICs of the rulebase are used to analyze the query and to translate it into SQL. This all takes place in main memory.

3.2 The Components of Carmin

Carmin's architecture, represented in Fig. 1, consists of five distinct components, and a sixth component outside of Carmin proper, the RDBMS itself. The components are 1) the pre-analyzer, 2) the SQL translator, 3) the RDBMS, 4) the post-analyzer, 5) the explanation and answer facility, and 6) the query formation facility. The components are somewhat independent of one another in their functionality, and can be discussed separately.

Input/output and flow of control are represented by the solid arrows in Fig. 1. A Datalog query first goes to the *pre-analyzer*. This checks the query for semantic and syntactic *well-formedness*. It checks for misconceptions and "short-circuits" the query if it determines that the query's answer set must be empty. Otherwise, it proceeds to the *SQL translator* which formulates an SQL query (or sequence of queries) to send to the RDBMS. The answer set is returned and the *post-analyzer* is invoked, if needed. The results of both analyzers and the answer set are shipped to the *explanation and answer facility*. This presents the answer set and/or any additional information and explanations to the user.

After the query has been processed and answered, the *query formation facility* may be invoked. It takes as input the previous query and the results of the analyses and processing. It finds "related" queries based on this information. These queries are returned to the user as possible queries to ask. The user may choose one of the selections, or to write a new query.[14]

The dashed arrows in Fig. 1 represent the flow of information. All the modules use the rulebase for the given database. Datastructures and information are also passed among the modules. The analysis of the query performed by the *pre-analyzer* is the most important of these.

The cooperative behaviors Carmin supports are divided primarily between the analyzers. Those needing only the rulebase are in the *pre-analyzer*. Those that may need subsequent information from the database or that rely on results of the query processing must go into the *post-analyzer*. The *post-analyzer* may need to query the database itself to obtain more information about the query.[15]

The components on the left-hand side of Fig. 1, the analyzers and the translator, are primarily algorithmic in nature. Each cooperative behavior to be supported needs to be given a clear, declarative meaning. Guarantees can then be

---

[13] The current system does not handle user constraints, but may in future versions.

[14] This facility is turned off when Carmin is used by an applications program.

[15] This is transparent to the user, except for the time it requires.

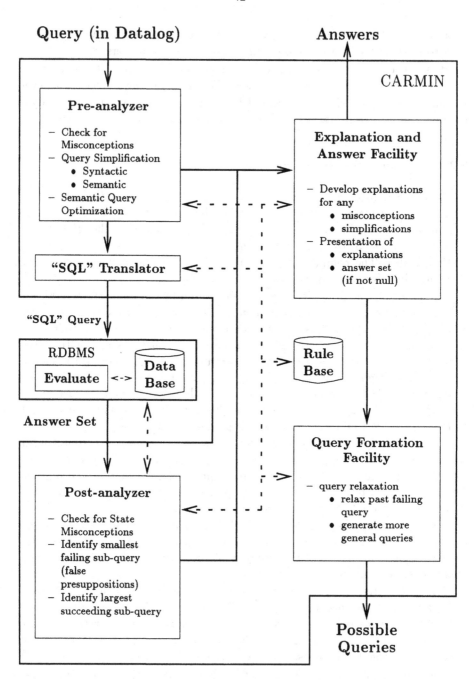

Fig. 1. Architechture of Carmin

made about the correctness of the cooperative answers found, and certain general guarantees about *which* meta-answers can be found (completeness). Work on these draws from logic programming and algorithms.

The components on the right-hand side, the explanation and query formation facilities, are heuristic in nature. They must incorporate judgement and prune away extraneous possibilities. Explanations can be too complex, so choices as to what to present must be made. In [21, 22, 23], Gal and Minker address some of these issues and present heuristics for making such choices. Gaasterland and Minker [14, 19] consider how to organize responses and explanations to be better understood. The query formation facility employs techniques to rewrite queries into related queries in which the user may be interested. (See [16].) Again, the number of choices must be limited so as not to overwhelm the user, and the possibilities ought to be evaluated for relevance *before* being offered. These components rely on artificial intelligence and natural language research and practice. (Cooperation based on user models also fall into this category.)

The Pre-analyzer. The primary task of the pre-analyzer is to check a query for misconceptions. An example of this was presented in Sec. 2. If a misconception is found, the result *plus* the analysis is sent to the explanation facility to generate an explanation for the user. It should be guaranteed that any misconception found is a *best*, or *strongest*, meta-answer. There are three criteria for ranking misconceptions. The first (and of highest priority) is the same criterion set for false presuppositions. If a subquery Q' of Q has a misconception, reporting that Q' must fail is more informative than just reporting that Q must fail. A *minimal* such subquery that must fail should be identified.

The next two criteria involve minimizing the complexity of the misconception (and, hence, the ensuing explanation). A misconception is called *simple* if the proof of failure can be derived from just the literals of the query. However, if some of the literals are views, it may be necessary to expand their definitions (to *unfold* some of the rules) before failure can be proven.[16] Query (4) exhibits this. When such unfolding is required, the misconception is called *complex*. It is necessary to account for *all* unfoldings. Carmin will produce *most general* explanations, which means that none of the unfolded queries could be refolded and still constitute a valid explanation.

The third criterion is to pick the simplest proof, measured by the length of the proof. To keep an explanation understandable, simpler proofs are preferred.

The analysis for misconceptions is the basis for other cooperative techniques as well. Carmin attempts to *simplify* a query whenever possible. A query is called *redundant* if some subquery is semantically equivalent; that is, it must return the same answer set. Redundant queries are detected and reported. (Redundancy can be considered to indicate a misconception on the user's behalf.) Syntactic analysis can be done on the query too in an attempt to reduce it, but it is necessary to limit the effort spent. (See [37], chapter 14, for a discussion of such techniques.) Carmin incorporates such analysis.

---

[16] A *closed world assumption* [36] is assumed over the rules.

The pre-analyzer can host other cooperative tasks. So far, the techniques discussed preserve the meaning of the query. However, there are reasons why the query might be rewritten in a semantically non-preserving manner to better accommodate a user's needs. Cuppens and Demolombe [11, 12] show how a query can be rewritten to return more information than the user originally requested. For instance, the system should always report price whenever anyone inquires about airline tickets. Gaasterland and Minker [14, 19] also consider how to rewrite the query to avoid answers in which it is known the user has no interest.

Some of the byproducts of the pre-analysis are useful for the purposes of semantic query optimization. Redundancy reduction over a query usually results in a query that is more easily evaluated. When the analyzer checks for misconceptions, it deduces generic facts that follow from the query. Many of these facts are selects (many of which are non-obvious because they do not derive directly from the query, but rather from the rules and ICs) which do not change the meaning of the query, but can be added to the query to gain potential optimization. Since the analysis explores unfoldings of the query, it sometimes eliminates entire branches of the query, yielding simpler queries for evaluation. In addition, more SQO methods could be incorporated into the pre-analyzer stage.

The SQL Translator and the RDBMS. We built Carmin around a RDBMS because this is the standard technology and is widely available and used. Thus, Carmin must convert its queries into SQL at some stage to send them to the RDBMS for evaluation. This translator raises a number of technical issues and research issues for deductive databases in its own right. Carmin's translator is superior to most direct, naïve approaches. It chooses to materialize intermediate stages of the query rather than simply to unfold the query in all ways. This almost always results in a simpler SQL to evaluate.

The SQL that Carmin generates for a query is in general comparable to what an SQL programmer would write given the query specification. The translator will sometimes do better because of SQO, unless the programmer is very familiar with the semantics of that database.

There is much room for improvement of the translator. It currently has no access to table sizes and other statistical information which an RDBMS keeps for its own optimization purposes. With such information, the translator could make more intelligent materialization decisions. However, this line of research is not central to the Carmin project, though relevant.

Post-analyzer. After the query is evaluated, there may still be a need for cooperative analysis. As seen with query 1 in Sec. 2, if a query fails, it is useful to identify a *minimum failing subquery*. There has been much research on this topic [10, 27, 29, 30, 31, 34, 35]. However, the complexity of finding a MFS has remained in question. The implicit assumption has been that it may cost exponential time in worst case even to find one MFS. We now know that, in fact, to find a MFS for a query costs at most N subsequent queries to the database, where N is the number of conjuncts in the query [26].[17]

Even after a query is evaluated, it is possible to be more informative than with false presuppositions. The query may still harbor misconceptions and must fail with respect to the current *state* of the database. A query is said to have a *state misconception* iff

$$\mathbf{DB} \vdash \not\exists q.\mathcal{Q}$$

Compare this to the semantics of pure misconceptions (3). It is strictly weaker. However, it is strictly stronger than false presuppositions (2). State misconceptions also have explanations and should be selected by the same criteria outlined above for (pure) misconceptions. Similar to the search for MFSs, to find state misconceptions requires subsequent queries to the database.

The post-analyser is intrinsically expensive because it requires those subsequent queries. Its results can sometimes be very useful, justifying this expense, but it is at the user's discretion whether to engage the post-analyser.

Explanation and Answer Facility. This facility takes as input the analyses of the query, the answer set from the query evaluation (if done), and any meta-answers generated along the way, and coordinates a response to the query for the user. As more cooperative behaviors are added to the system, it is necessary to upgrade the explanation facility to coordinate the different types of meta-answers into a cohesive response. Furthermore, there must be a strategy to present each type of meta-answer in a comprehensible fashion; otherwise the information is useless. In [14], Gaasterland considers some of the pertinent issues involved to coordinate such information in a response.

The Query Formation Facility. This facility can be engaged to help a user formulate subsequent queries. Information from the analyses of a query can be used to *relax* it into more general, related queries, as discussed above.

If the query fails, the post-analyser can be employed to identify MFSs. It is also worthwhile to identify the subqueries that *succeed*. The subqueries of interest are the *maximal succeeding subqueries* (MSSs). To know the MFSs of a query does not, unfortunately, tell one what the MSSs to the query are, contrary to one's initial impressions. Fortunately, a variation of the algorithm used for MFSs can be used to find MSSs. It too requires N subsequent queries to the database to find a MSS of the original query, where N again is the number of conjuncts in the query [26]. A MSS is returned to the user as a query which does lead to answers, in which the user may have an interest. Furthermore, identification of the MSS in itself is cooperative, as it informs the user of what information *is* in the database. For example, consider the failing query (1) seen in Sec. 2 again. The query

---

[17] To find a number of subsequent MFSs to a query can be expensive. It is shown that to find $\mathcal{O}(N)$ MFSs to a query of size N is **NP-*complete*** [26].

$\leftarrow$ **ward** $(P, \; maternity)$, **has_infection** $(P, \; I)$, **contagious** (I).

might be returned as a MSS. There are no patients on the maternity ward with contagious *staff* infections, however there *are* patients on the maternity ward with contagious infections.

4 Costs And Justification

4.1 Justification

A tool such as Carmin must be cost-effective and useful for users. Two aspects need justifying: 1) the notion cooperative answering itself; 2) and the Carmin architecture.

While many of the cooperative answering techniques proposed put forth appear very beneficial in theory, for most it remains to be seen whether they are beneficial in practice. To justify cooperative answering, two questions must be answered:

1. Are certain cooperative answering techniques useful within common database environments and applications?
2. Can those cooperative answering techniques be implemented cost-effectively?

Justifying Cooperative Answering. A CDBS must assure that the answer to the second question is yes. The Carmin project *is* an endeavor to see if certain fundamental cooperative answering techniques can be offered cost-effectively. Of course, the performance of a CDBS depends on the cooperative answering techniques the designers have chosen to support, and on the algorithms used to support them. The first question remains unanswered, and is justification in itself for why CDBSs are needed. They are needed so people may use them and evaluate the usefulness of cooperative answering in database environments in practice.

Justifying Carmin's Architecture. The design choices of Carmin must be defended too. Perhaps another architecture would be more cost-effective, or provide more useful functionality. The key design choice of Carmin most open to question is the choice to have a *pre-analysis* stage. Many have argued that cooperative behaviors should go in a *post-analysis* stage, after the query is processed. (For instance, see [34].)

This stems from the belief that the logical analysis of the query requires general theorem proving and would most always be too expensive. (It need not, so the cost remains in question.) Research in the Carmin project aims to dispell this belief. (For more, see the next section.) The cost of such analysis must be contained, and the analysis even curtailed in worst cases. Furthermore, it should be that the average case (almost all cases) has small, manageable cost. The Carmin system has demonstrated that the time of the pre-analysis of the query is, in practice, a magnitude smaller than the time of evaluating the query. Given this, the pre-analysis adds little overhead. (See the appendix for some initial results which support this.)

Next, the question can be raised, why pre-analyze *every* query? Consider the check for misconceptions. If, say, only ten percent of queries fail, the pre-analysis is wasted effort for the other ninety percent of queries. There are good arguments against this criticism. As database schema and semantics continue to become more complex, and as the types of "standardly asked" queries continue to become more complex, the percentage of queries that fail should increase. In addition, semantic query optimization cannot be done without pre-analysis.

It also must be recognized that the "wasted" cost of analyzing a non-failing, reasonable query is, in general, much less than that required for a failing query. If the system waits until after processing and checks only the failing queries for misconceptions, the cost of a failing query is the analysis *plus* the execution time. With pre-analysis, the execution cost is not paid for failing queries. Even if failing queries are a small percentage, it may still be more cost-effective to analyze all queries.

So if the goal is to minimize average response time to queries, the picture is far from clear. Given the potential cost savings via SQO in Carmin, the picture is even less clear. Only experimentation can settle these issues.[18]

4.2   Costs of the Components

The key expense in Carmin is the time the pre-analyzer spends on a query. Special care must be taken to control this cost, and to guarantee that it never is excessive. The check for misconceptions is a complex logical task, so estimating its time is difficult too. Central to the Carmin project has been to devise efficient, practical approaches to this analysis.

In Datalog without recursion, the misconception check is computable, but the task can be shown to be *coNP-complete*. This arises from the closed world assumption and the need to check a possibly exponential number of unfoldings of the query to verify it must fail over all of them.[19] At first, this may seem to be a fatal indictment. There is reason to believe, however, that in average case, the misconception check remains tractable. Very few of the possible unfoldings usually need to be explored, and most all complex misconceptions involve only a few unfoldings. In practice, the number is on the order of the size of the query.

In any case, the fact that the misconception check is, in worst case, intractable can be paid for by accepting *incompleteness* of the misconception check rather

---

[18] To be fair, since Carmin is also a research platform for cooperative answering, it must have a *pre-analyzer* stage anyway to accommodate those cooperative techniques that require it. Furthermore, it seems a realistic CDBS should support some of these other cooperative behaviors; for instance, query simplification.

[19] Without the closed world assumption, all misconceptions are *simple*. The misconception check in this case can be shown to be within polynomial bounds (further barring negation and inequalities in the rulebase and query).

than accepting unbounded complexity. (The check will still always be *correct* whenever it finds a misconception.) Since the check iterates through a query's unfoldings, the process can be curtailed should it ever explore too many (determined by a preset threshold). This guarantees performance at the cost of completeness. In average case (almost all cases), Carmin completes the analysis.

In [32], Levy, Mumick, Sagiv, and Shmueli show that the misconception check in Datalog with recursion is undecidable. With recursion, incompleteness *must* be accepted. Still, we believe that, in most all cases, the misconception check can be completed in reasonable time bounds. Good heuristics will be required in this case to curtail the misconception process appropriately.

The cost of a query's analysis depends on the complexity of the rulebase with respect to that query. All analysis of the query takes place in memory and the cost is *CPU* time. The overhead of the SQL translator in Carmin is negligible and bounded. The cost of evaluation is dictated by the complexity of the query and by the size of the database, and is dominated by disk *I/O* time. Given the assumption that the rulebase is much smaller than the database in size, and the fact that the query's analysis is *CPU*-bound whereas its evaluation is *I/O*-bound, evaluation time should greatly exceed analysis time.

As discussed above, the post-analyzer can be expensive. However the expense is due to the necessity of subsequent querying of the database. The analysis expense can be bounded in the same way the pre-analyzer is. Thus, the cost can be predicted in advance. Therefore, a user can reasonably decide whether to engage the post-analyzer.

The cost of the explanation facility is inconsequential compared to the time required for a user to read and interpret the response. All meta-answers are formulated by the analyzers and their transformation by the explanation facility is computationally simple.

The query formation facility is also controlled by the user. Some of the features are inexpensive, as the computational overhead was paid in analysis. Query relaxation exploits the analysis done of the query by the pre-analyzer. Finding MSSs to a query is expensive because of the database access costs. However, as with the post-processor, the time can be predicted. Thus, the user can decide when to invoke the MSS search.

4.3 Implementation Issues

The architecture of Carmin outlined in this paper has many ramifications for an implementation. We have focused to build a generic set of tools necessary to provide the type of cooperative behaviors discussed. Cooperative answering requires more than the standard deductive capacity found in deductive database systems to be implemented efficiently. The deductive mechanism has had to be extended, for instance, to allow for finding *all* the generic consequences of a query. Abductive inferencing is required to search for state misconceptions. A variety of specialty algorithms have had to be developed, for instance, to search for MFSs and MSSs and syntactic reduction of queries.

At the core of the pre-processor is the Carmin Engine. It is a bottom-up inference engine. The general strategy for misconception checking is as follows: an answer is presupposed to the query; all possible consequences are deduced from these "facts"; if inconsistency is found, a misconception has been identified.

The implementation phase of Carmin has brought many of the important algorithmic issues of cooperative answering to light. This has prompted a fair amount of effort to design algorithms that begin to address some of the surprisingly intricate computational issues raised by cooperative answering.

5   Conclusions

5.1   Status of the Carmin System

We are working to finish a stable prototype of the Carmin system in the near term that incorporates the features described in this paper. We plan to make it available to be used with actual database systems and databases, both to evaluate the system and, we hope, to gain the benefits of cooperative answering. We also plan to share the system as a research platform with others who are studying cooperative answering techniques and deductive databases.

The current Carmin system is available as a demonstration via *World Wide Web*. Our *URL* is *http://karna.cs.umd.edu:3264/*. This is also reachable through the *WWW* server for the Computer Science Department of the University of Maryland at College Park. Documentation is available on-line for how to run it. The current on-line prototype is limited, but will be improving.

5.2   Future work in the Carmin Project

There remains much to do in the field of cooperative answering, and the research agenda for the Carmin project is open-ended, with much important and beneficial work still to be done. A primary goal is to deliver a useful CDBS prototype in the near-term. Future research includes:

- further research in types of cooperative answering techniques and behaviors
  - incorporating other known cooperative answering techniques
  - devising new ones
- research in algorithms for semantic query optimization
- further research in the algorithmic support of cooperative behaviors
  - improving performance
  - supporting new cooperative techniques
- improving the explanation facility
- interfacing Carmin with a deductive database system

Carmin is a research platform. A cooperative technique can be implemented and tested in the system to see if it is effective. The system now offers a number of standard analysis tools that should help to implement new techniques, and to determine if a new technique can be made tractable.

The current SQO in Carmin is just opportunistic (what we saw we could do easily). Attention needs to be paid to how to accomplish SQO in such a system to full advantage. Especially since some cost for query analysis can be tolerated for the benefits of cooperative answers, it can be exploited for the purposes of SQO.

Explanation must be central to any CDBS. Any type of meta-answer to a query is only effective if it can be understood by the user. This means such answers cannot be too complex, and they must be represented in a fashion that is easy to read and interpret. Further explanation strategies should be developed for a number of cooperative behaviors.

We would also like to interface Carmin with deductive database systems. This raises issues of how Carmin's deductive capacities and a deductive database system's should be coupled. We believe tools such as Carmin are indispensable to the success of deductive databases. The schema and semantics of deductive databases are more complex in general than those of relational databases. Without cooperative analysis of queries, such systems may be too difficult to use effectively.

References

1. U. S. Chakravarthy. *Semantic Query Optimization in Deductive Databases*. PhD thesis, University of Maryland at College Park, Department of Computer Science, 1985.
2. U. S. Chakravarthy, J. Grant, and J. Minker. Foundations of semantic query optimization for deductive databases. In J. Minker, editor, *Proc. Workshop on Foundations of Deductive Databases and Logic Programming*, pages 67–101, Washington, D.C., August 18-22 1986.
3. U. S. Chakravarthy, J. Grant, and J. Minker. Semantic query optimization: Additional constraints and control strategies. In L. Kerschberg, editor, *Proc. Expert Database Systems*, pages 259–269, Charleston, Apr. 1986.
4. U. S. Chakravarthy, J. Grant, and J. Minker. Logic based approach to semantic query optimization. *ACM Transactions on Database Systems*, 15(2):162–207, June 1990.
5. W. W. Chu. CoBase: A cooperative database system. In Demolombe and Imielinski [13], pages 41–73. To appear.
6. W. W. Chu and Q. Chen. Neighborhood and associative query answering. *Journal of Intelligent Information Systems*, 1:355–382, 1992.
7. W. W. Chu, Q. Chen, and A. Hwang. Query answering via cooperative data inference. *Journal of Intelligent Information Systems*, 3:57–87, 1994.
8. W. W. Chu, Q. Chen, and R.-C. Lee. A structured approach for cooperative query answering. *IEEE Transactions on Knowledge and Data Engineering*, 1992.
9. W. W. Chu, M. A. Merzbacher, and L. Berkovich. The design and implementation of CoBase. In *Proceedings of the 1993 ACM SIGMOD: International Conference on Management of Data*, pages 517–522, Washington, D.C., May 1993. ACM Press.
10. F. Corella, S. J. Kaplan, G. Wiederhold, and L. Yesil. Cooperative responses to boolean queries. In *First International Conference on Data Engineering*, pages 77–85, Silver Spring, Maryland, 1984. IEEE Computer Society Press.

11. F. Cuppens and R. Demolombe. Cooperative answering: a methodology to provide intellegent access to databases. In L. Kershberg, editor, *Proc. of the Second International Conference on Expert Database System*, pages 333–353, George Mason University, Apr. 1988.

12. F. Cuppens and R. Demolombe. How to recognize interesting topics to provide cooperative answering. *Information Systems*, 14(2):163–173, 1989.

13. R. Demolombe and T. Imielinski, editors. *Non Standard Queries and Answers*. Oxford University Press, 1994. To appear.

14. T. Gaasterland. *Cooperative Answers for Database Queries*. PhD thesis, University of Maryland, Department of Computer Science, College Park, 1992.

15. T. Gaasterland, P. Godfrey, and J. Minker. An overview of cooperative answering. *Journal of Intelligent Information Systems*, 1(2):123–157, 1992. Invited paper.

16. T. Gaasterland, P. Godfrey, and J. Minker. Relaxation as a platform for cooperative answering. *Journal of Intelligent Information Systems*, 1:293–321, 1992.

17. T. Gaasterland, P. Godfrey, and J. Minker. An overview of cooperative answering. In Demolombe and Imielinski [13], pages 1–39. Appears orginally as [15].

18. T. Gaasterland, P. Godfrey, J. Minker, and L. Novik. A cooperative answering system. In A. Voronkov, editor, *Proceedings of the Logic Programming and Automated Reasoning Conference*, Lecture Notes in Artificial Intelligence 624, pages 478–480. Springer-Verlag, St. Petersburg, Russia, July 1992.

19. T. Gaasterland and J. Minker. User needs and language generation issues in a cooperative answering system. In P. Saint-Dizier, editor, *ICLP'91 Workshop: Advanced Logic Programming Tools and Formalisms for Language Processing*, pages 1–14, INRIA, Paris, France, June 1991.

20. T. Gaasterland, J. Minker, and A. Rajasekar. Deductive Database Systems and Knowledge Base Systems. In *Proceedings of VIA 90*, Barcelona, Spain, October 1990.

21. A. Gal. *Cooperative Responses in Deductive Databases*. PhD thesis, Department of Computer Science, University of Maryland, College Park, Maryland, 1988.

22. A. Gal and J. Minker. A natural language database interface that provides cooperative answers. *Proceedings of the Second Conference on Artificial Intelligence Applications*, December 11–13 1985.

23. A. Gal and J. Minker. Informative and cooperative answers in databases using integrity constraints. In V. Dahl and P. Saint-Dizier, editors, *Natural Language Understanding and Logic Programming*, pages 277–300. North Holland, 1988.

24. H. Gallaire and J. Minker, editors. *Logic and Databases*. Plenum Press, New York, Apr. 1978.

25. H. Gallaire, J. Minker, and J.-M. Nicolas, editors. *Advances in Database Theory, Volume 1*. Plenum Press, New York, 1981.

26. P. Godfrey. Minimal failing subqueries. In progress, 1994.

27. J. M. Janas. On the feasibility of informative answers. In Gallaire et al. [25], pages 397–414.

28. A. Joshi, B. Webber, and I. Sag, editors. *Elements of Discourse Understanding*. Cambridge University Press, 1981.

29. S. J. Kaplan. Appropriate responses to inappropriate questions. In Joshi et al. [28], pages 127–144.

30. S. J. Kaplan. Cooperative responses from a portable natural language query system. *Artificial Intelligence*, 19(2):165–187, Oct. 1982.

31. R. M. Lee. Conversational aspects of database interactions. In *Proceedings of the 4th International Conference on Very Large Data Bases*, Berlin, 1978.

32. A. Y. Levy, I. S. Mumick, Y. Sagiv, and O. Shmueli. Equivalence, query-reachability, and satisfiability in datalog extensions. In *Proceedings og the Twelfth ACM SIGACT-SIGMOD-SIGART Symposium on Principles of Database Systems*, pages 109–122, Washington, D.C., May 1993.

33. A. Motro. Extending the relational model to support goal queries. In *Proceedings from the First International Workshop on Expert Database Systems*, pages 129–150. Benjamin/Cummings, 1986.

34. A. Motro. SEAVE: A mechanism for verifying user presuppositions in query systems. *ACM Transactions on Office Information Systems*, 4(4):312–330, October 1986.

35. A. Motro. FLEX: A tolerant and cooperative user interface to databases. *IEEE Transactions on Knowledge and Data Engineering*, 2(2):231–246, June 1990.

36. R. Reiter. On closed world data bases. In Gallaire and Minker [24], pages 55–76.

37. J. D. Ullman. *Principles of Database and Knowledge-Base Systems, Volume II: The New Technologies*. Principles of Computer Science Series. Computer Science Press, Incorporated, Rockville, Maryland, 1989.

Appendix—Some Initial Timing Results

The Navy Database

A Navy database[20] has been used for testing Carmin. Characteristics of the Navy database are as follows. It is an INGRES database for keeping information on naval ships (sizes, capacities, etc.), port visits, port-to-port voyages, and position reports, installed weaponry, and so forth.

The database has 17 database relations which range in size from from 2 to 7565 tuples (average is 568) and the number of fields per relation range from 2 to 11 (average is 5).

The Rule Base

Rules and *integrity constraints* were added in the rulebase for the Navy database for testing Carmin. The full *rulebase* contains 19 rules and 18 integrity constraints. For these tests, three sizes of rulebases were used:

- **RB**$_A$ is the full rulebase.
- **RB**$_B$ has all the rules and 9 of the ICs.
- **RB**$_C$ has 10 of the rules and 9 of the ICs.

$$\text{RB}_A \supset \text{RB}_B \supset \text{RB}_C$$

The Queries

Q_1: simple select over a base relation

    ship(name: Name, num: ID, base: B), B\= 5, B\= 30.

Q_2: 5-way join over relations with a select

    opercom(fleet: _F, commander: Commander),
    ship(num: _S, fleet: _F),
    install(shipid: _S, weapon: _W),
    weapon(id: _W, rang: _R),
    _R > 1000,
    position(shipid: _S, ocean: Ocean).

Q_3: union view (not supported by INGRES's view facility)

    at_port(ship: Name, port: Port, purpose: Purpose).

Q_4: union view with a join and a select

---

[20] We thank Wesley W. Chu at UCLA for making the database available to us.

```
at_port(ship: S, port: Port, purpose: Purpose),
port(name: Port, country: CP),
ship(name: S, flag: CS),
CP \= CS.
```

Q_5: query with a non-trivial misconception

```
ship_type(shipid: ID_1, ship: SH_1,
   type: T_1, surface: 'subsurface'),
ship_type(shipid: ID_2, ship: SH_2,
   type: T_2, surface: 'surface'),
radar(type: T_1, radar: R),
radar(type: T_2, radar: R).
```

Q_6: second query with a non-trivial misconception

```
has_weapon(shipid: SID, ship: S, weapontype: rocket),
ship_type(shipid: SID, ship: S, surface: subsurface).
```

Timing Results

Stopwatch Times (sec)	Q_1	Q_2	Q_3	Q_4	Q_5	Q_6
Carmin **A**	2.17	4.79	18.34	29.39	1.77	1.35
with **B**	1.95	4.64	18.67	28.36	1.40	1.13
INGRES **C**	1.95	4.56	17.60	27.97	1.40	1.09
Pure INGRES	1.58	4.08	15.45	27.66	4.17	4.14
Percentage Overhead	37	17	19	6	-58	-67

Notes about the timing results:

- Percentage overhead is calculated against Carmin running with **RB**$_A$.
- Each time is the minimum of 10 trials. This is to help eliminate background noise from other processes.
- The *UNIX csh time* utility was used.
  For Carmin timing, the queries were piped to a running Carmin session.

Both Carmin and INGRES were run on the same system, a SUN SPARC IPX running UNIX, SunOS 4.1.3. The queries were piped to a standing Carmin interactive session, and the turn-around time measured. INGRES was called batch for each query. The start-up time of INGRES is small and is paid in both cases, so does not bias the comparison.

For more information such as the rulebase employed, the QUEL translation of the queries in the query suite, and so forth, please connect to our *WWW* server as described in the conclusions. This information is available on-line.

Database Management for Real-Time Applications

Alex Buchmann

Technical University of Darmstadt, Germany

Abstract. A growing number of applications require time-constrained access to data. For these applications, the timeliness of the data is part of the correctness criteria. Timing constraints can be derived from the temporal consistency requirements of the application and must be enforced by the DBMS. Examples of applications that require the processing of varying quantities of data with timing constraints range from chemical and power plant control, to network management, air traffic control, and multimedia systems.

The tutorial covers motivation and applications requiring real-time data management, and introduces the basic notions. We discuss the scheduling problem as one of the core problems in real-time systems, introduce a reference model and discuss the fundamental issues and alternatives in scheduling a variety of resources, ranging from CPU to I/O and data. We analyze the issues involved in real-time transaction processing and the trade-offs between flexibility and predictability. We address the issues of overload management as one of the critical components of real-time systems and propose alternatives for flexible overload management based on contingency plans. The tutorial concludes with an analysis of required operating system support and a discussion of what capability is actually offered by today's real-time operating systems. We conclude with a perspective of what is required to re-engineer a DBMS to meet the real-time requirements of modern applications.

Spatial Databases

Hanan Samet

University of Maryland, USA

Abstract. The ability to deal with spatial data is becoming increasingly important in applications in geographic information systems, computer vision, computer graphics, computer vision, image processing, solid modeling, robotics, and cartography. This manifests itself in the need to incorporate this data in existing database management systems.

This incorporation must result in the coexistence of the spatial data with the non-spatial data. The result is termed a spatial database. Spatial databases must deal with points, lines, rectangles, regions, surfaces, volumes, and other geometric data, as well as time and non-geometric data (known as attribute data). The implementation of spatial databases involves many issues including a choice among a number of different representations for the underlying data, as well as the types of queries to be supported,

In this tutorial we review some of the most recent representations and the type of operations that they are designed to support. We also discuss methods of integrating spatial and non-spatial data in conventional database management systems, as well as examine some existing spatial database systems.

The Evolution of User Interface Tools for Database Applications

Moshe Zloof and Ravi Krishnamurthy

Hewlett-Packard Labs, USA

Abstract. The recent advances in hardware and enabling software technologies are having profound effect on the development of UI tools for building database applications.

In this tutorial, we will first give a historical account of the evolution of DB UI tools since the early seventies in terms of database models, database languages, database development tools (Visual 4GL), and end user graphical tools. As the users of SQL were primarily application developers, the tools were built directed to this clientele. Therefore, the design factors for building programmers' tools were focused on increasing their productivity.

Advent of PC database management systems, saw the metamorphism of this clientele to less sophisticated users. These non-programmers (i.e., power users) who wish to build their applications required different kinds of tools and the PC database industry lead this thrust. We address the design factors in both these types of tools and contrast them.

In doing the above, we will review and compare some of the current environments in terms of their power, functionality, levels of abstraction and ease of use. This will include, but is not limited to, such products or research prototypes as: Paradox, Access, 4GL Windows, PowerSoft, Prograph, ICBE (being prototyped at HP Labs).

Finally, we will extrapolate on how this UI technology will be evolving in the future specifically into the areas of entertainment and mobile personal appliances.

Temporal Database Technology for Air Traffic Flow Management

S.M.Sripada[1], B.L.Rosser[2], J.M.Bedford[2] and R.A.Kowalski[3]

[1] European Computer-Industry Research Centre
Arabellastrasse 17, 81925 Munich, Germany. sripada@ecrc.de
[2] Ferranti International plc, Simulation and Training
Ty Coch Way, Cwmbran NP44 7XX, U.K.
[3] Imperial College of Science, Technology & Medicine
180 Queen's Gate, London SW7 2BZ, U.K. rak@doc.ic.ac.uk

Abstract. The function of air traffic flow management (ATFM) is to ensure that air traffic operates within adequate margins of safety. Existing ATFM systems are manual which are over-conservative in operation resulting in under-utilisation of available airspace. As well as being costly, such systems are unable to cope with increased demand for air travel in regions such as Europe. Attempts are currently being made to provide computer-based decision support for ATFM. Computerised decision support for ATFM ensures that safety margins are maintained while at the same time increasing the effective capacity of the airspace by more efficient flight scheduling. At the heart of such a system is active temporal database technology which aids the air traffic controllers by keeping track of airspace occupancy (a time-map of spatio-temporal trajectories of aircraft) in controlled regions of airspace, enabling flow managers to process requests for new slots for takeoff and to smoothen and optimise the flow of air traffic. The technology also aids air traffic controllers by alerting them to possible conflicts and by providing tools for re-routing aircraft to avoid mid-air collisions. The paper describes a large scale demonstrator for ATFM that has been developed at Ferranti Simulation and Training.

1 Introduction

In recent years, civil aviation has seen a rapid increase in demand calling for increased air-space utilisation. Existing systems for air traffic flow management (ATFM) are manual and are unable to cope with this increase in demand without compromising safety. Efforts are therefore underway to provide computer-based decision support for ATFM. The function of air traffic flow management is to ensure that air traffic operates within adequate margins of safety. This paper describes a large scale demonstrator for strategic and tactical flow management that has been developed at Ferranti Simulation and Training.

At the heart of the ATFM system is active temporal database technology which aids flow management by supporting the maintenance of a model of airspace occupancy for controlled regions of air space. The ATFM application provides a perfect case for the use of active temporal database technology. Some of the functionalities required by the application which highlight the need for active temporal database technology are described below.

Temporal Databases Flow Managers require a model of airspace occupancy in order to control air traffic. The model comprises a time-map of spatio-temporal trajectories of the various air-borne aircraft in controlled regions of airspace. This requires the ability to store and manipulate spatial and temporal data. In the ATFM application, temporal data is quite complex and requires special database functionalities to support temporal knowledge representation and reasoning.

Real-time updates Space-time coordinates of an aircraft along its route are periodically relayed back to Air Traffic Control units. Based on this input, the airspace occupancy table needs to be continuously and quickly revised to reflect the latest state of the airspace. Information from the airspace occupancy table is then used to allocate slots for new flights as well as to detect and avoid mid-air conflicts.

Integrity constraints Upon every update, the database has to ensure that capacity of a sector of airspace is not exceeded at any time; it should also enforce that a minimum safe separation distance is always maintained between all airborne aircraft.

Triggers Upon every revision, the database has to detect any violations of integrity constraints and automatically initiate actions that alert the flow manager and support remedial actions such as re-routing.

Past records A record of all the past data are to be kept so that analyses may be carried out for post-incident investigations, improving scheduling strategies, optimising the flow of traffic, and discover patterns in air traffic and airspace utilisation for strategic planning purposes. Thus the application requires bi-temporal databases handling both valid time and transaction time [3]. Valid time denotes the time at which information models reality (e.g. an aircraft being at a particular point in space at a certain time) whereas transaction time denotes the time for which the information is believed (or recorded) in the database (e.g. at the time of take-off, the flight is predicted to be at a certain point in space at a certain time; at a later time, this belief may be revised).

The rest of the paper is organised as follows: Section 2 describes the domain of Air Traffic Control (ATC) and specifically the problem of Air Traffic Flow Management (ATFM). The requirements of a computer-based decision support system for ATFM are also described in Section 2. A description of the temporal database technology used in the application and the domain modelling aspects are presented in Section 3. Implementation and performance of the ATFM system are sketched in Section 4. In view of the proprietary nature of the technology, only an outline of the implementation has been included in sections 3 and 4. Plans for commercial exploitation as well as ongoing work and conclusions are presented in Section 5.

2 The ATFM Application

2.1 The ATC Domain

In the early days of commercial air transportation, the skies and runways were relatively empty. Pilots were free to take off from an airport, choose their route to their destination, and land there as soon as they could see that the runaway was free. As both the volume of air traffic and the speed of aircraft increased, the risk of unfettered air travel became too great. First, it became necessary to control the use of runways to avoid problems at take-off and landing. Next, the busy zones in the vicinity of airports needed to be controlled to prevent accidents during approach and ascent. Finally, controls were extended to the enroute section of a flight, i.e. when the aircraft is flying at its cruising altitude and speed towards its destination. In this way, the industry of Air Traffic Control (ATC) evolved.

The means by which ATC functions to control air traffic depend upon

- an internationally agreed set of rules and regulations,
- an infrastructure of equipment, and
- human resources to put the system into effect.

The rules and regulations define safe flying practice. They constrain pilots to follow well-defined routes at definite altitudes (known as flight levels), to inform the authorities of these in advance, and to fly at defined minimum distances one from another. The infrastructure includes ground-based radar for tracking aircraft in flight, beacons which emit direction-finding and position-identifying signals to aircraft, and on-board equipment such as radio, transponders and an increasing array of electronic safety devices. The resources are the Air Traffic Controllers and associated staff. Their main function is to help pilots to follow the rules and regulations by monitoring flights and directing pilots to avoid conflicts (i.e. violations of the standards for safe separation).

The requirements of Air Traffic Control dictate that the controlled airspace is hierarchically divided into distinct three dimensional areas ranging from Flight Information Regions (FIRs) where specific procedures and standards apply to sectors which are the units of operational control.

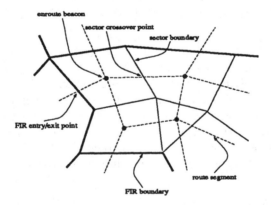

Fig.1. A highly schematic view of a part of an airspace

A highly schematic and simplified plan view of an airspace showing part of an FIRs and its constituent sectors is shown in Fig.1. The dotted lines are the routes that the aircraft actually travel along. They pass over waypoints, shown as heavy dots in the figure (enroute beacons are situated at ground level). Lines joining the waypoints form a grid of imaginary air corridors along which the aircraft travel. An aircraft flying along a route is always under the control of the Controller for the sector it currently occupies. When it passes from one sector to the adjacent one, it is explicitly "handed over" from the first Controller to his counterpart in the next sector.

2.2 The Role of Air Traffic Flow Management in ATC

The over-riding goal of Air Traffic Control (ATC) is maintaining safety in air transportation. It achieves this by a complex of control, management and planning procedures organised into several layers. The details of this organisation vary from country to country according to local conditions. However, a common factor is the fundamental division of the task into Strategic Planning, Radar Control, and Flow Management.

Strategic Planning is carried out often several years in advance. Its object is to ensure that the ATC infrastructure is adequate to meet expected demand. This may involve re-organising the route network, improving equipment levels, or training more Air Traffic Controllers. The Radar Control and Flow Management levels are both concerned with the operation of safety procedures within this infrastructure.

The Radar Controller bears the front line responsibility for maintaining safe separation between aircraft in flight. He does this by monitoring the positions of all aircraft in his sector (i.e. the volume of controlled airspace he is responsible for) on a radar screen, and by communicating instructions to pilots by radio when necessary.

A skilled Radar Controller is well able to perform this function as long as his workload remains within his capacity. If there is too much activity within his sector at a given time, he may become overloaded and risk making an error. Examples of potential errors are failing to observe an impending "conflict" (i.e. a violation of the separation standard applying to the sector), mis-directing a pilot, or failing to effect a smooth hand-over of control when an aircraft leaves his sector.

One measure employed to reduce the risk of such an overload is to predict the Radar Controller's workload for a short period ahead of real time (i.e. up to about 30 minutes), and to schedule his operations so that no two actions become urgent at the same time. (Often, this function is performed by a separate member of the Radar Control team called the Planning Controller.) However, this presupposes that the workload profile averaged over time remains below the limit set by his capacity. In the busier regions of the air transport network, where traffic loads vary widely over time and space, this requires Flow Management.

The need for Air Traffic Flow Management (ATFM) arose to remove all risk that any sector of (controlled) airspace could become overloaded for an extended period, with the consequent threat to safety. ATFM covers a range of activities which can be characterised as strategic, pre-tactical and tactical - according to the time-scales over which they operate. For all of these activities, it is necessary to carry out a prediction of traffic flows.

At the strategic level, these predictions are used to determine appropriate staffing levels for particular sectors and to set restrictions when necessary. Underloaded sectors can often be grouped together under one Radar Controller, thus freeing resources, while more heavily loaded sectors are assigned to the most experienced Radar Control teams in order to maximise their capacity.

When an overload is predicted - i.e. the predicted traffic flow will exceed the maximum safe capacity of the sector - the Flow Manager must plan measures to reduce the load. These measures are designed to re-distribute the traffic in time, in space, or both. When the overload is of relatively short duration (e.g. one hour or so at the peak of the daily traffic cycle), some of the peak traffic can be delayed, thus smoothing out the cycle. In other cases, it may be more effective to divert traffic from an overloaded sector through nearby sectors which are not overloaded.

The restriction is the strategic Flow Manager's main instrument to effect such re-distributions. A basic restriction is applied to a sector and specifies the maximum number of aircraft permitted to enter the sector over a specified period. Usually, restrictions are refined to take account of the distribution of flows through a sector. In this case, separate restrictions may be placed on the individual entry points to the overloaded sector.

A Flow Management policy (including restrictions and guidelines for re-routing or delaying flights) is initially set well in advance of real time (usually at the start of a busy season). This is reviewed and tailored, by adjusting the restrictions if necessary, one day before the day of operation. The restrictions, together with general principles of day-to-day flow management, are then enforced at the tactical level by the procedure of Slot Allocation. This takes place in a time window extending from about thirty minutes to about four hours before real time, when airlines and pilots log their flight plans and request permission to traverse controlled airspace. The Flow Manager will either approve the flight plan as requested, or will negotiate time or route changes in accordance with the restriction plan. It is at this point that air travellers all too frequently become aware of the Flow Management process, when the pilot informs them that the delay in their departure is due to "Air Traffic Control".

2.3 Requirements for Computer-Based Decision Support for ATFM

The ideal decision support system for ATFM must be both integrated and distributed. It must integrate all levels of the ATFM process - from strategic to tactical. It must be accessible to users and information suppliers throughout its geographical range. It must be responsive for interactive use, and reactive to frequent updates and data revisions. It must cater for the special requirements of each user in each sub-region, while at the same time integrating traffic predictions and flow management measures over the whole range. It must deal intelligently with the large volumes of data at its disposal, taking account of the reliability, precision, and temporal characteristics of the data.

Above all, the system must be reliable in use. In increasing the effectiveness and efficiency of ATFM, it must not introduce additional hazards which could affect safety. To this end, it must begin by automating the lower-level aspects of the flow management process using well-established technology, leaving the Flow Manager in full control of the task. Nevertheless, it must also have built-in flexibility and capacity for progressive task automation, so that it may be developed and extended incrementally as technology allows. Without this, the system could quickly become out-dated and impede further progress.

2.4   Characteristics of ATFM Data

An effective ATFM decision support system will inevitably centre on the prediction of air traffic in terms of its volume and its detailed spatio-temporal distribution. This depends upon the availability of suitable data, and also upon appropriate methods of handling this data. The data available to an ATFM system can be described in terms of three basic characteristics, namely: its level of abstraction, its accuracy and precision, its lead time, and its source.

Air traffic data presented to ATFM is at three main levels of abstraction:
• individual flights: flight plans describing routes and associated timing information,
• traffic flow rates: the number of aircraft crossing a point (e.g. a beacon) per unit time as a function of time, and
• traffic load rates: the number of aircraft in an airspace entity (e.g. a sector or a route segment) as a function of time.
These are genuine levels of abstraction since information is progressively lost at each level. (Thus, reasoning from individual flights to either flow or load rates is straightforward, but the inverse is not.) This temporal data makes reference to a structural description of the airspace, i.e. the route network, its sectorisation, and the various kinds of "fixes" - instrumented beacons, reporting points, etc.

Accuracy and precision are generally inversely related when applied to predictive information. For example, the prediction that a flight will take off at 10.19am exactly will prove inaccurate if the flight actually takes off at 10.21am, whereas "about 10.20am" would have been true. Of course, neither prediction would be accurate if the flight was cancelled. In fact, ATFM data is generally presented at a constant high precision, even if this means that the accuracy is low. For example, every flight plan includes a take-off time expressed in hours and minutes whether this time is confirmed or is just a pious wish. The main determinants of accuracy are the data's lead time and its source.

In general, the earlier an item of ATFM information is available, the less accurate it is likely to be. The range of lead times is wide - from about one year ahead of real time down to minutes or hours after real time. In the context of current ATFM practice, however, information received later than about 30 minutes before real time tends to be useless for flow management purposes because it is too late to act on it.

Sources of Information There are five main types of information source used in ATFM:
• Intentions: flights intending to use controlled airspace are required to log their flight plans well before scheduled take-off.
• Historical data: seasonal, weekly and daily patterns in the level of utilisation of airspace due to holiday and commuter traffic.
• Trends: longer term trends such as the growing demands on controlled airspace.
• Special factors: factors such as major sporting events, state visits which produce localised effects.

• Actual events: Ultimately, all predictions are confirmed, refined or corrected by what happens in the real world. Many real time events are relevant to tactical ATFM because they have enduring consequences which fall within the tactical ATFM time window (i.e. 4 hours to 0.5 hours in advance). Examples are take-offs, position updates, temporary runway or route segment closures, weather fronts.

2.5 Prediction and Data Manipulation

An essential requirement for the Decision Support System posed by tactical ATFM is the ability to maintain a consistent picture of the traffic over a moving time window (of four hours) in the face of a constant stream of updates and revisions. As well as providing tools for dynamically managing the traffic at the level of individual flights, it must actively warn of any impending overloads. It must also be able to recover the exact context in which a Flow Management decision was made for the purpose of Post-Incident Analysis.

An important attribute of the Decision Support System for all levels of ATFM is the ability to support hypothetical reasoning. The Flow Manager will frequently wish to evaluate a number of alternative solutions to a problem before committing to a single solution. For example, a Strategic Flow Manager may wish to compare different restrictions and choose the one whose effects are closest to the ones desired. Similarly, a Tactical Flow Manager may wish to allocate a take-off slot tentatively, and move it forwards or backwards in time to clear any restriction violations that it might otherwise induce. The integrity of the database must not be affected by such tentative operations especially in view of the fact that it will be accessed by several users simultaneously - and the alternatives tried should not interfere with each other.

3   Temporal Database Technology for ATFM

The temporal database technology that has been developed for the ATFM application is based on the research solutions developed by Sripada in [7]. In particular, Sripada proposes a declarative representation of temporal knowledge in a database and the pre-computation of appropriate derived relations (materialised views) so as to improve query-time performance. To improve performance at update-time, an efficient method for the maintenance of these derived views has been proposed [8]. The pre-computed relations are then stored in an extended relational database for efficient access.

The architecture of the ATFM temporal database system is shown in Fig.2. The ATFM system has been developed around a Temporal Database kernel: a proprietary database system for real-time applications (SoftRP of Ferranti International plc, denoted by DMS in Fig.2.) has been extended and optimised to handle temporal data with suitable indexing techniques for efficient storage and retrieval of temporal data [2]. A number of interfaces are supported by the temporal relational database including TSQL, a temporal extension of SQL (as illustrated in Fig.2). A Deductive Temporal Database is then developed by tightly coupling Quintus Prolog and the Temporal Relational Database kernel with various optimisations for temporal database access. Data modelling of the application domain has been done in the deductive framework of GRF (General Representation Formalism) based on an extended version of the Event Calculus [4], a logic based framework for representing and reasoning with time and change. Mechanisms for materialisation, triggers and efficient belief revision have also been integrated into the tightly coupled system. Various decision support modules have been developed in Prolog which are served by the deductive temporal database system.

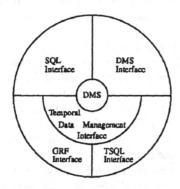

Fig.2. Architecture of the Deductive Temporal Database Management System. The DMS is the relational database kernel with SQL and TSQL interfaces. The DMS and GRF interfaces are deductive interfaces for the Prolog language.

3.1   Modelling Based on the Event Calculus

The deductive level of a DTDBMS calls for a suitable temporal knowledge representation formalism, for which there are many candidates (e.g. see [5]). The requirement here is for a temporal logic which can meet the requirements of "temporal projection" for industrial domains, and which can be provided with an efficient computational basis (temporal projection is model-based temporal reasoning which often equates to prediction in practice, but can equally well work backwards in time). The one chosen for the ATFM application was the Event Calculus because it enables the representation of events and processes (which abound in the ATFM application) plus its ability to deal with default persistence and continuous change and facilitate tasks such as abductive planning. Although the Event Calculus presents some computational problems for temporal reasoning in general, it proved possible to develop a very efficient implementation for temporal projection. Event Calculus was extended in the project with more powerful facilities (GRF) for modelling process-based domains such as air traffic.

The basic element of the ATFM domain is the *flight* process. As a physical process, flight is a continuous function that maps time to the position of the aircraft in space (altitude, latitude and longitude). This is modelled in the extended Event Calculus at a qualitative level, i.e. as a sequence of events (instantaneous changes in the qualitative state of the flight) and properties (persistent states of the flight). Typical events are *at_waypoint(flight,waypoint)* and *enter_sector(flight,sector)*. Typical properties are *enroute_between(flight,waypoint1,waypoint2)* and *in_sector(flight,sector)*.

The main model of the flight process model includes a unique identifier for the flight, an unambiguous representation of the flight path in terms of *take_off*, *at_waypoint* and *landing* events, and values for cruising altitude and cruising speed. From this, all other information concerning the flight can be recovered, sometimes with the aid of default information. For example, the *enter_sector* events can be found by solving for the intersections between the flight path and the sector boundaries, while the altitude at a point on the climb to cruising altitude can be found using a default climb profile.

Air traffic rates are deduced from the total set of known flights. If all of the *in_sector(flight,sector)* properties have been explicitly deduced, the sector load at any instant t can be easily recovered by the Event Calculus query *holds_at(in_sector(_,sector_name),⟨t⟩)* and counting the set of properties returned. To plot the sector load as a function of time, a simple mechanism can be defined which initialises the function with the above query, obtains all *enter_sector* and *exit_sector* events over the required time range (in time order), and increments or decrements the function at each such event.

Calculating flow rates at beacons or other waypoints can be done in a similar way. However, since flow is integrated over time, it is necessary to define a function for this integration. The simplest form of this is a time window. Thus, if the flow is to be expressed as number of aircraft per 10 minutes at time T, the time window will extend from T-5 minutes to T+5 minutes. For each event

happens(at_waypoint(flight,waypoint),⟨t⟩),

the events

happens(enter_time_window(flight,waypoint),⟨t-5⟩)   and
happens(exit_time_window(flight,waypoint),⟨t+5⟩)

are generated. These are then used exactly as the *enter_sector* and *exit_sector* events were to compute the required function.

Once generated in this way from the basic flight information, the rate functions can be themselves manipulated by the Flow Manager. For example, if the Flow Manager restricts the flow across a particular waypoint to 50% of its previous value, then 50% of the flights contributing to the value of the function at that point must be delayed to the end of the restriction period. Because of the heterogeneity (in respect of origin, destination and route) of the set of contributing flights, the system must select a representative subset to delay. This involves a degree of intelligent reasoning on the part of the system. In order to fine-tune the restriction, the Flow Manager must then be given the tools to modify the system's selection, i.e. by setting other restrictions or by explicitly applying the restriction to flights with specified destinations or origins. This is where the essential skill of strategic flow management lies. The problem is not yet sufficiently understood to be able to automate it, but the use of the ATFM system in manual mode will contribute to this understanding and permit automation in the longer term.

Integrity Enforcement through Triggers A flow management system must be able to maintain a consistent model of airspace usage in a changing world. To achieve this, the TDBMS must support consistency maintenance using integrity constraints. In the ATFM domain, the temporal database systems is required to enforce the following principal integrity constraints:

1. that the projected number of aircraft in a sector does not exceed the capacity of the sector at any point in time
2. that no two aircraft do not arrive at the same waypoint within a specified time window

Contrary to normal integrity constraints such as "an aircraft cannot be at two places in space the same time" which can be satisfied by deleting old conflicting information or rejecting the update, the above integrity constraints need to be maintained by the database system actively. When any revision to the database occurs that violates the above integrity constraints, the database should initiate a set of actions such as alerting the air traffic controller to the impending danger, invoking conflict resolution modules to present re-routing options to the controller.

The integrity enforcement mechanism is based on active database technology and is invoked by triggers from event-condition-action rules [1].

Real-time updates The projected trajectories of the aircraft need to be constantly revised with updates to a flights route or take-off time. The implications of the new time-space co-ordinates of the aircraft are then used to project the new (revised) trajectory of the flight, and integrity maintenance has to be carried out. All of this activity requires real-time belief revision capabilities. The belief revision not only involves deletion of old, incorrect data, but also the computation of new implicit data. Real-time updates are achieved through a novel technique for efficient belief revision based on transaction time stamping developed by Sripada [8].

4 Implementation

4.1 The Architecture of the ATFM system

The ATFM system that has been developed is called TIMS-ATM (Temporal Information Management System - Air Traffic Management). The TIMS-ATM architecture contains two distinct databases (see Fig.3). A "static" database stores the ATC infrastructure model. This needs to be optimised for fast retrieval, but updates are generally done off-line and infrequently. The other database stores the dynamically changing traffic predictions, and needs to be optimised for both retrieval and updates. The deductive level is provided by

1. a rule base and a data-driven inference engine for update time deduction, and
2. a goal-driven query processor for deduction at query time.

The nature of the application as essentially a monitoring system places a premium on update-time deduction. This means that as much information as possible is explicitly

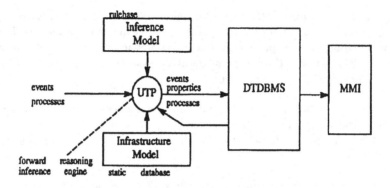

Fig.3. The TIMS-ATM system architecture

deduced from input messages by the Update Transaction Processor (UTP) and is stored in the temporal database as a time-map. This is then ready for access by the Flow Manager (or other reasoning agents) with minimal latency.

In the TIMS-ATM, a DTDBMS (Deductive Temporal Database Management System) forms the basis of a subsystem for inferring and storing temporal information (in this case, air traffic predictions). This subsystem acts as a server to a set of reasoning agents, which perform the ATFM tasks. These agents are initially human Flow Managers, interacting via specially designed MMI visualisation and input tools. However, the architecture supports the progressive automation of ATFM tasks by allowing additional task modules to be easily integrated. A few simple examples of these are demonstrated in the TIMS-ATM.

4.2 MMIs for Strategic and Tactical Flow Management

The TIMS-ATM demonstrator for Air Traffic Flow Management comprises a set of tools that aid the controller in performing both Strategic and Tactical Flow Management. These tools allow the controller to experiment with possible flow management actions before committing to a preferred decision. The flow management tools were developed to allow the flow manager to visualise and modify the information contained within the underlying temporal database via a Motif/X Window graphical user interface.

Strategic and Pre-Tactical Flow Management Given a projected airspace occupancy model for some time in the future, the TIMS-ATM tools for strategic and pre-tactical flow management allow the flow manager to visualise the impact of flow on air traffic controller's workload and to modify flows to alleviate this.

The two main approaches for displaying information contained within the temporal database are:

– plots of waypoint flow and sector load against time, and
– plots of Radar Controller's workload against time.

Radar Controller's workload is an additional level of abstraction which is implemented experimentally in the TIMS-ATM. It is calculated by summing the elements of workload generated by the several aircraft in the sector. As well as giving rise to a general workload increment for as long as it is in the sector, an aircraft generates additional workload according to its specific behaviour within the sector - e.g. as it is entering, leaving, or reaching a reporting point, if it is changing altitude, or if there is a prospect of conflict with another aircraft. The precise specification of these workload increments will require expert knowledge.

An additional display feature is the colour-coded analysis of a sector load by route. That is, the routes passing through a sector are coloured to indicate the volume of traffic using them. Saturated colours indicate heavy flows, while unsaturated colours indicate light flows. Numerical annotations are also used. This display gives the flow manager an immediate visual impression of the traffic pattern, which can help him identify the critical bottlenecks in the sector.

By clicking on the waypoints and selecting from a menu of operations, the Flow Manager can invoke a restriction setting tool. This enables him to alter the flow at the selected waypoint by a variable percentage. When he does this, a percentage of the traffic is automatically delayed. The tool also shows him the loads on all other sectors which might be affected by his action, so that he can check any knock-on effects produced by the delay.

Tactical Flow Management The Tactical Flow Management Tools provide support for the flow manager in the activity of slot allocation. The flow manager can select a flight from a list of flights awaiting slot allocation and a consistency check of the plan associated with the flight is performed. If the plan is valid then the flight is hypothetically projected into the airspace occupancy model of the temporal database. If no conflicts, congestion or restriction violations are detected by the system, the flow manager can commit to the slot allocation. Otherwise, the flow manager is provided with a set of tools to repair the conflict interactively. These tools include:

- a colour annotated display of the route on the geographical display, annotated with times at key points enroute,
- waypoint flow and sector load plots for the relevant parts of the route,
- a time map display showing all of the flights passing a selected waypoint, together with their altitudes,

The flow manager is able to reschedule a slot manually by using either mouse or keyboard interaction. An experimental automatic slot allocator is also provided. This works by moving the flight forward in time until a clear flight path is found (i.e. one free of conflicts, congestion and restriction violations).

4.3 Performance and Optimisation

The TDBMS has been developed for efficiency in updating and accessing temporal data. It has been implemented using a proprietary real time data management system that provides constant time access, query optimisation and high update performance. The constant time access means that the time to search for a record using a single unique index is independent of the number of entries in the database. The temporal database has been further optimised for manipulating temporal attributes by transparently incorporating a multi-index intersection operation and an optimised join.

The benefit of using this database technology for ATFM is that it is possible to project an average of 2000 flights per hour into the airspace usage model that covers a large section of European airspace.

To illustrate the performance of the database on multiple time attributes, Fig.4. gives the result of a set of range queries on a database containing 16758 records. Time is typically represented as an integer in the TDBMS and the data contains two integer time attributes labelled X and Y. The results of the benchmark show the superior and predictable performance of the intersection operation independent of the data distribution.

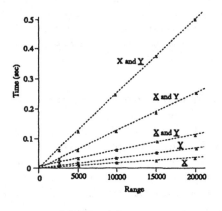

Range	Records returned		
	X	Y	X and Y
2500	424	852	23
5000	749	1696	52
10000	1670	3679	227
15000	2652	5700	972
20000	3662	7331	1827

(a) Time taken (b) Records retrieved

Fig.4. Range Select benchmark on one or two integer attributes. The select operations were performed on the X, Y and X and Y attributes. An underscore indicates that an index was used for that attribute. Timings were taken from a Sun 4/330(17.8 mips).

5 Conclusions

We have described a computerised decision support system for Air Traffic Flow Management developed at Ferranti International plc (UK). The potential benefits of such a system is higher capacity utilisation without a decrease in air safety, resulting in lower operational costs and lower air travel costs. One of the crucial enabling technologies in the development of the demonstrator was active temporal database technology.

The demonstrator has been successfully tested in simulated real-time with real flight information from the UK airspace. Negotiations are currently in progress for the commercial deployment of the ATFM system in Europe. The temporal database technology is to be further extended and exploited in another project involving several members of European aircraft manufacturers and software vendors to develop a commercial product for pilot procedures training.

Application of database technology in advanced applications such as ATFM also has potential research gains. Firstly, it validates the research results such as those in [7] as providing practicable solutions to real world problems. Secondly, it provides necessary application oriented feedback towards establishing appropriate database standards (e.g. [6]). Lastly, it stimulates further research in the area towards the development of advanced temporal database technology for more sophisticated applications such as Intelligent Vehicle Highway Systems [9].

Acknowledgements

The work of the first author was supported by a Doctoral Fellowship from the Jawaharlal Nehru Memorial Trust(UK). The development of the ATFM system at Ferranti International plc was supported by the ESPRIT project EQUATOR. Many thanks are due to Todd Ferguson for his invaluable help in integrating figures into the camera-ready version of this paper.

References

1. Bayer, P.: State-Of-The-Art Report on Reactive Processing in Databases and Artificial Intelligence. The Knowledge Engineering Review, Vol.8, No.2, 1993
2. Bedford, J.M.: EQUATOR Temporal Database Management System - User Guide and Report. Technical Report AMS&T/EQ/REP/33, Ferranti International plc, May 1992
3. Jensen, C.S. et al.: A Concensus Glossary of Temporal Database Concepts. ACM SIGMOD Record, Vol.23, No.1, March 1994
4. Kowalski,R.A., Sergot,M.J.: A logic-based calculus of events. In New Generation Computing. 1986
5. Maiocchi, R., Pernici, B., Barbic, F.: Automatic Deduction of Temporal Information. ACM Transactions on Database Systems. Vol.17, No.4, December 1992
6. Snodgrass, R.T. et al.: TSQL2 Language Specification. ACM SIGMOD Record, Vol.23, No.1, March 1994
7. Sripada, S.M.: Temporal Reasoning in Deductive Databases. Doctoral Thesis. Department of Computing, Imperial College of Science, Technology & Medicine, University of London, January 1991
8. Sripada, S.M.: A Temporal Approach to Belief Revision in Knowledge Bases. In Proc. 9th IEEE Conference on Artificial Intelligence for Applications, CAIA'93, Orlando, Florida, March 1993
9. Sripada, S.M.: The Design of the ChronoBase Temporal Deductive Database System. In Proc. International Workshop on Infrastructure for Temporal Databases (NSF Workshop), Arlington, Texas, June 1993

Using an Extended ER-Model Based Data Dictionary to Automatically Generate Product Modeling Systems

Olof Johansson
CAELAB
Department of Computer and Information Science
Linköping University
Email: ojo@ida.liu.se

Abstract. The complexity of industrial artifacts such as power plants, aircrafts etc., is continuously growing. Typically for such advanced products is that they are hybrids of various technologies and contain several types of engineering models that are related in a complex fashion. For power plant design, there are functional models, mechanical models, electrical models etc.

A product modeling system (PMS) is a computer integrated development environment for a specific class of advanced products. A well integrated PMS consists of a central product model database which is interfaced with CAD-applications that support graphical design of various engineering models.

This paper describes a successful approach to manage the development of a product modeling system for power plant design. The key idea is to store a high-level PMS design specification in the form of an extended entity relationship model in a data dictionary. Most of the source code for the PMS implementation is then generated automatically, using SQL-based code generators which are easy to develop. Our PMS-development system generates product model database schemas and user interfaces. It also generates high-level database schema related interface modules in the native application development language of a CAD-system. Through these, a CAD application developer has a high-level access to the object structures in the product model database.

Using the described approach, we have developed a power plant PMS which has been in production at the turbine manufacturer ABB STAL and the power plant engineering company ABB Carbon for more than half a year now. The PMS database is based on the Sybase SQL Server. AutoCAD is used for design of power plant schematics. Form based user interfaces and report generators are implemented in UNIFACE and Microsoft Access.

The data dictionary design and SQL-based code generation technique seems to be generally applicable and has been used for generating source code implementations in C++, LISP, SQL, and various textual form description languages.

The architecture of our PMS-development system is described together with the data dictionary schema and examples of generated source code.

We estimate that this software engineering approach reduces systems development costs about 5 - 10 times.

1 Introduction

The complexity in high-tech industrial artifacts such as power plants, aircrafts etc., is continuously growing. The product development times must be reduced and the designs become better engineered and more cost-effective.

Typically for high-tech products is that they are hybrids of different technologies and contain several types of engineering models that describe different aspects of a product. A steam turbine plant design for instance contains models of the functional behavior of its internal systems. These are typically turbine systems, steam systems, lubrication oil systems, electrical systems, etc. The plant design also has geometrical models of its mechanical parts, the layout of components in the plant etc. All of these models contain objects that have functional and geometrical representations and are interrelated in a complex fashion.

By using object-oriented product models, it is possible to model an artifact and its complex interrelationships in a way that naturally reflects the engineering models of several kinds of engineers, i.e. turbine designers, electrical- and mechanical engineers etc. An object-oriented product design can be more integrated, and thus facilitate efficient communication for concurrent engineering.

A product modeling system (PMS) is an object-oriented computer integrated development environment for a specific class of products. PMSs have a strong potential for increasing engineering productivity and ease the management of complex high-tech designs. There are however three major obstacles that severely prevent the development of long-term successful PMS.

I   The complexity of the product itself.

II   The extensive amount of software engineering skills needed for design and implementation of a PMS.

III   Computer technology is under continuous development and a PMS implementation will   become obsolete within a few years.

To overcome these, we have taken an approach which is depicted in Fig. 1.

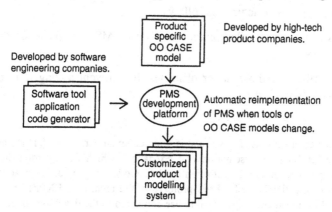

Fig. 1. Approach to overcome the three obstacles against PMS development.

The key idea to overcome the three obstacles is to separate the knowledge of product experts and software engineering experts with a clean and small interface. In our case, this is achieved by an object-oriented datamodel (OODM) which can be represented graphically by extended entity-relationship diagrams (EER-diagrams).

The core of a product specific object-oriented CASE model is the OODM. The OO CASE model serves as a PMS object system design specification which is expressed in a graphically representable formal language. Its semantic expressiveness is similar to the data definition constructs of the product data modeling language EXPRESS [EXPRESS88][STEP92a][1], but provides more flexible facilities for maintenance, documentation and code generation.

Our object-oriented data models have similarities with Chen's ER-diagrams [Chen76], but have their formal ground in the thorough theoretical work on infological models made by Sundgren [Sundgren73][Sundgren89][Sundgren92]. We use a compact graphical notation for our EER-diagrams, which is similar to the one used by Cattell for object-relational database schemas [Cattell 91]. (See Fig. **4**.)

EER-diagrams and reports generated from an object-oriented CASE tool can be understood by both product experts and software engineering experts and serves as communication medium between the two engineering disciplines.

Software engineering companies who develop tools such as databases, CAD-systems, user interface toolkits etc., can develop knowledge in how to transform an OO CASE model into a working implementation for their own specific software tools. Once the transformations have been formalized in a programming language, SE-companies can package and sell their software engineering knowledge in the form of application code generators.

If the design of the PMS development platform in Fig. **1** can be standardized, it would enable many software tool companies to implement applications code generators that would be applicable to many engineering companies' PMS, and thus open up a competitive and developing market.

The rest of the paper is structured as follows :

Section 2 gives a more detailed picture of what a PMS may be by describing our power plant PMS.

Section 3 describes the three major obstacles that prevent a long term successful PMS-investment in more detail.

---

[1] EXPRESS has an object-based flavor and is a fundamental part of the STEP standard ISO 10303, "Product Data Representation and Exchange" which has its roots in the early 1980's. The purpose of our object-oriented data models is primarily to accelerate the development of practically useful PMS-prototypes. We regard the EXPRESS-language as somewhat oldfashioned and impractical to use compared to the development environments we have available.

Section 4 shows the architecture of our PMS development system.

Section 5 introduces the easy and practical graphical notation of our EER-diagrams by describing a simple example of a PMS OODM. Such a model serves as a high-level design specification of a PMS and is stored in the data dictionary of the PMS-development system.

Section 6 shows an example of the kind of source code that can be generated automatically from the data dictionary. The source code example is generated from the OODM introduced in Section 5.

Section 7 describes our data dictionary as an EER-diagram, using the notation introduced in Section 5. The data dictionary schema is a step towards a core of a standardized PMS development platform.

Section 8 gives some facts and experiences we have gained from the development of a power plant PMS which now has been used in daily production by more than 10 engineers for more than half a year. The system is currently a very strong candidate for becoming a common platform for system design of industrial turbines in the size of 10-100 MW within ABB. One of the key reasons is its potential to continuously evolve and adapt to new demands.

Section 9 describe conclusions and future work.

2 Product Modeling System

Fig. 2 shows the structure of a product modeling system (PMS) for power plant design. The product model database manages object-oriented engineering structures which have a large and complex database schema. Different CAX[1]-applications need to manipulate and interact with these structures on an efficient abstraction level. Engineers must also be able to browse the product model database interactively, and create, update, and copy various complex product structures.

In the upper left corner of Fig. 2, we have a plant browser application. It allows a project manager to navigate and manipulate the major structures of plant models. He may for instance, create the structure of a new plant by creating and connecting the objects that constitute its major "part-of" structure. Some of the objects represent different systems in the plant, such as turbine system, lubrication system etc. Within the plant browser the project manager can assign *user access rights* to the substructures of, for instance a turbine system. In this way he can delegate the task and authority to develop the details of systems to different system engineers in his staff.

---

[1] CAX is a common name for CAD, CAE and CAM which stand for Computer Aided Design, Computer Aided Engineering and Computer Aided Manufacturing.

A turbine systems engineer, can use an AutoCAD application to draw diagrams which specify how different functional components in a turbine system are connected. These *Process and Instrumentation Diagrams* (P&ID) show how the steam is processed through different turbine components, and where instruments are placed that measure vibrations, temperature etc. There is an interactive interface between the P&ID CAD-application and the product model database. E.g. the systems engineer can select an instrument on the P&ID and bring up a form where specific data for that instrument can be entered into its corresponding database object.

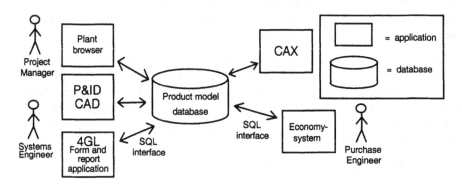

Fig. 2. Sample product modeling system for power plant design.

Client applications for data entry and report generation can be developed using modern 4GL-tools with an SQL-interface. Currently, we use Microsoft Access for user friendly data interaction and generation of reports.

There are however, other applications under consideration. This is symbolized by the right side CAX- and economy system application in Fig. 2. For a turbine that contains more than 20 000 details, the purchase process demands quite a lot of effort. Integrating logistics and purchase systems with the PMS can save large amounts of routine work, and can provide economic decision support to the engineers when choosing between different design alternatives. Today careful economic analysis of a design is often omitted because of the cost in time and effort to gather the needed economic data.

Integrated product modeling systems make it easier to reuse old designs and libraries of design components. Reusing designs has the same potential for speeding up development of mechanical artifacts as for VLSI-designs and object-oriented software.

An integrated PMS may allow a chief engineer to simulate within a few hours several hundred man-hours of engineering work by copying and assembling appropriate submodels within the PMS.

3 The Problem of Developing Large Scale Product Modeling Systems

When the potential benefits of product modeling systems are so high, why don't we see more of them in commercial use ? As indicated in the introduction, it is no easy task to develop a PMS which can be maintained as a versatile tool for a high-tech product engineering company. The following three sections give some details about why.

I) The complexity of the product itself.

Besides the different interrelated engineering models there are the scale and development time aspects. A typical steam turbine plant contains thousands of articles which are assembled and interconnected in a complex fashion. A project can take years to complete and may involve a hundred people who create and use different sorts of product related information.

Thus, the PMS must provide security functionality for authorization of access privileges for different user categories. It must also allow privilege assignments to individual users who shall work on a subset of several parallel product models that belong to concurrent development projects. E.g. a turbine systems engineer must be able to manipulate the turbine systems for the three turbine plants he has been assigned to, but not the other fifteen that are being developed in parallel and stored in the same database.

ISO 9000[1] puts demand on a secure system for quality control. Hence, the PMS must provide configuration and version management including locking of inspected and approved submodels to secure certified subdesigns from unauthorized changes.

II) The design and implementation of a PMS requires an extensive amount of software engineering skills.

The software engineering process of a PMS includes designing an adequate object-oriented data model for the product. This is a heavy and iterative process. Several engineering disciplines must work together and no single person has a complete understanding of all aspects of the product.

Without adequate CASE-tools the requirements- and design specifications become large and difficult to manage and understand. This is a threat, since the design documentation has to be iterated efficiently with knowledgeable product experts who are a scarce resource and do not have much time. If the project looses their interest and high quality influence it will severely affect the acceptance of the resulting PMS.

---

[1] ISO 9000 is a standard for quality assurance (QA). A product development company can be certified according to ISO 9000. To get the certification, the company has to provide proof that they manufacture their products according to procedures which guarantee an adequate QA. Part of the proof is given in the form of documentation of the QA-procedures, and these have to fullfill the requierements stated by the standard.

A PMS may need to integrate CAD, CAE, CAM and economic information systems. This requires software engineering skills in CAD, databases, user interfaces, different programming languages etc. Software engineers with this comprehensive amount of SE-knowledge are rarely available in enough quantity at the engineering company itself. Using consultants is expensive, and can make the company dependent and vulnerable.

III) The fast development of computer technology.

This is a problem which all developers of large scale software systems fight with today. New advances in software and hardware technology will in a few years render a developed system obsolete.

It is hard for an engineering company to decide which CASE-tools, database systems, UI-toolkits, etc. to purchase. An investment is expensive, and often ties the company to a certain set of software products for a long time. The software maintenance task quickly becomes a major problem. Leveraging a PMS to a new generation of computer technology may become an extremely expensive project. Especially if its design is stored in old-fashioned "closed" CASE-tools.

4 Architecture of a PMS Development System

Fig. 3 depicts the architecture of the PMS development system we are using for the power plant PMS. It can be divided into three parts. In the upper part there is OOCASE, our tool for interactive graphical design of object-oriented data models. In the center we have the data dictionary which is implemented on a relational database. The data dictionary can be read by source code generators written as SQL-scripts, which generate the parts of the database- and application source code that are specified by the data model. The bottom part is the generated PMS, which can be recognized from Fig. 2.

OOCASE is our interactive graphical CASE tool for development of object-oriented data models. It has its roots in an experimental system for testing the validity of a novel user interface software architecture, developed as a thesis project [Johansson91]. A special feature of OOCASE is that it allows several smaller EER-diagrams to depict related subsets of a larger object-oriented data model. In this way, a system designer can concentrate on a smaller diagram which only shows the subset of entities, attributes and relationships, that are interesting for a certain aspect of the data model. There is less need for the traditional "spaghetti" diagrams which "take up a wall" to get a grasp of the whole model. Printed out, our PMS data model consists of 18 EER-diagrams, defining different functional areas of the power plant product model.

From OOCASE, data models can be exported in a record format or as a batch file of SQL-insert statements. Currently, we use the relational database Sybase for implementing the data dictionary. Entities, relationships, attributes and other OO-data modeling object types have their corresponding relational tables. The SQL-

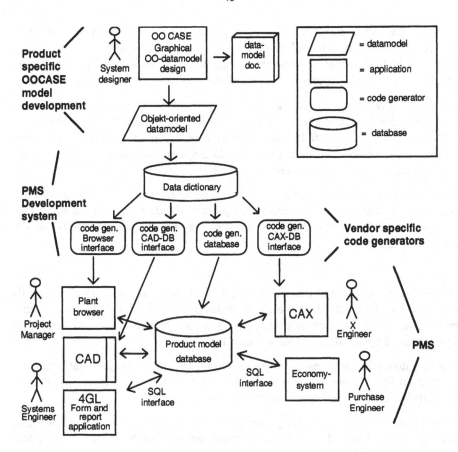

Fig. 3. Architecture of our PMS development system.

batch inserts tuples representing data modeling objects into these tables. A system designer can interact with the data dictionary directly using SQL, or indirectly through a 4GL-tool such as Microsoft Access.

Before code generation can be applied, the data model needs to be supplemented with implementation data that is dependent on the programming language of the target tools. Standard data types for instance, have different keywords in different target languages. The keywords are stored in the data dictionary, and have to be associated with attributes in the data model. We have a set of stored procedures that add this extra implementation information.

The code generators are SQL-scripts written in Sybase Transact-SQL[Sybase90a][Sybase91a]. They consist of **select** statements that combine literal source code text strings with data from the data dictionary and produces a set of string tuples that make up the generated lines of source code.

A code generation script can be seen as a source code template, which is instanciated with data from the data dictionary. When generating source code for a relational PMS database implementation the templates typically define different standard types of triggers and stored procedures.

For each entity in the data model P stored procedures are generated. These are typically procedures that create, update, or delete an instance of an entity in the PMS database. See Fig. **6** for an example. Stored procedures are pre-compiled within the DBMS and can be called from a CAD-system by a remote procedure call. Such communications give fast response times.

For a complex data model with E entities, the amount of generated procedures becomes P*E. Data which is stored in one place in the data dictionary is duplicated to a large number of places in the generated source code. Duplication factors of 100 are not unusual.

During the development of the data model, an attribute of an entity which is heavily inherited may be changed. If the PMS implementation is coded manually such a minor change may need manual changes on several hundred lines of source code spread around many different source code files.

Tracking down the locations and make the changes may take a significant number of hours even for a programmer who is familiar with the code. Some places will probably be forgotten and appear as bugs later on.

If the PMS is implemented using source code generators, the manual change and debugging work is saved. A complete re-implementation of the of the whole system may be done in a few hours. For our power plant PMS more than 40 000 lines of source code are generated and it takes some time to recompile and reload it, even if most of the work is done automatically.

The main advantage which really speeds up the PMS development process, is that the software engineer who performs the re-implementations does not have to refresh his/her understanding of the vast amount of details in the source code.

5 A PMS Object-Oriented Data Model Example

Object-oriented data models serve as a medium for communication between product experts and software engineers. Fig. **4** shows the EER-diagram of a small PMS data model, containing 5 entities, 4 relationships and 18 attributes. The example is used to introduce our graphical EER notation. It also gives the reader an idea of what is stored in the data dictionary (further described in section 7).

The data model describes a toy PMS database for a small company with several *Departments*. A *Department*-entity has the two attributes *department_id* and *department_name*.

Each department can be responsible for many products. Thus the entity *Department* has the one-to-many relationship *department_products* to the entity *Product*. As shown in the diagram a one-to-many relationship is represented by a fork with three sticks in the entity on the many side.

A product is described by an hierarchical structure of articles which has its root in a main article. This is represented by giving *Product* a one-to-one relationship *product_mainArticle* to *Article*. *Article* has a one-to-many relationship *mainArticle_subArticles* to itself, and thus an *Article* can own a hierarchical structure of sub articles.

On the right, we can see that a *Drawing* may be related to many *Articles* in the article structures of the products.

For the management of a PMS database we need some common database attributes on each product model object. These are gathered in the entity *DatabaseObject*, which is inherited by all other entities in the data model. More about *DatabaseObject's* attributes later.

Inheritance is represented by the name of the inherited entity in parentheses in the box right between the name of the entity and its attributes. Representing inheritance by a name-reference is easy to explain to non-software engineering people. Just say that *(DatabaseObject)* represents a copy of all attributes in *DatabaseObject*.

The representation also makes the diagrams look less messy than drawing lines with special inheritance symbols which inexperienced people easily confuse with ordinary relationships.

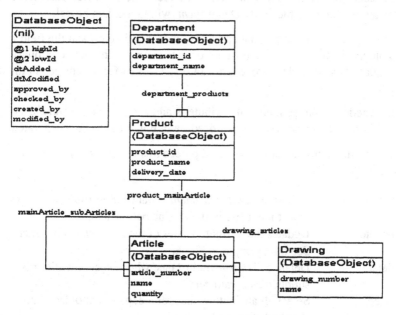

Fig. 4. Simple PMS data model example to describe the graphical syntax of our EER-diagrams.

Each object in the PMS-database needs a unique object identifier. Since we use a relational database for implementing PMS-databases, we have chosen 64-bit object identifiers divided into two 32-bit standard long integers in the key attributes *highId* and *lowId* of *DatabaseObject*. To ensure object identifier uniqueness amongst product models developed in parallel PMS's, each PMS-database gets a unique *highId*. *lowId*'s are generated from a counter that is ensured to always be larger that a certain value calculated from the current time. In practice this works as a good insurance that the same object identifiers will not be generated again, even after a server crash and later incomplete recovery or an accidental change of the counter. If one object identifier is generated every second, a 32-bit counter will last for 68 years.

The attributes *dtAdded* and *dtModified* are time stamp attributes which store the date and time when the object was first added to the database, and when it was last modified. These attributes are managed automatically by triggers in the generated PMS database implementation.

The attributes *approved_by, checked_by, created_by* and *modified_by* store a login-identifier for the user performing the corresponding task. Using triggers in a relational database, the modification of an object can be inhibited if it has already been checked or approved.

6 Code Generation Example

Fig. **6** shows an example of an automatically generated stored procedure written in Sybase's Transact-SQL. The procedure updates a row in the table *de_department* where instances of the entity *Department* are stored. "*de*" is a two character *prefix* which uniquely identifies the entity *Department* within the data model.

During code generation, the parameter names (@de_highid etc.) and the field names of the table are fetched from the attribute objects stored in the data dictionary. The same template type of update procedure can be generated for all entities in the data dictionary.

If the data model is changed, e.g. an attribute is added to the entity *DatabaseObject* which is inherited by *Department*, the procedure in Fig. **6** has to be regenerated.

Examples of other automatically generated procedures for the entity *Department* are given in Fig. **5**.

de_insert	Creates a new *Department* instance. Return its new unique object identifier in the l-value parameters.
de_update	Updates the attribute values of the *Department* instance. See the example in Fig. **6**.
de_delete	Delete a *Department* instance who's object identifier is supplied as parameters.
de_select	Select all attribute values for a department object with the supplied object identifier.

Fig. 5. Automatically generated stored procedures for the entity Department.

```
create proc de_update
                @de_highid obid ,
                @de_lowid obid ,
                @de_dtadded datetime null,
                @de_dtmodified datetime null,
                @de_approved_by char(5) null,
                @de_checked_by char(5) null,
                @de_created_by char(5) null,
                @de_modified_by char(5) null,
                @de_department_id char(8) ,
                @de_department_name char(20) null
as
                declare @result int
                begin transaction de_update
                update de_department
                set     /* key de_highid is not updated */
                        /* key de_lowid is not updated */
                        de_dtadded=@de_dtadded,
                        de_dtmodified=@de_dtmodified,
                        de_approved_by =@ de_approved_by,
                        de_checked_by =@ de_checked_by,
                        de_created_by =@ de_created_by,
                        de_modified_by =@ de_modified_by,
                        de_department_id =@ de_department_id,
                        de_department_name =@ de_department_name
                where   de_highid =@ de_highid
                  and   de_lowid =@ de_lowid
                execute @result = check_error_and_rowcount1 @@error,
                        @@rowcount, "de_update"
                if @result=0
                        commit transaction de_update
                else
                        rollback transaction de_update
                return @result
go
```

Fig. 6. Example of an automatically generated stored procedure.[1]

---

[1] In Sybase Transact-SQL, all parameters and local variables are preceded by '@'. 'obid' is a user defined type equal to a 32-bit integer. @@error and @@rowcount are Sybase system variables holding a possible error number and the number of rows that were affected in the last operation.

Procedures that manipulate relationships are bound to a particular entity. Examples of procedures that can be generated automatically for the 1-N relationship *department_products* in Fig. 4 are given below.

de_relAllProducts	Select all attribute values for *Product* objects that belong to the department who's object identifier is supplied as parameters to the procedure.
de_relCreateProducts	Create a new product object and connect it to the department object whose object identifier is supplied as parameters.
de_relDeleteProducts	Delete a product object which belongs to a particular department object.

The procedures are loaded into the PMS database server, and can be called from a client application, for instance when a user selects a command from a menu in the user interface of a generated browser application.

The technique of concatenating literal strings with data dictionary data in declarative SQL-scripts seems to be generally applicable for source code generation of all types of textual programming languages. We have used it for generating code in SQL, C++, LISP and textual user interface definition languages.

7 The Data Dictionary Data Model

In the same way as a PMS-database is an engineering database described by a *PMS data model*, the data dictionary is a software engineering database, described by a *data dictionary data model*. As a matter of fact, the data model for the data dictionary is actually stored in the data dictionary itself, and has been used for generation of stored procedures and data dictionary browsers.

Appendix A shows an EER-diagram for the data dictionary. It is helpful to keep a bookmark at that page for quick reference while we explain the some of the important characteristics of the different data dictionary objects.

The reader might wonder why the entities in appendix A are prefixed with "AX", and here is the explanation; When generating an implementation of a data model for an object-oriented language such as Smalltalk, C++ etc., it is useful to map each entity in the data model into two classes. One superclass, prefixed with "AX" which is generated automatically, and one immediate subclass of the AX class, prefixed with "X" where manually written code is added. In most OO-languages, the source code for each class has its own source code files. The two-class-implementation allows automatically generated code and user written code to be separated. When the data model is changed, e.g. when an attribute is added to an entity, only the AX source file is regenerated, and the manually written code is left intact.

The manually written X-class can easily access the member variables and the functions for relationship management, using automatically generated virtual accessor functions in the AX class.

AXDBObject

All data dictionary objects inherit from AXDBObject. It manages unique key attributes for object identifiers (*highId, lowId*) and time stamping attributes (*dtAdded,dtModified*). After each modification, the current users login-identifier is recorded in the *owner*-attribute.

AXObject

AXObject inherits AXDBObject via XDBObject. Data dictionary objects which are created by the user, inherit from XObject. Most data dictionary objects, such as AXEntity, AXAttribute etc. need a *name* and a short descriptive textual *definition*. When working with an international company such as ABB, the PMS data models have to be coordinated between different sites in different countries. Therefore it is useful to have an alternative name and an auxiliary name that can document names in other languages. In our case, we have used *name* for English names, *altName* for the Swedish names, and *auxName* for German names.

In our implementation, the English names can have about 30 characters and are used for code generation. Sometimes, however, older target languages don't allow such long identifier names, and then a *shortName* can be used instead.

AXDataDictionary

There is only one instance of XDataDictionary in the data dictionary database. This instance is used for holding "global" data dictionary variables, and represent a "root" object, from which the user can navigate down to other data model objects in an automatically generated browser.

AXDataModel

For each PMS-implementation, there is a corresponding data model. Instances of XDataModel represent the "root"-object of such a data model. The attribute *target_directory* contains a path to the directory where generated code for the PMS-implementation should be placed.

AXEntity

Instances of AXEntity hold entity related information. When generating code for a relational DBMS, the inheritance hierarchy is flattened, so that leaf-entities get all their attributes stored in the same table. It is only interesting to generate tables for leaf entities. To distinguish them from inherited ones such as *DatabaseObject* in Fig. **4**, leaf entities have their *genSqlFlag* set to TRUE.

The *prefix* holds a two to four characters prefix that uniquely identifies the entity within a data model. This is useful since many named code objects in generated code are related to a specific entity. Examples of named code objects are table related stored procedures, triggers, or user interface forms for editing entity instances. As presented in Fig. 5, stored procedure names such as de_create, de_update, de_delete etc., are generated for the entity *Department*.

If the name of a generated table for some reason cannot be the same as the English *name* for the entity, the system designer can override it by entering something in *tableName*.

AXRelation

A relationship is connected to two entities, called entity1 and entity2. For a one-to-many relationship, entity1 is on the one-side, and entity2 on the many-side. The relationship type, e.g. 1-1, 1-N or M-N is stored in *type*. AXRelation also has implementation descriptive attributes, such as *cascadeDelete2*. This flag tell the code generators that if an entity on the entity1-side of the relationship is deleted, then all related entities on the entity2-side should be deleted.

AXAttribute

An entity owns a set of attributes via the relationship *entity_attributes*. In the data dictionary it is possible to specify a *defaultValue* for an attribute and define if the value is *mandatory* i.e. NULL-values are not allowed etc.

AXProperty

While developing several larger data models within the same product domain, one discovers that there are attributes which appear over and over again. In the domain of turbine design, the attribute *article_number* is a good example of this. In such cases, it is useful to store a common definition for that "attribute type" as a standard *Property* in the data dictionary. This allows several attributes to share the definition of data type, default value etc. If a company implements several PMS databases from the same data dictionary, they can easily combine data from the different databases, by joining over standard attributes.

When several data models have been developed, a property library emerges. While developing new data models, company standard attribute names and definitions can be picked from the property library and thus enforce reuse of definitions. This gives an opportunity to gain control over diverging semantics for company information resources.

AXTypeDef

All variable and attribute implementations are based on some data type. A PMS may be implemented using several different programming languages which need to share data and thus type definitions. A *TypeDef* stores a standard type definition and has a set of *Declarations* for various programming languages. A signed 32-bit integer is declared as a `long` in C and C++, while the name of the same data type is `int` in Sybase' SQL. When generating code, especially for interface libraries between CAD-systems and databases, this kind of data type mapping information is necessary.

In our data dictionary, we have a set of standard data types defined, based on the ones available in OMG's Interface Definition Language (IDL) which is specified in [CORBA91].

AXDomain

A *Domain* defines a value domain. An example of a *Domain* is *week_number*. A week_number can have the *TypeDef* "Integer", and a range of values between 1 and 53, i.e. *minValue* = 1 and *maxValue* = 53. A PMS data model may have entities for project planning. An article entity may have a engineering project planning entity that contains the attributes *start_week* and an *end_week*. There may also be planning entity for the articles manufacturing process, which have the same week attributes.

Now it is possible to define the two properties *start_week* and *end_week* which both belong to the *Domain week_number*.

Through the relationship *property_attributes* the attributes of the articles entity's planning entities are connected to their corresponding properties *start_week* and *end_week*.

Later during the data model development, one may discover that the planned design period for certain large scale articles may last for more than a year. Hence the domain *week_number* also must include the number of the Year. All affected attributes in the data dictionary can be traced through the relationships *domain_properties* and *property_attributes*.

By changing the definitions in the domain, the change can be automatically propagated through the properties to attributes in all data models. Using the code generators, the PMSs can be reimplemented with the new data type.

This section gave a short description of some of the entities and relationships in the data model of our data dictionary. The complete data model consists of 23 entities, 29 relationships and 140 attributes. Most of the entities which are not described here are only used for storing abstract intermediate implementation models which aid the code generation.

8 Experience from the Power Plant PMS

The power plant PMS is developed iteratively using prototypes. Engineering experts in power plant design participate in the continuous development of the PMS data model. When a new version of the model is confirmed, a prototype is implemented in between a day and a couple of weeks, depending on how much code that has to be written manually.

Plant designers and other users work with the new prototype, get new ideas and give their suggestions on what should be included in the next prototype version. The suggestions are compiled, remitted and ordered according to priority to become the input specification for the next version of the PMS data model.

In our latest version of the turbine power plant PMS, the object-oriented data model contained about 70 entities, 40 relationships and 380 attributes. When the model was printed on paper in the form of EER-diagrams and reports, it produced about 170 A4 pages. The generated Sybase implementation of the PMS database builds 50 tables which contain about 1800 fields.

We have one AutoCAD-application for browsing the database on the plant level and drawing process and instrumentation diagrams over the power plant systems. Its drawing environment is based on a commercial product and has been extended with special drawing functionality by an AutoCAD application development company. This is a recommendable way to save researchers from spending most of their time doing painful, but necessary quality- and usability improving implementation work. Without a commercial status of the PMS, it is hard to keep up the interest from busy product engineers.

A few of our leading product engineers develop their own report- and search form applications in Microsoft Access with some support from the computer department of ABB STAL.

The computer department have also developed a form based browser application which has about 50 forms. There are many different types of workstations at our ABB-partners, so this implementation is done in the multiple platform 4GL-development environment UNIFACE. Since we currently have no code generators for UNIFACE, this application is comparatively expensive to maintain.

The software developed at Linköping University consists of about 60 000 lines of code, of which more than 60% is generated automatically from the data dictionary. It is developed on a Sun Sparc IPX with 1,5 GB of disk.

The power plant PMS has been in production for system development of power plants at ABB Carbon AB, and a new generation of gas turbines at ABB STAL since the fall of 93. Currently it has about 10 regular users. The hardware is a mixture of platforms, including IBM RS 6000, Sun Sparc and PC's.

9 Conclusions and future work

There is a large potential benefit in using object-oriented product models for engineering of high-tech mechanical artifacts. There are however three major obstacles that prevent development of successful product modeling systems (PMS).

I)   The design of the product models quickly becomes very complex.

II)   The implementation of a PMS requires extensive software engineering skills, and

III) Computer technology is under continuous development and a PMS implementation will become obsolete within a few years.

Our solution to overcome these problems is to use object-oriented CASE models which enable a clean separation of the domains of product specific engineering knowledge from software engineering implementation knowledge. The models are stored in a data dictionary from which source code implementations can be generated automatically. Following this approach means that :

I) The product specific engineering knowledge is documented as an object-oriented CASE-model which is stored in a data dictionary according to standard format. Object-oriented CASE-tools facilitate development and maintenance of large object-oriented data models for PMSs.

II) Different software vendors can package their software engineering knowledge for a particular software platform into code generators which transform standard format object-oriented CASE-models into working implementations on their specific software platforms. Typical targets for such implementations are databases, user interfaces, and interface libraries between CAD-systems and databases.

III) New generations of computer technology can be put into production when code generators for the new target technology has been developed. In the future we see SQL3-databases, a wide range of parametric CAD-software packages, and 3D-user interfaces where object-oriented product models can be developed in virtual 3D worlds.

The approach is successfully used for development of a power plant PMS. We expect this system to become easy to port to new generations of computer technology.

Future work will be to refine the data dictionary design to also include other modeling aspects such as data flow- and state transition models to increase the functionality space of the generated PMS-implementations. The data dictionary design for storing PMS-information models should be high-level and independent of any particular database-, CAD-system or user interface implementation. Thus, when new computer technology becomes commercially available, new code generators can be developed and used for generation of implementations of any kind of company specific PMS that has an established OO CASE model.

One of our first steps will be to work on a PMS development system implementation in AMOS [FahlRischSköld91]. This will allow us to, amongst other things, gain the power of AMOS declarative object-oriented query language for code generation.

Acknowledgments

This research project has been funded by the 4´th National Swedish program for Information Technology (IT4), ABB STAL AB, ABB Carbon AB and Association of Swedish Engineering Industries.

References

[Cattell91] Cattell, R.G.G., "Object data management : object-oriented and extended relational database systems", *Addison Wesley*, ISBN 0-201-53092-9

[Chen76] P.P.S. Chen, "The entity-relationship model: Towards a unified view of data", *ACM Transactions on Systems*, March 1976, pp 9-36

[CORBA91] Object Management Group, "The Common Object Request Broker: Architecture and Specification", *fax an order to OMG Publications +1-303-444 3850, cost ~$80*

[EXPRESS88] Information Modeling Language EXPRESS, ISO TC184/SC4/WG1 Report N268, August 1988, 112 pages

[FahlRischSköld91] G. Fahl, T.Risch, M. Sköld "AMOS - An Architecture for Active Mediators", *Proceedings of International Workshop on Next Generation Information Technologies and Systems*, June 28-30, Haifa, Israel, 1993

[Johansson91] O. Johansson, "Improving Implementation of Graphical User Interfaces for Object-Oriented Knowledge-Bases", Linköping Studies in Science and Technology, ISBN 91-7870-792-7, ISSN 0280-7971, 1991

[Sundgren73] B. Sundgren, "An Infological Approach to Data Bases", National Central Bureau of Statistics, Sweden, and University of Stockholm, Dept. of Administrative Information Processing, *Beckmans Tryckerier AB*, Stockholm 1973

[Sundgren89] B. Sundgren, "Conceptual Modeling for Statistical Databases", Central Bureau of Statistics, Sweden, 1989, ISSN 0283-8680

[Sundgren92] B. Sundgren, "Databasorienterad Systemutveckling", *Studentlitteratur*, ISBN 91-44-35991-8 (in Swedish)

[STEP92] "International Standard ISO 10303 - Industrial automation systems and integration - Product data representation and exchange."

[STEP92a] "International Standard ISO 10303 - Industrial automation systems - Product data representation and exchange. Part 11: Description methods: The EXPRESS language reference manual"

[Sybase90a] "Transact-SQL User's Guide", Release 4.2, *Sybase Inc*, 1990

[Sybase91a] "Commands Reference Manual", Release 4.2, *Sybase Inc*, 1991

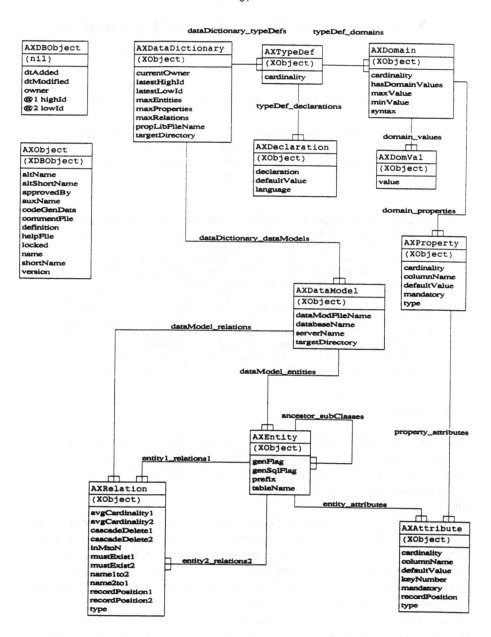

Appendix A. EER-diagram for the data dictionary.

A Notation for Describing Aggregate Relationships in an Object-Oriented Data Model[*]

Bryon K. Ehlmann[1] and Gregory A. Riccardi[2]

[1]CIS Department, Florida A&M University, Tallahassee FL 32307, USA,
ehlmann@cs.fsu.edu
[2]Computer Science, Florida State University, Tallahassee, FL 32306 USA,
riccardi@cs.fsu.edu

Abstract. The emphasis in object-oriented databases (OODBs) is on the inheritance, or "is a," type of relationship; yet, many relationships within databases are of the aggregate type—e.g., "is a part of" and "is associated with." While the semantics of the inheritance relationship is directly supported by OODB systems, the semantics of aggregate relationships must often be implemented again and again by application programmers.

To address this problem, this paper proposes a notation for describing the semantics of a taxonomy of aggregate relationship types. The notation can be incorporated into an Object-Relationship Diagram (ORD) and an Object-oriented Database Definition Language (ODDL) to provide enhanced conceptual models for OODB design and improved support of aggregate relationships by an extended OODB system. Such support can significantly ease database applications development and improve the integrity of database operation.

1 Introduction

Object-oriented database (OODB) systems combine object-oriented concepts with traditional database management system (DBMS) capabilities. Object-oriented concepts are generally defined to include object identity, abstract data types or classes, and inheritance [14]. A number of papers provide excellent surveys of OODB systems [2, 15, 28].

As part of the concept of inheritance, OODB systems provide for the specification and support of the "is a" type of relationship. Support means that the semantic integrity of the relationship is maintained by the database system. Often missing, however, from OODB systems is the specification and support of other types of relationships—e.g., the "is a part of," "is owned by", and "is (or may be) associated with" relationships between objects. These types of *non-inheritance relationships* characterize the vast majority of relationships in most databases. The lack of direct OODB system support for them places the burden on applications programmers. The code necessary to maintain their semantic integrity is complex and must be invented (or at least customized) over and over again by these programmers.

This paper specifically focuses on these types of relationships and shows how they can be better supported by OODB systems. More precisely, the types of rela-

---

* This research was partially supported by the National Science Foundation under grant CDA-9313299 and the U.S. Dept. of Energy under contract DE-FG05-92ER40735.

tionships to be addressed form the aggregation hierarchy [2] or the composition hierarchy [15] in OODBs. Their actual number and variety are quite amazing with just subtle semantic differences often distinguishing one from another. They are structurally represented at the conceptual level in OODBs by the aggregation of an object's attributes, specifically those whose values are themselves objects. These relationships are hereafter referred to as *aggregate relationships*. The paper proposes a notation for describing a taxonomy of aggregate relationship types.

The notation has some distinctive features. First, with relatively simple syntax and carefully chosen semantics, it captures the desired behavior of many common aggregate relationship types—more than just the "is a part of" type often found in non-traditional database applications and supported in some existing OODB systems. The notation can be used in an Object-Relationship Diagram (ORD) to identify and document relationship types during initial database requirements analysis and design. It can be used in an Object-oriented Database Definition Language (ODDL) to precisely specify relationship and inverse relationship semantics to an extended OODB system. Notation semantics provide for the implicit propagation of operations necessary to maintain and manipulate complex objects and for the enforcement of cardinality constraints, which are more precise than the "one" (meaning zero or one) and "many" (meaning zero, one, or more) that are common in existing OODB systems. The notation focuses on an important subset of the constraints and triggers specifiable in a more generalized, rule-based, integrity constraint mechanism, e.g., [7, 25], allowing this subset to be more easily specified and more efficiently implemented.

The ultimate benefit of the notation will be to significantly ease OODB development and enhance data integrity. For example, the notation when supported by an OODB system makes possible a simple, high-level database operation to delete a complex object. This operation automatically ensures that all objects that are "part of" the deleted object are also deleted and that all objects merely "associated with" the deleted object are no longer associated as such. Also, it ensures that objects that only exist in the database to describe other objects are automatically deleted when they are no longer being used for this purpose. Making such an operation the responsibility of the database system improves the integrity of the database and dramatically decreases the cost of applications code development and maintenance.

The remainder of the paper is organized as follows: Section 2 briefly discusses related research in semantic models and OODBs; Section 3 defines the relationship notation and its semantics; Section 4 illustrates how the notation can be used to specify a variety of aggregate relationships in the context of an ORD; Section 5 illustrates how the notation and relationships defined in an ORD map into an ODDL and into an OODB; and Section 6 concludes with some final remarks.

2 Related Work

This paper is relevant to certain OODB areas still requiring research even though many OODB systems have become commercially available in recent years. These areas are defining and perhaps standardizing the object-oriented data model; incorporating more data semantics into the model; and developing OODB design methodologies and tools [15].

The ideas presented relate to prior research on semantic data models [5, 6, 8, 11, 13, 24, 26]. The most modest objective of this research has been to provide improved models for database design. A more daring objective has been to incorporate more knowledge of relationship semantics into the database so that the semantics can be enforced by the database system rather than by the application.

Efforts have been made by others to extend object-oriented models to include additional semantic modeling concepts. Support for inverse relationships of the type one-to-one, one-to-many, and many-to-many is included in many OODB systems—e.g., IRIS [12], Object Store [18], Objectivity/DB [19], and Ontos [20]—as well as the recently proposed ODMG-93 Object Database Standard [4]. Also, as previously mentioned, a number of OODB systems support composite objects, i.e., the "is a part of" relationship [16, 18, 19, 23].

The notation proposed here for describing relationship semantics can be compared to other proposed schemes for defining similar semantics in the relational model [7, 17] and in proposed object-oriented data models that include relations [1, 22]. First, unlike these schemes, the proposed notation assumes a basic object-oriented data model where most relationships are represented *conceptually* as object attributes that may reference other objects. The notation provides OODBs with the equivalent of the declarative referential integrity rules that were first proposed in [7] for relational databases and then reduced in [17] for relational databases derived using an extended entity-relationship model. The notation also provides the equivalent of the null constraint on foreign keys. Like Rumbaugh [22], the authors of [1] argue for including a relation construct in the object-oriented model to better represent relationships—an issue likely to generate more debate. Assuming this construct, they propose declarative referential, surjectivity, dependency, cardinality, and constancy constraints to describe aggregate relationships. Again, the equivalent of these constraints is provided by the notation proposed here, though the packaging is radically different. The notation makes expedient use of more precise cardinality constraints in an attempt to minimize constraint inconsistencies, syntax, and the number and complexity of concepts that a user must confront. Unlike [1], it also allows shared class dependency via multiple prime classes, which provides automatic deletion of objects when they are no longer referenced.

3 Relationship Notation and Semantics

The notation given in this section defines a taxonomy of common types of aggregate relationships that exist between objects in some domain of interest, e.g., a database. The objects are assumed to be categorized based on common attributes and behavior into object *classes*. A class thus defines a set of objects of a particular type.

All relationships between objects are viewed as binary relationships. Relationships involving three or more objects or relationships having distinct attributes or behavior are considered objects having binary relationships with the objects they relate. Relationships are described in terms of a *subject class* and a *relative class*, and instances of these relationships exist between subject class objects and relative class objects. When such an instance exists, a *subject object* is related to a *relative object* and visa versa. The existence of a relationship instance is contingent on the existence of both objects in the database.

All relationships are bi-directional. Each relationship has an inverse where the relative class is viewed as the subject class and subject class as the relative class. For example, the classic relationship between a department and its employees where department is the subject class can also be viewed as a relationship between an employee and a department where employee is the subject class. The amount of internal database support given to a relationship direction, that is, indexes or structures that provide efficient access to related objects, varies considerably and is an implementation issue, not a conceptual issue.

Relationship types are defined at two levels. A `cardinality-relationship` defines a relationship type solely by subject and relative class *cardinalities*. A `relationship` extends this definition by indicating the level of *binding* between related objects, i.e., the destructibility of relationship instances and the implicit deletability of objects based on the relationship.

3.1 Cardinality Relationship

The notation for a `cardinality-relationship` is given by the syntax diagrams in Fig. 1. The `cardinality` before the `-to-` describes the cardinality for the subject class; the one after the `-to-` describes the cardinality for the relative class. The relative class cardinality is the number of objects of the relative class that can relate to a single object of the subject class. Likewise, the subject class cardinality is the number of objects of the subject class that can relate to a single object of the relative class. The / denotes "or" and the M denotes "Many", which is taken to mean one or more. The 0/, 1, and M notation is adequate to describe the cardinalities of most relationships.

As an example, the relationship between departments and employees could be described as `1-to-0/M`. Each department, the subject class object, relates to zero, one, or more employees. Each employee, the relative class object, relates to exactly one department.

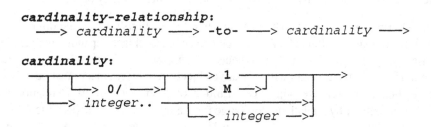

Fig. 1. *Cardinality-relationship* Syntax Diagrams

Though seldom required for conceptual design, the `integer..` and `integer..integer` notation can be used to describe cardinalities in greater detail. For example, `2..` means two or more, and `2..10` means two through ten. Each `integer` must be non-negative, and the second must not be less than the first. `0..` is equivalent to `0/M`, `0..1` is equivalent to `0/1`, `1..` is equivalent to M, and `x..` where x is greater than 1 and `x..y` where x is 1 or greater are special cases of M. For the most part, the level of detail afforded by the `..` notation is not germane to the discussion of relationships in the remainder of this paper.

An *intra-class relationship* occurs when the subject and relative class are the same class. An intra-class relationship cannot be `0/1-to-1`, `0/1-to-M`, or `1-to-M`. These are mathematically impossible, as shown in [10], though they can occur between subclasses of a class, which are discussed in Section 4.

The semantics prescribed for a relationship type, hereafter referred to as *relationship semantics*, place constraints on the state of the database and specify that certain database operations perform checks and have desirable side effects in order to maintain these constraints. Affected operations are:

- add a class object,
- delete a class object,
- create a relationship between two class objects,
- destroy a relationship between two class objects, and
- change a relationship for a class object so it relates to a different class object.

These operations are at a higher level than similar object-level operations that are typical in existing OODB systems. They are assumed to be publicly available in some form for a class or are used privately to build even higher-level class behavior. All constraints imposed by relationship semantics must be satisfied at the time a database transaction commits.

Relationship semantics as defined by a `cardinality-relationship` are derived from the semantics of the cardinalities for the subject class and the relative class. For example, the semantics of a `1-to-0/M` relationship type are the semantics of a `-to-0/M` specification plus the semantics of a `1-to-` specification. *Cardinality semantics* are given below in terms of a relationship R having the given cardinality for the relative class. The semantics in terms of an inverse relationship having the cardinality for the subject class are obtained by substituting the terms "relative" for "subject" and "subject" for "relative" wherever they occur below.

`-to-1` (inverse `1-to-`). The generic name for relationship R in the direction of the relative class is "defined by a." Each subject class object depends on a relative class object for its definition and existence. A subject object cannot be added without having an R relationship with a relative object. A subject object must be deleted if deletion of its relative object is permitted or destruction of its R relationship (either directly or by a relationship change for the relative object) is permitted.

For example, a `0/M-to-1` relationship between employees and departments means that each employee must have, i.e., is defined by, a department. Deletion of an employee's department or destruction of its relationship with a department if permitted would require deletion of the employee.

-to-M (inverse M-to-). The generic name for relationship R in the direction of the relative class is "defined by one or more." Each subject class object depends on one or more relative class objects for its definition and existence. A subject object cannot be added without having an R relationship with at least one relative object. A subject object must be deleted if deletion of its only relative object or destruction of its only R relationship is permitted.

-to-0/1 (inverse 0/1-to-). The generic name for relationship R in the direction of the relative class is "may be described by a." A subject class object does not depend on a relative class object for its definition and existence. Instead, a relative object serves only to further describe the subject object. Deletion of a subject object is never required by the cardinality of its relative class.

-to-0/M (inverse 0/M-to-). The generic name for relationship R in the direction of the relative class is "may be described by one or more." A subject class object does not depend on a relative class object for its definition and existence. Instead, relative objects serve only to further describe the subject object. Deletion of a subject object is never required by the cardinality of its relative class.

For specifications -to-M, -to-0/1, and -to-0/M, an R relationship that a subject object has with a relative object must be implicitly destroyed if deletion of the relative object is permitted and this deletion does not require the deletion of the subject object (as is possible in -to-M).

The four possible cardinalities—1, M, 0/1, and 0/M—for the two classes in a relationship result in ten distinct and basic relationship types. Six of the sixteen possible combinations are indistinct since relationships are bi-directional. Relationship semantics are more finely tuned and more relationship types result when a *cardinality-relationship* is extended to a *relationship*.

3.2 Relationship

A *relationship*, given in Fig. 2, provides a second, more detailed level of relationship type definition by indicating the level of subject and relative class *binding*. Bindings define the implicit and explicit destructibility of relationships and whether relationship destruction can result in the implicit deletion of related objects. All existing relationships involving an object must be implicitly destroyed before an object can be deleted. Implicit deletions resulting from object deletion and relationship destruction enforce cardinalities and can define the extent of a *composite object*. This in turn can define the meanings of other composite object operations—e.g., copy and print. A composite print on an object x would print x as well as all objects whose deletion would be attempted as a result of the deletion of x.

The *binding* before the < in a *relationship* indicates the binding for the subject class; the one after the > indicates the binding for the relative class.

relationship:
　—> *binding* < *cardinality-relationship* > *binding* —>

binding:

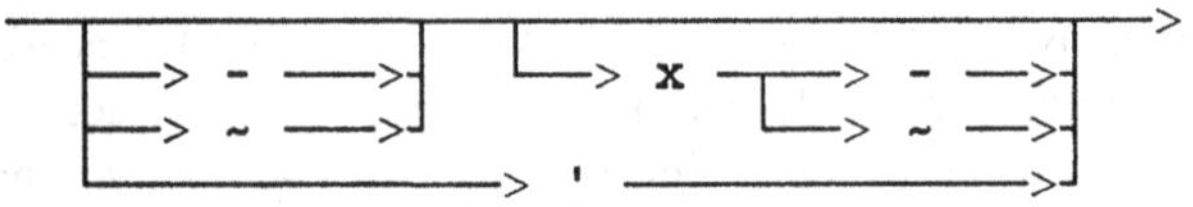

Fig. 2. *Relationship* Syntax Diagrams

Relationship semantics as defined by a *relationship* are derived from cardinality semantics and the semantics of the specified bindings.

Default Binding. The default binding for a class *C* in a relationship *R* denotes that existing *R* relationships are both implicitly destructible on deletion of a *C* object and explicitly destructible, provided this destruction does not violate the cardinality for *C* in *R*. That is, when a *C* object is deleted, implicitly or explicitly, each *R* relationship it has with another object is implicitly destroyed if the cardinality for *C* in *R* is not violated. If it is violated, the delete is disallowed. Also, an explicit destruction of a *R* relationship (either directly or via a relationship change) is allowed if and only if the cardinality for *C* in *R* is not violated. For example, the default binding for the employee class in a <0/M-to-1> relationship between employees and departments denotes that the relationship between an employee and a department is implicitly destroyed when the employee is deleted. Such destruction never violates the 0/M cardinality for the employee class. The default binding for the department class in the relationship denotes that a department cannot be deleted if it has any employees since implicit relationship destruction would violate the 1 cardinality for the department class, i.e., an employee must have 1 department. Also, a relationship between an employee and a department cannot be explicitly destroyed as this would violate the 1 cardinality, though an employee's department may be changed.

Implicit Destructibility Bindings. The bindings - and ~ pertain to the implicit destructibility of relationships. The - (minus) binding for a class *C* in a relationship *R* denotes that existing *R* relationships are never implicitly destructible on deletion of a *C* object. That is, deletion of a *C* object fails when it has an *R* relationship with another object. For example, if the relationship between departments and employees was <0/1-to-0/M>-, then an employee could exist without being in a department; however, if in a department, the employee cannot be deleted. A - binding is superfluous for a 1 cardinality since implicit destruction of an existing *R* relationship always violates the cardinality and fails with the default binding.

The ~ (tilde) binding for a class *C* in a relationship *R* is only meaningful for cardinalities 1 and M and denotes that existing *R* relationships are always implicitly destructible on deletion of a *C* object. When implicit destruction violates the cardinality for *C* in *R*, the related object is implicitly deleted—i.e., deletion effectively propagates like a wave (~). If deletion of the related object fails (because of constraints involving this or another relationship), deletion of the *C* object fails. For example, if the relationship between departments and employees was <1-to-M>~, then deletion of the last employee in a department would cause the deletion of the department. If the relationship was ~<1-to-M>~, then deletion of a department would cause deletion of all employees in the department.

Explicit Destructibility Bindings. The bindings x- and x~ pertain to the explicit destructibility of relationships. The x- binding for a class C in a relationship R denotes that R relationships are not explicitly destructible, either directly or via a relationship change. For example, if the relationship between departments and employees was <0/1-to-0/M>x-, then a relationship instance between an employee and a department once created cannot be explicitly destroyed. It can, however, be implicitly destroyed if the employee is deleted. The x- binding need be given only once in a `relationship` and applies to both classes. It effectively binds objects "until death do ye part."

The x~ binding for a class C in a relationship R is only meaningful for cardinalities 1 and M and denotes that R relationships are always explicitly destructible. When explicit destruction violates the cardinality for C in R, the related object is implicitly deleted. If the deletion of the related object fails, the explicit destruction fails. For example, if the relationship between departments and employees was <0/1-to-M>x~, then explicit destruction of the relationship between a department and the last employee in the department would cause the deletion of the department. If the relationship was x~<1-to-M>x~, then explicit destruction of a department and employee relationship would cause deletion of the employee. (This implicit deletion fails if the employee is the last one in the department, unless the relationship was x~<1-to-M>~x~. In this case the department would also be deleted!)

Prime Binding. A ' (prime) binding pertains to both implicit and explicit destructibility and can be given for only one class in a `relationship`. The ' binding for a class C in a relationship R denotes that C is the *prime class* and the other class is the *subordinate class*. When a C object is deleted, implicitly or explicitly, each R relationship it has with a subordinate object is implicitly destroyed, and an implicit delete is done on the subordinate object. Also, when an R relationship is explicitly destroyed, an implicit delete is done on the subordinate object. Failure of an implicit delete on a subordinate object will cause the failure of a C object delete or explicit R destruction if and only if the implicit deletion is needed to maintain the cardinality for C in R. These semantics assume that objects of a subordinate class are dependent or partially dependent on objects of the prime class for their existence. For a 1 cardinality, the ' binding is equivalent to a ~x~ binding.

To illustrate, if the relationship between departments and employees was '<1-to-0/M>, then department is the prime class and employee the subordinate. When a department is deleted, all of the relationships it has with its employees are implicitly destroyed and an implicit delete is done on all of these employees. If any of these deletes fail, the department delete fails since the 1 cardinality constraint must be maintained. The usefulness of the ' binding should become more apparent by additional examples given in the next section.

The possible bindings in a `relationship` result in many more distinct relationship types. Relationship semantics are complete and totally meaningful only when a `relationship` appears in a context where classes are designated as to whether or not their objects are "explicitly deletable." Such a context is supplied by an ORD.

4 Object-Relationship Diagram (ORD)

The Object-Relationship Diagram (ORD) provides an object-based, semantic data model and is based on the traditional Entity-Relationship Diagram (ERD) [5]. There are, however, some differences. For example, class attributes are omitted from the ORD since its main purpose is to identify object classes and relationships. Also, the ORD more precisely defines aggregate relationships. Like some extended ERDs, e.g., [27, 11], it includes precise relationship cardinalities. In fact, it includes the equivalent of a `relationship` for each relationship.

Figs. 3 and 4 show ORDs that model parts of a company database, and Figs. 4 and 5 show ORDs that model portions of a nuclear physics experiments database. An earlier version of the relationship notation and the ORD were originally developed to aid in the design of this database as an OODB [9, 10, 21]. The following paragraphs explain the ORD and then discuss some of the relationships shown in the ORDs. The purpose of this discussion is to further illustrate the relationship notation and show the variety of relationships that can be described by incorporating it into an ER-like diagram.

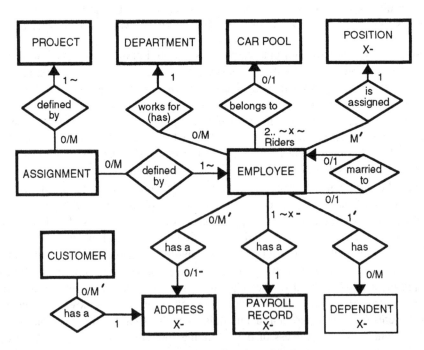

Fig. 3. ORD for a Company Database

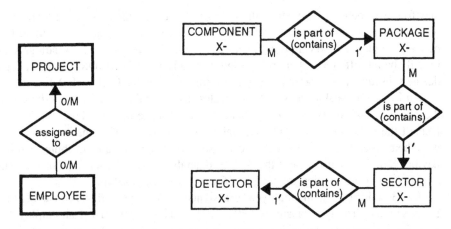

Fig. 4. ORD for Employees
and Projects

Fig. 5. ORD for the Detector in a Nuclear Physics
Experiments Database

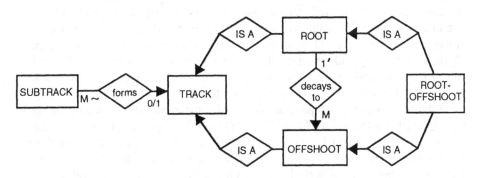

Fig. 6. ORD for Tracks in a Nuclear Physics Experiments Database

Rectangles in an ORD identify object classes. An X- within a rectangle indicates that objects of the class are not explicitly deletable, the default, X, being that they are. A rectangle with broader sides indicates a requirement for direct access to the objects of a class, which defines an entry point into the database. Fig. 3 indicates that employees are directly accessible, while dependents must be accessed via their relationship with an employee.

Two rectangles are linked via a diamond to identify a relationship between two classes. An arrow points from subject class to relative class, and the relationship name in the diamond identifies the relationship from this perspective, e.g., an employee "works for" a department. The inverse relationship may be obtained by reversing the arrow and supplying a name appropriate to this direction. Such a name may be given in parentheses after the relationship name, e.g., a department "has" employees. The *cardinality* given before the diamond in the direction of the arrow applies to the subject class; the one given after the diamond applies to the relative class. A name describing the role played by class objects in the relationship may follow or be given just below the `cardinality` for the class. The `binding` for a class is given after the `cardinality` or role name, e.g., the relationship between employees and car pools is `~x~<2..-to-0/1>`. If desired, bindings may initially be left off an ORD entirely, resulting in a Level 1 ORD (ORD_1), then added during subsequent analysis and design, resulting in a Level 2 ORD (ORD_2).

An IS A relationship in an ORD indicates that the subject class is a *subclass* of the relative class, the *superclass*. That is, objects of the subject class are also objects of the relative class. Subclasses inherit the attributes and behavior associated with their superclass(es). A subclass can also have its own unique attributes and behavior. Subclasses also inherit the explicit deletability and relationships of their superclass(es). Cardinalities are not given for the IS A relationship.

Fig. 3 indicates that an employee "is assigned" a position, perhaps consisting of a title and rank. The relationship is `'<M-to-1>`. This means that if an employee x is deleted, it's relationship with a position will be implicitly destroyed and an attempt will be made to implicitly delete the related position since EMPLOYEE is the prime class. If the position is also assigned to another employee, i.e., if there exists a relationship instance with another employee, the position is not deleted since the 1 cardinality would be violated and a default binding does not allow implicit destruction of this relationship. Employee x will still be deleted since its deletion does not violate the M cardinality. Only when a position is no longer assigned to any employee will it be implicitly deleted. (It can never be explicitly deleted.) This occurs when its only related employee is deleted or its only relationship with an employee is explicitly destroyed via a change of position for the employee.

If the desire was to have positions maintained independently of employees, then the relationship between EMPLOYEE and POSITION classes should be `<0/M-to-1>` and positions should be made explicitly deletable. Deletion of a employee would simply result in the implicit destruction of its relationship with a position. Deletion of a position would not be allowed if it were assigned to any employee.

An address, like a position, is dependent on one or more objects for its existence; however, unlike a position, the objects can be of different classes. The relationship types between ADDRESS and two prime classes EMPLOYEE and CUSTOMER ensure that an address is deleted if and only if it no longer relates to any employee or customer.

The ORD in Fig. 4 shows the classic `0/M-to-0/M` relationship between employees and projects. Since the relationship between an employee and a project is not modeled as an object in the ORD, it can have no attributes or behavior.

The ASSIGNMENT class in Fig. 3 models this `0/M-to-0/M` relationship as an object class, where an assignment object is actually a relationship instance between an employee and a project. Based on the given relationship specifications, if an employee or project is deleted, all related assignment objects are implicitly deleted. When an assignment is deleted, its relationships with a project and an employee are destroyed. Modeling the relationship as an object class provides for relationship attributes, e.g., the starting and expected ending date for an assignment, and behavior, e.g., extend an assignment for x days. A class like the ASSIGNMENT class is called a *relationship class*.

One last relationship in Fig. 3 deserving special note is that between employees and car pools. Because of the ~x~<2..-to-0/1> relationship, a car pool is implicitly deleted when its second-to-last relationship with an employee is destroyed, either because the employee is deleted or the employee's relationship with the car pool has been explicitly destroyed, i.e., the employee has quit the car pool.

The ORD in Fig. 5 models part of a detector used for an experiment conducted at a nuclear physics accelerator. In such an experiment, a particle beam is directed at a target—a slice of material whose nuclei are to be studied. Collisions between beam particles and target nuclei result in scattered particles whose tracks are recorded by various kinds of electronic components positioned within the detector.

Fig. 5 indicates that every detector component "is part of" a detector package, which "is part of" a sector within the magnetic field, which "is part of" a detector description. A detector can be implicitly deleted via its relationship with an experiment, which is not shown in the ORD. The semantics of the '<1-to-M> relationships dictate that if a detector is deleted, all related sectors, packages, and components are implicitly deleted. A component can be shifted from one package to another via a relationship change, but its relationship to at least one detector package cannot be explicitly destroyed without leading to its deletion.

Some slightly different relationship types could have been specified for package and component—variations on the "is part of" theme. For example, if the component rectangle did not contain an X-, then a component could be explicitly deleted provided it wasn't the only one in a package; and if the relationship was '<1-to-M>~, then the explicit deletion of the only component in a package would result in an attempted implicit deletion of the package.

Relationships involving particle subtracks and tracks that result from the analysis of an experiment are defined in the ORD in Fig. 6. Based on these definitions, deleting the last subtrack of a track results in the implicit deletion of the track. Also, deleting a track, either implicitly or explicitly, does not result in the deletion of any subtracks; however, it can result in the implicit deletion of a tree of tracks having the deleted track as its root.

The remaining relationships in the ORDs exhibit a variety of additional types with subtle differences in semantics denoted by their cardinalities and bindings.

5 Object-oriented Database Definition Language (ODDL)

This section provides an overview of ODDL. Its main purpose is to show how the relationship notation can be incorporated into an object-oriented, data definition language (DDL). A complete definition of ODDL including a discussion of its implementation can be found in [10].

ODDL is being developed both as a practical tool to facilitate the design and implementation of a nuclear physics experiments database as well as a research tool to experiment with possible OODB enhancements. One of its main objectives is to define a very basic, conceptual object-oriented data model that can be extended to provide additional semantic modeling features. To this end, ODDL incorporates the `relationship` notation for aggregate relationships. The basic data model defined by ODDL is very similar to the object-oriented data models defined by others, e.g., [3]. In fact, the data model and to a large extent the language itself is a compatible superset of the C++ binding of the ODMG-93 Object Database Standard [4].

ODDL will be implemented by extensions made to a commercially available OODB system. ODDL will provide the high-level operations, e.g., deletion, required to support each `relationship` defined in an ODDL specification. The implementation of these operations will use the primitive classes and object-level operations supplied by the OODB system.

Fig. 7 gives part of an ODDL specification that corresponds to the ORD in Fig. 3. The specification includes a number of class definitions, e.g., `employee`, and a number of *extents*, e.g., `Employees`. An extent allows all objects of a particular class to be directly accessible. C++ code is interspersed within ODDL to provide for the specification of user-defined attribute types, e.g., `date`, and object behavior as member functions, e.g., `RaiseSalary` for class `employee`. Not shown in Fig. 7 is that an `isa` (or `:public`) clause may follow the `class-name` in a class definition to specify the class as a subclass of one or more superclasses.

Attributes are defined for each class that serve to describe the objects of the class. An attribute is either *literal-valued*, e.g., `Name` in `employee`, or *object-valued*, e.g., `Dept` in `employee`. Object-valued attributes represent in ODDL most of aggregate relationships that are identified in an ORD. Object-valued attributes are *single-valued*, e.g. `Dept` in `employee`, or *multi-valued*, e.g., `Tasks` in `employee`. A multi-valued attribute is constructed as a set, or collection, of objects of a specific type. Single-valued attributes represent `-to-0/1` or `-to-1` relationships, and multi-valued attributes represent `-to-0/M` or `-to-M` relationships. A `relationship` is given for each object-valued attribute to define the relationship type.

The ODDL data model assumes that relationship creation, destruction, and change occurs via operations on object-valued attributes. A relationship instance is created when the value of a single-valued attribute that is null is set to (reference) a specific object or when an object (reference) is inserted into a multi-valued attribute. A relationship instance is destroyed when the non-null value of a single-valued attribute is set to null or when an object is deleted from a multi-valued attribute. And finally, a relationship instance is changed when the non-null value of a single-valued attribute is set to a different object or when an object in a multi-valued attribute is replaced by another.

An `attribute-name` given in an `inverse` clause for an object-valued attribute, e.g., `Employees` for `Dept` in the class `employee`, identifies the *inverse attribute*, the attribute that represents the inverse relationship. An inverse attribute permits the relationship to be meaningfully viewed from the context of the relative class, thus facilitating relationship manipulation and the specification of queries from this context. It also usually, but not necessarily, provides for efficient access of subject class objects from relative class objects. Inverse attributes are automatically maintained in the face of object deletions and relationship creations, destructions, and changes.

```
Database CompanyDB  // Company DataBase

$C++
class date {...};
typedef char* string;
...
$.
{
   ...
   class employee {
      string            SSN;           // Social Security Number
      string            Name;          // Last name, First name
      date              BirthDate;
      address           Address '<0/M-to-0/1>-;
      payroll_record    Payroll inverse Employee ~x-<1-to-1>;
      department        Dept inverse Employees <0/M-to-1>;
      position          Position '<M-to-1>;
      set<assignment>   Tasks inverse Employee ~<1-to-0/M>; [1]
      employee          Spouse inverse Spouse <0/1-to-0/1>;
      set<dependent>    Dependents '<1-to-0/M>;
      car_pool          CarPool inverse Riders ~x~<2..-to-0/1>;
$C++
      void RaiseSalary(int percentage);
      void CancelAssignments();
      ...
$.
   };
   extent set<employee>  Employees  key SSN; [2]

   class department {
      string            Name;
      string            Location;      // Building No.
      set<employee>     Employees inverse Dept <1-to-0/M>;
      ...
   };
   extent set<department>  Departments  key Name;

   class assignment {
      project           Project  inverse Tasks <0/M-to-1>~;
      employee          Employee inverse Tasks <0/M-to-1>~;
      date              StartingDate;
      date              TerminationDate;
      int               Duration; [3]  // in days
$C++
      void Extend(int days);  // Extend assigment.
      ...
$.
   };
   extent set<assignment> Assignments key (Project, Employee);
...
};
$footnotes
[1]  os_List
[2]  index on key, ordered index on (Department, Name)
[3]  derived
...
$.
```

Fig. 7. ODDL Example

The representation of relationships as object-valued attributes in ODDL is conceptual. They permit the user to conveniently view and manipulate a relationship from the context of a particular object and specify access to related objects in a query language.

Footnote references can be given for object-valued attributes and extents, e.g., [1] for Tasks in employee. Footnotes provide implementation aspects related to the conceptual database definition. These aspects are generally part of the internal schema.

6 Conclusion

This paper has proposed a notation for describing aggregate relationships in an OODB. The main features of this notation are summarized as follows.

- It incorporates the equivalent of referential integrity constraints as proposed for relational databases as well as null, key, and surjectivity constraints.
- It assumes a basic object-oriented data model where most relationships are represented as object-valued attributes.
- It can be integrated into an ER-type diagram and an object-oriented DDL, thus aiding database requirements analysis, design, and specification.
- It provides for automatic garbage collection of objects.
- It is based on and consistent with relationship cardinalities, a well-understood concept normally dealt with during requirements analysis.
- It permits specification of precise cardinality constraints, including lower and upper bounds.
- It can provide the basis for defining the extent of a complex object.
- It facilitates the implementation of a large variety of aggregate relationships in an OODB with minimal syntax and semantics.

References

1. A. Albano, G. Ghelli, and B. Orsini, "A Relationship Mechanism for a Strongly Typed Object-Oriented Database Programming Language," *Proc. of the 17th Int'l VLDB Conf.*, Morgan Kaufmann, San Mateo, CA, 1991, 565-575.
2. E. Bertino and L. Martino, "Object-Oriented Database Management Systems: Concepts and Issues," *Computer*, IEEE Computer Society Press, **24**(4), April 1991, 33-47.
3. E. Bertino, M. Negri, G. Pelagatti, L. Sbattella, "Object-Oriented Query Languages: The Notion and the Issues," *IEEE Trans. Knowledge & Data Eng.*, **4**(3), 1992, 223-237.
4. R.G.G. Cattel, ed., T. Atwood, J. Duhl, G. Ferran, M. Loomis, D. Wade, *The Object Database Standard: ODMG-93*, Morgan Kaufmann, San Mateo, CA, 1994.
5. P.P. Chen, "The Entity-relationship Model: Towards a Unified View of Data," *ACM Trans. on Database Systems*, **1**(1), 1976, 1-36.
6. E. Codd, "Extending the Database Relational Model to Capture More Meaning," *ACM Trans. on Database Systems*, **4**(4), Dec. 1979, 397-434.

7. C.J. Date, "Referential Integrity," *Proc. 7th Int'l VLDB Conf.*, IEEE Computer Society Press, 1981, 2-12.

8. C.J. Date, *An Introduction to Database Systems Volume II*, Addison-Wesley, Reading, MA, 1983, 241-289.

9. B.K. Ehlmann, L.C. Dennis, and G.A. Riccardi, "An Object-based Conceptual Model of a Nuclear Physics Experiments Database," *Nuclear Instruments & Methods in Physics Research*, Sect. A, Elsevier Science, North-Holland, **A325**, 1993, 294-308.

10. B.K. Ehlmann, "Applying an Object-Oriented Database Model to a Scientific Database Problem: Managing Experimental Data at CEBAF," Ph.D. dissertation, Florida State Univ., Tallahassee, FL, UMI Dissertation Services, Ann Arbor, MI, 1992.

11. D.W. Embley and T.W. Ling, "Synergistic Database Design with an Extended Entity-Relationship Model," *Entity-Relationship Approach to Database Design and Query*, F.H. Lochovsky, ed., North Holland, New York, NY, 1990, 111-128.

12. D.H. Fishman, et al., "Overview of the IRIS DBMS," *Object-Oriented Concepts, Applications, and Databases*, W. Kim and F. Lochovsky, eds., Addison-Wesley (ACM Press), Reading, MA, 1989, 219-250.

13. R. Hull and R. King, "Semantic Database Modeling: Survey, Applications, and Research Issues," *ACM Computing Surveys*, **19**(3), Sept 1987, 201-260.

14. S. Khoshafian and R. Abnous, *Object-Orientation Concepts, Languages, Databases, User Interfaces*, John Wiley & Sons, New York, NY, 1990, 257-321.

15. W. Kim, "Object-Oriented Databases: Definition and Research Directions," *IEEE Trans. on Knowledge and Data Eng.*, **2**(3), Sept. 1990, 327-341.

16. W. Kim, J.F. Garza, N. Ballou, and D. Woelk, "Architecture of the ORION Next-Generation Database System," *IEEE Trans. Knowledge & Data Eng.*, **2**(1), 1990, 109-124.

17. V.M. Markowitz, "Referential Integrity Revisited: An Object-oriented Perspective," *Proc. 16th Int'l VLDB Conf.*, Morgan Kaufmann, San Mateo, CA, 1990, 578-589.

18. Object Design Inc., *ObjectStore Technical Overview*, Burlington, MA, May, 1991.

19. Objectivity Inc., *Objectivity/DB System Overview*, Menlo Park, CA, March, 1990.

20. Ontologic Inc., *ONTOS Release 2.0 Product Description*, Burlington, MA, Oct. 1990.

21. G.A. Riccardi and B.K. Ehlmann, "Object-oriented Development of Scientific Databases, an Example from Experimental Physics," *Proc. of the First Software Eng. Research Forum*, Tampa, FL, Nov. 1991, 277-286.

22. J. Rumbaugh, "Relations as Semantic Constructs in an Object-oriented Language," *OOPSLA'87* as ACM SIGPLAN, **22**(12), Dec. 1987, 466-481.

23. J. Rumbaugh, "Controlling Propagation of Operations Using Attributes on Relations," *OOPSLA'88* as ACM SIGPLAN, **23**(11), Nov. 1988, 285-296.

24. H.A. Schmid and J.R. Swenson, "On the Semantics of the Relational Data Model," *Proc. ACM SIGMOD Int'l Conf. on Management of Data*, 1975

25. M. Stonebraker, L.A. Rowe, and M. Hirohama, "The Implementation of POSTGRES," *IEEE Trans. on Knowledge & Data Eng.*, **2**(1), March 1990, 125-142.

26. J. P. Thompson, *Data With Semantics*, Van Nostrand Reinhold, NY, 1989, 237-253.

27. D.C. Tsichritzis and F.H. Lochovsky, *Data Models*, Prentice-Hall, Englewood Cliffs, NJ, 1982.

28. S.B. Zdonik and D. Maier, eds. "Fundamentals of Object-Oriented Databases," *Readings in Object-Oriented DB Systems*, Morgan Kaufmann, San Mateo, CA, 1990, 1-32.

Modeling Activities of Application Domains

Mohammad Ketabchi, Nipun Sehgal,

Surapol Dasananda, Rani Mikkilineni, Xiangyang Li

ketabchi@otl.scu.edu
Object Technology Laboratory
School of Engineering
Santa Clara University
Santa Clara, CA 95053

Abstract. Modeling the activities of an application domain is a necessary extension of modeling the structure and behavior of objects in the domain. Object models capture the structure and behavior of components in the application domains, whereas activity models are used to describe the functionality of the domain. The integration of object and activity modeling is essential for producing complete domain models in which the objects and activities are mutually consistent. Realization of such domain models simplifies the development of sophisticated applications. Using a DBMS simplifies the realization of the model and further facilitates the development of multiuser applications.

The notion of Process is introduced as a modeling construct for activities. Process decomposition and Process hierarchies are introduced as mechanisms that allow abstractions of activities. The notion of Signal is introduced as a mechanism for Processes to communicate and exchange data. Language facilities for defining Process and Signal are presented.

Key words: Application domain modeling, object-orientation, and process

1. Introduction

Domain modeling consists of not only modeling the structure and behavior of objects in the domain, but also the functional aspects of the domain. The functional aspects of a domain manifest themselves as activities specific to the domain. Domain activities describe "what" is being done and "how" it is done whereas the objects describe "to what" it is done.

The notions of object, composition, aggregation, generalization/specialization[1], classification, and relationship types can be used to describe the structure of the domain under consideration. This in turn can lead only to structural abstractions. The notion of object behavior can be used to describe the state changes and protocols of objects where the protocol of each object defines the valid interactions with that object. Even though each object would encapsulate the behavior describing the protocol of the object, information about activities in the domain would not be captured. There should be a mechanism to capture such information because the modeling of activities of an application domain is as useful as the modeling of the objects in the domain. For a general discussion of object concepts, see [2, 3, 4].

Coupling object and functional modeling underlies many CASE tools [5]. The modeling facilities provided by such tools, however, are not uniform; different concepts, diagrams and symbols are used to model activities, behavior and structure of objects. Also, such tools cannot ensure the consistency of the functional and object models, because their underlying methodologies are only loosely coupled. Thus, while most structural constraints can be maintained by several database management systems, the functional constraints are lost once the design stage is complete [6]. CASE tools such as TI's IEF [7] provide an integrated layered approach to modeling and application development. While the coupling between structure and activities in IEF is strong, the emphasis is on automated application generation and the model is not uniform across the layers. Also, the data model is ER based [8], thus does not exploit the advantages of object-oriented models.

The integration of functional, structural and behavioral modeling has been the focus of many analysis methodologies [9]. The thrust of such efforts has been in capturing the static and dynamic features of a system at various levels of abstraction. An example of this is Object Modeling Technique [10] which includes an object diagram, data-flow diagrams and state-transition diagrams. These diagrams represent object model, functional model, and dynamic model of the system. However, these models are not well integrated. It is difficult to recognize how an object, operation or attribute in the object model relates to a data flow or data flow process in the functional model or to an event or state in the dynamic model. Also, these models are at different levels of granularity which makes it difficult to synthesize them into manageable and uniform application domain models. Another example is Objectory [26] which includes Entity, Use Case, and Service modeling in analysis phase, and system, block, and component level designs in design phase. The concepts of use case and service in the analysis phase of Objectory lead to a better understanding of activities associated with the target system. If they were employed as part of the domain analysis they can potentially lead to identification of processes and tasks in the domain. However, Objectory considers these analysis as part of top-down system development process and assumes component libraries which include only objects. We provide facilities to build application domain models that include the activities of the domain and facilitates the development of multiple model-based applications using the domain model. Methodologies such as Object Modeling Technique, Shlaer and Mellor[11] and Booch [12] emphasize modeling of the structure and behavior of objects but do not address domain-wide activities. The diagrams that supposedly represent inter-object communications or subsystem communications are just summaries of events external to objects. Attempts have been made to come up with an integrated design methodology that combines functional, behavioral, and structural modeling. Some of these efforts propose new constructs or extensions to the data flow oriented functional model and the ER data model to allow a tighter coupling of these models [6].

Design and specification languages such as CCITT's SDL (Specification and Design Language) [13] have incorporated modeling of activities as part of the description of the domain. SDL focuses on the procedural and declarative aspects of process description. SDL also emphasizes the communication between processes. The original SDL is not object-oriented. However, an object-oriented version of SDL is described in [14]. Process specification languages such as PML [15] focus primarily on modeling of processes without relating it to domain structure. The binding to structural abstractions is generally weak. Modeling of long-running activities has been the focus of nested and extended transaction management models such as [16] and workflow models such as [25]. Modeling of processes in the software domain as process-objects is discussed in [17].

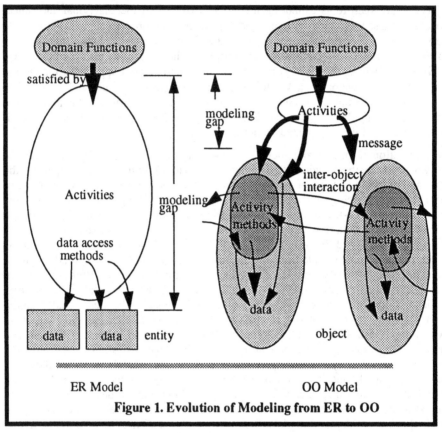

Figure 1. Evolution of Modeling from ER to OO

A framework to realize an integrated, consistent, closely knit conceptual model would include activity modeling as well as object modeling. The advantages of integrating object and activity modeling are:

1. Leads to a better and more complete understanding of the application domain. It also provides documentation for the domain.

2. Allows domain experts to verify the structure of the application domain by activity modeling. This forms the basis of object analysis methodologies where the validity of the objects is verified by simulating key processes (activities) in the domain.

3. Facilitates the application design and development. Complete domain models that include activity models simplify the development of model-based application systems by reducing the gap between the applications and the components (objects). If the notion of global schema in DBMS is generalized to support such domain models, sophisticated multi user database applications can be easily be developed

4. Application software maps the application domain to the software domain. It is only when the mapping involves the highest domain functions and activities, that it becomes easy to maintain software. This is especially true as changes with the greatest impact generally occur due to changing domain requirements.

In Section 2 it is argued that objects become manageable and more useful once concepts are introduced to model domain activities. Section 3 introduces the Process and Task modeling concepts that allow the modeling of activities as an extension to object modeling. Signals are introduced to allow interprocess communication. In Section 4, language facilities to define Process, Signal and Task are presented. Section 5 presents a summary and concluding remarks. Section 5 presents a summary and conclusion.

2. Object-Oriented Modeling

Model of an application domain consists of three components: activities in the domain, objects of interest and the structural and behavioral constraints placed on them, and the interdependencies between the objects and the activities. In the ER model, the structural component is modeled as entities and relationships. Entities have no associated behavior; thus modeling of activities, generally embedded in the applications, includes the behavior of objects and operations needed to access them. As a consequence, the "modeling gap" between the entities and the domain functions is large; activities have to incorporate a lot. The modeling gap is defined as that part of the domain which cannot be adequately modeled with the constructs of the meta model. This gap is then filled by the applications that are written to implement the activity. This is illustrated in figure 1.

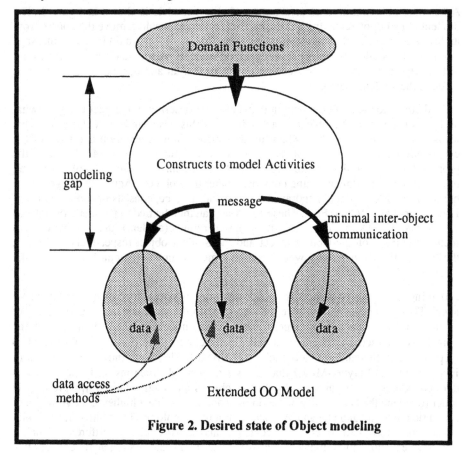

Figure 2. Desired state of Object modeling

The object-oriented paradigm introduced the "object" as a construct that combines structure and behavior. The structure of the object is described by attributes associated with the object. The behavior of the object is described by its operations. The "data" now is encapsulated with the access methods. As shown in figure 1, the modeling gap is larger for the pre-OO models (such as ER model). The introduction of the "object" concept has reduced the gap to the extent that the operations that are needed to access the data are no longer part of the activities; they are encapsulated with the object. But, in the current state of OO modeling, there is no concept that facilitates the modeling of the activities. As there is no concept that adequately models the activities, the objects end up encapsulating all the activities and interdependencies between objects and activities in addition to the operations. This results in models where activities and all the inter-object communications are embedded in individual objects rather than any other concept because there is no other concept in the OO paradigm. This leads to a dissolution of the activity model. As domain activities are not adequately modeled, the mapping of domain functions to components of the domain that realize them cannot be easily determined. There is a need to provide constructs that would facilitate modeling of activities. As illustrated in figure 2, a consequence of this would be that objects would diminish in size and the inter-object communication would be minimized. This leads to more reusable objects and well-defined activities among objects.

An example illustrating the current state of object models is shown in figure 3. The Student object upon receiving a drop_course() message would remove the course from its list of courses. To maintain consistency, the Course object would be sent a message to remove the student from its list of registered students. Also, the Course object would in turn send a message to the Account object so that an appropriate update would be made to the student's account.

Thus there is no clear cut distinction between what describes the object vis-a-vis what describes the use of the object in an activity, in this case Student Withdrawal. This leads to ambiguous modeling which in turn impacts implementation and reduces the extensibility and reusability of the objects in the model. Figure 4 illustrates the proposed alternative that would allow objects to remain autonomous while capturing the activities in the domain using constructs other than objects. Activities are generally hierarchical. The Student Withdrawal activity, for instance, consists of sub-activities of Drop Course and Refund Fees. These activities can then be tied to the methods defined on objects. The Drop Course activity maps to remove(student) and remove(course) methods defined on the Course object and the Student object respectively. Similarly, the Refund Fees sub-activity would invoke a method update(amount) defined on the Account object.

Providing modeling constructs to model activities is necessary but not sufficient by itself. These concepts should be tightly coupled to the structure at different levels of abstraction. This leads to a layered approach to modeling where dynamics of the domain is abstracted into activities and the structure of the domain is abstracted as HyperObjects. Semantic models such as HAMMER [18] have introduced notions of Hyper-Entity and Hyper-Model that allow structural abstractions. A Hyper-Entity is defined as a collection of logically related objects and their relationships grouped in order to reduce the complexity of the domain and to provide a higher level view. Other semantic modeling and OO analysis and design methodologies have introduced similar constructs referred to as clusters, contexts, and subsystems. In different domains, HyperObjects are called divisions, departments, blocks, etc. As a generic concept that

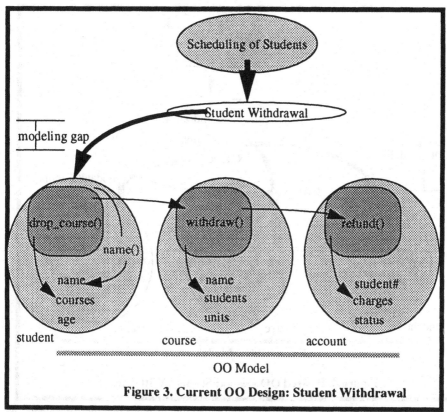

Figure 3. Current OO Design: Student Withdrawal

allows organization of objects, HyperObject is a useful concept in any domain model. A composite object is a restricted case of a HyperObject where the existence of component objects depend upon the existence of the composite object and the only relationship among the composite object and its parts is component relationship. Due to lack of space, the notion of HyperObjects described in [19] are not discussed in this paper in detail.

3. Concepts for Modeling Activity

Process and Task are introduced as two concepts that would facilitate modeling of activities and their interactions with objects, thereby reducing the modeling gap. A process is an activity integral to the complete description of the application domain. Examples of processes are the 'scheduling' activity of the school domain, the 'check-in, check-out' activities of the hotel domain and the 'patient registration' activity of the hospital domain. Processes can be viewed at different levels of abstraction where each process may be subdivided into other processes which in turn can be further decomposed into more fundamental processes. This corresponds to the activity hierarchy. A process is considered to be atomic when its decomposition is of no interest from modeling point of view.

An atomic process would be considered to be a task. A task is an indivisible unit of activity which would execute in its entirety, or not execute at all. A task can be viewed

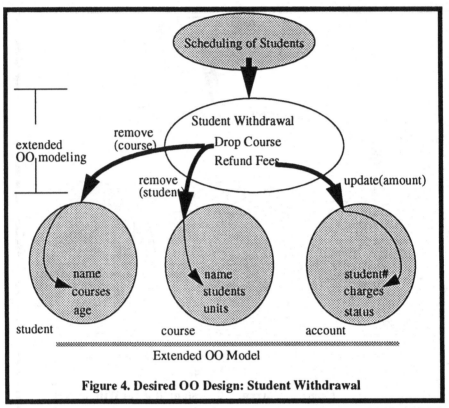

Figure 4. Desired OO Design: Student Withdrawal

as a logical transaction. A task could in turn invoke one or more methods of objects. A process, on the other hand, would invoke one or more tasks. As processes are long-running activities, their running to completion cannot be guaranteed. Figure 5 illustrates OO modeling with process and task. Note that processes focus on modeling of activities and therefore represent the functional components of the domain. Tasks, on the other hand, tie processes to objects, thereby represent the interactions between activities and objects of the application domain model.

An example of modeling the hotel domain with process and task is illustrated in figure 6. 'Room_Reservation' is a function which is realized by the 'Check-In' and 'Check-Out' activities. These long-running activities are modeled as processes. The 'Check-Out' process in turn can be viewed as a sequence of indivisible activities such as 'access guest details', 'bill and deallocate room' and 'update guest details'. These activities can be modeled as tasks. These tasks send messages to objects in the domain to realize their functionality. For instance, the 'bill guest and deallocate room' task would invoke methods charge_guest(amount) in the 'bill' object and the set_room_empty(room#) in the 'room' object. Other than the fact that the extended OO model leads to a better design, it can be seen that a change in the functionality, or other forms of maintenance can be handled conveniently. A change to the internal data of the room object would affect only the implementation of the methods that access the room data as long as the interface between the tasks and the methods is maintained.

In the next section we present an overview of an object-oriented high-level modeling

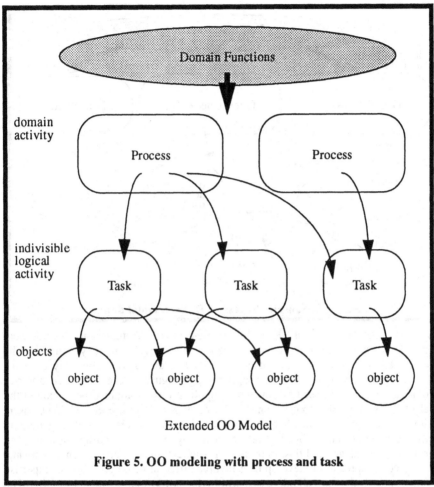

Figure 5. OO modeling with process and task

language that provides Process, Task, HyperObject, and Signal constructs for modeling activities in application domain. The language, referred to as OSL (Object Specification Language) [19, 20] is the host language of the OCADS (Object-Centered Application Development System) which supports layered model-based application development methodology[21].

4. Object Specification Language (OSL)

OSL is an object-oriented high-level language for modeling advanced application domains such as network management. OSL is different from common object-oriented programming languages such as C++ in that it provides extensive modeling facilities. It is different from data definition and semantic modeling languages such as SQL [22], OSQL (Object SQL) [23], and ER (Entity Relationships) [15] because it provides facilities for modeling interactions among objects and activities of application domains.

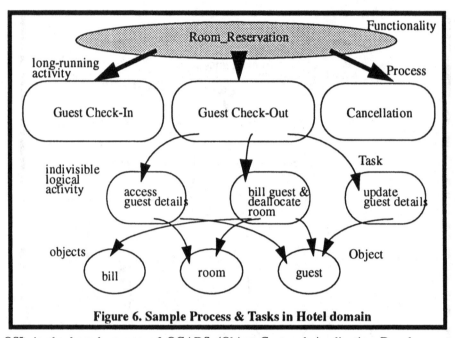

Figure 6. Sample Process & Tasks in Hotel domain

OSL is the host language of OCADS (Object-Centered Application Development System). OCADS is a layered model-based application development system [24]. The kernel of OCADS is a collection of classes which encapsulate technology domains such as operating system facilities, programming languages, user interface libraries and other software tools used in developing applications. Domain experts extend the kernel of OCADS by the application domain models defined in OSL. OCADS users develop applications on top of the application domain models by utilizing domain specific semantics and objects, rather than by using operating system and programming language facilities. In traditional application development environments, these aspects of application development involve different activities, people, expertise and tools. In OSL they are all addressed within the uniform object model of OSL. The OSL processor can generate executable code from the specifications of the applications developed on top of the domain model.

The main objectives of OSL are:

1. To facilitate the modeling of application domains by allowing the specification of not only the structure and behavior of application domain objects, but also the interactions among them and the activities of the domain.

2. To provide a high-level uniform interface to all the activities in a model-based domain specific application development process.

3. To provide direct manipulation object-oriented application builders with executable application domain models by generating code from the specifications of the domain models.

4. To provide encapsulation facilities to allow reuse of existing software libraries and components in developing applications.

OSL is a modeling language with a powerful logical meta model. The logical model of OSL is an extended object model where objects are not limited to classes and their instances. Relationships, events, rules, triggers, tasks, signals, processes, and their instances are first class objects in OSL. The OSL facilities that support static modeling are a super set of the capabilities of most conventional modeling languages because OSL provides facilities such as encapsulation, classification, specialization, state, hyperobject, and relationships. OSL supports dynamic modeling by providing facilities such as event that capture communication among objects. Modeling of constraints in a domain is supported by the OSL constructs rule and trigger. Activities are modeled using process and task whereas interaction between processes is captured using signal. In addition to these modeling primitives, OSL provides support for commonly used primitives such as repeater, selector and iterator which support a declarative rather than a procedural approach to set-oriented operations on large sets of data.

The key OSL feature which makes the specification of behavior possible is the set of powerful facilities that allows most common computations to be declared rather than embedded in code. Significant portions of conventional software systems consist of such things as rules, relationships, events, selectors, repeaters, iterators, tasks, and processes which are declared in OSL.

This paper focuses on the OSL mechanisms that support modeling of activities and interactions among them: Process, Task and Signal. A template like format is used to describe these constructs. Other OSL constructs, Class, Rule, Trigger, Event, Relationship, State, Selector, Repeater, and Iterator are described in [19, 20].

4.1 OSL Process

The process construct in OSL represents an abstraction of a collection of steps that realize functionality of the domain knowledge. For example, student admission, student registration and class scheduling are candidates for processes in University domain. All OSL Processes are refinements of the OSL kernel Process. All processes are instances of the single OSL Meta Process. Figure 7 shows the OSL Process template.

```
BeginProcessSpec
ProcessName        <Name>;
SuperProcess       <Name>;
Documentation      <Documentation>;
HyperObjects       <hyperObjectList>;
Parameter          <FormalParameterDeclaration>;
Signals
       Send        <Signals>;
       Receive     <Signals>;
Context            <VariableDeclaration>;
Steps              <Statements>;
EndProcessSpec
```

Figure 7 - OSL Process template

The HyperObjects section specifies one or more HyperObjects which provide the name scope for the process. A Hyper Object is an abstract object representing a collection of OSL constructs which together as a whole is semantically significant. A HyperObject may contain Classes, Relationships, Events, Rules and Triggers. HyperObjects provide an abstraction mechanism where domain knowledge can be structured into higher level objects. This allows the users to hide irrelevant details in the domain by grouping OSL constructs into HyperObjects and provides users with an abstract view of the domain knowledge. By including a HyperObject in a process specification, all member constructs of the HyperObject are accessible to the process. The Parameter section allows the Process to accept parameters from the invoker which may be another Process. OSL Processes use the signal construct described in the next section as a means of communication and synchronization with other processes. The Signals section specifies the lists of Signals the Process may send and receive. The Context section specifies the declarations of local variables used in this Process. The Steps section contains a sequence of statements to be executed when the Process is invoked. The statements are executed sequentially. An statement in this section may invoke other Processes, invoke Tasks or send messages to objects.

An OSL Process is independently executable. It may be invoked directly by the users or by another Process. Each Process is executed concurrently with other Processes in the same application. A Process has its own execution environment and a thread of control starting from the first statement in the Steps section. The environment of each Process contains all the constructs such as Classes, Relationships, Rules and Events that are needed for the Process to be executed successfully. An object instance created by a Process is added to the extent of the OSL construct of the instance. The extents of all constructs in the domain of the Process are part of the Process environment and last throughout the lifetime of the Process. Any Tasks or methods invoked directly or indirectly by the Process also have access to the same Process environment. In the current version of OSL, an OSL Process is implemented by a UNIX process.

The example in figure 8 shows the student admission Process in the university domain. The Process admits a new student to a department. The student information is provided by the user. The Process then assigns a new student Id and an advisor for the student. Finally, the Process sends a NewStudent Signal carrying the new student information.

BeginProcessSpec
ProcessName Admission;
SuperProcess Process;
Documentation
    Description
        Creates a new student object and assign a new student
        id. Admits the new student to a specified department.
        An Advisor is assigned to the student and the New
        Student signal is sent.
HyperObjects School;
Signals
    Send   NewStudent;
Context
    d : Department;
    dname : String;

```
            s: Student;
            name : String;
            phone : Phone;
            gpa : Real;
Steps
            InputDept(dname);
            d = Department.locate(dname);
            InputStudent(name, phone, gpa);
            s = Student(name, phone, gpa);
            s.set_id( generateNewId() );
            AssignAdvisor(s, d);
            NewStudent.send(s.get_id(), s.get_name(), phone, gpa);
EndProcessSpec
```

Figure 8 - An OSL Process example

4.2 OSL Signal

The Signal construct provides synchronization and communication capability among OSL Processes. All user-defined Signals are refinements of the OSL kernel Signal. All signals are instances of a single OSL Meta Signal. Figure 9 shows the OSL Signal template.

```
BeginSignalSpec
SignalName          <Name>;
SuperSignal         <Name>;
Documentation       <Documentation>;
Attributes          <AttributeDeclarations>;
Operations          <Refinements of send, register, wait,
                        and check operations>

EndSignalSpec
```

Figure 9 - OSL Signal template

The attribute section specifies the information which need to be passed via Signal construct from the sending Process to the receiving Process. Operation section specifies the send, register, wait, and receive operations provided by OSL kernel Signal shown in figure 10.

```
BeginSignalSpec
SignalName          Signal;
SuperSignal         Concept;
Documentation       OSL Kernel Signal;
Attributes
        sender : Process;
Operations
        send( ) : Boolean;
        register(receiver : Process, sender : { Process } );
        wait( sender : Process ) : Boolean;
        check( sender : Process ) : Boolean;
EndSignalSpec
```

Figure 10 - OSL kernel Signal

The send operation is used by the sender Process to send a Signal. When the send operation of a Signal is invoked an instance of that Signal is created. The sender Process must pass values for the attributes of the Signal. These values are passed as the actual arguments to the send operation. The system assigns these values to the attributes of the Signal instance object created as a result of invocation of send operation. Due to the limitations of the current implementation of interprocess communication the actual arguments of send operation can not be object references. The register operation is used by the receiver Process to indicate that it is ready to receive the Signal generated by the sender Process specified as the second argument of the register operation. If this argument is not specified, a Signal sent by any Process will be received. After registering to receive a Signal, the Process uses either the wait operation (blocking call) or the check operation (non-blocking call) to receive the Signal. These operations return the sender, and any Signal attributes that need to be passed from the sender Process. The Signal construct provides a flexible communication among OSL Processes. Figure 11 shows an example Signal called NewStudent. Note that NewStudent Signal inherits the sender attribute from the kernel Signal and redefines send, wait, and check operations.

```
BeginSignalSpec
SignalName          NewStudent;
SuperSignalName     Signal;
Attributes
        id : StudentId;
        name : String;
        phone : Phone;
        gpa : Real;
Operations
        send(id:StudentId, name:String, phone:Phone, gpa:Real);
        wait(p:process, id:StudentId, name:String, phone:Phone,
                    gpa:Real);
        check(p:process, id:StudentId, name:String, phone:Phone,
                    gpa:Real);
EndSignalSpec
```

Figure 11 - An OSL Signal example

An OSL Process must declare the Signals it may send or receive. The following example shows two Processes that use the NewStudent Signal in figure 11 to communicate with each other by passing information via a Signal.

```
BeginProcessSpec
ProcessName   Admission;
Context       .
              s: Student;
              .
Signals
        Send   NewStudent;
```

Steps

```
        // create a new student object
        s = Student( ... );
        .

        // send new student information via signal to another process
        NewStudent.send(this, s.get_id(), s.get_name(),
                s.get_phone());

        .
```

EndProcessSpec

BeginProcessSpec
ProcessName   StudentRecord;
Context   s: Student;
Signals
        Receive NewStudent;
Steps

```
        NewStudent.register(this, {Admission});

        .

        NewStudent.wait(sender, id, name, phone);
        // add the new student information to the permanent records

        .
```

EndProcessSpec
Figure 12 - Two OSL Processes communicating via an OSL Signal

4.3 OSL Task

The Task construct is an abstraction of a basic unit of work in a domain. All user-defined Tasks are refinements of OSL kernel Task. All tasks are instances of the single OSL Meta Task. A Task is performed in it's entirety or not at all. Figure 12 shows OSL Task template.

BeginTaskSpec
TaskName   <Name>;
SuperTask   <Names>;
Documentation   <Documentation>;
Parameter   <FormalParameterDeclaration>;
Context   <VariableDeclaration>;
Perform   <Statements>;
EndTaskSpec

Figure 13 - OSL Task template

The Parameter section allows the Task to accept parameters from the invoker which may be a process or another Task. The Context section specifies the declarations of local variables used in this Task. The Perform section contains a sequence of statements to be executed when the Task is invoked. The statements in the Perform section are executed sequentially. Figure 14 shows an example Task called AssignAdvisor. This Task accepts a student and a department. It selects a professor who is not on sabbatical and has the least number of advisees in the department and assigns him/her as the advisor of the student.

BeginTaskSpec
TaskName   AssignAdvisor;
SuperTask   Task;
Documentation
    Description
        Selects a professor who is not on sabbatical and has the least number of advisees and assigns him/her as the advisor of student.
Parameter
    s : Student;
    d : Department;
Context
    L : [Professor];
    p : Professor;
Perform
    L = selectAvailableProfs(d);
    sortByAdviseeCount(L);
    p = L.getFirst();
    s.set_advisor(p);
EndTaskSpec

Figure 14 - An OSL Task example

5. Summary and Conclusion

The modeling of activities along with objects of the application domains leads to complete domain models. This, among other things, results in objects that are more reusable, a model that is more extensible, implementable and verifiable. Activities are an integral part of the description of an application domain and can be modeled as Processes. Processes can be viewed at different levels of abstraction. Tasks, which are atomic units of meaningful work in the domain, tie together activities and objects. Domain models that include activities in addition to objects are generalized database global schemas which reduce the gap between the schema and applications and simplify the development of sophisticated database applications considerably.

The ideas described in this article have been incorporated in the OSL (Object Specification Language) which is the host language of the OCADS (Object Centered Application Development System). OCADS is a direct manipulation domain-specific application builder that is being developed at the Object Technology Laboratory at Santa Clara University. In addition to Process, Signal, Task, and HyperObject, OSL provides concepts such as relationship, rule, trigger, and event for modeling interactions and communications among objects. Moreover, OSL provides selector, repeater, and iterator for set-oriented manipulation of large sets of objects. OSL selector provides SQL-like functionality, OSL repeater allows distribution of operations over the elements of a set, and OSL iterator provides functionality similar to cursor functionality in conventional DBMS. The current version of the OSL implementation provides a full graphic interface, an encapsulator that encapsulates

C++ classes into OSL classes, and a translator that generates C++ code. The code generator of OSL will be modified to generate DDL for Fujitsu's OODBMSs ODBII to make application domain models persistent. The ABT (Application Building Tool) of OCADS can then be used for developing ODBII application systems using the persistent multiuser domain models.

6. Acknowledgments

The OCADS project including OSL design and development is sponsored by Fujitsu Limited, Fujitsu Network Transmission Systems, U S West Advanced Technologies, and Santa Clara University.

References

1. R. Hull and R. King, "Semantic Database Modeling: Survey, Applications, and Research Issues," ACM Computing Surveys, Vol. 19, No. 3, 1987, pp. 201-260.

2. S. Khoshafian and R. Abnous, "Object-Orientation: Concepts, Languages, Databases, User Intefaces," New York Wiley, 1990.

3. R. T. Bruce, "CASE Brought Down to Earth," Database Programming & Design, 1, 10, Oct 88, pp. 22-39.

4. King, "My cat is object-oriented," in Object-Oriented concepts, databases, and applications, Ed. by Won Kim and Frederick H. Lochovsky, Addison-Wesley, 1989, pp. 23-30.

5. O. Nierstrasz, "A Survey of Object-Oriented Concepts," Object-oriented concepts, databases, and applications, Ed. by Won Kim and Frederick H. Lochovsky, Addison-Wesley, 1989, pp. 3-21.

6. Victor Markowitz, "Representing Processes in the Extended E-R Model," Information Sciences, Vol 52, 1990, pp. 247-284.

7. Texas Instruments, "Information Engineering Facility"

8. P. Chen, "The Entity-Relationship Model - Toward a Unified View of Data," ACM Transaction on Database Systems 1, Mar 1976, pp. 9-36.

9. D. Monarchi and G. Puhr, "A Research Typology for Object-Oriented Analysis and Design," Communications of the ACM, Vol 35, Number 9, Sep. 1992.

10. J. Rumbaugh, et al., "Object-Oriented Modeling and Design," Prentice Hall, Feb. 1991.

11. S. Shlaer and S. Mellor, "Object-Oriented System Analysis: Modeling the World in Data," Prentice Hall,1988.

12. G. Booch, "Object-Oriented Design with Applications," Benjamin/Cummings,1991.

13. F. Belina, D. Hogrefe, "The CCITT-Specification and Description Language SDL," Computer Networks and ISDN System 16 (1988/89) 311-341, North Holland, Amsterdam.

94

14. Moller-Pederson et al., "Rationale and Tutorial on OSDL: An Object-Oriented Extension of SDL," Computer Networks, Vol. 13, No. 2, 1987.

15. R. F. Bruynooghe, J. M. Parker and J. S. Rowles, "PSS: A System for Process Enactment," First International Conference on the Software Process, pp. 128-141, Oct 1991.

16. U. Dayal, M. Hsu and R. Ladin, "A Transactional Model for Long-Running Activities," Proceedings of 17th International Conference on VLDB, pp. 113-122, Barcelona, Spain, 1991.

17. L. Osterweil, "A Process-Object Centered View of Software Environment Architecture," Univ. of Colorado, Boulder, CO 80309-0430.

18. Jianhua Zhu, Rodolphe Nassif, Pankaj Goyal, Pam Drew and Bertil Askelid, "Incorporating a Model Hierarchy into the ER Paradigm," U S WEST Advanced Technologies, 6200 South Quebec St., Englewood, CO 80111, 1990.

19. M. Ketabchi, et al., "Object Specification Language," TR#OTL-1994-05, Santa Clara University, Object Technology Laboratory, Feb. 1994.

20. M. Ketabchi, S., Dasananda, R., Mikkilineni, M., Aoshima, N., Sehgal, S., Suguta, P., Hinkson, "An Object Specification Language for Communication," Annual of Communication, 1993, also TR#OTL-1993-44, Santa Clara University, Object Technology Laboratory, Jan. 1994.

21. M. Ketabchi, K., Sadeghi, "Applying Object-Oriented DBMS Technology to Software Analysis and Maintenance," Presented at the International Conference on Database and Expert Systems Applications, Prague, Czech Republic, September, 1993, also TR#OTL-1994-02, Santa Clara University, Object Technology Laboratory, Jan. 1994.

22. R. Elmasri, S. Navathe, "Fundamentals of Database Systems," Benjamin Cummings, 1989.

23. D. Fishman, et. al., "IRIS: An object-oriented database management system," ACM Transaction on Office Information Systems, 5, 1, pp. 48-69, Jan. 1987

24. M. Ketabchi, et. al, "Composition Abstractions for an Object-Centered Application Development System," TR#OTL-1994-06, Santa Clara University, Object Technology Laboratory, Feb. 1994.

25. H. Wachter, A. Reuter, "The ConTract Model," Chapter 7, Database Transaction Models for Advanced Applications, A. Elmagarmid, editor, Morgan-Kaufmann, 1992.

26. I. Jacobsen, "Object-Oriented Development in an Industrial Environment," Proceedings of OOPSLA87.

27. R. Wirfs-Brock, B. Wilkerson, and L. Wiener, "Designing Object-Oriented Software," Prentice Hall, 1990.

Efficient Image Retrieval By Color Contents

Hongjun Lu   Beng-Chin Ooi   Kian-Lee Tan

Department of Information Systems and Computer Science
National University of Singapore

Abstract. Images are becoming an important asset and managing them for efficient retrieval poses challenges to the database community. In this paper, we proposed a novel three-tier color index that supports efficient image retrieval by color contents which is important to certain applications, especially when shapes and semantic objects cannot be easily recognized. A prototype painting database system is designed and implemented to demonstrate the effectiveness of the proposed indexing technique. Besides the color index, two other indexes, B^+-trees for structured attributes and a signature file for free-text descriptions, were also implemented. As a result, a wide range of queries, both text-based and content-based can be processed efficiently. We also look at existing image database systems based on their query retrieval capabilities.

1   Introduction

The traditional database management systems, which have been effective in managing structured data, are unable to provide satisfactory performance for images which are non-alphanumeric and unstructured. With the growing need for image information systems, researchers have begun to design and implement *image database systems*. To handle large unstructured images, such systems must possess more functionalities than the traditional database systems. These include (1) the capability to analyze the image to extract key features such as the shape of objects in the image and color components; (2) the support for feature-based indexing to facilitate efficient search of a collection of images and other related information based on the feature of the images; (3) the support for content-based retrieval; and (4) the ability to handle inexact queries to capture what we humans perceive as a similarity between two images.

A large number of work has been done to develop image database systems. However, though much progress has been made in image manipulation like zooming, rotation and reflection, little progress is made in key feature extraction which is crucial in supporting content-based queries. Current computer vision techniques are still incapable of extracting all key features and identify all the embedded semantics in an image relevant to the queries supported.

In this paper, we provide a taxonomy of existing image database systems based on their query retrieval capabilities. We also describe a prototype image database system that we have developed for a painting database. In particular, our prototype features a novel three-tier color index that effectively narrow the search space to minimize accesses to unqualifying images. Besides the color index

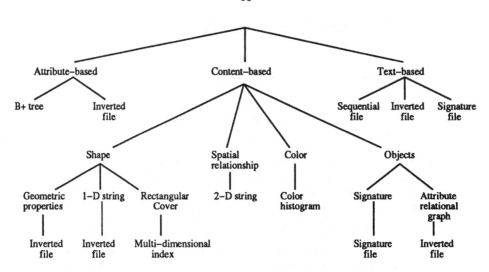

Fig. 1. A taxonomy of image database systems.

which is used for content-based queries, we have also implemented B$^+$-trees and
a signature file to facilitate retrievals based on attributes and text description.
Thus our system is able to support a wide range of queries.

2   A Taxonomy Of Image Database Systems

Existing image database systems can be classified based on the image features
used for indexing. For each image feature, further classifications can be made
with respect to the semantic representations used for the feature. A different
type of semantic representation entails a different type of indexing method. In
this section, we provide a taxonomy of image database systems based on such
classifications as depicted in Figure 1.

Attribute-based The most straightforward approach to support image objects
is to treat the images as large objects. A conventional DBMS, extended with the
capability to handle large objects, can be used to manage the images. Access
to the unstructured images is achieved through the structured attributes of the
image. Hence no special effort is required to design the organization technique,
indexing mechanisms (such as B$^+$-trees and inverted files) and query processing
methods of the systems. Because of its simplicity, early image database systems
are built based on this approach [4]. However, this approach is not capable of
handling the more user-friendly content-based queries.

Text-based Advances in text-retrieval research have prompted many researchers
to apply the concepts of Document Retrieval System to image database systems
[23]. Image database systems based on free-text retrieval attempts to provide

"content-based" functionalities by manual description of the image and treating the image description as a document. Image access is done through the accompanying image description. For example, for the query "Retrieve all paintings that show an Asian girl skating in an ice ring", the description "an Asian girl skating in an ice ring" is used to retrieve the images. The system attempts to match this description with that of images stored in the database. Indexing methods that can be used include signature file access methods [3, 17], inverted file access methods [23] and direct (or sequential) file access methods. Besides being unable to facilitate content-based queries, there are other limitations – (1) a free-text description of an image is highly variable due to the ambiguities in the natural language associated with annotating images with text and the different interpretations of the image; (2) image description is usually incomplete since an image is semantically richer than text description; (3) the vocabulary of the person creating the index and the user or even between users may not match.

Content-based To facilitate content-based retrievals, researchers have addressed the issue from several directions. The difference in these work lies in the content information (i.e. the image feature) that is being indexed on.

Shape Feature The shape feature is extremely useful for image database systems like an X-ray system or a criminal picture identification system. In an X-ray system, queries like "Retrieve all kidney X-rays with a kidney stone of this shape" are very common. For a criminal picture system, we expect queries like "Retrieve all criminals with a round face shape". The example shape, the shape of a kidney stone in the first case and *round* in the second, can be supplied using an example image. Shape features can be represented using (1) the geometric properties of the image [27], such as shape factors (e.g. ratio of height to width), mesh features, moment features and curved line features; (2) a collection of rectangles that forms a *rectangular cover* of the shape [19]; and (3) its boundary information (such as arc or a line) which can be compactly stored as a one-dimensional string [2]. Each of the above methods has its own index mechanism to faciliate fast access. For a systems that is based on the shape feature, unless the images have very distinct shape, the performance may suffer.

Semantic Objects If objects within an image are prominent and recognizable, retrieval can be achieved based on the objects. Queries can be performed by matching the object list of an image and the object lists of images in the database. In [12], the image is represented as an attribute relational graph (AGR) [12] that comprises a set of nodes that represent objects or parts of objects in the image, and edges that capture the relationships between the nodes. On the other hand, an image may also be represented by a signature which can be obtained by the composition of the signatures of the objects it contains [13]. The object-based approach is, however, limited by current image analysis techniques.

Spatial Relationship A more discriminating way to retrieve images is to specify both the semantic objects in the images as well as the spatial relationships between the objects. An example is "Retrieve all paintings with a house and a tree on its left". The house and tree are the objects while "to its left" is a spatial relationship between the two. In [6, 7], a semantic representation for spatial relationship using a two-dimensional string (2-D string) was proposed. During query processing, the 2-D string representation of the query and those of the database are compared. Similarity retrieval is supported using an exact representation and an approximate matching algorithm.

Color A natural way to retrieve colorful images would be to retrieve them by color. A semantic representation for color is the use of color histogram that captures the color composition of images (in percentages) [26]. The degree of similarity between two images is determined by the extent of the intersection between the histograms. Query by visual example is possible by matching the histograms. Object recognition is also achieved by using the color composition of the object. However, to support indexing using color histograms, a multidimensional indexing method is necessary and the number of dimensions required is of very high order (which is the number of distinct colors to be supported). Most of the existing multi-dimensional indexing methods do not perform well for high dimensionalities.

3 Color Index: A 3-Tier Approach

In this section, we describe a novel color-based index that comprises three levels of abstraction. Such an index facilitates content-based queries for colored images.

3.1 The Case For Color

Most of the existing indexes is based on objects since image identity is usually intrinsically related to the objects it contains [11, 10, 12, 13, 14, 16]. It has been widely recognized that people describe images based on the objects contained within the image. However, when a picture is abstract or contains no recognizable objects, people would describe it using color. As mentioned, indexing based on objects is limited by the capabilities of today's computer vision techniques. As such, most of the existing systems that index on objects have to resort to manual (interactive) object recognitions.

Color, on the other hand, is a local identifying feature that is independent of view and resolution. It is also widely used as a trademark in objects that occur in artificial environments, such as packaged goods, advertising signs, road signs, etc. Shape cue, in contrast to color, are highly resolution dependent. The major plus point for color indexing is that color identification algorithm can be carried out without image segmentation and analysis. In addition, access methods indexing on color are not limited by current image analysis techniques. Moreover, color recognition can be carried out automatically without human intervention.

3.2 Color Representation – Multi-level Color Histograms

A color histogram of an image contains the normalized count of the number of pixels in the image that has a particular color in a discrete color space. For example, an image which is half red and half blue will have a color histogram as shown in the top-left histogram (level 1) of Figure 3. The histogram defines an equivalence function on the set of all possible colors, that is to say, two colors are considered the same if they map to the same "bin". For example, the colors "light red" and "bright red" will be both mapped to the same position ("red") in the color histogram.

Recent studies [24, 25, 26] showed that *color histograms* are effective in characterizing the color of an image. While experimental results in [26] demonstrated that a color histogram can be used to discriminate among a large number of images, it also showed that as much as 10% of the images cannot be distinguished. This is because using a single histogram to represent the colors of an entire image suffers from a drawback – the positional information of the color is lost. Using the same histogram for illustration, we can only conclude that 50% of the image is blue color and 50% of it is red color. We, however, have no idea about the distribution of the color – the image could have its top-half red and the bottom-half blue, or its left-half red and its right-half blue, etc.

To handle positional information of color, we propose a complete quad-tree structure, called *multi-level color histogram*, based on the principle of recursive decomposition. The top level (root) of the tree corresponds to a histogram that gives the global color composition of the entire image. This is essentially what has been traditionally done. The second level comprises four histograms which give the color composition of the top left, top right, bottom left and bottom right quadrants of the image respectively. At the next level, each quadrant of the image is further subdivided into four quadrants, each of which has its own histogram. In other words, at the third level, there are sixteen color histograms. This process is repeated for the number of levels desired. In general, at the ith level, the image is subdivided into 4^{i-1} regular regions, and each region has its own histogram to describe its color composition. Figure 2 shows a 3-level color histogram. With the multi-level color histogram, we are able to discriminate between images where the traditional approach fails. As an example, consider two images – one has its top-half blue and bottom-half red, while the other has its left-half blue and right-half red. Figure 3 shows a 2-level color histogram for the images. By using only a single histogram (corresponds to the first level of the multi-level color histogram) for each image, we are unable to differentiate between the two images since both images have the same color composition. However, we can see a difference in the color composition of the images at the second level of histograms. The increase in discrimination power allows us to prune the search space of content-based queries. During query processing, the source and target images are compared based on the color composition of their histograms. The top-level histograms are first compared. If they match within some threshold value (as determined by the confidence level of the query), the next level will be searched, and so on. Only when the threshold value at the leaf

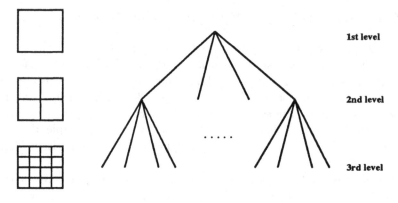

Fig. 2. A 3-level color histogram.

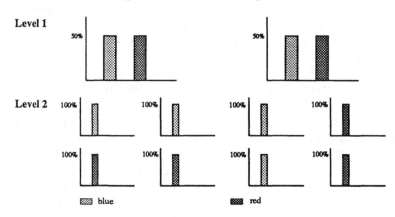

Fig. 3. The discriminating power of multi-level color histogram.

level is met then will the image be retrieved. The target image will be ignored if it fails to meet the threshold at any level of the tree. In this way, we minimize unnecessary accesses to images that do not satisfy the query.

The multi-level color histogram also provides us with an additional capability to support color distribution queries of the form "Retrieve all paintings with green grass land under the blue sky". Such a description can be formulated using $m \times m$ grid cells, and the users need to fill up the cells with the colors given in a color palette.

3.3 Similarity Of Images Based On Color

In order to use color for content-based queries, we need to have a method to determine whether two images are similar based on their colors. A straightforward approach is to compare the images pixel by pixel and when the difference in pixel values fall within a tolerance level, the pixels are considered matched. The degree of similarity between the images is then determined by the ratio of the number of matched pixels to the total number of pixels in the source image. The major drawback of such an approach, however, is that it not only requires the two images to be of the same dimension, it also incurs excessive processing of large volume of data (in the order of tera-bytes).

In this paper, we propose that the degree of similarity between two images be measured based on the color histograms since the color of an image is represented by a multi-level color histogram. We define the *histogram intersection* function, h, between two histograms as $h : A \times B \to H$ such that $H_i = min(A_i, B_i)$, $1 \leq i \leq m$ where A, B, H are histograms, *min* is a function that computes the minimum value of its input, m is the number of distinct colors allowed in the system, and A_i, B_i, H_i denote the percentage of the image with color i for histograms A, B, H respectively. The resultant histogram essentially tells us how similar, in terms of color composition, are the two images that are represented by the input histograms. To obtain a single similarity value, $\mathcal{S}$, we sum up the percentages of all the m colors of the resultant histogram, H, i.e. $\mathcal{S} = \sum_{i=1}^{m} H_i$.

With the multi-level histogram, since every level (of histograms) captures the color composition of the entire image, we can use any level to compute the histogram intersection in order to obtain an estimate of the similarity value. For the ith level, the corresponding pairs of each of the 4^{i-1} histograms of the two images are intersected. The resulting similarity value at the ith level is computed as $\mathcal{S}_i = \frac{1}{4^{i-1}} \sum_{j=1}^{4^{i-1}} \sum_{k=1}^{m} H_j^k$ where H_j^k denotes the percentage of the kth color in the jth histogram.

For the multi-level histogram, as we move from the root level to the leaf level, each level of histogram reflects more closely the color composition and distribution of the image. As such, the similarity value decreases as we go down the tree. However, the similarity value at the leaf level provides the best estimate to compare two images. On the other hand, processing time required to compute the similarity value increases with the level. This is because the number of histograms increases as we go from the root level to the leaf level.

We can use these observations to our advantage. For any image that may match the query, the similarity value obtained from the top level of histogram intersection is computed. If the degree of similarity is within the desired value, we proceed to compute the similarity value for the next level, and so on, until the leaf level. However, if the degree of similarity at any level is less than the desired value, this image is "discarded" since it can never satisfy the query. Since it costs less to compute the similarity value at the higher levels of the tree, a significant amount of processing time may be saved.

3.4 Dominant Color Classification

Color histogram is a multi-dimensional representation structure, where the number of dimensions is the number of colors in the discrete color space. Hence, to index on color using color histograms requires a multi-dimensional structure that performs well for high dimensionalities. Most of the prevailing multi-dimensional indexing methods, mainly the family of R-trees [20, 21, 15], linear quadtrees [22] and grid-files [9], lose their superior performance at high dimensionalities. To achieve high efficiency, we have to reduce the dimensionalities required for the index, without compromising on the number of dimensions needed by the color histogram. We analyzed a reasonably large collection of the color histograms of images and made several very interesting observations:

1. Most of the images are dominated by a small number of colors.
2. These *dominant* colors contribute more to the similarity of the image with other images, i.e. images which match only on the dominant colors tend to be more similar than images that match only on the less dominant colors.
3. The dominant colors can serve as a filter to prune away images that are not similar. That is, if a query image has certain dominant colors, we only need to search all images with the same dominant colors.

Based on the observations, we can classify images into *disjoint* classes with respect to the set of their k most dominant colors. For example, with $k = 2$, an image dominated by blue and red will be put into a different class than an image dominated by red and green. The number of classes depends on the value of k and is given by $^nC_k = \frac{n!}{(n-k)!k!}$ where n is the number of colors in the discrete color space. Note that the number of classes increases as k increases until k is half the value of n. Figure 4 shows the classification of images for various values of k. With the dominant color classification, we need to index on the dominant colors

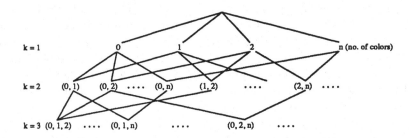

Fig. 4. Dominant color classification.

only. This allows us to reduce the high dimensionality of color histogram and avoid the problems related to multi-dimensional indexes with high dimensions.

3.5 The 3-Tier Color Index

We are now ready to look at the proposed 3-tier color index, which is shown in Figure 5. As shown in the figure, the first layer of the index is the Dominant Color Classification. It allows us to prune off images belonging to classes that would never satisfy the query, and narrows the search space to some classes.

Layer 2 is a multi-dimensional R-tree structure [21] that is used to organize the images within a class. R-tree is efficient in handling spatial data, and it allows

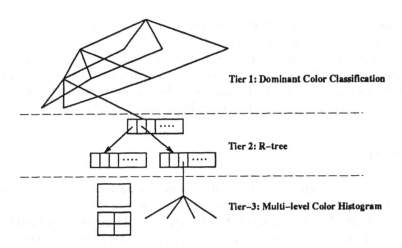

Fig. 5. The 3-tier color index.

range retrieval of all points within a distance from a particular fixed point. Hence, we would be able to use this functionality to retrieve all images within a distance away from the query image. The distance in our context would be the extent of dissimilarity. From the classes singled out by the first layer, images that are not similar to the query image can be further pruned from consideration.

Finally, the last layer, which is the multi-level color histogram, compare the histograms of the source image with each of the remaining potential candidate images. Images that fail the test need not be retrieved.

Thus, we see that the 3-tier color index minimizes access to the database to images that are most likely to satisfy the query.

4 A Prototype Image Retrieval System

A prototype image retrieval system supporting color content-based retrieval using the proposed 3-tier color index has been implemented. The system also supports attribute- and text-based retrieval.

4.1 The Database

To test the effectiveness of retrieval by color contents, we chose paintings as the image data. Paintings are ideal for testing a system supporting retrieval by color contents because of the following: The image population comes from different style of paintings, such as *Chinese* paintings, *impressionist* paintings, and *abstract arts*, etc. In addition, paintings encompass a wide variety of images – images with clear/unclear lines, images with distinct/non-distinct shapes, images which contains a lot of objects and images that are abstract and even human begins cannot make out what it contains or describe it. Furthermore, most paintings have a wide variety of colors and stress more on color tone, color composition, and form than features such as shape.

In the database, paintings are stored together with a number of structured attributes, such as the title, painter, the year the painting was completed, the size of the painting, etc. For each painting, a description of its contents is also provided so that paintings can also be retrieved from their descriptions.

4.2 Feature Extraction

In our current prototype, we indexed only on one image feature, which is color. Since all existing work that indexed on color uses a single color histogram, we cannot apply the feature extraction methods they used for our multi-level color histogram. Our algorithm is essentially a bottom-up approach that computes the leaf level histograms first, and proceed to compute the next higher level of histograms using the histograms of its children. The algorithm scans the image to count the number of pixels having a particular color. In this way, we can obtain the histograms for the leaf level. Next, each higher level of histograms is computed from its succeeding level. The algorithm is clearly efficient since it requires only one scan of the image.

4.3 Index Support

To efficiently support a wide range of queries, three types of indexes are implemented that targets at attribute-based, text-based and content-based queries.

Fixed Attribute Indexing – B^+-Trees The prototype also indexed on the fixed attributes **title, painter, location** and **year**. These are attributes that are most commonly used for retrieval. A B^+-tree index [8] is built for each of these attributes. B^+-tree is used to ensure optimum performance by maintaining its height balanced property since it is one of the most efficient index to support retrieval of alphanumeric or numeric data. Moreover, it also supports range queries. Hence, the system is able to provide fast access to single-valued queries like "Retrieve all images painted by Picasso", as well as range queries such as "Retrieve all images painted before 1900".

Free Text Indexing – A Signature File In order to allow users to retrieve the image based on descriptions in free text, such as "a lady in red", pictures in our database are also indexed on their descriptions which are in the form of free text. The index on free text description is implemented using the bit-sliced signature file access method [29]. An advantage of the signature file access method is its storage efficiency. Moreover, signature files, being much smaller than the inverted files or the sequential files, require less searching time.

Color Indexing – A 3-Tier Index Currently, the database only supports content-based queries by color similarity. To issue a content-based query, the user gives a sample image and specifies the color similarity of the image to be retrieved. The system will retrieve images whose color features are similar to the sample image within the specified range. (If no similarity value is given, the preset system default value will be used). The color features of pictures are indexed using the 3-tier index proposed in Section 3. To effectively implement the proposed index, the following issues are studied.

Optimal number of levels of multi-level histogram As pointed out earlier, increasing the number of levels of the multi-color histogram provides a better color composition of the image, and thus increases the power of discrimination. However, the cost to compute the histogram intersection increases too. In order to determine an optimal number of levels, a series of experiments were conducted by varying the number of levels, $\mathcal{L}$, and observing the effects to find a value of $\mathcal{L}$ that gives satisfactory discrimination power and requires an acceptable amount of storage and processing time.

In our experiments, the same expected degree of similarity was used. Both exact-match and partial-match queries are categorized into three groups:

1. Type $F_e(F_p)$: exact-match (partial-match) queries with images which are found in the database;
2. Type $R_e(R_p)$: exact-match (partial-match) queries with images which are rotated or reflected version of a database image; and
3. Type $N_e(N_p)$: exact-match (partial-match) queries with images which are not found in the database.

We found that both Type F_e and N_e queries were not sensitive to the values of $\mathcal{L}$, that is, correct images were retrieved or no images were retrieved from the database for all $\mathcal{L}$ values tested. However, for Type R_e queries, the system returned the corresponding upright version of the database image with single level histogram, i.e. $\mathcal{L} = 1$. This is an unsatisfactory result which indicates poor discriminating power. By increasing $\mathcal{L}$ to 2, the system is able to discriminate between the upright version and the rotated or reflected version of the images. For the partial match queries, the number of images returned decreases with increasing $\mathcal{L}$ value. This demonstrates the increase in discriminating power for larger values of $\mathcal{L}$. However, we found that the number of images returned by the system when $\mathcal{L}$ is set to 2 or more is about the same in the database tested. To reduce the cost, we set $\mathcal{L}$ to 2 in our prototype. This "magic" number could vary from one application to another. To achieve the desired balance between the cost and performance, some experiments should be conducted and the number of histogram levels becomes a configurable system parameter.

Limit the number of classes to be searched The use of the dominant color classification to retrieve images is complicated by partial-match queries and the degree of similarity that the user expects from the target images. As such, more than one class may have to be searched. We determine the classes based on the following heuristic:

> For an expected similarity value of $\mathcal{S}$, the color value of the target image, $\mathcal{T}$ must be within the range $[\mathcal{C} - \mathcal{D}, \mathcal{C} + \mathcal{D}]$ where $\mathcal{D}$ is the degree of mismatch, and equal $(1 - \mathcal{S})$ and $\mathcal{C}$ is the color value of the query image.

To illustrate, let us consider the normalized image histogram (sorted in descending order) shown in Table 1. Suppose the expected similarity value is 0.9. Then the maximum possible mismatch is 0.1. If any of the range is not satisfied, the expected similarity value of 0.9 can never be achieved. Values satisfying the range ensure that the mismatch value for the color is less than the maximum possible mismatch for the color. From Table 1, we see that the value of color 5 in any target image that satisfies the query image will never be lower than 0.4, and the values for other colors in the same target image will never be higher than 0.4. Thus, we can be sure that color 5 must be one of the dominant colors in the desired image, and so we can narrow our search to classes that contain color 5. Repeating the process and identifying the next dominant color will allow us to narrow our search space. For example, if the number of dominant colors used is 2, then since the possible target range values for colors 0 and 4 overlap, and no other (non-selected) colors has value higher than 0.12, both colors should be included as the next dominant color. Thus, we have two classes to be searched – class with dominant colors 5 and 0, and class with dominant colors 5 and 4.

Table 1. Possible range for target images.

Color	Value	Possible value range for target image
5	0.5	0.4–0.6
0	0.25	0.15–0.35
4	0.22	0.12–0.32
3	0.01	0–0.11
1	0.01	0–0.11
2	0	0–0.10
6	0	0–0.10

Optimal number of dominant colors The number of dominant colors affect the pruning ability of the Dominant Color Classification. This is because more dominant colors (up to at most half the number of colors in the discrete color space) results in a larger number of classes, and the effect is that more classes has to be searched during retrieval. To determine the pruning ability of the dominant colors, we conducted an experiment with different number of dominant colors, $\mathcal{D}$. We define the *prune_down* metric as the ratio of the number of histograms searched to the total number of histograms. Here, we would want the value of prune-down to be as small as possible.

Our results showed that, as expected, an increase in $\mathcal{D}$ increases the number of classes to be searched. However, due to a more significant increase in the total number of classes, the search space decreases with the increase in the value of $\mathcal{D}$. The value of prune-down, however, stabilizes after $\mathcal{D} = 3$. This is because the number of dominant colors is usually no more than 3. In the cases when the number of dominant colors is greater than 3, some of the dominant colors do not cover more than 10% of the image. As a result, these "dominant" colors do not contribute much to the similarity value. As such, a value of $\mathcal{D}$ exceeding 3 does not produce a lower prune-down value. We, therefore, restrict the number of dominant colors to 3 in our prototype.

Queries Using Multiple Indexes As can be seen, the three indexes allow us to answer a wide range of queries. In fact, with diverse attributes indexed on, composite queries are also answerable. For example, the query "Retrieve all paintings in 1990 (fixed attribute) which has a lady in red (free-text description) and looks similar to this image example (image-based)", requires us to combine the three types of indexes.

5 Conclusion

In this paper, we have provided a taxonomy of existing image database systems based on their query retrieval capabilities. We have also described the prototype image database system that we have developed for a painting database. A novel feature of our prototype is its three-tier color index used for content-based retrievals. To facilitate retrievals based on attributes and text description, we have also implemented B^+-tree indexes and a signature file. Thus, our system is able to support a wide range of queries.

Acknowledgement We benefited from discussions with Tat-Seng Chua. Ching-Ching Goh and Hai-Yong Chung implemented the system.

References

1. Christodoulakis, S., Faloutsos, C.: Signature Files: An Access Method for Documents and its Analytical Performance Evaluation. ACM Trans. Office Info. Syst. V2(4) (1984) 267–288
2. Jea, K-F, Y-C Lee, Y-C: Building Efficient and Flexible Feature-based Indices. Info. Syst. V15(6) (1990) 653–662
3. Faloutsos, C.: Access Methods for Text. ACM Comp. Surveys V17(1) (1985) 49–74
4. Chang, N.S., K.S. Fu, K.S.: Picture Query Languages for Pictorial Database Systems. IEEE Computer (1981) 23–33
5. Chang, S.K., Liu, S.H.: Picture Indexing and Abstraction Techniques for Pictorial Databases. IEEE Trans. Pattern Analysis and Machine Intelligence (1984) 475–484

6. Chang, S.K., Shi, Q.Y., Yan, C.W.", Iconic Indexing by 2-D String. IEEE Trans. Pattern Analysis and Machine Intelligence V9(3) (1987) 413–428

7. Chang, S.K., Yan, C.W., Dimitroff, D.C., Arndt, T.: An Intelligent Image Database System. IEEE Trans. Software Engineering V14(5) (1988) 681–688

8. Comer, D.: The Ubiquitous B-tree. ACM Comp. Surveys V11(2) (1979) 121–137

9. Nievergelt, J., Hinterberger, H., Sevcik, K.C.: The Grid File: An Adaptable, Symmetric Multikey File Structure. ACM Trans. Database Systems V9(1) (1984) 38–71

10. Eshera, M.A., Fu, K.S.: An Image Understanding System Using Attributed Symbolic Representation and Inexact Graph Matching. IEEE Trans. Pattern Analysis and Machine Intelligence V8(5) (1986) 604–618

11. Conti, P., Rabitti, F.: Retrieval of Multi-Media Document Images in MULTOS. The Esprit Conf '87 (1987) 1389–1412

12. Rabitti, F., Stanchev, P.: GRIM-DBMS: A Graphical Image Database Management System. The IFIP TCS Working Conf on Visual Database Systems (1989) 415–430

13. Rabitti, F., Savino, P.: Image Query Processing Based on Multi-Level Signatures. 14th Conf on R&D in IR (1991) 305–314

14. Rabitti, F., Savino, P.: Query Processing on Image Databases. "Proceedings of the IFIP 2nd Working Conf on Visual Database Systems", (1992) 174–188

15. Sellis, T., Roussopoulous, N., Faloutsos, C.: The R+-Tree: A Dynamic Index for Multi-Dimensional Objects. 13th VLDB Conf (1987) 507–518

16. Rabitti, F., Savino, P.: An Information Retrieval Approach for Image Databases. 18th VLDB Conf (1992) 574–584

17. Sacks-Davis, R., Ramamohanaras, K., Kent, A.J.: A Signature File Scheme Based on Multiple Organizations for Indexing Very Large Text Databases. Info. Syst. (1988)

18. Jain, R.: Visual Information Management Systems. SIGMOD Record V22(3) (1993) 56–75

19. Jagadish, H.V.: A Retrieval Technique for Similar Shape. 1991 SIGMOD (1991) 208–217

20. Beckmann, N., Kriegel, H.P., Schneider, R., Seeger, B.: The R*-tree: An Efficient and Robust Access Method for Points and Rectangles. 1990 SIGMOD (1990)

21. Guttman, A.: R-Trees: A Dynamic Index Structure for Spatial Searching. 1984 SIGMOD (1984) 47–57

22. Samet, H.: The Design and Analysis of Spatial Data Structures. Addison-Wesley (1989)

23. Al-Hawamden, Price, R., Tng, T.H.: Free-text Based Image Retrieval Systems. Institute of System Science, National University of Singapore TR 91-54-0 (1991)

24. Niblack, W., Barber, R., Equitz, W., Flicker, M., Glasman, E., Petkovic, D., Yanker, P., Faloutsos, C., Taubin, G.: The QBIC Project: Querying Images by Content Using Color, Texture and Shape. SPIE V1908 (1993)

25. Niblack, W., Flicker, M.: Find me the pictures that look like this: IBM's Image Query Project. Advanced Imaging (1993)

26. Swain, M.J.: Interactive Indexing into Image Database. SPIE V1908 (1993)

27. Tanabe, K., Ohya, J.: A Similarity Retrieval Method for Line Drawing Image Database. Progress in Image Analysis and Processing (1989)

28. Woelk, D., Luther, W., Kim, W.: Multimedia Applications and Database Requirements. IEEE CS Office Automation Symp. (1987) 180–189

29. Roberts, C.S.: Partial Match Retrieval via the Method of Superimposed Codes. Proceedings of the IEEE 67 12 (1979) 1624–1642

STAR - A Multimedia Database System For Trademark Registration

J.K. Wu, B.M. Mehtre, Y.J. Gao, P.C. Lam, A. Desai Narasimhalu

Institute of Systems Science, National University of Singapore, Singapore 0511

Abstract. *To ensure the uniqueness of all trademarks registered is very important. With ever increasing number of registered trademarks, this is becoming increasingly difficult. A system for search and registration of trademarks is presented in this paper. Trademarks are complex patterns consisting of various image and text patterns, called device-mark and word-in-mark respectively. Traditionally, only text part has been used for search and retrieval of such patterns. This was largely due to the diversity and complexity of image patterns occurring in trademarks. The System for Trademark Archival and Registration (STAR) presented here, uses features based on image as well as text components of trademarks and brings out the conflicting trademarks for the consideration of trademark officer. Thus, it simplifies the task of trademark office to a great extent. A structural representation consisting of image, graphics, text, and phonetics has been proposed to handle the diversity and complexity of trademarks. Based on this structural representation, an object-oriented database schema, a sophisticated segmentation technique, a composite similarity measure for searching conflicting trademarks, and an indexing scheme have been developed. Initial results are very promising. More testing is in progress.*

1 Introduction

The importance of trademark has increased with the successful agreement of GATT talks, wherein more countries will now protect the trademark and patent laws. The problem of trademark registration thus gets added importance. To ensure the uniqueness of all trademarks registered is very important. This is very daunting and challenging task due to ever increasing number of registered trademarks. The problem is further aggravated by the complexity and diversity of trademark patterns. Traditionally, database systems are employed to a limited extent for such purpose, as they still need to use manual paper based indexing method for searching the symbolic "device-marks" trademarks.

Recently much attention has been paid to the research of image databases [14, 15, 17, 18, 22, 20]. Research effort has mainly been focused at feature-based retrieval of images. For example, a Computer-Aided Facial Image Inference and Retrieval (CAFIIR) system in [22] provides four special image data access means, namely, visual browsing, similarity retrieval, fuzzy retrieval, and free text retrieval, for criminal identification. Kato et al[1] proposed a TRADE-MARK system, which allows design and retrieval of trademarks from a free hand sketch of a sample trademark. They used graphic patterns rather than actual trademarks for similarity retrieval.

Due to advances in imaging technologies and retrieval methods many new applications involving image information retrieval are emerging. Such applications exploit new features and functionalities of the image database systems. Unlike the commonality of images involved in other imaging applications like fingerprint or remote sensing, trademark images pose an altogether different problem. The single most important among them being diversity in the image types. Almost every trademark, by rule, has to be different from other trademarks. This rules out the possibility of having generic common features as used in any traditional pattern recognition application.

We have proposed a structural representation scheme to tackle the difficulties of trademark image archival and search problem. This scheme of representation consists of multimedia data types: graphics, image, text, phonetics; a sophisticated segmentation technique, a composite similarity measure and a complex indexing scheme. A prototype Trademark Archival and Registration System (STAR) has been developed at the Institute of Systems Science, National University of Singapore. A block schematic of STAR is shown in Fig. 1. There are two main functions, trademark archival and trademark search (for registration). Trademark archival is done in four steps: trademark image input, normalization, segmentation, and insertion. On the other hand, trademark registration involves five steps: trademark image input, normalization, segmentation, searching for similar trademarks, verification by trademark officer, registration and insertion of the current trademark.

When a trademark image is scanned in, it is normalized to a standard size and orientation. In the segmentation stage, user interactively fills in the structural representation frame, by typing in details such as trademark number, class, proprietor's name, company name, inputing word-in-mark, phonetics, and interpretation. The device-mark will be characterized by both meaning and shape measures. The meaning is entered by the operator, while the shape measures are automatically computed. After segmentation, the representation frame of a trademark has been completed. It is ready to be either inserted into the database, or can be submitted to search for similar trademarks.

The challenges in computerization of trademark registration arise due to the diversity and complexity of trademark images. These are approached as follows: a composite structural representation is used for trademarks, building this representation structure for each trademark images (through segmentation), and composite search techniques for retrieving similar trademarks. The following three sections will be dedicated to each of these three issues. Section 2 gives our scheme of trademark representation and matching, sections 3 describes the trademark segmentation and feature extraction, section 4 deals with searching of similar trademarks, and conclusions are given in section 5. The references are given at the end of the paper.

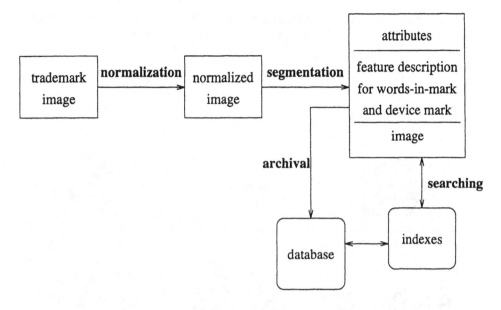

Fig. 1. Block Schematic of Trademark Archival and Registration System

2 Scheme of Trademark Representation and Matching

Among the technical difficulties of automated search of trademarks are the following: an unlimited variety of symbolic patterns, multi-lingual words, unlimited abbreviations, styled characters, importance of meaning of the words (rather than appearance), abstract graphics components. All these variations can occur singly or in any combinations of the above. We use the following structural classification of trademarks:

1. Trademarks with word-in-mark only.
   (a) Multi-lingual words;
   (b) Abbreviations;
   (c) Styled characters;
2. Trademarks with device mark only.
   (a) Abstract shapes;
   (b) Drawing of existing object, such as crown, animal;
   (c) Styled characters;
   (d) Composed of multi components;
3. Mixture of both word-in-mark and device mark.

Above structural classification can be illustrated by 12 trademark images of airline companies shown in Fig. 2. Trademark image (3,2) has word-in-mark only. Trademark images (1,1), (1,2), (1,3), (3,3), and (4,1) have device mark only. Image (4,2) can be considered as device mark, as character "M", is not just a character but has graphics. It looks a crown (conflicts with trademark (1,2), also a crown) and hence may be considered as device-mark. Trademark images (2,1), (3,1), (2,2) have both word-in-mark and device mark.

Fig. 2. Trademarks of airline companies. We use row and column number to label these trademark images. For example, Finnair will be labeled as (1,3) image.

We represent trademarks as structural patterns consisting of word-in-mark and device-mark. The word-in-mark is text, and the device-mark is graphic or image. Fig. 3 illustrates the structural representation. The detailed description of this representation is as follows.

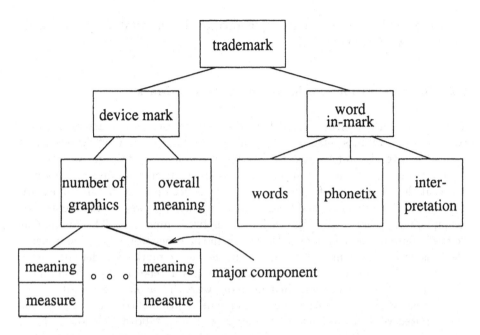

Fig. 3. Structural representation of trademarks

2.1 Representation and Matching of Word-In-Mark

According to trademark registration rules, word-in-mark similarity will be considered in three aspects: word-in-mark text, phonetics, and interpretation. To match the multi-lingual word-in-mark text, the similarity will be evaluated first against lingual type, and then the syntax in terms of the language. Word-in-mark text in all alphabetic languages will be matched using alphabetic matching rules. For ideographic languages such as Chinese word-in-mark text is matched using character code.

Word-in-marks will be considered similar if their phonetics are similar even if they are from different languages. We represent phonetics of all types of word-in-mark using 41 phonemes published by the National Technical Information Service of USA in document "AD/A021 929". As soon as the phonetics of the trademarks are obtained, similarity measures of phonetics for trademarks can be computed using the same method for words-in-mark text.

Interpretation is the third aspect to evaluate similarities between trademarks. The interpretation for abbreviations is straightforward. For example, "TWA" is Trans-World Airlines. Interpretation of word-in-mark in other languages to English is done by the user. Matching of interpretation of word-in-mark of trademarks is based on similarity between words. A synonyms dictionary is maintained which assigns degrees of similarity between pairs of similar words. The overall similarity will be the total similarity normalized by the total number of words within the word-in-mark.

2.2 Representation and Matching of Device-Mark

The device-mark is either a graphic or an image. Styled characters are also considered as graphics, such as "M" in image (4,2) in Fig. 2. Most device-marks consist of several components. To describe their shape or texture, we need to separate them by segmentation process. It is known from computer vision study [21] that the description of a graphic or image device involves the shape/texture description of components and the spatial relationship between components. For example, trademark image (3,3) in Fig. 2 has two components. The component "circle" contains the component "leaf". Or in the other words, the components "leaf" is within the component "circle". In the device-mark of trademark image (3,1) in Fig. 2, there are four components. The spatial relationships among these four components can be described in many ways. To avoid the complexity of spatial relationship description, we use coded description of component positions with limited vocabulary, such as "center", "outline", "above", "below", "left", and "right". With this scheme, the four components in trademark image (3,1) in Fig. 2 have position description of "outline", "above", "center", and "below". Here, the outline means bounding figure or enclosure. Many times the outline is a circle. Most device-marks of trademarks carry particular meaning. For example, image (4,1) is an eagle. When searching for similar trademarks, the meaning of device-marks is weighted quite high. For example, both image (1,2) and (4,2) in Fig. 2 have the meaning "crown". They are similar in the sense of meaning even though they are totally different as far as structure and shape are concerned. Of course, structure and shape are also important when computing the similarity. In case the device-mark does not have a particular meaning, then structure, shape, and texture measures are the only factors used to evaluate the similarity value. This is true, for example, for the trademark shown in (3,1) of Fig. 2.

3 Segmentation and Feature Extraction

Since the nature of trademark images is very complex and lack any commonality, fully automatic segmentation is almost impossible. Hence, we have adopted a semi-automatic and interactive segmentation. A partial automatic segmentation is performed by labeling the connected components, and the result is presented to the user, through an interactive user interface. The results of such a segmentation are presented in different colors for different components for easy identification (or grouping) by the user. The user-interface facilitates grouping of one or more components together. Once a component or a group of components is selected by the user, they are extracted and highlighted. The image features (measures for similarity) are computed.

3.1   Interactive Segmentation

A first level segmentation of trademark images is performed by labeling of connected components in the image. The partial segmentation results are presented to the user through an interactive user-friendly interface. Fig. 4 shows the segmentation module. Every Trademark that is submitted to trademark office is assigned a unique identification number. Also, trademarks are classified based on their business categories as defined by international classification of goods and services. As evident from the figure, this module facilitates entry of details of trademark owner, company, address etc. The device-mark details like position (left, right, center, etc), type of component (graphic, texture, stylized character etc), are entered by choosing the options provided through the pull down menu. The meaning of components (if available) is entered through the prompt dialog. Optionally, a component can be designated as major (important) component, when there are more than one components.

The details of word-in-mark like position, words, phonetics, and interpretation are similarly entered. The figure shows interactive segmentation of an airline trademark. This trademark has both device-mark, represented by flying bird, and the word-in-mark "Abu Dhabi". For the device-mark, whole bird image is selected. The shape measures are automatically computed as soon as the user completes selection. For the word-in-mark, the details are entered like-wise. In this case, of course, no features are computed, as the matching is based on words (text), phonetics and interpretation.

3.2   Image Features

There are many techniques of shape/texture analysis. Chain coding [4],fourier descriptors [6], invariant moments [7], autoregressive models [10], polar signatures [11] and syntactic approaches [12] are all well known methods of shape representation. Among them, Fourier descriptors, invariant moments, autoregressive models and polar signature methods are independent of translation and rotation.

For a two-dimensional digital image $f(x, y)$ the moment of order $p + q$ is given by [3]

$$\mu_{pq} = \sum_x \sum_y (x - \overline{x})^p (y - \overline{y})^q f(x, y). \tag{1}$$

The *normalised central moments*, denoted by η_{pq}, are defined as

$$\eta_{pq} = \mu_{pq} / \mu_{00}^\gamma \tag{2}$$

where $\gamma = (p + q + 1)/2$, for $p + q = 2, 3, \ldots$.

From the second and third moments, a set of seven *invariant moments* are computed as follows:

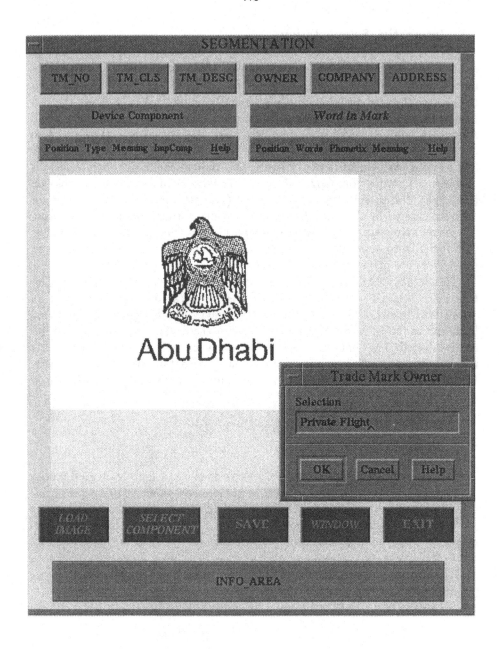

Fig. 4. Segmentation of trademark images

$$\phi_1 = \eta_{20} + \eta_{02}$$
$$\phi_2 = (\eta_{20} - \eta_{02})^2 + 4\eta_{11}^2$$
$$\phi_3 = (\eta_{30} - \eta_{02})^2 + (3\eta_{21} - \eta_{03})^2$$
$$\phi_4 = (\eta_{30} + \eta_{12})^2 + (3\eta_{21} + \eta_{03})^2$$
$$\phi_5 = (\eta_{30} - 3\eta_{12})(\eta_{30} + \eta_{12})[(\eta_{30} + \eta_{12})^2 - 3(\eta_{21} + \eta_{03})^2] + (3\eta_{21} - \eta_{03})(\eta_{21} + \eta_{03})[3(\eta_{30} + \eta_{12})^2 - (\eta_{21} + \eta_{03})^2]$$
$$\phi_6 = (\eta_{20} - \eta_{02})[(\eta_{30} + \eta_{12})^2 - (\eta_{21} + \eta_{03})^2] + 4\eta_{11}(\eta_{30} + \eta_{12})(\eta_{21} + \eta_{03})$$
$$\phi_7 = (3\eta_{21} - \eta_{03})(\eta_{30} + \eta_{12})[(\eta_{30} + \eta_{12})^2 - 3(\eta_{21} - \eta_{30})^2] + [(3\eta_{12} - \eta_{30})(\eta_{21} + \eta_{03})[3(\eta_{30} + \eta_{12})^2 - (\eta_{21} + \eta_{03})^2]$$

This set of moments has been shown [3] to be invariant to translation, rotation, and scale change. This was tested for a set of different trademark images, and was found to be true.

4 Searching Similar Trademarks

An important step in trademark registration is to ensure the uniqueness of all registered trademarks. To achieve this, we have to see that there does not exist similar or even distantly resembling trademarks in the database. If they exist, then they are conflicting and the current trademark may not be accepted for registration. Traditionally manual searches are carried out. Manual searching is extremely tedious and almost impossible for trademarks with device-marks which cannot be described precisely. For example, the device-mark of trademark shown in (3,1) of Fig.2. Manual searching depends on trademark indices. Indices are either built by categorization or based on letters of word-in-mark or textual description of device-mark. When a device-mark can't be described, it can't be put into the index. The problem becomes more difficult, when more and more trademarks adopt abstract graphics, the meaning of which are ambiguous. Fortunately, shape/texture analysis technique in computer vision provides means to describe various types of device-marks, as described in previous section. Iconic indexing method in [22] offers an ideal approach to create index on the extracted complex shape/texture measures.

From information retrieval point of view, searching for similar trademarks is a kind of similarity retrieval, which consists of two major techniques: defining similarity measures and building indices on the feature measures to accelerate the searching process. They are discussed in the following subsections.

4.1 Composite Similarity Measures

Complex structural representation of trademarks leads to composite similarity measure. The composite similarity measure for trademarks can be defined in terms of weighted distance and written as follows:

$$d_{cj} = w^w d_{ci}^w + w^d d_{cj}^d \tag{3}$$

where d_{cj} is the overall similarity measure for the "current" trademark and j-th trademark image in the archive, w^w, w^d and d^w, d^d are weights for word-in-mark and device-mark, respectively, and d^w, d^d are distances for word-in-mark and device-mark, respectively.

$$d_{cj}^w = \begin{cases} 0 & \text{if } wim_c = wim_j = false \\ \theta_w & \text{if } wim_c \neq wim_j \\ w_w^w d_{wcj}^w + w_p^w d_{pcj}^w + w_i^w d_{icj}^w & \text{if } wim_c = wim_j = true \end{cases}$$

where wim_j is a boolean function to represent the presence and absence of word-in-mark in the j-th trademark, w_w^w, w_p^w, w_i^w and $d_{wcj}^w, d_{pcj}^w, d_{icj}^w$ are weights and distances of words, phonetics, and interpretation between the current trademark and the j-th trademark, respectively. θ_w is the penalty when one trademark has a word-in-mark but the other does not.

Similarly, the similarity for device mark is defined as

$$d_{cj}^d = \begin{cases} 0 & \text{if } dev_c = dev_j = false \\ \theta_d & \text{if } dev_c \neq dev_j \\ \frac{1}{N_{comp}} \sum_k (w_m^d d_{mkcj}^d + w_p^d d_{pkcj}^d + w_g^d d_{gkcj}^d) & \text{if } dev_c = dev_j = true \end{cases}$$

where dev_j is a boolean function to represent the presence and absence of device mark in the j-th trademark, θ_d is the penalty when one trademark has a device mark but the other does not. w_m^d, w_p^d, w_g^d are weights for the meaning, position and shape/texture aspects for the device mark and $d_{mkcj}^d, d_{pkcj}^d, d_{gkcj}^d$ are distances of the meaning, position and shape/texture aspects of k-th components of the device mark of the current trademark and a component of the device mark of the j-th trademark. Notice that the graphics components of device mark do not have any particular order when they are segmented. Any graphics component in the current trademark can match any graphics component in the j-th trademark. The distance of the device mark is then defined as the minimum distance between these two device marks.

Notice also that graphics components are not necessarily treated equally. For example, in the trademark image (3, 3), the leaf graphic part is more important than the circle. Therefore, we distinguish such component as *major component*. If the major component of the device mark of the current trademark matches the major component of the device mark of the j-th trademark, more weight should be put to their distance than the distances of the other components.

$$d_{cj}^d = (1 - w_{imp})(d_{cj}^d - \frac{1}{N_{comp}} d_{imp-cj}^d) + w_{imp} d_{imp-cj}^d \tag{4}$$

where w_{imp} and d_{imp-cj}^d are the weight factor and the distance for the major component.

We can simply adopt the Euclidean distance to measure the distance between device marks because the shape/texture measures are represented as vectors after segmentation and feature extraction. Similarity measures for word-in-mark is measured by the number of same ordered characters in the two words [23]. The formula is:

$$d_w^w = 1 - sim_w = 1 - \sum_k w_k l_k / l_{word} \tag{5}$$

where s_w is the similarity measure, l_k, l_{word} are length of the k-th common factor between two words and the length of the whole word. Several cases will be checked when actually computing the length of common factors. The word length is taken to be the average length of two words. Following table lists similarity measures between two words, where sim_w, sim_p are similarities for word and phonetics.

word 1	word 2	sim_w	sim_p
asi	asea	0.750000	0.333333
foral	feral	0.975000	0.975000
cosmic	coshmick	0.937500	0.979167
armor	amor	0.975000	0.800000
creeza	kreeza	0.916667	1.000000
heart	hart	0.975000	0.968750
Chikngrillas	Chickutay	0.854167	0.825000
aero	aeron	0.975000	0.750000
gaynor	caynore	0.857143	0.833333
communication	com*tion	0.942308	0.932692
3M	Three M	0.142857	1.000000
Fujitsu	Kodar	0.000000	0.000000

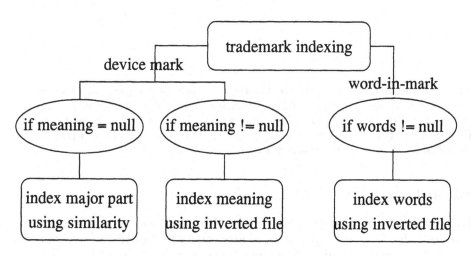

Fig. 5. Indices for trademark searching

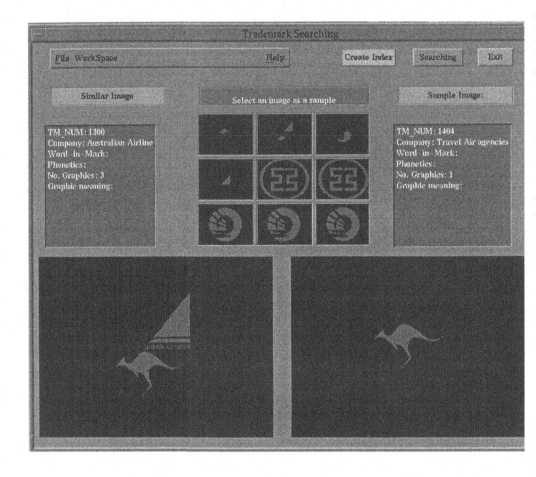

Fig. 6. Trademark searching results. On the right side of the panel are attributes and image of the sample trademark. 9 icon images displayed at the center part show searching results. They are arranged from the most similar (top-left) to the least similar (bottom-left). The detailed information of any of these 9 image can be displayed on the left side of the panel by clicking the corresponding icon image.

4.2 Indexing

For a trademark archive, there may be hundred thousands of trademarks. To accelerate the the searching process, indices should be created. As depicted in Fig. 5, there are three indices. The way to organize these three indices itself is a tree structure.

Similarity measures of device marks are vectors rather than primitive data types. The iconic indexing method in [22] is suitable to create index on this shape/texture measures.

4.3 Sample Search Results

Searching for the similar trademarks is carried out after presenting a completely segmented input trademark. Indices are used to narrow down possible candidates so as to reduce the searching time. All possible candidates will be examined using the composite similarity measure. Fig. 6 shows a preliminary result with a database of hundred trademark images. In all 9 trademarks have been listed as similarity search output. The distance measures for trademark images from top-left to bottom-right are: 0.000000, 0.300000, 1.031324, 1.082123, 1.356212, 1.356485, 1.356485, 1.358610, 1.358610. Note from the similarities that only two trademarks are very similar. Other trademark images are quite different from the sample trademark, and therefore can be considered not similar. They can be easily discarded by a registration officer or automatically with a threshold, for example, 1, for the similarity.

5 Conclusions

A system for trademarks archival and registration is proposed and a prototype has been developed. This system is capable of handling the twin challenges, diversity and complexity, in computerization of trademarks registration. Following are the three main contributions in the proposed system: structural representation, segmentation, and searching. The system has been tested for a variety of trademark images, and the results are promising. Future work plan includes large scale testing, performance improvement, and build a robust operational product.

References

1. T. Kato, H. Shimogaki and K. Fujimura, *Architecture and User Interface of Intelligent Multimedia Database System TRADEMARK*, Bulletin of the Electrotechnical laboratory, Vol. 52, No., 7, 1988, pp. 1-20.
2. W. Niblack, et al, *The QBIC Project: Querying Images by Content Using Color, Texture, and Shape*, SPIE Vol. 1908, 1993, pp. 173-187.
3. E. L. Hall, *Computer Image Processing and Recognition*, Academic Press, 1979, pp. 420-423.
4. H. Lynn Bues and Steven S.H. Tu: An improved corner detection algorithm based on chain coded plane curves, *Pattern Recognition*, Vol 20, No 3, pp. 291-296, 1987.
5. Herbert Freeman and Larry S. Davis: A Corner Finding Algorithm for Chain Coded Curves, *IEEE Trans on Computers*, 297-303, March 1977.
6. Chun-Shin Lin and Chia-Lin Hwang: New Forms of Shape Invariants From Elliptic Fourier Descriptors, *Pattern Recognition*, Vol 20, No 5, 535-545, 1987.
7. X.Y. Jiang and H. Bunke: Simple and Fast Computation of Moments, *Pattern Recognition*, Vol 24, No 8, pp. 801-806, 1991.
8. Jia Guu Leu: Computing a Shape's Moments From its Boundary, *Pattern Recognition*, Vol 24, No 10, pp. 949-957, 1991.

9. N.J.C. Strachan, P. Nesvadba, and A.R. Allen: A Method of Working Out the Moments of a Polygon Using an Integration technique, *Pattern Recognition Letters*, 11 (1990), 351-354, North Holland.

10. S.R. Dubois and F.H. Glanz: An Autoregressive Model Approach to two-dimensional Shape Classification, *IEEE Trans on Pattern Analysis and Machine Intelligence*, 8, 55-66, (1986).

11. W.N. Lie and Y.C. Chen: Shape Representation and Matching using Polar Signature, *Proc. Int. Computer Symposium*, 1986, Tainan, Taiwan, pp. 710-718, (1986).

12. H.H. Chen and J.S. Su: A Syntactic Approach to Shape Recognition, *Proc. Int. Computer Symp.*, 1986, Tainan, Taiwan, pp. 103-122, (december 1986).

13. S. K. Chang, C. W. Yan, D. Dimitrof and T. Arnd: An Intelligent Image Database System, *IEEE Trans. Software Engineering*, 14, 681-688 (1988).

14. Y.H. Ang, S.H. Ong, and C.T. Leung: Image Retrieval Based on Shape and Texture Features, 2nd*Singapore International Conference on Image Processing*, 7-11 Sept 1992, pp. 547-551.

15. H. V. Jagadish: A Retrieval Technique for Similar Shapes, *Proceedings of the ACM SIGMOD, International Conference on Management of Data*, Vol 20, Issue 2, pp. 208-217, June 1991.

16. F. Rabitti and P. Savino: Automatic Image Indexation and Retrieval, *Intelligent Text and Image Handling*, Proceedings of RIAO, pp. 864-884, 1991.

17. C.C. Chang and S.Y. Lee: Retrieval Of Similar Pictures on Pictorial Databases, *Pattern Recognition*, Vol 24, No 7, pp. 675-680, 1991.

18. William I. Grosky and Rajiv Mehrotra: Index Based Object Recognition in Pictorial Data Management, *Computer Vision, Graphics, and Image Processing*, 52, 416-436 (1990).

19. Suh Yin Lee, Man Kwan Shan and Wei Pang Yang: Similarity Retrieval of Iconic Image Database, *Pattern Recognition*, Vol 22, No 6, pp. 675-682, 1989.

20. Bach J, Paul S, Jain R (1993) An interactive image management system for face information retrieval, *IEEE Trans. on Knowledge and Data Engineering*, Special Section on Multimedia Information Systems

21. D. H. Ballard, C. H. Brown, Computer Vision, Prentice Hall Inc., New York, 1982

22. J. K. Wu, Y. H. Ang, C. P. Lam, H. H. Loh, A. D. Narasimhalu: Inference and Retrieval of Facial Images, *ACM Multimedia Journal*, to appear in 1994.

23. Meadow, Charles T., Text Information Retrieval Systems, Academic Press, Inc., San Diego, California. 1992.

Visualizing and Querying Distributed Event Traces with Hy+

Mariano P. Consens, Masum Z. Hasan, Alberto O. Mendelzon

Computer Systems Research Institute, University of Toronto, 6 King's College Road, Toronto, Ontario, canada, M5S 1A1

Abstract. A programmer attempting to understand and debug a distributed program deals with large volumes of trace data that describe the program's behaviour. Visualization is widely believed to help in this and similar tasks. We contend that visualization is indeed useful, but only if accompanied of powerful data management facilities to support abstraction and filtering. The **Hy+** visualization system and GraphLog query language provide these facilities. They support not just a fixed way of visualizing data, but visualizations that can be specified and manipulated through declarative queries, like data are manipulated in a database. In this paper we show how the **Hy+**/GraphLog system can be used by distributed program debuggers to meet their information manipulation and visualization goals.

The **Hy+**/GraphLog system can be used for observing behaviour of distributed and parallel applications by specifying normal or abnormal patterns that the programmer is looking for as declarative GraphLog queries and manipulating the resulting visualizations to understand the behaviour of the program.

1 Introduction

Distributed and parallel program debugging requires the analysis of large volumes of trace data. We show that a system that provides a convenient marriage of deductive databases and visualization technology is well suited for the specification and presentation services required for analyzing the behaviour of distributed and parallel programs. To understand the behavior of a complex system, visualization techniques are widely used. But simple and fixed ways of visualizing data are not well suited to our intended application domain. Our proposal allows the programmer not only to specify visualizations through declarative queries, but also to store and manipulate visualizations like data are manipulated in a database. These queries provide a powerful mechanism for *abstraction*, that is, defining higher level objects that match the programmer's understanding of the computation, and for *filtering*, that is, focusing on particular subsets of the trace data.

The **Hy+**/GraphLog system developed at the University of Toronto is a general purpose environment for visualizing structural data that has been applied to areas such as software engineering [6], hypertext [3] and network management [2]. GraphLog [4] is the visual query language for the **Hy+** system.

Debugging can be viewed as the detection and diagnosis of unexpected behaviour by examining actual behaviour at different levels of abstraction. The trace data can be viewed as a *causality graph*, as in [18], capturing information about interprocess communication events and their precedence. But a simplistic display of the causality graph to the user is impractical; there is too much information in it at too low a level. We propose instead a pattern-matching paradigm; the programmer can specify normal or abnormal patterns that he/she is looking for and, using filtering, ask the debugging tool to display them in various ways. In addition, the programmer can create new patterns at different levels of abstractions from existing data, providing alternative ways of looking at the same information. For example, one can create a *waits-for* graph, abstracted from the raw data, which makes deadlocks easy to see and whose size is proportional to the number of processes, not to the number of events in the computation.

In this paper, we will describe the use of the $\mathbf{Hy}^+$ data visualization system for postmortem debugging of parallel and distributed programs. $\mathbf{Hy}^+$ emphasizes visualization with analysis. Using GraphLog, we can filter raw trace data to focus on arbitrary subsets of the program; we can define new objects and relationships that embody our knowledge of the program's semantics and map the raw data into them; and we can observe program behaviour at varying levels of abstraction. With such a tool, the people who actually know the meaning of the computation are the ones who get to decide what is visualized and how to visualize it.

The rest of the paper is organized as follows. An overview of the $\mathbf{Hy}^+$ system and GraphLog is given in Section 2. In Section 3 we describe the methods of distributed trace analysis, and causality graph. The process of trace analysis with $\mathbf{Hy}^+$, the format of the traces used, the transformation of the traces to a causality graph, and the process and event abstraction with $\mathbf{Hy}^+$ are discussed in Section 4. We then discuss in Section 5, how the behavior of several different versions of the *Dining Philosophers Problem* has been analyzed with the aid of the $\mathbf{Hy}^+$ system. Section 6 provides a brief overview of dynamic analysis of traces with $\mathbf{Hy}^+$. We then conclude with a discussion of future work in Section 7.

2 Overview of the $\mathbf{Hy}^+$ System

The $\mathbf{Hy}^+$ system provides extensive support for query visualization, visualizing the input instance, and visualizing the output instance in several different modes. The visualizations manipulated by the system are labeled graphs and *hygraphs* [7].

Each tuple $(a_1, \ldots, a_i, b_1, \ldots, b_j, c_1, \ldots, c_k)$ in a relational database can be represented by a directed multigraph having an edge labeled $r(c_1, \ldots, c_k)$ from a node labeled $(a_1, \ldots, a_i)$ to a node labeled $(b_1, \ldots, b_j)$ corresponding to each tuple of each relation r in the database.

For example, suppose we have a database describing an execution of the *dining philosophers* program described in Section 5. The database has two relations, *left_fork* and *right_fork*, so that *left_fork(p,f)* means that philosopher p has fork f to its left, and similarly for *right_fork(p,f)*. Since philosophers and forks are both implemented as processes in this program, a philosopher is represented by a term of the form *process(philo, id1, id2)* where *philo* is a constant indicating the type of process and *id1* and *id2* are system- and programmer-defined process identifiers. Consider, for example, the tuples: *left_fork(process(philo,199,0)*, *pro-cess(fork,187,0))*, and *right_fork(process(philo,199,0)*, *process(fork,193,1))*. The first tuple says that the left fork of a philosopher process with process-id 199 and programmer-defined-id 0 is a fork process with identifiers 187 and 0. Figure 1(a) shows the graph representation of these tuples. The function symbol in the term (*process* in this case) is used to select the icon that represents the node. The

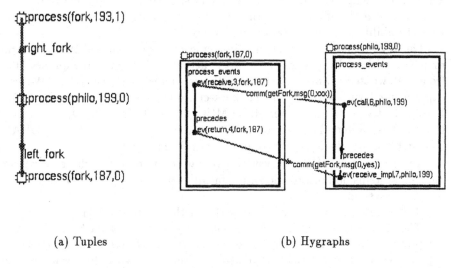

(a) Tuples   (b) Hygraphs

Fig. 1. Visualizing tuples and hygraphs.

data model we use is more general than graphs. Hygraphs, are a hybrid between Harel's higraphs [9] and directed hypergraphs. A hygraph extends the notion of a graph by incorporating *blobs* in addition to edges. A blob relates a contain-ing node with a set of contained nodes and is diagrammatically represented as a region associated with the container node that encloses the contained nodes. Figure 1(b) shows two blobs where the philo and fork processes (*blob nodes*) contain their respective communication events *ev(...)*. A node may have multi-ple blobs associated with it, and blobs may be arbitrarily nested. Extending the representation to hygraphs allows varying levels of abstraction in the display of hierarchical data and provides a flexible mechanism for clustering information. The **Hy⁺** system has browsers with extensive facilities for editing hygraphs (e.g., copy, cut, and paste; selective collapsing and exploding of blobs; panning and zooming; executing several layout algorithms; moving hygraphs to and from files;

editing node and edge labels; etc.).

The visual queries supported by the $\mathbf{Hy^+}$ system are expressions of the GraphLog query language [4]. GraphLog queries are graph patterns whose nodes are labeled by sequences of variables and constants and whose edges are labeled by *path regular expressions* on relations. The query evaluation process consists of finding in the database all instances of the given pattern and for each such instance performing some action, such as defining new edges, blobs, or nodes in the database graph (**Define** mode) or extracting from the database the instances of the pattern (**Show** mode). GraphLog has higher expressive power than first-order languages based on the relational algebra or calculus such as SQL. In particular it can express, with no need for recursion, queries that involve computing transitive closures or similar graph traversal operations. The language is also capable of expressing first-order aggregate queries as well as aggregation along path traversals (e.g., shortest path queries)[5]. It will be clear from the examples discussed in the paper that debugging requires a language with the ability to express transitive closures.

The $\mathbf{Hy^+}$ visual query system is implemented as a front-end that can communicate with multiple back-ends for the actual evaluation of the queries. The front-end, written in Smalltalk, includes the user interface of the system. We have experimented with several different back-end query processors: Prolog [8], the LDL deductive database system from MCC [13], and CORAL [14], the deductive database system from Wisconsin. The current implementation uses CORAL. The architecture of the $\mathbf{Hy^+}$ system is shown in Figure 2.

An examination of the survey [12] reveals that most distributed program analysis systems do not provide all the facilities provided by the $\mathbf{Hy^+}$ system in one single system.

$\mathbf{Hy^+}$ combines to a certain extent the methods proposed in [15], [18], and [1]. The system described in [15] uses the query language TQuel [16]. [18] does not provide a querying capability, and the abstraction, filtering and visualization capabilities are also limited. The EBBA system [1] provides higher-level event abstraction mechanism, but ignores precedence information and lacks visualization capability provided by $\mathbf{Hy^+}$. Furthermore, the visual and graphical nature of GraphLog queries allow the user to express intuitively appealing queries.

3 Methods of Program Trace Analysis

There are two ways of analyzing distributed program traces: *static* and *dynamic*. In static analysis, the execution traces of a program are collected and analyzed off-line on the whole trace database. Dynamic analysis can be performed in two ways: 1) *on-line*, through real-time feed of the event traces as the program executes; 2) postmortem *animation* of stored event traces, that is, the dynamic behaviour of the program is simulated by replaying the events in the collected traces. In the second method the stored trace data is fed to the database line by line (or in chunks of lines as specified by the user), thus giving the illusion that the trace data from the execution monitors are being fed to the database

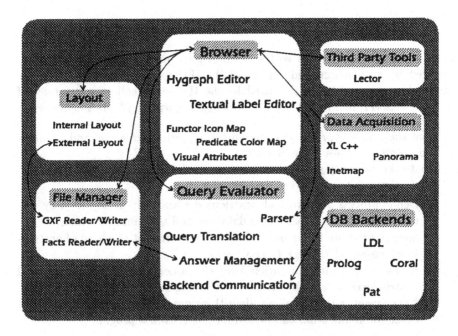

Fig. 2. Overview of the Hy$^+$ architecture.

in real-time. Real-time analysis, as opposed to simulating dynamic behaviour, is problematic for various reasons.

3.1 Causality Graph

In our model of distributed computation interprocess communication (IPC) is achieved only by synchronous or asynchronous message passing. The set of events (*send, receive, return* or *reply* and *implied receive* of the returned message) produced by an execution of a distributed system defines a *partial ordering*. A partial order of events in our system is determined by the total order of local events of each independent process, the precedence of a sending event in one process to the corresponding receive event in the receiving process, and the precedence of the return event to the corresponding implied receive event. Events that are incomparable in this partial order are (potentially) *concurrent*. The partial order is defined as follows.

Let $e_{i,k} \in S$ be the *kth* event in process i. Then we define $e_{i,k} \rightarrow e_{j,l}$, if $i = j$, and $k < l$ or if $i \neq j$ and $e_{i,k}$ is a *send* or a *return* event and $e_{j,l}$ is a *receive* or a *implied receive* event.

From this definition it follows that the set of events $e_{i,k} \in S$ forms a directed acyclic graph (DAG), called the *causality graph*. **Hy**$^+$ can be used effectively for dealing with graph structured databases. For example, the precedence relationship between two events can be decided by path traversals in a graph.

4 Process of Trace Analysis with Hy$^+$

We start the analysis process with a trace of program execution that could be generated by an instrumented version of the IPC package being used. In our experiments, we used traces produced by the IPC event collection modules of the *Panorama* [11] monitor. The steps of debugging with **Hy$^+$** are the following.

- Treat the traces of primitive communication, process creation, and termination events as tuples in the database.
- Create the causality graph through the use of simple GraphLog queries.
- Iterate through the following steps, in any order:
  - Define process and event abstractions declaratively at any level by creating hygraphs from the trace database and the causality graph.
  - Specify program behaviour as hygraph patterns (at any level of abstraction) expressed through GraphLog queries.
  - Focus on relevant information using GraphLog's filtering capability and control level of detail by interactively hiding and revealing blob contents.
  - Experiment with the layout algorithms provided by the system to discover communication and behaviour patterns in a program.

In dynamic analysis, each time the database is updated, the specified queries are evaluated. Details are discussed in Section 6.

4.1 Description of Traces

In this subsection we describe the trace formats we obtained from running *Hermes* [17] programs. Hermes is an experimental programming language for distributed computing developed at IBM Research. We shall use Hermes terminology for describing communication events, but the ideas are applicable in general, and the system is independent of any particular trace format.

In Hermes, synchronous communication is achieved by a call, which blocks the caller until the callee returns. There is also a send operation for asynchronous communication. A primitive event trace has the following format:

```
comm_event( source_process_name, destination_process_name,
            source_process_id, destination_process_id,
            source_event_serial_no, destination_event_serial_no,
            service_name, programmer_defined_id, message)
```

where comm_event stands for one of call, send, receive, return or receive_implied. (A receive_implied event is assumed to occur after each return.) Other events that may appear in the trace, with a slightly different format, are create and end.

The following are examples of two event traces, taken from a "Dining Philosophers" program described later:

```
receive_impl( philo, fork, 205, 196, 19, 10, getFork, 2, msg(3,yes) ).
call( philo, fork, 196, 205, 12, freeFork, 2, msg(3) ).
```

For example, the first event is a receive_impl by process 205, of type philo, from a corresponding return by process 196, of type fork, it is the 19th event within the philo process and the 10th event within the fork process. The receive_impl relates to a getFork service requested by the caller. The 2 is a programmer defined identifier. and msg(3,yes) is information associated with the message whose interpretation is application dependent. Note the second event, which is a call, has no destination sequence number, since this number is unknown at the time of the call.

4.2 Transforming the trace database

The trace as described above is the raw data that **Hy**$^+$ takes as input. The graphical representation of the initial trace database is shown in Figure 3. The

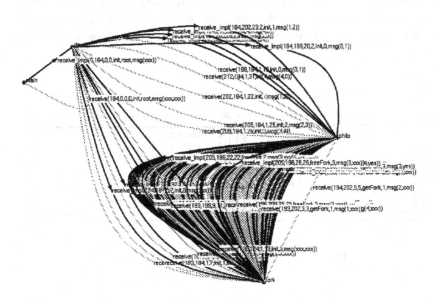

Fig. 3. Unusable **Hy**$^+$ representation of the initial trace database.

default interpretation of a tuple like p(X,Y,Z) in **Hy**$^+$ is as an edge from node X to node Y labelled p(Z); this is not very useful here, since the first two arguments of the communication event tuples are process types, not individual processes. Also, the long list of parameters associated with each event clutters the diagram, the layout superimposes many of the nodes and edges, and it is difficult to understand the relationship of the diagram to the program's execution.

To reshape the information into usable form, we issue a query containing a number of defineGraphLog boxes as shown in Figure 6, to define logical concepts of interest to the programmer. Before describing these queries, let us go over the process of query formulation in GraphLog. A GraphLog query is a set of boxes of two kinds: *define* and *show*. Both types of boxes contain a graphical pattern in which certain objects, shown thicker in the pictures, are *distinguished*. The meaning of a define box is: for each instance of the non-distinguished part of the pattern found in the database, define a corresponding instance of the distinguished object. The meaning of a show box is: for each instance of the pattern found in the database, add to the answer all the distinguished objects matched.

For example, box define1 in Figure 4 has a distinguished instance edge. The meaning is: for each process P that has received an initialization message from the root, create a process node and connect P to it with a new instance edge. We can think of this as a Horn clause or rule where the "if" part corresponds to the receive edge specialized to have init as a constant argument, and the "then" part to the distinguished instance edge. An example of a show box is shown in box show1 in Figure 4. The distinguished instance edge is to be shown whenever the first argument of its process endpoint is fork. Intuitively, this is simply a request to show all the instances of fork processes, and thus equivalent to a relational selection and projection. We will show more sophisticated uses of show boxes later on.

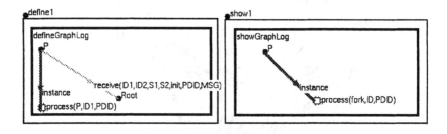

Fig. 4. Hy⁺ queries in define and show mode.

We now describe the queries we will use to form the *causality graph* from the raw trace data. The define1 query in Figure 4 just described is the first query of the preprocessing queries. The boxes labelled define2 and define3 in Figure 6 define *event* nodes (ev) and relate each process instance to all the events within that process instance by means of events edges. The box labelled define4 defines a new kind of edge (IPC edge) that relates each call event within a calling process to the corresponding receive event in the callee. Finally, boxes define5 and define6 define the precedence relationship precedes between events corresponding to the partial order defined in Section 3. Similarly the *return* and *receive_impl* events are defined. Thus these preprocessing queries construct the *causality graph*.

These transformations are somewhat complicated, but the programmer does not need to specify them each time he or she starts to analyze a new program.

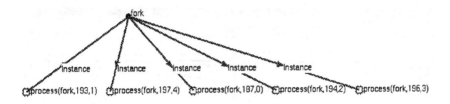

Fig. 5. Result of show query.

The transformations are not application dependent, they only depend on the trace format and the model of computation. Once formulated, they can easily be canned and applied to execution traces of any application.

4.3 Process and Event Abstraction

Now that we have reformulated the raw data, we are in a position to do some clustering. Figure 7 shows clustering of all events within a process P into a process blob owned by P (box **define1**). Note the events within each process will be linearly related by the **precedes** edges we defined in the last subsection, thus simulating the *timeline* in a *process-time* diagram. The "show" box labelled **show1** in Figure 7 asks the system to display all the process nodes, their **process_events** blobs, the **precedes** edges within the blobs, and the IPC **comm** edges between events. The **PT diagram** window is the result. The process blobs can themselves be clustered together if desired, thus achieving any level of abstraction. In Figure 7 seven of the ten blobs have been collapsed and their contents hidden to simplify the visualization and eliminate distractions.

An *abstract event* is a higher-level event consisting of primitive or other abstract events. For example, the set of communication events send, receive, return, and implied receive corresponding to a rendezvous-style synchronous event can be collapsed into a single abstract event. An example of event abstraction will be shown in next section.

5 Case Study: The Dining Philosophers Problem

The examples we have been using come from a Hermes implementation of a well known problem in concurrent programming, the *Dining Philosophers Problem*: N philosophers sit around a round table. There are N forks on the table. To be able to eat a philosopher must pick up the forks that are at his left and right. In a more elaborate version of the problem a philosopher may eat many times until his plate (of spaghetti) is finished. Between two eating events he releases the acquired forks, then thinks for a while.

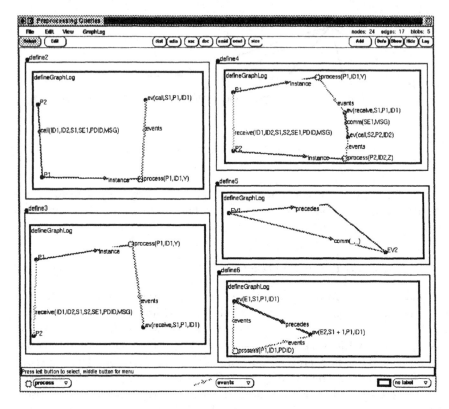

Fig. 6. Preprocess queries to form causality graph.

Let's see how a programmer might use **Hy$^+$** to observe his program's behaviour. The programmer first starts with the simple solution in Figure 8.

The root process dp creates 5 instances of the philo and the fork processes and passes the philosopher processes their corresponding left and right forks they are allowed to use. Left fork of philo[i] is fork_id[i] and the right fork is fork_id[(i+1) mod 5]. The fork processes provide two services: get_fork and free_fork.

There is a bug in this program; it wrongly specifies the right fork of a philosopher by writing (i+1) instead of (i+1) mod N in line 13 of the dp process above. The programmer will, in general, formulate a number of GraphLog queries to observe the behaviour of his/her program and evaluate them over the stored trace database. For example, in this particular case, programmer will formulate queries showing the left and right fork initialization pattern, fork holding and releasing patterns, deadlock pattern and the ordering of eating events by the 5 philosophers. The evaluation of the left and right fork initialization pattern query in Figure 9 reveals the bug as a hole in the pattern as shown in Figure 10(a). The query in Figure 9 operates on the message contents (msg(L,R)) of the initialization message received by the philosopher processes from the root process. For example, a left fork edge is created between philo(I) and fork(K), if

133

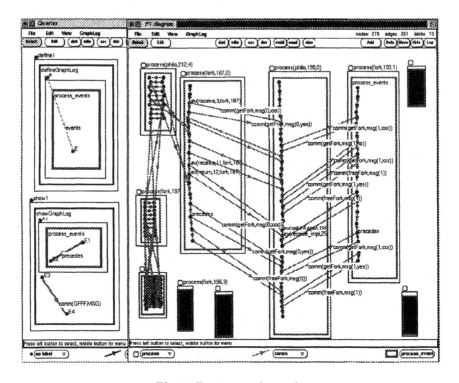

Fig. 7. Event trace hygraphs.

$K = L$, where L is the left fork id in msg(L,R) received by philo(I) during initialization. Correcting the bug produces instead the Figure 10(b) with the correct initialization pattern.

The program that results from correcting the first bug may cause a deadlock. This type of bug is called a *timing bug* and results from the nondeterministic nature of distributed programs running on a distributed network of processors. We will now see how the deadlock and its cause is observed. The query define1 in Figure 11 defines a holds edge between a philosopher and a fork process, if a getFork request is granted. If the request fails, the request_fails edge is created. The crossed out edge labelled ^precedes (representing negation) states that no return event followed the receive event in the fork. The query define3 in Figure 11 defines the *wait-for* cycle indicating deadlock, the result of which is shown in Figure 12(a). By showing the holds events in Figure 12(b) the real cause of the deadlock is observed. It shows that all the philosophers were able to simultaneously hold the left fork, thus waiting forever for the right fork.

The programmer now writes a third version by introducing a "fair policy" in the hope that it might avert the deadlock. In this solution, line 8 of the fork process is replaced with return("yes") and line 10 with return("no"), indicating explicitly that the fork is not available, so that the philo process frees the first acquired fork. A corresponding modification is introduced in the philo process. A

```
1 process dp:
2     --create 5 fork and philo processes
3     while i < 5 do
4         fork_id[i] := create("fork")
5         create("philo")
6         i := i + 1
7     endwhile
8     --initialize the philo processes
9     --by passing them appropriate
10    --left and right fork ids
11    while i < 5 do
12        left_fork := fork_id[i];
13        right_fork := fork_id[i+1];
14        call philo[i].init(left_fork, right_fork)
15    endwhile

1 process fork:
2     get_fork:
3         receive()
4         if fork available
5             available := FALSE
6             --give the fork to the
7             --requesting philo
8             return
9         else
10            --Block (do not return)
11    end get_fork
12    free_fork:
13        receive()
14        available := YES
15        return
16    end free_fork
1 process philo:
2     init:
3         receive(left_fork, right_fork)
4     end init
5     call fork[left_fork].get_fork()
6     call fork[right_fork].get_fork()
7     eat
8     call fork[left_fork].free_fork()
9     call fork[right_fork].free_fork()
```

Fig. 8. Dinning Philosophers Code.

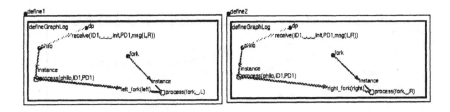

Fig. 9. Assigning Left and right forks.

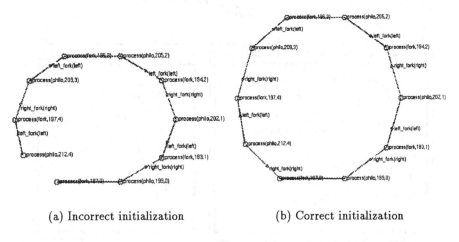

(a) Incorrect initialization   (b) Correct initialization

Fig. 10. Left and right fork initialization patterns.

bug is introduced in line 5 of the fork process, namely the programmer mistakenly writes TRUE instead of FALSE. This means that the fork is always available even though another philosopher might have acquired it.

The queries showing the ordering of eating events give a hint about the bug. To formulate the ordering queries we first create abstract events (abs_ev(getFork, ...) and abs_ev(freeFork, ...)) by collapsing the send, receive, return, and receive_implied events into one single blob through the query define1 in Figure 13. We then define the precedence abs_precedes between the abstract events using the queries define2 and define3 in the same figure. The ordering of eating events is defined in the query define1 in Figure 14. The query states that if the last getFork event of a philosopher transitively precedes (abs_precedes+) the same event in another philosopher, then create a eat_precedes edge between these two philosophers. The dashed line indicates transitive closure. The result of this query is shown in Figure 15(a). By complementing eat_precedes edges we get the philosophers who eat concurrently, shown as conc_eat edges in define2 query in Figure 14. The regular expression eat_precedes | -eat_precedes states that the eat_precedes edges are to be matched in the forward or the reverse direction. The visualization of conc_eat in Figure 15(b) shows that two neighboring philosophers, in this case philosophers 2 and 3 eat concurrently, thus indicating that the availability of the forks has not been checked properly.

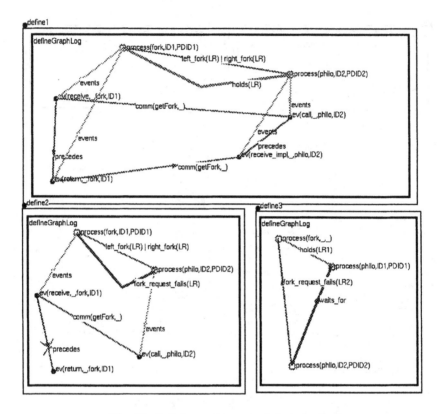

Fig. 11. Defining patterns to detect deadlock.

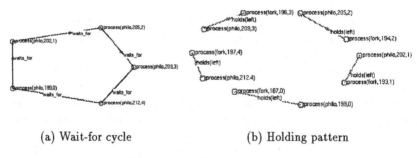

(a) Wait-for cycle   (b) Holding pattern

Fig. 12. Deadlock detection.

6 Dynamic Analysis

Using static analysis alone, it may be difficult to detect the real cause of a problem. For example, consider the bug in the initialization of the philosopher processes with correct left and right forks. It may be difficult to see immediately

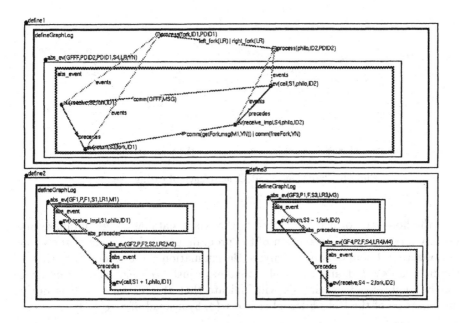

Fig. 13. Defining abstract events.

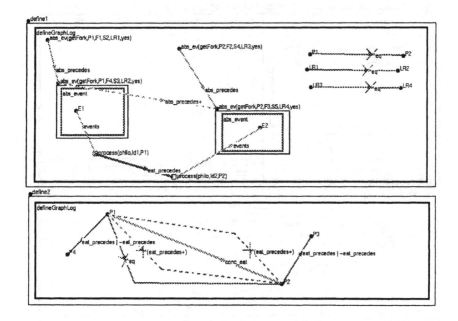

Fig. 14. Defining ordering of eating events.

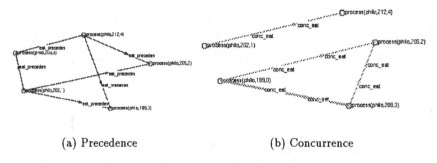

(a) Precedence   (b) Concurrence

Fig. 15. Precedence and Concurrence of eating events.

why the hole was formed by analyzing the whole database. The database may be very large, since the execution of the program proceeds in spite of the wrong initialization. Using dynamic analysis, the simulation can be stopped as soon as the hole is detected and the tuples that have just been fed into the database can be analyzed. The analysis will indicate that the message content during initialization of the last philosopher is $msg(4, 5)$ instead of $msg(4, 0)$.

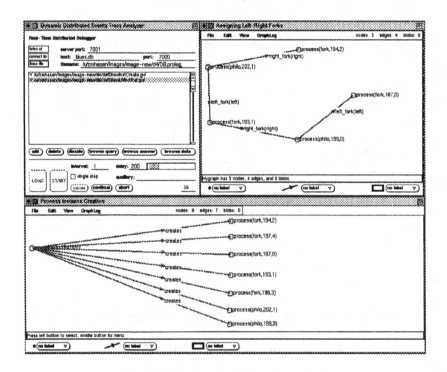

Fig. 16. Snapshot 1 of dynamic analysis.

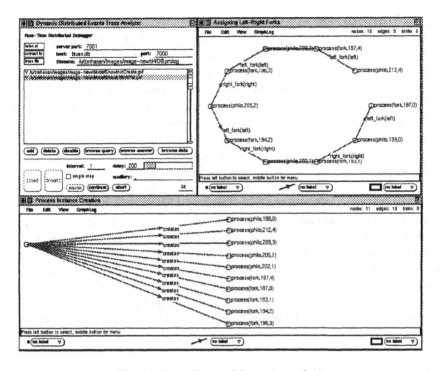

Fig. 17. Snapshot 2 of dynamic analysis.

Hy^+ supports a simple dynamic analysis facility, illustrated in Figure 16. The Window Dynamic Distributed Events Trace Analyzer in the figure shows the control panel for dynamic analysis. Traces are read in from a log file or from a (UNIX) socket. Trace data are fed into the database system tuple by tuple or grouped into sets at intervals specified by the programmer through the control panel. A delay can be specified to control the speed of simulation. Each time new data are fed in, a set of queries is evaluated. In Figure 16, two such queries have been specified by the programmer by giving their file names in the control panel. Snapshots of the latest results of the queries are shown in the other two windows in the figure. As the simulation progresses, at one point the user notices that even though all the process instances have been created, the left-right forks assignment pattern is not a cycle as it should have been. Figure 17 shows another frame where the user has detected the hole in the left and right forks assignment pattern and stopped the simulation for close observation of the trace.

7 Conclusion and Future Work

We have described how the Hy^+ data visualization system can be used for analysis of distributed event traces, in particular, for observing the behaviour of parallel and distributed programs. We have shown how   a combination of deductive database technology with novel visualization techniques can provide a useful tool for understanding distributed and parallel programs, by providing abstraction and filtering as well as visualization facilities.

In the current version of dynamic analysis, the queries are evaluated in a naive fashion, namely, each time the database is updated with a tuple (or tuples) all the selected queries are evaluated and results are recomputed from scratch. Ideally, we would like to have active database features, that is, firing only affected queries. The queries would be evaluated incrementally based on timestamps of events, instead of recomputing all results from scratch.

The expressive power of GraphLog can be enhanced by adding a temporal dimension. GraphLog augmented with temporal operators will be able to express important temporal properties of concurrent programs. Work is in progress to define a *temporal event and interval specification language* (TEISL) incorporating operators similar to interval operators in [16] and a visual equivalent of the proposed operators [10]. TEISL will be incorporated seamlessly into GraphLog. The proposed extension will be a vehicle for visual specification of temporal events in an active database and temporal queries in a temporal database. Work is in progress to add active database features as required by the dynamic analysis. The resulting tool will also be useful for behavior observation of active databases [10].

References

1. Peter Bates. Debugging heterogeneous distributed systems using event-based models of behavior. *Proceedings of the ACM SIGPLAN/SIGOPS Workshop on Parallel and Distributed Debugging, published in ACM SIGPLAN Notices*, 24(1):11–22, January 1989.

2. Mariano Consens and Masum Hasan. Supporting network management through declaratively specified data visualizations. In H.G. Hegering and Y. Yemini, editors, *Proceedings of the IEEE/IFIP Third International Symposium on Integrated Network Management, III*, pages 725–738. Elsevier North Holland, April 1993.

3. Mariano Consens and Alberto Mendelzon. Expressing structural hypertext queries in GraphLog. In *Proceedings of the Second ACM Hypertext Conference*, pages 269–292, 1989.

4. Mariano Consens and Alberto Mendelzon. GraphLog: a visual formalism for real life recursion. In *Proceedings of the Ninth ACM SIGACT-SIGMOD Symposium on Principles of Database Systems*, pages 404–416, 1990.

5. Mariano Consens and Alberto Mendelzon. Low complexity aggregation in GraphLog and Datalog. In *Proceedings of the Third International Conference on Database Theory, Lecture Notes in Computer Science Nr. 470*, pages 379–394. Springer-Verlag, 1990. A revised version has been accepted for publication in TCS.

6. Mariano Consens, Alberto Mendelzon, and Arthur Ryman. Visualizing and querying software structures. In *14th. Intl. Conference on Software Engineering*, pages 138–156, 1992.

7. Mariano P. Consens. Creating and Filtering Structural Data Visualizations using Hygraph Patterns. Fothcoming PhD Thesis, University of Toronto, 1993.

8. Milan Fukar. Translating GraphLog into Prolog. Technical report, Center for Advanced Studies IBM Canada Limited, October 1991.

9. David Harel. On visual formalisms. *Communications of the ACM*, 31(5):514–530, 1988.

10. Masum Z. Hasan. A visual and temporal framework for behavior observation of active databases. PhD Thesis Proposal, Department of Computer Science, University of Waterloo, Waterloo, Ontario, Canada, 1994.

11. W. Korfhage. The panorama monitoring system. Technical report, Polytechnic University, Brooklyn, 1992.

12. Charles E. McDowell and David P. Helmbold. Debugging concurrent programs. *ACM Computing Surveys*, 21(4):593–622, December 1989.

13. Shamim Naqvi and Tsur Shalom. *A logical language for data and knowledge bases.* Computer Science Press, New York, 1989.

14. R. Ramakrishnan, D. Srivastava, and S. Sudarshan. CORAL: Control, Relations and Logic. In *Proceedings of International Conference on Very Large Databases*, 1992.

15. Richard Snodgrass. A relational approach to monitoring complex systems. *ACM Transactions on Computer Systems*, 6(2):157–196, May 1988.

16. R.T. Snodgrass. The temporal query language TQuel. *ACM Transactions on Database Systems*, 12(2):247–298, June 1987.

17. R.E. Strom, D.F. Bacon, A.P. Goldberg, A. Lowry, D.M. Yellin, and S.A. Yemini. *HERMES: A Language for Distributed Computing.* Prentice Hall, Englewood Cliffs, New Jersey, 1991.

18. Dror Zernik and Larry Rudolph. Animating work and time for debugging parallel programs foundation and experience. *Proceedings of the ACM/ONR Workshop on Parallel and Distributed Debugging, published in ACM SIGPLAN Notices*, 26(12):46–56, December 1991.

Dynamic Maps as Composite Views of Varied Geographic Database Servers

Masatoshi ARIKAWA[1], Hideyo KAWAKITA[2], and Yahiko KAMBAYASHI[3]

[1] Hiroshima City University, Asa-minami-ku, Hiroshima 731-01, JAPAN
[2] Sharp Co., JAPAN
[3] Faculty of Engineering, Kyoto University, Sakyo, Kyoto 606-01, JAPAN

Abstract. This paper presents new style maps, called *dynamic maps*, based on view functions of geographic databases. The dynamic maps contain two basic components, (1) queries applied to geographic databases and (2) visualization methods for data derived by the queries. There are three major factors to change the content of dynamic maps, (1) data (unlike conventional geographic systems, we assume that up-to-date data are always used to generate maps), (2) query (a map for a specific purpose is generated by a query), (3) visualization method (even if a set of objects to be displayed is determined, the resulting map cannot be uniquely determined, since we have to distinguish important geographic objects and there is a limit caused by the size of a display). A prototype system **GeoProxy** was developed in order to prove that the dynamic maps are feasible and useful. This paper also describes the system organization and object management, and presents the demonstrations of interactions with users in **GeoProxy**.

1 Introduction

In this paper, we will discuss *dynamic maps* for geographic databases. In conventional map systems, geographic data are fixed like the current car navigation systems. Future systems must make use of up-to-date computer technologies. The computer networks must change the current style computer maps to more dynamic information products composed of many pieces of information derived from varied information sources, such as traffic information centers, map centers, commercial regional information services, and locations of people (Fig. 1).

The new style maps, called *dynamic maps*, should provide users with more flexible, specialized and reliable information than paper maps. That is,

(A) changes in the real world can be reflected in the contents of the maps immediately.

In conventional character-oriented database systems, such a requirement is satisfied. Furthermore, users can specify queries to obtain data suitable for their purposes. On the other hand, in conventional geographic systems, the variety of queries is limited. We cannot apply a query for car driving to land price databases. It is very important for geographic databases to support various kinds of queries.

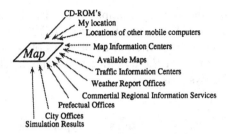

Fig. 1. A dynamic map as a composite of many pieces of information

(B) Users can easily and freely produce the maps which consist of the only data of their interests and which are visualized by their intended methods.

The above (A) and (B) are already satisfied by conventional character-oriented databases. Since we must handle various geographic objects, it is difficult to realize such functions.

The third requirement to be discussed is not considered by conventional character-oriented database systems. In the conventional systems, all the data will be printed in tabular forms after selected by a query. In geographic database systems, it is not simple to generate a final map from the selected geographic objects. For example, all the objects are not equally treated. Buildings at crossing points of roads may be more important than other buildings in drivers' maps. Due to the limit caused by displays, we must select objects according to the priority. Selection and placement of objects are determined by visualization methods. Visualization methods produce a map by a query, knowledge on geographic objects (if a small river is displayed, bigger rivers must be also displayed.), and display characteristics (resolution, color or black/white).

(C) Appearances of the maps can be changed to adapt to the changes of users' purposes, the results of users' operations, and the limitation of display devices.

Since it is very difficult to select a proper visualization method, dynamic maps should provide users various visual interfaces to adjust visualization methods. Selection of visualization methods is a new requirement which was not considered in conventional character-oriented databases.

As a summary, the dynamic map has the following three characteristics.

(A) On-line data can be used
(B) Query to be applied is not limited
(C) Visualization methods can be selected by a user through easy-to-use interfaces.

The following table shows rough comparisons with dynamic maps and typical information systems; Information Retrieval (IR) Systems, Database (DB) Systems, and Hypermedia, from the points of views of the above three characteristics. The characteristics of the dynamic maps should also be supported in geographic information systems.

	IR Systems	DB Systems	Hypermedia	Dynamic Maps
Data	fixed	on-line	fixed	on-line
Query	fixed form (restricted)	flexible	navigation (restricted)	flexible
Visualization Method	text (fixed)	table (fixed)	texts with pictures (fixed)	various

The principles of dynamic maps have not been formalized yet. We consider that *database views* and *views of interactive graphics* are key concepts to create a uniform model that deals with the above three characteristics (Arikawa 1992). View concepts have been used in some areas, such as database systems, computer graphics, user interfaces and natural language processing. The meanings of the view are different among those areas, and relatively clear in the areas of database systems and computer graphics because there are commercial systems which provide view functions. In the database systems, views are virtual databases defined by *queries* to real databases (Date 1990). The view functions provide both application programs and users with appropriate interfaces to real databases, and guarantee that all application programs and users can always obtain up-to-date data through real databases which generally have been updated in order to always store present and reliable data. If dynamic maps are defined as views of *geographic databases* which are considered the collections of varied kinds of databases concerning regions on the earth, the contents of the dynamic maps are also guaranteed to provide users with up-to-date information from the geographic databases. In the computer graphics, views are defined by *visualization procedures* to create visual objects on display screens. Examples of the visualization procedures are methods of projecting three dimensional geometric objects to two dimensional planes, rendering surfaces of visual objects and selecting lights (Foley et al. 1990). Usually, users freely decide the visualization procedures, those are views, according to their purposes. Objects referred to by views are called *models*. One model can be referred to by many views. Users often manipulate views directly by input devices, such as mouses, to change their models. The changes in the models automatically cause changes of all views referring to the models.

Query languages are considered useful for users to freely select their intended information from databases as components of maps (Roussoupoulos et al. 1988), however the query languages are not appropriate for users' controlling the appropriate amount of data for the fixed-sized display screen. Furthermore, when users change the size of the window which displays a map, the appropriate amount of data also should be changed. This paper proposes methods for users to create maps of their interests by means of (1) users' assigning importance levels to classes of the data selected by their queries and (2) user's selecting adaptive visualization methods for the selected data according to the importance levels and the limitation of displays.

Section 2 presents examples of users' interactions with dynamic maps in our prototype system "**GeoProxy**". Section 3 mentions the process of creating the dynamic maps from geographic databases by ad hoc queries and visualization methods. Section 4 describes a basic mechanism to select visualization methods for the data selected by ad hoc queries. Section 5 gives some concluding remarks.

2   Examples of Users' Interactions with Dynamic Maps

Figure 2 shows that a too dense map is not useful according to the users' requirement, regardless of the limitation of a display device. The constraints on the placements of characters for the legibility of maps, such as no overlaps among texts and graphic features, are not satisfied in this example (Robinson et al. 1978). There have been some researches on name placements for maps, however, most of the researches have focused on generating paper maps (Doerschler et al. 1992) and the legibility of maps has been considered the most important factor for the researches. On the other hand, we have focused on name placements for on-line maps (Arikawa et al. 1991). The on-line maps should require fast responses against users' queries and can have animation objects as their components. In our system, names can behave as animation objects which can have autonomy to avoid overlaps between other names and geographic features.

The amounts of data required by users are often too large to be visualized in a given window. Particularly, this situations must happen when all maps serve as scale-less (arbitrarily scaled) maps. Users will not be able to look up their intended information from such a dense map.

The constraints of the visualization for users to read maps correctly are solved in the Map window in Fig. 3 (Arikawa et al. 1994). The map satisfies the constraints which make the map legible in the condition that the data and the visualization methods required by users are the same as the previous example in Fig. 2. The content of the map in Fig. 3 is regarded as the result of finding a trade-off point between the users' requirement and the limitation of the visualization, using the constraints solver which executes a relaxation method (described in Sect. 4). These examples illustrate the environments where users can adjust the appearances of maps through some views (the amount of data and visualization forms of the data).

The window in the right of Fig. 3, labeled "V_Rank Function", displays the relation "VRankFunc" between importance levels and *visualization ranks* "VRanks" of this map. For examples, the numbers of VRanks may correspond to "nothing to display", "only black-colored point features", and "red-colored names and red-colored point features". The VRanks are set up by integer numbers. The higher the number of the VRanks are, the more informative the vi-

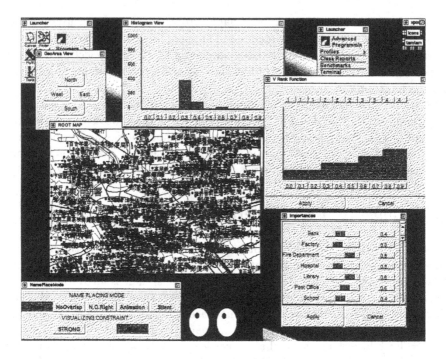

Fig. 2. A dynamic maps without considering its legibility

sualization of the objects is. Objects with the higher importance levels should be visualized as the higher VRanks. If objects with the less importance levels are visualized as the higher VRanks, the results of the visualization are much different from users' requirement and often cause users' misunderstanding due to incorrect information on the map.

The horizontal axis of the VRankFunc represents the importance levels, and the vertical axis represents the VRanks. The VRanks are displayed and set up for every 0.1 importance levels in this window. The set of the (short horizontal) black thin bars represents the VRankFunc expressing the requirement from users, and the black-filled areas represent the VRankFunc of the current displayed map. Users can set up the VRankFunc by means of moving the bars with the mouse. The compromise between the users' requirement and the visualization limitation can be visualized as the differences between two VRankFuncs represented by the black thin bars and the black-filled area. By clicking a number of some importance levels below the horizontal axis, the visual list of the classes for the number could be popped up. (A class is a collection of objects.)

Users will be able to display more objects if they enlarge the window of the map. Figure 4 illustrates the result of enlarging the window. More objects are displayed on the map (in Fig. 4) than in the previous example (in Fig. 3), and the content of the map becomes closer to the users' requirement than the previous

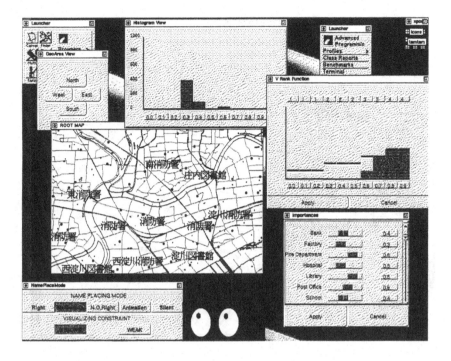

Fig. 3. A dynamic maps without overlaps among names

example. We can easily and quantitatively find the improvement of the content of the map by means of the window of "V_Rank Function". The compromise between the users' requirement and the visualization limitation becomes smaller than the previous example. From the viewpoint of the amount of displayed data, the threshold of importance levels has moved to a lower level in the current example than the previous one.

The window in the left of Fig. 4 labeled "Importances" is a window to set up the importance levels for each class of geographic objects. By clicking the name of a class in the window, the number of objects belonging to the class appears. The window labeled "Histogram View" in the upper right-hand corner of Fig. 4 is a window indicating the histogram concerning the number of geographic objects for classes required by users, and the window also shows the number of objects to be displayed and not to be displayed on the map, using different colors for bars. By clicking the number of an importance level, the visual list of the classes with the importance level could be popped up. The window labeled "GeoArea View" in the middle of the figure is a window to change the area displayed on the map. The buttons labeled "North", "South", "East" and "West" are used to shift the area towards a direction. The window labeled "Name Place Mode" in the left of Fig. 4 is a window to choose the modes for placing names on the map (the visualization constraints, animation, and so on). Such environments

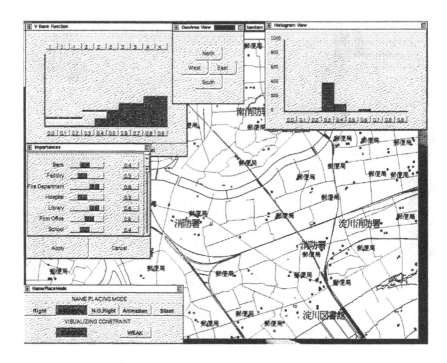

Fig. 4. A dynamic map with a large-sized window

composed of these windows assist in users' making maps for special purposes through many *views* to operate database views and visualization methods.

Figure 5 illustrates the derivations of a map. The top of Fig. 5 is the root map (labeled "ROOT MAP") which displays the area specified by users. The other two maps are derived from the root map. The objects with low importance levels that cannot be displayed in the root map can be displayed in the derived map labeled "MAP" in the lower right-hand corner of the figure. In order to derive the map, users only specify a geographic area on the root map. The *representing display objects* (ReprDOs) of the derived map are propagated and displayed in the other maps covering the areas of the ReprDOs (in the root map and the other derived map labeled "SUB WINDOW MAP"). The ReprDOs appear as the filled rectangles in both "ROOT MAP" and "SUB WINDOW MAP". The area of the derived map "MAP" is changed by moving one of the ReprDOs on the two maps "ROOT MAP" and "SUB WINDOW MAP". The changes of the derived map "MAP" propagate to all associated maps "ROOT MAP" and "SUB WINDOW MAP".

The area of the other derived map labeled "SUBWINDOW MAP" is specified by the area as the relative locations in the root map's window. This derived map is considered as a peephole of the root map's window. The ReprDO of the map "SUBWINDOW MAP" is displayed in the root map as the transparent rectangle (not filled). In this case, the derived map always shows the content zooming up the the central zone of the root map, unless the ReprDO is moved in the root map.

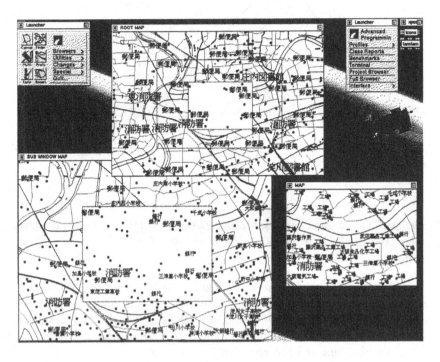

Fig. 5. Derived maps and their representing display objects on the maps

3   Dynamic Maps Derived from Geographic Databases

3.1   Process of Creating Dynamic Maps through Queries and Visualization Methods

There are two kinds of objects which are used in quite different purposes, those are *conceptual objects* (CO's) and *display objects* (DO's). CO's are stored as entries in databases and are designed for many purposes. On the other hand, DO's are results of visualizing CO's by certain visualization methods. Multiple DO's can refer to the same CO. A dynamic map consists of multiple DO's (Fig. 6). If CO's are updated, the changes would appear on all dynamic maps containing the DO's corresponding to the updated CO's.

The main process of creating dynamic maps from geographic databases is as follows (Fig. 7):

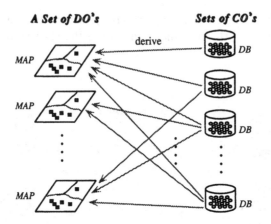

Fig. 6. A conceptual objects (CO) referred by multiple display objects (DO's), and a dynamic map composed of multiple DO's

1. retrieve CO's of users' interests from geographic databases by ad hoc queries;
2. select the methods to visualize the retrieved CO's as DO's on a dynamic map.

As the above, a map is mainly defined by two components, those are (1) *queries* and (2) *visualization methods*. Due to the limit of display screens, all CO's selected by queries could not be visualized as DO's on a map. The visualization methods decide what CO's should be visualized as DO's and not according to the users' requirement and the visualization limitation.

A sets of CO's selected from databases is called a *database view* (DV). The DV's are defined by *a set of queries Q*. The Q are decomposed into multiple simple queries, one of which can be only applied to a geographic database, such as a river database, and an administration area database. A *visual layer* (VL) corresponds to a DV. The VL may not include all DO's which corresponds to all CO's selected by the query applied to a geographic database. The VL is denoted as a pair of the DV and *a visualization method* (VM), that is, $\langle DV, VM \rangle$. The VM specifies the properties of DO's, such as patterns, colors, and behaviors against mouse clicks, according to all global relaxation among all CO's in all DV's for a map. A *dynamic map* (DM) is composed of multiple VL's. A DM is considered a snapshot of the result of queries applied to geographic databases. The DM itself can be a persistent object and be stored in *a map database*.

There are some common conditions (CC's) in queries of database views, such as *area* and *time*. The CC are introduced to a DM as additional components. The CC is a set of conditions which are common for conditions of queries to every database. The CC of a DM is a part of C of every DV which belongs to the DM. For example, if the *time* condition of the CC of a DM is changed from 1994 to 1990, all DV's of the dynamic maps are updated by the queries in

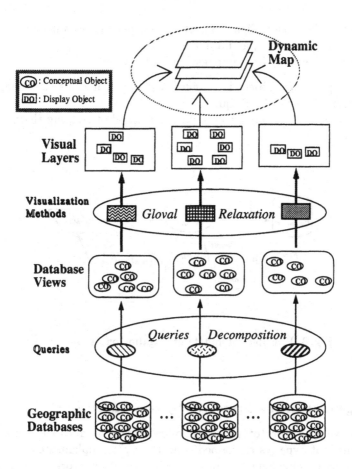

Fig. 7. The process of creating a dynamic map from geographic databases

which the *time* condition is 1990. If we add information of another new database *NDB* to the *DM*, the *DV* of the *NDB* is automatically created according to the *CC* "*time* = 1990."

3.2 Update Propagation on Dynamic Maps

The dynamic maps are views mainly defined by queries and visualization methods. This subsection shows the basic principles of update propagation on the dynamic maps. The queries create *database views* from geographic databases. The database views, therefore, depends on geographic databases. The dependence means that changes in geographic databases cause changes of the database views. The database views include candidates to display on a dynamic map. The visualization methods create a dynamic map from the database views. The dynamic maps depend on the database views. Thus, the dynamic maps depend on geographic databases. Figure 8 shows the dependencies among a geographic database, a database view, and a dynamic map.

The procedure of update propagation is followings.

step 1 If a particular object is changed, the object informs the change to all dependent objects. If not, quit.

step 2 The dependent objects execute the method of creating themselves. Go to **step 1**.

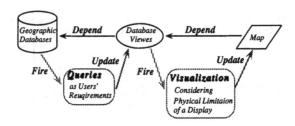

Fig. 8. Principles of update propagation on dynamic maps

3.3 Organization of a Prototype System "GeoProxy"

We have developed a prototype system of geographic databases to prove our approach. The prototype system named **"GeoProxy"** is implemented by an object-oriented programming language and environment, VisualWorks\Smalltalk (ParcPlace Systems, Inc.). Users can open various kinds of windows as views, such as the window displaying a map and the window displaying the saturation of the map, in order to view geographic information and to operate it. In the environments, users can change the appearances of maps by interacting with some of the windows providing various views of databases. Furthermore, users can derive new maps for smaller areas from the current displayed maps which usually have many hidden objects not to display on the screen.

Figure 9 illustrates the organization of **GeoProxy**. A GeoProject in the figure is an object corresponding to a view of geographic databases. A GeoProxy in the figure are derived from the GeoProject, and are visualized for special purposes.

A GeoProxy is an object which holds the information for the displayed map. Geographic display objects, the area of the map and the Visualization methods are stored in the GeoProxy. From the viewpoint of MVC(*Model, View,* and *Controller*) architectures of the GUI (Graphical User Interfaces) softwares (ParcPlace Systems 1992), the GeoProxy works as an *model*, and several *view-controller* pairs are attached to it. The displayed map (Map shown in Fig. 9) is one of its *views*. The environment for operating various parameters for the appearance of a map is also realized as a composite of *views*. The ImportanceLevel,

VRankFunction and so on shown in the figure are all *views* and components of the environment.

The tree structure shown in Fig. 9 represents the derivations of maps. The relationships of inclusions in terms of geographic areas are visualized by *representing display objects*(ReprDOs), for example, the rectangles in the "ROOT MAP" window in Fig. 5. The ReprDOs can be considered as units for cooperative works. The GeoProject is regarded as a shared data for the cooperative works and the GeoProxys are considered personal environments for operating the shared data. Using the shared data (GeoProject), users can operate the geographic information on each map (GeoProxy). The update such as addition and deletion of the data propagates to all GeoProxys that have been derived from the same Geo-Project. The some GeoProxys inherit the parameters for the visualization from other GeoProxys.

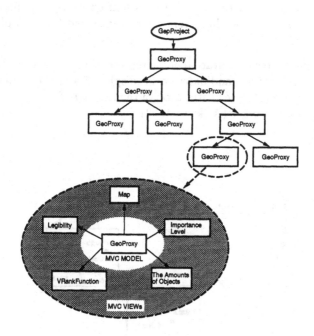

Fig. 9. Organization of **GeoProxy** system

4 Selection of Visualization Methods According to Importance Levels and Limitation of Displays

In order to process ad hoc queries prepared by users, which may require too many CO's as components of a map, independent of the physical limitation of display devices, we introduce importance levels to be assigned to the collections of CO's. Since users cannot predict the number of the CO's required by their ad hoc queries, the importance levels should be assigned to CO's in order to select CO's to be displayed. In this paper, the collections of semantically related CO's are called "classes". The prototype system **GeoProxy** selects visualization methods for classes according to the importance levels specified by users and the limitation of display. The visualization methods create DO's corresponding to CO's in higher importance levels. **GeoProxy** provides users with graphical user interfaces for observing the results of visualizing CO's and adjusting the importance levels of them.

One of the important problems of determining visualization methods is to decide the limitation of a collection of DO's in a window. There are many restrictions to relate the limitation. For example, the names of the objects (as texts) must never overlap the texts or graphics annotating other objects. The amount of characters to be displayed on a screen is limited by the condition that the whole area occupied by the characters can never exceed the area of the screen at least.

Figure 10 illustrates a saturation curve representing the relationship between the number of objects as candidates to be displayed and the number of DO's appearing on the screen. Such saturation of the number of the DO's on a screen is called *saturation of maps* (Arikawa 1992).

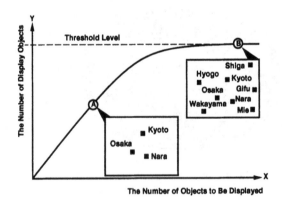

Fig. 10. Saturation of a map

This subsection describes basic principles to select visualization methods for classes, according to the importance levels assigned to the classes and the limitation of displays.

4.1 Basic Concepts for Display Complexity of Maps.

This subsection will define a criterion to distinguish between complex maps and sparse maps. Complex maps include too many DO's for users to look up their intended information. Before the definition of the criterion, several preliminary concepts concerning the complexity of maps are defined.

Definition of Displayed Map ($DispMap$).

$$DispMap = DO^* \tag{1}$$

Definition of Display Density for a Unit Area ($Density(UnitArea)$).

$$Density(UnitArea) = \sum_{DO_i \in UnitArea} DispCmpx(DO_i) \tag{2}$$

$UnitArea$ is a unit area on the display screen, and DO_i is the i-th display object. $DispCmpx(DO_i)$ is the display complexity for DO_i. Generally, $DispCmpx(DO_i)$ is defined for each class.

The display complexity may depend on areas and shapes of graphics. The display complexity of a map is naturally defined as the highest density among all densities, which are display complexities for unit areas in the map.

Definition of Display Complexity of a Map ($DispCmpx(DispMap)$).

$$DispCmpx(DispMap) = \max_{UnitArea_j \in SOUA} Density(UnitArea_j) \tag{3}$$

$$= \max_{UnitArea_j \in SOUA} \left\{ \sum_{DO_i \in UnitArea_j} DispCmpx(DO_i) \right\} \tag{4}$$

$\max_{x \in S}$: returns the element of maximum value in the set S.
$SOUA$: a set of unit areas in a map.

The display complexity of a map strongly depends on the definition of $SOUA$. The definition of $SOUA$ is related to the size and shape of a unit area and the placements of all unit areas. If the definition of $SOUA$ is too complicated, it takes much time to calculate the display complexity for each $SOUA$ and the systems cannot respond in real-time.

4.2 Saturation of Maps and Relaxation of Users' Requirement.

The saturation of maps is defined by *the threshold levels for the display complexity of maps*. The threshold levels are usually decided by the empirical laws which indicate the upper limits of the amount of display objects under a given condition (the size of display screen and so on.). For example, the empirical laws give the maximum percentage of areas occupied by texts.

The following is a basic algorithm to compute the displaying form (defined as VRankFunc) as a trade-off point between users' requirement (defined as VRank-Func) and the constraints of visualization.

$DispMap = \phi$
for $Class \in$ "a set of classes"
   in the decreasing order of "importance levels"
begin
 for $VRank$ **from** $VRankFunc(Class, DecCond, SatCond)$ **to** 0
 begin
   if $DispCmpx(DispMap \cup DO(Class, VRank)) < threshold$
   then $Class.VRank := VRank$; **exit.**
 end
 $DispMap = DispMap \cup GenDO(Class, Class.VRank)$
end

$GenDO(Class, VRank)$ is the function that returns a set of the DOs with the $VRank$ from the COs included in the *Class*. The *threshold* is a given threshold level for the display complexity of maps. *Class.VRank* is the VRank (representing the feasible displaying form) for the *Class*.

The above algorithm does not create maps with maximum number of DO's in the window of a limited size. Other algorithms are also necessary for various purposes. Users should be able to choose freely their intended algorithm from some algorithms prepared in the systems. There are several relaxation methods to find the trade-off point between users' requirement and the limitation on the visualization.

5 Concluding Remarks

In the research field of database systems, views of databases are considered as databases. This idea allows us to treat the source databases and the views (or the derived databases) uniformly. Application systems based on views of databases, however, must deal with display objects, such as windows, buttons and visual controllers, as proxy objects which have some components referring to and produced from views of databases (Maier et al. 1993). The proxy objects also have other components composed of additional attributes and methods in order to satisfy users' purposes and realize visual interfaces for special purposes. The basic architecture of implementing a prototype system **GeoProxy** considers display objects as views of databases. In this system, the definitions of the views are extended to general computing descriptions, including database queries and visualization programs. The architecture allows users to convert a set of geographic objects retrieved by a certain query to one or multiple display objects which usually serves as a map. Expanding the views of databases to general objects in the object-orientation, we succeeded in clarifying the system organizations and the management of objects for hypermedia applications which are strongly based on the views of databases. Geographic applications could provide good experimental objects and usages to prove the feasibility and usefulness of hypermedia systems based on the views of databases.

Acknowledgements

We would like to thank Mr. Hiroshi Kai (Canon Co.) and Mr. Ken'ichi Horikawa (Kyoto Univ.) for their cooperation to implement our prototype system **GeoProxy**. Miss. Kumiko Fukahori gave us good comments and corrections to our English. The digitized geographic data is supplied by the Geographical Survey Institute of Japan.

References

Arikawa, M. and Kambayashi, Y. : "Dynamic name placement functions for interactive map systems", *Australian Computer Journal*, Vol. 23, No. 4, 1991, pp. 133 - 147.

Arikawa, M. : "Studies on View Functions for Geographic Databases", Ph. D Dissertation, Department of Computer Science and Communication Engineering, Kyushu University, 1992.

Arikawa, M., Kawakita, H. and Kambayashi, Y. : "An Environment of Generating Interactive Maps with Compromises between Users' Requirements and Limitations of Display Devices", *Journal of the Geographic Information Systems Association*, Vol. 2, 1994 (In Japanese).

Date, C. J.: *An Introduction to Database Systems*, Addison-Wesley Publishing Co., 1990.

Doerschler, J. S. and Freeman, H.: "A Rule-Based System for Dense-Map Name Placement", Communication of ACM, Vol. 35, No. 1, pp. 68 - 79, 1992.

Foley, J. D., Dam, A. v., Feiner, S. K., and Hughes, J. F.: *Computer Graphics*, Addison-Wesley Publishing Company, Second Edition, 1990.

Maier, D. and Cushing, J. B. : "Treating Programs as Objects: The Computational Proxy Experience", *Proc. of Third Int'l Conf., Deductive and Object-Oriented Databases*, 1993, pp. 1 - 12.

ParcPlace Systems, Inc., *ObjectWorks\Smalltalk Users Manual*, 1992.

Robinson, A. H., Sale, R., and Morrison, J., *Elements of Cartography*, John Wiley & Sons, 1978.

Roussoupoulos, N, Faloutsos, C., and Sellis, T., "An Efficient Pictorial Database System for PSQL", IEEE Transactions on Software Engineering, Vol. 14, No. 5, 1988, pp. 689 - 650.

Limits Database for an
Environmental Information System
– A Fuzzy Set–based Querying Approach –

Ralf Kramer[1]* and Horst Spandl[2]

[1] Forschungszentrum Informatik (FZI)
Haid–und–Neu–Straße 10–14, D–76131 Karlsruhe, Germany
kramer@fzi.de
[2] Landesanstalt für Umweltschutz (LfU)
Griesbachstraße 1–3, D–76185 Karlsruhe, Germany
63_spa@lfu-bw.de

Abstract. This paper describes the design and implementation of the limits database for the environmental information system of Baden-Württemberg. Environmental legislation in Germany is based on numerous laws, decrees, and other regulations. Regulations of the European Union (EU) have a growing impact. Not surprisingly, terminology differs substantially among different regulations. Even for experts, it is impossible to keep track of all regulations and their specific terminology. Thus, two main problems had to be solved. The first challenge was to develop a conceptual model that captures the semantics of a broad collection of regulations. The second main requirement was to support (possibly non-expert) users in querying the limits database. Both challenges are met by an approach that can be characterized as a front-end to a conventional, state-of-the-art relational database system that accepts and processes fuzzy queries.

1 Introduction

Modern pre-emptive environmental politics crucially depends on up-to-date measurement data, as well as environmental monitoring and analysis, i.e., it depends on numerous and varied environmental information. To this end, the Ministry for the Environment of Baden-Württemberg, Germany, is currently building an Environmental Information System (Umweltinformationssystem, UIS [1, 15]). It defines a task-oriented technical and organizational framework for providing and processing environmental data. Besides defining standards and rules, UIS develops the means for the mutual use and exchange of information for the various users within the environmental civil service of Baden-Württemberg.

Environmental legislation in the Federal Republic of Germany is based on numerous laws, decrees and other regulations, influenced increasingly by laws of the European Union (EU) [14]. An important instrument to control environmental pollution, with the goal of minimizing the dangers to human beings and the

* Partially funded by Umweltministerium Baden-Württemberg grant No. U 15-93.01.

biosphere, is the definition of limits, e.g., for the dumping of harmful substances into the environment. These come in various flavours depending on their legal status and source.

Limits differ in their effects. There are *limits* that must strictly be obeyed. Others are *approximate limits, guideline values, reference values, values for comparison, warning values,* and many more that provide some guiding principle for making a decision. Unless indicated otherwise, in this paper the term *limit* is meant to encompass all of these meanings. Limits can be defined by legislation, they can be provisionally determined by scientists, or they can be proposed by committees or commissions. They differ with respect to their compulsory nature as well as their target and purpose. Limits are not static; they are constantly discussed and reviewed according to the current state of the art.

Many components of the environmental information system UIS use limits to process and compare measured environmental data. To ensure a consistent view on and use of limits within the UIS, a central database for limits and related values is needed. Ideally, this database should include as many different limits from as many different sources as possible, so as to provide a broad tool for environmental monitoring, analysis and assessment.

Due to the wide fluctuations of effects, status, origins, and force of limits, there is no universal semantics to the limits. Interpretation of limits is up both to the collector during data acquisition and to the user when trying to apply them. Thus, the main challenge is to provide the user with the means to extract meaningful information from the database under these conditions of imprecision.

The remainder of this paper is organized as follows. In Sect. 2, we describe the application's background, its current status, and the specific requirements for a limits database. Section 3 presents our data base design. Our solution to advanced querying of precise data, which includes fuzzy queries, is presented in Sect. 4 in greater detail. Based on the requirements and the logical database design, we develop the overall system design in Sect. 5. Section 6 surveys relevant work from the application and from the database solution point of view. Finally, we summarize the lessons learned so far and give an outlook on current and future research in Sect. 7.

2 The Application

2.1 The Environmental Information System UIS

The environmental information system UIS of Baden-Württemberg distinguishes among three levels of system categories (see Fig. 1). On the highest level, comprehensive components span the first two levels and bring together subject-specific information to provide an interdisciplinary view of environmental data. The main purpose is to support the (political) planning and decision making process by providing specially aggregated environmental data as well as relevant indicator values. On the strategic level, the management information system UFIS provides specially processed information on the status of entities across all environmental subjects. On the operative management level, TULIS is concerned

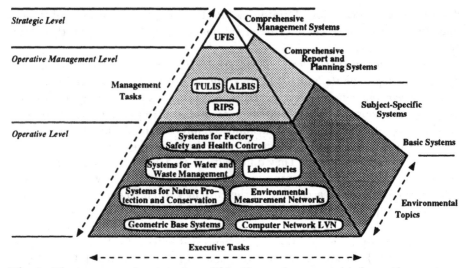

Fig. 1. The component categories within the environmental information system (UIS) of Baden-Württemberg, Germany

with technospherical (i.e., anything man-made) aspects and air pollution control – e.g., support for factory safety and health control. ALBIS, on the other hand, primarily deals with questions of nature protection and conservation. RIPS manages geographical data relevant to environmental topics.

On the lowest, operative level, subject-specific components support special tasks related to the environment, such as various measurement networks or special programs for specific controlling and monitoring tasks. These systems are the most important information sources for the comprehensive systems. Basic components provide the neccessary infrastructure for UIS – e.g., digital map data from the Baden-Württemberg land survey office, or the computer network LVN, which connects every office within the civil service of Baden-Württemberg.

2.2 Current Situation

The comprehensive report systems UFIS and TULIS have a particularly strong demand for a general server module for limits. Both systems provide a graphical user interface to the various measurement data in the topics air, ground and water collected in a central database (see Fig. 2). The graphs are drawn on a digital map; values exceeding a certain threshold, mostly some limit, can be highlighted. Currently, these systems use a simplified data model of limits. With the integration of more and more data sources from subject-specific components, a more sophisticated solution became neccessary.

When work on the comprehensive components of the environmental information system UIS began, many of the decentralized subject-specific components were already in place. Many of them incorporate some knowledge of limits. However, the solutions are very specific, targeted at specialists, with no comprehen-

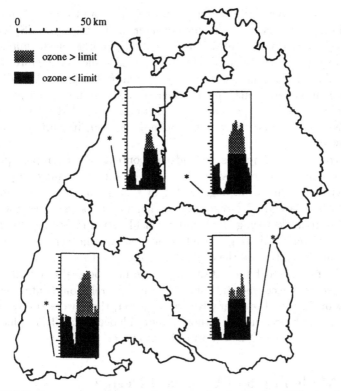

Fig. 2. Half-hour means of ozone during a day in Baden-Württemberg as presented by TULIS

sive presentation of measured environmental data in mind, thus presenting only a few limits for substances in one particular area of interest based on one explicitly named law or regulation. In many cases, the information is attached to a specialized database on chemical substances (see Sect. 6.1 for more details), and/or is hard-coded into the application. While such "decentralized" solutions solve detailed tasks quickly, they fail to address the need for a comprehensive view of environmental data, and thus cause the specialist responsible for a certain subject-specific component to miss many of the continuously, ongoing changes in environmental regulations – especially in fields that are only of partial interest for him or her. Consequently, the major goal for the limits database for UIS was a certain degree of integration in order to provide consistent and up-to-date information on limits using a single model and a single system for the different users of limits.

2.3 Requirements

The basic requirement for the limits database was the integration of the various subject-specific views on limits, in order to provide a consistent base for the evaluation of environmental data. The access module had to be implemented as a self-contained module within the client/server architecture of UIS. The data model had to take into account the fact that, depending on an application's context, there may be several limits for a given substance. Therefore, the user interface should only present those limits to the user that are technically sound in the given context (substance, environmental medium, measured parameter). For a certain substance, e.g., ozone in the air measured as half-hour means, the limits for monthly or yearly means should not be used, if limits for half-hour means are available.

The interpretation of queries depends on context. For example, queries to the limits database have to consider that a given substance may be present in different environmental media, e.g., nickel in the ground or in ground water. Depending on the law and/or regulation, different limits can exist for a given substance. The manufacturing plant under consideration may impose conditions that result in different limits, e.g., with heating systems whether the fuel is coal or oil. In addition, depending on the object to be protected (e.g., humans, animals, or plants), the risk posed by a certain substance may be evaluated differently.

The comprehensive components of the UIS use the relational database system Oracle (Version 7). For the interactive application, there were several requirements, such as hardware and operating system independence. To implement the interactive user interface, Oracle*Forms 4 was chosen.

3   Data Modelling and Database Design

The textual collection of a broad range of limits in regulations [14] – including laws, decrees and other legal texts – provided an excellent starting point for the conceptual database design. This collection covers a variety of topics such as air pollution, heavy metals in the soil, and the quality of drinking water. Regulations from different regions (e.g., Baden-Württemberg), countries (e.g., Germany, Switzerland, Netherlands), or country communities (e.g., UN, EU) differ considerably in their terminology. Thus, we had to address the challenge of developing an adequate conceptual model that allows to capture these semantics.

Entity-Relationship modelling is used as the standard method for conceptual database design within UIS. In the final ER-diagram [10, 11], all entities including **parameter** and **regulation** revolve around the entity type **limit**. In contrast to other models and systems, our model, and the system based on it, offers several advantages. In particular, the model captures the following semantics directly, and the system based on it allows for appropriate querying:

- Laws, e.g., regulations in the European Union, rarely change after their introduction. Instead, subsequent changes to limits (i.e., lower upper bounds), or limits for additional parameters, are always introduced by new regulations.
- In several regulations, the values for single parameters change over time – i.e., they depend on the date (e.g., a step-by-step tightening of a limit over a predefined period of time).

- Different regulations may use different names for the same parameter. Thus, synonyms for parameters have to be taken into account.
- Furthermore, parameters may be grouped according to certain criteria. Parameter groups are specific for individual regulations, even if the same terms are used. Limits are defined either for single parameters or for parameter groups. For example, one regulation might just mention *heavy metals*, while another might explicitly refer to *the heavy metals nickel, copper and lead.*

The conceptual model was transformed into a corresponding logical schema (i.e., relational schema) with the standard rules, thus achieving the third normal form. Declarative integrity constraints were added manually where appropriate and necessary.

4 Advanced Query Processing

4.1 Application Demands and General Approach

In the previous section, some peculiarities of our application should have become obvious. Besides regulations being changed by other regulations, parameter synonyms and parameter groups are modelled. They should be used, i.e., queried appropriately, at the request of the user. Obviously, user queries cannot be mapped to SQL queries directly. Instead, further computation to combine intermediate results from several SQL queries is necessary to answer a single user query.

Furthermore, as already mentioned in Sect. 3, the terminology differs considerably, even among different regulations in the same country. In general, average users will only know exactly about their specific application domains. Thus, they are faced with the problem of formulating queries for other domains, or just even regulations that they have not been working with so far or that may even be completely unknown to them. In short, it is simply impossible for a single user to keep track of all necessary information. With conventional systems, the user will get either no result (i.e., no tuples qualifying at all), or a huge, unsorted set of result tuples. Basically, (s)he will use a trial-and-error approach to obtain the desired information: (s)he will have to reformulate the query several times.

To obviate this problem, our system explicitly models the semantic similarities between different terms of the application domain. These terms correspond to attribute values in our conceptual and logical model. The approach is based on fuzzy set theory (see [6, 12, 21] for an introduction). Fuzzy sets provide an intuitive means for modeling what an end-user might call "vague semantic associations", and for extending the classical boolean framework of relational database systems. In the subsequent section, we focus on our solution to similarity queries.

4.2 Similarity Queries

Similarities are specified in each dimension of the search space (i.e., for each search parameter that corresponds to an entity (type) in the ER model) sepa-

Table 1. Similarities among several regions

original region	substitution	similarity
Baden-Württemberg	Germany	0.9
Baden-Württemberg	European Union	0.8
Baden-Württemberg	Switzerland	0.5

rately. This accords with the human ability (and tendency) to think in mono-causal chains rather than networks [5]. As the attribute domains are both textual and numeric, similarities cannot be defined, in general, as a mathematical function $f(x)$ that computes a value depending on some numeric input value x. Instead, similarities are defined explicitly for each pair of attribute values (see Table 1 for a simplified example). The multi-dimensional aspect remains to be computed by the system.

Our approach to this computation is based on fuzzy sets. Similarities in single dimensions are expressed between pairs of entities with numbers in the interval $(0.0, 1.0)$. In the literature on fuzzy sets, several solutions to compute the membership to a set are proposed. Technically speaking, we look for a t-norm if conjunctions are considered, and a t-conorm if disjunctions are required. For our application, conjunctions, and thus a t-norm, are deemed sufficient. Simple conjunctive predicates together with similarities substitute the need for complex predicates, i.e., combinations of AND- and OR-predicates.

A t-norm is a function $T : [0, 1]^2 \rightarrow [0, 1]$ that has to fulfill the conditions of monotonicity, commutativity, associativity and neutral element [12]. Although the min-operation (and the corresponding max-operation) have some nice algebraic properties, they do not match human thinking of equalities and similarities. Examples from our application showed that the computation of the product $T_{prod}(a, b) := a * b$ is more appropriate as a t-norm. Zimmermann [21] has arrived at the same result. For the implementation (see Sect. 5) and further optimization (see Sect. 7) of the sequence of similarity searches, the properties of $T_{prod}(a, b)$ such as commutativity and associativity are important.

Currently, similarity queries for six entity types are supported. For each of them, a so-called *similarity relation* is defined. In the remainder of this section, we will illustrate the processing of similarity queries with a fairly simple example.

Table 1 shows similarities for the region *Baden-Württemberg*, Table 2 similarities among different types of limits. While processing a user query that includes a predicate **region = Baden-Württemberg** and another predicate **type = limit**,

Table 2. Similarities among different types of limits

original type	substitution	similarity
limit	approximate limit	0.9
limit	guideline value	0.8
limit	reference value	0.7

Table 3. Similarities (T_{prod}(region, type)) as computed during query processing

type	region			
	B-W	G	EU	CH
limit	1.00	0.90	0.80	0.50
approximate limit	0.90	0.81	0.72	0.45
guideline value	0.80	0.72	0.64	0.40
reference value	0.70	0.63	0.56	0.35

these similarity relations are used to extend the set of regions and the set of types of limits taken into account. In the example of Table 1, the similarity search looks for regulations in *Germany*, the *EU*, and *Switzerland* as well. Because of Table 2, the **types** *approximate limit, guideline value,* and *reference value* are considered as well. During query processing, the similarities $\mathsf{T}_{prod}(\textbf{region}, \textbf{type})$ are computed as shown in Table 3. The qualifying tuples – eventually limit values in our application – are sorted according to decreasing similarities. Note that, depending on those tuples that actually exist in the database and those search attributes that were not used in this example, there might be 0, 1 or more result tuples for every potential result tuple shown in Table 4.

4.3 User Configuration

The alert reader will have noticed that instead of changing one regulation with another, or instead of defining synonyms and groups for parameters (as sketched in Sect. 3) we do not model exact correspondences when introducing similarities among the values of an entity. Thus, the individual user may either agree or disagree with a definition of similarity between two entities. Most likely, the user would like to omit certain substitutions, to introduce individual substitutions for the current working context, or to change existing ones. Other standard substitutions may be just right. These demands can only be incorporated if both standard (default) substitutions and individual substitutions are supported.

Therefore, every similarity relation is augmented by a further attribute indicating the user who introduced the substitution. These individual substitutions

Table 4. The first potential result tuples and their relevant attribut values

region	type	parameter	value	...	similarities
Baden-Württemberg	limit	...	...		1.00
Baden-Württemberg	approximate limit	...	...		0.90
Germany	limit	...	...		0.90
Germany	approximate limit	...	...		0.81
Baden-Württemberg	guideline value	...	...		0.80
European Union	limit	...	...		0.80
...	...				

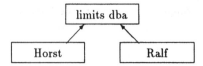

Fig. 3. A simple 2-level substitution and search hierarchy

are organized in a tree hierarchy. Currently, three levels, including the root, are assumed to be sufficient, whereas the implementation supports an arbitrary number of levels. At the root, we have the standard substitutions, which are used as default. On the next level, we find the substitutions for specific environmental subjects (air, water, soil etc.). On the third level, we find substitutions for individual users. The search for every single substitution starts at the level chosen by the user and proceeds towards the root, until a substitution is found.

Figure 3 shows an example of a 2-level substitution hierarchy. Table 5 extends the example of the previous section; similarities as defined in Table 1 are taken as default substitutions and are thus attributed to the limits database adminstrator (*limits dba*). If user *Horst* searches for limits in *Baden-Württemberg*, his individual substitutions, i.e., the regions *Germany* and *Sweden*, are considered. In this case, default substitutions are modified. For *Ralf*, there are no individual substitutions for *Baden-Württemberg*. Thus, if *Ralf* searches for limits in *Baden-Württemberg*, the standard substitutions, i.e., those of the *limits dba*, are used according to the search hierarchy of Fig. 3.

5   System Architecture

Based on the logical database design and the query processing demands, the application system has to fulfill several requirements that strongly influence its software architecture. Interactive and non-interactive (program) database accesses must be supported. An interactive end-user front-end to the query functionality as described in the previous section is required. This front-end should either be used as a stand-alone application, or be called by other applications. For constructing complete results, i.e., for the projection of all important attributes

Table 5. User-specific similarities among several regions

user	original region	substitution	similarity
limits dba	Baden-Württemberg	Germany	0.9
limits dba	Baden-Württemberg	European Union	0.8
limits dba	Baden-Württemberg	Switzerland	0.5
Horst	Baden-Württemberg	Germany	0.9
Horst	Baden-Württemberg	Sweden	0.7
Ralf	Germany	European Union	0.9
Ralf	Germany	Sweden	0.6

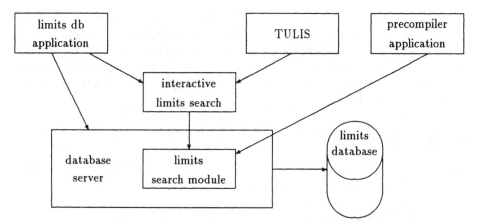

Fig. 4. System architecture with call hierarchy

from all relations, the central relation **limits** has to be outer-joined with several other relations keeping in mind that Oracle limits the number of relations with which a single relation can be outer-joined in a single query, to just one. The result tuples should be sorted, taking into account their final similarity values to be computed during query processing.

Again, these demands require a single user query to be mapped to a sequence of SQL queries. Thus, the challenge is to find an efficient implementation for this mapping. Our solution is based on stored procedures, i.e., procedures running within the database server. This search module was implemented using PL/SQL, the vendor-specific procedural extension to SQL. It is implemented as a package containing the stored procedures required for query processing. Because these (precompiled) procedures are executed within the database server, communication overhead in a client/server environment is minimized. The package's procedures can be used from conventional programming languages like C with a precompiler without using SQL, or directly from a graphical user interface, which was implemented using Oracle*Forms. This provides both flexibility and convenience for programmers who want to use the limits database in their specific applications.

Figure 4 shows the overall system architecture. The call hierarchy is sketched as well. We have the following modules (see [10] for more details):

- the limits search module implements the advanced querying functionality (including querying based on fuzzy sets), provides a procedural interface for user queries, and maps a single user query to a sequence of SQL queries;
- an interactive user interface to the search module;
- the general limits database application includes the graphical user interface to the search module;
- non-database applications like TULIS may call the interactive user interface; and
- precompiler applications containing direct calls to the search module.

When the graphical user interface for the interactive search of limits is called from systems like TULIS, an application context that supersedes user- or application-specific default search parameters may be transferred via parameters to the interactive search. Due to restrictions imposed by Oracle*Forms, result tuples must be transferred to the calling application via a relation specially created for this purpose.

6 Related Work

In this section, we place our work into the context of related work in two areas: limits databases, and fuzzy (or imprecise, vague) querying techniques.

6.1 Limits Databases

Our solution to a limits database for an environmental information system differs substantially from other systems that model limits data. The focal point of our data model is the entity type `limit`. Other systems containing limits (e.g., [4, 7, 19], to list just a few) are mostly substances databases, with the central entity of a chemical substance, that focus on chemical and physical properties. Because the number of substances is enormous, many of these systems concentrate on particular substance classes – e.g., toxic substances, pesticides, dangerous substances in building and construction industry, etc.. Information on limits is generally restricted to few selected values from the most relevant regulations for the particular application domain. Our system, on the other hand, offers a general view on limits across most relevant regulations.

We model different types of limits and capture their semantics, e.g. *limits, approximate limits, guideline* and *reference values* etc.. This approach can be viewed as introducing a meta-level to the limits.

Our system has been carefully crafted to allow its easy integration into the client/server environment, which forms the foundation of the environmental information system UIS. In contrast, most substance databases are stand-alone applications, which quite often are only available for PC-systems.

The intended use of our limits database within the comprehensive report systems of UIS made it neccessary to provide context-sensitive querying techniques (e.g., looking for a limit on arsenic in ground water) suitable for non-experts. In contrast, existing substance databases are aimed at experts in certain specialized topics, such as water and waste management. These people usually know exactly, which regulation to use. Our system is able to inform the user that various limits, coming from possibly many regulations, exist. Due to the implicit ordering via the similarity relation, we can order the search results by their (semantic) closeness to the search parameters.

One representative example of a substance database with a strong bias on regulations is the LIS system [13], a PC-based Clipper application. It records general information for a huge number of chemical substances. The focus is on the entity of a substance. LIS tries to provide as much information from a given regulation as possible, with limits being just another entity. The system, which presents a uniform, easy-to-use interface, is targeted at an audience of expert users. The user typically searches for a substance, the system lists some of its basic properties, and produces a list of those regulations that contain a reference to the substance. The user can then pick one of the regulations and is presented with more detailed information from that regulation. Basically, this approach lacks a unifying conceptual and logical data model on limits. Instead, each regulation is modelled separately, which makes it difficult for the (non-expert) user to compare, and even to query, the information stored in the database. There is no possibility to direct a query based on semantic context, e.g., by specifying that only limits for arsenic in water are of interest. The user needs to know, which of the regulations might be appropriate.

6.2 Fuzzy Queries

To classify our approach, we have to distinguish between fuzzy data (bases) and fuzzy, flexible or imprecise queries (e.g., [3, 8, 18]). We are concerned with the latter – i.e., imprecise querying of precise data.

Early approaches to this problem relied on distance metrics. VAGUE [17] is one of those systems. Our limits database and VAGUE share a common characteristic: they both allow for user-specific substitutions and multiple metrics for the same domain, respectively. One of the most important advantages of our system is that, even for application experts, let alone average users, it is much easier to define similarities for search parameters separately than to define complex (multidimensional) metrics like $\sqrt{(1.83\,d)^2 + (1.47\,c)^2 + (2.20\,r)^2}$, where d equals some distance, c a category, and r a rating from the application [17]. Furthermore, as pointed out in [3], in contrast to fuzzy set approaches (see the definition of the t-norm), metrics in general may lead to discontinuities if conjunctions are used, and if the individual terms are fulfilled to differing degrees.

In contrast to other approaches that are based on fuzzy sets as well, extending the relational query language SQL was not an issue for our application, because SQL is not used directly by end-users. Instead, we either use a graphical user interface to express the query, or we provide a procedural interface that comprises the parameters necessary for fuzzy queries (and, of course, all other advanced query features). Nevertheless, extending a declarative query language is interesting, because it allows for further query optimization.

With respect to the implementation, we rely on advanced relational database system technology, i.e., we use (precompiled) stored procedures as the application interface to the database instead of SQL. In contrast to application level solutions in client/server environments, we are able to perform complex computation on the database server itself, thus avoiding network communication overhead. Where implementation concepts are discussed at all in the literature, client/server issues are neglected; e.g., [2] concentrates on query optimization when discussing implementation aspects, and [20] just distinguishes among database, knowledge base, and inference engine.

To the best of our knowledge, our solution is unique with respect to the several modes of usage (see Sect. 5 and Fig. 4).

7 Conclusions, Enhancements, and Future Research

In this paper, we have presented the design and implementation of the limits database for the environmental information system UIS of Baden-Württemberg. The system is a general server module of limit values for measured environmental parameters that can be used to supplement many types of interactive or non-interactive applications. After an introduction to UIS, we emphazised the advanced query processing functionality of our system. We are able to process fuzzy, i.e., semantically imprecise, queries depending on their subject-specific context via a procedural front-end to a conventional relational database system.

In less than a year, we have modelled the relevant data, designed and implemented a system for querying the limits database, and for storing data in it. When we presented the data model and the solution based on it to the application experts, only minor corrections, e.g., changing an entity's name, had to be incorporated into the model. We were able to integrate further examples taken from regulations not included in [14], and other types of limits, into our model instantaneously. The system is nearly fully operational with respect to query processing, as described in this paper. Current limitations (calling interactive database applications from C-programs) are due to using β-releases of the GUI tool. Below, we summarize some of the lessons learned so far, and we describe our short term research agenda.

Although [14] provided a good starting point for data modelling, it does not make sense to insert the data automatically due to their complexity and lack of homogeneity. Thus, we need the support from experts in different application domains in order to avoid mistakes and misinterpretations, and to discuss contradictions among different regulations.

Several disadvantages of the relational data model became obvious. For instance, it would be advantageous to define a data type *similarity relation*, and to create instances of this data type for each entity. Similarly, an object-oriented programming language would be most appropriate to implement just *one* generic similarity search, and then to create several instances of this method.

Furthermore, the implementation effort revealed some deficiencies in the current implementation of the SQL standard. An efficient main-memory implementation of temporary base relations, as defined in the SQL-2 standard [16], would allow for an easy-to-program (i.e., declarative instead of procedural style), yet run-time efficient implementation of the search module, that still uses stored procedures. We plan to study performance issues in more detail when the system contains more data.

Currently, we are investigating other application areas where our general approach to fuzzy query processing as an extension to conventional, exact query processing is applicable as well. Furthermore, we currently develop a run-time scheduler (optimizer) for the front-end, which chooses among different execution sequences depending on the search parameters supplied by the user and the relations' size. Another future enhancement is to exclude tuples below a certain threshold in their similarity value when the number of result tuples would become too large otherwise.

Acknowledgements. S. Hemmer was involved in data modelling and the implementation effort. His support, discussions with B. Boss on fuzzy databases, and P. Lockemann's comments on an earlier draft of this paper are gratefully acknowledged.

References

1. Land Baden-Württemberg: *Umweltinformationssystem Baden-Württemberg.* Reihe Verwaltung 2000, Band 6, Hrsg.: Innen- und Umweltministerium, Stuttgart, 1991
2. P. Bosc, M. Galibourg, G. Hamon: *Fuzzy Querying with SQL: Extensions and Implementation Aspects.* Fuzzy Sets and Systems, Vol. 28, 1988, pp. 333-349
3. P. Bosc, H. Prade: *An Introduction to Fuzzy Set and Possibility Theory-based Approaches to the Treatment of Uncertainty and Imprecision in Data Base Management Systems.* 2nd UMIS Workshop, Catalina, California, USA, April 1993
4. *CCINFOdisc,* Canadian Centre for Occupational Health and Safety
5. D. Dörner: *Die Logik des Mißlingens – Strategisches Denken in komplexen Situationen.* Rowohlt, Reinbek, 1992
6. D. Dubois, H. Prade, R.Y. Yager (Eds.): *Readings in Fuzzy Sets for Intelligent Systems.* Morgan Kaufmann, San Mateo, California, USA, 1993
7. *European Inventory of Existing Chemical Substances (EINECS)*
8. N. Fuhr: *Anfragefunktionen für Umweltinformationssysteme.* in: W. Pillmann, A. Jaeschke (Hrgs.): *Informatik für den Umweltschutz.* Proceedings 5. Symposium, Wien, Austria, September 1990; Springer, 1990, pp. 27 – 37
9. S. Hemmer, R. Kramer: *Limits Database for UIS – Users' Guide Query Module (in German).* FZI Bericht 20/93, Forschungszentrum Informatik (FZI), 1993
10. R. Kramer: *Limits Database for UIS – Project Documentation (in German).* Forschungszentrum Informatik (FZI), November 1993
11. R. Kramer, H. Spandl: *Limits Database for an Environmental Information System – A Fuzzy Set based Querying Approach.* FZI Report 25/93, Forschungszentrum Informatik (FZI), December 1993
12. R. Kruse, J. Gebhardt, F. Klawonn: *Fuzzy-Systeme.* Teubner, Stuttgart, 1993
13. Landesanstalt für Immisionsschutz Nordrhein-Westfalen: *Organismen- und Stoffliste, Version 3.1.* 1993
14. Landesanstalt für Umweltschutz Baden-Württemberg, L. Roth: *Grenzwerte - Kennzahlen zur Umweltbelastung in Deutschland und in der EG, Tabellenwerk.* Ecomed Fachverlag, Landsberg, 1992
15. R. Mayer-Föll: *Zur Rahmenkonzeption des Umweltinformationssystems Baden-Württemberg.* in: O. Günther, H. Kuhn, R. Mayer-Föll, F.J. Radermacher (Hrsg.): *Konzeption und Einsatz von Umweltinformationssystemen,* Proceedings, Informatik Fachberichte 301, Springer-Verlag Berlin Heidelberg, 1991, pp. 3-19
16. J. Melton, A. R. Simon: *Understanding the New SQL: A Complete Guide.* Morgan Kaufmann Publishers, San Mateo, California, USA, 1993
17. A. Motro: *VAGUE: A User Interface to Relational Databases that Permits Vague Queries.* ACM Trans. on Office Information Systems, Vol. 6(3), 1988, pp. 187-214
18. A. Motro: *Accomodating Imprecision in Database Systems: Issues and Solutions.* ACM SIGMOD Record, Vol. 19(4), December 1990, pp. 69 – 74
19. *Pest Bank,* (CD-ROM) Center for Environmental and Regulatory Information System (CERIS), Environmental Protection Agency (EPA), USA
20. M. Zemankova: *FIIS: A Fuzzy Intelligent Information System.* IEEE Data Engineeering, Special Issue on Imprecisions in Databases, Vol. 12(2), 1989, pp. 11-20
21. H. J. Zimmermann: *Fuzzy Set Theory and its Applications.* Kluwer, Boston, 2nd edition, 1991

An Intelligent Database System Application: The Design of EMS

Elena Baralis[1], Stefano Ceri[2], Gabriella Monteleone[3], Stefano Paraboschi[2]

[1] Politecnico di Torino, Dipartimento di Automatica e Informatica,
Corso Duca degli Abruzzi 24, 10129 Torino, Italy
baralis@polito.it
[2] Politecnico di Milano, Dipartimento di Elettronica e Informazione,
Piazza L. da Vinci 32, 20133 Milano, Italy
{ceri,parabosc}@elet.polimi.it
[3] TXT Ingegneria Informatica, Via Socrate 41, 20128 Milano, Italy
monteleone@txt.it

Abstract. Intelligence in database systems is the capability of modeling both the complex structure of data and its dynamic evolution. The Chimera intelligent database prototype, designed in the context of the IDEA Esprit project, provides an object-oriented data model, deductive rules to express computations, and production rules to implement active reactions to database events. We present in this paper a high-level description of the main features of the Chimera conceptual interface, and we describe the design of the Energy Management System application in Chimera.

1 Introduction

Intelligence in database systems is the capability of modeling both the complex structure of data and its dynamic evolution. Deductive Object-Oriented Database systems provide an object-oriented data model combined with rules to express complex computations. Chimera, an intelligent database prototype designed in the context of the IDEA Esprit project, substantially extends in this direction, by providing passive (deductive) rules to express computations, and active (production) rules to implement reactions to database events.

The availability of passive and active rules allows the database designer to incorporate into the database system knowledge that was previously contained in the applicative software. Thus, after physical independence and logical independence [2], it is possible to achieve *knowledge independence*, i.e. extract the knowledge from the applications and introduce it into the database schema. Knowledge independence presents some advantages:

- it "factorizes" knowledge and makes it available to all applications, thus simplifying the application design, specification, and coding
- it simplifies the management of changes, because change in knowledge is centralized and automatically reflected at the application's level
- it simplifies the specification of knowledge itself, by means of specific tools and compilers which are currently being designed

– it contributes to the formal definition of knowledge, thus enabling the proof of important properties such as correctness, completeness, termination, confluence, non-redundancy, consistency

Knowledge independence, as physical and logical independence, requires a body of theoretical research to provide methodologies and tools. It requires, at the same time, practical design experience to gain a deep understanding of the problems connected to complex database system applications design.

The work in this paper is focused on the design of a complex application using the Chimera intelligent database system: the Electrical Management System, that manages the static and dynamic evolution of an electrical network. To our knowledge, even if some applications are now being proposed [4, 7, 8, 6, 3], no established design methodology is available to the intelligent database systems designer. In this paper, we present the case study development as a collection of design activities, that we espect to evolve in a complete design methodology.

1.1 The Energy Management System

The EMS database application has been designed in cooperation with the Italian Electricity Board, ENEL (for a complete description see [5]). It manages the evolution of the dynamic description of the Italian power distribution network. The EMS database provides:

– a description of the network topology, i.e. of its static structure,
– a description of the network dynamic operation, i.e. the way power is actually distributed through the network.

The EMS network is composed by *sites* and *branches* connecting site pairs. Figure 1 provides an example of a network topology. Sites can be:

– *primary stations*, where power is generated, or voltage is transformed (e.g. from high voltage to low voltage)
– *nodes*, where power is supplied to the users connected directly to the node, and distributed among all the outgoing branches to supply depending nodes

Sites are interconnected by branches. Branches have two *switch gears* located at their ends. The open or closed state of each branch is determined by the state of its two switch gears. The network dynamic operation is completely described by the state of all its switch gears and the direction of the current flow associated to all active (i.e. with both switch gears closed) branches.

Currently, the power distribution network is managed by a network database and the network description is divided in 200 separate areas that cover Italy. In Tables 1 and 2 are given some figures for the size of ENEL network.

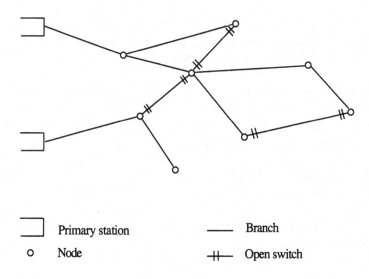

Fig. 1. EMS network topology

Table 1. Number of sites and connections in the network

Object	Number
Primary substations	1600
Nodes	500000
Branches	550000

1.2 Outline of the Paper

In Section 2 we present an overview of the Chimera conceptual interface and we describe all the distinctive features of the language. In Section 3 we describe the design process for the EMS application and present some relevant aspects of the application. In Section 4 we draw conclusions and outline future work.

2 Chimera

Chimera is the conceptual interface of IDEA. Chimera supports object-oriented, deductive, and active database features. It consists of:

– a *conceptual model*, called Chimera Model (CM), providing object-oriented modeling facilities

Table 2. Frequency of transactions in the network

Transaction type	Frequency
monitoring the operating condition of the network	daily
network dynamic reconfiguration	2 days per week
topology modifications	monthly

– a *conceptual language*, called Chimera Language (CL), providing data definitions, declarative queries, procedural primitives for database manipulation, as well as various forms of rules and constraints

Chimera is extensively described in [1]. In the following we provide an informal overview of its main features. We describe in Section 2.1 the Chimera concepts, i.e. all the items available to the database designer to describe the features of a complex application, while in Section 2.2 we outline the language constructs allowed in the Chimera language.

2.1 Chimera Concepts

A schema definition in Chimera is a collection of targeted and untargeted definitions. Each type or class definition is a target, that is, a unit of abstraction and modularization. Features (such as attributes and operations) that are defined in the context of a given target have a scope that is limited to that target. Thus, targets enable a modular design and some degree of information hiding that is typical of object-oriented design.

However, some information in the schema cannot be targeted; for instance views combining information from several classes, or triggers affecting multiple classes, or constraints relating the state of objects from several classes. Therefore, some definitions cannot be expressed in the context of types and classes and are called untargeted definitions.

Given that targeted definitions are usually easier to understand, control, and evolve, a good design principle for Chimera applications is to choose an appropriate collection of targets, so that most of the definitions in the schema can be targeted.

Objects and Object Classes. Every entity of an application domain that is to be represented in the database should be modeled as an object. An object is described by its identity and its state. The *identity* allows to uniquely identify an object and is internally represented by means of an immutable object identifier (OID) automatically assigned to each object at object creation time. All information semantically meaningful to the object characterizes its *state* and it is described by its attributes. State changes are manipulation of an object's attributes performed by operations.

All objects in a Chimera application must belong to an object class. Object classes may be recursively specialized into subclasses, resulting in a taxonomic hierarchy of arbitrary depth. A subclass inherits all attributes and operations from its superclasses, but may redefine their implementation. Moreover, a subclass may introduce additional attributes that are applicable only to the objects in that subclass. It is possible to define multiple superclasses, with some restrictions on multiple inheritance.

The definition of an object class is performed in two separate steps, that allow an incremental development of the schema design process:

1. the definition of the *signature*, i.e. of all names and domains associated with the class
2. the definition of the *implementation* of the concepts associated with the class

When defining a new class, all concepts related to individual instances of that class have to be introduced:

- *attributes* of individual instances of the class, that can be either extensional attributes permanently stored in the database, or derived attributes computed at run time;
- *operations* causing state changes to individual objects;
- *constraints*, i.e. conditions restricting attribute values of individual objects;
- *triggers* establishing reactions to arbitrary events affecting class members.

In addition, several concepts related to the entire class (but not to individual instances) are introduced as well:

- *c-attributes* associating values with the entire class rather than with individual instances (extensional or derived);
- *c-operations* changing the state of (extensional) c-attributes;
- *c-constraints* that apply to the entire class rather than to individual instances.

Finally, all superclass relationships between the newly defined class and previously defined classes have to be stated at class definition time.

All the concepts introduced in the signature of a class are associated to their implementation, that depends on the particular nature of each concept. Classes can be populated either by explicitly creating each individual instance, or by implicitly and collectively defining all instances by means of deductive rules. The same applies for attributes and class attributes: attribute values can either be introduced individually during object creation (extensional attributes), or defined collectively by means of passive rules (derived attributes). Constraints (and class constraints) are always implemented by passive rules. Operations and triggers are implemented by means of different imperative constructs (see Section 2.2).

Values and Value Classes. Values are a means of describing objects, thus they are concrete symbols, or structures composed from symbols by applying the set, list, or record constructors. Values can belong to predefined or user-defined types. Predefined basic value types are system-defined and include object identifiers, integers, and strings. User-defined value types allow the database designer to explicitly define the structure of a value type and to restrict the range of its instances by specifying constraints.

Predefined and user-defined value types are considered as "abstract domains" in Chimera, in the sense that the set of instances of the type is never made explicit by enumerating the individual instances. Value classes are introduced to control the extent of a user-defined value type by enumerating its values. In this way, additional storage for an explicit value set is allocated and successively populated by means of individual insertions.

Constraints. Constraints provide a means for restricting the content of the database. Constraints consist of conditions expressed in CL: they have a name, and they may have output parameters. In case of violation of a constraint, the output parameters return values specific to the cause of the particular violation. Constraints can be either targeted or untargeted. When they are targeted to a particular class, they may either restrict the set of legal values of its attributes, or restrict the extent of the respective class (c-constraints).

Chimera also supports some built-in constraints, for which it is not necessary to define an implementation, such as *key* and *notnull* specifications for given attributes.

Triggers. Triggers provide active behaviour to the database by introducing specific reactions to particular events relevant to the database. Chimera supports set-oriented triggers, that follow the *event-condition-action* paradigm of active databases. *Events* are database specific operations (i.e. queries and updates), or operation calls. When any of its triggering events occurs, a trigger becomes active. *Conditions* are declarative formulas, that are evaluated in the current state. *Reactions* are calls to procedures written in the Chimera language.

Trigger processing is system-initiated after the execution of the action that generates the event (immediate triggers), or at the end of the transaction (deferred triggers). It is an iterative cycle, in which: (i) one trigger is chosen among all active triggers (ii) the selected trigger's condition is evaluated, and (iii) if the condition is satisfied, then the reaction is executed. The trigger processing cycle continues until no trigger is active. When multiple triggers are active at the same time, one is randomly selected, but it is possible to specify priorities, thus forcing a partial ordering among triggers.

The trigger specification language in Chimera presents a rich variety of options:

− all the *complete sequence* of occurred events can be examined, or only their *net-effect* (i.e. the cumulative effect of successive operations on the same data) can be considered

– events can be *consumed*, i.e. discarded after the consideration of the trigger, or *preserved*, i.e. all events since the transaction start are considered at each trigger's consideration

The preceding options are orthogonal: for instance, the net-effect can be computed either on new events generated after the last trigger's consideration, or on all events since transaction start. The rich semantics of the trigger specification language allows the use of triggers for a variety of different applications, e.g. static and dynamic constraint checking (net-effect and preserving, respectively), logging of individual changes (complete sequence), alerting (consuming).

Views. Views are used to specify derived concepts (referring to several classes) from concepts already present in the database, thus presenting information in a format that is most suited to specific user needs. Views can be interpreted as "predefined queries", whose definition is included in the schema of a Chimera database. Each view has a signature (a user defined value type) and an implementation (a collection of passive rules.

2.2 Chimera Language

The Chimera language serves two main purposes: to define the implementation of schema components (e.g. passive and active rules) and to describe data manipulation by means of queries, updates, and transactions.

The Chimera language is a logic-based language, supporting declarative queries, declarative rules for data definition (passive rules), as well as declarative conditions for controlling imperative (active) rules and imperative operations. It is composed by *terms*, that denote either values or objects, and *formulas* that express propositions about individuals, that can be true or false and are evaluated over a database state. We do not elaborate on the features of the logic language here; the interested reader can refer to [1].

Passive Rules. Passive rules are used for the declarative definition of intensional subclasses and derived attributes. Furthermore, they are used to define views and constraints. They are expressed in the form

$$head \leftarrow body$$

where the head is an atomic formula, the body is an arbitrary formula, and each variable in the head occurs also in the body. Rules are stratified with respect to sets and negation, thereby ensuring that the computation of their fixpoint converges to a unique minimal model.

Active Rules and Operations. Two different categories of imperative constructs are defined in Chimera: active rules, that implement triggers and operation implementations, that implement operations. Both constructs contain a procedural expression that defines the actual actions to be executed, and a declarative pre-condition that must be satisfied over the current database state for the actions to take place. The invocation style is different: operations require an explicit operation invocation, and control is locally transfered from one operation call to the next. Triggers are implicitly invoked by a system component that monitors actions and determines appropriate reactions.

Queries, Updates, and Transactions. Chimera supports the conventional notions of query, update, and transaction. *Queries* can be submitted from a user-friendly interface (UFI) or from an application program interface (API). Query primitives include: `display`, `select` and `next`. Each primitive consists of a Chimera formula and a target list. The formula is evaluated over the current state of the database, returning either each individual binding (`next`) or the set of all bindings (`display` and `select`) for the target list variables. *Updates* in Chimera support object creation and deletion, object migration from one class to another, state change or change of persistency status of objects, and value class population and modification. A Chimera *transaction* is user-controlled by means of commit and rollback primitives that either atomically execute the changes defined in the transaction boundaries, or restore the transaction initial state.

3 Designing the EMS Application

We now turn to the description of a substantial application, EMS, through the Chimera model and language. In order to develop the EMS application, we enucleated the following design activities:

1. The first basic task in the application design is the identification of all the important entities, that will become targets in Chimera. As targeted definitions are usually easier to understand, this is a key activity in the design process: the choice of an appropriate collection of targets simplifies the understanding and evolution management of the schema.
2. The subsequent task is the definition of the untargeted concepts (constraints, triggers, views), that involve the reference to more than one target in their definition. This activity provides a first feedback on the adequacy of the target collection: if an excessive number of constraints and triggers cannot be accommodated in class definitions as targeted concepts, the selection of targets can be revised.
3. The last task is the identification of applications. In this activity the advantage of embedding and factorizing knowledge into the database system becomes evident. Most complex computations are already defined as intentional attributes or views, while active rules take care of the propagation of all data modification operations to maintain the database consistency. Thus, applications are normally reduced to the description of state changes performed on the database.

The complete design process is cyclical, as each activity provides useful feedbacks to improve the other activities' effectiveness.

The first activity is the most significant one, and can be further divided in some relevant steps:

- give an abstract definition of targets and relationships among targets (e.g. hierarchies or part-of relationships); such definitions can be represented with an (extended) ER diagram
- give a definition of relevant domains, in which value types and value classes
- give the operational description of each target, in terms of its implementation (derived attributes and operations)
- give a definition of the constraints targeted to a class
- give a definition of each trigger targeted to a class

In the following we present a subset of the EMS application (the complete application is described in [5]), that exploits the features provided by the Chimera conceptual interface presented in Section 2. To describe the EMS application, we initially define (a subset of) the *schema* of the EMS application by individuating all relevant targets and providing the definition of some value and object classes in Section 3.1. Then, we augment the data model with untargeted concepts, such as untargeted constraints and triggers in Section 3.2. We finally discuss how the knowledge embedded into the database schema can be exploited when performing complex data modification operations (transactions) in Section 3.3.

3.1 Designing the targets

Abstract representation definition. In the EMS application some fundamental entities can be easily identified: sites, branches connecting sites, and switches determining the state of each branch (open or closed). The entity **site** represents a generic node in the network and it can be further specialized in **station**, representing the generators in the network, and **node**, representing all nodes used for power distribution. A high-level entity-relationship representation of the database schema is given in Figure 2.

Value type definition. Switch gears and branches in the EMS application may assume any of the two values **OPEN** and **CLOSED**. This requirement can be enforced by defining a value type constrained to the two values, as represented in Figure 3. The restriction on the domain is specified through the constraint **ImproperStatus**, that detects when an incorrect value is assigned to any attribute of type **switchStatus**. This choice does not require any explicit insertion of values performed by the user, but prevents the domain evolution during the application lifetime (e.g. the definition of a new switch state **OUT-OF-ORDER**). If domain evolution is required, it can be implemented by defining a value class for **switchStatus** and then explicitly inserting all the allowed values.

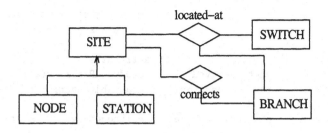

Fig. 2. EMS entity-relationship schema

```
define value type switchStatus: string(6)
    constraints
        ImproperStatus(status: switchStatus);
define implementation for switchStatus
    constraints
        ImproperStatus(S) <- S \= "OPEN", S \= "CLOSED"
end
```

Fig. 3. Definition of the switchStatus value class

Class signature definition. The Chimera object-oriented data model provides a natural representation for class hierarchies. In Figure 4 the signature definition for the three classes site, node, and station is presented. In the two subclasses node and station, the class definition is refined by adding attributes and constraints specific to each subclass. In particular, let us consider the site class: all the attribute names are listed with their respective type declarations. Derived attributes, such as powerOut, are followed by the keyword derived. Their evaluation is defined by a passive rule in the implementation section. Observe the use of the set type constructor set-of that defines the attribute branches as a set of OID's.

Derived attributes implementation. The definition of derived attributes allows the designer to represent explicitly the dependency of a given attribute value on some other attribute values: derived attributes are implemented by declarative expressions, that describe the computation of the actual attribute value. In Figure 5 is gioven the implementation of the site attributes branchOut and suppliedNodes, whose signature is defined in Figure 4. branchOut is an object-valued attribute that computes all branches outgoing from a site. Its implementation defines a view on the branch class that computes the OID's of all branches currently outgoing the given site (represented by the special variable Self). The suppliedNodes attribute computes all nodes supplied by the site. A node is sup-

```
define object class site                    define object class station
 attributes                                  superclasses
  name: string(20);                           site
  description: string(40);                    attributes
  branches: set-of-branch, derived;           producedPower: real;
  branchOut: set-of(branch), derived;         availablePower: real, derived;
  powerOut: real, derived;                    constraints
  suppliedNodes: set-of(node), derived;      NotEnoughPower(S: station);

define object class node
  superclasses
    site
  attributes
    absorbedPower: real;
    branchIn: branch, derived;
    powerIn: real, derived;
    absorbedPower: real;
    supplyingNodes: set-of(node), derived;
    supplyingStation: station, derived;
    possibleSupplyingNodes: set-of(node), derived;
    possibleSupplyingStation: set-of(station), derived;
constraints
    WrongPowerBalancement(N: node);
```

Fig. 4. The site hierarchy

plied by a site if (a) its incoming branch is one of the site's outgoing branches, or (b) it is supplied by some node supplied by that site. The two passive rules in Figure 5 implement the two above conditions.

```
define implementation for site
   ...
Self.branchOut <- branch(B), B.orientation.from=Self;
(N in Self.suppliedNodes <- node(N), branch(B), (B in Self.branchOut),
                          (B=N.branchIn), B.status"CLOSED"
(N in Self.suppliedNodes <- node(X), node(N), (X in Self.suppliedNodes),
                          (N in X.suppliedNodes);
   ...
```

Fig. 5. Implementation definition for attributes branchOut and suppliedNodes in site

Operation definition. Operations allow the database designer to specify procedures that change the database state in the definition of classes (similar to methods in object-oriented databases). Operations are defined in the class signature and their implementation is defined in the implementation section. The implementation consists of a procedure name, possibly with input and output parameters, a "guard condition", expressing a condition on the database to be verified for the actual operation to be performed, and the code describing the operation itself. We give in Figure 6 two examples of implementation of simple operations changing a branch and a switch state to CLOSED. When a branch close() operation is issued, if the branch is open, a state change of its switches to CLOSED is performed by calling the corresponding operation. The implementation of the switch class close() operation, if the switch is open, simply calls the predefined modify operation that performs the modification of attribute status to the new CLOSED state.

```
define object class branch            define object class switch
 operations                            operations
  close()                               close()
  ...                                   ...
define implementation for branch      define implementation for switch
 ...                                   ...
 operations                            operations
  close():                              close(): Self.status="OPEN"
    Self.status="OPEN",switch(S),          -> modify(Self.status,"CLOSED");
    S.switchedBranch=Self -> S.close     ...
 ...
```

Fig. 6. The close() operation in switch and branch

Targeted constraints definition. In the EMS application, a number of design constraints on the network structure are defined. The WrongDesign constraint represented in Figure 7 is targeted on the node class and detects when more than one branch connects any two site pairs. The output parameter is the list of all branches violating the constraint. Note that the use of deductive rules with both head and body, and of denial form for expressing the body, adopted in Chimera, generates bindings for the variables in the head when the constraint is violated; bindings correspond to data violating the constraint. The NotEnoughPower targeted constraint represented in Figure 8 detects when a station's output power exceeds its produced power. The condition detecting the constraint violation is simple, because of the use of the derived attribute powerOut, which computes the dynamic value of the output power.

3.2 Designing untargeted concepts

Constraints definition. The untargeted constraint WrongSwitch is represented in Figure 9. It detects when a switch is associated to a (node, branch) pair,

```
define object class branch
  ...
constraints
  WrongDesign(B:branch);
define implementation for branch
  ...
constraints
  WrongDesign(Self) <- branch(B), B\=Self, Self.site1=Self.site2,
                       Self.site2=Self.site1;
  ...
```

Fig. 7. Implementation definition for constraint WrongConstraint in node

```
define object class station
constraints
  NotEnoughPower(S:station);
  ...
define implementation for station
constraints
  NotEnoughPower(Self) <- Self.producedPower-Self.powerOut<0;
```

Fig. 8. Constraint NotEnoughPower in station

in which the node is not connected to the branch. Its definition involves the classes **node**, **branch**, and **switch**. It produces the list of all switches violating the constraint, that can be used for the constraint enforcement.

```
define constraint WrongSwitch(switch: S, node: N, branch: B);
  WrongSwitch(S, N, B) <- node(N), branch(B), switch(S), S.node=N,
                          S.switchedBranch=B, B.site1\=N, B.site2\=N;
```

Fig. 9. Untargeted constraint WrongSwitch

Triggers definition. In the EMS system, many network management tasks can be automatically performed by defining active rules. In particular, untargeted triggers can be defined to perform static and dynamic network reconfiguration tasks, such as insertion and deletion of nodes, or the network load recomputation after a switch state change.

The **DelBranches** trigger represented in Figure 10 enforces a static network reconfiguration after the deletion of a node: all branches connected to the node are deleted as well. This trigger is executed at the transaction's end if any node deletion occurred during the transaction. The `NoCurrentFlow` trigger in Figure 11 resets the branch orientation when a switch is opened (i.e. no current is flowing in the branch). In this case, the net-effect of all occurred events is considered: multiple changes to a switch status during a single transactions are disregarded and only the final switch state is considered.

```
define trigger DelBranches
events     delete(node)
condition branch(B),node(N),occurred(delete,N),B in N.branches
actions    delete(branch,B);
end
```

Fig. 10. Definition of the DelBranches trigger

```
define trigger NoCurrentFlow
events     modify(switch.status)
condition switch(S), branch(B), net-occurred(modify(status),S),
          S.status="OPEN", S.switchedBranch=B
actions    modify(branch.orientation,B,(NULL,NULL));
end
```

Fig. 11. Definition of the NoCurrentFlow trigger

3.3 Defining Transactions

We present in the following two different types of EMS database transactions, that are user-initiated modifications of the EMS static and dynamic description.

Deletion of a node in the network. A network static reconfiguration task requires the deletion of a node with name **Milano Centro** (node N), and the reconnection of the two isolated nodes **Milano Nord** (node N_1) and **Milano Sud** (node N_2) by a new connection, as shown in Figure 12. This requires the deletion of the given node N and the successive creation of a new branch connecting the nodes N_1 and N_2. The transaction that performs this task from the UFI interface is given in Figure 13. The first three **select** statements identify the nodes on which to operate, while the next two delete node N and create the new branch connecting N_1 and N_2 respectively. Observe that, at this point, the database in an inconsistent state:

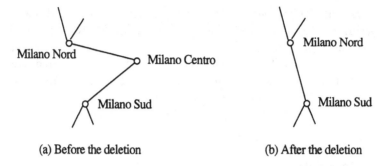

(a) Before the deletion (b) After the deletion

Fig. 12. Network reconfiguration due to the deletion of an intermediate node

- all the branches connected to the deleted node are dangling
- switches are associated to a non-existing node
- the new branch does not have switches at its two ends

The task of restoring database consistency is automatically implemented by two untargeted triggers that delete all the branches connected to the deleted node (see Section 3.3 and Fig. 10), and all the switches defined over these branches. Further, two switches associated to the newly created branch are created. While the delete/create operations are fairly simple, the propagation of the update would have required the knowledge of the entire structure of the network to be correctly performed.

```
begin-transaction;

select(N1 where node(N1), N1.name="Milano Nord");
select(N2 where node(N2), N2.name="Milano Sud");
select(N where node(N), N.name="Milano Centro");
delete(node,N);
create(branch,(N1,N2)));

commit;
```

Fig. 13. Transaction to delete an intermediate node in the network

Network reconfiguration after a branch fault. A branch failure interrupted power supply to some node in the network. The transaction required for reconfiguring the network in order to guarantee power supply to all its nodes is extremely complex. It requires the recomputation of the dynamic state of the network after the failure, and the evaluation of possible alternative connections by using the appropriate strategy. Let X be the node isolated because of the branch fault: a new path must be selected to supply node X. We show how the selection of a new propagation path can be performed under a restriction: the new path must require the state modification of at most one branch. The transaction can be divided in the following two steps:

1. if there exists one (or more) node N directly connected to node X and supplied by a station with available power larger than the power required by X, close the branch connecting the two nodes N and X
2. if the first step fails, search all the nodes N supplied by X that also have an alternative supplying node N_1 not supplied by X and supplied by a station with available power larger than the power required by X. Close the branch connecting the two nodes N and N_1

If both steps fail, more complex strategies (that are not presented in this paper) can be implemented.

In Figure 14 the first step above is specified for the UFI transaction interface, while in Figure 15 the second step is specified. Owing to the definition of several derived attributes, among which **powerOut** in **site** and **supplyingStation** in **node**, it is possible to express rather simple criteria on the new configuration of the network. The query to find appropriate branches to be closed could provide more than one branch, thus a non deterministic choice among all selected branches is performed to choose the branch to be closed (through the nondeterministic choose literal, see [1]).

```
begin-transaction;

select(N, SC
       where node(X), node(N), branch(B), branch(BC),
             B in N.branch, B in X.branch, B.status="OPEN",
             {N} * X.suppliedNodes = {};
             N.supplyingStation.availablePower >=
             X.powerOut+X.absorbedPower,
             choose(B,1,BC));
BC.close;

commit;
```

Fig. 14. Network reconfiguraton after a fault (first step)

```
begin-transaction;

select(N, SC
       where node(X), node(N), node(N1), branch(B), branch(BC),
             N in X.suppliedNodes, {N1} * X.suppliedNodes = {},
             B in N.branch, B in N1.branch, B.status="OPEN",
             N1.supplyingStation.availablePower >=
             X.powerOut+X.absorbedPower,
             choose(B,1,BC));
BC.close;

commit;
```

Fig. 15. Network reconfiguraton after a fault (second step)

4   Conclusions and Future Work

We have presented in this paper an intelligent database system application: the Energy Management System. This is a large, complex application that fully exploits the features presented by intelligent dabatase systems, i.e. the capability of representing both data and knowledge in the same database schema. This application highlights the main features of the Chimera intelligent database system, most notably its active features. Active rules extend the functionalities provided by a traditional Object-Oriented batabase system by allowing the designer to define actions automatically executed by the DBMS to react to the occurrence of specific database events. The EMS application was originated in the context of the IDEA Esprit project, in order to drive-test the language expressiveness and its power and usability from the designer's perspective. Its development provided encouraging results.

At the same time, we have sketched a sequence of activities which are required in order to develop an application, and outlined how such activities were performed in the case study. Far from being a consolidated methodology, this paper presents an attempt of systematically listing the novel design steps that are required to make a good use of intelligent technology. As future work, we intend to focus on this issue in greater depth: we are convinced that intelligent database technology will not become successful until design problems are deeply understood and application design techniques are able to exploit the enhanced power of these systems.

Accordingly, we plan in the context of the IDEA project to perform a significant effort towards the establishment of a solid methodological framework for application design support. In particular, we plan to:

- define a complete methodological framework
- identify a set of "good properties" of intelligent database systems designs

– provide a collection of design support tools to allow the designers to establish the above properties in real-life applications.

Acknowledgements

We thank all the ENEL engineers for their cooperation in the design of the EMS application, particularly Leonardo Dalle Rive, Diego Balboni, Piergiorgio Pacquola and Francesco Cazzola.

References

1. Ceri, S. and Manthey, R.: Consolidated specification of Chimera (CL and CM). Technical Report IDEA.DE.2P.005.01 (1993)
2. Date, C.J.: An Introduction to Database Systems. Addison-Wesley, Reading, Massachusetts (1990)
3. Hearne, C.,Parsons, S., Sikeler, A., Jonker, W., Cui, Z., Fox, J.: Object-oriented analysis in molecular biology: A Chimera case study. Technical Report IDEA.DE.1C.009 (1993)
4. Harland, J., Ramamohanarao, K.: An Aditi implementation of a flights database. Proceedings of the Workshop on Programming with Logic Databases, Vancouver, British Columbia, (1993) 6–17
5. Monteleone, G., Baralis, E.: A dynamical electric network description: Analysis and design. Technical Report IDEA.WP.1T.005.01, (1993)
6. Muntz, R.R., Shek, E.C., Zaniolo, C.: Using LDL++ for spazio-temporal reasoning in atmospheric science databases. Proceedings of the Workshop on Programming with Logic Databases, Vancouver, British Columbia (1993) 74–86
7. Roth, W.G., Ramakrishnan, R., Seshadri, P.: MIMSY: A system for analyzing time series data in the stock market domain. Proceedings of the Workshop on Programming with Logic Databases, Vancouver, British Columbia, (1993) 33–43
8. Shaw, S., Foggiato-Bish, L., Garcia, I., Tillman, G., Tryon, D., Wood, W., Zaniolo, C.: Improving data quality via LDL++. Proceedings of the Workshop on Programming with Logic Databases, Vancouver, British Columbia, (1993) 60–73

Using Next Generation Databases to Develop Financial Applications

Rakesh Chandra[1] and Arie Segev[2]

[1] Bond Portfolio Analysis Group
Salomon Brothers Inc.*** , 7 World Trade Center, New York, NY 10048
[2] Walter A. Haas School of Business
University of California at Berkeley
and
Information and Computing Sciences Division
Lawrence Berkeley Laboratory
Berkeley, CA 94720
email: rchandra@sp_server.sbi.com, segev@csr.lbl.gov

Abstract. Conventional database systems lack temporal, object and rule support to model financial database applications. In [CS93a], we described the complexity of financial applications and studied the database requirements of such applications. We argued that next-generation databases are an appropriate platform for developing database applications. In this paper we build upon this research by studying strategies to model entities commonly encountered in financial applications. Specifically, the financial entities discussed in this paper are financial instruments and portfolios. Positions in financial instruments and the trading strategies that give meaning to these positions are also modeled. The paper proposes class definitions to model the structural and dynamic properties of financial entities and the interactions between them. These class definitions describe a generic set of attributes and operators for the financial entities discussed. Examples from the financial domain are used to illustrate the modeling constructs and class definitions proposed.
Keywords: Financial Applications, Next-Generation Databases, Modeling Financial Entities.

1 Introduction

The breakdown of the Bretton-Woods agreement on a fixed system of exchange rates [Man92] in 1971, resulted in an increase in the fluctuation of exchange rates and interest rates. This event when coupled with the advances in information technology, sophistication of financial theory and a decrease in regulation in the 1980s, created a marketplace of a vast array of financial instruments that caters to different investment and risk management objectives. Financial database applications, which are meant to facilitate trading and research in these financial

---

*** Part of the research by this author was done while at the University of California at Berkeley and Lawrence Berkeley Laboratory

instruments have also become complex because: (a) there are a variety of complex financial instruments. The dynamic nature of the marketplace often forces new instruments to be introduced and old ones to be discontinued, (b) trading in these instruments is based on numerically intensive procedures and complex mathematical relationships between financial instruments, (c) the decrease in the cost of telecommunications and the increased reliability of networks make profitable opportunities available only for short periods of time.

In [CS93a], we studied the database requirements of financial applications and showed that conventional database systems are unable to handle the complexity of financial applications because they are specialized for the creation, manipulation and processing of fixed format snapshot records. We argued that next-generation database systems provide an appropriate platform for the development of efficient financial applications. Next-generation databases provide facilities to (a) add complex types to the base types of *float, int* and *char*, (b) declare new operators on base and complex types, (c) implement new access methods designed to optimize user-defined operators and (d) define rules that represent application semantics in the database. These facilities can be used to model financial objects in the database, e.g., financial instruments and portfolios, define functions or operators that take these financial objects as arguments, e.g., computation of the term structure of interest rates based on a set of bonds, create indexes that improve the efficiency of operators on financial objects and define rules that express the price relationships between financial instruments.

Even though next-generation databases offer a large set of features, our study of database requirements for financial applications [CS93a], led to the proposal of three constructs that are required to model financial objects in next-generation databases. These features are briefly summarized below and are used extensively in the class definitions developed in this paper.

In applications like financial trading, time based predicates in queries and rules are very important. There is also a need to define lists of time points or intervals. We refer to these lists as calendars. In [CS93a] and [CSS94], we developed a system of calendric abstract data types (ADTs) that allowed the creation and manipulation of user defined calendars. A simple list based language was proposed to define, manipulate and query calendars. This system allows the specification of natural-language time-based expressions, maintenance of valid time in databases, specification of temporal conditions in database queries and rules, and user-defined semantics for date manipulation. Periodicity of temporal data is an important aspect of many applications and is of special importance to financial trading. In [CSS94], we developed a system of time-based rules that allowed the specification of periodic events in rules. Since the calendar language described above provides the flexibility of specifying time-based events, an architecture for integrating time-based rules with the active database component of next-generation databases was also proposed. The dynamic nature of financial applications makes it very important for financial researchers to study the structural and behavioral properties of financial objects over time. For example, it is useful to know the composition of a portfolio (a structural property) at a specific time and also important to know how it has changed over a time interval. In addition, behavioral properties like the price of a financial instrument, interest rates and numerical measures that are valuable to traders must be studied over time. To model these properties, in [SC93] we developed a time-series class based on a study of the generic attributes and operators of time-series. In [CS93a], we showed how the constructs of calendric ADSts, time-based rules and time-series facilitated modeling financial applications.

Relevant Research

Rapid advances in technology have changed the way investment firms do business. This has been well documented in [BL92] and [Vea88]. [BL92] discuss the impact that computers have had on the ability of investment firms and trading houses to quickly analyze numerous trading strategies. [Vea88] discuss the role computers and trading systems had in the Oct. 19, 1987 crash. The presence of databases in trading systems was discussed in [AGM88], [PS88] and [Sam87]. [AGM88] point to the response time requirements of a database that facilitates stock-trading. [PS88] and [Sam87] present real-life experiences gained from a study of a large, high volume stock trading system that used a standard relational DBMS. [RS89] describe a bond trading system developed for a trading firm using a commercial relational database. They illustrate the difficulty in building efficient applications using commercial databases due to the lack of support for complex objects and time-based logic. In this paper we provide solutions to some of the problems outlined in [RS89]. As mentioned above, tracking financial entities over time is an integral aspect of financial applications. [SS87] provided a convenient way to look at this kind of temporal data through the concepts of *Time Sequence* and *Time Sequence Collection*. Temporal data modeling and representation have been extensively studied in the literature in [CC87], [Gad88], [SS88], [Sno87], [WD92]. A glossary of temporal concepts can be found in [JCG+92]. The main focus of this paper is to demonstrate how next-generation databases can be used to build reliable, high-performance financial trading applications. There are many prototype extensible systems including POSTGRES [Sto90], Exodus[Car90], Starburst[Lin87] and Ode[AG90]. A complete discussion of the capabilities of extensible databases can be found in [Car87].

2   Financial Applications

Financial database applications encompass trading and research activities. In this section, we provide a brief description of financial entities and give examples of important queries. The basic building block of a financial application is a financial instrument. A financial instrument gives its owner the right to receive a set of cash flows over time. Financial trading involves buying and selling these instruments based on specific objectives. Trading strategies are used to accomplish these objectives. Portfolios describe the financial instruments that traders and fund managers invest in. The composition and numerical measures of a portfolio are used to characterize the effectiveness of trading strategies and the performance of a trader. Typical queries in a financial application include computing the numerical measures of a financial instrument, e.g., theoretical value, sensitivity to price movements of the instrument, and/or a portfolio at a specific point in time or within a time interval. If financial instruments are complex (have cash flows that are not deterministic at all times), complex numerical techniques are required to compute these measures. Another example of a complex query is to select a portfolio of financial instruments from the available set such that constraints on the composition and expected future performance of the portfolio are satisfied. Horizon analysis, which involves assessing the performance of a portfolio based on hypothetical market scenarios is another computationally intensive query. Based on these queries, it is clear that queries in financial applications are complex. In addition, the dynamic nature of the application demands quick response times to these queries.

There are two important aspects to developing financial applications. The first aspect deals with modeling the behavioral, structural and dynamic properties of entities encountered in the application domain. The second aspect is optimizing the performance of queries on the modeled entities. This paper deals with the aspect of modeling and examines techniques for modeling financial entities in next-generation databases. The paper describes modeling strategies for financial applications that make use of the modeling constructs offered by next-generation databases, e.g., complex types, user-defined operators, access methods and rules, and modeling constructs developed using building blocks provided by the database, e.g., time-series, calendric ADTs and time-based rules. Issues of performance optimization are highlighted and are discussed in greater detail in [CS93b] and [Cha94]. The rest of this paper is organized as follows. Section 3 discusses the modeling of financial instruments as a class in next-generation databases. A generic set of attributes and operators are defined for the class of financial instruments. A *position* is defined as a contractual obligation in a fixed number of units of a financial instrument and a *trade* is defined as a collection of *positions*. A *trading strategy* gives meaning to the organization of positions in a trade. This strategy is used to attain a portfolio objective. Trades, positions and trading strategies are discussed in Section 4. Portfolios are discussed in Section 5. Section 6 concludes the paper with a summary. In the paper, class definitions are based on C++ [Str85] and when referring to the capabilities of next-generation databases, our focus is on the features offered by the extensible database, Postgres [Sto90], object-oriented systems and other similar systems.

3 Financial Instruments

As described above, financial instruments are the fundamental entity encountered in financial applications. Trading, trading strategies and portfolios will be modeled by using financial instruments as the building block. In this section, we discuss modeling financial instruments in next-generation databases. A financial instrument gives its owner the right to a set of cash flows over time and can be viewed as a complex object with simple and composite attributes. Since next-generation database allow the attriobjects.

In the past few years, there has been a proliferation of financial instruments introduced by investment banks and trading houses. These instruments are often classified based on their design. Thus, the first basis for classification is whether the instrument is derived from another instrument (a derivative) or is a base instrument. A derivative instrument is one where the set of future cash flows are derived from some fundamental source of uncertainty. The most common categories of derivative instruments are options, futures, forwards and swaps. Within each category, financial instruments can be further classified based on the risk/reward associated with the instrument and the attributes of the instrument. The following discussion on financial instruments includes (a) modeling financial instruments in next-generation databases and (b) an example of a bond instrument that illustrates the use of composite attribute types, inheritance, polymorphism and rules in modeling financial instruments.

Modeling Financial Instruments

Each financial instrument is modeled as an object with simple and complex attributes. The main attributes of a financial instrument are:

1. *Object Id* : Identifier of the instrument for purposes of retrieval and manipulation.
2. *Asset* : The underlying asset of the financial instrument. For a non-derivative instrument like a government bond, the value of the attribute is the bond itself. For a derivative instrument like a stock option, it is the underlying stock.
3. *Agents* : Models the fact that the financial instrument is a marketable commodity. The agents are the buyers and sellers that are involved in the market transaction.
4. *Measures* : is a collection of time-series that is composed of the numerical measures relevant to the instrument. For example, in a bond contract, the relevant measures would be the price, theoretical value, duration and convexity of the bond. Each of these is a time-series. In the case of an option, the relevant measures would be the price of the option, its theoretical value and the measures used to describe the sensitivity of the option to risks due to interest rate, volatility and time to expiration.
5. *Market Scenario* : is a structure that shows all the variables that determine the future cash flows and hence the value of an instrument. In the case of a bond, it would be the term structure of interest rates (the term-structure describes the relationship between the yield of bonds and their maturities). For a stock option, it would be the price of the underlying stock.
6. *Cash flow pattern* : One of the most fundamental aspects of a financial instrument is the set of cash flows that characterize it. The cash flow pattern is a set of future cash flows. For a simple zero-coupon bond, a bond that pays no interest during its lifetime, the cash flow for an investor is a cash

outflow at the time the bond is bought and a deterministic cash inflow when the bond matures. In cases where cash flows are deterministic, the cash flow pattern could be modeled as a time-series. But in cases where cash flows are contingent upon state variables like the interest rate or exchange rate or contingent upon the price of other financial instruments (e.g., options), the cash flow pattern must be modeled as a user-defined function. This function would have input arguments of the current time, the maturity date of the instrument and user-defined values for variables in the market scenario. The output would be a time-series (a set of future cash flows).

7. *Risk-profile* : of a financial instrument shows the cash flow pattern of an instrument under different market scenarios. In most cases, this is also modeled by a user-defined function. In the simplest case, such as a stock or a zero-coupon bond, the risk profile is a straight line.

8. *Valuation algorithms*: are a set of algorithms used to compute measures relevant to the financial instrument. We note that there may be several algorithms available for computing a particular measure. For example, the theoretical value of a financial instrument can be computed by a range of techniques which include analytical formulas, simulation, differential equations and lattice methods. Each algorithm would have different performance characteristics based on the expected time to complete and the accuracy of the result. In most situations it is possible to rank algorithms based on the expected accuracy of the result. But there are some situations in which two algorithms are based on different assumptions and it is likely that a user would like to compare the result of both algorithms, since they cannot be ranked by accuracy.

A partial class definition (in C++) of financial instruments is shown below.

```
class fin-inst{
 fin-inst      * asset[];//derived from one or more financial instruments
 char          * agents[];// thee specific exchange, financial institutions
 time-series   * measures[];
 void          * market-scenario[];// a set of variables that act as sources of
                    // uncertainty for the price process of the instrument
 time-series   * cashflow;
 double        ** riskprofile;// pointer to two dimensional array of double
 time-series   * value;
public:
  fin-inst(args,...);//constructor
  virtual time-series  cash-flow;// returns the set of cashflows over the
                      // life of the instrument
  virtual double**     risk-profile;// that computes the profit/loss under
                      // different market scenarios
  virtual VDPTR        valuation[];//functions used to value the
                      // instrument
  }
```

VDPTR is the name for a type that points to a function that returns the type void. In the definition above, the *asset* is modeled as an array of financial instruments since a derivative financial instrument can be derived from one or more financial instruments. *Agents* is defined as an array of text, since there can be many parties involved in a transaction with a financial instrument. *Measures* is a co that contains all the numerical measures used to monitor the performance of the instrument. The *market-scenario* is modeled as a pointer to the type void, since it will be a structure of varying complexity for different instruments. *Cash-flow* and the instruments' *value* are time-series. *risk-profile* is a two dimensional array of type double and thus is shown as a pointer to a pointer to a double. The public functions in the definition include the constructor for the class and routines to compute the cash-flow, risk-profile and value. The *virtual* keyword in the definition indicates that the actual routine for computing the cash-flow, risk-profile and value will be defined in derived classes of *fin-inst*. Derived classes of *fin-inst* would include *bonds*, which can be further classified into *govt. bonds*, *corporate bonds, mortgage bonds* and *high-yield (or junk) bonds*. This feature of overloading functions give the designer the capability to define a generic function, say *valuation()* for the class *fin-inst* and then define specific functions in classes such as *mortgage bonds* and *high-yield bonds*. When the function *valuation()* is called, the compiler will determine the exact function to use based on the class of the argument in the function call. In this section, we created a class definition for a financial instrument by modeling a generic set of attributes and operators. The next section uses the example of a financial instrument, a bond, to illustrate the above discussion.

Below, we model a bond as a sub-class of *fin-inst* (A partial class definition in C++ is shown). Note that several attributes including *Name, Agents, Cash flow, Risk-profile, Valuation-algorithms* and *Measures* are inherited from the class *fin-inst* since these are features common to all financial instruments. A more detailed discussion on the class definition can be found in [Cha94].

```
class bond_measures {
    double_time_series    duration, convexity, yield_to_maturity;
    double_time_series    vrealized_cmp_yield, olatility, theoretical_value;
        }

DBLPTR bond_value_ops[] = { // valuation schemes used to value bonds
    cox_ross_ingersoll, brennan_schwartz, binomial, simulation, finite_diff
        };

class bond : public fin-inst {
    float               face_value;/* of the bond */
    char              * issue_type; /* govt, corporate, mortgage, high-yield */
    char              * issuing_party[];
    double           ** coupon;/* pointer to two dimensional array of double */
    calendar            payout_dates;
    calendar            term;
    rating            * bond_rating; /* there may be many rating agencies */
    time-series       * call_schedule;
    bond_measures     * measures;
    double_time-series * price;
```

```
DBLPTR    * valuation_schemes = bond_value_ops; /* allows dynamic choice*/
  public:
    virtual double **    coupon();
    calendar             term_to_maturity();
    virtual VDPTR        call_provision;
    virtual DBLPTR       duration, convexity, yield_to_maturity;
};
```

4 Quotes, Positions, Trades and Trading Strategies

Modeling Quotes and Positions

Financial markets bring together traders with different long-term/short-term goals and trading styles. Some traders enter the market based on an opinion on which way the market will move and hope to profit from this expectation while others use trading strategies as insurance against adverse price movements in their existing trading positions. A different class of traders are arbitragers who hope to take advantage of price discrepancies between similar or related financial instruments trading in the same or different markets. Another class of traders are essentially middlemen who buy and sell as an accommodation to other market participants and hope to profit from the differences in bid and ask prices. To model the fact that financial instruments are bought and sold on the market by traders based on *quotes*, we define a *quote* as:

```
class quote {
    double-time-series * bid,  * ask;
    fin-inst            * instrument;
    int                 units;
    calendar            time-exp, time-range;
}
```

Whenever a trader makes a quote, he specifies a bid and/or ask price. This is modeled as a pointer to time-series since bid and ask prices are recorded. The quote is made for a specific number of *units* of *instrument* and is sometimes made effective within a *time-range*. The time the quote was registered is also stored in *time-exp*. Traders survey quotes available on the market to enter into trades based on specific trading strategies. To model the different trading strategies and styles, we consider the basic element in a trading strategy as a *position* and model it as a 4-tuple consisting of a financial instrument, the number of units of the instrument, an integer variable to indicate a long or short *position* (long indicates buying and short indicates selling) and a calendar expression that indicates the time point/interval when the *position* is effective. Thus, a *position* can be written as:

```
class position {
        quote  *   instrument-quote;
        float      units;
```

```
        bool        long;
        calendar    time-exp;
    public :
        position(char *,float, int, char *);//constructor
        //..
        }
position::position(quote * name, float units, int long, char* time)
{
    strcpy(instrument-quote,name);
    position::units = units ? units : 1; // give a default of 1
    position::long  = long;              // default position is long
    position::calendar = calendar(time); / constructor for class calendar
        }
```

Position is expressed as a class with the attribute *instrument-name*. *Instrument-quote* is a pointer to a *quote* and models the fact that the position is entered into based on a quote placed by another trader. *Units* and *long* indicate the number of instruments that the trader has a long or short position in and *time-exp* is the attribute which indicates the time point at which the position becomes effective. The default value of *time-exp* is *Now*. *position*() is a constructor that creates an instance of the class *position* given the arguments of *instrument-name*, *units*, *long* and *time-exp*. Thus, a trader's long position in an IBM-June-70 Call option could be expressed using the constructor of the class *position*:

```
position * position(''call-option-001'',''IBM-June-70'',1,''Now'');
```

Note that the *position* constructor applies some defaults when creating positions. The default for the number of units is 1, the default position is *long* and the calendar constructor provides a default of *Now*. We note that a *long/short* position refers to buying/selling an asset and not to the investment horizon of a trader, which can be long term or short term.

Modeling Trades and Trading Strategies

As discussed above, a *position* is a contractual obligation in a fixed number of units of a particular financial instrument. Thus, a *long position* in 10 option contracts means that the trader has purchased 10 option contracts while a *short position* in 10 option contracts means that the trader has contracted to sell 10 option contracts without necessarily having possession of the option contracts. A *trade* is defined as a linear collection of *positions*. A *trading strategy* gives meaning to the organization of *positions* within a *trade* and is used to achieve a *trading objective*. The simplest trade is a trade with 1 position where the position is long/short 1 unit of a financial instrument. An example of such a trade is buying a simple call option. (A *call option* on an underlying asset grants the purchaser the option to purchase a specified number of units of the asset at a specified time from the seller of the option). A complicated trading strategy for protecting against large volatility changes is a *butterfly spread*. This trading strategy is used when a trader expects price stability and will be discussed below. Thus, a trade can be modeled as:

```
class trade {
  position      * position-name;// array of positions
  comp-measures * trade-measures;// metrics for measuring the effectiveness
                                 // and risk of a trade
public :
  DBLPTR        * valuation-schemes[];
  trade(position*); // default constructor requires only 1 position
  //..
};
```

In this class definition, *trade-measures* is a collection of time-series that contains the set of numerical measures that express the market value of the trade, theoretical value and risk measures such as duration. These measures are time-series. DBLPTR is the name for a pointer to a function that returns a value of type double. *Valuation schemes* are used to get the measures of the trade and return values of type double.

5 Portfolios

Alongwith financial instruments, portfolios are the most important aspect of financial applications that we will discuss. A portfolio is modeled as a collection of trades. The main attributes of a portfolio are:

1. *Object Id* : used for querying and manipulating portfolios.
2. *Components* : collection of trades. This attribute is defined as an array of type *trade*.
3. *Arrival and Lifetime distribution of trades*: These parameters are useful in characterizing a portfolio management strategy. For example, if the arrival process has a high mean and the mean lifespan of a trade (the average time it is in the portfolio) is low, we can characterize the portfolio as an aggressively managed portfolio. A lifetime distribution that remains constant over time reflects a consistent portfolio management strategy. These measures are used to develop a model that can estimate the size of queries on portfolios [Cha94]. Since the arrival and lifetime distributions of a portfolio are dynamic measures, temporal rules are used to periodically recompute them.
4. *Measures* : A large set of numerical measures are used to characterize and measure the performance of the portfolio. Not all measures are relevant to a portfolio manager or trader at all times and thus, the database must offer the flexibility of associating a dynamic set of numerical measures with a portfolio. The dynamic nature of the application requires these measures to be stored over time. Thus the set of measures associated with a portfolio can be modeled as a history of a collection of time-series.
   Some measures are observed directly from market transactions while other measures are computed. For example, the market value of a portfolio is the sum of the value of each trade in the portfolio and is obtained from market data. The yield of the portfolio, on the other hand, is a computed measure.

Computed measures are modeled in next-generation databases through user-defined functions written in high-level programming languages (these functions are declared to the database as functions or operators). In addition to being numerically intensive, measures used to monitor the performance of a portfolio must be computed based on a user-defined monitoring policies. An additional complexity is that the monitoring policy can vary with market conditions. For example, if a portfolio manager executes a trade based on a particular trading strategy, in periods of low market volatility, the measure that computes the effectiveness of the trading strategy should be computed less often than in more turbulent economic times. This feature can be implemented using temporal rules [CSS94].

Portfolio measures are different from measures for instruments since portfolios are aggregations of trades. For example, the yield of a bond is the interest rate(y) that satisfies the equation: $P = \sum_{t=1}^{N} \frac{CF_t}{(1+y)^t}$. Here CF_t is the cash flow of the bond in period t and N is the number of periods till maturity. But the yield of a portfolio is not simply the weighted average of the yield of each instrument in its component trades. Rather, it is determined by generating and aggregating the cash flows of each component trade and then solving for y based on the above equation. Overloaded functions can be used to implement this feature. The function *yield()* could be defined as overloaded and a routine with the same name defined separately for the class *fin-inst* and *portfolio*. At runtime, the system would determine the correct algorithm to use based on the class of the argument to the function *yield()*.

5. *Cash Flow*: The cashflow of a portfolio is essentially the aggregation of the cash flows of each component trade. Unfortunately the diverse range of instruments in a portfolio can lead to a situation where some trades have deterministic cashflows, e.g., trades that involve simple bonds with fixed coupons, and some trades with contingent cash flows, e.g., stock options. Thus, to correctly compute the cash flows of a portfolio, a *market scenario* must be passed as an argument to the procedure that computes the cash flow for the portfolio. As described in section 3, a *market scenario* for a financial instrument is a collection of financial parameters that affect the price process of the instrument. But a union of *market scenarios* for all instruments that underlie the trades in the portfolio cannot always be used to derive the *market scenario* for a portfolio. Financial instruments in the portfolio may have common dependencies and in some cases, the dependencies of instruments may cancel out because of the way trades are structured. For example, a portfolio with a single trade involving a government bond would have the interest rate as an integral part of the *market scenario*. On the other hand, a portfolio with two trades, one the aforementioned govt. bond trade and the other a trade involving a foreign exchange option, would have the interest rate and exchange rates as integral components of the market scenario. But a portfolio with three trades such that the third trade completely hedged against the risk of foreign exchange fluctuation due to the trade involving the foreign exchange option, would just have the interest rate as part of the

market scenario. It should be noted that unlike the *market scenario* of an instrument, the *market scenario* of a portfolio is dynamic, both in terms of the values it can take and in terms of the variables that are part of it. For example, in the portfolio with 3 trades discussed above, if the third trade is not a perfect hedge and the effectiveness of the hedge varies with market conditions, then there will be instances where the *market scenario* contains both interest rates and exchange rates (when the hedge is not effective) and instances where only the interest rate is part of the *market scenario* (when the hedge is effective).

6. *Risk-profile*: of a portfolio is useful in implementing several portfolio management strategies such as hedging, immunization and indexing. Since the portfolio is an aggregation, the risk profile of a portfolio is constructed by using the risk profiles of the component trades in the portfolio.

A partial class definition (in C++) of portfolios is given below. A more detailed discussion of the class definition is found in [Cha94] :

```
class comp_measures {      /* numerical measures of the portfolio */
   double_time_series    theta; /* measures time risk */
   double_time_series    gamma; /* measures sensitivity of delta */
   double_time_series    vega;  /* measures volatility risk    */
   double_time_series    delta; /* measure price risk          */
   double_time_series    duration;/* measures interest rate risk */
   double_time_series    value, yield, convexity;
};

class portfolio {
  trade           * components;// array of trades
  comp-measures * measures;//for measuring the performance of a portfolio
  time-series     * cash-flow;
  double          * risk-profile[];
  stat-dist       * arrival;// distribution of arrival process of trades
  stat-dist       * lifetime;// distribution of lifespan of trades
    public :
  portfolio(trade*); // constructor
  VDPTR             * trading-operators = trading-ops;
  VDPTR             * portfolio-operators = portfolio-ops;
  double_time_series  cashflow(args...);   /* returns contingent cashflows */
                      /* over time based on a variable number of arguments */
  double          ** risk_profile(va_alist);
  DBLPTR            duration, delta, gamma, vega, convexity;
  DBLPTR            theta, value, yield;
    };

VDPTR portfolio_ops[] = { // operations used to manipulate portfolios
  openportfolio, closeportfolio, saveportfolio, compute_param, portfoliosize
      };
```

6 Conclusion

The complexity of financial instruments, advances in technology and increased uncertainty in the financial marketplace have made financial applications difficult to model. In this paper we argued that next-generation databases were an appropriate platform for the development of financial applications. The paper studied important aspects of financial applications and showed how financial entities such as financial instruments, portfolios, trades and trading strategies could be modeled in next-generation databases. The modeling used the features provided by next-generation databases such as an extensible type system, capability to create customized operators and access methods and rules. We showed how additional constructs such as calendric ADTs, time-series and time-based rules (proposed in [CS93a] and [CSS94]) were essential to the modeling exercise.

This paper identified a generic set of attributes and operators for financial instruments, trades and portfolios. Class definitions for each object were presented along with typical queries. The discussion also focussed on expressing these queries in the extensible query language. Specifically financial instruments were modeled as complex temporal objects and the example of a bond was used to illustrate important aspects of the discussion. A position was defined as a contractual obligation in a financial instrument. Collections of positions were defined as trades and collections of trades were defined as portfolios. Examples were discussed to illustrate the concepts.

References

[AG90]   R. Agrawal and N. H. Gehani. ODE (Object Database and Environment): The Language and Data Model. In *Proceedings of ACM SIGMOD International Conference on the Management of Data*, pages 36–45, May 1990.

[AGM88] R. Abbott and Hector Garcia-Molina. Scheduling Real-time Transactions. *ACM SIGMOD Record*, 17(1):71–81, March 1988.

[BL92]   R. J. Bauer and G.E. Liepins. Genetic Algorithms and Computerized Trading Strategies. In D.E. O'Leary and P.R. Watkins, editors, *Expert Systems in Finance*, pages 89–100. Elsevier Publishers, 1992.

[Car87]   M (ed.) Carey. Special Issue on Extensible Database Systems. *Database Engineering*, June 1987.

[Car90]   M. Carey. The Architecture of the EXODUS Extensible DBMS. In Stonebraker M., editor, *Readings in Database Systems*, pages 488–501. Morgan Kaufman, 1990.

[CC87]   J. Clifford and A. Croker. The historical relational data model HRDM and an algebra based on lifespans. In *Proceedings of the Third International Conference on Data Engineering*, pages 528–537, February 1987.

[Cha94]   R. Chandra. Managing Temporal Financial Data in Extensible Databases. Technical report, University of California, 1994.

[CS93a]   R. Chandra and A. Segev. Managing Temporal Financial Data in an Extensible Database. In *Proceedings of the 19th Int. Conf. on Very Large Databases, Dublin, Ireland*, August 1993.

[CS93b]   R. Chandra and A. Segev. Performance Optimization of Financial Database Applications. In *Proceedings of the 3rd Workshop on Information Technologies and Systems*, December 1993.

[CSS94]   R. Chandra, A. Segev, and M. Stonebraker. Implementing Calendars and Temporal Rules in Next-Generation Databases. In *Proceedings of the 10th Int. Conf. on Data Engineering*, February 1994.

[Gad88]   S.K. Gadia. The Role of Temporal Elements in a Temporal Database. *Database Engineering*, 7(2):197–203, 1988.

[JCG^{+}92]   C.S. Jenson, J. Clifford, S.K. Gadia, A. Segev, and R.T. Snodgrass. A Glossary of Temporal Database Concepts. *ACM SIGMOD Record*, 21(3):35–43, 1992.

[Lin87]   B. Lindsay. A Data Management Extension Architecture. In *Proceedings of ACM SIGMOD International Conference on the Management of Data*, May 1987.

[Man92]   G. Mankiw. *Macroeconomics*. Worth Publishers, New York, 1992.

[PS88]   P. Peinl and H. Sammer. High Contention in a Stock Trading Database: A Case Study. In *Proceedings of ACM SIGMOD International Conference on the Management of Data*, pages 260–268, May 1988.

[RS89]   S. Rozen and D Shasha. Using a Relational Database on Wall Street, The Good, the Bad and the Ugly. *Communications of the ACM*, 1989.

[Sam87]   H. Sammer. Online stock Trading Systems: Study of an application. In *Proceedings of Spring COMPCON 87 San Francisco*, pages 161–163, 1987.

[SC93]   A. Segev and R. Chandra. A Data Model for Time-Series Analysis. In N. Adam and B. Bhargava, editors, *Advanced Database Systems*. Lectures Notes in Computer Science Series, Springer Verlag, Nov 1993.

[Sno87]   R. Snodgrass. The Temporal Query Language TQuel. *ACM TODS*, 12(2), 1987.

[SS87]   A. Segev and A. Shoshani. A Logical Modeling of Temporal Databases. In *Proceedings of ACM SIGMOD International Conference on the Management of Data*, May 1987.

[SS88]   A. Segev and A. Shoshani. The Representation of a Temporal Data Model in the Relational Environment. In M. Rafanelli, J.C. Klensin, and P. Svensson, editors, *Lecture Notes in Computer Science No. 339*, pages 39–61. Springer-Verlag, 1988.

[Sto90]   M.R. Stonebraker. The Implementation of POSTGRES. *IEEE Transactions on Knowledge and Data Engineering*, 2(1):125–142, March 1990.

[Str85]   B. Stroustrup. *The C++ Programming Language*. Addison-Wesley Publishing Company, 1985.

[Vea88]   J. Voelcker and et. al. How computers helped stampede the stock market. *SPECTRUM*, Oct 1988.

[WD92]   G.T.J Wuu and U. Dayal. A Uniform Model for Temporal Object-Oriented Databases. In *Proceedings of the 8th Int. Conf. on Data Engineering*, pages 584–593, February 1992.

A Multidatabase Solution for a Financial Application

Munir Cochinwala, John Bradley, Ram Tanamy
and Raghu Subramanian

Dow Jones Telerate, Harborside Financial Center
Jersey City NJ 07311

Abstract. We have built a multidatabase system to support a financial
application that provides access to real-time and historical financial data
concerning stocks, bonds, options and mutual funds. The arrival rate of
data is 500 items per second, each of which may be saved in a DBMS.
Sub-second response time is required for queries.

The consistency and performance of real-time data differs from those of
historical data. Real-time data is non-persistent but requires database
consistency. Historical data is persistent and requires serializability on
< *instrument, timestamp*> pair. Since real-time data reflects current mar-
ket activity, it must be delivered to users faster than historical data. Historical data has sub-second response requirements for queries. A typical
query for historical data requests between 100-1000 records.

We could not find a single DBMS or even a multidatabase system that
met our performance requirements and consistency definition. In this
paper we define the characteristics of the application, the multidatabase
system we used to support the applications, and some requirements for
DBMS's in financial applications.

1 Introduction

We have implemented a multidatabase [12, 4, 1, 3, 2, 7, 9] system and financial
application, the Platform that provides access to real-time data, historical data
and value-added calculations (user-defined or programmed) over the different
types of data. The real-time data concerning equities, bonds, options, mutual
funds and currencies originates at various stock exchanges and brokerage houses.
It is sent over multiple real-time feeds, MarketFeed [5] and Ticker [6], that can
deliver data in compressed form at the rate of 56 Kilobits per second (Kbps)
or 19.2 Kbps. Historical data is either the summary of real-time data over an
interval or all of the data that is produced over an interval.

The data is sent on a per instrument basis. An instrument is identified as an
entity that has a price and is capable of being traded. All issues on exchanges
are identified as instruments. Data coming from the real-time feeds are ticks,
baselines, or correction. A tick is either a trade of an instrument, a bid for an
instrument, an ask for an instrument or a bid and ask for an instrument. A
baseline is a message received when a significant event occurs, like an exchange

open or close. It consists of the instrument name, type and current price. A correction is a message to correct an erroneous tick.

The universe of instruments consists of 500,000 instruments. The updates for instruments generally follow a 90-10 rule. 10% of the instruments are 'hot', i.e., 90% of the updates are for 10% of the instruments. 60% of user requests are for the 'hot' instruments.

We found that the application posed interesting problems. The challenge of the application is to reconcile conflicting consistency and performance requirements for data storage. Individual DBMS's are optimized for particular requirements. Each DBMS has serializability as a consistency criterion. Our broad approach was to incorporate fundamentally different DBMS's into a multidatabase to exploit the unique aspects of each DBMS, while presenting the appearance of a single entity to users. Using this approach we have built an application and system that meets our unique requirements.

The rest of the paper is organized as follows: Section 2 outlines the services provided by Platform and in Section 3, the architecture of the Platform is described. Section 4 defines the various components of the Platform. We first describe the multidatabase component and then describe how the services use the multidatabase component to implement their requirements. Section 5 is the conclusion.

2   Platform Services

The Platform provides three primary services to financial applications that deal with storage and retrieval of static information of instruments and their relation to producers, storage and retrieval of dynamic information about instruments, and storage and retrieval of historical data. These services are implemented as applications on several DBMSs. We also provide support for value-added calculations. However, value-added calculations are not implemented using DBMS's and are beyond the scope of this paper.

The system maintains a list of available instruments, current value and historical data for instruments. Each instrument needs to be identified uniquely within the system. Each instrument has static and dynamic data. Trades, quotes and corrections contain dynamic information about instruments. Data that is not changed as a result of a single trade is considered static. For instance, Dividends and instrument name are both static data. Data that may change as a result of a single or compound trade is considered dynamic. Price and Volume are dynamic data.

Users can request static or dynamic data for instruments. For dynamic data, the request can be for a snapshot of dynamic data or continuous updates of the dynamic data. The latter is known as registration. Users can register for instruments based on patterns on the instrument name or by predicates on the static data like 'maturitydate >2005'. Users can also request the system to summarize data (history) over intervals and retrieve the summary.

We have strict requirements based on speed, breadth and accuracy. Users must receive the current value of an instrument within 200 milliseconds of the receipt of a tick by the Platform. It must be possible to get the current value for any instrument and historical data for any instrument. At peak time, the system should be able to handle registrations from several hundred users each requesting registrations for several hundred instruments. The Platform is currently capable of handling 500 ticks a second. Timely updates of corrections is important since trades can be reported incorrectly and arbitragueurs (users doing arbitrage) trade on small deviations in price.

The application should also be scalable and reliable. Scalability must be possible to provide adequate performance and volume of data storage by installing additional processors and disks. Redundancy is necessary to provide sufficient reliability by maintaining replicated data.

3 Platform Architecture

An individual Platform may have one or several sites. The Platform facilitates effective use of the several DBMSs by providing multidatabase functionality. The multidatabase library contains a uniform API to access all DBMSs and atomic commitment to ensure consistency between the various DBMSs. The multidatabase system may be distributed across all sites of the Platform. In Fig. 1, we show the architecture of the Platform.

Each Platform site contains several data storage facilities: a relational DBMS (InterBase), an ISAM file system (C-Tree) and a memory resident DBMS (Smallbase). Use of a single type of DBMS would be unsuitable for this application as the various types of data stored on the Platform have different requirements. For example, static data and historical data require the persistence and atomicity provided by InterBase and C-Tree. However, historical data also requires faster access provided by C-Tree, while static data must be accessible via complex queries supported by InterBase. Smallbase provides very fast access and update times for non-persistent data, such as the current value of instruments, and cached data.

The diversity of our requirements precluded use of any proposed or existing multidatabase. We required main memory speed to gain performance and did not need durability. We also did not require global serializability and in some cases, did not even need local serializability. Our consistency criteria were application-defined.

4 Platform Components

Each application had different requirements for consistency, persistence, and performance. These requirements were met by the different DBMSs in the multidatabase system and by the flexibility provided by the multidatabase component. In Fig. 2, we show the different DBMSs used by each application. These DBMSs were accessed via DBAL, the multidatabase component in the Platform.

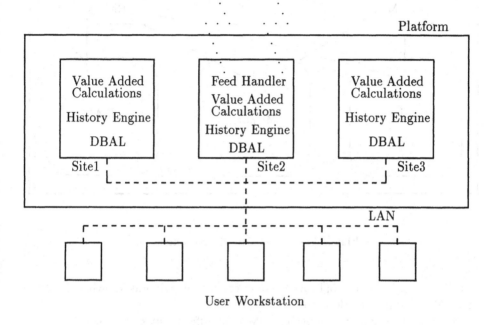

MarketFeed Ticker

Platform

Value Added
Calculations

History Engine

DBAL

Site1

Feed Handler

Value Added
Calculations

History Engine

DBAL

Site2

Value Added
Calculations

History Engine

DBAL

Site3

LAN

User Workstation

Fig. 1. Platform Architecture

4.1 DBAL

In order to use effectively several different DBMSs, a multidatabase component
was necessary. Using several DBMS interfaces increases the complexity of application programming. This problem is exacerbated by the non-SQL API provided
by C-Tree. A more important requirement was that consistent data would be
maintained across different DBMSs and sites.

The Database Access Library (DBAL) provides a uniform API to all supported DBMS's, location transparency for all Platform data, atomic commitment
of distributed transactions and enforcement of global consistency.

The DBAL API hides syntactic differences between the API's of the various DBMSs by defining all DBMS operations in terms of a dynamic SQL-like
language. Queries submitted to the DBMS and data returned from the DBMS
are represented as ASCII strings. However, the semantics of each operation is
limited by the functionality of the target DBMS. For example, an application
would view an ISAM file as a relation via DBAL. However, complex relational
operations, such as a join, would fail on ISAM files, because the operation is not
supported by the file system.

Location transparency is provided by a single global namespace encompassing
all nodes and DBMSs. Since we require that a relation name be unique across

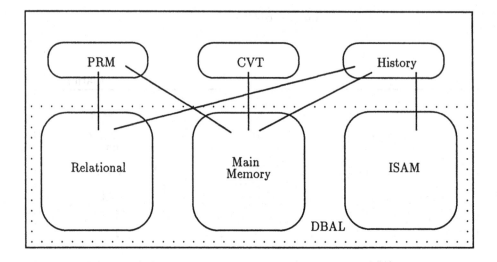

Fig. 2. Application DBMS Associations

the entire Platform, an application can query a table without knowing the site or DBMS in which it is located.

A transaction can span multiple DBMSs on different sites; two phase commit is used to guarantee atomicity. Global consistency is maintained via distributed certification [1] by ensuring that the local orders are compatible with a global serial order.

In addition, DBAL supports user defined Alerts. An Alert is a rule that consists of *event, condition and action*. Alerts in DBMSs often are expressed by rules [3] defined using languages such as relational query languages and object-oriented languages [10, 11]. Supported events are changes (insert, update, delete) to particular attributes of a relation. When a rule fires, DBAL notifies registered users of the event.

The implementation of DBAL uses several different types of processes (Client, Agent and Server) interacting within and across Platform sites. Client processes can access the DBMSs by calling functions in the DBAL run-time library, which forward DBMS requests to Agent processes to be executed. A single Server process performs resource allocation on each site.

Agents execute DBMS operations on behalf of Clients. Each Agent is linked to the run-time library of a particular DBMS and only executes requests for that DBMS. A fixed number of Agent processes are forked during system startup and are assigned to one Client at a time on a need basis. The Agents are actually transaction managers; a transaction model may be encapsulated in an Agent. Control information is stored in shared persistent storage to allow concurrent access by Agents.

When a Client requests access to a particular DBMS, UNIX Inter-Process Communication (IPC) will be used to link the Client and Agent processes. Each

Client's request is translated into the particular syntax of the target DBMS and DBMS output is translated to attribute/value pair format.

The DBAL runtime library provides functionality to act as a *coordinator* for a distributed commit protocol. A Client can request the coordinator to connect it to multiple DBMSs. The coordinator can request the Server to allocate remote Agents to it. The remote Agents are called *participants*. The Client can then issue operations through the coordinator to any of the connected DBMSs. The coordinator and participants execute the distributed commit protocol when the Client issues a commit.

An individual Agent performs transaction management for local transactions and interacts with the coordinator as part of the two-phase commit protocol for transactions across multiple DBMSs. An Agent does not know a global schema. To provide a robust, transaction management system, the Agent maintains transaction state in the persistent store. The persistent store contains enough information about the state of the transaction so the transaction could be restarted or aborted by another Agent. On each site, the persistent store is shared by all the Agents and the Server at that site.

An Agent-based approach to multidatabase transaction management along with Alerts and shared control information in the persistent store can provide support for multiple transaction models and access mechanisms [1]. Each Agent can implement a different transaction model and the multidatabase component can enforce global consistency since the control information is shared. Access control can be enforced by specifying Alerts on the shared control information.

4.2 Producer Resource Manager

The Producer Resource Manager (PRM) stores static information about instruments. The data originates from different sources that describe trades involving different types of financial instruments. Different types of instruments come from different sources. Equities are generally traded at an exchange, while bonds are traded through a short number of primary brokers. Each source may potentially be a different producer.

PRM also ensures the uniqueness of instruments. If a producer produces a new instrument, then it has to register that instrument with PRM. In addition, symbology inconsistencies must be resolved. For example, the same instrument may have different names from different sources. Platform must allow consumers to access instruments using a consistent naming scheme.

PRM also needs to keep the status of instruments. An instrument can be produced, available but not produced, or not available. The status of an instrument depends on the status of the producer. If the producer is currently active then all of its instruments are capable of being produced. Thus, if a producer state changes, PRM has to update the status of all instruments that belong to the producer.

All registrations for instruments go through PRM. Thus, if an instrument can be produced by multiple producers, PRM can do load balancing by choosing one of the multiple producers.

PRM has performance requirements for registration and update of instrument status. It is essential that response to registration be accomplished in less than a second. The status of instruments does not need to be persistent but the static part of instruments need to be persistent. PRM has to be available on each node of the Platform.

All of the static data for instruments is stored on InterBase using DBAL. For each type of instrument, we have a relation since the static data for a bond is significantly different than an equity. However, instrument name and instrument status are also replicated in Smallbase. All writes are to disk but a write for instrument status or instrument name also goes to Smallbase. The instrument name and status are maintained in Smallbase for fast access during registration and startup. At startup, a producer may update the status of all of its instrument. This could be significant since the universe of instruments is 500,000.

Different producers and products assign different names to the same instrument. Since the Platform gets instrument information from multiple sources, a many to one mapping between instrument names across sources to a unique instrument name has to be provided. For each instrument, an alias list is maintained. Users can request instrument information based on either the unique name or any of the aliases. The aliases are provided to be upwardly compatible with existing products.

PRM also provides an ability to define Alerts on instrument additions and deletions. The Alerts are used by the History Engine and are implemented using DBAL.

4.3 Current Value Table Handler

The Current Value (CV) Table Handler maintains dynamic data for instruments. Besides supplying information on current trading activity, the Platform maintains the current value of all registered instruments. Current value is nonpersistent data. If a site failure occurs, some real time trade data will be missed. Therefore, the correctness of current value data cannot be guaranteed across a failure.

The CV Table Handler also maintains statistical information about the instruments. This includes instruments that were the Most active, Most changed (gainers and losers) and most percentage volume changed. DBAL Alerts are used by the CV Table Handler to detect when the price of an instrument reaches a given level.

CV Table Handler will detect loss of data integrity by detecting lost messages. The Feeds deliver data for instruments with sequence numbers. If a sequence number is missed, then the CV Table marks the data as 'suspicious' so that users are aware of missed trades. The CV Table also applies corrections that come off the feed for particular instruments.

The CV Table is implemented using Smallbase. The data does not need to be persistent. The Feed subsystem delivers data to the CV Table Handler. The CV Handler does an update or insert of the values in the CV Table. The CV Table Handler also updates the statistical information for every update.

4.4 Historical Data Storage

The Platform History Engine stores data concerning the status of financial instruments at earlier periods of time. Historical data is defined by an abstraction called a history track consisting of a series of summaries associated with a particular financial instrument, the starting and ending time when data is being collected and the amount of time spanned by each summary. For example, the price of IBM stock may be tracked from 1/1/80 until the present time at 5 minute intervals.

Each interval summary contains the opening price (start of interval), closing price (end of interval), high price (peak during interval), low price (nadir during interval) and volume (number of units traded during interval). History users may retrieve data for any interval defined in units of seconds, minutes, hours, days, weeks, months, years or by tick (individual trade).

In addition, each user has access to the history inventory, which is a catalog of all history data stored at a Platform installation.

Historical data and inventory require different notions of consistency. Since inventory is replicated at all Platform sites, transactions on inventory must be serialized. However, a weaker *Append Only* transaction can be defined on history data, because modifications to history data are almost always insertions of a summary for a new interval. Therefore, appends need only be serializable in *<instrument, timestamp>* order. Transactions for different instruments are commutative.

The History Engine is the heaviest DBMS user on the Platform as measured by the amount of data stored and volume of data being retrieved by each query. Consequently, numerous optimizations were necessary to achieve the stated performance requirements.

Append only transactions were implemented by the History Engine to avoid the overhead of global serialization of its schedule. Serializability on *<instrument, timestamp>* is maintained by always inserting instruments in timestamp order. Global consistency is maintained by satisfying local consistency, since all tracks for an instrument will be stored in a single DBMS on a single site. When a track is created, it is assigned to the site that is storing tracks for that instrument already. Otherwise, the site with the least load is selected.

Minimization of disk I/O is critical to attaining fast response time to queries and processing of a large number of DBMS insertions. Intelligence was added to the component that collects real-time data and builds summaries to cluster data within a single track on disk. By clustering data, the number of disk blocks that must be read per query is minimized. This optimization also improves application performance for insertions. Newly arrived ticks and recent intervals are cached in Smallbase. Cached intervals will be inserted to InterBase as a single transaction, when a predetermined number of intervals have been collected ("hot" instruments) or a timer expires ("cold" instruments). Most queries are executed against the memory resident DBMS or the disk DBMS. Queries that cannot be completely satisfied by going against the memory resident DBMS have to be executed against both the memory resident DBMS and the disk DBMS.

Further performance improvements are obtained separating intraday data from interday data to reduce conflicts between DBMS resources. At the end of a trading day, data for that day (intraday) is moved from InterBase to C-Tree. Interday data is almost exclusively read-only, since all inserts are done for a particular day. Updates are infrequently applied to the previous day's DBMS in response to corrections to ticks.

Although users may submit queries defined by any interval, the History Engine only defines tracks in terms of relatively few standard intervals that encompass data that is most likely to be accessed. Standard intervals include ticks, 1 minute, 5 minutes, etc. By storing only standard intervals, the amount of disk space required for historical data as well as disk I/O volume is reduced. Queries on non-standard intervals are satisfied by building the requested data from standard intervals.

Query response time is also improved by storing a shadow of history inventory in the memory resident DBMS as all queries must access inventory. The memory resident copy is kept consistent by defining Alerters on modifications to the disk resident copy. All changes on disk are replicated in main storage.

Alerts are also effective in detecting the addition of new instruments that match a previous definition of history track. A user can create tracks for all instruments that match the pattern now or in the future. Since the names of all defined instruments are stored by Platform, the addition of instruments can be detected by monitoring changes to the DBMS. When the Alert fires, a new history track will be created.

5 Conclusion

Table 1. Application Characteristics.

Application	Persistence	Consistency	Read Item	Write Item
PRM	Yes	Serializability	Millisecs and Microsecs	Millisecs
History Data	Yes	By Application	Millisecs	Millisecs
History Inventory	Yes	Serializability	Microsecs	Millisecs
Current Value	No	None	Microsecs	Microsecs

We have built a multidatabase system to support an application that has diverse requirements for consistency and performance. We could not find a multidatabase system that satisfied our requirements for consistency and performance. In Table 1 we summarize the application characteristics.

We feel that a DBMS where application-defined semantics could be maintained would be extremely useful. In particular, DBMSs have serializability as the consistency constraint. We did not need strict serializability. We needed atomicity, durability, isolation but the definition of consistency was defined by the application. In fact, we had to implement our notion of application-defined consistency on top of serializability. We feel that this may restrict the set of schedules we could accept in our multidatabase system. If we could use the DBMS with our own scheduler, we may gain in performance. We need to explore this notion further.

The performance requirements of the applications dictated that we access a subset of the data in memory. We would have liked to have control of the cache of InterBase. Control of the cache includes replacement of the frames in the cache. We had to use Smallbase as the cache.

We would have liked an object-oriented DBMS. Our definitions of instruments can be defined as object classes. However, we had to have an unnatural decomposition of the instrument definitions when we had to decompose them into relations. This also added complexity to the queries and hindered performance. We plan to incorporate an object-oriented DBMS as part of the multidatabase.

We have to analyze the performance of the system. We also need to evaluate the performance of a transaction in memory, the cost of writing to multiple DBMSs and the cost of multidatabase transactions. We need to also look into the notion of synthetic securities, i.e. a security composed of multiple securities and analyze how load balancing and consistency are affected.

Aside from performance, we need to introduce recovery for the entire system. Currently, we recover using a tick log that is maintained both by Platform processes and the originating Exchanges. We need to explore the correctness of the DBMS and the application data when the real-time feeds are down, a DBMS crashes or a particular site is unavailable. We also need to explore dynamic load balancing of history tracks (when a site crashes) and its effect on correctness as well as performance.

We need to evaluate the requirements on DBMS systems to support financial applications. Our application focused on real-time data and historical data. We recognize the need for batched append-only transactions, support for 'hot instruments' in a cache, support for fast access non-persistent data and the need for application defined consistency. However, we have to explore financial data used by investment banks and financial data used in analytics. The data used by investment banks includes all the data about companies. This data is not easily modeled by a relational model. The data used in analytics is voluminous and is accessed multiple times for the same calculation. We do not 'know' the consistency or performance requirements for these two types of data. We need to explore these types of data so that we can gain some insight on the 'ideal' DBMS for financial applications.

Acknowledgements

We would like to thank the other implementors, Lloyd Fernandes, Bruce Holenstein and Rick Kerman. We would also like to thank John Bopp and Jeff Carvalho for multiple discussions that improved the system and application. Finally, we would like to thank Marie-Anne Neimat for providing us with Smallbase and with suggestions on improving the focus and presentation of this paper.

References

1. M. Cochinwala, K.C. Lee, W. Mansfield, Jr., and M,Yu: A Distributed Transaction Monitor. Proc. of RIDE-IMS 1993 April 1993
2. P. P. Chrysanthis and K. Ramamritham: A Formalism for Extended Transaction Models. Proc. of the 17th International Conference on VLDB September 1991
3. U. Dayal, M. Hsu, and R. Ladin: Organizing Long-Running Activities with Triggers and Transactions. Proc. of the ACM SIGMOD 1990.
4. A. K. Elmagarmid, Y. Leu, W. Litwin, and M. Rusinkiewicz: A Multidatabase Transaction Model for InterBase. Proc. of the 16th VLDB 1990
5. MarketFeed The Telerate Consolidated Feed: Technical Specifications August 1993
6. Telerate Ticker Feed Specification: Technical Specifications August 1993
7. I. Greif and S. Sarin: Data Sharing in Group Work. Computer-Supported Cooperative Work ed. Irene Greif Morgan Kaufman Publishers, 1988
8. J. Pons and J. Vilarem: Mixed Concurrency Control: Dealing with Heterogeneity in Distributed Database Systems. Proc. of the Fourteenth Conference on VLDB Los Angeles 1988
9. Calton Pu: Superdatabases for Composition of Heterogeneous Databases. Proc. of the Fourth International Conference on Data Engineering Los Angeles, 1988
10. Tore Risch: Monitoring Database Objects. Proc. of the Fifteenth Conference on VLDB 1989
11. A. Rosenthal, S. Chakravarthy, B. Blaustein, and J. Blakeley: Situation Monitoring for Active Databases. Proc. of the 14th VLDB 1989
12. Yuri Breibart, Hector Garcia-Molina and Avi Silberschatz: Overview of Multidatabase Transaction Management. Stanford Technical Report No. STAN-CS-92-143 May 1992
13. Michael Heytens, Sheralyn Listgarten, Marie-Anne Neimat and Kevin Wilkinson: Smallbase: A Main-Memory DBMS for High-Performance Applications. Unpublished Draft October 1993.
14. M. Stonebraker, A. Jhingran, J. Goh, and S. Potamianos: On Rules, Procedures, Caching and Views in Database Systems. Proc. of the ACM SIGMOD 1990.

Applying Next Generation Object-Oriented DBMS to Finite Element Analysis

Kjell Orsborn

Linköping University, S-581 83 Linköping, Sweden

Abstract. Scientific and engineering database applications put new requirements on database management systems that is usually not associated with traditional administrative database applications. These new database applications include *finite element analysis (FEA)* for *computational mechanics* and usually have a high level of complexity of both data and algorithms, as well as high volume of data and high requirements on execution efficiency. This paper shows how *next generation object-oriented database technology* that includes a *relationally complete* and *extensible object-oriented query language* can be used to model and manage FEA. The technology allows the design of *domain models* that represent application-oriented conceptual models of data and operators. An initial integration of a *main-memory object-relational database management system* with a state-of-the-art FEA program is presented. The FEA program integrates the complete FEA process and is controlled completely through a graphical user interface. Examples are included of the conceptual model and its manipulation along with some initial performance measures. It is shown that the integrated system provides competitive performance and is a promising alternative for design and implementation of future FEA software.

1 Introduction

The importance of scientific and engineering data management is more and more emphasized in both industrial and scientific communities [1] [2]. This paper describes an ongoing interdisciplinary research work that covers the fields of scientific and engineering database management and computational mechanics. More specifically, we use a *next generation object-oriented database management system (OO DBMS)*, also referred to as *object-relational (OR)* DBMS [3] including a *relationally complete* and *extensible OO query language*, to model and manage *finite element analysis (FEA)*. The discussion in the paper is based on an initial implementation of a system called FEA-MOS, which is an integration of a main-memory OR DBMS, AMOS [4], with a FEA program, TRINITAS [5]. AMOSQL, the query language of AMOS, is used to represent and manage the FEA domain model. AMOSQL is a derivative of OSQL [6] but is also influenced by SQL3 [7]. TRINITAS, representing the state-of-the-art within the field of FEA software, completely integrates the entire analysis process and is completely controlled through a graphical user interface. A typical TRINITAS session includes a generation of a finite element model from a specification of geometry, domain properties and boundary conditions, a solution phase, and an evaluation of numerical results. The data representation and its related operators in TRINITAS are piece by piece replaced by a corresponding representation in AMOS. Examples in the paper show typical needs for data modelling and initial performance measures comparing the original FEA software with FEAMOS. Main ideas included are the modelling and management of both structure and process of finite element methodology by the use of an extensible OO query language.

Our idea is to increase the conceptual level in the design of FEA software by using an OO query language to build *domain models* which represent application-oriented conceptual models of data and operators. Class structures and operators are defined to represent finite element (FE) methodology, i.e. FE models and solution algorithms. The extensible query language allows domain-specific FE operators to be included in the system. The user can define queries in terms of the FE model, and the queries may contain FE specific operators. The query optimizer thus needs to understand how to choose among several FE domain-specific operators to answer a query as efficient and as numerically stable as possible. The software developer can take advantage of general and predefined facilities of the OR DBMS for data modelling and management and does not need to write dedicated data structures and access procedures for FEA. Thus, by using declarative modelling techniques through the query language, the complexity of the system can be decreased together with an increased transparency and flexibility.

A database-based FEA application will further facilitate an integration or communication with other parts of the global *computer aided engineering (CAE)* system. It will then be possible to accomplish a global improvement of the efficiency of FEA software from the point of view of the developer, the maintainer, and the user. This will result in an increased life time of the software and an enhanced analysis quality. This has advantages for both industrial and scientific use of the software. Industrial users might emphasize integration and data management whereas flexible and transparent design might be emphasized by scientific users. The research work is expected to generate insight and experience to both scientific disciplines, i.e. general database technology can be expanded through generic requirements of the application domain (here computational mechanics) as well as the generic scientific database models and systems will extend the field of scientific and engineering computing.

2 Finite Element Analysis Based on Next Generation Object-Oriented DBMS Technology

2.1 Finite Element Analysis and Software

The *finite element method (FEM)* is a general numerical method for solving differential equations. It can be applied to problems within several engineering fields, such as mechanical, civil, and electrical engineering. Within mechanical engineering FEA is used for analyses of designs involving different characteristic design criteria, such as strength, stiffness, stability, resonance, etc. [8]. A typical analysis model includes data of the domain (geometry, material), boundary conditions (forces, prescribed displacements), and of the solution algorithm. The central part of a FEA is the solution of systems of equations of different levels of complexity depending on the phenomenon studied. In the case of a linear static stress analysis, as illustrated in Fig. 1, the central analysis step consists of a solution of a single system of equations. However, even the most basic cases of a FEA involves a large set of data with a high level of complexity. For example the number of unknowns in the equations can range from 100 to several 100 000.

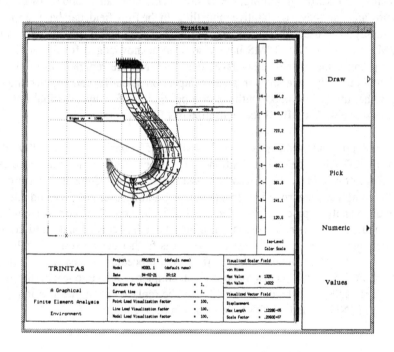

Fig. 1. An example of a FEA model of a hook analysed by a linear static stress analysis

The application of the FEM is mainly achieved by special-purpose programs where the analysis model can be specified in domain-specific terminology. Modern commercial FEA programs have integrated the complete analysis process from modelling to evaluation and also take advantage of graphical user interfaces in this process. However, the basic structure of commercial FEA software and its development have not gone through any dramatic change since its origin, in contrast to the exceptional development in hardware performance during the last 30 years which has been easier to take advantage of by application builders. Conventional FEA software is usually implemented as monolithic programs with various levels of integration of modelling and evaluation phases. The relatively low level of structure in these programs introduces large costs for maintenance, further development, and for communication with other subsystems in the CAE environment. This is motivating research on new software architectures for scientific and engineering computing.

Modern programming techniques, such as OO programming techniques, have also started to influence the area of FEA [9] [10] [11] [12] [13] [14] [15], and has been suggested for design and implementation of FEA software in order to reduce program complexity. In the main part of these works, Smalltalk or C++ have been used for implementation.

Compared to OO programming, OR DBMS techniques can extend software design further towards high-level declarative modelling. In the FEA field, database support has so far mainly been used for storage and retrieval of data and results using relational (R)DBMS. However, OO DBMS have also been acknowledged for the engineering field [16], and some of their advantages over RDBMS are reported on in [17]. OR DBMS will probably have an even greater impact on scientific and engineering computing in the future. This paper outlines the opportunities for, and potential impact of, using an extensible OR DBMS for realisation of FEA software.

The FEA program used in this work, TRINITAS [5], consists of about 2200 subroutines of FORTRAN code and is positioned somewhere between medium- and large-sized FEA software [18]. It can also be classified as a state-of-the-art FEA program, since it is completely controlled by an interactive graphical user interface and integrates the complete analysis process from modelling to evaluation. This process includes geometry modelling, domain properties definitions, boundary condition definitions, mesh generation, analysis, and result interpretation. It is further designed in a highly structured, "object-based", manner with specific sets of procedures for each concept class, such as point, line, etc. This has made it much simpler to integrate it with the AMOS DBMS, since subsets of the domain model can be replaced at a time. The initial integration of TRINITAS and AMOS is described in Sect. 2.4.

2.2   Object-Oriented Databases and Query Languages

Classical DBMS technology concentrated on supporting administrative applications. However, with the advent of OO DBMS there has recently been much DBMS research and development for developing database techniques to support also engineering activities, such as CAD, CAE, and CAM. We distinguish between the *first* and the *next* generation OO DBMS:

The first generation OO DBMS [19] (e.g. ObjectStore, Versant, Gemstone, Ontos) extend an OO programming language (usually C++) with *persistence*, i.e. the possibility to permanently retain C++ data structures on disk. Thus complex engineering data structures (e.g. representing a design) can be built within the C++ programming language by some tool, and then stored on disk. This allows sharing of design data structures between engineers and tools. Access to the database is usually by C++ programming (normally within some tool).

The success of today's RDBMS is largely due to the availability of query languages that allow non-expert programmers to query and update the database. Query language capabilities are only supported to a limited extent in first generation OO DBMS. The *next generation OO DBMS* [20] or *OR DBMS* [3] (e.g. OpenODB and Montage) also include relationally complete OO query languages to search and update object data structures. The query processors for an OO query language can use most of the techniques developed for relational query processors, but will also need new techniques [21]. Extensibility of the query language will also make it possible to make optimizations over the domain model and thereby domain-related operations [22].

Domain Modelling Using Query Languages. The extensibility of AMOSQL allows the design of *domain models* that represent application oriented models and operators, i.e. FEA models in our case. Domain models allow knowledge and data now hidden in application programs to be extracted from the applications and stored in next generation object databases with domain-specific models and operators. The benefits of using domain models include easier access and management through a query language, better data description (as schemas), and other benefits currently provided only by advanced DBMS such as transaction capabilities and ad hoc query processing. The query processing must be about as efficient as customized main-memory data structure representations to allow the use of local embedded domain models linked into applications without substantial loss of efficiency. Domain models often need to be able to represent specialized data structures for the intended class of applications.

Important research problems in developing domain models for mechanical design and analysis, e.g. using FEA, are to investigate:

- How is the domain modelled using an OO query and modelling language?

- Which domain-oriented data structures are required, and how should they be represented?

- What domain-oriented operators need to be defined?

- How are queries accessing domain-oriented data structures optimized?

- How can AMOS be integrated within a domain-oriented tool, e.g. for FEM analysis?

It is possible to use both programmed procedures and high-level query languages for accessing domain models. A query language is used to define, manipulate and retrieve information in a database. For instance, for retrieving some specific result from an analysis, a query can be formed in the high-level and declarative query language returning the information that satisfies the specified conditions. Combining general query-language constructs with domain-related representations provides a more problem-oriented communication. This approach to data management is more effective compared to the use of conventional programming languages [23][17]. The combination of programming and query languages and their pros and cons for data management is further discussed in Catell [24].

Object-oriented techniques, including object-oriented databases and query languages, are well suited to reduce system complexity. Their applicability are especially suitable to engineering applications which consist of large amounts of complex data and relationships. Specifically, a main-memory object-relational database, like AMOS, is combining high-level modelling with high execution efficiency. The use of declarative object-oriented queries for domain modelling and management offers several advantages over conventional programming:

- *Declarative models* are easier to describe, inspect and understand than procedural programs and thus become more transparent and flexible. A declarative modelling with an object-oriented query-language is compact and (de)composable and makes the domain modelling very flexible and powerful. This problem-oriented modelling approach will naturally produce a representation that is isomorphic to the problem domain.

- Advanced object-oriented query-languages also provide *object views* [25] [26] capabilities. In AMOSQL, views are supported through derived functions, where a function is uniformly invoked independently of whether it represents stored or derived data. This makes it possible to change the underlying physical object representation without altering the access queries. Thus, data independence and evolution are supported.

- The *extensibility* of AMOSQL provides powerful means for flexible domain modelling. A user/programmer can use very high level declarative query specifications, thus letting the DBMS do data access optimization. AMOSQL also provides extensibility of the query optimizer, which permits an introduction of more complex domain specific cost models that reflect certain aspects of the application domain. For example, solution costs for numerical operations, solution accuracy of numerical calculations, etc., can be included in the cost models. Thus, the query optimization can influence the choice and tuning of operators in FEA.

- Query languages also makes it possible to make advanced *ad hoc queries* concerning the contents of the database. This might be demanded by advanced users and is quite useful since it is impossible to foresee the complete information needs.

- Including a rule system in the query language provides a mechanism for constraint management. Actually, there is an ongoing work aiming at integrating active rules in the AMOS DBMS [27].

The advantages of these features are, of course, varying for different phases in the system or application life-cycle and for different types of application users and system developers. However, the methodology supports an incremental and iterative development, maintenance and evolution of domain models as well as domain modelling systems. It facilitates reuse and evolution of design, including domain conceptualizations and knowledge, by its ability of application and data independent representation.

2.3 Data Modelling and Management in AMOS

AMOS (Active Mediators Object System) [4] is a research prototype of an OR DBMS and a descendant of the WS-IRiS DBMS [21]. WS-IRiS is further a derivative of Iris [28]. AMOS is a main-memory database, i.e. it assumes that the entire database is contained in main-memory and uses disk for backup only. It includes an object-oriented extensible query language, AMOSQL, a derivative of OSQL [6], that is used to model and interface the database. AMOSQL is a functional language, originating from DAPLEX [29] and is also influenced by SQL3 [7]. The data model consists of the basic constructs *objects, types,* and *functions*.

The AMOSQL language is also extensible by calling external programming languages like C or LISP, and AMOSQL statements can also be embedded within program procedures.

Objects, Types, and Functions. Concepts in an application domain are represented as *objects*. There are two types of objects in AMOS. *Literal objects,* such as boolean, character string, integer, real, etc., are self identifying. The other type is called *surrogate object* and has unique object identifiers. Surrogate objects represent physical or abstract and external or internal concepts, e.g. mechanical components and assemblies such as skin panel or wing in an aircraft design, finite elements, geometrical elements, etc. System-specific objects, e.g. types and functions, are also treated as surrogate objects.

Types are used to structure objects according to their functional characteristics, in other words it is possible to structure objects into types. Types are in themselves related in a type hierarchy of subtypes and supertypes. Subtypes inherit functions from supertypes and can have multiple supertypes. In addition, functions can be overloaded on different subtypes (i.e. having different implementation for different types).

Functions are defined on types, and are used to represent attributes of, relationships among, and operations on objects. Examples of functions for these different categories might be diameter, distance, and move_point. It is possible to define functions as *stored, derived, procedure* or *foreign*. A stored function has its extension explicitly stored in the database, whereas a derived, procedure, or a foreign function has its extension defined in an AMOSQL query, an AMOSQL procedure, or a function in an external language, respectively. Furthermore, functions can be defined as one- or many-valued and are invertible when possible. Stored and some derived functions can be explicitly updated using update semantics but other functions need special treatment for updates.

Data Management in AMOSQL. AMOSQL provides statement constructs for typical database tasks, including data definition, population, updates, querying, flow control, and session and transaction control. Selected parts of these constructs is presented by means of the example in Fig. 2, which will be used in subsequent sections. The figure shows a rectangular plate that is fixed on a wall at its left side and is further exposed to a tension load through a wire connected at the upper right corner. A simple finite element model corresponding to this physical device consists of 9 bilinear elements and 16 nodes and is presented in Fig. 3.

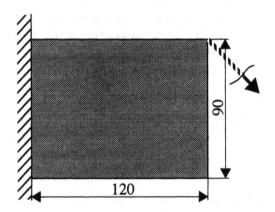

Fig. 2. A simple physical structure consisting of a plate that is exposed to a tension load

Data schemas can be defined, modified, and deleted by means of AMOSQL statements both statically and dynamically. The definition of types, functions, and objects is made through a `create` statement. For example, types may be defined by a `create type` statement as:

```
create type named_object(name charstring);
create type fea_object subtype of named_object;
create type element subtype of fea_object;
create type node subtype of fea_object;
```

where a stored function, `name`, is defined within the parentheses of the `named_object` type. A new type becomes an immediate subtype of all supertypes provided in the `subtype` clause, or if no supertypes are specified, it becomes an immediate subtype of the system type `UserTypeObject`.

Functions can also be defined separate from the types by a `create function` statement, exemplified by the `nodes` function that relates elements to nodes:

```
create function nodes(element el) -> node n as stored;
```

A database for the example in Fig. 3 is populated with objects with a `create type` statement with or without initialization of functions, and where *type* stands for the specific type to be instantiated. The database example can be created by the following statements:

```
create node (name)      :node_1 ("n1"),
                        :node_2 ("n2"),
                        ...
                        :node_16 ("n16");
create element (name, nodes)
   :element_1 ("e1", <:node_1, :node_2, :node_6, :node_5>),
   :element_2 ("e2", <:node_2, :node_3, :node_7, :node_6>),
                        ...
   :element_9 ("e9", <:node_11, :node_12, :node_16, :node_15>);
```

Derived functions are defined in a similar manner as stored functions with a single AMOSQL-query as the function body. An example of a derived function is presented as the topology function below:

```
create function topology(element e1) -> element e2 as
     select unique e2
            for each element e2
               where nodes(e1) = nodes(e2) and
                     e1 != e2;
```

The topology can be identified in Fig. 3, and defines how elements are related to each other. When the topology function is accessed, it derives the elements e2 that have some common node with element e1, i.e. the elements that are connected to a given element. An example shows the topology for element 1 and 5 respectively.

```
name(topology(:element_1));
<"e2"> <"e4"> <"e5">

name(topology(:element_5));
<"e1"> <"e2"> <"e4"> <"e6"> <"e8"> <"e9"> <"e7"> <"e3">
```

Querying a database for objects having specified properties is made using a select statement. For instance the nodes of :element_1 in the example earlier can be retrieved by the following query:

```
select name(nodes(:element_1));
<"n1"> <"n6"> <"n5"> <"n2">
```

Functions are also invertible (not always) and it is therefore possible to use the nodes function in the opposite direction which can be expressed as:

```
select name(e) for each element e where nodes(e) = :node_1;
```

Another example shows how boundary conditions defined on the geometry, as the fixed edge in Fig. 3, can be identified on the mesh by a connectivity function. All elements affected by this boundary condition can then be retrieved as follows:

```
select unique name(e) for each element e, node n, curve c where
            name(c) = "14" and nodes(e) = n
            nodal_to_curve_connectivity(n) = c;
<"e1"> <"e4"> <"e7">
```

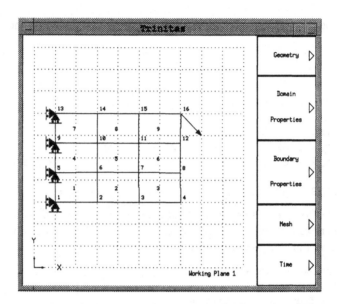

Fig. 3. A simple FE mesh consisting of 9 bilinear elements including node and element numbers. Rigid boundary conditions are introduced for the left edge and the loading condition is modelled by a point load. Note that node and element numbers are included only for facilitating interpretation of the examples and is not required (but optional) by the FEAMOS system

Deletion of types, functions, and objects is made through a `delete` statement as:

```
delete type element;
delete function nodes;
delete :element_1;
```

In addition to database population by object creation and attribute assignments it is possible to use *function update statements* set, add, and remove, and *type update statements* add and remove. Examples of update statements for functions are:

```
set nodes(:element_1) = <:node_1, :node_2, :node_4>;
add nodes(:element_1) = :node_5;
remove nodes(:element_1) = :node_2;
```

A more complete presentation of data management capabilities in AMOS and AMOSQL is presented in [30].

2.4 Domain Modeling of Finite Element Analysis in FEAMOS

An initial integration of TRINITAS and AMOS has been implemented. Data structures and corresponding procedures implemented in TRINITAS (written in FORTRAN) are incrementally replaced by schemas and operators in AMOS. TRINITAS has originally been designed in a highly structured, "object-based", manner with specific sets of procedures for each concept class, such as point, line, etc. This makes it easier to replace subsets of the FEA program part by part incrementally, and a demonstrable system exists at every stage. The programs are linked together and communication is done by transferring parameters between FORTRAN and C procedures using the AMOS C-interface. Concurrently with the normal TRINITAS interface it is possible to query the contents in the database through a database monitor that currently is a standard textual AMOS window.

Currently, the representation of the FEA domain in AMOS mainly covers geometry-related concepts. The classification of these are presented in Fig. 4. An abstract class geometry_object holds the basic geometry classes that include volume, surface, curve, and point. Corresponding subclasses in TRINITAS exists for the curve class and include straight_line, parabola_cubic_section, circular_segment, and bezier_cubic_segment. All these classes are modelled as types and subtypes in AMOS.

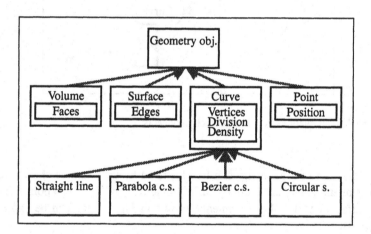

Fig. 4. Partial type structure for the geometry-related subset of the concept domain. Arrows denote is-a (subtype to supertype) relations

Topology relations faces, edges, and vertices are modelled as stored functions between basic geometry classes as illustrated in Fig. 5. For example, the function vertices defined by

```
create function vertices(curve c) -> vector as stored;
```

provides a relation from a curve instance to its points. In addition, the curve type currently has a division and a density function implemented. The division function represents the number of subdivisions a specific curve is divided into and the density function represents a node density along a curve. The point class has a function position that stores the x, y, and z spatial coordinates of a point instance.

When a geometry is modelled in TRINITAS, an object structure is then generated in an AMOS database by means of interface functions defined in AMOSQL providing encapsulation and data independence. Likewise, a manipulation of an object, as moving a point on the screen, implies a direct update of the database object. There are, for instance, functions and procedures for *constructing* and *destructing* objects as well as for *accessing* and *updating* functions.

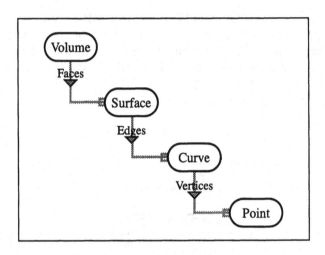

Fig. 5. Topological relations between geometry concepts

The modelling of a geometry can be illustrated by the example shown earlier in Fig. 2. The resulting model is built by basic geometric elements, i.e. 4 points, 4 straight lines, 1 surface, and 1 volume elements, shown in Fig. 6. This can be expressed in AMOSQL as:

```
create point(name, position)
        :point_1("p1", <0.0, 0.0, 0.0>),
        :point_2("p2", <0.0, 120.0, 0.0>),
        :point_3("p3", <90.0, 120.0, 0.0>),
        :point_4("p4", <90.0, 0.0, 0.0>);

create straight_line(name, vertices, division, density)
        :line_1("l1", {:point_1, :point_2}, 3.0, 0.0),
        :line_2("l2", {:point_2, :point_3}, 3.0, 0.0),
        :line_3("l3", {:point_3, :point_4}, 3.0, 0.0),
        :line_4("l4", {:point_4, :point_1}, 3.0, 0.0);

create surface(name, edges) :surface_1("s1",
        {:line_1, :line_2, :line_3, :line_4});

create volume(name, faces) :volume_1("v1", {:surface_1});
```

This modelling technique then makes it possible to put queries to the model about its structure and content, i.e. basic geometrical and topological information in this case.

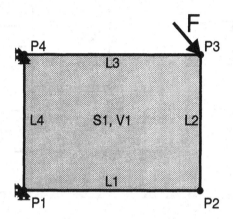

Fig. 6. Basic geometrical model of the structure in Fig. 2 including boundary conditions

For example the edges of `:surface_1` can be extracted by:

```
select edges(:surface_1);
<{OID[0x0:294], OID[0x0:295], OID[0x0:296], OID[0x0:297]}>
```

The `edges` function is modelled to store object identifiers internally for generality and efficiency reasons. However, the `name` function can also be used on each element of the vector for name reference. The preceding example would then look like:

```
select name(elements(edges(:surface_1)));
<"line_1"> <"line_2"> <"line_3"> <"line_4">
```

It is also possible to invert functions, i.e. apply the function in the opposite direction as in the following query that tells which surfaces a specific edge belongs to:

```
select name(s) for each surface s
              where elements(edges(s)) = :line_2;
<"s1">
```

In TRINITAS, the modelling of the example results in a geometry model as in Fig. 7. The geometry model is thereafter used as the basis for the specification and generation of a finite element mesh. If we specify a mesh with three bilinear elements per edge of the rectangular the resulting mesh is shown in Fig. 3. Figure 8 presents a view of the results from a linear static stress analysis of the model where a contour plot of iso-stress curves is included.

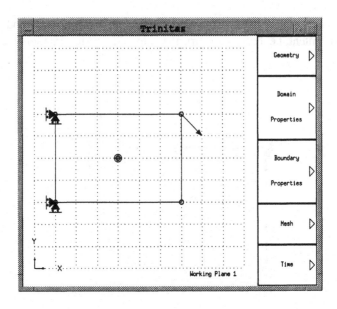

Fig. 7. The geometry model, of the example, with boundary conditions modelled in TRINITAS

The functionality of geometry-related concepts that are related to the user interface management is currently not modelled in the database. This includes finding the nearest point to a specific position, calculating distances between positions and points, etc. For this purpose, it would also be interesting to investigate how spatial indexing techniques could be used to support efficient processing of these types of queries. However, these operations can also be transferred into the database. These operators are expressed in AMOSQL as:

```
create function distance(real x1, real y1, real z1,
                    point p2) -> real d as
        select d for each real x2, real y2, real z2,
                    real t1, real t2, real t3
        where
            position(p2) = <x2, y2, z2> and
            t1 = (x2 - x1) and
            t2 = (y2 - y1) and
            t3 = (z2 - z1) and
            d = sqrt((t1*t1) + (t2*t2) + (t3*t3));

create function find_nearest_point(
                real x, real y, real z) -> point p1 as
        select p1
            where distance(x, y, z, p1) =
                    minagg((select distance(x, y, z, p2)
                        for each point p2));
```

And an application of these functions looks like:

```
distance(100.0, 100.0, 0.0, :point_3);
<22.3607>
name(find_nearest_point(100.0, 100.0, 0.0));
<"p3">
```

As the implementation continues, it will be possible to transfer more and more functionality to the database and large parts of the processing can be kept within the database system. The database model will be further developed to eventually include a complete FEA. This includes modelling of concepts and functionality related to the finite element mesh, domain properties, boundary conditions, the actual analysis, and result interpretation. Some simple examples of the concepts and relations that are apparent for the mesh was illustrated in Sect. 2.3. The analysis step involves the solution of a system of equations that requires the representation of matrices and matrix operators in the database. The processing of numerical calculations can be made by extending the query language with numerical operators as foreign functions.

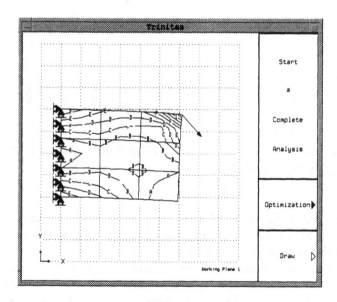

Fig. 8. A contour plot for the example showing iso-stress curves resulting from a linear static stress analysis

The current implementation, FEAMOS, has also been evaluated with respect to its execution performance. FEAMOS has been compared with TRINITAS, the original FEA program. Since execution performance is quite critical for these kinds of systems it is important that new software design principles are able to scale up with the application. To traditionalists it might be surprising that the evaluation result showed that the FEAMOS system scaled up better than TRINITAS. Especially, since the original TRINITAS system has acceptable response times and processing efficiency when it is used. The performance test measured the time for creation of objects including an initialization (update) of a stored function. In this case this corresponds to point objects and a position attribute with three coordinates. We also measured the access time for random access of the same number of objects including the function access. These results are presented in Fig. 9. The access phase is more critical than the creation phase since it has a higher frequency in a real application situation.

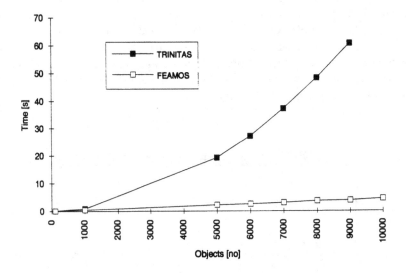

Fig. 9. Performance measures of TRINITAS and FEAMOS. This diagram shows the real access time for accessing the position of point objects

The improved performance of FEAMOS compared to TRINITAS is explained by the lack of dedicated storage structures in TRINITAS. TRINITAS performs linear search over the point object set, whereas FEAMOS takes advantage of built-in storage structures of AMOS, such as hash tables, for efficient access. These kinds of storage structures can, of course, also be implemented in TRINITAS, which should result in similar inclination of the TRINITAS performance curves. At small sets of objects (about <500), TRINITAS has better performance than FEAMOS which is due to the interface overhead in accessing the database. However, the processing performance is no real bottle-neck at these object volumes.

The quite encouraging performance measures of FEAMOS are also due to the fact that the database is embedded (shares the same address space) in the application and that the database is in main-memory. Disk access and process or network communication would severely slow down the system.

3 Summary

Results from the initial implementation of the FEA application treated in this paper show that the use of an OR DBMS including an extensible OO query language is a promising direction/competitive alternative in designing future FEA software. Both requirements on domain modelling and execution efficiency can be met by this approach.

High-level declarative modelling is supported by the extensible OO query language which makes development, maintenance, and use of the applications more effective. Furthermore, initial performance measures show that the overhead of using an embedded database is quite low, in particular if the database can be run in the same address space as the application. More specifically,

- It is not necessary to re-implement low-level dedicated data structures, such as indices, for each new system. Such re-implementation not only duplicates implementation efforts but, as our example shows, may prove less efficient than the highly optimized data management provided by an embedded DBMS.

- By providing access to other databases, e.g. relational DBMS [4], from the domain model it is possible to build models and ad hoc queries that combine data from other databases, e.g. from other components of a CAE system.

- Domain models can provide a generic model, here a FEA model, that can be used by many applications, providing design re-use and simplifying the combination of data from several systems.

- Extensibility of a query language, such as AMOSQL, will also make it possible to make optimizations over the domain model and thereby domain-related operations.

Future work will investigate these issues in greater detail. This aiso involves an inclusion of matrices and matrix procedures for modelling numerical algorithms.

Thus, using next generation OO DBMS and extensible OO query languages can renew development, maintenance, and usage of FEA software. The benefits of using domain models include easier access through a query language, better data description (as schemas), and other benefits currently provided only by advanced DBMS, such as transaction capabilities and ad hoc query processing. We believe that tools like object-relational database management systems and extensible query languages can provide a solid base for future scientific and engineering data management.

References

1. French, J. C., Jones, A. K., Pfaltz, J. L.: Summary of the Final Report of the NSF Workshop on Scientific Database Management. SIGMOD Record, 19(4), December 1990, 32-40.

2. IEEE Computer Society, The Bulletin of the Technical Committee on Data Engineering (TCDE), Special Issue on Scientific Databases, 93(2), 1993.

3. DBMS: A New Direction in DBMS. Interview with Michael R. Stonebraker in DBMS, February 1994, 50-60.

4. Fahl, G., Risch, T., Sköld, M.: AMOS - An Architecture for Active Mediators. The International Workshop on Next Generation Information Technologies and Systems (NGITS' 93), Haifa, Israel, June 28-30, 1993, 47-53.

5. Torstenfelt, B.: An Integrated Graphical System for Finite Element Analysis, User's manual. Version 2.0, LiTH-IKP-R-737, Linköping University, January 1993.

6. Lyngbaek, P.: OSQL: A Language for Object Databases. HPL-DTD-91-4, Hewlett-Packard Company, January 1991.

7. Beech, D.: Collections of Objects in SQL3. Proceedings of the 19th VLDB Conference, Dublin, Ireland, August 24-27, 1993, 244-255.

8. Becker, E. B., Carey, G. F., Oden, J. T.: Finite Elements: An Introduction. Prentice-Hall, Inc., Vol. 1, Texas Finite Element Series, 1981.

9. Baugh, J. W., Rehak, D. R.: Object-Oriented Design of Finite Element Programs. Computer Utilization in Structural Engineering Proceedings of the Sessions at Structures Congress '89, San Francisco, CA, USA, May 1-5, 1989, 91-100.

10. Fenves, G. L.: Object-Oriented Programming for Engineering Software Development. Engineering with Computers 6, 1990, 1-15.

11. Forde, B. W. R., Foschi, R., Stiemer, S. F.: Object-Oriented Finite Element Analysis. Computers & Structures 34(3), 1990, 355-374.

12. Filho, J. S. R. A., Devloo, P. R. B.: Object-Oriented Programming in Scientific Computations: the Beginning of a New Era. Engineering Computations 8, 1991, 81-87.

13. Dubois-Pelerin, Y., Zimmermann, T., Bomme, P.: Object-Oriented Finite Element Programming: II. A Prototype Program in Smalltalk. Computer Methods in Applied and Engineering 98, 1992, 361-397.

14. Williams, J. R., Lim, D., Gupta, A.: Software Design of Object Oriented Discrete Element Systems. Proceedings of the Third International Conference on Computational Plasticity, Barcelona, Spain, April 6-10, 1992, 1937-1947.

15. Tworzydlo, W. W., Oden, J. T.: Towards an Automated Environment in Computational Mechanics. Computer Methods in Applied and Engineering 104, 1993, 87-143.

16. Ahmed, S., Wong, A., Sriram, D., Logcher, R.: Object-Oriented Database Management Systems for Engineering: A Comparison. Journal of Object-Oriented Programming, 5(3), June 1992, 27-44

17. Ketabchi, M. A., Mathur, S., Risch, T., Chen, J.: Comparative Analysis of RDBMS and OODBMS: A Case Study. IEEE Computer Soc. Int. Conf. 35 San Francisco 1990 Digest of papers/ Compcon spring 90, February 26 - March 2, 1990, 528-537.

18. Cook, R. D.: Concepts and Applications of Finite Element Analysis. 3rd, John Wiley & Sons, Inc., 1989.

19. Atkinson, M., Bancilhon, F., DeWitt, D., Dittrich, K., Maier, D., Zdonik, S.: The Object-Oriented Database System Manifesto. in Kim, W., Nicolas, J-.M., Nishio, S., eds., Proceedings of the First International Conference on Deductive and Object-Oriented Databases (DOOD), Elsevier Science Publishers, Amsterdam, 1989, 40-57.

20. The Committee for Advanced DBMS Function: Third-Generation Database System Manifesto. SIGMOD Record, **19**(3), September 1990, 31-44.

21. Litwin, W., Risch, T.: Main Memory Oriented Optimization of OO Queries using Typed Datalog with Foreign Predicates. IEEE Transactions on Knowledge and Data Engineering, **4**(6), December 1992, 517-528.

22. Wolniewicz, R., Graefe, G.: Algebraic Optimization of Computations over Scientific Databases. Proceedings of the 19th VLDB Conference, Dublin, Ireland, August 24-27, 1993, 13-24.

23. Takizawa, M.: Distributed Database System JDDBS. JARECT Computer Science & Technologies. **7**, OHMSHA & North Holland (publ.), 1983, 262-283.

24. Catell, R. G. G.: Object Data Management: Object-Oriented and Extended Relational Database Systems. Addison-Wesley Publishing Company, Inc., 1991 (reprinted with corrections 1992).

25. Abiteboul, S., Bonner, A.: Objects and Views. Proceedings of the ACM SIGMOD Conference, 1991, 238-247.

26. Bancilhon, F., Delobel, C., Kanellakis, P. (eds.): Building an Object-Oriented Database System: The Story of O2. Morgan Kaufmann Publishers, Inc., 1992.

27. Risch, T., Sköld, M.: Active Rules Based on Object-Oriented Queries. LiTH-IDA-R-92-35, Linköping University, 1992. Also in a special issue on Active Databases of IEEE Data Engineering, **15**(1-4), December, 1992.

28. Fishman, D. H., Annevelink, J., Chow, E. Connors, T., Davis, J. W., Hasan, W. Hoch, C. G., Kent, W., Leichner, S., Lyngbaek, P., Mahbod, B., Neimat, M.A., Risch, T., Shan, M. C., Wilkinson, W. K.: Overview of the Iris DBMS. in Kim, W., Lochovsky, F. H. (eds.): Object-Oriented Concepts, Databases, and Applications, ACM Press, Addison-Wesley, 1989, 219-250.

29. Shipman, D. W.: The Functional Data Model and the Data Language DAPLEX. ACM TODS, **6**(1), March 1981, 140-173.

30. Karlsson, J., Larsson, S., Risch, T., Sköld, M., Werner, M.: AMOS Users's Guide., CAELAB Memo 94-01, Linköping University, March 1994.

A Physician's Workstation as an Application of Object-Oriented Database Technology in Healthcare

Philippe De Smedt, Jurgen Annevelink, Thuan Pham, Philip Strong

Hewlett-Packard Laboratories, Palo Alto, California 94304

Abstract. We describe solutions to practical database problems encountered during the implementation of a prototype Physician's Workstation (PWS) at Hewlett-Packard Laboratories: (i) the integration of legacy data repositories using an object-oriented database management system; and (ii) the development of a clinical information model which logically encapsulates potentially heterogeneous underlying data sources, and presents a unified view of relevant patient information to the application layer. This model is a first step towards an Electronic Medical Record (EMR). In addition, we show how the system has been architected to yield substantial performance gains by applying smart caching and data staging techniques, as well as how these techniques can be used to improve availability of data. The prototype is at present being evaluated in a clinical setting at the Veterans Administration's Medical Center in Palo Alto (PA-VAMC), where we have integrated their legacy Decentralized Hospital Computer Program (DHCP). The integration approach described is equally suited to the integration of other legacy systems. The PA-VAMC prototype provides access to over 30,000 patients, of which 5,500 are cached in PWS.

1 Introduction

The Physician's Workstation (PWS) project [1-5] investigates the use of a set of cooperative, knowledge-based information management tools and interfaces in a clinical information system by physicians in ambulatory care.

Our goals were to design the database component to

1. effectively support the requirements imposed by the application layer, and

2. efficiently access clinical data stored in legacy data repositories.

At the PA-VAMC, the underlying data management system is the Decentralized Hospital Computer Program (DHCP). OpenODB, HP's object-oriented database management system[1], was chosen to implement the database component of PWS, because of the expressiveness of its object-oriented model; its powerful application call interface, on top of which the end-user applications can be built; and because it supports external functions, which are crucial in providing access to legacy data systems. Furthermore,

---

1. OpenODB is based on the Iris model, described in [6].

OpenODB fully supports the functionality expected from an object-oriented database system, such as storage of data and methods, function overloading and multiple inheritance.

An essential component of the project is the definition of a comprehensive *clinical information model*. This model represents clinical data and behavior underlying the PWS applications. Examples of such clinical data are patient demographics, laboratory test results for a patient, medication data for a patient, information about individual medications and tests, etc. The model also defines a core set of functions that can be called by the applications. Examples include a function to find all test results for a patient over a certain time interval, and a function to evaluate patient compliance with medication orders. The idea is to build a model general enough to be accessed by a wide range of applications with their own special data requirements, capable of providing a sufficient level of abstraction to integrate data from a variety of heterogeneous data sources, but that at the same time captures enough clinical detail to be useful.

The clinical information model is the outcome of a detailed ongoing study of physician usage scenarios and how they impact the design of the end-user applications and interfaces, and what information model is needed to support them[1]. Based on our continuing research, we hope to generalize our model towards a more comprehensive Electronic Medical Record (EMR), an indispensable technology for providing effective healthcare through efficient access to a patient's entire medical history [7].

The paper is organized as follows: first, we describe the general architecture and functionality of PWS. Second, we focus on the clinical information model. Third, we show in detail how a legacy data repository with unique characteristics has been integrated into PWS, providing transparent access to its data. Finally, we address issues of performance and availability, and we conclude with a discussion of current and future extensions to our work.

2   PWS Architecture and Functionality

Figure 1 shows the logical structure of PWS. From the usage scenarios, we have derived

1. a set of applications (displays, reports, knowledge-based applications, etc.);

   and

2. the clinical information model that is representative of the data and functions required to support those applications[2].

---

1. More accurately from a database point of view, the term schema, rather than model, should be used here.

2. Those are the subject of some of the papers referenced, and will not be further discussed here.

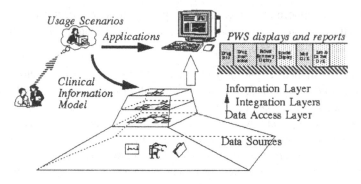

Fig. 1. Logical structure of PWS

To implement the clinical information model, a supporting structure was developed that can logically be described as follows: at the lowest level are the *data sources* that need to be accessed. Above that is the *data access layer*, which contains the functionality to query[1] the data and schema of the underlying data sources, a detailed example of which will be shown in a later section. The next level up is the *data integration layer*, which maintains the individual schemas associated with the underlying data sources, as well as the global schema, i.e., a schema representation of the clinical information model. This model semantically integrates the individual schemas, and provides a unified view to the upper layer, the *information layer*, which consists of the end-users applications and interfaces.

The PWS architecture corresponds to this logical view. Figure 2 shows a high-level picture of the architecture. At the core is the database component, which corresponds

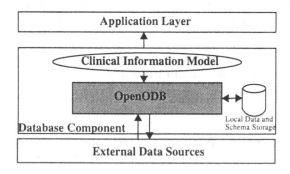

Fig. 2. High-level PWS architecture

to the data access and integration layers just described. This component is now described in more detail.

The purpose of the data access layer is to hide complex or awkward interfaces to leg-

---

1. At this point, PWS provides query access to the underlying data sources. For now, updates will be deferred, for medical/ethical reasons as well as technical.

acy data sources from higher layers, and to allow the transparent mapping of their schema and data into the OpenODB model. For each of the components of interest of the underlying data sources, a representative model is built inside of PWS: examples are the medication component, which covers areas such as medication orders and medications prescribed for a patient; and the laboratory test component, which deals with laboratory test orders and results for a patient, as well as maintains infomation about each type of test.

While providing access to the legacy data is critical, another crucial step is to integrate the various schemas obtained from all of the underlying sources, or even locally stored data, by mapping them into the global clinical information model, described in the next section.

As we pointed out, the clinical information model was derived by looking at how physicians would use a system like PWS, and what the data and functional requirements are. Physicians are not concerned with what repository data comes from. Rather, they deal at a higher level of abstraction: for instance, a physician does not care whether a test result comes from DHCP or from another source. Therefore, the clinical information model contains higher-level constructs which are visible to the end-user applications, but maintains information on how to map those constructs into the types and functions that correspond to each of the individual data sources. This is accomplished through multiple inheritance and overloading. Here are some examples: the clinical information model knows about patients, while each of the underlying data sources has their own notion of patients and their attributes. By making the different patient types subtypes of the generic patient type, references to a patient from within an application will be automatically mapped to the right specific patient subtype. Similarly, attributes of patients, which may have different names in different data repositories (e.g., date-of-birth in one, and dob in another), can be represented by the same overloaded function in PWS (e.g., birthdate). A function call will then be resolved based on the type of its argument.

In summary, we can present a unified clinical information model to end-user applications, by making use of the function overloading and inheritance properties of Open-ODB, as well as its capability to call external functions.

3 PWS Clinical Information Model

An initial prototype for the PWS project was developed based on a list of prototypical information requests that followed from an intensive study of work practices of physicians in ambulatory care [5]. To insure that the system fits into the workflow at the PA-VAMC, a collection of usage scenarios was developed. These scenarios were then used to create an object-oriented clinical information model, according to the informal process described in [8].

Our model was created using the declarative, object-oriented database language Object SQL (OSQL) [9]. The developers of OSQL actively participate in the SQL3 standardization efforts. However, neither OSQL nor SQL3 are universally accepted as a standard through which we could communicate our model. Furthermore, OSQL only partially addresses the problem of representing an object-oriented analysis and design. In particular, it does a very good job of characterizing the static aspects of the model, but provides limited support for representing dynamic aspects such as the possible state transitions that objects can be subjected to.

Accordingly, we continue to search for better methods, capable of completely characterizing and communicating our design. We discuss aspects of the clinical information model here. To represent the model, we draw on several sources. For static aspects of the design, we adopt the extended entity-relationship diagrams, as described in conjunction with the Fusion method [10]. For dynamic aspects, we adopt state diagrams, as described in conjuction with the Object Modeling Technique [11].

We do not present the complete PWS clinical information model in this section. Figure 3 contains a schematic for the class hierarchies of the system. This is fairly detailed and complete (omitting, however, class attributes). In addition, Fig. 3 contains relationships necessary to describe test ordering and result reporting using the system. Figure 4 contains a state diagram for test Order objects. Test result reporting (which we model as part of the test ordering process) is the subject of detailed examples used elsewhere in this paper, and we will include this here to illustrate the operation of the model. It turns out that the relationships and states required to support test ordering are typical of those required to support other aspects of system operation.

We begin by describing the class hierarchies. The two principal aggregate classes contained in Fig. 3 are illustrated using nested boxes labelled "PWS Provider" and "PWS Patient". Connections to their common superclass Person are shown with lines that meet in a triangle beneath the corresponding "Person" box. The open triangle here signifies that Provider and Patient do not partition the Person object space; in other words, the same person can be both provider and patient. We also show that DHCP_Provider and DHCP_Patient, corresponding to providers and patients in the legacy DHCP system, are subclasses of PWS_Provider and PWS_Patient[1]: what applies to objects of types PWS_Provider and PWS_Patient thus automatically applies to objects of types DHCP_Provider and DHCP_Patient, through OpenODB's multiple inheritance mechanism. Obviously, the same can be done for providers and patients of other legacy systems as well. By defining generic classes such as PWS_Provider and PWS_Patient, and specific subclasses corresponding to entities in the particular legacy systems being integrated, the approach described effectively supports schema integration.

Pws_Provider has component classes Patient List and Alert List. Each of these component classes in turn is itself an aggregate class, consisting of Patients and Alerts, respectively. Immediately to the upper left of the component classes is a symbol that describes the cardinality of the component. The "+" to the left of the "Patient List" box means that every Provider has one or more associated Patient List components. The "1" to the left of the "Alert List" box means that every Provider has exactly one associated Alert List component.

---

1. They are subclasses of other classes as well, as will be described in more detail in Sect. 4.

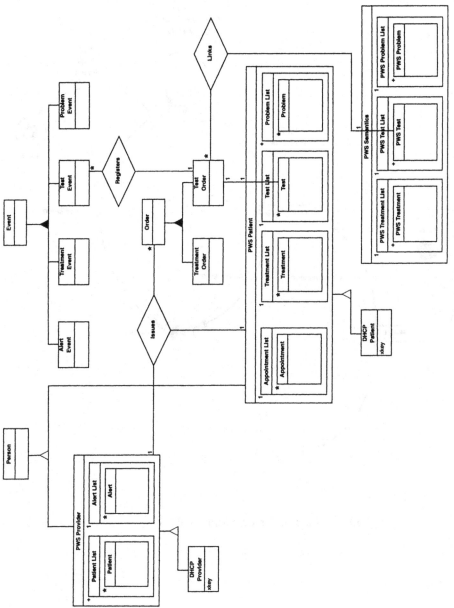

Fig. 3. Class hierarchy chart showing relationships for test ordering in PWS

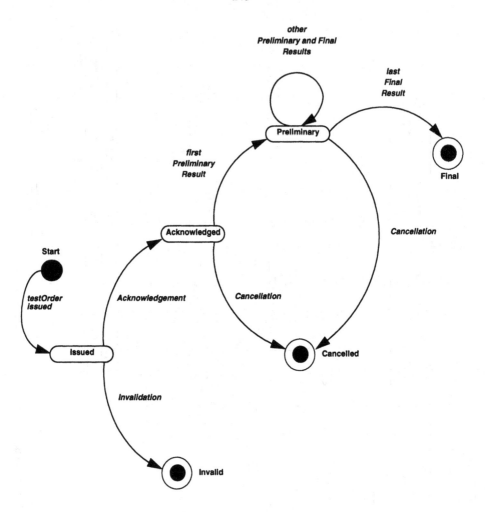

Fig. 4. State chart for test ordering in PWS

PWS_Patient has four component classes: exactly one Appointment List, exactly one Treatment List, exactly one Test List, and one or more Problem Lists (one master problem list, then an additional provider-specific problem list for each provider involved in the care of the patient). Here, too, each of these component classes is itself an aggregate class, consisting of Appointments, Treatments, Tests and Problems, respectively.

The relation Links (shown in Fig. 3 using a diamond-shaped box labelled "Links") illustrates the semantic links used by PWS. In particular, for every test Order object, there is exactly one linked object of the PWS Test sub-component class of the PWS Test List component class from the PWS Semantics table. The "cardinality" of the Links relationship is shown with symbols near its attached objects in the figures. "*" near the "Test Order" box and "1" near the "PWS Test" box implies that Links is a many:one relation between associated objects. Note also that there is a 1:1 association between test Order objects and objects from the Test sub-component class of the Test List component class for each patient. This (indirectly) provides the semantic link between tests (associated with an individual patient) and their associated PWS tests (the test descriptor).

Test Orders and treatment Orders partition the space of order objects, and this is shown in Fig. 3 with a black triangle on the lines linking the Order, Treatment Order and Test Order boxes. The ternary relation Issues demonstrates that, for every order, there is exactly one responsible provider, and exactly one patient subject to that order.

Alert Events, treatment events, test events, and problem events partition the space of event objects. The binary relation Registers shows that, for every test Event, there is exactly one associated test Order object.

Figure 4 contains a state chart for describing state transitions that occur during the lifetime of a test Order object. As mentioned above, test result reporting occurs as part of the test ordering process. We now describe this.

When a provider issues an order for a test[1] to the system, this is registered as a test Order Issued event. The corresponding test Order object passes into the Issued state, as illustrated in Fig. 4. Parties responsible for scheduling or carrying out the test can take one of two actions: they can either acknowledge receipt of the order, or they can invalidate the order (e.g., if the request was not appropriately authorized). In the first case, an acknowledgement event would be registered, and the test Order passes into the acknowledged state. In the second case, an invalidation event would be registered, and no further state transitions for the test Order could occur.

After receipt of the test has been acknowledged, it is still possible for a provider or other party to cancel the test. Under these circumstances, a cancellation event would

---

1. Please note that we do not make any updates to the legacy system, i.e., we do not create test orders ourselves. Rather, they are obtained from the legacy system, cached locally and turned into test Order objects within PWS.

be registered, and the test Order passes into the cancelled state. No further state transitions could occur for the test Order.

Typically, however, the test is performed, and results are reported. Test results become available within the legacy system asynchronously with respect to our system. Ultimately, they become available to our system as test Event objects. There are many complex issues involved in creating these objects, beyond the scope of the present discussion. In addition Test Result objects can either encode preliminary results or final results. Furthermore, test Order objects can specify either single tests or panels (sets) of tests. So a test Order object can, and typically does, have multiple test Events of various types registered against it.

When the first Test Result event is registered, the test Order object passes into the preliminary state. As long as additional results are outstanding for this test (e.g., it is a panel, or there are both preliminary and final results), the test Order remains in the preliminary state. When the last result becomes available, a last Final Result is registered, and the test Order makes the transition to the final state. At this point, too, no further state transitions could occur.

To reiterate, this is not the complete clinical information model for PWS. Other components operate similarly, however. The complete model is the subject of a forthcoming paper. In addition, we are currently exploring how the techniques that we used can be adapted to the field of work flow management.

4 Integration of Legacy Data Sources

We earlier mentioned multiple inheritance and overloading as essential integration mechanisms. OpenODB also provides support at the language level to facilitate integrating legacy data sources: the declarative OSQL language interface can be used both as a DDL and a DML, and can be used interactively and programmatically. By extending OSQL with procedural constructs, it combines the expressive power of a declarative language with the computational power of a procedural language. The procedural extensions are used to implement complex interfaces into legacy systems, while the declarative nature of the language hides that complexity from end-user applications. Examples of this are given throughout this section.

The PWS prototype provides access to a number of heterogeneous data sources, including legacy systems such as the DHCP system discussed in this paper and text retrieval systems, e.g., as discussed in [8]. Data residing in these external sources can be transparently combined with locally stored data using OpenODB's declarative query language constructs. PWS also provides access to other types of multi-media data, including radiology images and EKG waveforms.

In this section we focus on the integration of PWS with DHCP, as an example of how schema and data from an underlying legacy data repository can be selectively imported into an integrating database through the use of an external key mechanism where the external keys are the local representatives of the underlying data.

The Decentralized Hospital Computer Program (DHCP) was originally developed in 1982 by the Veterans Health Administration[13]. It is now used at close to 200 medical centers and many more outpatient clinics for a variety of applications ranging from payroll to order entry and result reporting. DHCP is implemented in MUMPS (Massachusetts General Hospital Utility Multi-Programming System). In what follows, we only describe DHCP to the extent necessary for the discussion.

In order to integrate DHCP into PWS, a number of OpenODB functions had to be implemented to facilitate the importation of both schema and data from the underlying system. At the lowest level, we implemented a (small) set of external functions that allow us to set up a connection to a MUMPS interpreter and send commands and receive replies. A DHCP database consists of a set of structured *files* and *sub-files*, where a file corresponds to a major entity of interest and can be used as an entry point into the DHCP database. Examples are the patient file, the file of all laboratory test specifications, the file of laboratory test orders, etc. A file is essentially an array of records, each of which is defined by one or more attribute values. Attributes can be either single-valued, e.g., the name attribute of a patient record has a string as its value, or multi-valued. A multi-valued attribute is in effect an array of pointers to records in a sub-file. The attributes of multi-valued attributes are defined similar to the attributes of files, thus providing a powerful data model that allows for the definition of arbitrarily nested structures. For example, a patient has a prescription profile attribute, which is a list of prescription records, each of which has several attributes (e.g., the drug prescribed, the prescribing physician, the number of refills allowed, etc.). In general, information in DHCP is accessed by traversing chains of pointer references and iterating over the components of multi-valued attributes.

Information about the file and sub-file structure is available in DHCP and is stored in two meta-files, for files and attributes respectively. These meta-files can be accessed like all other files and the process of importing DHCP files into OpenODB is bootstrapped by creating the OSQL types and functions to access these meta-files. The functions accessing the meta-files provide the functionality needed to look up what files are present, what attributes a file has and what the properties are of these attributes, e.g., what file they point to, or whether the attribute has a character string as its value. One can also query which file attributes have an index defined over them. On some attributes, a range index has been defined, which is particularly useful when doing queries involving time intervals, for instance.

Using the functions that access the meta-files, we can define a single function, called CrDHCPTypeandFuncs, to create the OSQL types and functions needed to access data stored in a DHCP file. The body of this function specifies the algorithm used to map DHCP files, sub-files and attributes of these to OSQL types and functions. For example, to access the DHCP Patient file and access the name, date of birth and laboratory reference attributes, one can call the function CrDHCPTypeandFuncs, as follows:

```
CrDHCPTypeandFuncs ('PATIENT',
                List('PWS_PATIENT'),
                List(
                    Tuple('NAME','NAME',0,''),
                    Tuple('DOB','DATE OF BIRTH',0,''),
                    Tuple('LAB_REF','LABORATORY REFERENCE',3,'')
                )
            );
```

The function CreateDHCPTypeandFuncs is an example of how the procedural aspects of the OSQL language are used to full advantage. It shows how most of the aspects of mapping the DHCP data model into the OSQL model can be abstracted in a single function call.

Figure 5 shows the types and functions created by the call above and their relationships to other, pre-existing types and functions. The arrows represent type-subtype relationships.

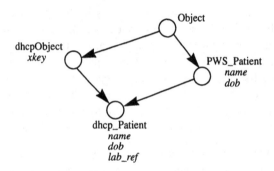

Fig. 5. Importation of DHCP files

Any type corresponding to a DHCP file is made a subtype of dhcpObject. This is done so that we can associate an external key (a MUMPS string) with the object. The external key or xkey of an object is used to locate and identify the record in a DHCP file corresponding to the OSQL object. In the example shown, dhcp_Patient is also made a subtype of PWS_Patient, as specified by the second argument of the call above. As a result, attribute functions whose names are identical to the corresponding attribute function of PWS_Patient are overloaded, thus immediately achieving a degree of integration, as shown for example by the name function. Note that other subtypes can be added to PWS_Patient, similar to dhcp_Patient, and that instances of these types may represent objects residing in other repositories. The attribute functions of dhcp_Patient are implemented as a call to a function that will look up the value of a specific attribute of an object, given the xkey of that object. The detailed implementation of the attribute functions depends on the third element of the tuples specifying what attribute to import (0 or 3 in the example given). For example, the difference between specifying a 0 or a 3, is that in the former case, the attribute function will look up, and if necessary create, the object corresponding to the xkey returned by the DHCP interface routines.

In the latter case, the attribute function simply returns the xkey, which is obviously more efficient, since it avoids the lookup and possibly the creation of an additional object.

The schema developer is free to specify additional OSQL functions. We use that frequently to be able to upload data from the DHCP database and make it available locally, which in turn enables us to define indexes that are not provided by the underlying legacy system. Uploading and caching data from a legacy data source obviously introduces the problem of keeping that data current. To solve those problems we again use the procedural extensions of OSQL, essentially programming the cache consistency algorithm into the functions that access the cache. Caching is discussed further in a later section.

To be able to start accessing objects corresponding to entries in DHCP files, we have implemented a special iterator function that will return the identifiers of the objects according to the value of a key attribute. In our prototype, we assume this attribute to be the first attribute in the list of attributes passed to the function CrDHCPTypeand-Funcs. Consequently, the first attribute for which a function is defined has to have an index defined over it. When the type is created, CrDHCPTypeandFuncs finds out what that index is (again, a MUMPS character string), and stores that as an attribute of the type. With that information, the function DHCP_Listtype can be called to return instances of that type. For instance, to create OpenODB objects for patients in DHCP, one can invoke it as follows:

```
DHCP_ListType('DHCP_PATIENT','PATIENT1',5);
```

The function call above will return a list of at most five objects, whose names are equal to or follow (in lexicographic order) the string specified as the second argument.

The function CrDHCPTypeandFuncs uses the function CrAttrF internally to create the attribute functions. This function can also be called independently to create additional attribute functions. Let us add function Provider, which corresponds to the primary physician assigned to a patient:

```
CrAttrF('PROVIDER',type DHCP_PATIENT','PROVIDER',0,'');
```

This is a function of type 0, which means that it is called with an object of type dhcp_Patient as its sole argument, and that the result, a pointer in this case, is stored in the database as an object of type dhcp_Provider. This type is automatically created when the Provider function is defined, because a corresponding type is created for the (sub-)file pointed at by the chosen attribute.

Obviously, it is useful to permanently store objects representing providers. However, when the pointer is of only immediate value (i.e., part of a chain to be followed to get to an end result), it is useless to create an object for it. For example, Lab_Ref by itself has very little contents of interest; however, it points into the file of laboratory test results (Lab Data), and is thus a necessary link in retrieving test data for a patient. To show this, let us first define a time range function over dhcp_Lab_Data (which was automatically created when the Lab_Ref function was defined):

CrAttrF('CHEM_TEST_RANGE', type DHCP_LAB_DATA,'CHEM',2,'');

Chem_Test_Range is a function that corresponds to the Chem (clinical chemistry tests) attribute in the Lab Data file. It is created as type 2, i.e., it takes an object of type dhcp_Lab_Data and a time interval as its arguments and returns a list of pairs of time values (in descending order) and the OID's of the objects corresponding to the test results. The detailed test results can then be found by further function calls over each of the test result objects. The process of getting to a patient's test results is thus to first find his/her laboratory reference, and then to call Chem_Test_Range over that reference and the desired time interval, e.g.,

:results := CHEM_TEST_RANGE(LAB_REF(patientOID), t1,t2);

(where patientOID is a Patient object, and t1 and t2 are the end-points of the time interval of interest). As can be seen here, Lab_Ref is only an intermediate function, and its result pointer can be passed immediately to Chem_Test_Range. If Lab_Ref were implemented in such a way as to create an object, the object would be wasted, as Chem_Test_Range would have to look up its xkey to proceed anyway. The only requirement is to allow functions to be overloaded to be called either with an OID as their (first) argument, or with a character string (an xkey). When functions are created through CrDHCPTypeandFuncs or CrAttrF, they are automatically overloaded to support this.

This section has concentrated on showing how a particular legacy data repository was integrated into PWS by writing procedures that encapsulate the actual mapping of the data models, and how one can selectively choose the extent to which data from that repository is represented as objects in the integrating database, through the use of external keys. This mechanism can be used to integrate any legacy database in which individual data items can be accessed through unique identifiers. In effect, by mapping the underlying data sources into the common PWS model, we achieve seemless interoperability among those data sources.

5 Performance and Availability Issues

The PWS prototype is expected to provide fast access to clinical data on a large number of patients. The local PA-VAMC knows about more than 30,000 patients. Based on an analysis of scheduled appointments at the General Medicine Clinic over the course of the past year, we derived which patients can be considered active. With that information, we decided to create a database of approximately 5,500 patients.

As discussed previously, a large number of relevant reports can be generated for a patient. The resident physicians helped us decide which reports were most important. The PWS clinical information model was built around those requirements, and currently comprises of a schema to support, among others, the following patient reports or displays:

1. medications prescribed for a patient, including possible interactions;

2. clinical chemistry test orders and results for a patient;

3. microbiology test orders and results, including bacteriology, mycology, parasitology, TB and virology;

4. electrocardiogram interpretations for a patient;

5. pulmonary function test results;

6. radiology reports;

7. surgical pathology reports;

8. cytopathology reports;

9. discharge diagnoses;

10. laboratory tests pending.

We achieved substantial performance gains and improved availability of data by bringing some of the data into the local OpenODB repository, in effect creating local caches of the data of the underlying system and drastically reducing the number of accesses to the legacy system[1]. Further performance improvements were obtained by building suitable indexes on these caches.

A conscious choice had to be made as to which data to cache. Clearly, caching all data would be prohibitive in terms of storage, and also defeat the purpose behind the layered architecture that we proposed. It was decided to cache all medication and clinical chemistry test data (orders as well as results) for a patient, and specification data for all tests (such as normality values, specimens over which the test can be performed, etc.). Based on observed performance, however, other types of data may be added as well.

For the 5,500 patients, the resulting local database has a size of about 820 Mbytes. Whether the data is cached or not is transparent to the end-user applications (except for noticeable performance differences): when an application requires data for which a cache exists, the cache will automatically be incrementally updated with the required data that had not been cached yet. This is accomplished by keeping track of the time interval for which data has been cached before[2]. As an example, clinical chemistry test results can be brought into the cache by specifying a patient name, and the desired time interval over which to retrieve the results (much like the Chem_Test_Range function defined earlier). If part of the specified interval has already been cached, only the non-cached fraction will be brought into the cache. In fact, if no data for a patient has been cached before, the same end-user functions can still be called, though obviously performance will be much affected as all data has to be retrieved from the underlying system, as opposed to the cache.

---

1. The actual number of accesses is dependent on the type of report and the level of detail required.

2. This scheme can only be used for data that is not modified in DHCP after it has been cached. Much clinical data is of this type, where data is usually added, instead of modified. More general schemes are being looked at, but are not further described in this paper.

For each of the 5,500 patients, clinical chemistry test data and medication data were uploaded into the cache from time 0 (set to January 1, 1901) to the current time. We have observed that for a patient with 2,500 test results, a query to retrieve all the detailed results goes down from 10 minutes in non-cached mode, to about 5 seconds with the data cached. While not all results may be of immediate interest to the physician, there still is a benefit in caching them, for instance to facilitate decision support queries, such as outcomes management, or the analysis of critical values over time as a function of medications prescribed.

The mechanism to keep the caches synchronized with DHCP is to find out which patients are scheduled to be seen by any of a list of resident physicians the next day. An overnight process is then run to update the caches with the necessary data. The next morning, the data is efficiently available. Furthermore, at the time of the visit, the physician can click on a box to get the latest test results, which will be brought into the cache, and displays are updated as necessary.

In addition to improved performance, an obvious advantage of this approach is availability of the data. Even if the underlying system becomes unavailable, the local database contains the critical data necessary to proceed, at least with the most important functions. Clearly, this factor also contributes to the choice of which data to cache.

On the downside, as already mentioned, caching large amounts of data takes up substantial storage space. The availability, performance and storage characteristics of a candidate for caching thus have to be weighed carefully against each other.

The clinical information model that we are currently using is a first step towards an Electronic Medical Record (EMR). In very large clinical environments, potentially having millions of patients, the issues of performance and availability become even more important, as issues of geographic distribution of the data, and distributed access to it, compound the problem. As an outgrowth of the PWS project, we are embarking on a study to define an EMR and the necessary supporting architectural infrastructure. The PWS testbed has helped us in terms of understanding the attendant data staging and availability issues. Data staging deals with the problem of where to most effectively store the data, in order to guarantee "optimal" performance and availability (the "meta"-equivalent of the micro-analysis done in PWS).

As an added benefit, caching data locally allows us to maintain a more extensive set of patient data than that available in DHCP: (test) ordering information, for instance, is purged from the active DHCP data repository after 60 days. Once it is brought into the PWS cache, it is available until explicitly deleted. By keeping this history, the PWS functionality can be expanded to perform analyses such as outcomes management, where the outcome of a treatment is compared against the prescribed treatment, or to assist in protocol-based decision making.

In summary, the clinical information model dictates the possible choices of data to cache. The scenarios identify which types of information physicians are most interested in, and therefore need optimized performance and availability. We have identified medication data and clinical chemistry tests as examples of such information. The benefits of caching are:

1. improved performance;

2. increased availability of data in case of failure;

3. access to historical data for analysis.

6 Current and Future Extensions

During the development of the PWS prototype, we identified a number of potential areas for further investigation. In order for a system like PWS to be successful in very large clinical environments, the following core set of requirements need to be satisfied (among others):

1. the system has to be scalable, i.e., it should be architected to be transparently adaptive to the growth of an organization;

2. it has to provide high-performance access to clinical information across the entire architecture; and

3. it has to provide support for declarative querying of the data, so that applications do not have to deal with the issues of where to find the data or how to get to it.

Clearly, for the distributed environments envisioned, a client-server architecture has to be put in place, which we briefly describe here.

Since the deployment of PWS at the PA-VAMC, a version of PWS has been created to run on OSF's Distributed Computing Environment (DCE). A large part of this work involves the implementation of a DCE/database interface component, which enables OpenODB to be accessible by DCE client programs via remote procedure calls (RPC), in a client-server fashion.

The move to DCE allows PWS components to leverage the distributed computing services (such as directory, distributed file, and security services) and infrastructure (such as threads and RPC). With the DCE/database interface component, the database can use these services and infrastructure without losing any of its functionality. For example, the database can accept multiple and concurrent RPC requests for queries, authenticate the identity of the caller, and even invoke data encryption on query results. Figure 6 illustrates the database and its DCE interface wrapper in the PWS DCE environment.

In our current implementation, the DCE/database interface component is a DCE server process. When this process receives an RPC call, it either invokes a query or a command over the database. The results are then packaged by the interface component, and returned to the calling process. This implementation allows us to rapidly make use of the database in the distributed computing environment without having to modify its implementation. Furthermore, different interface components can be constructed to make use of the database in different environments.

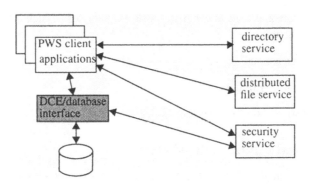

Fig. 6. The PWS DCE environment

For example, we have components that can interface with BMS (Broadcast Message Server) tools in the HP Softbench environment [14], as well as with CORBA (Common Object Request Broker Architecture) tools [15].

7 Conclusion

PWS was designed to provide physicians with efficient graphical access to patient information. The use of scenarios helped determine which user interfaces to provide, and which data schema to develop to support the end-user requirements. Analysis of these scenarios led to the development of a clinical information model, which is used in a dual capacity: as an integrating mechanism for legacy data sources, and as a comprehensive representation of patient information that can be accessed by applications.

We presented the general architecture and functionality of PWS, and the role of the clinical information model therein. We then gave a detailed description of the model.

As a prototype implementation of PWS, an agreement was worked out with the PA-VAMC to integrate their legacy DHCP data repository into PWS. This paper reports on the technical challenge of integrating the DHCP system, and suggests that the approach is general enough to be applied to integrating other legacy systems as well.

We described how a caching mechanism can be used for improved performance and increased availability. Through the discussion, it was shown how the scenarios were used in determining candidate data for caching.

We currently have a running prototype with access to a live system with over 30,000 patients, 5,500 of which have been cached in PWS, with a resulting database size of 820 Mbytes, and additional patients can be transparently added.

We also discussed some of the requirements for PWS in large-scale environments, and a prototype client-server implementation based on OSF's Distributed Computing Environment (DCE).

The experience from designing and developing this PWS prototype will be invaluable in defining an Electronic Medical Record and a supporting architecture.

Acknowledgements

We wish to acknowledge Danielle Fafchamps for her helpful comments on earlier drafts of this paper, and the other PWS team members, Curt Kolovson, Jaap Suermondt and Charles Young for their many contributions to the project. Barry Rotman at the PA-VAMC provided us with valuable feedback throughout the development of the prototype. Paul Tang deserves a special thanks for getting us involved in this challenging area.

References

[1] P.C. Tang, J. Annevelink, D. Fafchamps, W.M. Stanton, and C.Y. Young. Physician's Workstations: Integrated Information Management for Clinicians. In: P. Clayton, ed., Proceedings of the Fifteenth Annual Symposium on Computer Applications in Medical Care. McGraw-Hill, New York, 1991, pp. 569-573.

[2] W.M. Stanton and P.C. Tang. Knowledge-Based Support for a Physician's Workstation. In: P. Clayton, ed., Proceedings of the Fifteenth Annual Symposium on Computer Applications in Medical Care. McGraw-Hill, New York, 1991, pp. 649-653.

[3] J. Annevelink, C.Y. Young, and P.C. Tang. Heterogeneous Database Integration in a Physician Workstation. In: P. Clayton, ed., Proceedings of the Fifteenth Annual Symposium on Computer Applications in Medical Care. McGraw-Hill, New York, 1991, pp. 368-372.

[4] C.Y. Young, P.C. Tang, and J. Annevelink. An Open Systems Architecture for Development of a Physician's Workstation. In: P. Clayton, ed., Proceedings of the Fifteenth Annual Symposium on Computer Applications in Medical Care. McGraw-Hill, New York, 1991, pp. 491-495.

[5] D. Fafchamps, C.Y. Young, and P.C. Tang. Modelling Work Practices: Input to the Design of a Physician's Workstation. In: P. Clayton, ed., Proceedings of the Fifteenth Annual Symposium on Computer Applications in Medical Care. McGraw-Hill, New York, 1991, pp. 788-792.

[6] D.H. Fishman, et al. Overview of the Iris DBMS. In: W. Kim and F.H. Lochovsky, ed., Object-Oriented Concepts, Databases and Applications. ACM Press, New York, 1989.

[7] Institute of Medicine. The Computer-Based Patient Record: an Essential Technology for Health Care. National Academy Press, Washington, D.C., 1991.

[8] P.C. Strong, et al. Methodology for Developing a Physician's Workstation Using an Object-Oriented Clinical Information Model. Hewlett-Packard Laboratories Technical Memo HPL-DTD-93-5.

[9] J. Annevelink, et al. Object SQL - A Language for the Design and Implementation of Object Databases. Submitted for publication.

[10] D. Coleman, et al. Object-Oriented Development: the Fusion Method. Prentice-Hall. Englewood Cliffs, N.J., 1994.

[11] J. Rumbaugh, et al. Object-Oriented Modeling and Design. Prentice-Hall. Englewood Cliffs, N.J., 1991.

[12] T.W. Yan and J. Annevelink. Integrating a Structured-Text Retrieval System with an Object-Oriented Database System. Hewlett-Packard Laboratories Technical Memo HPL-DTD-94-11.

[13] Department of Veterans Affairs - Veterans Health Administration. Decentralized Hospital Computer Program, 1993.

[14] M. Cagan. The HP Softbench Environment: an Architecture for a New Generation of Software Tools. Hewlett-Packard Journal, June 1990, pp. 36-47.

[15] Object Management Group: Common Object Request Broker Architecture and Specification. Document Number 91.12.1, Revision 1.1, 1991.

Fast Document Ranking for Large Scale Information Retrieval

Michael Persin[1] and Justin Zobel[1] and Ron Sacks-Davis[2]

[1] Dept. of Computer Science, RMIT, GPO Box 2476V, Melbourne 3001, Australia.
[2] Faculty of Applied Science, RMIT, GPO Box 2476V, Melbourne 3001, Australia.

Abstract. For large document databases, evaluation of ranked queries can be expensive in cpu time, memory usage, and disk traffic. It has been shown that memory usage can be dramatically reduced by use of a simple filtering heuristic that eliminates most documents from consideration. In this paper we show that, by designing inverted indexes explicitly to support filtering, cpu time and disk traffic can also be dramatically reduced. The principle of the index design is that inverted lists are sorted by in-document frequency rather than by document number. In the context of compressed indexes such a re-ordering could result in a large increase in index size. We show, however, that it is possible to use the re-ordering to achieve a net reduction in index size, regardless of whether the index is compressed. Together, these techniques simultaneously achieve savings in cpu time, disk traffic, memory usage, and index size.

1 Introduction

Ranking techniques are used to evaluate informally-phrased queries on document databases [11, 12]. For the gigabyte databases now available, ranking is considered the best option for data access: Boolean queries require expert formulation, and techniques such as browsing are ineffective for the initial location of answers from among millions of documents. The need for ranking has led to efforts such as the international TREC project—a cooperative experiment involving twenty research groups, a two gigabyte database, and manual checking of over 300,000 documents for relevance to a test query set—intended to promote development of effective large scale information retrieval [9].

In comparison to Boolean queries, which retrieve exactly those documents that contain the specified query terms, ranked queries are statistically compared to the documents. The statistical *similarity* of a document to a query is assumed to correspond to the likely relevance of the document to the query, so the answers to the query are the documents with the highest similarity values. Many functions have been proposed for the computation of similarities. One of the most successful functions—in terms of *retrieval effectiveness*, or ability to locate answers that humans judge to be correct—is the cosine measure [11, 12]. This measure computes similarities by combining information such as the overall importance of each query term, co-occurrence of terms in document and query, and the frequency of the term in document and query.

For a large document database, the cost of evaluation of functions such as the cosine measure can be prohibitively high. This cost—in memory, cpu time, and disk traffic—arises because ranked queries are usually expressed in English and therefore contain a large number of terms, some of which will occur in many of the database's documents, and because ranking techniques assign a similarity value to every document containing any of the query terms. As a consequence, typically most of the documents in the database will have non-zero similarity, and will hence be candidates for presentation to the user.

In a straightforward implementation of a similarity measure such as the cosine measure, the document database has an inverted index that contains, for each term in the database, an *inverted list* of the identifiers of the documents containing that term. The costs of ranked query evaluation on such an index are: memory, to store the similarity values, usually requiring one accumulator per document in the database; disk traffic, to transfer inverted lists for each query term from disk to memory for processing; and cpu time, to process this index information. These costs make ranking impractical on small machines, a significant shortcoming given that text databases are now widely available for access on PCs and desktop workstations.

There have been many attempts to improve the efficiency of ranked query evaluation [2, 4, 5, 6, 8]. Most of these are based on some form of stopping condition; that is, they cease processing of query terms when some predefined condition is met. An better method is to process every query term and inverted list, but apply a filter to each list. The effect of the filter is that a document's accumulator is updated only if the combination of the frequency of the term in the document and the term's importance is large enough to be likely to have an impact on the final ordering of documents. Thus the inverted list of even a common term may be processed, but only for those documents in which the term is frequent will the accumulator be updated. This filter dramatically reduces the number of accumulators required to compute the cosine measure, without an adverse effect on retrieval effectiveness [10].

In this paper we show how to re-organise inverted files to support the filtering heuristic. Inverted lists are generally sorted by document identifier, but for the filter this implies that the whole of each list has to be processed, even when there are only a few documents in which the term is frequent. By sorting inverted lists by decreasing within-document frequency, the identifiers of the interesting documents are brought to the start of the list, also yielding a reduction in disk traffic because only part of each inverted list must be retrieved. However, such a reorganisation can potentially have an adverse impact on index size, because index compression techniques rely on the small differences between adjacent documents in longer inverted lists to achieve size reductions [7, 13]. We show, however, that it is possible to use the re-ordering to achieve a net reduction in index size, regardless of whether the index is compressed. Together, these improvements allow ranking to be performed on a small machine such as a PC, allowing users to take advantage of the availability of large text databases on cheap media.

Document databases and the cosine measure are described in Section 2. The filtering heuristic is described in Section 3. In Section 4 we show how to structure inverted lists to support filtering. Experimental results, for both compressed and uncompressed inverted files, are given in Section 5. Conclusions are given in Section 6.

2 Document databases and the cosine measure

An inverted index for a document database typically has two components: a *vocabulary* containing each term in the database; and, for each term t, an *inverted list*, of the identifiers of the documents containing that term and, with each identifier d, the in-document frequency $f_{d,t}$ of t in d. The inverted lists are usually sorted by document identifier, not only for convenience of processing but because such sorting allows index compression—once sorted, the differences (or *run-lengths*) between adjacent identifiers can be computed, yielding small integers that are suitable for compression. For example, consider the list consisting of the following ⟨document identifier, in-document frequency⟩ pairs

$$\langle 5, 3\rangle\langle 9, 2\rangle\langle 12, 2\rangle\langle 16, 5\rangle\langle 21, 1\rangle\langle 25, 2\rangle\langle 32, 4\rangle,$$

which represents the fact that the term being indexed occurs three times in document 5, twice in document 9, and so on. This list can be converted into the sequence of run-lengths

$$\langle 5, 3\rangle\langle 4, 2\rangle\langle 3, 2\rangle\langle 4, 5\rangle\langle 5, 1\rangle\langle 3, 2\rangle\langle 7, 4\rangle.$$

Given that the number of documents containing a given term can be used to compute the average run-length, using a parameterised code the run-lengths can be efficiently compressed, as the run-lengths will conform to a known distribution with a known mean. For high-frequency terms, often only 1 or 2 bits are required to represent a run-length. The $f_{d,t}$ values are already a skew distribution of small integers, and can be effectively represented in unary or in an Elias code [3]. Overall, such inverted index compression techniques can reduce index size by a factor of six or more [1, 7, 13].

For a large document database with an inverted file index, the similarity of each document to a query can be computed as follows. An accumulator is created for each document, either by initially allocating an accumulator for every document in the database or by dynamically adding an accumulator for a document when it is allocated non-zero similarity. The similarities of every document to the query are then computed simultaneously, by retrieving the inverted list for each query term and updating the accumulator for every document in the term's inverted list. Thus the main costs of query evaluation are memory space, for the accumulators; disk traffic, to retrieve inverted lists; and cpu time, to decode inverted lists. Reducing all of these costs to levels suitable for a small machine is the subject of this paper.

In this paper, we use the cosine measure to demonstrate our techniques. For the cosine measure, the similarity of document and query is given by

$$C_{q,d} = \frac{\sum_t f_{q,t} \times f_{d,t} \times I_t^2}{W_q \times W_d},$$

where W_x is the length (in some measure) of document or query x, I_t is the *a priori* importance of term t, and $f_{x,t}$ is the frequency of t in document or query x [11]. The importance of a term is usually computed from its overall frequency—often with $I_t = \log(N/f_t)$, where N is the number of documents in the database and f_t the frequency of the term in the database—so that the important terms are those that are rare. The accumulators are used to hold the running totals for the expression

$$sim_{q,d,t} = \sum_t f_{q,t} \times f_{d,t} \times I_t^2$$

for each document. The information for these totals is extracted from the inverted lists; W_d values are precomputed and stored elsewhere.

The retrieval effectiveness of a ranking mechanism—its ability to retrieve answers a human judges to be relevant—is computed from the recall (proportion of relevant documents retrieved) and precision (proportion of retrieved documents that are relevant). The expense of performing the necessary relevance judgements is the main reason that ranking experiments must be on established test databases such as the TREC collection.

3   Filtered evaluation of ranked queries

One of the main costs of ranked query evaluation is the memory required for the accumulators. They cannot be effectively compressed, because they are unpatterned real numbers, so the only way of reducing the space requirement is to reduce the number of documents for which an accumulator is required. Most techniques for limiting the number of accumulators are based on deciding whether to process or ignore an entire inverted list [2, 5, 6, 8]. These techniques range from use of a list of stop-words, usually common or closed-class words, to on-the-fly techniques that use statistics about the current state of evaluation to decide whether to proceed. The factors common to all of these techniques is that they may process the inverted list for a term even if it is not particularly important in any document, or discard a discriminating term simply because it is fairly frequent, and that they abruptly switch from free addition of accumulators to allowing no addition of accumulators at all.

We propose that it is more appropriate to use a *filtering* technique that provides a gradual transition from inclusion to omission of accumulators, as follows. Query terms are sorted by decreasing I_t, so that important terms are processed first. Then, before each term t is processed, two thresholds are computed, an insertion threshold f_{ins} and an addition threshold f_{add}, where $f_{add} \leq f_{ins}$. As the inverted list for t is processed, each $f_{d,t}$ is compared to the thresholds. If $f_{d,t} < f_{add}$, no action is taken. If $f_{add} \leq f_{d,t} < f_{ins}$ and d already has a non-zero accumulator, $sim_{q,d,t}$ is added to d's accumulator. If $f_{ins} \leq f_{d,t}$ then $sim_{q,d,t}$ is added to d's accumulator, and if necessary an accumulator is created. The thresholds are computed by

$$f_{ins} = c_{ins} \cdot S_{max}/(I_t^2 \cdot f_{q,t}) \quad \text{and}$$
$$f_{add} = c_{add} \cdot S_{max}/(I_t^2 \cdot f_{q,t}),$$

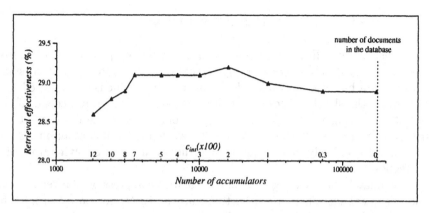

Fig. 1. Number of accumulators versus retrieval effectiveness

where c_{ins} and c_{add} are predefined constants, $c_{add} \leq c_{ins}$, and S_{max} is the current maximum accumulator value. The values of the thresholds are constant during processing of an inverted list.

The effect of this filtering is to make it progressively more difficult for accumulators to be added or updated. For the first terms processed—that is, the rare terms—the value of S_{max} is small and the value of I_t is large, so that most documents are considered. As S_{max} rises and I_t falls, the thresholds rise, until, in the limit, all $f_{d,t}$ values are less than f_{add}, so that processing an inverted list has no effect on accumulator values. The constants should be chosen so that the discarded information would, if included, have minimal impact on the final ordering. Typical values are $c_{add} = 0.005$ and $c_{ins} = 0.07$. The filtering technique is described in detail elsewhere [10].

The main saving yielded by this technique is a sharp reduction in the number of accumulators. This is illustrated for the Wall Street Journal database (described in Section 5) in Figure 1. On the horizontal axis we vary c_{ins}, which affects the number of accumulators; for example, c_{ins} of 0.07 results in roughly 4,000 accumulators, whereas c_{ins} of 0 results in every document having an accumulator, or almost 200,000 accumulators in total. The vertical axis is retrieval effectiveness, which remains high even when the number of accumulators is small; c_{ins} of about 0.02 results in 20,000 accumulators and better retrieval effectiveness than having 200,000 accumulators, and even at 4,000 accumulators retrieval effectiveness is still high. The technique also yields a small saving of cpu time, as we do not have to compute the $sim_{q,d,t}$ values for document identifiers that are filtered out.

However, the filtering technique as it stands does not yield substantial savings in either disk traffic or cpu time. To perform a ranking we still have to fetch and process the whole inverted list for every query term, comparing $f_{d,t}$ for every document to the current threshold values. For the long inverted lists only a few $f_{d,t}$ values pass the thresholds, so that most of the time spent processing these lists has no effect on the final ranking. The main topic of this paper is avoiding this waste of time, and our techniques for doing so are given in the next section.

4 Inverted file structures for filtering

Inverted lists are usually sorted by document identifier. We propose that inverted lists instead be sorted by decreasing $f_{d,t}$, so that the time wasted processing small $f_{d,t}$ values can be entirely avoided. First, once an $f_{d,t}$ value is encountered that is below the threshold, processing of the inverted list can stop. Second, if the inverted list is longer than a disk block, only one block of the list needs to be retrieved at a time: since the tail of a long inverted list will contain only small $f_{d,t}$ values, it is unlikely to be required, and there is no cost to leaving it on disk until requested.

Unfortunately such sorting is incompatible with compression of inverted lists. If the document identifiers are unsorted, run-lengths cannot be taken and the index size will dramatically increase. Besides the impact on space requirements, an immediate effect of this increase is in the real time required to compute a ranking: inverted lists become more expensive to retrieve from disk. For some queries this penalty will outweigh the gain of re-ordering.

Thus it is crucial that we find some way of maintaining the compression performance. A simple way of having some compression while sorting inverted lists by decreasing $f_{d,t}$ is to, within a re-ordered inverted list, sort the document identifiers with the same $f_{d,t}$ value. Inverted lists then consist of a series of *sequences*, where each sequence consists of: a frequency; the number of document identifiers in the sequence; and the identifiers themselves. For a sequence of several documents with the same frequency there is a potential space saving, as the frequency only has to be stored once, and the identifiers in a sequence can be sorted, allowing run-lengths to be taken and hence allowing compression. For example, the inverted list illustrated in Section 2 would be represented as

5, 1, (16)	4, 1, (32)	3, 1, (5)	2, 3, (9,3,13)	1, 1, (21)

in which each box is a sequence, the first number is the frequency, the second is the number of documents in the sequence, and the expression in brackets is the documents in that sequence. The expression $(9, 3, 13)$ represents the document numbers 9, 12, and 25 after run-lengths have been taken—these are the documents that contain the term with frequency 2.

However, the above method is unlikely to yield such good compression as for inverted lists that are sorted by identifier. One reason for increase in the size of the compressed inverted file is poorer compression of document identifiers within sequences. A run-length of k can typically be compressed to a little over $\log_2 k$ bits; since the average run-length between identifiers in a sequence is larger than the average run-length in the sorted inverted list, compression performance degrades.

Another reason for increase in size is that, although many sequences are only one or two documents long, the per-sequence parameters still have to be stored. The problem is most acute for higher frequency terms—a typical long inverted list will refer to many documents that each have one or two occurrences of the term, and a small number of documents that each have many occurrences of the term. That is, for the high frequencies, many sequences will have only one or two documents and the overheads of representing a short sequence (the need to store the number of documents and the loss of compression due to the large run-lengths) are high. For the low frequencies, the sequences are longer, but a small frequency can usually be represented in one or two bits, so the saving may not be large.

These problems can be overcome by selective application of the idea of sequences. As we have seen, there are advantages to the long sequences of low frequencies, but short sequences are inefficient. It follows that an efficient form of inverted list is an initial sequence of ⟨document identifier, frequency⟩ pairs, for the high frequencies that would lead to short sequences, followed by a series of sequences, one for each of the low frequencies. The structure within such an inverted list is quite complex, requiring several parameters to describe the components and their position within the list; we must be careful to ensure that the cost of storing these parameters does not outweigh the potential gain.

We propose the following structure for representing an inverted list. Each list is split into n sequences (the problem of choice of n is discussed later). The *leading sequence* is of ⟨document identifier, frequency⟩ pairs, for all documents with $f_{d,t} \geq n$. Each remaining sequence is of documents of some frequency $f_{d,t} < n$, and the sequences are ordered by decreasing frequency. Within each sequence, the entries are sorted by document identifier. Within the leading sequence, rather than storing $f_{d,t}$ values we store $f_{d,t} - n + 1$. The minimum value of n is 1, in which case the whole list is stored in one sequence.

The reason that such a scheme should be effective is that, for even the longer inverted lists of more common terms, the distribution of $f_{d,t}$ values is highly skew. Thus, in the above scheme, each of the low $f_{d,t}$ values would have its own sequence, which would be long; whereas the high $f_{d,t}$ values would share a sequence.

At the start of each inverted list that has been grouped into sequences we store a *list descriptor*, which is a string of n bits, each bit of which indicates presence or absence of a corresponding sequence. The frequency of a sequence is determined by the ordinal number of the bit, so that the number of sequences in an inverted list is limited by the size of the list descriptor n. This method means that, for all but the leading sequence, frequencies are not explicitly stored, and also means that we do not have to store the number of documents for an empty sequence; that is, in our code for the number of documents in a sequence, we do not have to allow for zero. An example of this descriptor method of storing inverted lists, using $n = 3$, is as follows.

| 111 | ⟨5, 1⟩⟨11, 3⟩⟨16, 2⟩ | 9,3,13 | 21 |

This example corresponds to the inverted list shown above. The first box is a string of bits indicating that each of the three sequences is present. The second box is the leading sequence and the third and fourth boxes are the sequences for frequencies 2 and 1 respectively.

The method of re-ordering inverted lists into sequences of documents of the same frequency is not the only possible solution to the problem of ignoring the majority of document identifiers. Moffat and Zobel have proposed that inverted lists be ordered by identifier, but also contain pointers into the inverted list at evenly-spaced intervals, to allow the search to "skip" sections of the list without decompression [8]. Such skipping provides the benefit of random access (usually impossible in the context of compression) while maintaining reasonable compression performance. In conjunction with their scheme of a small, fixed number of accumulators, the skipping reduces cpu time without degrading retrieval effectiveness; as we show in Section 5, however, their gain is limited compared to that given by the scheme we describe here.

In the remainder of this section we consider how, for inverted lists compressed with the descriptor method, to optimise for index size and query evaluation time.

4.1 Indexes with fixed-size descriptors

Consider the effect of having the same n for all inverted lists, and of the inverted file that results from varying this n. As we increase n, we increase the number of sequences in each inverted list. There are two consequences. On the one hand, increasing the number of sequences allows storage of more document identifiers without their corresponding frequencies. On the other hand, we have to store a sequence length for each sequence; and the length of each sequence decreases, which implies an increase in the average run-length and, hence, a worse rate of compression. We found that, for our test database, these phenomena are almost in balance, so that the difference in the sizes of compressed inverted lists (omitting list descriptors) does not exceed 1% for different sizes of descriptors. However, the descriptors are a significant overhead on the size of the inverted file, and as n increases they quickly become unacceptably large.

We have argued that the small n implies a small inverted file. But now consider the problem of a proper choice of n from the point of view of speed of query evaluation. The essence of the filtering method for fast query evaluation is to stop processing documents (ordered by decreasing $f_{d,t}$) as soon as a document with $f_{d,t} < f_{add}$ is found. Suppose that we are processing an inverted list which has a non-empty leading sequence. If the value of filter f_{add} is less than the minimal frequency n of documents in the leading sequence, we process the whole of the leading sequence, and possibly some subsequent sequences, and for all documents processed we update their accumulators; thus no decoding time is wasted. But if f_{add} is more than n we must process the whole of the leading sequence, even though some of the documents in the sequence will be ignored. This can be a substantial overhead on processing time, particularly for common terms, whose inverted lists can have long leading sequences.

So, using a fixed value of n, to achieve fast query evaluation we have to increase the size of n, which will however increase the size of the inverted file. The other possibility to allow n to vary between lists, which we will now consider.

4.2 Indexes with variable-sized descriptors

Consider the problem of choice of n to minimise index size, where n is allowed to vary between inverted lists. A simple method would be to, for each list, set n

to 1, compress the list; then increment n and compress it again; and so on until a minimum is found. The existence of a minimum is guaranteed, as the size of the list descriptor will, in the limit, be dominant. (Note that, in a scheme with varying n, in addition to the list descriptor the value of n must be stored in each list.) However, such a scheme is impractical, as the computational cost of finding the optimal value of n would be prohibitively high. As we do not have any more efficient mechanism for identifying the optimal n for each list, we are forced to investigate heuristics for choosing n.

The scheme we use for choosing n is based on the observation that using a separate sequence for each $f_{d,t}$ value, particularly when $f_{d,t}$ is high, is expensive because of the per-sequence overheads. For our method of compression, we have observed experimentally that the overheads are compensated by a better compression rate once the number of identifiers in a sequence is sufficiently large; around 30 identifiers is typical. Let us call the number of identifiers at which compression gains outweigh overheads the *sequence threshold* T.

To achieve good compression, we should avoid sequences of a length less than T. We determine the size of n for the inverted list for a term t using the following procedure. Initially, for each distinct value of $f_{d,t}$, we find the number of documents that contain t this number of times. Then we find the highest $f_{d,t}$ for which the number of documents is at least T. Let us denote this frequency as f_T. We then create the inverted list by having per-frequency sequences for frequencies from 1 to f_T and a leading sequence that contains documents with all remaining frequencies. The value of n for such an inverted list is $f_T + 1$. For example, if T is 1 then every frequency in every inverted list will have its own sequence, and the value of n for an inverted list will be the highest $f_{d,t}$ value in that list. On the other hand, for (say) a database of a million documents, if T is 100,000 then most inverted lists will have n of 1, and thus have only one sequence; but the inverted lists for the commonest terms will probably have several sequences, because these terms would in a typical database occur in almost every document.

The above method of constructing the inverted file allows us to achieve two aims simultaneously. On one hand, we avoid creation of inverted lists containing many short sequences that cannot be effectively compressed, and similarly avoid long list descriptors. On the other hand, we are able to keep the leading sequences short and, hence, have fast query evaluation.

We believe that, with this scheme, the costs of query evaluation will be sublinear in the size of the document database. Suppose for example that the database doubles in size. Then the number of documents in a typical inverted list will also double, but the number of frequencies with at least T documents will grow, taking documents that would otherwise be in the leading sequence; as a consequence the length of the leading sequence will grow more slowly than the database. The amount of index that must be fetched and processed to compute a ranking should, similarly, grow slowly, particularly since the rarest query term should become relatively more rare as documents are inserted, thus lifting both the importance of the term and the values of the filters. We are currently conducting experiments to test this theory.

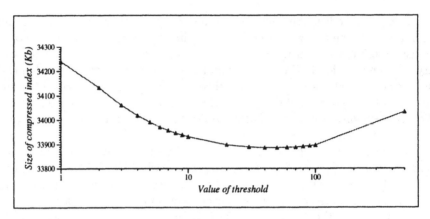

Fig. 2. Size of compressed index for different values of sequence threshold

5 Experimental results

The database we have used in our experiments is a database of articles from the Wall Street Journal, extracted from the TIPSTER collection for the TREC project [9]. Its parameters are shown in Table 1. The value of this database is that it has a set of queries with manual relevance judgements, which can be used to determine retrieval effectiveness. We have used queries 1–100, after removing SGML markup and stemming words to remove suffixes such as "ed" and "ing".

Size	532 Mb
Number of documents	173,255
Number of distinct terms	158,245
Average number of documents per term	255
Average $f_{d,t}$ value	2.17
Average maximal $f_{d,t}$ value	3.79

Table 1. Parameters of the Wall Street Journal

Using this database, we built a series of indexes using different values of the sequence threshold T, to experiment with the effect of different values of T on performance. In all of these experiments we used the filter values $c_{ins} = 0.07$ and $c_{add} = 0.005$, as these gave good retrieval effectiveness while requiring only a small number of accumulators. All times and volumes of disk traffic are per query, averaged over the 100 TREC queries, on a Sun SPARC 10, model 512, using local disks.

The size of an inverted file is shown as a function of the sequence threshold T in Figure 2. At one extreme, assigning T to 1 forces creation of a separate sequence for every frequency with at least one document. Inverted lists in such a file do not have leading sequences. This leads to an increase in index size because of the shortness of the sequences and because the descriptors are longer. Large

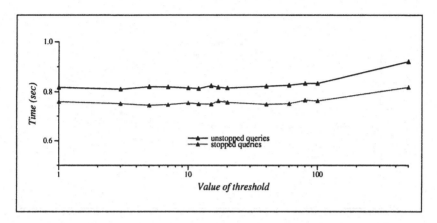

Fig. 3. Query evaluation time for different values of sequence threshold

values of T also lead to a gradual increase in inverted file size, as the leading sequences becomes long and we have to compress many large frequencies in these sequences. Note, however, that the size of a conventional compressed inverted file, in which documents are ordered by their identifiers, is 35.4 Mb; that is, even the largest inverted file created by our technique is smaller than the usual compressed inverted file [7, 13]. This surprising result is because, in our method, the number of stored frequencies is far less than in the usual method; this saving more than compensates for the decline in compression due to greater run-lengths and storage of sequence parameters.

The upper line in Figure 3 shows average query evaluation time for inverted files built using different values of T. The time is almost constant for small values of T since the difference in size of leading sequences is small. Performance deteriorates slightly for large values of T because, during processing of common terms, we have to process long leading sequences, searching for the documents that pass the filter and ignoring the rest. Even so, these times compare well to those of conventional compressed inverted lists, which require 5.82 cpu seconds; our methods require less than one sixth of this figure. Figure 3 also shows the time for queries after stop-words (that is, closed-class words that do not convey information, such as "the") have been removed; this removal can be justified by the fact that they have little impact on retrieval effectiveness. The times are very similar, demonstrating that the filtering method almost completely excludes stop-words from consideration. That is, our method obviates the need to manually select a list of stop-words. For conventional compressed inverted lists, the query evaluation time for stopped queries is 2.91 seconds.

The volume of inverted lists fetched and decompressed during query evaluation is shown in Figure 4, again for both stopped and unstopped queries. Inverted files built with small values of T provide an almost constant amount of decompressed data. This is because, on the one hand, the smaller the value of T the smaller the leading sequence and, hence, the smaller the number of documents which have to be decompressed but ignored; on the other hand, small

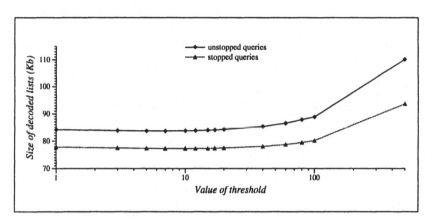

Fig. 4. Volume of inverted lists decoded during query evaluation

values of T give rise to inverted lists consisting of many small sequences, so that the overheads for storing sequence parameters increase and the same number of compressed identifiers occupy more space. For small values of T these phenomena are almost in balance, producing a plateau in the graph. On the other hand, inverted files built with large values of T have long leading sequences, leading to a steep increase in the amount of data that is fetched and processed.

Re-ordered inverted files require far less data to be fetched from disk than do conventional compressed inverted files. For unstopped queries, the amount of data fetched was 731 Kb; for stopped queries, it was 422 Kb. In contrast, using our technique the volume of index fetched was, for T of 10, 84 Kb and 77 Kb respectively.

Overall, performance is excellent across a wide range of T values from perhaps 8 to 80, and for all T values performance is better than for conventional compressed inverted files. Retrieval effectiveness is maintained; index size is reduced; cpu time is smaller by a factor of six; and disk traffic is smaller by a factor of eight. We expect that these figures would improve further with growth in the database size.

These results compare well to those of the "skipping" scheme of Moffat and Zobel [8], who on a larger database are only able to halve cpu time, and actually increase disk traffic slightly. However, their scheme is also applicable to Boolean queries, for which they achieve much greater performance gains; whereas we would expect that Boolean query performance would be largely unchanged with our indexes, which are designed purely for ranking.

5.1 Uncompressed inverted files

Our structure for inverted files, where documents in inverted lists are ordered by decreasing $f_{d,t}$, would also be effective in systems that use uncompressed inverted files. Using this structure yields significant reduction in the size of inverted files. Typically, a ⟨document number, frequency⟩ pair occupies 6 bytes:

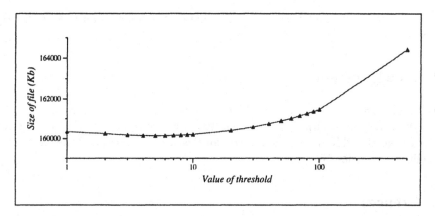

Fig. 5. Size of uncompressed index for different values of sequence threshold

4 bytes for storage of the document number and 2 bytes for storage of the term frequency. Using our structure of an inverted file allows decrease in the size of the inverted file from 238 Mb for the basic structure to 160 Mb; that is, we can almost completely avoid storing $f_{d,t}$ values. The size of the uncompressed inverted file for different values of the sequence threshold is shown in Figure 5.

6 Summary

We have shown how to make dramatic reductions in the major costs of ranking a query on a large document database—that is, in disk traffic, cpu time, and memory usage—without degrading retrieval effectiveness. The basis of these reductions is the filtering method, in which only the documents with high within-document frequency are considered as candidate answers; it is this technique that reduces memory usage, as having fewer candidates means that fewer accumulators are required to store information about these candidates.

The reductions in disk traffic and cpu time are based on the simple observation that, by ordering inverted lists by decreasing within-document frequency, only the first part of each list will contain high frequencies, and so the rest can be ignored. This simple observation, however, is complex to translate into practice, as the reordered lists cannot be compressed by existing techniques; the loss of compression can easily outweigh gains yielded by the reordering. We have nonetheless managed to compress reordered inverted lists, by, among documents of the same frequency, ordering by identifier, and for the higher, less common frequencies, not using frequency ordering at all.

For our test database, these techniques maintain retrieval effectiveness; reduce memory requirements from 173,255 to 4,000 accumulators; reduce the quantity of data requested from disk from 731 Kb to 83 Kb; and reduce cpu time from 5.8 to 0.8 seconds. There is also a small reduction in index size, from 35.4 Mb to 33.9 Mb, which is already a massive saving on the 238 Mb required for an uncompressed index. Together, these dramatic improvements allow ranking to be performed much faster, and on much smaller machines, than was previously possible.

Acknowledgements

We would like to thank Alistair Moffat. This research was supported by the Collaborative Information Technology Research Institute, the Key Centre for Knowledge-Based Systems, the Australian Research Council, and the Centre for Intelligent Decision Systems.

References

1. T.C. Bell, A. Moffat, C.G. Nevill-Manning, I.H. Witten, and J. Zobel. Data compression in full-text retrieval systems. *Journal of the American Society for Information Science*, 44(9):508–531, October 1993.
2. C. Buckley and A.F. Lewit. Optimisation of inverted vector searches. In *Proc. ACM-SIGIR International Conference on Research and Development in Information Retrieval*, pages 97–110, Montreal, Canada, June 1985.
3. P. Elias. Universal codeword sets and representations of the integers. *IEEE Transactions on Information Theory*, IT-21(2):194–203, March 1975.
4. W.B. Frakes and R. Baeza-Yates, editors. *Information Retrieval: Data Structures and Algorithms*. Prentice-Hall, New Jersey, 1992.
5. D. Harman and G. Candela. Retrieving records from a gigabyte of text on a minicomputer using statistical ranking. *Journal of the American Society for Information Science*, 41(8):581–589, 1990.
6. D. Lucarella. A document retrieval system based upon nearest neighbour searching. *Journal of Information Science*, 14:25–33, 1988.
7. A. Moffat and J. Zobel. Parameterised compression for sparse bitmaps. In *Proc. ACM-SIGIR International Conference on Research and Development in Information Retrieval*, pages 274–285, Copenhagen, Denmark, June 1992. ACM Press.
8. A. Moffat and J. Zobel. Fast ranking in limited space. In *Proc. IEEE International Conference on Data Engineering*, pages 428–437, February 1994.
9. National Institute of Standards and Technology. *Proc. Text Retrieval Conference (TREC)*, Washington, November 1992. Special Publication 500-207.
10. M. Persin. Document filtering for fast ranking. In *Proc. ACM-SIGIR International Conference on Research and Development in Information Retrieval*, 1994. (To appear).
11. G. Salton. *Automatic Text Processing: The Transformation, Analysis, and Retrieval of Information by Computer*. Addison-Wesley, Reading, MA, 1989.
12. G. Salton and M.J. McGill. *Introduction to Modern Information Retrieval*. McGraw-Hill, New York, 1983.
13. J. Zobel, A. Moffat, and R. Sacks-Davis. An efficient indexing technique for full-text database systems. In *Proc. International Conference on Very Large Databases*, pages 352–362, Vancouver, Canada, August 1992.

Text / Relational Database Management Systems: Harmonizing SQL and SGML

G. E. Blake, M. P. Consens, P. Kilpeläinen, P.-Å. Larson,
T. Snider, and F. W. Tompa

UW Centre for the New OED and Text Research,
University of Waterloo, Waterloo, Ontario, Canada N2L 3G1

Abstract. Combined text and relational database support is increasingly recognized as an emerging need of industry, spanning applications requiring text fields as parts of their data (e.g., for customer support) to those augmenting primary text resources by conventional relational data (e.g., for publication control). In this paper, we propose extensions to SQL that provide flexible and efficient access to structured text described by SGML. We also propose an architecture to support a text/relational database management system as a federated database environment, where component databases are accessed via "agents": SQL agents that translate standard or extended SQL queries into vendor-specific dialects, and text agents that process text sub-queries on full-text search engines.

1 Introduction

The application of database technology is seen as essential to the operation of a conventional business enterprise. However, there is a universe of business information, namely text, which is currently stored, accessed, and manipulated in an *ad hoc* fashion with none of the consistency and discipline of the database approach. Environments supporting both text and relational data are implemented through application programs within which separate repositories are accessed explicitly. Not only is this inconvenient for application programmers, but the disjointness of the data impedes data administrators' efforts to ensure data consistency. Furthermore, the difficult task of query optimization becomes the burden of every application programmer and the benefits of database transparency are impossible to realize. Ongoing work at the University of Waterloo has laid the foundations necessary for building an alternative to this disorder and lost potential.

The objective of the research is to design and implement a multidatabase system supporting text and relational data (T/RDBMS) that will better address the needs of these enterprises. We start with the requirement that the application program interface must be an extension of both SQL, the industry standard for relational data [ISO90], and SGML, the industry standard for structured text [Gol90, ISO86].

The T/RDBMS can be built as a federated database system with the actual data stored and managed by standard (relational and text) data management systems. Queries expressed in terms of the external data model are parsed, and the relational and text components identified. Query strategies can then be analyzed so that an efficient access plan can be identified. This plan can subsequently be executed under the control of a database monitor, which distributes parts of the query task to component database systems as needed, and integrates the results before they are returned to the application.

Several approaches to text management have been proposed by others. Customized document storage management systems, including text-specific access languages, have been implemented on top of commercial relational database systems (see, for example, [Wei85, Mar91]); these systems are incapable of simultaneously supporting conventional data. Alternatively, text storage has been provided by conventional systems, where long data fields are used for large objects or "blobs" [Bil92], but operators to support text manipulation have not usually been provided and these systems do not support SGML-like structured text.

At least three systems have been proposed within which structured text can be fragmented into relational fields and SQL queries can be applied against the resulting text subfields in conjunction with record-oriented data. The Air Transport Association has proposed the Structured Full-text Query Language (SFQL) as an extension to SQL incorporating SGML-based formatted text types [ATA91]. More recently, Oracle Corporation's SQL*TextRetrieval Version 2 provides a text retrieval product, supported by inverted indexing and a thesaurus capability, to be used in conjunction with the Oracle DBMS [Ora92]. Similalry, IDI's BASISplus supports structured full-text retrieval in conjunction with relational database functionality [Sey92]. Although each system provides a mechanism to assemble larger text units from the constituents, this is not provided within SQL. Thus, for example, such larger units cannot be presented as fields within an SQL view.

In order to maintain structured text in a single relational field, researchers at Australia's Collaborative Information Technology Research Institute have designed and implemented a nested relational database system (Atlas) and an extended SQL language to provide text support [Sac92]. Similarly there is a recent proposal to extend an object-oriented SQL dialect to support SGML documents [Chr94]. In both these approaches, the relational model has been extended to encompass structured data of arbitrary type, and subsequently structured text has been supported as a special case. We instead wish to explore a direct extension of SQL to support structured text in the hope that our proposals will suit text, and particularly SGML applications, more closely.

2 Example Text Database

To illustrate our proposed text extensions to SQL, we will use a simplified version of a database management system required for an encyclopedia, and describe our extensions in terms of this example.

Such a database requires management of both administrative records and text. Information about contributors and their articles, including tracking the development of the articles, must be maintained. In addition text management involves key-word generation, cross-reference maintenance, maintaining consistency of style, and maintaining consistency of bibliographic data.

Standard SQL type queries against this database are to be supported, to extract contributor addresses in order to generate address labels or to extract information about articles having due dates in a given time range, and to check information about payments to contributors. In addition, queries are to be expected against the bibliographic data using a variety of criteria based on authors, dates, and number of citations. Similarly, queries posed against the content of articles must be supported.

The articles themselves contain primarily prose text, but consider the form of the bibliography. Bibliographic data can be presented in a list format, a prose format or a combination of these two. For example, the bibliography for the article entitled "Canada, History of" in *The New Encyclopæaedia Britannica — Macropaedia* Vol. 3, p. 751, reads:

W.L. MORTON, *The Kingdom of Canada*, 2nd ed. (1969), is the fullest one-volume history and the most traditional.... To understand the place of the colonies that became Canada in the British Empire, the following are most useful: H.A. INNIS, *The Fur Trade in Canada*, 2nd ed. (1956), and *The Code Fisheries*, rev. ed. (1954);... The following works both introduce and analyze the development of the remaining British colonies to self-governing communities and their union in confederation. W.S. MACNUTT combines in a single narrative the histories of the Atlantic provinces in *The Atlantic Provinces, the Emergence of Colonial Society, 1712-1857*(1965). FERNAND OUELLET in his *Histoire 'economique et sociale du Qu'ebec, 1760-1850* (1966; Eng. trans. in prep.), applies with great success the demographic method of French historiography to the little known domestic development of that province....

A requirement for this database is that we must be able to retrieve the articles and bibliographies in their text form as crafted by the encyclopedia's contributors and editors. Thus, for example, we must be able to deal with the bibliography *as a single structured textual unit* and yet extract individual authors or citations as structured texts.

To illustrate our proposed language extensions, we will define one simplistic table with the following schema.

Encyclopedia

aid	title	cid	req_date	req_wc	due_date	article	biblio

where *aid* is the article identification, *title* is the proposed article title, *cid* is the contributor identification, *req_date* is the date the article was solicited from the author, *req_wc* is the requested word count for the article, *due_date* is the requested date for the article's completion, *article* is the text of the completed article, and *biblio* is the accompanying bibliography. For the sake of brevity and clarity, we will describe constructs in the DDL and DML in terms of this example; formal definitions and more detailed explanations can be found elsewhere [Bla94].

3   Data Definition Language

In our example the *article* and *biblio* fields are of a new data type TEXT. Fields of this type contain structured text and have an associated grammar to describe their content. Queries involving this new data type may use this grammar. The grammar for any of these TEXT fields must therefore be made known to the database.

The following SGML Document Type Declarations (DTDs) describe the grammar of *article* and *biblio* TEXT fields in our example. Note that the article may consist of a cross reference to another article or may itself be a complete article. The body of the article is followed by some keywords and some summary information that contains data such as birth place and dates of the article's subject, as appropriate. The bibliography allows free text to be intermingled with bibliographic fields as desired.

```
<! DOCTYPE article_information [
    <! ELEMENT article_information -- (detailed_article|xref)>
    <! ELEMENT xref -- ("see", article_title)>
    <! ELEMENT detailed_article -- (title,paragraph+,keywords*,summary)>
    <! ELEMENT summary -- (birth|death|parents|occupation|children)*>
    <! ELEMENT (title,keywords,paragraph,article_title) -- PCDATA>
    <! ELEMENT (birth,death,parents,occupation,children) -- PCDATA>
]>


<! DOCTYPE biblio_information [
    <! ELEMENT biblio_information -- (citations)>
    <! ELEMENT citations -- (citation+, (";" | ".")*>
    <! ELEMENT citation -- (author|ref|date|free_text)+>
    <! ELEMENT ref -- ( "in"?,work,edition?) >
    <! ELEMENT date -- ( "(", PCDATA , ")" )>
    <! ELEMENT (author,free_text,work,edition) -- PCDATA>
]>
```

To make known the grammar for any defined TEXT fields, we use a CREATE GRAMMAR statement, which incorporates standard SGML notation for this purpose.

```
CREATE GRAMMAR (<! ENTITY %example SYSTEM "/usr/dtd/art_inf"> %example;);
```

where the article-information DTD is assumed to be stored in the file named "/usr/dtd/art_inf". Such a statement informs the system where an SGML document entity is located. The document entity contains the SGML declaration (if necessary) and a prolog containing a DTD. A similar statement is required to introduce the grammar for the biblio-information DTD.

Now we can define the database table in the following CREATE TABLE statement.

```
CREATE TABLE Encyclopedia (
            aid INTEGER, title STRING, cid INTEGER,
            req_date DATE, req_wc INTEGER, due_date DATE,
            article TEXT GRAMMAR article_information,
            biblio TEXT GRAMMAR biblio_information
            PRIMARY KEY (aid)
            );
```

This statement defines a table called *Encyclopedia* with eight columns. Two are of the new type TEXT, for which we must give the name of an associated grammar.

In this case the primary key is an INTEGER column. However, the primary key for a table may instead be declared to be a subfield described by a nonterminal in the grammar associated with one of the TEXT columns.

We may want to extract certain subfields of TEXT columns in order to define a view. Consider, for example,

```
CREATE VIEW cited_auths AS
    (SELECT aid, title, biblio..author FROM Encyclopedia);
```

which defines a three column table containing the article's identification, title and cited authors. The semantics of elements such as biblio..author appearing in a SELECT are given in the next section.

In summary, the CREATE TABLE statement has been extended to accept a new data type for a column, namely TEXT. Unlike previous proposals, the type TEXT refers to *structured* searchable text, with an associated grammar. To comply with emerging text standards, we assume the grammar to be an SGML grammar, either one described by a DTD or derived as a sub-grammar of a given DTD, rooted at one of its elements. Elements of the grammar will also be available to be used in a query to refine a text search or to recover information about the grammar itself. Finally, primary and foreign keys may refer to data within a nonterminal in the grammar associated with a TEXT column.

4 Data Manipulation Language

In our attempts to combine the concepts of text and relational databases we have taken the approach that the text is embedded in relations rather than the other way around. Thus in our DDL we allow a field in a relation to be of type TEXT (i.e., structured text), with an associated grammar. In the DML we continue on this course: operations are typically applied to one structured field at a time.

For the purposes of the DML, an instance of a structured text field is considered to be a contiguous text string and a parse tree. Previous authors have proposed extensions to traditional SQL operators to include operations on *unstructured* text fields, in particular concatenation and pattern matching [ATA91, Ora92, Sac92]. For now we will accept those extensions and propose an operator and alternative notation for *structured* text manipulation suitable for extending SQL.

4.1 Examples of the Proposed DML

Before we explain the details of our proposed DML, we give two examples of its use. For convenience, we introduce a notation for projecting text subfields from attributes of type TEXT. In the next section we introduce a mechanism for selecting nodes in a parse tree, and we introduce a new operator, EXPAND, to extract some data from the paths to those nodes into a relation. Once we have described EXPAND, the semantics of this first notation will be formally specified, after which we will return to these sample queries.

In our example database we might want to answer the question

Who contributed articles for which the proposed titles do not match the titles included in the article's body?

With our extended SQL, we can formulate this query as

```
SELECT cid, aid
FROM Encyclopedia
WHERE title ≠ article..title;
```

Within the TEXT attribute named "article", title is a text subfield identified by an element of the associated SGML grammar. The dot notation gives direct access to such fields, and is available anywhere within the SELECT statement.

As a second question, consider

Find proposed titles and lengths of long articles on Canada.

Using our DML the answer can be obtained with the query

```
SELECT title, req_wc
FROM Encyclopedia
WHERE req_wc > 5000 AND SOME article..keywords CONTAINS "Canada";
```

Notice that an article having more than one keyword is selected if any one matches the given search string.

4.2   Converting Parse Trees to Relations

For some queries we wish to convert parts of a TEXT column into a relation so that we have the full power of SQL to manipulate subfields. An instance of a structured text field is a contiguous text string together with a parse tree [Gon87]. In order to minimize the size of the relation formed from this parse tree we wish to select nodes in the parse tree to indicate the components of the text that we wish to retain.

Consider the first example above. We wish to compare the value in one attribute against the value stored within a subfield of another attribute. To extract the title element from the article column, we can use the EXPAND operator as follows:

```
SELECT cid, aid
FROM Encyclopedia
WHERE title ≠ (EXPAND article INTO title AS contrib_title BY
                (SELECT nodeid FROM TEXT_NODES WHERE genid = "title"));
```

The EXPAND statement processes a parse tree and returns a relation. In this example, because one field is named between INTO and BY, the resulting relation will have a single column, populated by string(s) subsumed by node(s) of type title but renaming the single column as contrib_title.

Since in general we might not want to extract every node of a given type, the body of EXPAND consists of a SELECT statement that identifies desired nodes in the parse tree. So as to allow node selections to be written in full SQL, we define three *virtual* tables as follows:

TEXT_NODES (nodeid, genid, content)
TEXT_ATTRIBUTES (nodeid, attr, value)
TEXT_STRUCTURE (a_nodeid, d_nodeid)

where TEXT_NODES contains one tuple per node in the parse tree, consisting of a unique nodeid, the type of node ("generic identifier" in SGML), and the TEXT content subsumed by that node; TEXT_ATTRIBUTES relates SGML's attribute-value pairs to corresponding nodes; and TEXT_STRUCTURE contains nodeid pairs representing all ancestor-descendant relationships in the parse tree. Because these tables merely provide a notation to access data of type TEXT, the values for nodeid are undefined outside the EXPAND statement; within the EXPAND statement, however, nodeids can be compared for equality or for relative magnitude, where $n_1 < n_2$ if n_1 occurs first in a preorder traversal of the parse tree.

We illustrate the use of these tables with several examples, each returning a set of nodeids for selected nodes from the parse tree:

- *Select all nodes of type "paragraph" and containing substring "Canada".*

```
SELECT nodeid
FROM TEXT_NODES
WHERE genid = "paragraph" AND content CONTAINS "Canada"
```

Pattern matching uses the clause CONTAINS from previous SQL extensions.

- *Select all nodes having an ancestor of type "chapter".*

```
SELECT d_nodeid
FROM TEXT_STRUCTURE, TEXT_NODES
WHERE a_nodeid = nodeid AND genid = "chapter"
```

- *Select all nodes that have children.* (i.e., mark all *structured* fragments.)

```
SELECT DISTINCT a_nodeid
FROM NODE_STRUCTURE
```

- *Select all nodes where the parent has an (SGML) attribute of type status and value "Obs."*

```
SELECT d_nodeid
FROM TEXT_STRUCTURE
GROUP BY d_nodeid
HAVING max(a_nodeid) IN SELECT nodeid
                        FROM NODE_ATTRIBUTES
                        WHERE attr = "status" AND value = "Obs."
```

Having selected desired nodes in a parse tree, users might wish to extract any values along the paths from the root to those nodes. For example, having identified nodes corresponding to certain cited authors, a user might wish to extract complete citations as well as the authors' names. A corresponding subquery would be

```
EXPAND biblio INTO citation, author BY SELECT ...
```

where the SELECT clause identifies nodeids for nodes corresponding to relevant authors. If the SGML grammar defines the attribute "status" for elements with generic identifier "citation", the value of the attribute can also be extracted into a separate column:

```
EXPAND biblio INTO citation [status], author BY SELECT ...
```

In general, the EXPAND operator takes the form

```
EXPAND <col_reference>
INTO ([<node_name> [ <attr_list> ] AS] <col_name>)+
BY <select_stmt>
```

where attr_list is "[" ([<attr_name> AS] <col_name>)+ "]" . Thus several nodes' contents and their attribute values can be extracted, and each can be renamed.

To populate the resulting relation, we trace the paths from the root to each selected node in the parse tree and form one tuple for each such path (i.e., one tuple per selected node). Specifically, for each selected path, nodes on the path are examined in order from the root to the leaf and the node name list on the EXPAND line is scanned from left to right: as a node of the same type as specified in the list is found, its *content* (of type TEXT) is transferred to the associated column in the row and any designated attribute *value* is extracted as well. Any fields in the generated row for which there is no match along the path is given a NULL value.

4.3   Examples of SQL Queries Using EXPAND

For our example we continue to use the sample bibliographic database.

Find the article identification, title, contributor, and bibliography for entries where the bibliography has more than one citation but all are from the same author.

```
SELECT aid, title, cid, biblio
FROM Encyclopedia
WHERE 1 <SELECT COUNT(citation)
        FROM (EXPAND biblio INTO citation BY
            SELECT nodeid FROM TEXT_NODES WHERE genid = "citation")
AND 1 = SELECT COUNT(DISTINCT author)
        FROM (EXPAND biblio INTO author BY
            SELECT nodeid FROM TEXT_NODES WHERE genid = "author");
```

The EXPAND statement forms the basis of the dot operator used to simplify access to text subfields as in the examples shown earlier. For the expression $F..a_1..a_2...a_{n-1}..a_n$ describing a path in the parse tree of an instance of a TEXT field F in some table, we give the semantics:

```
EXPAND F INTO a_n BY

SELECT nodeid FROM TEXT_NODES, TEXT_STRUCTURE
WHERE nodeid = d_nodeid AND genid = "a_n"
AND a_nodeid IN (

            SELECT nodeid FROM TEXT_NODES, TEXT_STRUCTURE
            WHERE nodeid = d_nodeid AND genid = "a_{n-1}"
            AND a_nodeid IN (

        ...

                    SELECT nodeid FROM TEXT_NODES, TEXT_STRUCTURE
                    WHERE nodeid = d_nodeid AND genid = "a_1"

    ) ...)
```

Extraction of attribute value b from the selected node can be simply specified as $F..a_1..a_2...a_{n-1}..a_n[b]$.

Consider again the second example from Section 4.1:

```
SELECT title, req_wc
FROM Encyclopedia
WHERE req_wc > 5000 AND SOME article..keywords CONTAINS "Canada";
```

This is now well-defined as:

```
SELECT title, req_wc
FROM Encyclopedia
WHERE req_wc > 5000
AND SOME (EXPAND article INTO keywords BY
          SELECT nodeid FROM TEXT_NODES WHERE genid = "keywords")
          CONTAINS "Canada";
```

Complete semantics for uses of the dot notation throughout the SELECT statement (including in the SELECT and FROM clauses) have also been defined [Bla94].

5   Federated Database Architecture

Potential clients of the text/relational database management system have typically relied on conventional relational databases for conventional needs. Therefore we propose not to develop a wholly new database management system, but instead to integrate commercial relational database systems and commercial full-text search engines. To this end we define the following architecture:

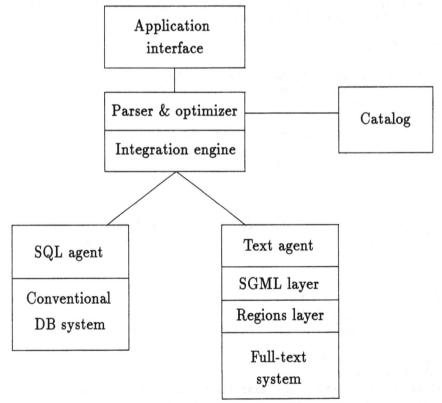

Application interface: This component provides an interface through which an application program interacts with the T/RDBMS system. It consists of a set of functions for submitting requests and retrieving the result of a request. In support of a data model integrating text with conventional relational data, requests are expressed in a version of SQL extended with features for text searching and text manipulation.

Parser & optimizer: When a request arrives from an application program, it is first parsed and semantically analysed. The next step is query optimization, that is, determining an efficient way of servicing the request, which is crucial to achieving good performance. These two steps require access to text and relational data descriptions, which are stored in a catalog (also called data dictionary). The output of these steps is a self-contained access plan that specifies how to evaluate the request: what requests (queries) to submit to each component system and what operations to perform to integrate the data from the various sources.

Integration engine: The access plan is passed to the integration engine which performs the computation specified in the plan. This consists of retrieving data from the underlying data sources (i.e., relational database system and text management system) by submitting requests specified in the plan and performing the processing required to integrate data from the several sources. Integration typically requires joins, but other operations may also be involved. The result is then returned to the application.

SQL agent: The system should not be dependent on any particular database system. The purpose of an SQL agent is to hide the specifics of the underlying database system and present a standard interface. We have already developed such agents for several database engines [Lar89a, Lar89b] and expect to develop additional ones in the near future. Each agent has a call-level interface based on Microsoft's Open Database Connectivity (ODBC) specification [Mic92].

Text agent: Similarly, the system should not be dependent on any particular text management system. Text agents providing a common interface to different text systems are being developed. However, no widely accepted, common interface exists in this area. We are currently implementing two layers between the central component and flat-text engines, one that converts our grammar-based queries into a form based on simpler "regions" or "zones" (such as those supported by PAT [Sal92]), and a second one that eliminates dependence on any structural capabilities being provided by the text search system. With this three-layer approach to text agents, the system will be compatible with text systems having varying degrees of obliviousness to structure.

The proposed architecture is based on our experience with multidatabase systems that integrate more traditional database system. Its main design objectives are flexibility and independence of underlying data sources (conventional database systems and text systems). Independence is achieved by providing agents that present a standardized interface and hide the details of of the underlying system. There is a price to be paid for this: the translation performed by an agent requires some extra processing, and, more significantly, the system may not be able to exploit some of the features of an underlying database or text system. However, the overall system is greatly simplified by isolating the rest of the software from the details of those systems. Not only is this good software practice, but it allows the integration of commercial database management systems into the architecture, where those systems can retain their independence and integrity. Furthermore, the architecture supports distribution: various components may be implemented as separate processes, possibly running on different machines.

Given performance estimates for each client subsystem, the central database engine must choose in which order and by which means to process the user's request. Consider again the simple query for long articles on Canada. If the requested length is stored in a traditional relational database (as a field in En-cyclopedia_relation) and keywords are stored in a text database (in Encyclope-dia_text), this could be implemented by

```
SELECT title, req_wc
FROM Encyclopedia_relation
WHERE req_wc >5000 AND aid IN (SELECT aid
                               FROM Encyclopedia_text
                               WHERE article..keywords CONTAINS "Canada");
```

Is it more efficient to find the relational records for long articles and then retrieve corresponding text records that include "Canada" among the keywords; or to find all text records that include the keyword "Canada", extract the article identifier and use that as part of a conventional relational subquery; or to execute both subqueries in parallel and then join the results? At least superficially, these choices correspond to those faced by global query optimization algorithms for conventional distributed and federated database systems, but we have learned from past experience that text brings its own needs and surprises to traditional database problems.

6   Conclusions and Further Work

We have developed a single model within which both text and relational data can be described so that users can access and manipulate all their data meaningfully. Our proposed extensions to SQL are modest, yet they are powerful enough to handle SGML-based data simply, to support extractions from highly structured text into relations, and to preserve the integrity of complex text units. We have designed a data description language and a query language integrating SQL with text search and text manipulation features, addressing the following questions:

- How can an SGML-defined description of text be integrated with SQL's DDL?

- Which text manipulation operators should be included in an extended SQL DML?

We have not yet designed update extensions to SQL that permit text subfields to be modified.

We have designed an architecture to support integrated text-and-relational databases using a federated database system. We have begun to implement and test the architecture and language, supporting data stored partially in an Oracle relational database and partially under the control of the PAT text engine. We will test all three text interfaces (SGML, regions, and flat-text) against PAT, and we expect that our experience will be transferrable to other engines with various capabilities. We do not expect full-text search engines to have sufficiently fast update characteristics to support transaction rates common to relational database environment, and we plan to investigate the development of faster and more flexible text update algorithms.

In further research, a primary problem to be addressed is execution planning. Before access strategies can be selected on the basis of expected performance, estimates of costs must be made available to the query optimizer. To achieve this end, traditional approaches require that we first develop cost models for text processing systems. In particular, for each class of operations, we must be able to determine upper and lower bounds on access time as well as expected access time to complete an operation in that class. We must then devise query optimization and data integration strategies that take advantage of such information.

References

[ATA91] ATA 89-9C SFQL Committee, "Advanced Retrieval Standard —SFQL: Structured Full-text Query Language," *ATA specification 100, Rev 30, Version 2.2, Prerelease C*, Air Transport Association, ATA 89-9C.SFQL V2.2/PR-C (October 1991) 84 pp.

[Bil92] A. Biliris, "The Performance of Three Database Storage Structures for Managing Large Objects," *Proc. Sigmod 92*, ACM, *Sigmod Record*, Vol. 21, No. 2 (June 1992) 276–285.

[Bla94] G.E. Blake, M.P. Consens, P. Kilpeläinen, P.-Å. Larson, T. Snider, and F.W. Tompa, "Text extensions to SQL," internal report, Univ. of Waterloo Centre for the New OED and Text Research, 1994.

[Chr94] V. Christophides, S. Abiteboul, S. Cluet, and M. Scholl, "From Structured Documents to Novel Query Facilities," To appear in *Proc. 13th. ACM SIGMOD Conf.*, (May 1994).

[Gol90] C. F. Goldfarb. *The SGML Handbook*. Oxford University Press, Oxford, 1990.

[Gon87] G. H. Gonnet and F. W. Tompa, "Mind Your Grammar: a New Approach to Modelling Text," *Very Large Data Bases* (VLDB), Vol. 13 (September 1987) pp. 339–346.

[ISO86] International Organization for Standardization, *International Standard 8879: Information Processing — Text and Office Systems — Standard Generalized Markup Language (SGML)*, first edition — 1986-10-15(Ref. No. ISO 8879-1986(E)), 155 pp.

[ISO90] International Organization for Standardization, "Information technology – Database Language SQL 2 Draft Report", ISO Committee ISO/IEC JTC 1/SC 21, 1990.

[Lar89a] P.-Å. Larson, "Relational Access to IMS Databases: Gateway Structure and Join Processing," Project report, (available from the author), 1989.

[Lar89b] P.-Å. Larson, H. AboElFotoh, M. Dionne, and F. Wang, "SQL Access to VAX DBMS Databases: Strategy Generation and Query Execution for Basic SFW Queries," Project report (available from the first author), 1989.

[Mar91] C. C. Marshall, F. G. Halasz, R. A. Rogers, and W. C. Janssen Jr., "Aquanet: a Hypertext Tool to Hold Your Knowledge in Place," *Proc. 3rd ACM Conf. on Hypertext: Hypertext 91*, San Antonio (Dec. 1991) 261–275.

[Mic92] Microsoft Corporation, *Microsoft ODBC Application Programmer's Guide*, Microsoft Corporation, 1992.

[Ora92] Oracle Corporation, *SQL*TextRetrieval Version 2 Technical Overview*, Oracle Corporation, 1992. 45 pp.

[Sac92] R. Sacks-Davis, A. Kent, K. Ramamohanarao, J. Thom, , and J. Zobel, "Atlas: a nested relational database system for text applications", Technical Report CITRI/TR-92-52, Collaborative Information Technology Research, Victoria, Australia, July 1992.

[Sal92] A. Salminen and F.W. Tompa. "PAT Expressions: an algebra for text search," *Papers in Computational Lexicography: COMPLEX '92*, Proc. 2nd Int. Conf. on Computational Lexicography (F. Kiefer, G. Kiss, J. Pajzs ed.), Linguistics Inst., Hungarian Academy of Science, Budapest (October 1992), 309–332.

[Sey92] Seybold Publications, "IDI Pursues Document Management," *Report on Publishing Systems*, Vol. 21, No. 16, May 1992.

[Wei85] E.S.C. Weiner. "The *New OED*: Problems in the Computerization of a Dictionary," *University Computing*, Vol. 7 (1985) 66-71.

[Zlo75] M.M. Zloof. "Query-by-Example: Operations on the Transitive Closure," IBM Research Report RC 5526, Yorktown Heights, N.Y., 1975.

Acknowledgements

This work has benefited from discussions with Tim Bray, Gordon Cormack, and Gaston Gonnet. The financial assistance of the University of Waterloo, the Natural Sciences and Engineering Research Council of Canada, and Open Text Corporation are gratefully acknowledged.

A DBMS-Based Multimedia Archiving Teleservice Incorporating Mail*

Heiko Thimm and Thomas C. Rakow

GMD - Integrated Publication and Information Systems Institute (IPSI)
Dolivostr. 15, 64293 Darmstadt, Germany

Abstract. In this paper, a teleservice for archiving and retrieving multimedia documents using public networks is described. This teleservice encourages a broad range of multimedia archiving applications. The described implementation is based on standardized multimedia mail and suitable for an asynchronous access mechanism. The originality of this work is the integration of multimedia mail with simple standalone archive clients for heterogeneous platforms and an archive server which is based on an object-oriented DBMS. The modeling of the server is described in-depth showing the contributions of object-oriented database technology for the realization of generic electronic archives that deal with structured multimedia documents. Helpful hints and important design suggestions for the implementation of advanced archive functionality are provided. Furthermore, functionality for efficient access on the client side is outlined. A sample application showing a Multimedia Calendar of Events is sketched as well.

1 Introduction

Advances in hardware technologies for multimedia applications have emerged in recent years and enabled the usage of images, graphics, audio, video, and digital animation sequences within information systems. There are already solutions from the area of data communication allowing to interchange these multimedia data. The introduced multimedia archiving teleservice for public networks demonstrates the integration of information systems and data communication technology for multimedia data. As access mechanism, it exploits standardized multimedia mail which is widely available and provides means for connection-less, asynchronous communication. Archiving and retrieval of multimedia documents is possible by an architecture that integrates multimedia mail with standalone archive clients and a multimedia archive server. A broad range of public multimedia applications is encouraged, e.g. a product catalog for teleshopping, virtual travel agency, subscription services for multimedia documents, cooperative authoring of multimedia documents, ... etc. suitable for an *asynchronous* access mechanism which can cope with the mail delay.

Our proposed teleservice supports both interchange mechanisms of the applied multimedia mail system [6, 15] which is based on the principles of CCITT Recommendation X.400 Message Handling System [2]: (1) *Store-and-forward* allows to interchange

---

* This work is partially granted by the German Telekom's DeTeBerkom GmbH, Berlin, under contract number 2038/2.

complete multimedia documents, while (2) *referenced-object-access* (ROA) is for high volume document parts. The main point of the latter is, that mails, instead of the data of a document component itself, may include a *global reference*, called *Distinguished Object Reference* (DOR) [9], that points to the data deposited on a specialized *global store*. When the presentation of the document component is requested, the data is retrieved from this store using a *synchronous* access protocol.

The archive server's modeling based on the VODAK DBMS is described in-depth. It shows the application of an object-oriented database management system for the realization of a *generic archive* that deals with *structured multimedia documents*. An adequate object-oriented approach for the modeling of these documents and the realization of the archiving functionality is discussed. This functionality includes recognition of replicated data which are reflected by *shared (multimedia) objects* saving storage capacity. It includes as well *dynamic document composition* which allows for users to retrieve a multimedia document composed from an original archived one including *format* as well as *quality transformations* for document parts. An object-oriented query language is used for selecting multimedia documents based on descriptive search arguments addressing contents as well as structure. Since even complex so-called *archive orders* to be performed by the server can be mapped almost completely into regular query statements, our clients could be kept simple. This is important for support of heterogeneous platforms. This also reduced the complexity of the server which primarily has to submit the queries to the query interpreter. A concrete sample application showing a *Multimedia Calendar of Events* (CoE) is sketched as well.

The paper is organized as follows. In section 2, the modeling of the multimedia archive is described. Section 3 provides the proposed teleservice architecture. Our sample application is outlined in section 4, while related work is addressed in section 5. We conclude this paper with a discussion of the experiences made and try to point out the benefits of our work for others. We also provide a summary of our future work.

2 Modeling the Multimedia Information Archive

The object-oriented design of the archive server using the VODAK DBMS is discussed in this section. First we give an overview of VODAK's data modeling language and its query language followed by an introduction of the document model of the utilized multimedia mail teleservice. Then we outline the main elements of the server's processing before the database schema and the archive's functionality are described. We conclude with a discussion of control and data flow and the organization of transactions.

2.1 Data Modeling and Querying Based on VODAK

VODAK is a research prototype of a distributed object-oriented DBMS which has been developed at GMD-IPSI within the past six years. It provides the data modeling and programming language VML [11, 12], the object-oriented query language VQL [1, 4], an advanced transaction model [16], support for heterogeneous storage devices, and it is currently extended in order to support multimedia data [14, 22, 23]. Efficient storage management for persistent objects is realized by the usage of the C++ ObjectStore^{TM} DBMS [17].

In VML structure and behavior of objects are described by *properties* and *methods*, respectively, which are defined in *object types*. An object type can be a subtype of another which *inherits* its properties and methods to its *subtypes*. Individual objects are instances of exactly one *class* which is associated with an object type specifying the class's *instance type* and another object type specifying the class's *own type*. An own type determines the structure and behavior of a class as an object itself, while an instance type defines structure and behavior of a class's instances. Classes itself can be instances of *metaclasses* that can be applied to model user-defined *semantic relationships* (e.g. part-of, role-of, ... etc.) on the instance level.

Query statements written in the declarative query language VQL are similar to SQL statements and have the following general form: "ACCESS ... FROM ... WHERE". VQL allows the specification of method calls in query statements. It is a helpful feature, that VQL statements can be directly included in VML, e.g. in a method body defined in an owntype querying the corresponding class's instances. Query optimization is currently under development.

2.2 Document Model of the Utilized Multimedia Mail System

The mails to be interchanged in a multimedia mail system have to carry multimedia documents structured according to an underlying document model. The document model relevant for our work permits hierarchical multimedia documents that consist of several *contents parts* providing document components and a *link part*. The latter describes the hierarchical organization and the layout of the document. Contents parts may contain instead of the data itself a *global reference*, called *Distinguished Object Reference (DOR)* [9], pointing to the corresponding data deposited on a *global store* which is accessible by the referenced-object-access (ROA) mechanism. All contents parts and the link part of a document are gathered in separate *mail body parts* which are typed parts of a mail. Mails exchanged within the context of our teleservice always include a mail body part of type *ARCHIVE* providing archiving specific information.

2.3 Archive Order Processing

Our teleservice provides the notion of an *archive order* which yields an *order result*. Using the client's order generation functionality, users can issue individual orders of the following predefined types: (1) INSERT - inserting an attached multimedia document, (2) SEARCH - querying the document base, (3) READ - retrieving documents based on their identifiers, (4) UPDATE - modifying contents identification data of certain documents, and (5) REMOVE - removing certain documents. Order results depends on *archive order parameters* which provide flexibility with respect to the order execution functionality. The processing of archive orders is coded within an *archive order processing loop* which comprises (1) receiving new order mails, (2) identifying and registering the archive orders, (3) processing the orders incl. generation of order result mails (4) sending the result mails.

2.4 Database Schema of the Mail Archive

The archive keeps track of received and sent multimedia mails, multimedia documents, document parts, and archive orders by mapping these artifacts into VML objects. Mail body parts, i.e. document parts, are mapped into objects of types corresponding to leaf nodes of the object type lattice shown in figure 1. Objects of those types which are sub-

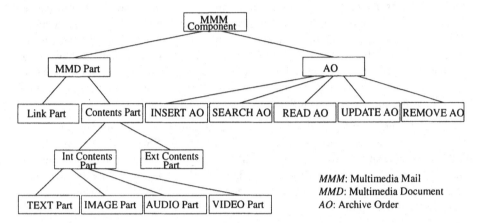

Fig. 1. Object Type Lattice for Multimedia Mail Components

types of *Int Contents Part* (*Int/Ext* stands for *internal/external*) model document parts that contain the contents data itself. These data are stored in VML's long fields. If available, specific *multimedia datatypes* are used e.g. for audios and images. Thus, *format and quality transformations* can be performed (see 2.5, SEARCH (c)). Objects of type *Ext_Contents Part* model document parts which contain instead of the data itself a reference to that data deposited on an external store specialized for high volume data (see section 3 for more details).

The owntypes of those classes that collect archive order objects include a query statement that evaluates the class's *pending* order objects. The class triggers the execution of each selected individual order by a method call. This complete procedure, i.e. selection and execution triggering, is encapsulated in the owntype's public method *anorder-classobj->execute_ArchiveOrders()*.

Figure 2 illustrates classes that collect those objects in which the multimedia documents are mapped. Multimedia documents are modeled as *complex objects* aggregating corresponding document part objects which are modeled as objects itself. Thus, *dynamic document composition* is supported. For the *part/whole* semantic relationship, existing between a multimedia document and its document parts, the predefined VML metaclass *HolonymicMeronymic Metaclass* (*HM* for short) [5] is applied by defining the relevant classes as instances of this metaclass and specifying the relationship's inherent semantics. Thus, we need not to implement ourselves the aspects of part-whole semantic relationships, which would require adequate pointer connections and methods managing the relationship and enforcing semantic integrity. By defining a class as an instance of the predefined *HM* metaclass, such methods are inherited. This furnishes the class with methods which capture the creation and deletion semantics of the part relationship and others that establish and dissolve part-whole connections. Furthermore, it allows the relevant classes to be queried in regard to their part relationships. The *HM* metaclass is applied for the definition of the part-whole semantic relationship

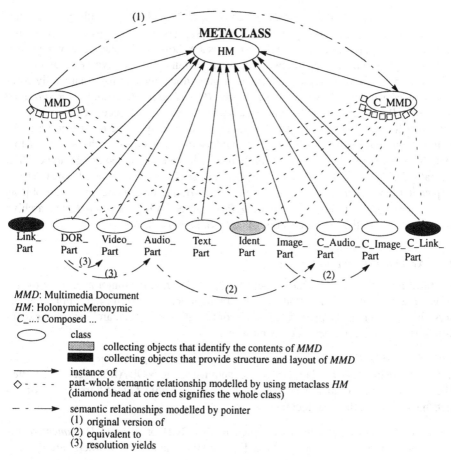

Fig. 2. Classes collecting document and aggregated document part objects

between multimedia documents and their parts as originally archived, i.e. between class *MMD* participating as whole and the shown seven other classes (connected by dotted line) participating as parts. It is also used to model the part-whole semantic relationship between dynamically composed documents and its component parts, i.e. between class *C_MMD* participating as whole and the shown nine other classes participating as parts. With respect to the former, there are two additional part classes called *C_Audio_Part* and *C_Image_Part*, since the document composition procedure can include format and quality transformations which result is modelled by a new object (see 2.5). *C_Link_Part* is for objects modeling a composed document's link Part. The class *Ident_Part* collects those objects that provide information identifying the corresponding document's individual contents. Thus, its instance type contains general and application specific properties which have to be adapted to the concrete application context. With respect to our sample application Multimedia Calendar of Events outlined in section 4, the event descriptions to be dealt with are identified by attributes like e.g. *ECategory, ECity, EFee, Keywords, ...* etc.

For other semantic relationships which are very specific and not generally applied a metaclass is not used, instead they are modelled by pointers from one instance to the other participating one. In figure 2, these relationships are shown at the class level which indicates their potential existence between concrete instances of the involved classes. The relationship *original version of* (1) relates original documents to its dynamically composed other versions. Between class *Audio_Part (Image_Part)* and *C_Audio_Part (C_Image_Part)*, there is a relationship called *equivalent to* (2) since the latter is different to the former only with respect to the format or quality of the document part. For example, while the object in *Image_Part* models an image coded in the sun raster format, the related object in class *C_Image_Part* models a compressed image in the JPEG format [25]. Thus, reuse of already available converted parts is supported. The relationship called *resolution yields* (3) between *DOR_Part*, addressing document part objects that contain a global reference, and *Video_Part*, respectively, *Audio_Part*, is an archive internal pointer to the reference's raw data if available in the archive.

2.5 Archive Order Fulfillment

For the different order types mentioned in 2.3, we describe the major aspects of the archive order execution which is always producing at least one result mail. For some orders, this mail contains a predefined order confirmation text. If an archive order execution fails, the mail provides an error message.

SEARCH and UPDATE orders contain VQL queries. The query statement is extracted from the remaining order data prior to its submission to VODAK's query interpreter. The evaluation of our queries always results in a set of *object identifiers* (OIDs) of objects modeling multimedia documents.

Search result constraint values contained in SEARCH orders and *Document transformation directives,* possibly contained in SEARCH and READ orders, are derived from information on the users preferences and the workstation environment modeled in the archive client. *Read variant determination statements* contained in READ orders are explicitly specified by the order originator. Likewise, *DOR creation instructions,* possibly contained in SEARCH and READ orders, as well as *DOR resolution instructions* possibly contained in INSERT orders are also specified by the order originator.

INSERT. The multimedia document accompanying the order is decomposed into its parts and mapped into the corresponding instances. Three objects are instantiated first. One modeling the multimedia document as a whole, another capturing document contents identification data, and a further one modeling the document's link part. The latter object provides methods for analyzing the document structure. Using these methods, the document parts can be mapped into the corresponding objects.

For document parts that contain a reference instead of the data itself, it is checked if an object with an identical reference value already exists in the database. If this check fails, a new object is instantiated, otherwise the preexisting one is shared. If a *DOR resolution instruction* is issued and an object containing the data referenced by the DOR is not existing in the database the DOR is resolved, i.e. the data is fetched from the referenced external store and included in the database (see section 3).

SEARCH. Four issues are discussed within the context of the fulfillment of SEARCH archive orders.

(a) Selection of Multimedia Documents Based on Descriptive and Multimedia Specific Data. Figure 3 shows two sample query expressions. In (1) the selection criteria does

ACCESS i–>getWholes()
 FROM i IN Ident_Part
 WHERE
    (i–>Get_ECategory() == 'concert') AND
    (i–>Get_ECity() == 'Darmstadt') AND
    i–>Get_EFee() <= 40;
	ACCESS d–>oid()
	 FROM d IN
	      (ACCESS i–>getWholes()
	      FROM i IN Ident_Part
	      WHERE
	         (i–>Get_ECategory() == 'concert') AND
	         (i–>Get_ECity() == 'Darmstadt')
	 WHERE
	    (EXISTS (a IN d–>getParts()):
	      a–>class == Audio_Part) AND
	    EXISTS (v IN d–>getParts()):
	      v–>class == Video_Part AND
	      v–>Get_Duration <= 180;

Selection of multimedia event descriptions concerning concerts, taking place in Darmstadt with a max. entrance fee of 40 DM	*Selection of multimedia event descriptions concerning concerts, taking place in Darmstadt which at least include one audio component and at least one video component with a max. duration of three minutes.*
(1) selection based on descriptive application specific search attributes	(2) selection based on descriptive application specific search attributes and search criteria addressing multimedia specific data

Fig. 3. Sample Query Expressions

not address multimedia specific aspects, like in (2). The method invocation *obj–>get-Wholes()* defined in the *HM* metaclass returns object identifiers of instances that participate in a part-whole relationship as whole, while the receiver object participates as part. In (2) the selected document objects, resulting from the nested inner statement, execute the method *obj–>getParts()* which is also defined in the *HM* metaclass. It evaluates the corresponding part objects. By using the existential quantifier, it is checked if among the whole object's part objects, there is at least one of class *Audio_Part*, and at least one of class *Video_Part*. The latter is further restricted by a max. duration time of three minutes in order to exclude long video clips resulting in high network and storage costs. The object identifiers of matching objects are returned as query result.

The resulting object identifiers belong to instances of class *MMD* and identify the multimedia documents to be returned. However, the actual contents of the modelled result mail(s) depends also on the aspects described in (b), (c) and (d).

(b) Constraint Dependent Search Result Variants. Each SEARCH order includes two search result constraint values denoted by C1 and C2 (C2 $\geq$ C1). If the number of object identifiers resulting from the query evaluation is smaller than C1, result mails that completely contain the original multimedia documents are modelled. If only C1 is exceeded, the modelled result mails contain only the application specific attribute values, while, if C2 is exceed too, a single result mail containing the total number of matching documents is modelled. In both cases it is assumed that the user will refine the original query.

(c) Dynamic Multimedia Document Composition. Figure 4 shows a sample query that

```
ACCESS (i->GetWholes())->Compose("maxLayer=2,maxVideo=0,exImageForm=GIF,
                                   exAudioForm=SUN-8")
FROM i IN Ident_Part
WHERE
        (i->Get_ECategory() == 'concert') AND
        (i->Get_ECity() == 'Darmstadt') AND
        i->Get_EFee() < 40;

selection of multimedia documents with subsequent creation of new documents composed from
the selected ones
```

Fig. 4. A sample query triggering dynamic document composition

contains in the *access* clause the invocation of the parameterized method *aMMD_obj->Compose(...)* which is executed by the selected objects contained in class *MMD* (Note, *obj->getWholes()* returns the object identifiers of instances of this class). This method instantiates an object of the class *C_MMD* modeling a new multimedia document that is composed by executing the *transformation directives* specified as method parameters. In figure 5, for a given multimedia document, the impact of the directives specified in the sample query is illustrated. The goal of this transformation is that the order result meets the user's environment, restrictions for network and storage costs, as well as his preferences with respect to the document's level of detail (It can be imagined, that overview information are contained in upper layer parts, while lower layer parts provide more details). The transformations neither influence the original document nor its components. Instead, a new link part for the composed document is created modeled by an object of the class *C_Link_Part*. If for image and audio parts another coding or quality, not already contained in the database, is required, a copy is transformed into the demanded coding, respectively, into the demanded quality. New objects of class *C_Audio_Part* and *C_Video_Part*, respectively, are instantiated modeling the transformed copies. Instead of object identifiers of the matching original document(s), the object identifiers of the dynamically composed objects, which are instances of class *C_MMD*, are returned as query result.

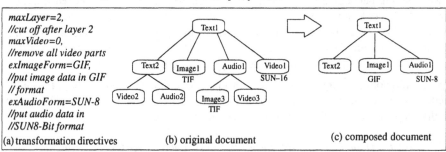

Fig. 5. Dynamic Document Composition based on transformation directives

(d) DOR creation request fulfillment. It is specified if those document parts which contain audio and video, respectively, should be interchanged via the *referenced-object-access* mechanism. For the relevant document parts, the archive has to satisfy the following precondition: The contents data has to be deposited on the global store and the archive has to contain an object providing the corresponding DOR. Note that this pre-

condition is satisfied by default for those document parts archived via a DOR. Otherwise, the archive has to perform the necessary actions. Instead of the contents data itself, the DORs are included into the order result mail.

READ. The objects modeling the multimedia documents to be read are identified in the order. Note, only identifiers of objects collected in class *MMD* are necessary. A *DOR creation instruction* can be included which is handled as described in SEARCH (d). What actually has to be read and returned depends on the following:

(a) Read Variant Determination Statements (explicitly defined):

i) *read: MMD;* (retrieve original multimedia document completely)
ii) *read: Attributes;* (retrieve application specific search attributes values)
ii) *read: Structure;* (retrieve document structure description)

(b) Document Composition Directives. Only if (a) i) is specified, dynamic document composition is performed. In figure 5 sample document transformation directives are shown as well as their impact on a given multimedia document. The processing is the same as for SEARCH (c).

REMOVE. Those instances of class *MMD* which object identifiers are specified in the order are removed. All of their corresponding part objects are removed as well, except shared ones. The deletion also includes the objects related to by the semantic relationship *original version of* which are instances of class *C_MMD* incl. their non-shared part objects.

UPDATE. An individual UPDATE order aiming on the alteration of some application specific attribute values of concrete documents consists of an usual query. The relevant property values are updated by corresponding method calls included in the *access* clause of the query (fig. 6).

```
ACCESS i–>Set_EFee(60)
FROM i IN Ident_Part
Where
            (i–>Get_ECategory() == 'concert') AND
            (i–>Get_EZIP() == 64293) AND
            (i–>Get_ELocation == 'Festhalle') AND
            (i–>Get_BDate() == [10/8/94])
```
The entrance fee of the concert at 10/8/94 given in the Festhalle in the city with ZIP code 64293 is changed to 60 DM.

Fig. 6. Sample Update Query

2.6 Control and Data Flow

The archive server's order execution functionality is encapsulated in methods of those object types which model archive orders. These methods are invoked from a database application program, called *Archive Agent* (AA), that coordinates the complete processing.

Figure 7 shows the cooperation between the object-oriented database, the database application program, and the *Multimedia Mail User Agent* (MMM-UA, see 3). Circles

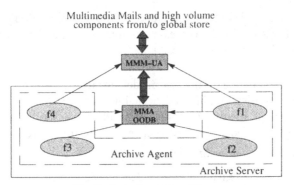

Fig. 7. Control and Data Flow

correspond to functional units of the AA that are continuously executed according to a predefined execution model. In f1-f4 the following tasks are performed:

f1: Incoming Mail Handler. The MMM-UA is instructed to receive new multimedia mails. For each received one, a new instance modeling the received mail is instantiated.

f2: Archive Order Registrar. The archive orders of the new multimedia mails are identified. For each identified order which does not violate the senders permissions, a new instance of the corresponding archive order class with state *pending* is instantiated. If an order could not be identified or the permission check failed, predefined mails are prepared and corresponding objects modeling these mails with state *not sent* are instantiated.

f3: Archive Order Handler. For each archive order in the state *pending* its archive order execution method is called. This method includes the preparation of result mails to be sent and the instantiation of corresponding objects modeling these mails. Then, the order object's state itself is changed to *completed.*

f4: Outgoing Mail Handler. For all objects modeling outgoing mails not sent yet, the MMM-UA is called to perform a send procedure. If this procedure successfully completes, the state of the objects is changed to *sent*, otherwise a new attempt is made in the next execution of f4.

2.7 Organizing Transactions

From the user's point of view, every archive order should be treated as a single transaction. Every INSERT, UPDATE, or REMOVE order changes the archive from one *consistent* state to another by inserting one document sent by a mail, updating a document by a new version, or by removing several documents according to a search expression. A mail document has to be inserted as a whole, but in case of errors (e.g. authorization check fails) nothing of the document should remain in the archive (*all or nothing*). Additionally, updates must be executed completely or the document still remains unchanged. Retrieval orders must be fulfilled by sending complete documents or composed documents based on complete documents, i.e. retrieval and modifying orders must be *isolated* from each other. In the case a modifying order is confirmed, the archive system is responsible for the *durability* of the existence of the sent document in the archive. Documents with unresolved DOR's, i.e. the corresponding contents data is not contained in the database, are already complete documents. Thus, DOR resolution is executed as a separate transaction.

As a drawback of this approach, a coarse granularity of units for concurrent execution appears. Especially, hot spot operations like the creation of instances (for received mails, order classes) and time-consuming operations like waiting for answers of the mail system (new mail?, send confirmation) may result in unfair scheduling of transactions. Orders with read or simple search requests must wait on long-duration insert and compose orders. Thus, a low degree of parallelism will be achieved. Using an object-oriented DBMS like VODAK allows the implementation of advanced transaction concepts. Semantic lock modes allow more concurrency than with the simple Read/Write Model for locking [16]. For example, the creation of an instance of a class commutes with the creation of another instance of the same class and can be executed in parallel. The VODAK DBMS supports commuting operations on its datatypes, e.g. the insertion of two different values in a SET commute. Additionally, the application programmer can specify that two methods of an object type commute under certain conditions. For example, retrieving application specific search attributes values *(read: Attributes)* and document structure descriptions *(read: Structure)* of the same document commute unconditionally.

Currently, we investigate our approach to balance the more parallelism against the more overhead for semantic transaction management.

3 Architecture for Multimedia Archiving by Multimedia Mail

Figure 8 shows the central components of our architecture which is based on a *client-server* approach. The archive server and each client are directly connected to a *Multimedia Mail User Agent* (MMM-UA) which supports the usual *store-and-forward* interchange mechanism via a connection to a *Message Transfer Agent* (MTA, X.400 signifies that it follows the standard X.400 [2]). Additionally, for high volume document parts, it also supports a *referenced-object-access* interchange mechanism (ROA). Here the document part to be interchanged is deposited on a *global store* and a *global reference* to that data, called *Distinguished Object Reference* (DOR) [9], is included in the mail instead of the data itself. Upon a *DOR resolution request*, the corresponding data is fetched from the global store applying OSI services and using a *synchronous* transport protocol on a broadband network. In contrast to the server's database which contains *completely* structured multimedia documents for an undefined period of time, the global store only contains *document parts* which are automatically removed after the *guaranteed access time* specified in the DOR value is exceeded. As shown in figure 8, in our test configuration the global store is located together with a client on the same node. However, other configurations are possible.

Access to archived data is based on the Data Manipulation Language supported by the VODAK DBMS. This is not a constraint. In fact, a standardized language like SQL [8] or "mailadopted" standards for synchronous client-server access, e.g. DFR [10] or RDA [7], could also be supported. However, the lack of application defined method calls and deficiencies with respect to that, respectively, in currently available versions of such languages has to be compensated by more sophisticated client functionality.

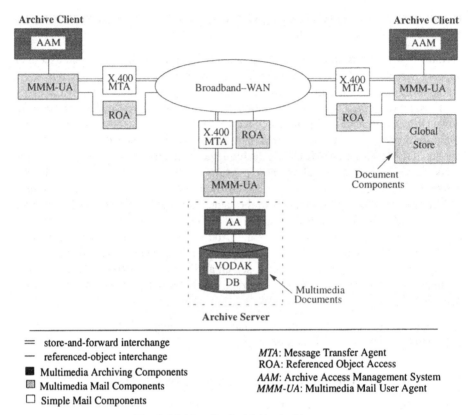

Fig. 8. Multimedia Archiving Architecture

The provided *descriptive access* includes access to a set of *application specific search attributes* that serve as predefined search criteria for the client. This necessitates that for every unit of archived multimedia data, these search attribute values are specified.

3.1 Multimedia Archive Client

Archive clients consist of *Archive Access Management Systems* (AAM) providing functionality which depends on the archive service profile and the kind of user.

A high level graphical user interface allows direct manipulative creation of archive orders. Some order components result from information on the user's preferences and the workstation environment accessible for the client.

For each READ order, the client makes sure that only those documents are retrieved, that are currently not available at the client's site by cross-checking the involved document identifiers.

After its specification, the AAM encapsulates an archive order in a multimedia mail which in turn is sent to the server. Sent archive orders are collected in an order list that is part of the client's user interface.

Result mails are dispatched, unpacked and shown to the user by an entry in the corresponding order's result list. Furthermore, the client persistently stores orders and results on the filesystem for reuse in other sessions.

3.2 Multimedia Archive Server

When an archive order mail is received and the originator has the permissions required for the order execution, the archive order is interpreted, i.e. it is mapped into a database operation. Its result is encapsulated in *1..n* single multimedia mails separating the multimedia documents to be delivered. This separation is necessary due to the possibly high data volume of multimedia documents.

A user interface for typical archive administrator tasks is provided by the server. It includes functions for the administration of the archive users, the management of the billing process, and for the direct insertion of multimedia data. Furthermore, it allows at runtime to alter and fine tune the server's current configuration, to connect/disconnect the server to/from the mail system, to activate/deactivate the archive server, and to bring the archive server down.

3.3 Archive Access Protocol

The archive access protocol, illustrated in figure 9, consists of rules that precisely define how an archive client can communicate with the server and vice versa.

Archive orders are issued to the archive server in separate order mails, i.e. a mail may only contain a single individual order. Each order includes an *order type identifier*, the client's own *order identifier* necessary for the management of its individual orders, and the actual order. The server returns *1..n* order result mails, that each include an *order result type identifier*, the total number of order result mails, and the mails own order result number.

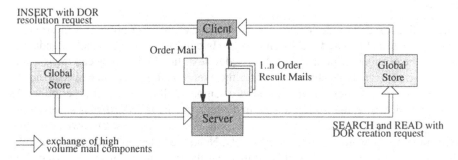

Fig. 9. The Archive Access Protocol

For those INSERT orders, that contain a *DOR resolution request*, some components of the document contained in the insert order mail are interchanged via the ROA mechanism, i.e. the server automatically fetches the raw data from the global store. High volume document components included in SEARCH and READ order result mails are interchanged in the same way, if the corresponding order contained a *DOR creation request*. However, the server automatically creates a new DOR only if for the involved document component a DOR is not already available yet.

4 Sample Application "Multimedia Calendar of Events"

For demonstration purposes, we built a concrete prototype showing a *Multimedia Calendar of Events* (CoE) which fits very well to the characteristics of applications encouraged by our proposed teleservice.

Figure 10 provides a screendump of the main window of our archive client's user interface. In the upper list, the user's orders are collected, while in the lower one, the result

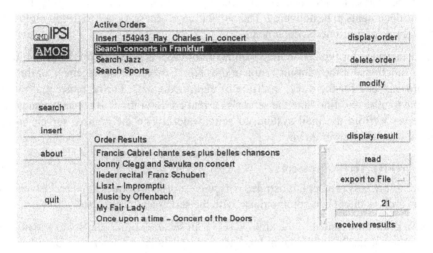

Fig. 10. Main window of the archive client.

of a selected order is listed. Note, a result can comprise a set of multimedia documents, e.g. there are already 21 resulting documents that belong to the highlighted order of figure 10.

The archive server provides to the users multimedia event descriptions, i.e. information relevant to attract people for a specific event. In contrast to conventional calendars of events, the event descriptions are not limited to text. In addition, they can include pictures (e.g. some pictures characteristic for the event), audio pieces (e.g. a sequence of a song), and video clips. Figure 11 shows a sample multimedia event description. As usual, by clicking at the icons included in the text, the multimedia data is presented by using adequate media specific presentation tools. For audio, we use our own audio tool which offers a powerful editing functionality. Note, the video presentation initiated by clicking at the icon with the label *DOR* involves the ROA mechanism. The window at the bottom shows the CoE-specific attributes and corresponding individual values.

5 Related Work

Multimedia database systems are a relatively new field due to the fact that the necessary hardware became available only recently and is still developing [3, 14, 23]. The first approaches were database systems for specialized data such as spatial databases [18, 20] and pictorial databases [24]. Spatial databases were attractive because the semantics of the objects and operations were clearly defined and their properties can be

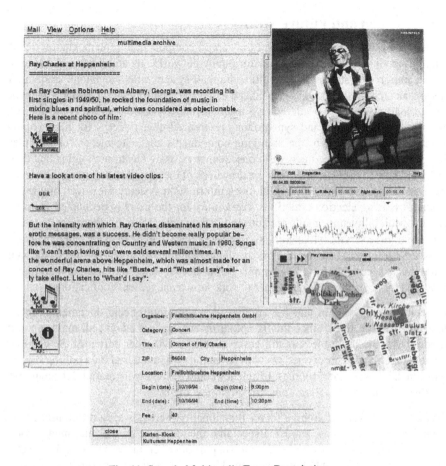

Fig. 11. Sample Multimedia Event Description

derived from geometry. One of the first multimedia efforts in managing multimedia data was the Multimedia Information Manager in the ORION object-oriented database system, developed at MCC [26]. The integration of the new data types is accomplished through a set of definitions of class hierarchies and a message passing protocol not only for the multimedia capture, storage, and presentation devices, but also for the captured and stored multimedia objects. This way a high degree of flexibility is achieved since new storage or presentation devices are easily included by providing the corresponding classes as subclasses of the existing classes. Another project is MINOS, the multimedia object presentation manager developed at the University of Crete [3]. Synchronization mechanisms for distributed multimedia systems are addressed in [21]. An approach for an integration of multimedia into a distributed office application environment based on a multimedia database is described in [19]. The utilization of a multimedia DBMS for the realization of a multimedia archiving teleservice, as described in this paper, is a new approach, not followed in any previous work.

6 Conclusion and Future Work

We described the concept, usage and the central component's implementation details of a multimedia archiving teleservice for public networks. Its architecture is based on the integration of a standardized multimedia mail system with standalone archive clients and an archive server which is realized using an object-oriented DBMS. The incorporated mail system's two interchange mechanisms, asynchronous store-and-forward for complete documents and synchronous referenced-object-access for high volume document parts, provide to the archiving components adequate means for the interchange of multimedia documents. A consequence of using electronic mail is that there is no guaranteed *response time*. This is a drawback of the proposed archiving teleservice implementation, especially if used for kiosk information systems. However, on the other hand, by using electronic mail, its *availability* for the users is decoupled from the server's availability since mails are buffered in the mail system. Furthermore, automatic *active* archive services, like e.g. a subscriber service, can be realized since mails can be issued regardless if the receiver is available. Another advantage of electronic mail is that it is is accessible for a large number of users. We suggest to use the mail implementation for *asynchronous* cooperative work flow management applications.

Between the mail system and the archive server the multimedia documents are exchanged based on files. Since this is not sufficient, a more advanced, main-memory based interface is desirable, but still not available yet. Another deficit of the coupling is that the archive server cooperates with its mail user agent based on a polling mechanism which is a waste of resources. Efficiency could be largely increased if the mail user agent would trigger the server upon arrival of new mails.

The described advanced archive server functionality prerequisites a differentiated and semantically rich database model. Especially, the structure of the multimedia documents must not be transparent in order to support query arguments that explicitly take the document structure into consideration. This is also necessary in order to facilitate dynamic document composition. With a powerful object-oriented modeling language like VODAK's VML, this requirement can be adequately met. The application of the predefined *Holonymic-Meronymic* VML metaclass for modeling the part-whole semantic relationships for dealing with structured multimedia documents relieved us from an explicit implementation of the relationships semantics. It turned out, that with VODAK's object-oriented query language VQL even complex archive orders can be almost completely mapped into regular query statements which have just to be submitted to VODAK's query interpreter. Thus, both, the clients and the server, are easier to implement. With a less powerful query language, not allowing method calls in query statements, this deficit has to be compensated by additional functionality. The contents of the multimedia documents are treated as database instances in order to facilitate format as well as quality transformations of document parts necessary to satisfy the user's preferences and reflect the client's workstation environment. For audio data, we could apply VML's built-in audio datatype that provides built-in methods for such transformations. Since other built-in multimedia datatypes are not available yet, for other document parts, the required transformation methods were implemented in the corresponding object types. This shows that for multimedia applications DBMS which explicitly support multimedia data by adequate datatypes are demanded.

The described teleservice architecture is highly generic. The customization to a concrete multimedia archiving application requires only a few adaptations for the client and the server while the client-server protocol remains the same.

The current state of our prototypical implementation includes the described archiving functionality almost completely. Only dynamic composition of multimedia documents and the DOR creation as well as DOR resolution instruction are still not supported. A future goal of our work is an upgrade of the archiving teleservice's profile by functionality for work flow management to support the distributed authoring, composition, and management of multimedia documents, i.e. support for *asynchronous* cooperative work. As sample application, we will use the *Multimedia Calendar of Events* for which the event descriptions are cooperatively created following a formal specification of sequential and parallel steps executed by several information suppliers.

Acknowledgement

Thanks to K. Hofrichter, P. Höpner, E. Möller, H. Pusch, K. Röhr and G. Schürmann of GMD-FOKUS for providing comprehensive support with respect to our multimedia mail implementation. We would also like to thank Steffen Jakob, who implemented the archive client. Thanks go out as well to Gisela Fischer, Wolfgang Klas and Peter Muth, who made helpful comments on an earlier version of this paper.

References

1. Aberer, K., Fischer, G.: Object-Oriented Query Processing: "The Impact of Metods on Language, Architecture and Optimization", *Arbeitspapiere der GMD No. 763*, St. Augustin, 1993

2. CCITT Recommendation X.400 series: 1988, Data Communication Networks, Message Handling Systems, Blue Book

3. Christodoulakis S., Ho F. and Theodoridou, M.: "The multimedia Object Presentation Manager of MINOS: A Symmetric Approach", *Proc. Int. Conf. on Management of Data*, Washington, 1986, pp. 295-310.

4. Fischer, G.: "Updates in Object-Oriented Database Systems by Method Calls Queries", *Proc. of 3rd ERCIM Database Research Group Workshop*, Pisa, Sept. 1992

5. Halper, M., Geller, J., Perl: "An OODB 'Part' Relationship Model", in Y. Yesha (ed.), *Proc. of First Int. Conf. on Information and Knowledge Management*, Baltimore, MD, 1992, pp. 602-611

6. Hofrichter, K., Möller E., Scheller, A., Schürmann, G.: "The BERKOM Multimedia Mail Teleservice", *Proc. of the Fourth Workshop on Future Trends of Distributed Computing Systems*, Lisbon, Portugal, September 1993, IEEE Computer Society Press, Los Alamitos, California, 1993, pp. 23-30

7. Information Processing Systems - Open Systems Interconnection - Remote Database Access (RDA), Part 1: Generic Model, Service, and Protocol, 1991

8. ISO/IEC, Database Language SQL2 and SQL3, international commitee document, JTCI/SC21, WG3 DBL SEL-3b, April 1990

9. ISO/IEC, Information Technologie - Text and office systems - Distributed Office Applications Model (DOAM), Part 2: Distinguished-object-reference and associated procedures, International Standard 10031, 1991

10. ISO/IEC, Information Technology - Text and office systems - Document Filing and Retrieval (DFR) - Part 1 and Part 2, International Standard 10166, 1991

11. Klas, W., Aberer, K., Neuhold, E.J.: "Object-Oriented Modeling for Hypermedia Systems using the VODAK Modeling Language (VML)", *Object-Oriented Database Management Systems*, NATO ASI Series, Springer Verlag Berlin Heidelberg, August 1993

12. Klas, W., et al.: "VML - The VODAK Model Language Version 3.1", Technical Report, GMD–IPSI, July 1993

13. Multimedia information systems - An international workshop, participant proceedings, Tempe, Arizona, February 7, 1992.

14. Moser, F., Rakow, T.C.: "Datenbankeinsatz für standardisierten Zugriff auf multimediale Archive", *Beiträge zur GI-Fachgruppentagung Datenbanken*, Jena, September 1993, Datenbank-Rundbrief, only available in German, Sept. 1993

15. Möller, E., Neumann, L., Schürmann, G., Thomas, S., Weber, R., Wolf, F.: "The BERKOM Multimedia-Mail Teleservice", to be published in Computer Communications

16. Muth, P., Rakow, T.C., Weikum, G., Broessler, P., Hasse, Ch.: "Semantic Concurrency Control in Object-Oriented Database Systems", *Proc. of IEEE Ninth International Conference on Data Engineering*, Washington DC, 1993, pp. 233-242

17. Object Design Inc.: ObjectStore Reference Manual, Release 2.0, Object Design Inc., Burlington, MA, October 1992

18. Orenstein, J., Manola, F.: "PROBE Spatial Data Modeling and Query processing in an Image Database Application", *IEEE Trans. Software Eng. 14*, No. 5, 1988

19. Rückert, J., Paul, B.: "Integrating Multimedia into the Distributed Office Application Environment", *Datenbanksysteme in Büro, Technik und Wissenschaft*, GI-Fachtagung Braunschweig, 3.-4. März 1993, Springer-Verlag

20. Stonebraker, M., Rowe, L.: "The Design of POSTGRES", *Proc. ACM SIGMOD 1986*

21. Steinmetz, R.: "Synchronization Properties in Multimedia Systems", *IEEE Journal on Selected Areas in Communications*, Vol.8 No. 3 April 1990.

22. Thimm, H., Rakow, T.C.: "Upgrading Multimedia Data-Handling Services of a Database Management System by an Interaction Manager", *Arbeitspapiere der GMD No. 762*, St. Augustin, July 1993

23. Turau, V., Rakow, T.C.: "A Schema Partition for Multimedia Database Management Systems", *Arbeitspapiere der GMD No. 729*, St. Augustin, February 1993

24. Tamura, H. and Yokoya, N.: "Database Systems: A Survey", *Pattern Recognition*, Vol. 17 No. 1 1984.

25. Wallace, G.K.: "Overview of the JPEG (ISO/CCITT) still image compression standard", Image Processing Algorithms and Techniques, *Proc. of the SPIE*, Vol. 1244, Feb. 1990, pp. 220-233

26. Woelk, D., Kim, W.: "Multimedia Information Management in an Object-Oriented Database System", *Proc. of the 13th VLDB Conference*, Brighton 1987.

A Zoomable DBMS for Brain Structure, Function and Behavior

J. Carlis, J. Riedl, A. Georgopoulos, G.Wilcox, R. Elde, J. Pardo, K. Ugurbil,
E. Retzel, J. Maguire, B. Miller, M. Claypool, T.Brelje, C. Honda

University of Minnesota
Computer Science Department and Medical School

Abstract. We have begun a long-term project to build a new kind of database and its enhanced, supporting database management system (DBMS) for international neuroscience research. Because brain research occurs world-wide, our database will be distributed, encouraging rapid, open dissemination of results to a broad audience of neuroscientists. It will conjoin information and experimental results from many disciplines. We envision a zoomable database of the brain tissue itself, in large part embedded in three dimensions (3D), through which one can "fly." Within this coarse structure, the database will also organize fine-structural, functional and behavioral data. As often as possible, the database will express experimental data in its purest, least analyzed form, so that expensive raw data can be analyzed and reanalyzed by researchers worldwide.

We believe that our project will profoundly effect the way in which neuroscience is done, while providing key areas for database research and distributed computing.

1 Introduction

We have begun a long term project to build a new kind of neuroscience research database and its enhanced, supporting database management system (DBMS). Our goals are: to connect neuroscience subdisciplines at a data level, to develop novel ways of examining the data, and to provide the neuroscience community distributed access to it.

We will have, for one rodent species, integrated data bridging three neuroscience subdisciplines: structural, functional and behavioral. We will thereby link: a) different scale imaging modality data, in particular, gross anatomic high field MRI, Positronic emission tomography (PET), and microscopic (confocal) static, anatomic images; b) static images to dynamically changing indices of neural responses; and c) macroscopic experimental behavior and functional imaging. So far we have developed data models for each subdiscipline, and implemented, in the Montage DBMS, the structural subdiscipline model and begun testing it. We will decorate (a neuroscience term) these structural maps with: neuroanatomic localization of neuronal transmitter, receptor and transducer molecules; neurophysiological determination of neuronal behavior in time; and functional imaging and other studies relating organismic behavior to regions of the nervous system.

In addition, the database will contain behavioral, cognitive and pharmacological research results that cannot be easily ascribed to any particular location. (This high resolution image database will require about 10 terabytes to fully describe one prototype rodent brain. In a sense we will have about 20 gigabytes of MRI data for the rodent serving as an index to the mass of confocal data. Confocal data is acquired in (.4 mb) overlapping rectangular units that are then "montaged" together.)

Given that the structural imaging data will be at several different scales, but will be linked, or anchored, together, we envision a zoomable 3-D database through which one can "fly." We are developing a graphical user interfaces (GUI) that allows a user to start on the outside of the brain and to direct the flying through it. One starts with an atlas view and can ask to zoom in, which means either taking a closer look at this level, or changing microscopy modalities (to MRI, or from MRI to confocal). One moves through the brain either via a joystick-indicated direction or towards a named brain location, or along a predefined pathway. While parked at a place in the brain a user may query the database about functional or behavioral data ascribed to the place (within some distance). For example, since some neuroscientists listen to the waveforms of neuron firings, one might ask to hear the waveform of a nearby neuron.

For several reasons we believe the project will be eminently useful to a broad range of clinical and basic neuroscientific disciplines.

1. Since the data will be "pristine," that is, as close to raw data as practical, neuroscientists will be able to examine and re-examine the data. For example, filled axons can be traced post hoc by following the trail of intracellular dye injected through completely serially sectioned and registered confocal images. Such post hoc analyses are not possible with the derived and processed images and temporal summaries found in the neuroscientific literature.

2. For the first time, high resolution MR images of rodent and primate nervous systems will be used to register consecutive confocal microscopic images to a single, anatomically relevant, globally contiguous, unperturbed frame of reference. To this registered data we will add functional data collected with multiple techniques along with associated uncertainties. Functional imaging will add another level to this structure-function relationship.

3. The data will be high quality, because it will be screened into the database by an editorial board equipped with workstations capable of high resolution display of the data. This peer review will be conducted over networks by an editorial structure similar to respected journals.The database will be built initially in Minneapolis but will be progressively distributed to Stockholm and other sites. The public, peer-reviewed component of the database will be broadly available to neuroscientists with access to Internet.

While its value is clear, the project presents challenging problems to neuroscientists and computer scientists alike. Section 2 of this paper describes our progress in logical design for the database. Section 3 describes our progress in

physical design for neural data. Section 4 outlines our support for worldwide
distribution for this zoomable database. Section 5 describes the cooperating set
of tools that will provide the graphical user interface to the database. Section 6
introduces some preliminary analysis on the feasibility of our design.

2 Data Modeling

In this section we present one of the preliminary data models developed so far.
Computer scientists built the models by examining manuals, source code, and,
most importantly, interviewing knowledgable neuroscientists and their technical
staff. The models are not finished. They reflect the current decisions made by
neuroscientists. The models came from an ongoing learning process conducted
during the last several months. Neuroscientists, via the models, are engaged in
articulating, for themselves, across subdisciplinary areas, and for the computer
scientists, how they, collectively, view a part of their world. The models name
types of data that neuroscientists want to remember. The models are not couched
in terms of files and headers, or integer and char. Those details are important,
but are covered at a different level. Models not shown are for functional and
behavioral data. (Note that these other models join the one described below via
relationships to the named brain location, cell, and pixel group entities.) Already,
the data models have been valuable as a communication tool. Specialists, via the
modeling process, have learned about other specialties and about their own.

2.1 Specific Goals

1. Our data model must accommodate the views of all involved neuroscientists.
2. We must determine exactly what consitutes raw, pristine data.
3. We must express montages of confocal microscopy images, assembled to depict large regions of the brain.
4. We must express the relationship between gross-scale (MR) images and fine-
   scale (confocal) images
5. We must distinguish between data about regions of the brain and data representing images of those regions.

2.2 Design Issues

Several of our specific goals exert noteworthy forces on the data modeling effort. Although every data modeling effort gathers information from many users
with different and conflicting views of the data, this project is special because it
includes users who view the data from profoundly different scales. Some neuroscientists examine individual neurons, while other consider entire regions of the
brain. Our data model must relate data from such different scales.

We want the database to contain raw, pristine data. However, many laboratory machines collect raw data bearing little resemblance to the ways scientists
typically visualize the data. MRI machines, for example, generate raw data in

the form of free induction decays, rather than in the form of images. Because we hope our database will encourage neuroscientists to share raw data, our data model must express exactly what constitutes raw data.

Because our database will support spatial display of brain tissue and locomotion ("flying") through it, our data model must express how neuroscientists think of the structure of the brain. Furthermore, our model must separate this common conception of the brain's structure from particular images of the brain.

2.3 Preliminary Design

We assume that readers are familiar with data modeling using a logical data structure, or LDS [20, 9, 14, 1, 8]. The model in Figure 1 focuses on MRI and Confocal notions plus their "Connections." To save space we have not displayed some straightforward types of data, and have used acronyms liberally. Our intent in this section is to rather plainly read the data models, in order to give a sense of the data involved.

A Magnetic Resonance Imaging (MRI) experiment comprises one or more episodes in which the investigator(s) induces the MRI machine, with a single command and a single set of acquisition parameters, to collect a sequence of free induction decays (FIDs). With this collected data (an FID acquisition), software can generate one or more displayable images. Note that the displayable images are not the raw data of the experiments. For each FID acquisition, the raw data are: acquisition parameters; a sequence of free induction decays; for each acquired spatial dimension, the location of the axis and the resolution; and gradient value and other machine settings A free induction decay is a sequence of complex numbers that describe the measured exponential decay as more and more hydrogen nuclei drop from an excited energy state to the ground state within the examined tissue.

One creates a displayable image by performing Fourier Transformations (FTs) to an FID acquisition. The image creator can, when applying the FT, supply one weighting function for each spatial dimension in the image. These applied functions are recorded with the saved image, because the resulting image depends on the set of parameters. Thus the image cannot be properly interpreted without them. This is an example of the pristine data principle repeated throughout this application. Each image derived in the pristine FID data has a set of slices perpendicular to the x-y plane. Thus each slice has a relative z value. Each slice comprises a set of (x,y,intensity) triplets, where intensity is the voxel gray-scale value for that slice at that 3D location.

A Confocal Microscopy experiment produces images from one or more physical slabs of tissue, each of which is extracted from a subject of a particular species and subspecies. The investigator(s) can treat any slab with one or more probe-flourophore combinations. We define a probe to be any histochemical, immuno-histochemical, or molecular biological reagent that recognizes a constituent or constituents of the tissue. We use the term flourophore loosely to describe another molecule that imparts optical detectability to a probe.

During the confocal microscopy process, each slab is optically divided into a set of slices; each slice is perpendicular to the z-axis and so has a relative z value. Associated with each slice is a set of parameters, such as excitation emission wavelength, lens-power and magnification, and a set of explanatory notes describing other pertinent details of the data collection. Each slice can have a number of displayable images associated with it; each image represents the illumination part of the slice with a laser beam modified by a particular filter. In other words, investigators can use several different filters to generate several different images for one region of a particular optical slice. An image is comprised of a set of (x,y,intensity) triplets with an associated z component describing the focal plane being imaged (termed an optical section). The intensity of each pixel is comprised of the gray-scale value for that image at that 3D location.

We need to register, or anchor, MRI and Confocal pixels to each other. Note that an anchored pixel implicitly anchors its (x,y) neighbors, and, perhaps, its z neighbors. Biologists sometimes call these anchoring points "fiduciary points". Cartographers sometimes call anchor points "tics."

Two kinds of anchor points need to be remembered within Confocal data. One kind, for image tiling, is where a pixel from each of two neighboring, slightly overlapping images are paired. The second kind connects slabs, or tissue sections. Two pixels in adjacent slabs are said to have a distance and orientation with each other. We have just completed capturing and anchoring a dozen or so images for one slice for a rodent. That task took about nine hours. While experience will speed up the manual task somewhat, we will have thousands of images and must automate both image capture and anchoring.

More problematic from a neuroscience point of view, and crucial to our notion of a zoomable DBMS, is the connection between an MRI voxel and a Confocal voxel. An MRI-Confocal anchor point pair consists of a voxel from each modality, an anchor specification and an asserter. An anchor specification reflects the state of knowledge of neuroscientists. Some pixel pairs will, via relatively large epsilon values, be loosely anchored, others with smaller epsilons are more tightly anchored. An asserter is a neuroscientist authorized to make connections. As the project progresses we expect this anchoring notion to be refined. For now, in addition to x, y and z epsilons, we have added kind and comment attributes to allow neuroscientists to record the reasoning behind an anchor.

The LDS defines connections among named and positional places in the brain. An asserter anchors an atlas pixel by pairing it with an MRI pixel. "Pixel group" is a convenient name for just one or a collection of MRI or Confocal pixels. An asserter may assert that a named location or a cell appears at a pixel group.

In addition to individual locations, neuroscientists are interested in pathways in the brain. A pathway for a named location or a cell (we use the same fragment of the data model for both) consists of a set of pathway nodes. A node is a place where a pathway ends or splits. Each node may be associated with a named location or a cell part, such as axon, axon hillock, axon-process dendrite, or nucleus. A pathway node has pathway arcs. A pathway arc is a logical connection between two nodes; it is realized by a sequence of "mileposts." Each pathway

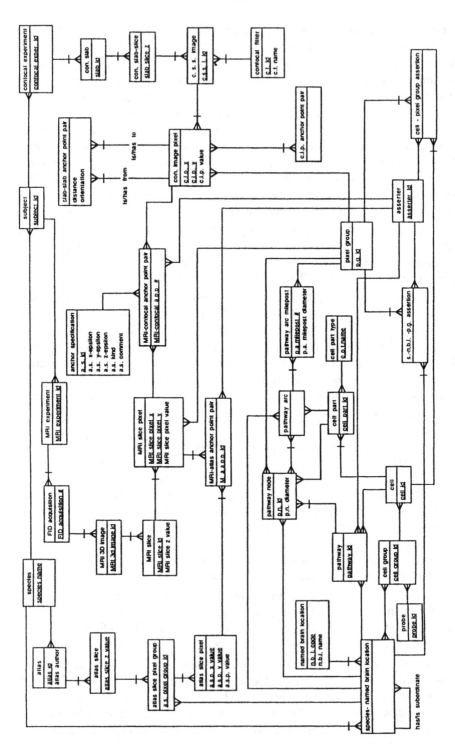

Figure 1. The Connections Logical Data Structure

milepost can be associated with a pixel group. A node or milepost, at least for cells, has a diameter. For example, the hippocampal formation contains neurons whose axons exit this named brain structure as a large pathway named the fornix. The axons within the fornix take a circuitous course and terminate in another named brain location, the mammillary nuclei of the hypothalamus. Along this pathway, some axons branch and issue collaterals that terminate in the septal nuclei and in other hypothalamic nuclei.

3 Physical Data Design

In this section we discuss the preliminary physical design decisions.

3.1 Specific Goals

We have identified several specific aims for physical database implementation.

1. Accommodate the large volume of data produced by the laboratory imaging equipment. The imaging equipment produces large amounts of data ranging from tens of gigabytes for MRI to tens of terabytes for confocal. The sheer size of the database alone makes building an effective and efficient zoomable DBMS hard.

2. Accommodate multi-dimentional scientific data. The data is n dimensional. Images are 2-d or 3-d, or larger, when we consider images captured through time (Functional MRI), with multiple filters (Confocal), and for multiple variable, behavioral studies.

3. Manage the data from the project's inception. We cannot wait until the DBMS extensions are implemented to manage the image data from the various modalities. At first, we will store image data just as it is currently being stored. In the database we will keep track of the files where the image data is stored. When the extensions are developed we will migrate the data into the database.

4. Manage irregular data. Some data, such as MRI, consists of regularly spaced thin slices. However, with confocal we will have locally dense data within a slab; initially large but decreasing distances between adjacent slabs in heavily analyzed regions; and long distances between slabs in sparsely analyzed regions. Furthermore, the size and shape of the data do not mesh readily with the secondary storage devices on which they will be stored.

5. The difficulty of registering data within and across imaging modalities complicates the task of connecting and searching the data. In particular, "warping", is needed (1) to meld data across different subjects, and (2) to counter tissue distortion across imaging modalities and treatments.

6. Users have conflicting patterns of access, which means that no one way of storing the data is ideal for all users. Examples of uses that conflict are:

   - Nucleus discovery primarily processes image (thin) slices while flying through the brain needs small 3-d collections of voxels within which much movement occurs. Furthermore, flying will vary in the zoom level, and the means of controlling direction. In addition some users will request that the system to go to a named brain location, in a 3-d compass direction, or along a pathway.

- Some users will search starting from experiments or probes in towards the structural voxels associated with interesting behavior; others will fly to a location and then want to look at behavioral and functional experimental data associated with that location; still others will search across species. Users examining images will want to see non-image data, e.g., neurophysiological time series data, associated with places in images. On the other hand, users looking at the effect of drugs will want to see images for possible locations where drug effects are mediated places.

3.2 Physical Data Design

It is clear to us that there is no one best mechanism for storing, processing and evolving the collection of neuroscience data for this application. We will build a suite of extensions to a commercially available DBMS that has been designed to be extended, and to compose effective solutions to each portion of the database from components provided with the DBMS and components that we create.

There are four parts to our local zoomable database solution:

1. Data Model. We will modify our techniques of mapping an LDS to schema and access paths, as put forth in [10, 18, 9, 11].
2. Chunks. To effectively and efficiently store and process the zoomable database, we will develop DBMS extensions to support transparent (to the program or human user) chunking of multi-dimensional data with several alternatives available for intra-chunk element order and with several alternative indexing schemes available. Chunks will be allowed to overlap [19].
3. Commercial, extensible DBMS. We are now implementing our zoomable DBMS using the new Montage DBMS [24], [23].
4. Tools. As we proceed with this project we will develop migration tools to convert neuroscience data that is in file format into a DBMS-loadable form. However, until we build our extensions, we will store image data as it is now in files, and within the DBMS refer to the data by file name.

4 Distributed Zoomable Database Support

We will use distributed computing technology for the database to achieve high availability and fast access. Since scientists will generate data in labs spread across the world, each laboratory will have a local database, including parts of the public data it uses regularly, and all private data. Accesses to data that are not in the local database will be automatically transformed into accesses to one of the remote databases containing the needed data. Several copies of the database (replicas) will be stored in different sites, so even catastrophic failures cannot destroy the data.

4.1 Specific Goals

We have identified four specific aims for distributed computing support for the zoomable neural database:

1. Very high availability. Leslie Lamport says of distributed systems "You know you have one when the crash of a computer you've never heard of stops you from getting any work done." The core database must always be available to scientists who are connected to any of the machines maintaining replicas, even during failures of parts of the network, or of some of the attached computers.
2. Local copies of data. Users must be allowed to store frequently used data locally. This will increase performance for updates and user interface accesses. Local data will also give users control and autonomy of their private databases.
3. Eventual consistency of all sites. Updates to data in a replica must be eventually transmitted to all replicas, despite failures before, during, or after the update.
4. High-quality data. Data in the database must be known to be of high quality so scientists can safely rely on it in their research. Data must be peer reviewed to the same standards applied to journal papers. In this way, scientists will be able to perform new studies on existing data with confidence in the raw data.

4.2 Design Issues

1. The network is varied and only occasionally connected. The database is distributed over unreliable networks. Machines housing replicas may go down because of bugs or for maintenance. Some sites may connect only once per day. Also, network speeds may vary from very fast ATMs to slow modems. Still, users demand quality service at all times.
2. Updates are very large. Each update is on the order of 100 Mbytes. 100 MB takes a significant amount of time to transmit from one station to another. Strict consistency would require that all stations wait until the data had propagated completely, making the system inaccessible to users for large periods of time [12, 4].
3. Strict consistency is not essential. Traditional distributed database systems maintain a consistency requirement called 1-copy serializability [3]. 1-copy serializability means that no user can observe even temporary inconsistencies caused by multiple users accessing and updating data on multiple replicas. 1-copy serializability is a theoretically [17, 15] and practically [7] well-understood consistency model. It is appropriate for applications that cannot tolerate any inconsistency in their data, no matter how modest or short-lived. Examples include financial databases and medical records databases. 1-copy serializability is implemented using powerful concurrency control techniques such as two-phase locking [13] or timestamp ordering [2] in conjunction with

a distributed commit protocol such as two-phase commit [22] or three-phase commit [21]. These protocols involve rounds of messages exchanged between all the sites of the distributed system. During the time the messages are being exchanged, no access may be made to affected data. Further, even the best such protocols must sometimes block access to part of the database if computer or network failures occur during the commit process [21]. For these reasons, we look to explore less strict consistency rules for the neural database.

4. Most operations are insertions. The most common operation on the database is adding new information. The collaborative review process will delete data rejected on grounds of scientific merit. Accepted data will be of high quality, and will seldom need to be modified after acceptance.

4.3 Preliminary Design

Distributed naming is an application domain that shares the high availability and eventual consistency characteristics of the zoomable neural database application [6, 10]. We borrow the basic update model from naming systems such as Grapevine [6], modifying it as necessary for the neuroscience application domain. The methods work on any of the types of data that will be stored in the zoomable database; we explore the model with image data as an example because its large size renders it the most difficult to handle.

Each update operation consists of a globally-unique timestamp and a database identifier for the actual data. The timestamps reflect causal ordering: an update with a larger timestamp cannot have depended on an update with a smaller timestamp [16, 5]. Each replica contains an update table to keep track of which update operations it has performed. For example, Figure 2 includes replica A, with an update table. Timestamp 54 corresponds to the first Add operation, and timestamp 55 corresponds to the second Add operation. Each Add operation is linked by location to its appropriate image montage in the database.

After all updates propagate to all replicas the data at each replica will be the same. For example, in Figure 3 replica B is identical to replica A. However, authors may submit updates directly to the replicas, or replicas may receive updates from other replicas. As in Figure 3, a globally inconsistent state may develop [22].

Replicas A and B exchange update information. The entire update tables are exchanged. Because the updates do not include image data, this exchange is fast.

Upon receiving the update table, each replica determines which updates it does not have using an efficient set difference algorithm. Replica A concludes it needs operations 60 and 61, while replica B needs only operation 56. Each replica then sends its request for the updates it needs, and the other replica returns the appropriate image data.

Both replicas then perform the insert, delete or modify operations on their local database. Once again, the replicas are in a consistent state (Figure 4).

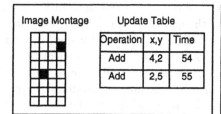

Figure 2: Two databases in an initial, consistent state. Each has identical update tables and database of image montages. The timestamps are globally ordered. Associated with each timestamp is an operation, linked by location to the image montage. Grey boxes represent additions to the image database.

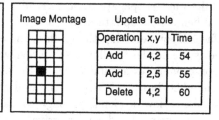

Figure 3: Two inconsistent replicas, resulting from authors submitting updates directly to particular replicas or from updates propagating independently from other replicas.

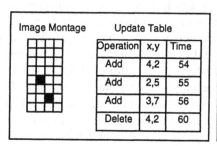

Figure 4: The once-again consistent replicas after merging their data.

4.4 Collaborative Reviewing

Overview Collaborative reviews ensure the quality of the data in the public database, much as journal reviews ensure the quality of journal articles. Authors submit new material to an editor of their choosing. The editor distributes the material to a set of reviewers. The reviewers assess the material's scientific merit and rate it with scores and comments. Upon receipt of all reviews, the editor makes the final decision about whether or not to include the material. Rejected material is returned to the client. Accepted material is added to the current material.

Design Ideas After preparing data suitable for submission to the database, the author submits an update to the nearest replica, indicating which editor should coordinate the reviews. A special update header is created that permits only the author or editor to see the new material. The update material then propagates to the other replicas normally. (For private databases the material is not reviewed, and does not propagate to other replicas.)

When a new update arrives the editor is notified through a review user interface. Upon receiving the update, the editor uses the review user interface to modify the header to allow a set of reviewers to also see the update. This modification propagates normally around the database. Updates to the review headers are handled independently by the update propagation mechanism, so only the modified review header is propagated, rather than the entire image.

When the modified header arrives at a replica used by a reviewer, the reviewer is notified through the review user interface. The reviewer evaluates the update based on the scientific merit and registration of the material. The reviewer must give a low score if any component is not scientifically satisfacory. The reviewer attaches the rating and a textual description of comments to the header. The system propagates the reviews back to the editor.

After receiving all reviews, the editor makes the final decision about rejection or acceptance of the material. In the case of acceptance, the editor modifies the header so that all clients have permission to view the update. This new header propagates normally around the database, making the newly approved data visible to other users. In the case of rejection, the editor submits a deletion request to the database, removing the partially visible update from the public database. (The private database of the submittor, however, remains intact.) The reviews return to the author, who may fix the problems and re-submit the update. It is the job of the author, not the reviewers or editors to fix any problems.

5 A User Interface for Browsing and Investigating the Nervous System

The goal of the user interface is to clearly and quickly display, at each step of an investigation, a manageable amount of data. A user starts a typical investigation by navigating through a coarse 3D model of the brain to a site of interest. The user then focuses on an interesting area and zooms to high-resolution images. Then follows an analytical phase, during which the user perhaps compares different types of data or data of the same type from different subjects or scans. The product of the session may include a log of the user's actions, snapshots of the data presented, and user-supplied judgments on the data, which may become part of the database.

5.1 Specific Goals

1. 3D view of brain structure. The user interface must provide a three-dimensional view of brain structure, that is as close to in situ appearance as possible. The user can navigate through low-resolution MR images and can zoom in to confocal images.
2. Embedded functional and behavioral data. The user interface must present functional and behavioral data embedded within the structure provided by the MR and confocal images.
3. Views of pristine data. The user interface must allow the user to select data from the 3D viewer to view in pristine form with traditional viewing tools.

5.2 Design Issues

1. Very high data volume. The user interface must provide reasonable performance in flying through different resolution views by appropriately filtering the amount of data processed during image computation. Filtering can occur in two ways. First, the user can select the types of data that should be presented. One user may wish to see only structural data, while another may prefer to see certain types of behavioral data in its appropriate location within the brain. Second, the DBMS should provide the user interface with appropriate mechanisms to select the granularity of data returned for a query.
2. Adaptability to available resources. The database must provide access to laboratories with a spectrum of computing resources, ranging from (a) high-performance workstations with terabytes of storage and high-speed connections to the Internet backbone to (b) personal computers running the X Windows system with one hundred megabytes of storage and periodic modem connection to a replica.

5.3 Interface Design

The interface will comprise several programs. Here we describe only the 3D Browser, which will display volume-rendered and polygon graphics in a natural 3D setting. It will be based on the interactive volume rendering program BoB (Brick of Bytes) created at the Army High Performance Computing Research Center. The 3D Browser will initially display a perspective volume rendering of the entire nervous system using MRI data. The user will then be able to "fly" into the data, navigating by familiar landmarks in the three-dimensional view. Simple markers, such as translucent planes and boxes, will indicate the presence of high-resolution confocal data, functional data, or behavioral data in a given region. As the user nears the region of interest the area of view can shrink, until only a small volume of the brain is displayed. As the user's view shrinks confocal data becomes visible, first as point locations of neurons and other features, then supplemented with outlines of features, and finally at the smallest sizes volume-rendered images of the original confocal data. The Browser will have two goals: to place high-resolution confocal and functional data in a 3D context, and to navigate to regions of interest. Once the user finds an interesting region other types of analysis become important.

We now have a prototype BoB viewer that enables a user to fly through 256x256x256 views of an MR brain image. We also have a prototype tool that aids in creating montages by making it possible to overlay images transparently to align them by landmarks. We have created a Mosaic server that includes an example of such a montage of confocal micrographs. We are working on tools for aligning confocal images with 3D MR images.

6 Preliminary Performance Analysis

We have done some preliminary performance analysis of update propagation and flying using the best disk and network performances known to us. There are also many forms of compression that can be applied to the data. Possibly, compression could reduce data sizes by a factor of 2 to 20. For flying, compression must be done in real-time. But because the effects of compression are hard to predict, we leave them out of the present estimates. Preliminary estimates convince us that we can easily achieve satisfactory performance for update proprgation. However, quick flying is more difficult.

6.1 Flying

Flying is a means by which a user can navigate through brain images in real-time. We assume 3 to 4 frames per second will be an acceptable rate to the user. Because flying involves rapid movement to a new brain location, the frames can be imprecise. Before sending the data, the server can reduce the frame resolution in each dimension by one-half to a one-fourth, reducing the data needed by one-eighth and one-sixty-fourth respectively. We call these Half-Flying and Quarter-Flying, respectively.

From the system view, flying requires several steps: image computation, data transfer and image display. Data transfer is the process of sending data from the server to the client. Image display is the process of the client drawing the data on the screen. Image computation is the process of determining what pixels to display from 3D confocal montages. There are two different methods of image computation that determine the amount of data transferred:

1. Remote image processing (Remote Flying). The server does the image computation and transfers only the 2D frame to the client. The server must be fast enough to handle all client requests. Furthermore, the network must deliver data at an acceptable flying rate. The client is only responsible for displaying the images. We estimate Remote Flying will require 8 Mbits (a mega-pixel) of data.

2. Local image processing (Local Flying). The server transfers the 3D data and the client does the image computation. The network must deliver the data at an acceptable rate and the client must do image computations sufficiently fast. We estimate Local Flying will require 128 Mbits (a 256-byte 3D region) of data.

Although we hope to make estimates for image computation and image display in the near future, currently we give estimates for only the data transfer portion of flying. Data transfer breaks down into two components: database retrieval and network delivery.

Database retrieval is the process of obtaining stored data though queries. Ultimately, query speeds are limited by disk rates. Recent studies at the Army High Performance Computing Research Center at the University of Minnesota (AHPCRC) have measured the performance of single disk arrays. When going through a file system, normal I/O runs at about 6 MB/second. Direct I/O which bypasses the file system buffer cache and beams data directly to the user's application buffer, which has been measured at 14.5 MB/sec on a non-fragmented file. Using direct I/O and striping across multiple disk arrays the AHPCRC can achieve up to N times 14.5 MB/sec where N is the number of arrays to stripe over. The AHPCRC currently stripes over 4 or 8 arrays, producing transfer rates in the neighborhood of 40MB/sec over 4 arrays using SGI's striping driver. In the 3-5 year time frame they expect to see the single array speed go to 100 MB/sec and possibly 1 GB/sec for large file transfers. If the physical design matches users' needs effectively, the database retrieval rate may approach the maximum disk rate. Table 1 shows our predictions of the maximum flying rates based on maximum disk speeds. Applications cannot exceed this retrieval speed.

Database Operation	Single SCSI	disk array	Direct I/O 1 array	Direct I/O 4 arrays	Direct I/O 8 arrays
Nominal Rate (MBytes/s)	1	6	14.5	58	116
Remote Flying (frames/s)	0.125	6	14.4	58.4	120
Remote Quarter-Flying (f/s)	8	400	880	3680	7440
Local Flying (f/s)	0.0078	0.376	0.88	3.6	7.28
Local Half-Flying (f/s)	0.063	3.04	7.2	28.8	58.4
Local Quarter-Flying (f/s)	0.5	24	58.4	232	464

Table 1. Predicted Disk Performance for Various Forms of Flying

All Normal and Direct I/O numbers are on disk arrays. Nominal Rate is the maximum data delivery rate on an unfragmented file. Flying is the rate frames are delivered when sending the exact confocal images. Half-Flying is when frames are delivered compressed one-half in each dimension. Quarter-Flying is when frames are delivered compressed three-fourths in each dimension. Local is when image computation is done at the client. Remote is when image computation is done at the server.

We predict only Remote Quarter Flying will be possible on a SCSI disk. Local Flying will only be possible with Direct I/O with 4 or more disks. Local Half-Flying and Remote Flying will only be possible on disk arrays using Normal I/O or direct I/O. Local Quarter Flying and Remote Half and Quarter Flying will be effective for all disk configurations.

Network delivery is the process of shipping the server data over the network to the client. Table 2 shows the maximum flying performance for various networks at the highest measured data rates under TCP/IP.

	9600B	T1	Ethernet	T3	FDDI	ATM	OC3
Nominal Rate (Mb/s)	0.08	1.5	10	45	100	155+	600
Actual Rate (Mb/s)	0.08	1.5	8	45	48-64	100+	200+
Remote Flying (frames/s)	0.01	0.19	1	5.7	6.3	12	25
Remote Half-Flying (f/s)	0.08	1.5	8	45	50	100	200
Remote Quarter-Flying (f/s)	0.64	12	64	360	400	800	1600
Local Flying (f/s)	0.0006	0.0126	0.06	0.36	0.40	0.75	1.6
Local Half-Flying (f/s)	0.0048	0.1	0.5	2.9	3.2	6	13
Local Quarter-Flying (f/s)	0.0384	0.81	4	23	26	48	100

Table 2. Predicted Network Performance for Various Forms of Flying

Nominal Rate is the maximum bandwidth. Actual Rate is the effective data rate under TCP/IP. We predict Local Flying will not be effective under any network configuration in the foreseeable future. Local Half-Flying will be effective on a FDDI or faster network. Local Quarter-Flying will be effective only on networks at least as fast as the Ethernet. Remote Flying will be effective on a T3 or faster network. Remote Half-Flying will be effective on any network faster than a T1. Remote Quarter Flying will be effective on any network. There is no type of Flying effective over a modem. Quarter-Flying performance will be acceptable for an Ethernet or faster network. Unfortunately, access from the internet is limited by the slowest link, often a T1. Thus, even Quarter-Flying will be unsatisfactory over the internet. Under Local Half-Flying and Local Flying even the Ethernet is not sufficient.

7 Conclusion

To the neuroscientist, databases like ours may become as important to as the laboratory. Because scientists with access will be "in" and those without access will be "out," distributed availability via computer networks is crucial. Our preliminary work encourages us. Neuroscientists found data modeling an effective means of communicating with each other and with computer scientists. We have begun implementing. The overall project capitalizes on the close collaboration and interplay among the members of a computer science team, a neuroscience team and exceptional imaging and computing facilities to develop database management techniques capable of bridging disciplinary (and continental) boundaries and facilitating interdisciplinary collaboration. By bridging the gap between neuroscience and computer science, we hope to shrink the gaps between the subdisciplines within neuroscience.

References

1. L. Barnett and J. Carlis. Feature information support and the sdts conceptual data model: Clarification and extension. In *Proceedings AUTO-CARTO 11, Eleventh International Symposium on Computer Assisted Cartography*, 1993.

2. P. Bernstein and N. Goodman. An algorithm for concurrency control and recovery in replicated distributed databases. *ACM Transactions on Database Systems*, 9(4):596–615, December 1984.

3. P. Bernstein, V. Hadzilacos, and N. Goodman. *Concurrency Control and Recovery in Database Systems*. Addison-Wesley, 1987.

4. P. Bernstein and Goodman N. An algorithm for concurrency control and recovery in replicated distributed databases. *ACM Transactions on Database Systems*, 9(4):596–615, 1984.

5. Ken Birman. Replication and availability in the ISIS system. *Operating System Review*, 19(5):79–86, December 1985.

6. A.D. Birrell, R. Levin, R.M. Needham, and M. Schroeder. Grapevine: An exercise in distributed computing. *Communications of the ACM*, 25:260–274, April 1982.

7. Michael Carey and Michael Stonebraker. The performance of concurrency control algorithms for database management systems. In *Proceedings of the Tenth International Conference on Very Large Data Bases*, Singapore, August 1984.

8. J. Carlis. *Data Modeling*. 1994. Book manuscript, in press.

9. J. Carlis and S. March. Multi-level model of physical database design problems and solutions. In *IEEE COMPDEC Conference*, February 1984.

10. J. Carlis, S. March, and G Dickson. Physical database design: A dss approach. *Information and Management*, August 1983.

11. S. M. Carlton, C. C. Lamotte, C. N. Honda, D. J. Surmeier, N. Delanerolle, and W. D. Willis. Ultrastructural analysis of axosomatic contacts on functionally identified primate spinothalamic tract neurons. *J Comp Neurol*, 281(4):555–66, 1989.

12. Jim Gray. The transaction concept: Virtues and limitations. In *Proc of the VLDB Conference*, Cannes, France, September 1981.

13. J.N. Gray, R.A. Lorie, G.F. Putzolu, and I.L. Traiger. Granularity of locks and degrees of consistency in a shared data base. In G.M. Nijssen, editor, *Modeling in Data Base Management Systems*. North Holland, Amsterdam, 1976.

14. J. Held and J. Carlis. Conceptual data modeling of an expert system. *IEEE Expert*, Spring 1989.

15. P. Kanellakis and C. Papadimitriou. The complexity of distributed concurrency control. *SIAM J. Comput.*, 14(1):52–74, February 1985.

16. L. Lamport. Time, clocks, and the ordering of events in a distributed system. *Communications of the ACM*, 21(7):558–565, July 1978.

17. C. Papadimitriou. *The Theory of Database Concurrency Control*. Computer Science Press, 1986.

18. K. Ryan and J. Carlis. Automatic generation of representative query sets. In *Proceedings of the 1984 Trends and Applications Conference, N.B.S.*, May 1984.

19. S. Sarawagi and M. Stonebraker. Efficient organization of large multidimensional arrays. In *Proceedings of the International Conference on Data Engineering*, Houston, TX, February 1994.

20. M. Senko. *Data Structures and Accessing in Data-Base Systems*. IBM Systems, January 1973.

21. D. Skeen. Nonblocking commit protocols. In *Proceedings of the 1981 ACM-SIGMOD International Conference on Management of Data*, pages 133–142, Ann Arbor, Michigan, 1981.

22. D. Skeen and M. Stonebraker. A formal model of crash recovery in a distributed system. *IEEE Transaction on Software Engineering*, SE-9(3):219–227, May 1983.

23. Michael Stonebraker. An overview of the sequoia 2000 project. Sequoia 2000 Technical Report 91/5, University of California, Berkeley, CA, December 1991.

24. Michael Stonebraker, James Frew, and Jeff Dozier. The sequoia 2000 architecture and implementation strategy. Sequoia 2000 Technical Report 93/23, University of California, Berkeley, CA, April 1993.

Combining Computation with Database Access in Biomolecular Computing

Graham J.L. Kemp[1], Zhuoan Jiao[1], Peter M.D. Gray[1] and John E. Fothergill[2]

[1] Department of Computing Science, University of Aberdeen, King's College,
Aberdeen, Scotland, AB9 2UE
[2] Department of Molecular and Cell Biology, University of Aberdeen, Marischal
College, Aberdeen AB9 1AS

Abstract. Protein structure analysis is a very important application for database technology, with industrial spinoffs. It is also very demanding because sequence search is so very different from 3-D structure search. We have developed a common data model for integrating sequence and structure data, and for relating different sequence numbering schemes to 3-D structures. We have been able to use our high-level functional language Daplex to express queries of both kinds, but using alternative storage schemas to get good performance in a way that is transparent to the user. Daplex functions can be stored in the database and associated with sub-types in an object-oriented fashion. This architecture allows practising scientists to combine complex geometric calculations with data access, which they need in order to search for complex relationships in the data which may validate or modify their hypotheses.

1 Introduction

The field of 'bioinformatics' covers all kinds of computer systems that manage biological data. Within this field, we are particularly interested in studying three-dimensional protein structures with a view to gaining a better understanding of the biological function of these important molecules and guiding experimental work.

Database management systems can be used to organise protein data, providing convenient access for a variety of studies. Two major projects, BIPED [11] and SESAM [10], have used the ORACLE and SYBASE relational databases, respectively, for storing protein structure data. While well suited to particular categories of protein structure queries, relational systems have limitations. As users of databases become more demanding in the kinds of queries which they wish to ask, these limitations become apparent and queries not anticipated by the database designer may be difficult, or even impossible to express. In our

* We are grateful to our partners in the European Biotechnology (BRIDGE) project, at ULB (Brussels), EMBL (Heidelberg), UCL (London) and ICRF (London), for discussions on protein schema design and help with fitting routines. Much of this work has been supported by the SERC.

protein work, we encounter many examples of this. We frequently want to include arbitrary geometric calculations in a query, measuring distances and angles, and applying three-dimensional transformations to structural fragments. Using a relational system, complex calculation cannot be combined easily with data retrieval, so queries can only use values which are explicitly stored in the database. Sequences are another aspect of protein data that does not fit well with relational storage – sequence information cannot be stored straightforwardly, and queries relating to sequence require several expensive join operations to be performed.

We have implemented an object-oriented database, P/FDM [9] [8], based on the functional data model (FDM) [18]. This system is implemented in a combination of C and Prolog, and data can be interrogated using Prolog and the query language Daplex. P/FDM has been used in scientific domains, principally in biotechnology [9] and geology [17]. In the work presented here, we have integrated antibody structure and sequence data to develop a system tailored to antibody analysis and modelling.

In this paper we describe the antibody application, and give examples of the kinds of search needed. We discuss the advantages of using an FDM database which has Prolog as its implementation language.

2 The Application Area

We have focused on a particular class of protein molecule – antibodies (or *immunoglobulins*). These molecules are of particular interest because they have a high degree of specificity which provides a wide range of therapeutic and other applications. Experimental developments over the past few years have led to new techniques for constructing artificial molecules based on natural antibodies. The function of these new molecules is determined by their three-dimensional structures. Therefore, insights into structure-function relationships gained through computer-based studies can be of direct value to experimentalists.

The functional data model is an example of a semantic data model. The basic concepts in the functional data model are *entities*, which are used to represent real world objects, and *functions*, which are used to represent entity properties including scalar attributes and relationships between entities. A benefit of using a semantic data model is that important concepts in the application domain can be mapped directly onto entity classes and relationships. In this section we describe the antibody application, outlining how data are represented in our database.

2.1 Antibody Sequences

The term "bioinformatics" is most widely used in relation to protein and DNA sequence data. DNA and protein molecules are natural polymers. In proteins there are 20 different kinds of amino acid residues (or "residues") forming chains usually many hundreds of residues in length. Using a different letter of the alphabet to represent each different kind of residue, a string of letters describes the composition of a protein chain (i.e. the chain's "sequence").

Antibodies normally consist of four chains of amino acid residues – two long chains of around 400 residues (referred to as "heavy" chains) and two shorter chains of around 220 residues (referred to as "light" chains). Several thousand antibody sequences have been determined experimentally. These have been collected and organised by Kabat *et al.* [13] and are available on-line. We have taken sequence data from this collection (which we will refer to as "Kabat data bank") and loaded this into our object-oriented database in accordance with the schema shown in the lower part of Fig. 1. The Daplex definition of this schema is shown in Fig. 2. In the Kabat data bank, the sequences are organised in "groups" with strong similarities. We currently store sequences in 34 of these groups, storing on average around one hundred sequences for each group.

Within each group, Kabat *et al.* [13] have identified positions at which a particular residue, or residues with similar chemical properties, invariably or very frequently occur. These positions can be grouped together into contiguous blocks referred to as framework regions. In addition to these relatively conserved regions there are others where there is no apparent "preference" and any residue type is found. These are sometimes described as the "hypervariable" regions. The entity class called kabat_group_region is used to record the extents of these regions, and the familiar codes used to refer to them. These groups and regions are well known to scientists working in this field.

When the sequences are entered into the Kabat data bank, they are compared with one another, and aligned to give the best match. An extract from such a multiple alignment is shown in Fig. 3. Since the sequences will sometimes differ in length, it is often necessary to introduce artificial breaks in the string of characters representing a sequence to maximise the number of residue matches with other sequences and thereby achieve the best possible alignment (differences in the lengths sequences are expected to have arisen through evolution, and "gaps" correspond to insertions and deletions in the genetic material). While it may be useful to know what residue is, say, the 40th in a chain it is generally more useful to know what kind of residue is at, say, position 45 in the multiple alignment. There is one kabat_group_position entity instance per multiple alignment position (i.e. alignment column) within each subgroup and both the well known Kabat data bank code for each position and the ordinal number of this position within a multiple alignment (contiguous numbers, starting at one) are recorded as attributes of this class.

2.2 Antibody Structures

While sequence data is important, we are particularly interested in studying three-dimensional antibody structures since it is a molecule's three-dimensional shape that determines its biological function. Structures of large molecules like proteins are determined experimentally by X-ray crystallography. This is a more difficult process than determining a protein's sequence, so although several thousand antibody sequences are known, only a small (but rapidly growing) number of antibody structures are known. The Protein Data Bank (PDB) [1] was established in 1971 at Brookhaven National Laboratory and has become the main

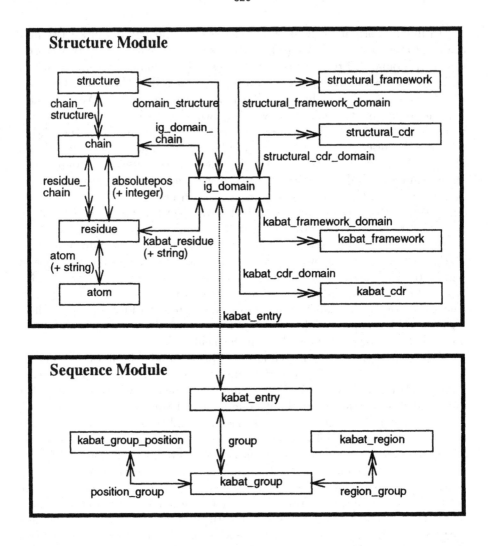

Fig. 1. Schema diagram. Object classes are represented by rectangular boxes. Labelled arrows represent relationships between objects. The dotted line represents an optional (partial) relationship.

declare structure ->> entity
declare protein_code(structure) -> string
declare protein_name(structure) -> string
declare source(structure) -> string
declare authors(structure) -> string
declare resolution(structure) -> float
declare ig_name(structure) -> string
declare class(structure) -> string
key_of structure is protein_code

declare chain ->> entity
declare structure_chain(chain) -> structure
declare component_id(chain) -> string
declare pdb_chain_id(chain) -> string
declare num_residues(chain) -> integer
declare chain_class(chain) -> string
key_of chain is key_of(component_protein),
    component_id

declare residue ->> entity
declare pos(residue) -> integer
declare name(residue) -> string
declare residue_chain(residue) -> chain
declare author_id(residue) -> string
declare kabat_position(residue) -> string
key_of residue is key_of(has_component), pos

declare atom ->> value_entity
declare x(atom) -> float
declare y(atom) -> float
declare z(atom) -> float
declare accessibility(atom) -> float
declare atom(residue, string) -> atom

declare ig_domain ->> entity
declare domain_structure(ig_domain) -> structure
declare name(ig_domain) -> string
declare ig_domain_chain(ig_domain) -> chain
declare domain_type(ig_domain) -> string
declare source(ig_domain) -> string
declare subgroup(ig_domain) -> string

declare start(ig_domain) -> integer
declare end(ig_domain) -> integer
declare kabat_entry(ig_domain) -> kabat_entry
key_of ig_domain is key_of(domain_structure), name

declare structural_framework ->> entity
declare structural_framework_domain(structural_framework) ->
    ig_domain
declare name(structural_framework) -> string
declare start(structural_framework) -> integer
declare end(structural_framework) -> integer
key_of structural_framework is
    key_of(structural_framework_domain), name

declare structural_cdr ->> entity
declare structural_cdr_domain(structural_cdr) -> ig_domain
declare name(structural_cdr) -> string
declare start(structural_cdr) -> integer
declare end(structural_cdr) -> integer
declare canonical_conformation(structural_cdr) -> integer
key_of structural_cdr is
    key_of(structural_cdr_domain), name

declare kabat_framework ->> entity
declare kabat_framework_domain(kabat_framework) ->
    ig_domain
declare name(kabat_framework) -> string
declare start(kabat_framework) -> integer
declare end(kabat_framework) -> integer
key_of kabat_framework is
    key_of(kabat_framework_domain), name

declare kabat_cdr ->> entity
declare kabat_cdr_domain(kabat_cdr) -> ig_domain
declare name(kabat_cdr) -> string
declare start(kabat_cdr) -> integer
declare end(kabat_cdr) -> integer
key_of kabat_cdr is key_of(kabat_cdr_domain), name

declare absolutepos(chain, integer) -> residue
declare kabat_residue(ig_domain, string) -> residue;

declare kabat_entry ->> entity
declare entry_code(kabat_entry) -> string
declare sequence(kabat_entry) -> string
declare group(kabat_entry) -> kabat_group
key_of kabat_entry is entry_code;

declare kabat_region ->> entity
declare region_group(kabat_region) -> kabat_group
declare region_name(kabat_region) -> string
declare region_start(kabat_region) -> integer
declare region_end(kabat_region) -> integer
key_of kabat_region is key_of(region_group), region_name

declare kabat_group ->> entity
declare group_code(kabat_group) -> string
declare chain_type(kabat_group) -> string
key_of kabat_group is group_code

declare kabat_group_position ->> entity
declare position_group(kabat_group_position) -> kabat_group
declare line_number(kabat_group_position) -> integer
declare position_name(kabat_group_position) -> string
declare invariant_residue(kabat_group_position) -> string
key_of kabat_group_position is
    key_of(position_group), line_number

Fig. 2. Daplex declaration of antibody structure and sequence data.

```
      *  *      *  *            ** **       *  **
 ... SSLSASLGDRVTISCRASQ------DISNHLNWYQQKPDGTVKLLIYY ...
 ... AIMSASPGEKVTMTCSASS-------SVSYMHWYQQKSGTSPKRWIYD ...
 ... SSLAVSVGEKVTMSCQSSQSLLYNSNQKNFLAWYQQKPGQSPKLLIYW ...
 ... SSLSASVGGRVTITCRASQ------GISNNLNWYQQKPGKTPKLLIYA ...
 ... LSLPVSLGDQASISCRSSQSLVHS-NGNTYLHWYLQKPGQSPKLLIYK ...
```

Fig. 3. Extract from a multiple alignment showing parts of five protein sequences. Asterisks mark the 11 of the 48 alignment positions at which all five proteins have the same residue. Hyphens represent gaps which have been introduced artificially to improve the alignment by increasing the number of matches found elsewhere.

depository for protein structure data. In our database we currently store data on 29 antibody structures taken from the PDB. The ball-and-stick picture of an antibody fragment (Fig. 4) shows the size and complexity of these molecules.

The schema for the structural part of the database is shown in the upper part of Fig. 1. We represent each antibody structure as a *structure* object in our database, and each structure is uniquely identified by its PDB code. Each structure is related to a set of *chain* objects, which are in turn related to the residues they contain. An amino acid residue has a main chain part and a side chain part. The 20 different amino acid residues have a common backbone composition, but differ in the side chains that are attached. For each residue we store data on its atoms, recording atom names and three-dimensional coordinates.

In addition to these entity classes which are relevant to all kinds of protein, antibodies have particular structural features that are recorded in our database and which form the basis for many searches. Each antibody chain folds in three dimensions to form globular domains. In each antibody chain there is a variable domain with around 110 residues. Three hypervariable regions, as described in the previous section, are located in each variable domain. Within a variable domain, the protein chain threads back and forth from one end of the domain to the other, traversing the domain nine times. Five of the strands form a sheet that faces another sheet made up of the other four strands. Adjacent strands in the same sheet are held together by a regular hydrogen bond pattern: thus the strands provide a stable framework from which loops emanate at either end. The connectivity of the strands in a heavy chain variable domain ("VH domain") is shown in Fig. 5. The connectivity of light chain variable domains ("VL domains") is the same. There is one *ig_domain* instance for each antibody domain (or "immunoglobulin domain") stored.

Several different numbering conventions are used by scientists to identify particular residues in an immunoglobulin domain. The most widely used numbering convention is that used in the multiple alignments produced by Kabat *et al.* [13]. These codes are assigned so that residues at equivalent positions in different structures have the same position code. However, crystallographers will be familiar with the residue codes assigned by the authors in the PDB files.

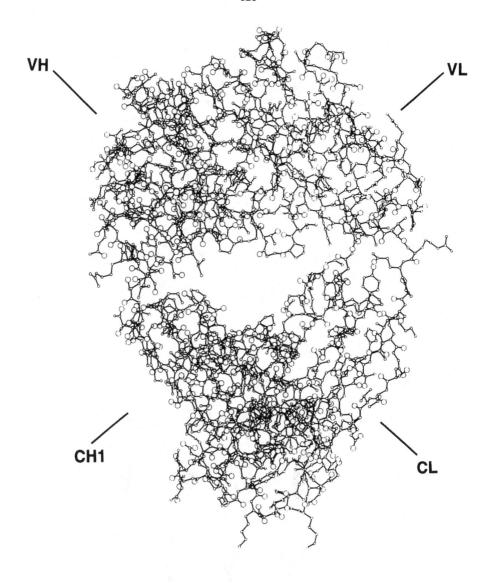

Fig. 4. Ball-and-stick model of part of an antibody molecule. Each ball represents the position of an atom; sticks represent covalent bonds between atoms. Four immunoglobulin domains are shown. The two light chain domains are on the right, with the VL domain at the top right. Two domains from the heavy chain are on the left, with the VH domain at the top left. The complementarity determining regions are at the top of the picture. (Fig. 4 and Fig. 5(a) were prepared using the QUANTA molecular modelling package, written by R.E. Hubbard, University of York.)

5(a)

5(b)

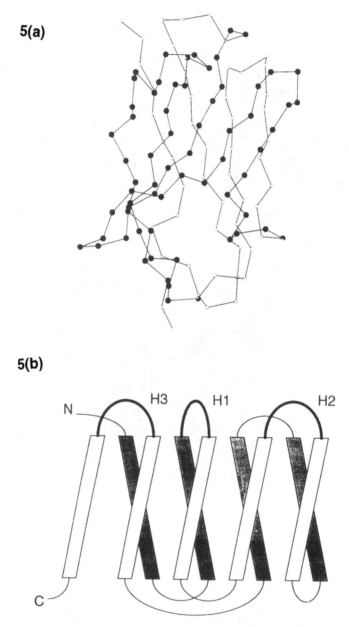

Fig. 5. Connectivity of strands in a VH domain. (a) Protein backbone trace of a VH domain. Each circle represents the position of a residue. Black circles represent residues nearest the viewer. (b) Schematic representation of a VH domain (in the same orientation as (a)). The five white rods represent strands in the larger sheet and the four shaded rods represent the strands in the other sheet. Arches at the top and bottom represent the "loops" of protein chain that link the strands. The three structural CDRs are labelled H1, H2, and H3.

These are sometimes the same as those used by Kabat, but not always. A third way to number residues is to start at one end of the chain, and to assign consecutive numbers to the residues starting at one. Therefore, three code numbers are recorded with each residue from an antibody chain – the residue identifier used in the PDB entry; the Kabat position code; the ordinal position within the chain. Our schema includes a two-argument function called *absolutepos* that takes a chain and an integer representing an ordinal position as its arguments and returns the residue object found at that position in the given chain. This function provides an index for accessing particular residues within a chain quickly, enabling navigation from a chain to particular residues of interest directly, compared with join operations that would be necessary if we were using relational storage. An important requirement for structure searches is that residues at topologically equivalent positions in different structures can be identified easily and quickly. Therefore, another index function *kabat_residue* takes an *ig_domain* object and a Kabat position code as its arguments and gives direct access to the residue at that position in the given domain.

Antibodies are the first line of the immune response system, able to bind foreign bodies like viruses and toxins. These molecules recognised by antibodies are called *antigens*. A VL domain usually lies beside a VH domain in such a way that they each contributes three loops to form a surface patch that is directly involved in binding the antigen. Structural studies of variable domains [5] [6] have shown that these loops can adopt very different conformations from one antibody structure to another, while the framework of strands remains relatively conserved. In Fig. 5, the three heavy chain variable loops are marked H1, H2 and H3. The three variable loops in VL domains are referred to as L1, L2 and L3. These structurally variable regions roughly correspond to the hypervariable regions in sequences listed by Kabat *et al.* [13], but the endpoints are often different. These variable regions, sequence-based or structure-based, are commonly referred to as the complementarity determining regions (CDRs), and it is these regions that normally establish direct contact with the antigen. It is these regions that give an antibody its specificity, and sequence modifications to an antibody in these regions may result in a molecule that binds more strongly or more weakly, or even binds to a different antigen. Structural CDRs and framework regions (established by Chothia and Lesk [5]) and sequence-based CDRs and framework regions (established by Kabat *et al.* [13]) are stored in the structural module of the database.

3 Antibody Data Searches

Sequence and structural data are analysed in very different ways. In searching sequence data we are basically performing string searches, trying to identify sequences which match a particular profile, or which have particular residues at key positions. In searching for patterns in three-dimensional structures, we frequently want to perform on-the-fly geometric calculations that may include calls to foreign code.

The main query language used with our database is Daplex. The syntax of Daplex is given in [8]. It is very general, including functions, sets, existential quantifiers, object identifiers, subtypes, multi-argument functions and recursive functions. Daplex queries are strongly type-checked and translated to Prolog for execution. Daplex can also call functions written in Prolog or C, provided they have a Daplex type definition.

3.1 Antibody Sequence Searches

A query against the sequence data typically tries to find sequences with particular characteristics, e.g. certain residues at particular positions, and then prints additional information about these sequences, or prints the number of such sequences found. Recalling that each residue type can be represented by a single letter, the one-letter code for the residue at a particular Kabat position in a sequence can be found using the function *residue_code*. Values for this function are not stored directly, but are derived by mapping to the appropriate position in the sequence when this function is called. This function takes a kabat_entry object and a (usually numeric) string representing a Kabat position code as its arguments and retrieves the one-letter code of the residue at the requested position.

The following Daplex query finds the entry codes for all light chain sequences that have a valine residue (code "V") at Kabat position 33 and an alanine (code "A") residue at Kabat position 71:

```
for each e in kabat_entry such that
    chain_type(group(e)) = "light" and
    residue_code(e, "33") = "V" and
    residue_code(e, "71") = "A"
print(entry_code(e));
```

This query is optimised and translated to Prolog code that processes the query by first iterating over all kabat_group objects, and testing these to see whether their chain type is 'light'. For those that are, the related kabat_entry objects are retrieved. For each candidate kabat_entry object, the sequence is retrieved and the function residue_code retrieves the one letter code of the residues at the requested positions. Each time the function residue_code is called, the sequence of the kabat_entry given as an argument must be retrieved from disc (or disc buffer). The sequence is then converted to a list of characters, which is passed to another Prolog predicate that processes the list recursively to find the position in the list corresponding to the given Kabat position.

This approach can answer all queries expressed in Daplex, but performance is disappointing – many of the queries relating to the sequence data are slow compared with answering these queries simply by searching flat files using standard string searching techniques or UNIX commands. However, formulating UNIX scripts to answer these queries is awkward and the scripts are devoid of any biological meaning.

To get efficient performance for these queries while continuing to express queries in Daplex with reference to the biochemical concepts described in the database schema, a program was written that attempts to generate a UNIX script from a Daplex query automatically. To see how this translation is done, let us consider how Daplex queries are normally processed in P/FDM. A Daplex query is first translated to a "list comprehension" as in functional programming, containing the essential elements of the query in a simple regular format that provides a convenient starting point for query optimisation [12]. The optimisation stage tries to improve query performance by altering the navigation path, changing the order in which objects are retrieved so that selections can be applied as early as possible. Prolog code which includes calls to primitive data access routines is generated based on the optimised list comprehension. However, list comprehensions can also be used as the basis for *application-specific optimisation*. The idea is to recognise list comprehensions for queries that perform a straightforward sequence search, and to translate these to a UNIX command that performs the same operation on the flat files of sequences.

The list comprehension for the above query is as follows:

[f | a ← kabat_entry; b ← group(a); c ← chain_type(b); c = 'light';
d ← residue_code(a,'33'); d = 'V'; e ← residue_code(a,'71'); e = 'A';
f ← entry_code(a)]

The qualifiers on the first line (generating values for variables a, b and c, and testing c) recognise that the file containing light chain sequences should be searched. The second line of qualifiers (generating and testing values for d and e) define the pattern that will constrain the search. The final line shows how the result will be generated, and is translated to a UNIX command that can extract the entry code from lines matching the search criteria. This translation is implemented easily in Prolog since items in the list of qualifiers can be matched with template queries using Prolog's unification mechanism. The two alternative routes for processing this query can be seen in Fig. 6. A variation on this kind of query is to count the number of sequences satisfying a particular pattern. This can also be translated to a UNIX script.

We accept that schema-specific optimisations like this are rather *ad hoc*. However, each optimising transformation implemented can deal with a class of queries, and are not restricted to answering only one particular query, retrieving a particular set of data values. Further, each class of query optimised in this way is one identified as important to the users, thus a small number of *ad hoc* optimisations can improve processing of many user queries since the sequence-based queries have a similar form.

The ability to introduce optimisations is a benefit of having data independence, and being able to hide the storage implementation details from users and user applications. All of the optimisations are done below the level of the conceptual schema. The point is that from the outset arbitrary queries can be formulated and answered using the system's standard data access operations. As particular kinds of query are identified as important, useful, and amenable to

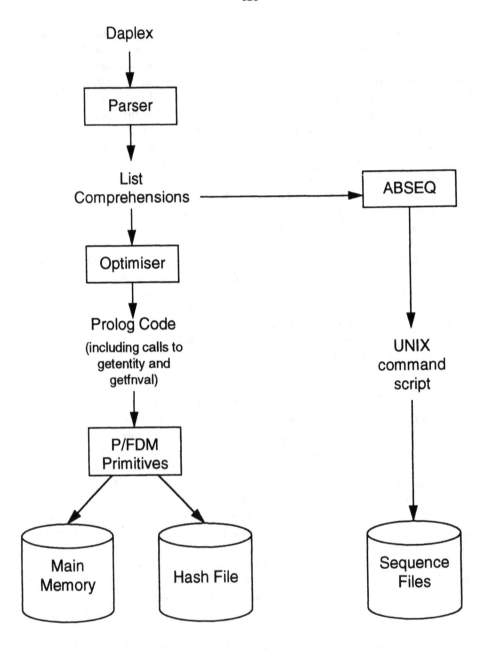

Fig. 6. Processing Daplex queries. Following the route on the left, any list comprehension can be translated to Prolog code accessing any kind of storage module. List comprehensions for simple queries against sequence data can be translated directly to a UNIX command script operating on flat files by the program ABSEQ.

being optimised by using alternative (or additional) data representations, then this can be done. Users don't lose the investment made in developing and storing queries prior to the optimisation strategies being implemented – pre-existing Daplex code will be able to take advantage of later processing improvements, since optimisation is done using the list comprehension version of queries to which all Daplex queries are first translated. The idea of storage-specific optimisation is also used in our experiments with relational storage modules, where list comprehensions relating to data stored in a relational module are translated to SQL [15].

The UNIX scripts operate on flat files that contain a copy of the sequences stored in a hash file. This requires extra storage space, but we believe this to be a worthwhile trade-off for improved performance for common sequence queries. Having an alternative stored version of the data may make schema changes more difficult – again a reason for first using standard P/FDM system facilities while experiments with prototype schemata are carried out. Only when we have established a schema to be successful for all applications initially envisaged (and we believe that it is sufficiently well structured to cope with future needs) do we turn our attention to optimising frequently asked queries. Also note that sequence data never changes unless there has been an error. Hence there is no problem of updating duplicate copies.

3.2 Antibody Structure Searches

The following examples are representative of the kinds of structural queries asked, and demonstrate calculation combined with data retrieval.

3.2.1 Arrangements of Strands within an Immunoglobulin Domain

The database can be used to examine spatial relationships between strands within a domain. Looking at the three-dimensional structure of the antibody with PDB code 7FAB, we observe that the valine residue at Kabat position 33 and the alanine residue at position 71 in the light chain are in different sheets but are adjacent in space with their side chains directed towards each other. We may speculate that the separation between the two sheets at this point may be related to the kinds of residues at these positions. The following Daplex query examines all VL domains and prints the PDB code, the names of residues at (Kabat) positions 33 and 71 and the distance between their $C\beta$ atoms:

```
for each d in ig_domain such that
   domain_type(d) = "variable" and chain_type(d) = "light"
print(protein_code(d),
   name(kabat_residue(d, "33")),
   name(kabat_residue(d, "71")),
   distance(atom(kabat_residue(d, "33"), "CB"),
           atom(kabat_residue(d, "71"), "CB")));
```

We find that when the residue at Kabat position 33 is valine, which has a small branched side chain, or methionine, which has an unbranched side chain, then the separation is between 4.15 and 4.56 Angstroms. However, when leucine, which has a larger branched side chain, is at position 33 we find the separation between the $C\beta$ atoms to be greater in all cases. In all of the VL structures in the database that have leucine at position 33, a large aromatic residue is present at position 71. The two other structures that have an aromatic residue at position 71 have a methionine residue at position 33, and their separation is small.

The function *distance* calculates the distance between the two atoms given at its arguments. It would be impractical to store the distance between all pairs of atoms in the database, so it is vital that quantities can be calculated when needed.

3.2.2 Orientation of Complementarity Determining Regions

We are interested in the orientation of the CDRs because these regions are important for specificity in binding antigen. Chothia and Lesk [5] and Chothia *et al.* [6] have made careful studies of these regions, and have identified groups of variable domains whose CDRs have similar conformations. They observe that in a particular class of VL domains (called Vλ domains), the first five residues of the L1 region have a similar conformation, and that the side chain of the isoleucine residue at the fifth position in the L1 region points inwards towards the centre of the domain. We can query the database to investigate this observation.

First we must devise a way to express "side chain pointing inwards". The first bond in the side chain connects the alpha-carbon ($C\alpha$) atom to the beta-carbon ($C\beta$), and the direction of this bond can be used as the direction of the side chain. Now, VL domains have a disulphide bond connecting the cysteine residues at Kabat positions 23 and 88. Visual inspection of any one of the known VL domain structures shows this disulphide bridge to be located in the middle of the VL domain, between the two β-sheets. Therefore, the angle defined by the $C\beta$ of the fifth residue in the L1 loop, the $C\alpha$ of that residue and the $C\alpha$ of residue 23 will be acute if the fifth residue in the L1 loop is directed towards the centre of the VL domain. A function called *angle* takes three atoms as its arguments and returns the angle (in degrees) defined by their centres. This function calls out to a routine written in C to calculate this value. The following query finds all L1 regions from Vλ domains and prints their PDB code, the names of the residues at the relevant positions and the calculated angle:

```
for each c in structural_cdr such that name(c) = "L1"
    for the d in structural_cdr_domain(c) such that
        chain_class(d) = "lambda"
      for the r1 in residue(c,5)
        for the r2 in kabat_residue(d,"23")
    print(protein_code(d), name(r1), name(r2),
      angle(atom(r1,"CB"), atom(r1,"CA"), atom(r2,"CA")));
```

The results for this query are as follows:

```
1FB4 ILE CYS 19.3
2FB4 ILE CYS 19.3
2RHE ILE CYS 18.8
3FAB ILE CYS 16.6
7FAB ILE CYS 15.8
8FAB ASN CYS 116.2
```

The first five results support the observations made by Chothia and Lesk [5]. The structure 8FAB has been determined since that earlier study. It has a very different L1 conformation and its fifth residue is an outward-pointing asparagine rather than an inward-pointing isoleucine.

An alternative way to compare the L1 conformations of the L1 regions is to superpose a pair of L1 regions and measure how well they fit. Fitting is done using a FORTRAN implementation of an algorithm for fitting two sets of points [16]. This routine calculates the transformation that best fits the first set of points onto the second and measures the root mean square (RMS) distance between the two sets. The following query finds each pair of Vλ domains in turn and for each pair prints their codes and the RMS distance calculated when main chain atoms of five residues starting at Kabat position 26 (the start of the L1 loop) in the first domain is fitted to the corresponding atoms in the second domain.

```
for each d1 in ig_domain such that
    chain_class(d1) = "lambda"
  for each d2 in ig_domain such that
      chain_class(d2) = "lambda" and d1 <> d2
print(protein_code(d1), protein_code(d2),
  main_chain_similarity(d1, d2, "26", 5));
```

We find that, apart from 8FAB, these have a similar conformation giving an RMS distance less that 0.6 Angstroms when compared. When 8FAB L1 region is compared with any of the others, the RMS distance is greater than 1.7 Angstroms.

Rather than superposing L1 regions on each other, a variation on this query is to superpose the two strands flanking this loop from two different domains to find the three-dimensional transformation that achieves the best fit. Applying this transformation to L1 loop atoms and comparing their transformed positions with the corresponding atoms in the target L1 loop shows this conformational difference more strongly.

4 Discussion

The present antibody database occupies around 60Mb and contains data on 29 structures and over 3500 sequences.

Computers are being used increasingly in protein structure studies. Computer-based structure analysis features strongly in over half of all research articles in recent issues of protein engineering journals. To date, most of this analysis has been done with interactive molecular graphics packages for visually inspecting and modelling structures, and molecular mechanics programs for performing energy calculations. Other interesting analysis is typically done using *ad hoc* software operating on "flat files". Until recently, the number of known proteins has been "manageable", with many individual researchers interested in only a small subset of these, so molecular graphics and other programs processing raw data files have been satisfactory for most studies.

Some recent projects have produced systems for querying protein structure data. A system using parameter relation rows [20] has been incorporated in the molecular modelling package WHAT IF. This makes a sequential pass through files of structure data stored as ordered sequences. Predicates over these sequences are represented as matrices of boolean flags. There is one row of flags per atom, with each flag representing a different property. Rows can be combined using logical operators to answer queries. The Iditis system [19] is based on the relational model, but the search engine has been customised for order-based queries, enabling queries about a residue and others at nearby positions specified by offset values to be answered without expensive joins. An interface to the SESAM database [10], called ALI, also enables order-based queries to be processed efficiently. Iditis and WHAT IF are not database systems in the sense that they cannot be updated and extended by users – systems are delivered with data pre-loaded. Nor can they include function calls of the kind shown in section 3.2. Nevertheless, these customised systems do give good performance for simple structure queries that require scanning large tables but do not require user-specified computations. (While we have focused on data retrieval in this paper, updates are important for some applications of protein databases, e.g. [14].)

We showed in section 3.1 how P/FDM can make use of alternative storage and searching strategies for simple sequence queries. We can envisage generating calls to tailored systems like Iditis or ALI for simple structure searches by producing code for these systems directly from list comprehensions, as described above. We should continue to use standard P/FDM access routines for more sophisticated searches and queries requiring calculation, and for data obtained locally.

The number of known structures is increasing rapidly. In 1977, there were only 77 known structures in PDB. This rose to 655 by April 1991, 1055 by January 1993, and the current release (October 1993) contains 1727 structures. This rapid rise in the number of known structures will bring new opportunities for systematic studies, while requiring better data management to provide easy access to data. Therefore, we anticipate databases playing an increasingly important role in this area, and consequently we need high-level query languages that can compute with such data.

Databases complement molecular graphics as a tool for protein structure analysis. Visual inspection of a known structure can suggest hypotheses about protein structure. Queries can then be formulated to test a hypothesis by systematically searching all other known structures to see if the hypothesis holds for these. Additionally, molecular graphics can be used to inspect the results of a database search. We have implemented an interface between the database and the molecular modelling package QUANTA that enables parts of a structure to be highlighted or molecular fragments satisfying the search criteria to be transferred and displayed automatically as the result of a database search. Using Prolog, a query can arrange to send the first result for display, and then send subsequent solutions for display as backtracking is forced.

Where an antibody sequence has been determined but its structure is unknown, it is possible to construct a hypothetical three-dimensional model based on the known structures of other antibodies. This process is known as *homology modelling*. Modelling antibody variable domains is a problem well suited to a homology modelling approach since analysis of known antibody structures has suggested procedures for modelling these with greater confidence than is generally possible for other classes of proteins. A homology modelling system has been implemented as an application of the P/FDM database [14] and has been used in modelling "humanised" mouse monoclonal antibodies. Visual inspection of these models has suggested structural reasons for observed differences in binding affinity [3] [4]. We intend developing the modelling system further, based on structural studies.

5 Conclusions

Protein structure analysis is a demanding application for database technology. Protein sequence search has very different requirements from structure search. Initially, we used hash files for storing both the structural data and sequence data, but were able to process sequence queries more efficiently by transforming and optimising the queries to work on a sequential file storage representation. This saves the user from having to learn a new query language, or use UNIX commands or C. We retain the hash file storage which is well suited to our structural work where queries tend to be more navigational. The P/FDM database provides full database facilities [8]. By adhering to a strong conceptual schema and using a high-level language like Daplex, we can use alternative physical storage schemas [7]. In addition to the hash file store used in this work, we have experimented with relational storage for storing selected object classes [15] and could similarly use a C++ object store as our storage schema.

It is our experience that the combination of semantic data model and stored method code in P/FDM provides a good foundation for developing user applications. Thus, it is encouraging for the proposed SQL3 language standard, which is moving closer to Daplex. The formal schema diagram helps in query formulation, as does the clarity and expressiveness of the query language, which is strongly typed. The database provides full functionality in accessing and manipulating data, while the data independence inherent in the system architecture means that we can improve performance incrementally, making the system a more useful tool for protein scientists. This has been further enhanced by the development of a graphical front-end that generates Daplex [2].

It is vital to be able to combine geometric calculations with data access when searching a structural database, since it is not possible to pre-compute all

conceivable distances and angles. The intermediate results of a calculation can
themselves be stored in the database if these are identified to have long-term
value and are expensive to calculate. Furthermore, the routines such as *angle*
and *main_chain_similarity* (in section 3.2.2) are integrated as methods in the
database and can be re-used by others instead of being locked up in packages.
This is one of the virtues of object-oriented technology.

Structural studies have identified structural patterns that are useful when
constructing three-dimensional models of antibodies (e.g. the effect of residues
at key positions on structural geometry). Database queries can play a role in
such studies, which can validate or modify scientific hypotheses. The increase in
the number of known antibody structures will lead to further structural patterns
being identified and this will be facilitated by good data models and high-level
querying systems.

References

1. Bernstein, F.C., Koetzle, T.F., Williams, G.J.B., Mayer, E.F., Jr., Bryce, M.D., Rodgers, J.R., Kennard, O., Shimanouchi, T. and Tasumi, M. : The Protein Data Bank: A Computer-based Archival File for Macromolecular Structures. Mol. Biol. **112** (1977) 535–542

2. Boyle, J., Fothergill, J.E. and Gray, P.M.D.: Design of a 3D user interface to a database. In Proc. Workshop on Database Issues for Data Visualization, San Jose (1993)

3. Carr, F., Tempest, P., Forster, S., Kemp, G. and Harris, W.: Development of humanised antibodies for therapeutic applications. Pharmaceutical Manufacturing International (1992) 81–83

4. Carr, F., Tempest, P., Kemp, G. and Harris, W.: Human antibodies for therapeutic application. Industrial Biotechnology International (1993) 49–51

5. Chothia, C. and Lesk, A.M.: Canonical Structures for the Hypervariable Regions of Immunoglobulins. J. Mol. Biol. **196** (1987) 901–917

6. Chothia, C., Lesk, A.M., Tramontano, A., Levitt, M., Smith-Gill, S.J., Air, G., Sheriff, S., Padlan, E.A., Davies, D., Tulip, W.R., Colman, P.M., Spinelli, S., Alzari, P.M. and Poljak, R.J.: Conformations of immunoglobulin hypervariable regions. Nature **342** (1989) 877–883

7. Gray, P.M.D. and Kemp, G.J.L.: In Praise of Daplex. Technical Report, Department of Computing Science, University of Aberdeen (1994)

8. Gray, P.M.D., Kulkarni, K.G. and Paton, N.W.: Object-oriented databases: A semantic data model approach. Prentice Hall International (UK) Ltd., Hemel Hempstead (1992)

9. Gray, P.M.D., Paton, N.W., Kemp, G.J.L. and Fothergill, J.E.: An object-oriented database for protein structure analysis. Protein Engineering **3** (1990) 235–243

10. Huysmans, M., Richelle, J. and Wodak, S.J.: SESAM: a relational database for structure and sequence of macromolecules. Proteins: Structure, Function and Genetics **11** (1991) 59–76

11. Islam, S.A. and Sternberg, M.J.E.: A relational database of protein structures designed for flexible enquiries about conformation. Protein Engineering **2** (1989) 431–442

12. Jiao, Z. and Gray, P.M.D.: Optimisation of methods in a navigational query language. In Delobel, C., Kifer, M. and Masunaga, Y. (eds.) Proc. 2nd International Conference on Deductive and Object-Oriented Databases, Springer-Verlag (1991) 22–42

13. Kabat, E.A., Wu, T.T., Perry, H.M., Gottesman, K.S., and Foeller, C.: Sequences of Proteins of Immunological Interest, 5th edit., Public Health Service, NIH, Washington D.C. (1992)

14. Kemp, G.J.L.: Protein modelling: a design application of an object-oriented database. In Gero, J.S. (ed.) Artificial intelligence in design '91, Butterworth-Heinmann Ltd., (1991) 387–406

15. Kemp, G.J.L., Iriarte, J.J. and Gray, P.M.D.: Efficient Access to FDM Objects Stored in a Relational Database. To be published, Proceedings BNCOD-12 (1994)

16. McLachlan, A.D.: Gene Duplication in the Structural Evolution of Chymotrypsin. J. Mol. Biol. **128** (1979) 49–79

17. Owens, J. Gray, P.M.D. and North, C.P.: The Stochastic Modelling Toolbox. Proceedings EUROCAIPEP 93, PSTI (1993)

18. Shipman D.W.: The Functional Data Model and the Data Language DAPLEX. ACM Transactions on Database Systems **6** (1981) 140–173

19. Thornton, J.M. and Gardner, S.P.: Database Analysis for Protein Engineering. CDA News, Molecular Modelling and Protein Engineering Series, Part 7 (1993)

20. Vriend, G.: Parameter relation rows: a query system for protein structure function relationships. Protein Engineering **4** (1990) 221–223

An Object-Oriented Database of Protein Structure Data

Michio Nakanishi[1], Minoru Ito[2] and Akihiro Hashimoto[1] *

[1] Department of Information and Computer Sciences, Faculty of Engineering Science, Osaka University, Toyonaka, Osaka 560, Japan

[2] Graduate School of Information Science, Nara Institute of Science and Technology, Ikoma, Nara 630-01, Japan

E-mail : naka@ics.es.osaka-u.ac.jp

Abstract. An object-oriented database system is being developed, which is used to store protein three-dimensional structure data. Proteins from Brookhaven's Protein Data Bank (PDB) are classified by their enzyme code numbers and each protein is represented as a composite object. The system provides a number of methods to avoid writing lengthy Object-SQL (OSQL) statements for complex queries. Furthermore, fixed views are also provided to achieve efficient query processing.

Keywords: object-oriented database, view, protein structure, protein modeling

1   Introduction

Computer-aided molecular modeling, protein structure predictions, molecular mechanics, and dynamics calculations are widely used for understanding three-dimensional structures of proteins and their relationships to biological functions [1, 2]. These interest and the increase in the number of known protein structures have created a demand for convenient access to protein structure data. Brookhaven's Protein Data Bank (PDB) has become established as a main repository for crystallographically determined protein structure data [3]. It contains flat files in a "standard" format, which are typically accessed using Fortran programs.

However, the need for more convenient access led to projects for storing protein structure data in relational databases. There are two major projects: Birbeck Integrated Protein Engineering Database (BIPED) [4] and SESAM [5]. The former uses ORACLE as a relational database management system. In BIPED, protein data of PDB are organized into ten relations that reflect hierarchical

---

* We would like to thank Prof. M. Kusunoki at the Institute for Protein Research, Osaka University, Japan, for his helpful advice on our database. We also thank K. Katano, M. Yoshida and A. Chimura in our research group for writing elegant C++ code.

Structure relation

BRCODE	PNAME	PFUNCTION	PSOURCE	. . . . . .
4HHB	HEMOGLOBIN	TRANSPORT	HUMAN..	. . . . . .
2PAB	PREALBUMIN	TRANSPORT	HUMAN..	. . . . . .
. . .	. . .	. . .	. . .	. . .

Chain relation

BRCODE	CHAINID	NRES	. . .
4HHB	A	141	. . .
4HHB	B	146	. . .
4HHB	C	141	. . .
4HHB	D	146	. . .
2PAB	A	127	. . .
2PAB	B	127	. . .
. . .	. . .	. . .	. . .

Residue relation

BRCODE	RNAME	POSITION	CHAINID	. . .
. . .	. . .	. . .	. . .	. . .
4HHB	SER	3	A	. . .
4HHB	PRO	4	A	. . .
4HHB	ALA	5	A	. . .
. . .	. . .	. . .	. . .	. . .
4HHB	VAL	17	A	. . .
4HHB	GLY	18	A	. . .
. . .	. . .	. . .	. . .	. . .

Figure 1. Data representation in BIPED

information at the protein structure, chain, residue (amino acid), and atom levels. A part of the relations are shown in Figure 1. On the other hand, SESAM implemented a protein database using SYBASE. The database is an integration of structural data obtained from PDB with sequence information from other databanks such as SWISS-PROT. It also contains higher level of topological properties, as well as a molecular dictionary and an interface to conventional molecular graphics.

While these are well suited to particular kind of queries for protein data, there are still drawbacks in relational systems, as follows:

1. Sequence data must be expressed explicitly by serial numbers, and join operations are necessary to evaluate queries relating to such a sequence. Common key attributes between relations, such as BRCODE in Figure 1, require extra storage space.

2. It is difficult to deal with text data of variable length such as remark field in PDB.

3. It is not easy to write a complex condition in a where clause of SQL.

These problems can be solved using object-oriented databases (OODBs). Problems (1) and (2) are solved by defining each protein as a composite object. The feature of modeling composite objects enables a database designer to reflect the

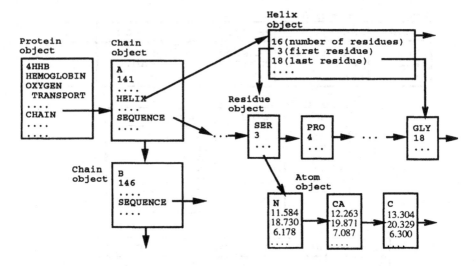

Figure 2. The conceptual structure of a protein

structure of a protein on a database schema in a natural and intuitive way. A residue sequence of variable length can be represented as a set of objects threaded by pointers, and thus space redundancy of key attributes should be reduced. Other data of variable length can also be represented as constituent objects of composite objects as mentioned above. As for problem (3), methods can be provided in OODB, which are frequently used or which require complex calculations. By providing appropriate methods, users can write a query with a complex condition succinctly. P/FDM is the first OODB system to store protein data [6, 7, 8]. Most of the data from BIPED are stored in the system. Since P/FDM is an integration of Prolog with a functional data model (FDM) database, its data can be accessed using prolog, and thus applications requiring data retrieval and calculation can be prototyped rapidly. OOPDB is another project using object-oriented approach [9, 10]. PDBlib and PDBtool are being developed and extended as parts of the project; the former is an object-oriented class library written in C++ for representing protein structures, and the latter is a prototype structure verification tool with graphical user interface (GUI).

In this paper we present a protein database system using VERSANT, which is a commercially available OODB management system. Protein data are classified by their enzyme code (EC) numbers[1] and are stored in our database accordingly. Figure 2 illustrates the conceptual structure of a protein that is modeled as a composite object in our system.

Section 2 gives a definition of our database schema including attributes and

---

[1] The EC number enables a systematic classification of enzymes, which consists of 'E.C.' and four digits. For example, the EC number of an isonicotinimidylated liver alcohol dehydrogenase is E.C.1.1.1.1.

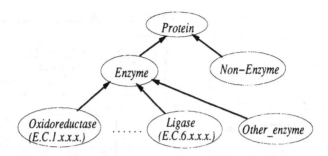

Figure 3. A class hierarchy (*isa* relationships)

methods. In section 3, we discuss the methods, by which a typical retrieval can be expressed succinctly. Section 4.1 presents implementation issues related to performance. Section 4.2 gives two major differences between P/FDM and our system, and section 4.3 presents the view mechanism provided in our system. Our conclusions are mentioned in Section 5.

2 The database schema

2.1 A class hierarchy and composite objects

The class hierarchy of our database schema, shown in Figure 3, is based on the EC numbers. Each class is represented by an oval, which contains the class name. Each arrow between ovals denotes an *isa* relationship between the corresponding classes; that is, the "to" class is a superclass of the "from" class. For convenience, class names are given in italic. All proteins are in class *Proteins*, which is categorized into two subclasses, *Enzyme* and *Non-Enzyme*. The

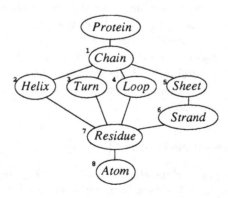

Figure 4. A composite object (*is-part-of* relationships)

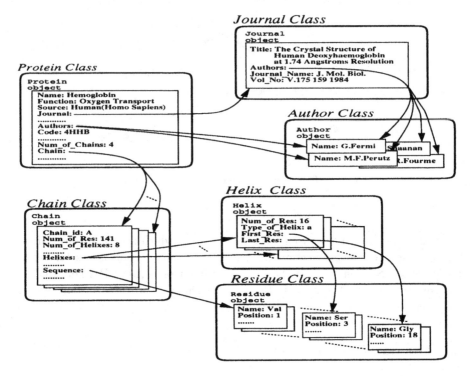

Figure 5. An example of a protein structured as a composite object

two classes inherit all attributes and all methods from *Proteins*. Enzymes are categorized into seven subclasses by EC numbers, thereby the class *Enzyme* has seven subclasses accordingly. Each protein must belong to a leaf class in Figure 3.

Each protein consists of a number of chains, and a chain consists of four kinds of secondary structure: helix, turn, loop, and sheet. Each secondary structure is a sequence of residues, and each residue consists of a number of atoms. It is natural to represent each protein as a composite object that reflects the protein structure explained above. Figure 4 briefly shows *is-part-of* relationships between classes forming a composite object. A more detailed figure of a composite class structure is shown in Figure 5 including bibliographic data classes such as *Author* and *Journal*, where each rectangular box denotes an object and each arc denotes a pointer to the constituent object.

2.2 The attributes of each class

There are two types of class attribute; one is a key word in PDB and another is not a key word but a data item, such as "resolution", extracted from the commentary in the PDB file. This section describes some of the characteristic attributes. Each attribute is written in bold face and followed by a brief explanation.

1: *Proteins* has 24 attributes. Six of them are listed below. (The attributes of *Proteins* are given in Appendix A.)

- **Name** : the name of the protein.
- **Functional_Classification** : the functional name of the protein.
- **Authors** : the names of researchers who analyzed the protein.
- **Structure_Analysis_Method** : the method used to analyze the protein three-dimensional structure.
- **Resolution** : the wavelength of X ray used to analyze the protein three-dimensional data.
- **Refinement** : the method of the refinement after analyzing the protein three-dimensional structure.

2: *Enzyme* inherits all the attributes from *Proteins* and has **EC_number** as an additional attribute.

3: *Oxidoreductase, Transferase, Hydrolase, Lyase, Isomerase, Ligase, Other_enzyme* are the subclasses of *Enzyme* and inherit all the attributes from *Enzyme*. They have no additional attributes.

4: *Non-Enzyme* is another subclass of *Proteins* and inherits all the attributes from *Proteins*. There is no additional attribute.

2.3 The methods of each class

There are three types of method, as follows:

Type A: Display the primitive value of the attribute.

Type B: Get the object identifier (OID) that is a means of navigating through a complex network of objects.

Type C: Examine whether or not the protein satisfies a particular condition. (This type of method returns a Boolean value: true or false.)

This section describes a number of interesting methods. (Some of the prototypical methods of *Proteins* are given in Appendix B.)

1: *Proteins* has about 50 methods. Some of them are listed below. Here, the first three methods are of type A, **get_chain** is of type B, and the remainings are of type C.

- **display_all** : Display all the attribute values of the protein.
- **display_name** : Display the value of **Name** attribute.
- **display_3D** : Display the three-dimensional structure of the protein.
- **get_chain** : Get all the OIDs of the chain objects that compose the protein object.
- **judge_sequence** : For a given residue sequence, examine whether or not the protein contains the residue sequence in its chains. For example, suppose that "Ala–{Gly, Ser}– ?–Ala–*–Gly" is given as a residue sequence. This means that the first residue is alanine, the next is either glycine or serine, the third is an arbitrary residue, the forth is alanine, and the last is glycine. Furthermore, by the symbol "*" there may be an arbitrary number of residues between the fourth and the last residues.

- **judge_structure** : For a given secondary structure pattern, examine whether or not the protein contains the secondary structure pattern in its chains.
- **judge_structure** : For example, suppose that "bab" is given as a secondary structure pattern. Then the method examines whether or not the protein contains a β-sheet, followed by an α-helix and a β-sheet.
- **judge_keyword_in_authors** : For a given string, examine whether or not the string occurs in an object in *Author* pointed by the **Authors** value.

2: *Enzyme* inherits all the methods from *Proteins*. There are two additional methods **display_EC_number** and **display_all** of type A, as follows:

- **display_EC_number** : Display the value of the attribute **EC_number**.
- **display_all** : Display all the attribute values of the protein including the EC_number. Note that the method overrides the method **display_all** defined in *Proteins*.

3: *Oxidoreductase, Transferase, Hydrolase, Lyase, Isomerase, Ligase, Other_enzyme* inherit all the methods from *Enzyme*.

4: *Non-Enzyme* inherits all the methods from *Proteins*.

3 Retrievals

A query with a complex condition tends to have a lengthy **where** clause, if it is written in usual SQL. However, using object-SQL (OSQL), which is one of the main query languages of VERSANT, a query may contain methods in **select** and **where** clauses. Thus, if appropriate methods are provided to compute complex calculations, users will be able to write queries succinctly using the methods. To show how methods are useful in our database compared to the retrievals from BIPED, let us illustrate two example queries. Suppose that we want to retrieve proteins whose resolution is less than 2.0 Å. In BIPED, the query can be written in SQL, as follows:

```
select  p.PNAME
from    Structure p
where  p.RESOLUTION < 2.0
```

On the other hand, the query can be written in OSQL, as follows:

```
select  p.get_name()
from    Proteins p
where  p.get_resolution() < 2.0;
```

In this case, there is no significant difference between the queries. Let us next consider a query to search for a residue pattern "Ala-Gly-Ala". The query may be written in SQL, as follows:

```
select  s.BRCODE, s.PNAME
from    Structure s, Chain c, Residue r₁, Residue r₂, Residue r₃
where   s.BRCODE = c.BRCODE          and  c.BRCODE = r₁.BRCODE
  and   c.CHAINID = r₁.CHAINID       and  r₁.RNAME = "Ala"
  and   c.BRCODE = r₂.BRCODE         and  c.CHAINID = r₂.CHAINID
  and   r₂.RNAME = "Gly"             and  c.BRCODE = r₃.BRCODE
  and   c.CHAINID = r₃.CHAINID       and  r₃.RNAME = "Ala"
  and   r₁.POSITION + 1 = r₂.POSITION and  r₂.POSITION + 1 = r₃.POSITION
```

In our database, however, using the method *judge_sequence* given in Section 2.3, we can write the query in a very succinct form, as follows:

```
select  p.get_code(), p.get_name()
from    Proteins p
where   p.judge_sequence("Ala–Gly–Ala");
```

Figure 6 shows how this query is executed on VERSANT-Screen. The back window shows the query written by a user and the front shows the corresponding result.

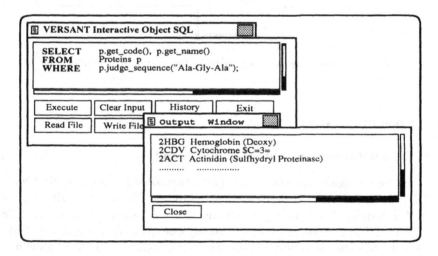

Figure 6. Execution of a query on VERSANT-Screen

We are also designing a GUI using X-window. Figure 7 shows a sample browser window for our database. Note that the application program that implements the GUI makes good use of views (which will be discussed in Section 4.3) in order to execute a given query efficiently.

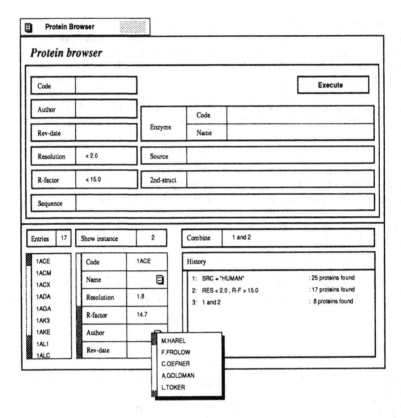

Figure 7. An example of a window in the graphical user interface

4 Implementation

4.1 The database size and its improvement

We have been implementing our protein structure database under VERSANT on a SUN SPARC station. Methods are coded in C++. The database size is about 500 MegaBytes, while the original October 1992 release of PDB is about 280 MegaBytes. The increase in the size is mainly due to our design policy that each atom is represented as an object. Note that atom data (coordinates) amount to 90 percent of the whole PDB data and that each atom data takes only 80 bytes. Thus, overhead of making an object for each atom becomes tremendous. Because the atom data are usually unnecessary for retrieval, we are now changing the schema, in which all the atom data of one protein are gathered, compressed, and then stored as a single object (see Figure 8). This results in reducing the database size to 200 MegaBytes. Furthermore, the reduction will make it faster to visualize the three-dimensional structure of a protein, because the visualization program will be able to have the whole atom data of a protein at once.

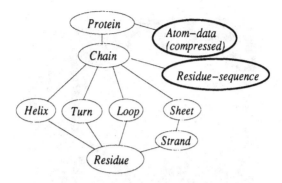

Figure 8. Revised composite object schema

It is expected that queries to search for residue sequences are very frequent, but such queries require only residue names. Thus, in order to retrieve residues, it is inefficient to navigate the pointers as shown in Figure 2. By adding a new class, *Residue-sequence*, that holds the residue name sequence (amino acid sequence), we will be able to improve the search speed of a given sequence. From our experience, these kind of care should be necessary when an object is composed of many smaller objects.

The molecular structure of the retrieved protein can be visualized on a screen in a variety of representations, such as wire-frame, backbone, union-of-spheres, sticks, ribbons, and ball-and-stick. The visualization can be implemented by dynamically linking the public domain visualization software, RasMol [11]. Figure 9 shows human hemoglobin structure represented as a union-of-spheres surface. This kind of graphics interface will give users intuitive understanding of modeling proteins.

4.2 Differences between P/FDM and our system

There are two major differences between P/FDM and our system. First, all proteins are classified into eight leaf classes as shown in Figure 3 in our system (that is, each object expressing a protein must belong to a leaf class), while they are not classified in P/FDM. This classification will reduce the retrieval time for those queries specifying enzyme classes. Secondly, our system provides views. Though the views should be prepared in advance by a database designer and may not be defined by users, they will also lead to fast retrieval since they restrict the objects to be searched. Detailed discussion on the views will be given in section 4.3.

4.3 View

Most of the relational databases provide the ability to create a view which is a "virtual" relation defined by a query from one or more stored relations. The

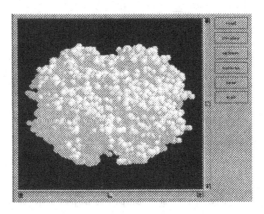

Figure 9. A molecular structure generated by RasMol

relational operations such as join, select, and project may be used to define a view. A database administrator can define views to protect some data from unauthorized accesses and to be able to change the conceptual schema without affecting users' applications. Each view can also be used as a short hand (macro) constructed from stored relations. While the concept of view has been studied extensively in relational databases, it is largely unexplored for OODBs [12]. To the authors' knowledge, no commercial OODB management system supports views except O_2 [13, 14]. Tanaka et al. proposed a way to support views in the environment of Smalltalk [15]. They define a new class called "View" to manage views, and each instance of "View" holds a view definition.

In our database, we provide a kind of view by defining a new class. Let us consider a query in which an EC number is specified. Since the proteins are classified and stored according to their EC numbers, it suffices to search the class of proteins having the specified EC number, e.g. *Oxidoreductase* for "EC1xxx," and thus the query can be evaluated efficiently. For a query in which no EC number is specified, however, we have to search all proteins in all leaf classes. For example, a query for finding the proteins whose sources are "human" will require exhaustive search in the database. In order to avoid such a situation, we provide a kind of view in our system. To implement views in our database, we define a new class *"View,"* make an instance in *View* for each view, and store the set of OIDs satisfying the specified view definition in each instance. In this sense, our view is considered as a kind of *materialized view* [13, 16], or can be regarded as an index in relational databases. In Figure 10, an example view is illustrated, which contains the set of OIDs of protein objects whose sources are "human."

There is no need for users to update our database, thereby no update operations are supported in our system. Furthermore, since the update of PDB is done by releasing a new version of PDB, the corresponding update of ours can

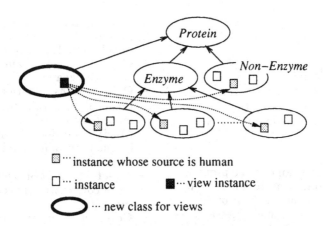

Figure 10. View implementation

be done by reconstructing the whole database from the PDB quarterly release. Thus we are free from the problems relating to update (including update through a view).

5   Conclusion

We have presented a protein structure database under VERSANT. The proteins are classified and stored according to their EC numbers. Each protein is modeled as a composite object in an intuitive and natural way. A number of useful methods are implemented and enable users to write queries succinctly. View function is also provided, which will lead to efficient query processing. It is not difficult to add methods that will be used frequently to our system. (Such a method can be found by interviewing protein researchers.)

Since PDB contains inconsistent data and has a variety of data formats, it was very difficult to convert the PDB data accurately into ours. It took a lot of time to remove the inconsistency in PDB, since we must do by hand. Two data formats, Abstract Syntax Notation 1 (ASN.1) and Crystallographic Information File (CIF), are going to be used in order to remove the ambiguity of the current PDB format. The new release of PDB will include data in these formats. We hope the standardization will greatly help both protein researchers and database designers to deal with protein structure data.

Appendix

A Attributes

The appendix gives the attributes of *Proteins*, *Chain*, *Helix*, and so on.

Proteins

- **Name** : the name of the protein.
- **Functional_Classification** : the functional name of the protein.
- **Authors** : the names of researchers who analyzed the protein.
- **Structure_Analysis_Method** : the method used to analyze the protein three-dimensional structure.
- **Resolution** : the wavelength of X-ray used to analyze the protein three-dimensional structure.
- **Refinement** : the method of the refinement after analyzing the protein three-dimensional structure.
- **Source** : species, organ, tissue and mutant from which the protein has been obtained.
- **Journal** : the literature citation that defines coordinate set.
- **References** : the important papers relating to the structure which originate from the depositor's laboratory except the paper in Journal.
- **Remarks** : general remarks.
- **Sites** : the identification of residue groups comprising the various sites.
- **Code** : the name of the PDB file containing the protein data.
- **Heteros** : the identification of non-standard residues, prosthetic groups, inhibitors and solvent molecules (except water), etc.
- **Number_of_Chains** : the number of the chains forming the protein.
- **Chains** : the pointers to the chain objects.
- **Date** : date when the protein was originally entered in PDB.
- **Revision_Date** : revision date.
- **Footnotes** : footnotes relating to specific atoms or residues.

- **Scale** : transformation from orthogonal Å coordinates into fractional crystallographic coordinates.
- **Cryst** : unit cell parameters, space group designation.
- **Origx** : transformation from orthogonal Å coordinates into submitted coordinates.
- **Mtrix** : transformations expressing non-crystallographic symmetry.
- **Tvect** : translation vector for infinite covalently connected structures.
- **Connects** : connectivity attributes.

Class attributes of constituent objects are listed below.

1. *Chain*

- **Chain_id** : the chain identifier.
- **Number_of_Residues** : the number of residues forming the chain.
- **Number_of_Helixes** : the number of helixes forming the chain.
- **Number_of_Turns** : the number of turns forming the chain.
- **Number_of_Loops** : the number of loops forming the chain.
- **Number_of_Sheets** : the number of sheets forming the chain.
- **Helixes** : the pointers to the helix objects.
- **Turns** : the pointers to the turn objects.
- **Loops** : the pointers to the loop objects.
- **Sheets** : the pointers to the sheet objects.
- **Sequences** : the pointer to the first residue object in the chain.

2. *Helix*

- **Number_of_Residues** : the number of residues forming the helix.
- **Type_of_Helix** : type of the helix (e.g., α-helix, π-helix).
- **First_Residue** : the pointer to the first residue in the helix.
- **Last_Residue** : the pointer to the last residue in the helix.

3. *Turn*

- **Number_of_Residues** : the number of residues forming the turn. type of the helix (e.g.,
- **First_Residue** : the pointer to the first residue in the turn.
- **Last_Residue** : the pointer to the last residue in the turn.

4. *Loop*

- **Number_of_Residues** : the number of residues forming the loop.
- **First_Residue** : the pointer to the first residue in the loop.
- **Last_Residue** : the pointer to the last residue in the loop.

5. *Sheet*

- **Number_of_Strands** : the number of strands forming the sheet.
- **Strand** : the pointers to the strand objects.

6. *Strand*

- **Number_of_Residues** : the number of residues forming the strand.
- **Parallel** : parallelism or anti-parallelism of the strand with respect to the previous strand.
- **First_Residue** : the pointer to the first residue in strand.
- **Last_Residue** : the pointer to the last residue in the strand.

7. *Residue*

- **Name** : the name of the residue.
- **Position** : the position of the residue in the chain.
- **Ssbond** : the pointer to the partner residue of disulfide bond.
- **Number_of_Atoms** : the number of atoms forming the residue.
- **Atom** : the pointers to the atom objects.

8. *Atom*

- **Name** : the name of the atom. weight of the atom.
- **Coordinate_X, Y, Z** : coordinate set.

B   Methods

The appendix gives some of the protypical methods of type C in Section 2.3.

- **judge_keyword_in_name** : For a given set of keywords, examine whether or not the protein's attribute **Name** contains all the keywords.
- **judge_keyword_in_title** : For a given set of keywords, examine whether or not the title of the reference about the protein contains all the keywords.
- **judge_keyword_in_authors** : For a given name, examines whether or not the attribute **Authors** of the protein contains the name.
- **judge_keyword_in_source**: For a given set of keywords, examine whether or not the protein's attribute **Source** contains all the keywords.
- **judge_keyword_in_refinement**: For a given set of keywords, examine whether or not the attribute **Refinement** of the protein contains all the keywords.
- **judge_residue_in_site**: For a given residue, examines whether or not the protein's attribute **Sites** contains the residue.
- **judge_hetero_in_protein**: For a given set of names, examine whether or not the attribute **Heteros** of the protein contains all the names.
- **judge_sequence**: For a given sequence of residues, examine whether or not the protein contains the sequence in the chain.
- **judge_sequence_in_helix, judge_sequence_in_loop, judge_sequence_in_turn, judge_sequence_in_strand**: For a given sequence of residues, examine whether or not the protein contains the sequence in each secondary structure.
- **judge_structure**: For a given pattern of the secondary structure, examine whether or not the protein contains the pattern in the chain.

References

1. Pattabiraman, N., Namboodiri, K., Lowrey, A., and Gaber, B.P.: "NRL_3D: a sequence-structure database derived from the protein data bank(PDB) and searchable within the PIR environment," Protein Sequences and Data Analysis, vol. 3, pp.387-405 (1990).
2. Clark, D.A., Barton, G.J., and Rawlings, C.J.: "A knowledge-based architecture for protein sequence analysis and structure prediction," Journal of Molecular Graphics, vol. 8, pp.94-107 (1990).
3. Bernstein, F.C., Koetzle, T.F., Williams, G.J.B., Meyer, D.F., Brice, M.D., Rodgers, J.R., Kennard, O., Shimanouchi, T., and Tasumi, M.: "The Protein Data Bank: A computer-based archival file for macromolecular structures," Journal of Molecular Biology, vol. 112, pp.535-542 (1977).
4. Islam, S.A. and Sternberg, M.J.E.: "A relational database of protein structures designed for flexible enquiries about conformation," Protein Engineering, vol. 2, no. 6, pp.431-442 (1989).
5. Huysmans, M., Richelle, J., and Wodak, S.J.: "SESAM: A relational database for structure and sequence of macromolecules," Proteins, vol. 11, pp.59-76 (1991).
6. Gray, P.M.D., Paton, N.W., Kemp, G.J.L., and Fothergill, J.E.: "An object-oriented database for protein structure analysis," Protein Engineering, vol. 3, no. 4, pp.235-243 (1990).
7. Gray, P.M.D. and Kemp, G.J.L.: "Finding hydrophobic microdomains using an object-oriented database," Computer Applications in the Biosciences, vol. 6, no. 4, pp.357-363 (1990).
8. Gray, P.M.D., Kulkarni, G.K., and Paton, N.W.: "Object-oriented databases: A semantic data model approach," Prentice Hall (1992).
9. Chang, W., Shindyalov, I.N., Pu, C., and Bourne, P.E.: "Design and Application of PDBlib, A C^{++} Macromolecular Class Library," CABIOS (to appear).
10. Pu, C., Alessio, E., Groeninger, A., Shindyalov, I.N., Chang, W., and Bourne, P.E.: "PDBtool: An Object Oriented Toolkit for Protein Structure Verification," (draft).
11. Sayle, R. and Bissell, A.: "RasMol: A program for fast realistic rendering of molecular structures with shadows," Proceedings of 10th Eurographics Conference (1992).
12. Rundensteiner, E.A.: "Multi-View: A methodology for supporting multiple views in object-oriented databases," 18th International Conference on Very Large DataBases, pp.187-198 (1992).
13. Mamou, J.-C. and Medeiros, C.B.: "Interactive manipulation of object-oriented views," 7th International Conference on Data Engineering, pp.60-69 (1991).
14. Abiteboul, S. and Bonner, A.: "Objects and views," SIGMOD, pp.238-247 (1991).
15. Tanaka, K., Yoshikawa, M., and Ishihara, K.: "Schema design, views and incomplete information in object-oriented databases," Journal of Information Processing, vol. 12, no. 3, pp.239-250 (1989).
16. Bertino, E.: "A view mechanism for object-oriented databases," 3rd International Conference on Extending Database Technology, Lecture Notes in Computer Science #580, pp.136-151 (1992).

Active Database Technology Supports Cancer Clustering

H.-J. Appelrath[1], H. Behrends[2], H. Jasper[2], V. Kamp[1]

[1] Kuratorium OFFIS e.V., Westerstr. 10-12, 26121 Oldenburg
[2] Universität Oldenburg, Fachbereich Informatik, Abteilung Informationssysteme,
Postfach 2503, D-26111 Oldenburg,
e-mail: [jasper,behrends]@informatik.uni-oldenburg.de

Abstract. Our research group is considered with the definition, implementation and application of novel concepts for database management systems. Here we present the joined experiences of introducing active capabilities on top of a relational database system and its application in the context of cancer clustering. Active databases provide rules in order to enhance conventional databases by mechanisms for detecting events and triggering the corresponding actions. Events are raised due to state changes in the database, by a clock or by external components. Actions manipulate the database, trigger external tools, signal to the user etc. Clustering cancer cases in time and space is the basis for empirical studies on their determinants. We present our approach for detecting clusters in tumour registries. The latter provide information about national or area-wide cancer cases. In the system presented here hypotheses on cancer clusters are generated as soon as significant events have encountered.

Keywords: Healthcare, Medical Information Systems, Active Databases, Event Management and Monitoring

1 Introduction

The project Active_INEKS aims at novel cancer clustering techniques using active database technology. A conventional, relational database documents cancer cases in a predefined area, here the Weser-Ems-Region in North-West Germany. Incoming data is stored and epidemiologists are allowed to use it for testing hypotheses on cancer clusters and their determinants. Additional, e.g. spatial data can be related to data about cancer cases. The behaviour of such a passive cancer registry is not very sufficient because no relationships are detected by the system itself although all data and necessary statistical tests are available within the system. Epidemiologists utter always similar queries in order to find significant relationships. This could at least be automated by periodical statistical tests and informing the epidemiologists about the findings. We tried to incorporate some of this automatic "active" behaviour into the cancer registry in the project Active_INEKS. The resulting system is designed to inform some epidemiologist on findings about cancer clusters or determinants in the stored or incoming data, respectively (see Figure 1 for a scetch on the scenario).

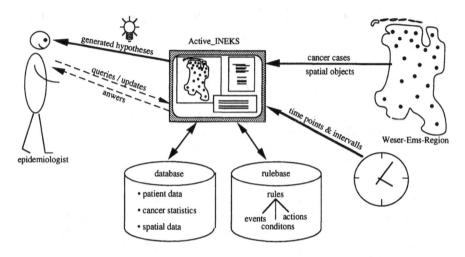

Fig. 1. Active_INEKS Scenario

The approach pursued in Active_INEKS should support cancer research mainly in two areas: In the first place, it should automatically generate hypotheses about cancer-clusters for epidemiologists. Events in time and space are used to find time-space-configurations that are candidates for such clusters. Secondly, it uses periodical statistical tests in order to evade the need for (re-) computing totally new statistics each time an update on cancer data arrives. These periodical tests are long lasting processes that are informed about relevant events and thereafter decide on new statistical evidences. The active database development environment AIDE is applied for realising Active_INEKS. It provides event-condition-action-rules, called (EC)*A-rules, for the specification of events and corresponding actions. An integrated component for statistical tests implements periodical methods and provides events as a result of detected significance. This paper is organised as follows. First we give more details on the application domain, i.e. cancer clustering. Thereafter, some basics on active databases are given. Our prototype implementation of an active database toolbox is presented in the following section. Some aspects on the implementation of Active_INEKS with this toolbox are detailed in the fifth section. The paper finishes with concluding remarks and an outlook on further research.

2 Cancer Clustering

To overcome cancer is not only still an immense medical task but also an increasing interdisciplinary task, see [12] and [13]. The main aim of investigating causality is to improve prevention. Therefore computer supported population-based cancer registries are an important foundation. They improve methodical founded cancer research providing the possibility to manage huge and differentiated data about cancer diseases, death and complementary health-related data. Besides they offer new chances and methods to support epidemiological research for monitoring the development of diseases especially cancer by modern database technology and interactive and appropriate visualisation mechanisms.

Indispensable for modern health reports are descriptive epidemiological studies which are used to evaluate the data. Descriptive epidemiology is population-based and not related to individual cases. It deals with the occurrence of diseases, their respective accumulations, especially their spatial and / or temporal distributions in comparison to standardised populations. A continuous description of the development of cancer diseases in the population depends on an operating epidemiological cancer registry and is based on the periodical computation of quantified indicators. Indicators like mortality describe the health state of the population and are strongly related to the living environment and therefore can be influenced by collective and social activities. Public health policy and activities change with changing technology and social values, but the goals remain the same, for example: to reduce the amount of disease and premature death.

Analysing the spatial distribution of regional health data is a common way to detect possible health risks within a population. Those investigations are based on a systematic analysis of mortality data. Cluster analysis belongs to this set of statistical methods used to group variables or observations into strongly interrelated subgroups. To detect regional patterns in health data it is necessary to define measures of spatial clustering and to use significance tests evaluating the similarity of adjacent data values. The patterns may represent various environmental effects like relation to socio-economic status and urbanisation. In general the interpretation of health data efforts additional knowledge. Therefore, environmental data has to be integrated, like: socio-demographic data, geographic data and data describing the health risks resulting from the technical and social environment. For example the event of an increased cancer rate around an incineration plant for garbage can only be estimated in the right way if data concerning the pollutants, the kind of disease and the age composition of the population is available. In routine vital statistics there are already measures or indicators like population density, urbanisation, medical health services, area usage, social and economic data or the living quality. To support epidemiological research these indicators have to be integrated into an environmental-related information-system. Interrelation between the data serve to generate hypotheses concerning striking temporal or spatial situations and their causalities. Often the hypotheses are already known and are verified by the data. Such a verification, often periodical, is carried out only on special database queries of the epidemiologists although all relevant data is available. With modern "active" database technology the available data can be evaluated by automated instructions.

Using "passive" database technology for rare health events like cancer the rate of occurrence in a region could increase without being easily recognised. An "active" system enables for example earlier detection of such increases in the rate of incidence. An incidence rate is a measure of the rate at which new events occur in the population. The number of new cases of a specified disease reported during a defined period of time is the enumerator, and the number of persons in the stated population in which the cases occurred in the denominator. Therefore an event like an increased incidence rate of leukaemia around an incineration plant for garbage can be detected at the time of its occurrence. Because of the generated hypotheses of a possible increased rate an immediate reaction like special follow-up studies can succeed. To explore relations between cases and environmental influences the database has to manage geographic data as well. On the top of geographic information geo-operators, for example **around**, have to be defined in order to specify spatial events like in the previous example.

The "active" informationsystem seems to be able to generate hypotheses pointing to statistical significant and striking temporal respectively spatial situations. Epidemiological knowledge is coded in rules to detect striking temporal or spatial situations in the corresponding database. The rules are tested continuously whether they match the data. Matching the data means that the variables in the conditional part of the rule are instantiated with concrete cases. Subsequently the rules can fire and appropriate hypotheses are automatically generated. The significance of the hypotheses has to be proofed by a statistical test.

3   Active Databases

Traditional databases (i.e. relational and object-oriented databases) are called passive, because they react only on queries and update requests. Most database systems provide consistency checking that results in additional reactions but only due to violations of the logical consistency of the database. Active databases need enhancements of passive database features, in order to

- react on changes in the status of objects managed within the database or
- react on time events, e.g. when reaching a predefined time point for a periodical statistical test (figure 7) or after any time interval has elapsed or
- react on other application specific events, e.g. occurrence of a specific number of cancer cases or defining new regions or intervals for clustering.

These enhancements concern especially the language necessary for describing active behaviour as well as the implementation of the corresponding runtime system. Active databases (ref. e.g. [3], [4], [5], [6], [7], [9], [14], [15]) provide means for specifying active behaviour and monitoring incoming events. They supply rule based languages, as e.g. introduced in [5]. Each rule consists of three parts, describing events, conditions and actions (ECA-rule for short). The semantics is as follows: each time an event is detected and the conditions are satisfied the corresponding action will be performed. Since these ECA-rules have their roots in the database community, they usually concentrate on update and time events. Therefore, the ECA-rules introduced so far are extensions of the older trigger languages for consistency checking in databases. The basic components of an active database are visualised in Figure 2. The darker shadowed rectangles in the upper right part of Figure 2 show the three major components for the implementation of active databases, namely:

- **Rule management**

  The rule management component is the core of an active system. Those parts of the process model that should be handled automatically are implemented by rules within the active database. Rules are specified in the form of situation-action pairs. Generally, a situation is described by a first order expression, but here we are interested in the appearance of situations. Therefore, a situation is described by events and conditions. Events are happenings of interest (see [6]). Our rule language must be expressive enough to model the events relevant for cancer clustering and corresponding statistical actions. Conditions are expressions on the state of the database about cancer cases etc. Actions are activities that should be carried out automatically when the corresponding situation has been detected. Actions may be database updates, triggering of statistic tools or notification of the users of Active_INEKS, i.e. epidemiologists.

- **Event monitoring**

  This component registers atomic events that occur as update requests on the database, result from attaining defined time stamps or from elapsing predefined time intervals or come from external systems like statistic package as described in the next section. It proves whenever such an atomic event encounters whether a complex situation described by the rules has occurred and, if positive, triggers the corresponding action. The conditions are usually tested by querying the database. Actions may result in additional events, which again are monitored by this component. Events are persistently stored for both, monitoring complex situation and explaining system behaviour to the user.

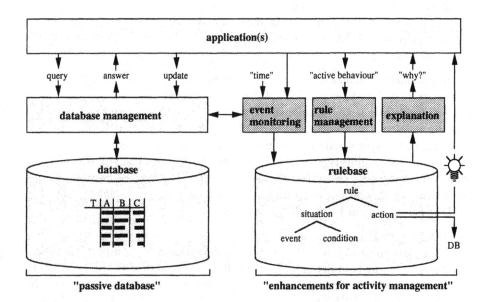

Fig. 2. Components of an active database

– **Explanation**

This component is necessary for the user of an active cancer clustering system in order to follow the systems actions and reactions. Whereas in a passive environment the user triggers e.g. the statistic tools and therefore expects the system to behave in some or the other way, in an active environment the system may behave in an unforeseen way displaying messages about hypotheses or some computed value. Being faced with this eventually unexpected behaviour the need for a sophisticated explanation facility is obvious.

The implementation of an active cancer clustering system following the given scenario uses our environment for building active information systems which incorporates an extensible active database management system and a development environment.

4 AIDE: An Environment for Implementing Active Databases

Our active database management system and active database engineering environment is called AIDE (Active Information Systems Development Environment). We support active behaviour of databases especially via complex, external events, that may occur e.g. in statistic tools, user interfaces or other plugged in devices. Therefore, we propose an extensible approach for event description, that allows for intermixing atomic as well as complex events and conditions. Atomic events may occur

– in the database as result of update requests,
– as time stamps from a clock,
– as call-backs due to interactions at the user interface of applications,
– as signals from plugged in devices or
– as messages from other software components, here especially statistic tools.

AIDE provides interfaces to the different external components through so-called active abstract datatypes (AADT). Like abstract datatypes (ADT) AADT describe the interface of any component as a set of procedures (here called actions) that encapsulate the module. Additionally, an AADT specifies the set of event types for the atomic events that may occur at the components interface, therefore we call such a datatype active. Following the discussion above it is obvious that AIDE must provide active abstract datatypes for the database, the clock, the user interface and for the statistic tools and spatial data management. The AADTs for AIDE can be detailed as follows:

– **DATABASE**

This component provides the usual data definition and manipulation procedures including transactions. Additionally, for each state-changing procedure an event type is defined in the interface of the module DATABASE, e.g. INSERT(Object), DELETE(Object) and MODIFY(Object), where "Object" is the parameter for events of this type, i.e. a real or virtual database relation.

- **TIME**

  The clock provides procedures for setting and querying the actual date and time. Operators like BEFORE, AFTER and BETWEEN, DURING, AT, EVERY allow for the specification of timing constraints for complex events. The TIME component signals e.g. arrivings of time marks and elapsing of time intervals to the event manager.

- **USER_INTERFACE**

  This modul provides access to all features of a graphical user interface management system (we will use X_Fantasy, see [8], an in-house developed extension of the X-Window System). The call-backs of the window system due to object or menu selection are interpreted as events in our AIS environment.

- **STATISTIC TOOLS**

  There are several statistical methods available in the statistic package. Worthy to notice is the index-of-dispersion test that has been implemented as a joined approach with the faculty of mathematics. This test is e.g. periodical performed as result from sufficient new data and signals events about significant findings regarding anormal distribution of cancer cases.

- **SPATIAL DATA**

  An additional component is implemented for handling spatial data (in the database as well) in order to relate hypothetical cancer-clusters to environmental data, ref. [1].

Figure 3 shows our layered approach for the implementation of the AIS environment AIDE. The active abstract datatypes are provided on the basic I-AIS-layer. The different active datatypes are joined together in the language layer of the AIDE-architecture, called ADL. Besides the traditional data definition and data manipulation statements the languages of the L-AIS layer provide so-named (EC)*A rules in the activity description language ADL, see the discussion below. On the top layer of our AIS prototype we develop tools for engineering active databases (ref. 10], [11]). These include browsers, editors and visual programming tools.

ADL

The core of active database technology is the introduction of event-condition-action-rules. Our AIDE toolbox provides ADL (Activity Description Language), which is the major extension w.r.t. conventional database technology. ADL provides an enhanced dialect of the ECA-rules known in the literature. We call the constitutens of ADL "(EC)*A-rules" in order to point out that events and conditions may be arbitrarily intertwined. Each (EC)*A rule consists of two parts, the "(EC)*" part describes an event type and the "A" part describes the actions to be performed when a matching event of the corresponding event type occurs.

The (EC)* part specifies an atomic or complex event. Each complex event type in turn is specified by combining either atomic event types that are provided by the various AADT of the I-AIS layer or already specified complex event types. Atomic event types can be combined via boolean operators, see left part of Figure 4. The (n-ary) AND-operator defines a new event type that specifies that at least one matching event of each constituent must be detected before the

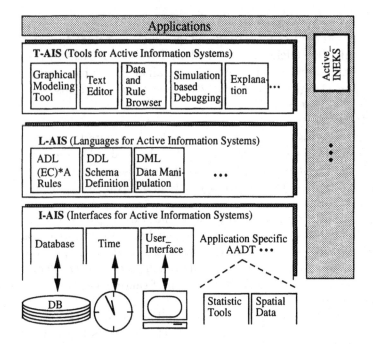

Fig. 3. The AIDE Toolbox

complex event of this type is recognised. The (n-ary) OR-operator realises the corresponding OR-semantics. The (n-ary) SEQ-operator specifies a sequence, i.e. has AND-semantics and an additional ordering in time on the elements of the complex event. The COUNT-operator specifies a complex event as the occurrence of a predefined number of some other event. The NOT-operator is allowed only in special cases, i.e. in combination with fixed time constraints. The right part of figure 4 depicts the tree structure of a complex event description without additional constraining conditions. Each E defines some arbitrary type of atomic or complex event. The corresponding ADL expression (see figure 5 for an excerpt of our language) is as follows (note the infix-notation for 2-ary AND -/OR -operators):

```
EVENT Complex = AND (E,  SEQ(E, COUNT 3 OF E) OR E),  E AND E) END EVENT
```

Atomic and complex events can be constrained, especially by boolean expressions on database states and by temporal expressions. For example, the AADT TIME provides the operators BETWEEN, DURING and AT that allow for constraining complex event types using other basic or complex event types from arbitrary AADT, since each event has appropriate time information attached.

Actions are either basic procedures of one of the active datatypes of the I-AIS layer or combined expressions consisting of such basic procedures interconnected by sequencing conditional and repetition operators. Figure 5 depicts some syntactic definitions of our language.

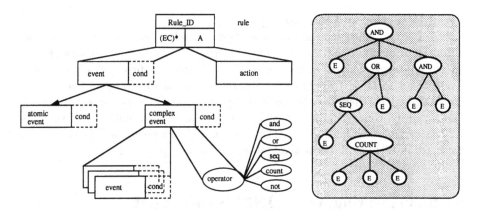

Fig. 4. Structure of (EC)*A-rules in ADL and complex event type

```
rule_spec          ::= "RULE" rule_id
                       "ON" event_id
                       "DO" action_id expr_list [";"]
                       [ "STATE" ("active" | "nonactive") ";"]
                       [ "PRIORITY" num ";"]
                       [ "VERSION" num ";"]
                       [ "EXPLAIN" string ";"]
                       "END_RULE".
generic_event_spec ::= "GENERIC_EVENT"
                       generic_event_id "("formal_parameter_list ")" "="
                       alias_decl
                       event_type
                       "END_GENERIC_EVENT".
event_spec         ::= "EVENT" event_id "="
                       ["FIFO" | "LIFO"]
                       ("GENERIC_EVENT_INSTANCE"
                       generic_event_id  "("actual_parameter_list"))
                         | (alias_decl
                            event_type)
                       "END_EVENT".
event_type         ::= atomic_event ["ALIVE" num time]
                       | comp_event
                       | "[" atomic_event ["ALIVE"num time] "WHERE" condition"]"
                       | "["comp_event "WHERE" condition "]".
comp_event         ::= event_id
                       | "(" event_type ")"
                       | "COUNT" num "OF" "(" event_type ")"
                       | event_type "AND" event_type
                       | event_type "OR" event_type
                       | ["SOFT"] "SEQ" "(" event_list ")"
                       | event_type ["NOT"] "BETWEEN" interva
                       | "(" "NOT" event_type ")" "BETWEEN" : terval
                       | event_type ["NOT"] "DURING" num time
                       | event_type ["NOT"] "AT" time_stamp
                       | "EVERY" num time "BETWEEN" interval:
                       | "TRANSACT" "(" "TBEGIN" "," event_l: t "," transact_end ")".
action_spec        ::= "ACTION" action_id form_list [ ":" tyr ] "="
                       var_decl
                       statement_seq
                       "END_ACTION".
...
```

Fig. 5. An extract of the ADL-syntax

Event Detection and Processing

For each (EC)* expression in an application, i.e. ADL program, there exists an automaton for detecting the matching complex events. The semantics of such an automaton is defined in the sense of a coloured Predicate/Transition Net. Events lead to state transitions in automatons until the complex events that are described by them are detected. Thereafter, the corresponding actions are performed. Of course, cyclic invocations of event detection and action execution may occur and must be eliminated (in a test and debug phase, see the simulation approach in [2]) before the active database goes into production.

5   Implementing Active_INEKS with AIDE

The Active_INEKS application for cancer clustering consists mainly of four parts:

- The **database** contains data about cancer cases and environmental facts in the Weser-Ems-Region (North-West Germany, Lower Saxony State, 2.2 million inhabitants).
- The **statistic package** provides several statistical tests, i.e. index-of-dispersion test, exposition-test and community-dependency-test.
- The **rule base** specifies the active behaviour of Active_INEKS, especially when to perform a statistical test and when to inform the epidemiologists.
- The **user interface** provides a sophisticated graphical presentation of data and findings to the user.

Each of this components is presented in more detail in the sequel.

The Active_INEKS database

The Active_INEKS database concentrates on information about cancer cases, i.e. patient and treatment data, and about the environment in the Weser-Ems-Region. For each patient detailed information about diseases is stored, besides the usual personal data like age, sex, living place, etc. For each disease of a patient the corresponding treatments are noticed. Additionally, information about deaths are stored. Each patient is related to the corresponding administration area. These in turn are defined as spatial objects, using polygons (i.e. ordered sets of BorderPoint). Arbitrary information is related to the administration areas, e.g. age-specific rates, industries, pollutions, neighbourhood, etc. Figure 6 depicts the entity-relationship schema (normalised w.r.t. n-m-mappings) of Active_INEKS. The database itself is encapsulated via the aforementioned AADTs `Database` and `Spatial Data`. Additional access to aggregated data is possible via the statistic package, i.e. the AADT `Statistic Tools`.The actual extension exists of 13.400 patients, 14600 primary tumours, 5000 secondary manifestations, 3900 deaths, 9100 treatments, 160 Industrial areas, 5 major cities, 12 counties, 134 communities.

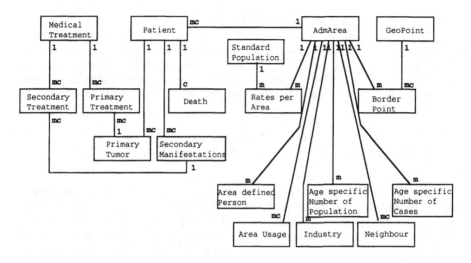

Fig. 6. Part of ER-Schema of Active_INEKS

The Active_INEKS statistic package

The statistic package has been implemented in C++. One class for mathematical standard distributions (Normal, Poisson and χ^2), one for testing significance of values and one for accessing the test data from the database have been implemented. These classes use the three existing test methods, i.e. index-of-dispersion test, exposition-test and community-dependency-test, each one implemented as a class of its own. These set of test-classes can easily be extended by additional

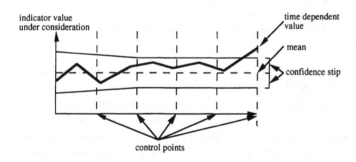

Fig. 7. Periodic statistic test

test methods. Figure 7 shows the characteristics of such a statistic test. The confidence stip is computed by methods of the class for testing the significance depending on the according test. The actual time dependent value is computed from the tuples in the database.

Aspects of ADL-rules in Active_INEKS

Such a test is periodically performed by specifying a corresponding ADL rule. In this case we can define a periodic event using the EVERY-clause and call the test with corresponding parameters in the action part. Other rules in the rule base mirror special interest of epidemiologists. Consider a specialist for leukaemia. Of course, she is interested in leukaemia cases. The following event reflects her interest:

```
EVENT Leukaemia_Case(Patient) = INSERT(primaertumore, Patient)
    WHERE (Patient.ICD_Code >= 204 AND Patient.ICD_Code <= 208)
END EVENT
```

Whenever such an event encounters she wants to be informed and a community-dependency-test to be performed. Therefore, an action has to be specified, that calls the corresponding method from the statistic-AADT. Additionally, the industries in the community are looked for an exposition test, if the leukaemia-case showed significance for a cluster. This looks like the following:

```
ACTION TEST_COMMUNITY( Com: COMMUNITIES, ages: TUPLE OF INT,
                       ICDs: TUPLE OF INT) =
PRINTINFORMATION("Leukaemia-case in %s", Community);
IF STAT_COMM_TEST(Com, ages, ICDs)>=STAT_COMM_TEST_SIGNIFICANCE_THRESHOLD
THEN PRINTINFORMATION("Significant Comm. Dep and exposition test
                      is %i",STAT_EXPOS_TEST(Com, ages, ICDs))
END IF
END ACTION
```

Event and action specification are combined in the following rule called "Leukaemia", in which the test is called with the community, the patient is living in, low age classes (special interest: children) and the according ICD codes:

```
RULE Leukaemia = ON Leukaemia_Case(Patient)
    DO TEST_COMMUNITY(Patient.community,
                      [0,5,10,15],[204, 205, 206, 207, 208])
END RULE
```

Generally, the rules in Active_INEKS are of various categories. There are rules for consistency definition, just like triggers in ordinary database applications. In these consistency rules only database updates are used for specifying events. One other major class of rules represent the epidemiologists methods of investigation. Typically, those cases in which statistical tests are meaningful are defined by events. These events are specified by database updates and conditions on the state of the database (mostly number of stored cases of interest), sometimes with additional time constraints.

The Active_INEKS user interface

Answers and findings are presented to the user of Active_INEKS via a sophisticated user interface. This interface is accessible from ADL-rules, i.e. user-interface-events can be defined as events in ADL and methods of the user-interface-tool kit may be called in action-parts of ADL-rules. The following Figure 8 shows the

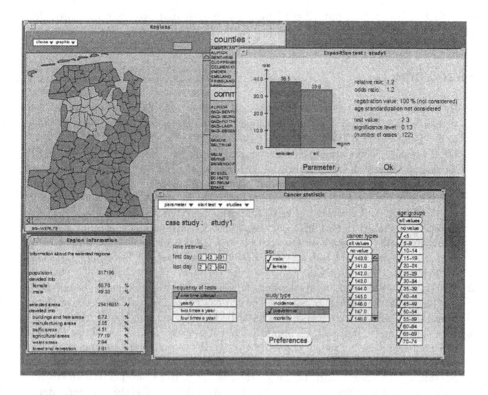

Fig. 8. Typical Active_INEKS user interface configuration

interface of a typical session of an epidemiologist. There are 4 coloured windows. In the upper left part the Weser-Ems-Region is presented, showing the areas and communities. These are coloured in correspondence to a just performed statistical exposition test, see the upper right window. More information about the selected regions (lighter polygons in the map of the Weser-Ems-Region) is given in the lower left window, e.g. area size, population, area usage etc. The lower right window shows the various buttons and panels used by the epidemiologist for tailoring the actual statistic test.

6   Concluding remarks

In this paper we present our prototypical implementation of the extensible active database management environment AIDE and its application to cancer epidemiology in the Active_INEKS project. The prototype is realised in a relational environment. Active behaviour is integrated through (EC)*A-rules which allow for describing complex application-specific events by intermixing basic events and conditions from integrated, application specific active abstract datatypes. Up to now, the data are managed within the relational prototype. The implementation of a first version of the (EC)*A rule language has been carried out by a project team with about 12 students. A sophisticated user interface provides the graphically definition of interesting regions and displaying statistical data.

References

1. H.-J. Appelrath, H. Behrends, H. Jasper, H. Ortleb: "Die Entwicklung aktiver Datenbanken am Beispiel der Krebsforschung", Proc. Datenbanken für Büro, Technik und Wissenschaft, BTW'93, Springer Verlag, 1993.
2. H. Behrends: "Simulation-based Debugging of Active Databases", Proc. IEEE Workshop "Research Issues in Database Engineering, RIDE 94", Houston, TX, 1994.
3. H. Behrends, H. Jasper, H. Ortleb, A. Beesten, K. Dargel, J. Friebe, R. Ihmels, G. Kempen, J. Kuth, F. Laskowski, I. Luers, J. Rettig, A. Robbers, F. Wietek, C. Wobbe, H.-J. Appelrath: "Aktive Informationssystem: Endbericht der Projektgruppe", Technical Report IS/15/A, Dept. of CS, Universität Oldenburg, 1993.
4. S. Chakravarthy: "Making an Object-Oriented DBMS Active: Design, Implementation, and Evaluation of a Prototyp", EDBT'90 Int. Conf. on Extending Database Technologie, 1990.
5. U. Dayal, B. Blaustein, A. Buchmann, U. Chakaravarthy, M. Hsu, R. Ledin, D.R. McCarthy, A. Rosenthal, S. Sarin: "The HiPAC Project: Combining Active Databases and Timing Constraints", SIGMOD RECORD, Vol. 17, March, 1988.
6. N. Gehani, H. V. Jagadish, O. Shmueli: "Event Specification in an Active Object-Oriented Database", Proc. of the ACM SIGMOD International Conference on Management of Data, 1992.
7. S. Gatziu, A. Geppert, K.R. Dittrich: "Integrating Active Concepts into an Object-Oriented Database System", Proc. 3rd. Int. Workshop on Database Programming Languages (DBPL), Nafplion, 1991.
8. R. Götze: "Object-Oriented Specification of Complex Dialogues", Proc. Eurographics Workshop on Object-Oriented Graphics, Champery, 1992.
9. R. Hull, D. Jacobs: "Language Constructs for Programming Active Databases", Proc. of the 17th International Conference on Very Large Data Bases, Barcelona, 1991.
10. H. Jasper: "Aktive Informationssysteme und ihr Entwurf", Proc. 4th GI-Workshop "Grundlagen von Datenbanken", Technical Report, ECRC, TR ECRC-92-13, Munich, 1992.
11. H. Jasper: "Active Databases for Active Repositories", Proc. 10th IEEE Conf. on Data Engineering, "ICDE 94", Houston, TX, 1994.
12. B. MacMohan, T.F. Pugh: "Epidemiology", Little, Brown and Co.,Boston, 1970.
13. G. Mann, R. Haux: "Database Schema Design for Clinical Studies Based on a Semantic Data Model", Computational Statistics and Data Analysis, Vol. 15, North Holland, 1993.
14. D.R. McCarthy, U. Dayal: "The Architecture Of An Active Data Base Management System", Proc. of the ACM SIGMOD Intern. Conference on Management of Data, 1989.
15. M. Stonebraker, A. Jhingran, J. Goh, S. Potamianos: "On Rules, Procedures, Caching and Views in Data Base Systems", Proc. of the ACM SIGMOD International Conference on Management of Data, 1990.

A Gateway from DBPL to Ingres [*]

Florian Matthes[1], Andreas Rudloff[1], Joachim W. Schmidt[1], Kazimierz Subieta[2]

[1] University of Hamburg, Dept. of Computer Science, Vogt-Kölln-Straße 30, D-22527
Hamburg, Germany, e-mail: J_Schmidt@informatik.uni-hamburg.de
[2] Polish Academy of Sciences, Institute of Computer Science, Ordona 21, PL-01-237
Warszawa, Poland, e-mail: subieta@wars.ipian.waw.pl

Abstract. A gateway from DBPL (being a superset of Modula-2) to the
commercial database system Ingres is described. DBPL extends Modula-
2 by a new bulk data type constructor "relation", persistence, and high-
level relational expressions (queries) based on the predicate calculus,
thereby maintaining the basic concepts of the language like strong typing and orthogonality. The gateway enables the user to write *normal*
DBPL programs for accessing Ingres databases. This is in contrast to
typical implementations that embed SQL statements into a programming language and results in a fully transparent interface for DBPL programmers. DBPL queries and statements referring to Ingres tables are
automatically converted into corresponding SQL statements, are evaluated by the Ingres database server and the results are transferred back
under the control of the DBPL program. This procedure also resolves
queries referring to both Ingres and DBPL tables. The design assumptions of the gateway and the used implementation methods are presented
as well as design and implementation difficulties.

1 Introduction

The coupling of programming languages with relational database systems is
based conventionally on embedding a query language into a programming language. The border distinguishing querying and programming languages has become, however, more and more fuzzy. Many functionalities typical for programming languages and programming environments were fixed in the SQL standard as capabilities of the "query language". Besides the impedance mismatch,
this approach involved yet another disadvantage known as *bottom-up evolution*,
i.e. extending incrementally and *ad hoc* the functionalities of query languages
with the result that many positive features that were the reason for the initial development were lost. This concerns mainly SQL which recently evolved
in the direction of programming languages (which is especially striking in the
INGRES/Windows4GL [Ingr90] and Oracle PL/SQL [Orac91]).

Initial motivation and trends in the development of query languages were
different from those of programming languages. One basic assumption was simplicity and naturalness of the whole query interface, called *user-friendliness*.
The positive aspects of user-friendliness include data independence, declarativity,

---

[*] This research was supported by ESPRIT Basic Research (FIDE)

simplification of notions concerning data views, macroscopic operations allowing the user to determine extensive computations in a compact form, and a syntax similar to a natural language. However, user-friendliness also means the restriction of the language' s functionality and power as well as non-orthogonality of the language' s constructs (e.g. due to syntax). Real applications may consist of a large number of queries and other constructs with the consequence that other interpretations of user-friendliness are of vital importance such as preventing the user from his/her own errors, computational completeness, and support of various programming abstractions.

Database Programming Languages (DBPL-s) are to be distinguished from these pure query languages. DBPL-s are strongly and statically type checked (allowing the removal of many errors before a program is executed) as well as syntactically and semantically orthogonal (leading to a reduction of the number of necessary primitives in the language, as well as the size of manuals). They support full computational and pragmatic universality as well as various programming abstractions and have clean semantics. DBPL-s adopt the concept of a query language as a powerful construct of a programming language. The language DBPL [ScMa91, ScMa92, MRSS92] extends Modula-2 in several directions. In particular, it introduces persistence, bulk data (relations) and high-level relational expressions (equivalent to queries), which allow declarative and associative access to relation variables.

Despite the various advantages of DBPL, we are aware that it has little chance of success in the commercial world as a complete system. As observed in [Banc92], products of research activity suffer from the "new programming language syndrome": very few organizations are ready to adopt a new programming language or a new system. DBPL is a new product working with its own database format produced at a university. Clients of database systems usually prefer the long existence of the databases, since investment in gathering data, writing programs, education of staff, organization of technological routines of data processing, etc. is high. Commercial systems are equipped with a large family of utilities which are not implemented in DBPL since (however very useful) they do not present scientific problems. We do not expect, therefore, that potential clients of database systems will decide to use DBPL as the only tool for the full development of database applications.

University software such as DBPL and their concepts, however, can be transferred to the commercial world as a supplement on top of popular and widely distributed systems. Many professionals who are dissatisfied with the capabilities and the programming style offered by languages such as SQL embedded in some host language delivered with commercial database systems are potential DBPL clients. Direct use of the high level language with its clean concepts is at hand with storage and access of the data, for example, in an Ingres database, thereby allowing the use of all the tools supported by the system. This was the main reason for deciding to create the gateway. Vice versa, the implementation of the gateway allows the DBPL community - students and researchers - to access large commercial database systems and thereby use, within the DBPL programming environment, their various capabilities.

There are several possible approaches in designing a gateway. In this project we decided to couple the DBPL run-time system with the Ingres SQL machine [IngrA89, IngrB89]. All references from DBPL programs to Ingres databases are transformed during run-time into dynamic SQL statements. This permits the use of the SQL optimizer and all capabilities of Ingres that are "below" the SQL machine (concurrency, indices, views, Ingres/Star, gateways, etc.). The interface is fully transparent to DBPL programmers: knowledge of SQL and Ingres is not necessary. This approach does not support the opinion that SQL should be the "intergalactic language" [SRLG+90] for the next database era, but only accepts a widely used standard. We do not believe that SQL, as a programming language, has reached its maturity (despite fixing it in huge standards).

The paper is organized as follows. In Section 2 we present briefly similarities and differences between DBPL and Ingres SQL. In Section 3 we discuss possible methods of mapping DBPL constructs into SQL statements and present the methods chosen. In Section 4 we present architectural assumptions of the gateway in connection with the architecture of DBPL. In Section 5 implementation difficulties are discussed.

2 Similarities and Differences of DBPL and Ingres SQL

There are significant differences in the available types for structuring data offered by Ingres and DBPL. Full orthogonality of type constructors is a leading principle in DBPL which results in the possibility of defining nested relational structures whereas Ingres allows flat relations only. On the level of queries orthogonality of DBPL f.e. allows range relations of queries to be described by queries itself, in SQL this is not possible. Persistence in DBPL is also introduced as a orthogonal property of modules (DATABASE MODULEs) allowing variables of every type (except pointer-variables) to become persistent. INGRES only supports persistent relations.

Primary keys of relations in DBPL are considered as a structural property of a relation and as such they are declared in the definition of the relation type. The semantics of some operators depends on them. In contrast to this primary keys in Ingres are defined for relation variables and used only internally (for creating an index structure). For querying the information about primary keys is irrelevant. As a consequence DBPL does not allow duplicate tuples either in stored relations or in intermediate query outputs, but Ingres does so. So efficient programming of some tasks in DBPL may prove impossible.

Both Ingres SQL and DBPL make the distinction between querying a database and processing a database. SQL was designed for retrieval and then extended by some programming capabilities, that is, inserting, deleting and updating. It is not computationally complete: more complex (but still typical) programming tasks require a classical (host) programming language. In DBPL the main reason for the distinction between queries and other constructs of the language is query optimization. DBPL is based on the assumption that queries problematic for query optimizers should be forbidden syntactically. As a consequence, functions and operators are not allowed within DBPL predicates. This restriction results in a potential for good performance, however, it violates the orthogonality principle. As consequence it is practically impossible to utilize in DBPL queries requiring capabilities available in SQL like arithmetic operators, aggregate functions and grouping.

By high-level constructs we denote such programming capabilities which support data independence and follow the "many-data-at-a-time" principle. We list all high-level constructs of DBPL that may concern Ingres databases with short comments concerning their semantics and possible equivalents in SQL. All examples refer to the classical supplier-part database defined as follows (whereby the primary key is determined by the attributes following the RELATION-keyword in the type definition):

```
TYPE suppRel = RELATION sno OF
          RECORD sno:...; sname:...; status:...; city:... END;
     partRel = RELATION pno OF
          RECORD pno:...; pname:...; color:...;
                 weight:...; city:... END;
     spRel   = RELATION pno OF
          RECORD sno:...; pno:...; qty:... END;
VAR supp: suppRel; part: partRel; sp: spRel;
```

1. Quantified boolean expressions, for example:

   ```
   ALL X IN part (SOME Y IN sp (X.pno = Y.pno))
   ```

   Quantifiers have several counterparts in SQL; we will discuss them later.

2. Selective access expressions, for example:

   ```
   EACH X IN supp: SOME Y IN sp (X.sno = Y.sno)
   ```

   Selective access expressions can be used inside the FOR iterator; in this case the range variable has the status of an updatable programming variable. Selective access expressions have a direct counterpart in SQL.

3. Constructive access expressions, for example:

   ```
   {X.sname,Y.pno} OF EACH X IN supp, EACH Y IN sp:
   (X.sno = Y.sno) AND (Y.qty > 200)
   ```

   They have a direct counterpart in SQL.

4. Aggregate expressions used to construct tuple and relation values have no counterpart in SQL. One example is: for example:

   ```
   partRel{{"P7", "bolt", "green", 65, "London"},
           {"P8", "nut",  "red", 11, "Rome"  }}
   ```

5. Relation expressions for describing relation values by combining an access expression with a compatible relation type (which determines the primary key), for example:

   ```
   JoinRelType{{X.sname,Y.pname} OF
     EACH X IN supp, EACH Y IN part: SOME Z IN sp
     ((X.sno = Z.sno) AND (Y.pno = Z.pno) AND (Z.qty > 200))}
   ```

Relation expressions can be used in all contexts allowed for stored relations, i.e. they follow the orthogonality principle. SQL does not allow expressions as range relations under a **from** clause.

6. Union operator, for example:

```
suppRel{EACH X IN supp: X.city = "London",
        EACH Y IN supp: Y.status > 10,
        {"S8", "Miller", 20, "Paris"}}
```

Ingres SQL also supports union, but only on the top nesting level.

7. Relational operators $=$, $\#$, $<$, $<=$, $>$, $>=$ denoting relation equality, non-equality and set-theoretic inclusions, for example:

```
suppRel{EACH Y IN supp: Y.status > 30} <=
    suppRel{EACH X IN supp: X.city = "London"}
```

SQL does not support these comparisons.

8. Assignments on relations realizing all updates: := (assign), : − (delete), : + (insert), and :& (update), for example the insert operation:

```
supp    :+ suppRel{{"S1", "Schmidt", 25, "Berlin"}};
```

All operators follow the "many-data-at-a-time" principle (both operands are relation-valued; in the example the right-hand side expressions is a relation value of cardinality one). They can be implemented by SQL high-level "update", "insert", "delete" statements, or by fetching the required tuples from Ingres tables to a DBPL buffer, doing the required operations and shipping them back to Ingres.

The standard DBPL functions CARD (the number of relation elements) has a direct counterpart in SQL whereas the "one-data-at-a-time" functions EXCL and INCL (exclude/include one tuple) present a problem, because their semantics is based on primary keys (discussed later). No SQL equivalent exists for the low-level standard procedures LOWEST, HIGHEST, THIS, NEXT and PRIOR. They enable processing of DBPL relations in a tuple-by-tuple fashion. Some tasks cannot be programmed without them, for example, merging of relations or a browsing utility for visualizing the contents of a database.

SQL views are special objects with independent existence in the database. They can be dynamically created and deleted. In DBPL similar notions are called "constructors" and "selectors" [ERMS91]. They are not, however, properties of the database but rather properties of the source text of programs. They are first-class objects and may exist in the database as values of variables, but only when proper assignments are executed in the user program. Both, selectors and constructors, may have parameters and so they are different from SQL views. Beside this selectors could be considered as updatable views whereas the constructors (pure query expressions) could be recursive (with a fixed-point semantics). Since the mapping of selectors and constructors into views implies problems, we have chosen to construct the gateway between DBPL and Ingres on architectural levels that are below these abstractions (still allowing to evaluate recursive queries on Ingres tables).

DBPL does not deal with null-values. In Ingres SQL null-values are associated with special facilities (a comparison operator *is [not] null* and *indicator variables* in embedded SQL) and with a special treatment in aggregate functions. Null-values are captured in DBPL by variant records; however, there is no simple systematic mapping from existing SQL databases to semantically equivalent DBPL type definitions. Ingres types such as *date, money, table-key,* and *object-key* could be represented in DBPL but they require special functions to serve them and are currently not available.

Both DBPL and Ingres are multi-user database systems and employ their own methods for dealing with transactions, locks, deadlocks, logs, etc. There is no danger of improper interference of these mechanisms since from the point of view of Ingres, a DBPL application is one of its clients, and a Ingres application cannot be a client of DBPL.

3 Mapping DBPL into SQL

Since the gateway from DBPL to Ingres is a generic application which must work for all types of relations and for any DBPL high-level expressions the use of dynamic SQL was necessary. It is an extension of the capabilities in embedded SQL allowing to write SQL statements as strings which can be manipulated during run-time. Basic component is the so-called SQL Description Area (SQLDA), which allows a communication between the application and the Ingres server through pointers. It is a dynamically created data structure consisting of explicit typing information and pointers to data. The pointers are counterparts of the host variables in embedded SQL. They have two kinds of applications. In the first case (used by **select** statements) they determine places, where the attributes of a retrieved tuple are to be written. In the second case, they determine actual parameters of an SQL statement. This technique assumes application of statements containing question marks as "formal parameters" which will be substituted by the values referenced through the pointers at execution time.

In the following the basic methods that have been used to map DBPL constructs referring to Ingres relations are presented. For most DBPL constructs such a mapping exists, but in some cases there is no convenient solution, thus we needed some escape methods. Although being not very efficient, they allow the completion of computations. There are several such methods; in this project we use only one of them, namely copying DBPL relations to the Ingres side.

3.1 Unproblematic Cases

DBPL expressions without quantifiers: Consider the following DBPL expression:

{*projection list*} OF
EACH X_1 IN Rel_1,..., EACH X_n IN Rel_n: $p(X_1,...,X_n)$

If the predicate p does not contain quantifiers and all comparisons in p are available in SQL, then this expression is equivalent to the following SQL query:

```
select projection list
from Rel₁ X₁, ... , Relₙ Xₙ
where p(X₁,...,Xₙ)
```

DBPL predicates returning boolean values: SQL has no semantic domain with boolean values, thus we convert a DBPL predicate p into the following SQL statement:

```
select * from AuxRel where p
```

where AuxRel is the name of an auxiliary Ingres table containing exactly one tuple. We need only a simple procedure returning TRUE if the select statement will return a non-empty result, and FALSE otherwise. The DBPL predicate ("Do all suppliers have a status higher than 10?")

```
ALL X IN supp (X.status > 10)
```

is converted to the following SQL query:

```
select * from AuxRel where not exists
  (select * from supp X where not( X.status > 10 ) )
```

DBPL expressions with quantifier SOME in the prenex form: If a DBPL expression contains only SOME quantifiers in the prenex form, the conversion is simple. The DBPL expression

```
{projection list} OF
  EACH X₁ IN Rel₁,...,EACH Xₙ IN Relₙ:
    SOME Y₁ IN Relₙ₊₁,...,SOME Yₘ IN Relₙ₊ₘ (p)
```

where p contains no quantifiers, can be directly mapped to the following SQL query:

```
select projection list from
  Rel₁ X₁, ..., Relₙ Xₙ, Relₙ₊₁ Y₁, ..., Relₙ₊ₘ Yₘ where p
```

DBPL projection lists into SQL equivalents with no change, since syntax in both cases is the same.

3.2 Predicates with Universal Quantifiers

SQL supports several methods for expressing queries which require the use of universal quantifiers when formulated in other languages [Frat91]. These are the following:

Quantified comparisons They are normal comparisons followed by the key words all or any, for example, =all, <any, >=all, etc. Because of the lack of universality of quantified comparisons the automatic conversion of DBPL' s universal quantifiers is problematic.

Function "count" Since it requires materialization of its argument, this method may lead to performance problems.

Operator "exists" The predicate ALL X IN R (p(X)) can be expressed in SQL as

```
not exists (select * from R X where not p(X))
```

The method seems to be the most promising because of its universality and potential for optimization; thus it is used in the implementation. The DBPL access expression and the corresponding SQL statement for the query ("Suppliers supplying all parts") are

```
EACH X IN supp: ALL  Y IN part
  (SOME Z IN sp ((X.sno = Z.sno) AND (Y.pno = Z.pno)))

select * from supp X1 where  not exists
(select * from part X2 where  not exists
  (select * from sp X3 where X1.sno = X3.sno and X2.pno = X3.pno))
```

3.3   DBPL Expressions Mixing DBPL and Ingres Relations

Two kinds of mixing can be distinguished. In the first case, a DBPL statement contains sub-statements independent of external variables. As an example, consider the expression

```
EACH X IN supp: SOME Y IN sp (Y.pno = "P1")
```

Assume that supp is an Ingres table and sp is a DBPL relation. Since the internal sub-predicate does not reference the external variable X, we can evaluate it on the side of DBPL, and then generate a proper SQL statement. This method is applied in the implementation: using a procedure that recursively scans a predicate tree, discovers independent subpredicates, evaluates them, and then modifies the tree by reducing it and inserting the calculated truth values resp. temporary relations. In other cases mixing requires the application of escape methods.

3.4   Predicates with a Range Relation Given by a Subpredicate

SQL does not allow select blocks in the from clause, thus direct mapping of predicates with range subpredicates (range relations described by relation expressions) is impossible. There are several methods of solving this problem, in particular unnesting and creation of a view on the Ingres side. In this project we decided to create a temporary range relation on the Ingres side.

3.5   FOR EACH Construct

Mapping the FOR EACH construct of DBPL was the most difficult implementation problem. The semantics of the construct

```
FOR EACH variable IN relation: predicate DO
  sequence of statements
END
```

can be explained as follows. The *sequence of statements* is executed for each tuple in *relation*, for which *predicate* is true. The *sequence of statements* may contain arbitrary DBPL statements, in particular other "FOR EACH" statements. The *variable* inside the *sequence of statements* is considered as a normal programming variable. In particular, all updates of the *relation* can be done by this variable. The updating semantics is, however, not straightforward: the variable contains a main memory copy of the processed tuple and all updates modify the copy only. At the end of each loop the original tuple in the relation is modified according to the values of this eventually modified copy.

An example of the FOR EACH construct follows:

```
FOR EACH X IN supp : X.city = "London" DO
  X.status := X.status + 10;
  FOR EACH Y IN sp : X.sno = Y.sno DO
    WriteString(X.sname); WriteString(Y.pno); WriteInt(Y.qty);
  END;
END;
```

The above semantics has a direct counterpart in SQL relying on the application of cursors. Dynamic SQL assumes that the buffer for fetching/flushing a tuple is organized through SQLDAs. DBPL allows nested FOR EACH and recursion, thus SQLDAs, names of cursors and SQL *PREPARE* statements must be managed by a special stack, which we implemented in SQL+C.

The dynamic SQL version is neither clear nor well specified in SQL manuals; there are also some bugs. Thus the final solution is the result of experiments rather than careful reading of manuals. To serve the FOR EACH construct we need the following steps:

1. Generate a SQL query from the argument of the FOR EACH statement. The statement presented above will produce the query

   ```
   select X1.* from supp X1 where X1.city = "London"
   ```

2. Execute *PREPARE* and *DESCRIBE* SQL commands with the the query generated in the previous step as argument. This step is necessary to obtain the attribute names of the relation.

3. Generate an extended SQL query

   ```
   <previous query> FOR DIRECT UPDATE OF <list of all attributes>
   ```

   The statement presented above will produce the query

   ```
   select X1.* from supp X1 where X1.city = "London"
   FOR DIRECT UPDATE OF sno, sname, status, city
   ```

4. Generate a new statement name and push it on the stack. Then create a new SQLDA and push it also on the stack.

5. Execute *PREPARE* and *DESCRIBE* SQL statements for the given extended query, statement name and SQLDA.

6. Generate a new cursor name and push it on the stack. Then declare the cursor.

7. Open the cursor. This is the preparation step for fetching tuples from the Ingres relation.

8. Extract the relation name from the query and generate the SQL update statement

    UPDATE relation name
    SET attribute$_1$ = ?,..., attribute$_n$ = ?
    WHERE CURRENT OF cursor name

   For the example above we generate the statement

    UPDATE supp SET sno = ?, sname = ?, status = ?, city = ?
    WHERE CURRENT OF dbcurs$_i$

9. Generate a new statement name and push it on the stack. Then execute the SQL *PREPARE* statement w.r.t. the generated UPDATE statement and the new statement name.

Now, on the top of the stack we have two statements, one cursor and one SQLDA. Fetching tuples requires the SQL *FETCH* command (with the cursor addressing the first statement), while flushing requires the SQL *EXECUTE* command addressing the second statement.

The above procedure is complicated, although the task is typical. In our opinion, design solutions concerning cursor processing in embedded SQL were burdened by attempts to hide the fact that cursors are pointer-valued variables. In effect, this programming interface is more difficult than it should be.

3.6 Implementation of High-Level Relational Assignments

For each of the four kinds of high-level relational assignments in DBPL (assign, insert, update, delete) we must consider four cases, depending on the status of the left-hand and right-hand side relations (DBPL/DBPL, DBPL/Ingres, Ingres/DBPL, Ingres/Ingres). Each case implied specific methods. Even in the Ingres/Ingres case not all operations can be executed by SQL because of the lack of power. An example of these problems is the *delete* operation for the Ingres/DBPL case. In DBPL the construct $R_1 : - R_2$ means removing from R_1 all those tuples whose primary keys are the same as for one of the R_2 tuples; values of other attributes of R_2 are not taken into account. The SQL method of passing parameters to statements through question marks requires filling in values of *all* attributes. As follows from DBPL semantics, some of attributes of R_2 tuples may be meaningless. To ignore them, we generate the SQL statement

    DELETE FROM R$_1$ WHERE p$_1$ AND p$_2$ AND ... AND p$_n$

where n is the number of attributes. Predicate p_i has the form **attribute$_i$ =** ? for key attributes, and the form ($1 = 1$ OR **attribute$_i$ = ?**) for non-key attributes. For example, the DBPL statement

    supp :- suppRel{{"S1","",0,""}, {"S2","",0,""}};

generates the SQL statement

    DELETE FROM supp WHERE sno = ? AND (1=1 OR sname = ?)
         AND (1=1 OR status = ?) AND (1=1 OR city = ?)

This statement is executed for each tuple of the right hand side relation. The example clearly shows the disadvantage of the SQL *ad hoc* approach to generic programming.

3.7 Relational Comparisons

Since DBPL does not allow duplicate tuples, all comparisons can be performed by one operator *contains* (denoted $>=$). Equality and strong comparisons are obtained by comparison of the numbers of tuples and *contains*. Semantics of relational comparisons in DBPL assumes that only primary keys are taken into account. That is, the DBPL predicate $R_1 >= R_2$ means

$$\pi_{primarykeys}(R_1) \supseteq \pi_{primarykeys}(R_2)$$

where π denotes projection, and $\supseteq$ is an inclusion of sets. As in the previous case, we must consider four cases of relational comparisons, dependingly whether the left-hand side and right-hand side relations are on the DBPL or Ingres side. In the case when one relation is DBPL and another is Ingres, we apply a sequential scan through the right hand side relation and check if the primary key of the tested tuple is present in the left hand side relation. If both relations are from the side of Ingres, we change predicate $R_1 >= R_2$ into a quantified predicate

```
ALL Y IN R₂ (SOME X IN R₁
    ((X.key₁ = Y.key₁) AND ...AND (X.key_last = Y.key_last)))
```

and then transform it in a corresponding *select* statement (see sec. 3.2).

4 Architecture of the Gateway

The general architectural view of the gateway, DBPL and Ingres is presented in Fig. 1. The entry Ingres interface is embedded SQL. We wrote a package of procedures in embedded SQL + C capable of mapping all DBPL constructs (unfortunately the dynamic embedding is not standardized until now). The procedures are also available in a normal DBPL module. They allow the user to write SQL statements inside DBPL programs, an advantage for some kinds of applications.

Exit points in DBPL implied more problems. We assumed that the DBPL compiler should not be changed; all connections to Ingres should be done from the existing run-time system. The DBPL run-time system consists of several layers and features of DBPL are tailored to parts of different layers. Some work was necessary to make the architecture of the run-time system cleaner. Afterwards it was possible to determine exit points "below" the transaction processing system (thus the gateway does not deal with locking, unlocking, log, recovery, etc.) and "below" the system responsible for evaluation of DBPL selectors and constructors (thus the gateway also does not deal with them). Exit points to Ingres are in the module responsible for evaluation of DBPL predicates and sometimes in the lower layer responsible for tuple-oriented processing of relations.

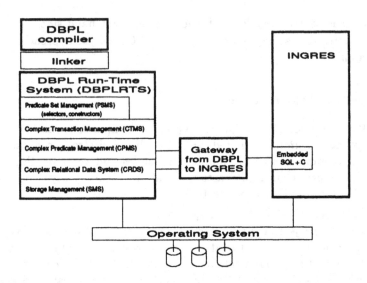

Fig. 1. General view on the gateway, DBPL and Ingres

We introduced a change to the DBPL data dictionary allowing to distinguish between DBPL and Ingres relations. Since the compiler is unchanged, a DBPL program processing Ingres relations is exactly the same as that required for DBPL relations. This means that each Ingres relation which has to be processed by DBPL should have a "twin" relation on the DBPL side. Normally this twin is empty and not used but it must be declared and stored. Twin DBPL relations allow the user to retrieve typing information and sometimes they are internally used for storing intermediate results. The architecture of the gateway is presented in more detail in Fig. 2. A special utility is written to change the status of DBPL relations. This utility compares types of corresponding DBPL and Ingres twin relations. If the types are fully compatible, it allows the user to change the status of the DBPL relation so that further processing will be performed on the Ingres relation.

Generation of SQL queries from DBPL predicates is done by a recursive scan of the DBPL predicate tree. During the scan a list of SQL lexicals is built. Roots of the tree corresponding to access expressions cause pushing lexicals *select*, *from* and *where* to the list. Then, projections in the tree insert proper lexicals after *select*, range relations in the tree insert proper lexicals after *from*, and conditional expression insert proper lexicals after *where*. The list works as a stack: to take into account nested select blocks, the insertions are done after this *select*, *from* or *where*, which is the nearest from the top of the list. When the select block is completed it is "masked" (so it is not seen by further insertions). This algorithm is modified for *exists* and other lexicals to take into account all situations that can occur in DBPL predicate trees. The final SQL query is obtained by direct generation of the query text from the list of lexicals.

For evaluating DBPL predicates containing mixed references to DBPL and

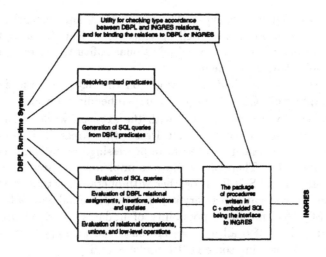

Fig. 2. Architecture of the gateway

Ingres relations the corresponding predicate tree is recursively scanned and one of the following answers is produced: *pure dbpl, pure ingres, top dbpl, top ingres, mixed joins, badly mixed*. The answer *pure ingres* means that the predicate contains only references to Ingres relations and can be converted into a SQL query. *Top dbpl* means that the predicate contains independent subpredicates that are *pure ingres*. They can be evaluated internally and the whole predicate becomes *pure dbpl*. Similarly, *top ingres* means that the predicate contains subpredicates that are *pure dbpl*; they can be internally evaluated on the side of DBPL, then the resulting temporary relations are copied to the Ingres side, thus the whole predicate becomes *pure ingres*. In the case of *mixed joins* we send the participating DBPL relations to the Ingres side (the escape method), thus the predicate becomes *pure ingres*. The result *badly mixed* means that all good methods fail, and the only method is copying Ingres relations to the DBPL side. For performance reasons we prefer to generate in such a case a run-time error in the current implementation.

5 Implementation Difficulties

A few problems were caused on the side of DBPL. On the language level the missing possibility of using arithmetic and other operators inside the high-level constructs limits the utilization of the full power of SQL. On the system level the use of Modula-2 as system-programming language requires that all advanced data structures are stored in dynamic memory. This concerns, in particular, syntactic trees for high-level expressions and predicates, type descriptors, and the data dictionary. Receiving information from these structures requires navigation via pointers, a feature which is cumbersome and error-prone. In Modula-2 there is no alternative solution. This is an argument in favour of languages having the possibility to define bulk types. The construction and semantics of internal DBPL structures is not always well specified and clear. Small optimizations concerning syntactic trees introduced additional difficulties in recognizing their semantics and in traversing them.

Most of the problems had their origin on the SQL side especially in bad design assumption of SQL and its (dynamic) embedding concept.

1. Communication of dynamic SQL with the external world is based on prepared statements, cursors, and SQL Description Areas. This interface is not well prepared for nested and recursive processing, which is inherent for languages like DBPL. Therefore we have to implement a special stack of statements, cursors and SQLDAs together with operators acting on this stack.

2. Although the concept of primary keys is a fundamental part of the relational model, SQL has no direct possibility of updates based on primary keys. In contrast, in DBPL all updates are based on primary keys. This causes problems in expressing some DBPL updates in SQL.

3. The missing orthogonality of the language leads to problems in the automatic generation of SQL queries. For example there is no nested union, there are no range expressions described by queries, all this must be done on the DBPL side. Another example is the **select count(*) from** ... statement where we would prefer the syntax **count(select** ... **from** ...).

4. No queries returning boolean values, they must be simulated by counting the number of elements of a corresponding select-statement. The missing truth values requires the substitution by formulas like 1=1 or 1=0.

Sometimes it is also difficult to retrieve internal information from the system which is necessary for writing generic applications. May be the ongoing standardization work (f.e. for the data dictionary) will lead to a better situation.

1. There are difficulties in retrieving all information about Ingres tables; in particular, this concerns recognizing which attributes are forming the primary keys.

2. No comparison of tuples for equality, and no (officially supported) explicit tuple identifiers and operations on them.

3. In programming of generic applications we need to "capture" some system reactions to errors. These reactions and error codes are not well specified in the documentation of Ingres. In this context the automatic generation of the *SQL STOP* statement, in all possible places where an error is expected, is controversial. STOPs after errors are frequently unacceptable, because before the stop some operations must be performed. This forces use to use the statement *WHENEVER SQLERROR CONTINUE* after each SQL statement, which makes the text of the program longer and less readable. SQL itself gives poor testing capabilities for programmers, e.g. about names of available relations, about their ownership, status, number of tuples, etc.

With new releases (and realizations) of the SQL-standard, which will also cover dynamic SQL, some of the following problems will hopefully become obsolete.

1. The system of navigation through cursors gives no possibility to navigate to the *prior* tuple, making the implementation of browsing capabilities extremely difficult.

2. SQL dynamic statements use question marks as "formal parameters". This is inconvenient and error-prone.
3. To open a cursor for updating in dynamic SQL, the programmer must generate the statement *select ... from ... FOR DIRECT UPDATE OF ...* which is not described in the manual (we invented it by experiments).
4. There are some not well-justified syntactic features of SQL statements; for example, an *update* statement through a cursor requires the relation name despite the fact that it was determined previously during declaration of the cursor.
5. Direct update through cursors may change the order of rows, what means that the processing may lose consistency (e.g. the same row will be updated two times).

Surprisingly there also have been technical problems with bugs in the used version of the Ingres system. So opening a cursor for a query returning an empty result causes a run-time error. Because normally it is impossible to predict whether the result of a user query is empty or non-empty a special handling of empty query results is necessary. Another example was the *WHENEVER SQLERROR CONTINUE* statement that does not work in all cases, requiring the manual correction of the C programs generated by the ESQL-precompiler.

6 Conclusion

The implementation of the gateway from DBPL to the commercial Ingres system achieves several results. A direct pragmatic result is that Ingres databases are now transparently accessible within DBPL programs. This allows the user to build up modular designed applications using a type-safe language with orthogonal language constructs thereby significantly reducing the risk of run-time errors and increasing the maintainability and extensibility of the application while using the reliability and effectiveness of a commercial database system developed and improved over years. It has also uncovered some limitations and disadvantages of both DBPL and SQL. When considering DBPL, we recognized limitations of high-level constructs which may produce problems for users especially if they come from the SQL world. The advantage of DBPL - strong typing - may become a hindrance to the development of some applications requiring generic procedures mainly because of its monomorphic type system. This shows directly the need for new languages with polymorphic type systems as a base for persistent programming and system construction [ScMa93].

The majority of problems were connected, however, with SQL. In contrast to the enthusiasm found in popular database textbooks, our experience with SQL as a programming language indicated that SQL is below the state-of-the-art. Many *ad-hoc* solutions, irregularity of syntax and semantics, limitations, unclear rules of use, an approach to user-friendliness which forbids untypical (but still reasonable) situations, lack of programming abstractions, etc. make the programming of generic programs difficult and frustrating.

This clearly emphasizes the necessity and usefulness of our approach to view database systems simply as external servers which can be accessed via powerful languages like DBPL. We feel that SQL has yet to achieve the maturity necessary for next-generation databases. It is our hope that this paper helps clarify some design pitfalls in database languages and offers a way to solutions for avoiding these problems.

References

[Banc92]   F. Bancilhon. Understanding Object-Oriented Database Systems. Advances in Database Technology - EDBT '92, Proc. of 3rd International Conference on Extending Database Technology, Vienna, Austria, March 1992, Springer LNCS 580, pp.1-9, 1992

[Date87]   C.J. Date. A Guide to Ingres. Addison-Wesley 1987.

[ERMS91]   J. Eder, A. Rudloff, F. Matthes, J.W. Schmidt. Data Construction with Recursive Set Expressions. Next Generation Information System Technology. Proc. of 1st East/West Database Workshop, Kiev, USSR, Oct.1990, Springer LNCS 504, 1991, pp.271-293

[Frat91]   C. Fratarcangeli. Technique for Universal Quantification in SQL. SIGMOD RECORD Vol.20, No.3, Sep. 1991, pp.16-24

[IngrA89]   Ingres/SQL Command Summary for the UNIX and VMS Operating Systems. Release 6, Relational Technology Inc., August 1989

[IngrB89]   Ingres/SQL Reference Manual. Release 6, Relational Technology Inc., August 1989

[Ingr90]   Language Reference Manual for INGRES/Windows 4GL for the UNIX and VMS Operating Systems. INGRES Release 6, Ingres Corporation, August 1990.

[Orac91]   PL/SQL, User Guide and Reference, Version 1.0, June 1991. Oracle Corporation 1991.

[MRSS92]   F. Matthes, A. Rudloff, J.W. Schmidt, K. Subieta. The Database Programming Language DBPL, User and System Manual. FIDE, ESPRIT BRA Project 3070, Technical Report Series, FIDE/92/47, 1992

[ScMa91]   J.W. Schmidt, F. Matthes. The Rationale behind DBPL. 3rd Symposium on Mathematical Fundamentals of Database and Knowledge Base Systems, Springer LNCS 495, 1991.

[ScMa92]   J.W. Schmidt, F. Matthes. The Database Programming Language DBPL, Rationale and Report. FIDE, ESPRIT BRA Project 3070, Technical Report Series, FIDE/92/46, 1992

[ScMa93]   J.W. Schmidt, F. Matthes. Lean Languages and Models: Towards an Interoperable Kernel for Persistent Object Systems. Proceedings if the IEEE International Workshop on Research Issues in Data Engineering RIDE'93 Vienna, Austria, April 1993

[SRLG+90]   M. Stonebraker, L.A. Rowe, B. Lindsay, J. Gray, M. Carey, M. Brodie, P. Bernstein, D. Beech: The Committee for Advanced DBMS Function. Third-Generation Data Base System Manifesto. ACM SIGMOD Record 19(3), pp.31-44, 1990.

Federation and Stepwise Reduction of Database Systems

Elke Radeke[1] and Marc H. Scholl[2]

[1] Cadlab (Cooperation Uniniversity of Paderborn & SNI AG),
Bahnhofstr. 32, 33102 Paderborn, Germany, e-mail: elke@cadlab.de
[2] University of Ulm, Faculty of Computer Science,
89069 Ulm, Germany, e-mail: scholl@informatik.uni-ulm.de

Abstract. Many enterprises suffer from the problems of heterogeneous data (base) systems, such as redundancy and lack of control. Existing approaches either try to couple the database systems into a federation (FDBS) or migrate data to a single (often new) database system. This paper proposes an integration of both concepts by incorporating migration facilities into an FDBS. General FDBS concepts couple the multiple database systems and allow several degrees of global *control* over heterogeneity and redundancy. In addition, new migration concepts enable data and applications to move from one component database system to another. This supports the requirement of industrial users to stepwise *reduce* heterogeneity and redundancy in a controlled way. It allows to decrease the number of database systems as much and as fast as the enterprise areas can bear it.

1 Introduction

Today, many data management systems exist for different purposes. Within an enterprise or cooperation different database systems or different releases of a database system are in use. This **heterogeneity** primarily has *technical reasons* since no database system is general enough to be appropriate to all application domains. Moreover, it has *economical reasons* because there are various database systems on the market suitable for the same application domain which differ in service support and price. In general, also *organizational reasons* exist if each department can choose on its own a database system without a global strategy. Huge investments have already been realized for the multiple database systems in the enterprises: many database tools and programs are self-implemented or acquired and gigabytes of data are stored in the databases. But in most enterprises, links between heterogeneous systems are missing. Such a situation induces serious **problems**, as already discussed in the scientific world, but also recognized by industrial organizations. Concerning this problem, we are in contact with two departments of Cadlab's industrial partner Siemens Nixdorf Informationssysteme (SNI). Many organizations and also both industrial project partners requested a reduction of heterogeneity as future global enterprise strategy due to the following problems:

– There are applications that need to access more than one database system. So, application programmers have to use *various database interfaces*, need to know the databases (*location*) of required data, and if the database systems support different data models, also a *conversion* from one model to the other has to be implemented. This increases the code and decreases its clarity. Both of our project partners require such multidatabase applications.

– Some data may be stored *redundantly* in many databases, possibly in *different representations*. Hence, the risk of *data inconsistency* is huge and the risk for wrong decisions increases. Updates on redundant data have to be invoked in multiple database systems by the user. By analyzing the data of one of our project partners, we found geometry information for hardware components both in a PCB layout system and in a part library. Corresponding data of these systems were identified in a self-implemented cross reference list. Updates on hardware components have to be executed on several systems and concurrency conflicts as well as incomplete operation sequences result in inconsistent data.

In order to improve the situation and to fulfill the requirements of industrial users, **our solution** proposes to stepwise *reduce* heterogeneity under the *control* of a federated database system (FDBS). First, existing (and new) database systems are coupled to an FDBS [17] which commonly offers a uniform transparent interface for all database systems and allows to control some kind of redundancy. To enhance performance and decrease (uncontrolled) data redundancy as well as database system heterogeneity, we introduce migration mechanisms for an FDBS. They support an enterprise in minimizing the number of database systems as much and as fast as the areas can bear it. In the long run, it allows to eliminate database systems of antiquated technology (where possible) or to reduce the number of database systems appropriate for the same application domain. To achieve this, their data and applications are migrated (Fig. 1).

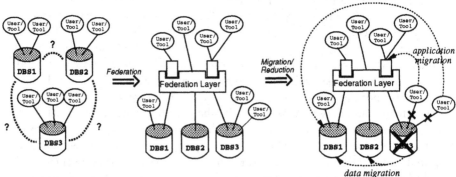

Fig. 1. Stepwise federation and reduction of database systems

In contrast to our approach, some database vendors propose to directly switch from the multiple heterogeneous systems to their single database system. Although a single database system would provide a more performant access to all data than in an FDBS containing multiple DBS, it is neither financially nor organizationally advisable to migrate all existing data and applications to a new

DBS at once, especially in large enterprises. This was also validated by our industrial project partners. Such a migration, in general, lasts several months or even years where the various enterprise areas realize the migration [10]. In this critical phase where data are duplicated to the new database system the enterprise would have no control over these redundant data.

To enable global control when migrating from multiple heterogeneous information systems to a single database system, Drew [4] developed five steps: (1) integrated data access, (2) consistency between redundant data, (3) data migration to a new DBS, (4) application (interface) migration to this DBS, (5) DBS evolution. FDBS were sketched as appropriate solution, but without presenting concrete concepts. Therefore, we close this gap, but regard a more general approach which does not necessarily end in a single new DBS. In many cases and also in one of our industrial projects a single database system will not fit all application domains (see above: technical reason for heterogeneity).

Existing FDBS, e.g. Pegasus [13], Multibase [8], and Carnot [20], all provide a uniform global interface for multiple heterogeneous DBS and support some kinds of redundancy control (detailed comparison below). But no existing FDBS approach elaborates on the reduction of component database systems, which is a typical global enterprise goal.

Gateway database systems, e.g. Oracle, also allow to access data of some different DBS and, in addition, support the importation of foreign data. But they do not control the redundancy between connected database systems. Hence, the risk for data inconsistency is huge.

The **structure of this paper** is as follows: Section 2 presents **step one** in overcoming database system heterogeneity: The database systems are coupled to an FDBS which *controls* heterogeneity with general FDBS mechanisms. **Step two** is then realized by a new FDBS concept, object migration, introduced in Section 3. We demonstrate how this can be used to *reduce* heterogeneity and redundancy in an FDBS in a controlled way. The number of database systems can be decreased preserving data and applications. Finally, Section 4 concludes and gives an outlook on future activities.

2 Building a Federated Database System

A federated database system brings the multiple heterogeneous database systems of an enterprise under a global control. It represents an important first step to overcome the heterogeneity and builds the basis of our work. Section 2.1 presents required concepts of an FDBS in form of a global functional model. It is illustrated by specific user requirements that we got from our project partners. While a homogenization layer on top of the database systems hides heterogeneity, specific techniques are required to identify and control data that is redundantly stored in the multiple component database systems (CDBS). They are presented in Section 2.2, based on our prior work. Here, we also show the problems in guaranteeing consistency between redundant data of different CDBS which may result in temporary inconsistencies. Beside the global strategy of many enterprises to reduce heterogeneity, this is a main reason why additional FDBS migration concepts are required. Before these new concepts are introduced in Section 3, the base concepts of an FDBS are illustrated by a simplified scenario of one of our project partners in Section 2.3.

2.1 Global Functional Model

During the requirement specification with our two project partners, we developed a global functional model for an FDBS (Fig. 2).

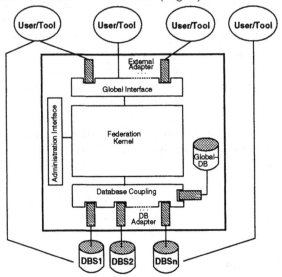

Fig. 2. FDBS architecture

A software layer is built on top of multiple heterogeneous, autonomous, distributed data management systems. Our project partners require to couple hierarchical, relational, and object-oriented database systems as well as file systems. One of them, for example, has 20 different data management systems. While object-oriented database systems are not yet in use at them, all other data management systems already contain a huge amount of data and have multiple applications. Due to lack of resources, these (local) applications should first continue running on their data management systems. This will be achieved by preserving the autonomy of the data management systems. Later on, these applications may be migrated, see Section 3.4.

For new applications accessing data of multiple data management systems, an interface is requested enabling transparent and uniform access to all data. We chose a multi-lingual interface similar to HD-DBMS [2] with a *global interface* and some *external interfaces/adapters*. It was required by our project partners to support their own application interfaces as well as various standard interfaces like STEP (data exchange format), SQL (relational query language), and ODL/OQL/OML (proposed standard of ODMG for object-oriented DBS) which open a wide market of standard software. In Section 3.4, we will see that a multi-lingual interface also eases the migration of applications.

Administration functionality is offered by an *administration interface*. It allows to start, stop, and initialize an FDBS as well as to to couple/decouple the data management systems to/from the FDBS. A dynamic extension of the FDBS with new data management systems is especially requested by CAx[3] tools of one project partner. CAx tools are often delivered by suppliers with new data libraries at one shot containing new hardware component data.

The coupling software to the component database systems consists of a generic part, the *database coupling* where specifics are realized in some *DBS adapters*. This eases implementation effort, in particular with respect to dynamic extensions with new data management systems.

The *FDBS kernel* handles general required mechanisms like global access control, global transaction management, query/update processing and optimization, data redundancy control (see also Section 2.2), and object migration (see Section 3.1). Meta information as well as global data that do not map to any DBS are stored in an auxiliary database, the *Global-DB*. In Section 3.5 we will see how all existing DBS of an FDBS may be reduced to an integrated DBS in some cases and all data are migrated to the Global-DB.

2.2 Redundancy Control

After the presentation of a functional model for FDBS to globally control heterogeneous database systems, in this section we point out specific techniques to control redundant data. It represents the basis for our migration facilities.

When database systems are coupled to an FDBS, in general they contain many redundant data. Kent [7] called it a mapping from many proxies to one real world entity which require specific object identification techniques [5, 6]. For example, one of our project partners stores geometry information for hardware components redundantly in a layout system and a part library because it is needed by their local applications. In order to reduce the risk for data inconsistency and ease global enterprise management, the redundancy need to be controlled globally within the FDBS.

Redundancy control consists of two steps: (1) identification of redundancy and (2) consistency control of the identified redundancies. Based on our previous work [16, 19], we present two mechanisms to identify redundancy: schema integration and object integration. Afterwards, we mention some techniques for consistency control between redundant data.

Redundancy Identification

Schema Integration:

For hiding heterogeneity and identifying redundancies among schema data, in [19] we developed concrete schema transformation processors. They allow to integrate flexibly the schemata of multiple component database systems (CDBS) and build up the 5 level schema architecture for FDBS [17] (see also Fig. 7). It considers also an incremental evolution of the FDBS, e.g. by extending it with

---

[3] Computer Aided x where x is a place-holder for Design (CAD), Manufacturing (CAM), Concurrent Engineering (CACE), etc.

new database systems (required by our project partners).

By schema integration, those data *redundancies* can be controlled that result from *globally created* objects. Assume a new object $g1$ is created via the global interfaces of a global type T of a federated/external schema and T was mapped by schema integration to multiple local types $T1, ..., Tn$ $(n > 1)$ of some local schemata. Then the FDBS stores this logical global object $g1$ as multiple local objects $l1, ..., ln$ in the corresponding component databases of $T1, ..., Tn$ (Fig. 3). This kind of data redundancy is automatically identified and the mapping between them is managed by the FDBS. By building an FDBS for our project partner that integrates schemata of the layout system and part library such that geometry information of both systems are represented by a single global type, we enable to create new hardware geometry data at one shot in both systems. At present, two separate create-operations have to be invoked and corresponding data is identified by inserting them in a self-implemented cross reference list.

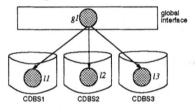

Fig. 3. Object creation for a global type mapped to multiple local types

Object Integration:

Since the database systems of an FDBS were populated independently before the federation, there is already redundant data in the various DBS. In order to supplementary control data *redundancy* that was *created before federation resp. by local applications* in the FDBS, we additionally offer techniques for object integration. They allow to identify existing data of different CDBS as a single entity for the FDBS [7]. For that, we developed a global operation 'same' for the global/external interface [16]. It enables a user/administrator to select some objects via queries and unify them to a single logical global object (Fig. 4).

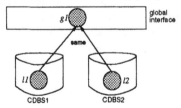

Fig. 4. Identifying two local objects as a single global object

In the FDBS of our project partners, a chance exists to formally specify redundancies among the component systems, e.g. by announcing the self-implemented cross reference list, and let the FDBS control its consistency.

Consistency Control Between Redundant Data

After some objects were identified as same/redundant, global queries will only deliver them as a single global object and the FDBS controls consistency between their data. This is an important advantage for our project partners. One of them currently handles data consistency of geometry information stored both in the layout system and the part library by hand. By scanning the self-implemented cross reference list from time to time, values of related objects are compared and inconsistencies are corrected by hand. If redundancy is identified in the FDBS, Updates are propagated to the corresponding objects for some degree. This controls consistency and will free our project partners from checking it by hand.

Update propagation is relatively easy for FDBS-global updates but induces some problems for CDBS-local updates. Due to autonomy, local CDBS applications may update objects without effecting the same-objects in the other CDBS. Proposed solutions are to lose the autonomy, using triggers [5], or allowing temporary inconsistency in the FDBS and, for example, specify time frames when data consistency is checked [20]. But some systems of our project partners require autonomy and only a few offer a trigger mechanism (neither IMS nor file system). Thus the FDBS can only support globally controlled, periodic consistency check. That is, data may remain somewhat inconsistent, though identified by the FDBS as redundant. This is an important reason to apply, in a second step, migration concepts (Section 3) to reduce redundant/same objects, after it was brought under global control in the FDBS. Nevertheless, the required global enterprise strategy to reduce heterogeneity is more important.

2.3 Example

Before the migration concepts are introduced, the base concepts of an FDBS are illustrated by a simplified scenario of one of our project partners. It originates from Computer Aided Concurrent Engineering (CACE) [3].

Fig. 5 illustrates a situation in an enterprise containing three database systems for the production life cycle: *ProductionDBS* in the production department with *Machine*, *Material*, and *Product* information; *SalesDBS1* in the first sales department and *SalesDBS2* in the second sales department, both storing data about *Articles*, *Costumers*, and *Depots* of their district.

These three database systems are federated into an FDBS and heterogeneity is hidden by a transparent global interface (object-oriented) and an external interface with SQL syntax for ad-hoc queries. There are several local applications for *ProductionDBS*, *SalesDBS1*, and *SalesDBS2*, but the enterprise also developed a global application that browses all enterprise information. This global application accesses data from all three database systems through the global interface in a uniform and transparent way.

Redundancy among the database systems is identified by schema and object integration so that the FDBS may control consistency among them to some degree. By *schema integration* we combine the local types *Product* of *ProductionDBS* and *Article* of *SalesDBS1* and *SalesDBS2* to a single global type, named *Product* while all other local types are directly mapped 1:1 to a global type in the federated schema. After schema integration, product data can be created at one shot in all three databases systems. When a global application creates an object *g1* of a global type *Product* this is automatically stored as three local objects, *l1* in *ProductionDBS*, *l2* in *SalesDBS1*, and *l3* in *SalesDBS2* (Fig. 3).

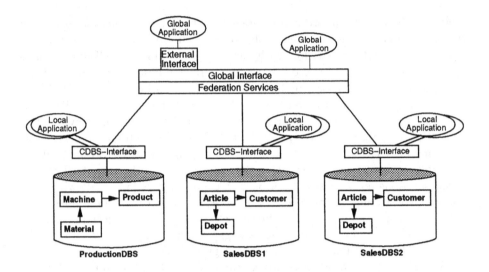

Fig. 5. FDBS for Computer Aided Concurrent Engineering

Moreover, object integration allows to supplementary identify redundant data that was already stored in the database systems before federation or during federation by some local applications. Assume that *ProductionDBS* and *SalesDBS1* both contain a product "SGI-screen" before federation. To let the FDBS know that these two local objects represent a single entity for the FDBS, they are identified as same by object integration (Fig. 4).

While in this section we showed how some concrete database systems get under the global control of an FDBS, in the following we extend the example by demonstrating the reduction of heterogeneity/redundancy.

3 Migration within an FDBS

In this section, we extend the FDBS with new capabilities to migrate objects from arbitrary CDBS to another one. We first introduce base concepts for migrating objects within an FDBS and show how data that was already identified as redundant can be reduced to less local objects using object migration. Then we point out the use of object migration to minimize the number of CDBS. This represents the important second step in overcoming heterogeneity and easing enterprise management. It supports the global strategy of many organizations including our project partners to reduce heterogeneity in a controlled way.

While we restrict on base concepts for object migration in this paper, we present more details in a companion paper [12], e.g. underlying algorithms or an analysis of migration for other objects than those mapped directly 1:m to local objects.

3.1 Base Model for Object Migration in FDBS

By object migration, data is transferred from one component database system of the FDBS to another. Users can initiate object migration by an operation of the FDBS global (and external) interface. Therefore they have to specify the (global) object and, in general, source as well as target CDBS.[4]

We extend the CACE FDBS example of Section 2.3 in order to illustrate this:

EXAMPLE 2: Assume a new product is released for sale in district 1 and, hence, migrates from ProductionDBS to SalesDBS1 (Fig. 6).

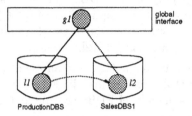

Fig. 6. Object migration from ProductionDBS to SalesDBS1

Here, global object *g1* that was stored in ProductionDBS as local object *l1* shall be migrated through the global interface to SalesDBS1. We also see that object migration requires additional capabilities for object identification. The assignment of global to local objects must be updatable dynamically. In the example of Fig. 6 global object *g1* was first assigned to the local object *l1* and after object migration also/instead to local object *l2*.   ◇

What data migrates of an object depends on the canonical data model of the FDBS and the object definition within this data model. Our solution is based on an object-oriented data model fulfilling the requirements for an FDBS canonical data model [15]. An upcoming standard for an object-oriented data model is fixed in [14] with the following object notion:

An object consists of several attributes that express its structure (data attributes and relationships) and owns some methods describing the object's behavior. To formally define the attributes and methods of objects, types are used. Generally, an object is migrated with the following data to a target CDBS:

- All *data attributes* are migrated.
- Attributes representing *relationships* and related objects are not migrated. When two related global objects and their relationship were all mapped to the same CDBS and object migration changes the locality for one of the objects then the relationship becomes an interdatabase relationship between objects of different CDBS and is now stored in the Global-DB. Although the relationship may be deleted in the source CDBS by DBS referencial integrity rules it will be preserved in the FDBS to enable compatibility to existing global applications. In [12] we also consider the migration of object graphs, i.e. objects with related objects.
- *Methods* are only supported by a few DBS, e.g. object-oriented DBS. So they are migrated only in few cases. Since all objects of the same type own the same methods, method migration is coupled with type migration (s.b.).

---

[4] In some cases also transparent object migration is possible, see below.

– The *type* of an object has to be migrated as a prerequisite if there does not exist an equivalent type in the target CDBS. Two local types of different CDBS are equivalent, if they were mapped during schema integration to the same global type.

A type migration, in general, induces schema evolution within the FDBS. This decreases the autonomy of the FDBS. But since schema evolution is reduced to schema extension, local applications of the CDBS are further on executable without any modification. There are also some special cases that do not need any type migration at all [12].

When an object is transferred from one CDBS to another, data has to be transformed according to the FDBS architecture. In Fig. 7 we see how an object migration is processed using the 5 level FDBS schema architecture of [17].

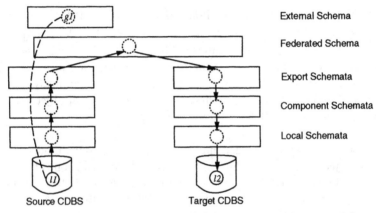

Fig. 7. Object migration according to the 5 level FDBS architecture

Here, a global object *g1* that is accessed according to a specific external schema shall be migrated from a source CDBS to a target CDBS. Our object migration mechanism, first, locates the corresponding local object(s) in the source CDBS. Then these local objects are transformed from the local schema of the source CDBS through a federated schema to the local schema of the target CDBS. Finally these data are stored into the TargetDBS as local object(s). This scenario is similar to reading data from one CDBS and writing it to another CDBS. But object migration is executed as one atomic global operation and it allows to retain the global identity of the migrated object (detailed differences see below).

3.2 Base Operations for Object Migration

We offer three kinds of operation primitives for object migration (Fig. 8):

1. *Absolute movement*: Objects are transferred into the target CDBS as shown in the base model and are deleted in the source CDBS. Object identity at the global interface remains the same. Shared information, e.g. type information, cannot be migrated by absolute movement.

2. *Replication*: Objects are transferred to the target CDBS but not deleted in the source CDBS. The duplicates represent a single global object and the FDBS may guarantee data consistency between them (see also Section 2.2).

3. *Independent copy*: Objects are also duplicated to the target CDBS, but get a different global identity. Data consistency is not guaranteed between the duplicates.

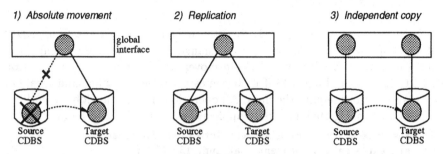

Fig. 8. Migration functionality: (1) absolute movement, (2) replication, (3) independent copy

These migration functionalities are offered at the FDBS global interface and possibly at some external interfaces by (1) explicit migration operations 'move', 'replicate', and 'copy' and the first two also by (2) operations for class change, 'shift' and 'add'.

Explicit Migration Operations

The explicit migration operations, in general, require as input the object to be migrated as well as source and target CDBS. The FDBS generates an identifier for each CDBS to enable the specification of the CDBS (similar to [9]).

EXAMPLE 3: Within the CACE FDBS, single objects can be moved, replicated, and copied across component database systems as follows using a C++ global interface where identifiers for the CDBS are offered by predefined variables:

```
obj->move (SalesDBS1,SalesDBS2);            //absolute movement of 'obj'
                                            //from SalesDBS1 to SalesDBS2
obj->replicate (ProductionDBS,SalesDBS1);  //object replication          ◇
obj2 = obj->copy (ProductionDBS,SalesDBS2);//independent copy
```

These migration operations are, in general, not transparent because they require location information for the source and target CDBS. But we allow to configure some parts. For example, the administrator may fix a specific CDBS resp. the Global-DB as target for object migration through the administrator interface. This is ingenious when migration is constantly realized from some legacy CDBS to a single CDBS of new technology. If we may also configure the source CDBS in an FDBS, all migration operations are quasi transparent. That means no CDBS has to be specified in any migration operation call. In [12] we identified further cases of transparent explicit migration operations.

Implicit Migration Operations

Implicit migration operations provide another kind of transparent migration. It can be induced by modifying the object's class. We offer a global operation to 'add' an object to another class. This results in a replication migration in case both classes are mapped to different CDBS. By 'shift', moreover, an object may change into another class corresponding to an absolute movement, if the classes map to different CDBS.

EXAMPLE 4: In a university FDBS with two database systems *StudentDBS* and *EmployeeDBS*, we may arbitrarily change persons from a student to an employee at the end of study (absolute movement), or replicate his data from StudentDBS to EmployeeDBS if he becomes a student assistant and local employee applications require the data. All operations retain the global identity of the person so that global university applications do not have to be modified.

```
//absolute movement of a student into class Employee
any_student = select (Student, matr_nr, 1333333);
any_student->shift (Employee);

//a student additionally is in class Employee but remains in Student
another_student = select (Student, matr_nr, 1555555);
another_student->add (Employee);
```
◇

The implicit operations are transparent because the user has to specify neither source nor target CDBS. But in contrast to the explicit migration operations, it supports fewer cases of object migration. The user has to specify two different classes as source and target and in addition both classes have to be mapped to different CDBS. For the CACE FDBS example, product data cannot migrate from *ProductionDBS* to *SalesDBS1* or *SalesDBS2* using implicit migration operations. The reason is that only a single global type exists for product data though mapped to three local types of different CDBS (*Product* of *ProductionDBS* and *Article* of *SalesDBS1* and *SalesDBS2*). This would have been possible, if these local types were mapped to different global types.

Class change in FDBS was also considered in O*SQL [9] and COCOON [18] and build the starting point for development of our object migration mechanism.

Migration of Object Classes and Databases

Beside migrating single objects, we also provide mechanisms to migrate whole object classes[5] or databases with a single operation. For this, we provide the explicit migration operations also for classes and databases. This corresponds to an iterative execution of object migration for all objects of a given class or database. Although the operations need not be realized as atomic operations because it may imply migration of some thousand objects, it makes the use of object migration easier and more convenient, in particular the reduction of DBS.

EXAMPLE 5: We may replicate all product data of *ProductionDBS* to *SalesDBS2* at once or completely move all data of *SalesDBS1* to *SalesDBS2* with the following operations using a C++ binding where classes and databases are specified by predefined variables:

---

[5] A *class* comprises some objects of a given type.

```
Product->replicate (ProductionDBS, SalesDBS1);
SalesDBS1->move (SalesDBS2);
```

3.3 Reduction of Redundant Data

A special case of object migration exists for those objects that were stored redundantly in the source and target CDBS and the redundancy was already identified within the FDBS by schema or object integration (Section 2.2). This case can be used to decrease redundancy in the FDBS and may become necessary during the reduction of DBS.

To analyze how migration works for objects that were identified as redundant and stored in source and target CDBS, we regard the three migration operations:

1. Absolute movement: The redundant data of the object only has to be removed from the source CDBS, but, in general, no transfer of redundant data has to be realized.[6] This achieves a reduction of redundant data where the number of CDBS the data is stored in decrements for one.
2. Replication: No transfer of redundant data has to be realized.
3. Independent copy: The copy function operates as usual. A global new object is created and the data is duplicated in the target CDBS. Now, the redundant data will be stored twice in the target CDBS, but since it is an independent copy with different global identity both may change differently.

EXAMPLE 6: Assume a global object $g1$ of type Product is stored as three local objects $l1$ in *ProductionDBS*, $l2$ in *SalesDBS1*, and $l3$ in *SalesDBS2*. They were identified as redundant and consistency between their data was controlled as far as possible from the FDBS. If a global application requests to replicate $g1$ from *SalesDBS1* to *SalesDBS2* then no action has to be invoked because such a replica already exists. If it should be migrated by absolute movement, e.g. when both database systems are reduced to a single one, then the product data is deleted in the *SalesDBS1*. Now, $g1$ is only stored redundantly in two CDBS (instead of three) and the risk for temporary data inconsistency decreases. ◇

Sometimes, not all data of an object is redundant in source and target CDBS but only a subset. Then, non-redundant data of the source-CDBS are migrated as usual. In [12], we differentiate some object kinds dependent on how much data is redundant and where it is stored and show object migration for these kinds. In this section, however, we focus on those objects that were already managed by the FDBS as completely redundant/same. We have seen that they are automatically reduced during object migration. This decreases redundancy and facilitates DBS reduction.

---

[6] Exceptions may be required if redundant data were not consistent in source and target at the time of object migration. If the data from source CDBS was chosen as correct during conflict solution, however, a migration of redundant data is necessary.

3.4 How Object Migration Supports Application Migration

Increasing requirements of applications to a database system can make it necessary to switch application systems partly or completely to a new database system. Meier and Dippold [10], for example, describe a change of a banking system from hierarchical to relational database technology. Existing literature, e.g. [1, 4, 11], focus on application between isolated database systems. But also in FDBS, application migration is required if existing local applications require to change to newer database technology. We distinguish the following two cases of application migration (Fig. 9) which sometimes require a migration of their application data (object migration):

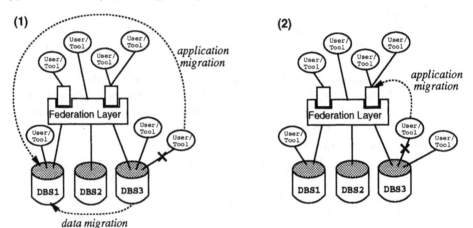

Fig. 9. Application migration (1) to a CDBS interface and (2) to an FDBS interface

1. An application may become a local application of another CDBS. For this, either the application has to be adapted to the new DBS interface or its application interface is previously realized on top of this CDBS. To enable its execution after migration, all its data has to be migrated to the target CDBS, too.
   EXAMPLE 7: In our CACE FDBS we may migrate/replicate a sales application primarily acquired for *SalesDBS1* to *SalesDBS2* in order to locally benefit in both database systems from it. Since both database system are relational and offer the same SQL interface, the application can directly be used in *SalesDBS2* without any recoding after its data was migrated through the FDBS global interface.   ◇

2. An application may also get a global application, since FDBS and their global interface mostly underly new database technology. For this, the application is either adapted to the global resp. an existing external interface of the FDBS or the application interface is realized as new external interface and the application remains unchanged. The application data may remain in its source CDBS. Then the migrated application accesses its data through the 5 schema levels of the FDBS (see Section 2.2).
   EXAMPLE 8: If a graphical data monitor of *ProductionDBS* is well known and accepted in the enterprise and also suited as an FDBS monitor, this

local application can be migrated/replicated from the *ProductionDBS* to the global/external interface of the FDBS. In case the application interface is different from the global and any existing external interface, we have to either recode the application to one of these interfaces or realize the application interface as new external interface in the FDBS. ◇

More performant access may often be achieved for an application that becomes a global application if its data are migrated into the Global-DB due to easier mappings.

An easy application migration can be realized when the target CDBS has a similar data model and functionality than its source. If both offer exactly the same interface, the application is directly executable after its data were migrated. The possibility for same interfaces increases if standard interfaces are provided, e.g. SQL of ANSI/ISO for the relational data model.

Application migration and object migration may in particular serve to reduce the number of CDBS in an FDBS. While the general FDBS capabilities presented in Section 2, e.g. schema integration and object integration, allow to control heterogeneity and redundancy in some cases, object and application migration can be used to stepwise reduce heterogeneity and redundancy. This is explained in more detail in the following section.

3.5 Reduction of Component Database Systems

In many enterprises or cooperations there is a multitude of database systems, some ten or hundreds. Such a situation also exists at our project partners. By coupling database systems to an FDBS, heterogeneity is hidden while preserving their autonomy. But for the long term, a reduction of this big number of database systems is desirable. This was in particular formulated as global enterprise strategy at our project partners. A reduction of database systems will result in the following advantages for an enterprise:

- Less effort for database administration if the number of databases decreases.
- In general, there is less redundant data in the FDBS. If redundancy was already identified (by schema/object integration), the effort for consistency control will decrease and the remaining temporary inconsistencies are reduced. For redundant data not yet identified as same, the risk for general data inconsistency will decrease.

In general, no database system can be eliminated together with all its data and applications because some of it is still required somehow. In order to reduce the number of database systems in an FDBS without eliminating relevant data or applications, we recommend migration techniques. Before eliminating a database system from an FDBS, all still required applications are migrated from this CDBS to some arbitrary CDBS or the FDBS interfaces (see previous section) and all corresponding data is migrated by our object migration mechanism to the other CDBS resp. the Global-DB (Fig. 10).

Those data that were already stored redundantly in source and target CDBS and where redundancy was controlled by the FDBS are reduced during object migration. It will not be duplicated in the target (see Section 3.3).

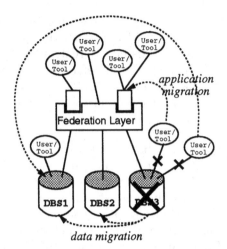

data migration

Fig. 10. Database reduction in an FDBS by object and application migration

DBS candidates to be eliminated are those with obsolete database technology that do not fulfill the requirements of today's enterprises [10]. Moreover, multiple database systems supporting the same data model and offering similar functionality may be reduced to a single database system. The latter case particularly eases application migration (see Section 3.4).

EXAMPLE 9: When the two districts corresponding to *SalesDBS1* and *Sales-DBS2* are composed together to a single enterprise district, we may also reduce both database systems to a single one. This is quite easy in our example since both DBS are relational with an ISO-SQL interface. After all data of *SalesDBS1* is migrated by absolute movement for databases to *SalesDBS2* or vice versa, the applications are directly executable on the target CDBS.   ◇

Our project partners emphasized that not all database systems can be reduced at once. Although the reduction of heterogeneity is the global enterprise strategy, not all enterprise areas may fulfill this goal immediately. Instead a stepwise approach is requested by which the various enterprise areas may reduce heterogeneity and redundancy as much and fast as they bear it. So, global enterprise heterogeneity reduces step-by-step.

Migration Paths

In the following, we discuss by three migration paths in which order data and applications may be migrated to reduce the number of database systems in an FDBS. We show also how our object migration functionality is used for this. Exemplary, we took the Global-DB as migration target.

Path 1 : First, all data of the source CDBS is replicated into Global-DB using the 'replicate'-operation for databases. Afterwards applications of the CDBS may stepwise be migrated by either adapting them to an external/global interface or realizing the application interface as a new external interface.
Advantage: During the migration of the applications (in general some months or years) data consistency may be controlled by the FDBS.

Disadvantage: High expense to manage a completely replicated database. In case of all data not being required any longer, e.g. because some applications will be eliminated, more data than necessary were migrated.

Path 2 : Applications are first migrated to global/external interfaces and data access is realized through the 5 level schema architecture during this time. After all applications were migrated from a CDBS, all the data is migrated via 'move'-operation for databases into the Global-DB.

Advantages: (1) consistent data during the migration of the applications; (2) no data replication and thus no additional effort for replication management.

Disadvantage: Migrated applications run with lower performance as long as data are not migrated to the Global-DB. A heuristic that migrates performance-critical applications at the end weakens this disadvantage.

Path 3 : As a mix of 1. and 2., an iterative process migrates stepwise an application or application set with selected objects to the Global-DB. First, we analyze the schema of the application (set) and then migrate all objects that correspond to the schema information via 'replicate'-operation for classes. Afterwards the application resp. application set is migrated. Thus, stepwise more and more objects are migrated to the Global-DB and managed as replicas by the FDBS. When all applications using a specific type/class of the CDBS schema are already migrated, all objects of this type/class can be eliminated in the source CDBS. To further minimize the number of current replicas, a heuristic based on connectivity components identifies application sets that possess many types together but have less in common with other applications. These application sets should be migrated in connection.

In some cases, by using the technique of database reduction, we may reduce from a multitude of heterogeneous distributed autonomous database systems to a *single integrated database system*. For example, if all CDBS are eliminated, their data is migrated to the Global-DB, and still required applications are adapted to the global or an external interface of the FDBS (Fig. 11).

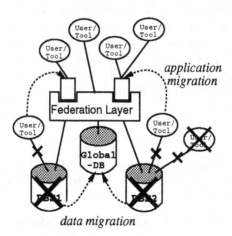

Fig. 11. Database reduction in an FDBS resulting to a single integrated DBS

This new database system still includes federation services. Later on new database systems, e.g. of future database technology, may be coupled together with these data and applications. So, this approach tries to eliminate current heterogeneity in a smooth way but does not represent an isolated system for the future.

In contrast to [4], our projects with two industrial organizations showed that not all enterprises or cooperations will go for only a single database system because a single database system may not fit all their application domains.

4 Conclusion

This paper presented an approach of how enterprises may stepwise overcome the problems of database system heterogeneity. In particular it supports the global goal of our industrial project partners to reduce heterogeneity in a controlled way. The essential idea is the tight integration of migration facilities into an FDBS. General FDBS concepts first *control* heterogeneity and redundancy while the migration facilities allow to *reduce* them under control of the FDBS step by step. We presented object migration concepts for an FDBS which allow to move data from one component database system to another without coercion to change global identity (global data independence). Redundant data is not duplicated in the target CDBS but is automatically reduced (redundancy reduction). We showed how object migration supports enterprises in decreasing its number of database systems while retaining still required data and applications of eliminated DBS. Each enterprise area can choose as much and fast as it bears some database systems to be eliminated. So, the global enterprise goal of heterogeneity minimization can be achieved step by step.

In general, building an FDBS is not as expensive as heterogeneity problems cost an enterprise. Federation services do not represent an enterprise-specific software, but contain many generic parts which can be implemented for several enterprises in common. At Cadlab, we are currently developing federation services containing a generic kernel and plan to realize with our industrial project partners some customers specific FDBS.[7] In order to fulfill our partners' requirements, we will also implement object migration capabilities in our prototypes. While this paper derived from users' needs rough concepts for object migration in FDBS and showed the benefits, more precise concepts as well as realization aspects are elaborated in a companion paper [12]. To further support database reduction, more work is needed to ease the adaptation of applications to new database interfaces. Some approaches already exist in this field [10] which consider application migration between isolated DBS.

References

1. M.L. BRODIE. The promise of distributed computing and the challenges of legacy systems. In *10th British National Conf. on Databases, Advanced Database Systems (Aberdeen)*, pages 1–28, 1992.

---

[7] This work is granted by the ESPRIT project JESSI COMMON FRAME No. 7364.

2. CARDENAS, A. Heterogeneous distributed database management: The HD-DBMS. *Proc. IEEE 75*, pages 555–600, 1987.

3. CHAPPELL, C., STEVENSON, C. *Concurrent Engineering: The Market Opportunity.* OVUM, 1992.

4. P. DREW. On database technology for information system migration and evolution. In *Proc. Workshop on Interoperability of Database Systems and Database Applications (Fribourg, Switzerland)*, pages 121–130, 1993.

5. ELIASSEN, F., KARLSEN, R. Interoperability and Object Identity. *SIGMOD RECORD 20(4)*, pages 25–29, 1991.

6. HAERTIG, M., DITTRICH, K.R. An object-oriented integration framework for building heterogeneous database systems. In *Proc. IFIP-DS5 Semantics of Interoperable Database Systems (Lorne)*, pages 32–61, 1992.

7. KENT, W. The breakdown of the information model in multi-database systems. *SIGMOD RECORD 20(4)*, pages 10–15, 1991.

8. LANDERS, T., AND ROSENBERG, R. An overview od Multibase. In *Proc. 2nd Int'l Conf. on Distributed Databases*, pages 153–184, 1982.

9. LITWIN, W. O*SQL: a language for multidatabase interoperability. In *Proc. IFIP-DS5 Semantics of Interoperable Database Systems (Lorne)*, pages 114–133, 1992.

10. MEIER, A., DIPPOLD, R. Migration and co-existence of heterogeneous databases; practical solutions for changing into the relational database technology (in german). *Informatik-Spektrum 15(3)*, pages 157–166, 1992.

11. NETZE, J., SEELOS, H.-J. Scenes and strategies of data migration (in german). *Wirtschaftsinformatik 35 (4/93)*, pages 320–324, 1993.

12. RADEKE, E., SCHOLL, M.H. Object migration in federated database systems. Cadlab Report 3/94, 1994.

13. RAFII, A., AHMED, R., DESMEDT, P., DU, W., KENT, W., KETABCHI, M.A., LITWIN, W.A., SHAN, M.C. Multidatabase management in Pegasus. In *Proc. 1st Int'l Workshop on Interoperability in Multidatabase Systems (Kyoto). IEEE Comp. Soc. Press*, pages 166–173, 1991.

14. CATELL R.G.G., editor. *The object database standard: ODMG'93.* Morgan Kaufmann Publisher, 1994.

15. SALTOR F., CASTELLANOS M., GARCIA-SOLACO M. Suitability of data models as canonical models for federated databases. *SIGMOD RECORD 20(4)*, pages 44–48, 1991.

16. SCHOLL, M.H., SCHEK, H.J., TRESCH, M. Object algebra and views for multi-objectbases. In *Proc. Int'l Workshop on Distributed Object Management (Edmonton)*, pages 352–372, 1992.

17. SHETH, A., LARSON, J. Federated database systems for managing distributed, heterogeneous, and autonomous databases. *ACM Computing Surveys 22(3)*, pages 183–236, 1990.

18. TRESCH, M. Dynamic evolution in object databases (in german). PhD thesis, University of Ulm, Germany , Feb. 1994.

19. TRESCH, M., SCHOLL, M.H. Schema transformation processors for federated objectbases. In *Proc. 3rd Int'l Symp. on Datebase Systems for Advanced Applications (Daejon, Korea)* , 1993.

20. WOELK, D., SHEN, W.-M., HUHNS, M., CANNATA, P. Model driven enterprise information management in Carnot. MCC Technical Report, Nr. Carnot-130-92 , 1992.

Methods and Tools for Data Value Re-Engineering

Daniel Aebi and Reto Largo

Institut für Informationssysteme
ETH Zürich
8092 Zürich, Switzerland

Abstract. Existing information system applications are regularly subject of change. They have to evolve according to changed needs. Almost always, meta-data as well as data values are involved in this process of change. This paper characterizes some of the repeatedly encountered problems and proposes a general data re-engineering model. The architecture of an experimental toolkit which facilitates the application of this model for a broad range of situations is presented and discussed.

1 Introduction

A regularly encountered labour-intensive activity in information systems (IS) maintenance or migration is the adaption of the data according to new or changed needs. This task, which can be associated with the term *data re-engineering* [1], includes a reverse engineering step to recognize structures and semantics, followed by a forward engineering step during which the data must be appropriately converted for the new or changed system. While improvements in software engineering technologies facilitate the design and implementation of new IS applications, the problem of managing the evolution of existing applications remains. Almost any adaptive maintenance task involves substantial changes to the data, often not only to data structures but to data values, too. This becomes especially important when a legacy system should be migrated into a new environment, which often includes a change of the underlying data model. Such migration tasks have crucial consequences on data.

Considering the proliferation of methods and tools in the field of database design, the forward engineering step seems to be much more mature than its reverse counterpart. It is interesting to notice, that up to now, data re-engineering has got little interest in the database scientific community [23]. Moreover, the few studies that can be found [26], [27], [28], concentrate on the problem of reconstructing the database *design*. Data *values* are at most considered for the reconstruction of dependencies and keys [24]. The contribution of this paper goes beyond that point of view in setting the focus of attention to data value problems, too. This also includes aspects of data quality as we showed in [14].

For the rest of the paper our focus of attention is the situation where data of an existing (old) information system application has to be changed to be reused in a new environment. We do not distinguish between migration, systems replacement and adaptive maintenance as long as data aspects are considered.

The structure of the paper is as follows: in Section 2 some regularly encountered data definition as well as data value problems are shown. A simple example for some of these problems is given in Section 3. Section 4 presents our model for the data re-engineering process in general. Section 5 describes the architecture of an experimental toolkit which can support this process.

2 Data Re-Engineering Problems

Data re-engineering problems can be divided into three classes: data *model* problems, data *definition* problems and data *value* problems. Data model problems occur, if the data model of the old system is different from the data model of the new one (e.g. migrating from a hierarchical data model to a relational one). In these cases, a translation of the different data models into a common data model has proven useful [21]. This class of problems is beyond the scope of this paper.

The remaining two classes, data definition problems and data value problems are strongly interrelated, i.e. changes in the definition of an attribute also demand data values to be changed. Data definition problems have to be solved during data engineering as well as during data re-engineering, whereas data value problems only occur during data re-engineering.

Data definition problems stem primarily from the fact, that the new system will offer improved or changed functionality. This might yield changed data structures and, often more severe, changed consistency constraints. Data value problems may also occur in existing systems resulting from domain evolution [12].

In the following subsections we present some examples of data definition and data value problems. We use notions from the relational [16] as well as the entity-relationship terminology [22]. A more systematic classification approach can be found in [35].

2.1 Data Definition Problems

D1 *Schema mapping*: The different attributes and entities from the old schema have to be mapped to a new schema according to the requirements of the new system [13].

D2 *Consistency constraints*: The new system might have new, changed or dropped consistency constraints.

D3 *Entity-sets and relationships*: New entity-sets might be introduced and interrelated with existing ones. To establish the appropriate relationships the corresponding data values must be provided somehow. Current relationships might no longer exist in the new system or have changed cardinality [12].

D4 *Identification heterogenity*: Entities are identified by different key constructs, e.g. entities might be identified by a combination of several attributes in the old system, whereas a special key-attribute is introduced in the new system.

D5 *Attributes*: Attributes in the new system might use different base types and domains. Addition and removal of attributes might yield differences between the entity-sets in the new system and the ones in the old system.

D6 *Coded semantics*: The old system might use literals or field recycling (e.g. coding additional information in an existing attribute because of the inflexibility of the old system) to represent the desired semantics [13],[12].

...

2.2 Data Value Problems

V1 *Objectidentification*: The same entity might appear twice in the same context. Such duplicates have to be identified and removed to avoid redundancy.

V2 *Identification heterogenity*: An entity represented in two different relations might have the same key structures but not the same key values, e.g. a foreign key in a relation has to be changed according to the changes of the appropriate primary key.

V3 *Range conflicts*: Values of an attribute do not match with the defined range, e.g. negative numbers in fields which should only contain positive ones.

V4 *Unit, scaling and granularity differences*: Some calculations might have changed over time, but the former calculated data has not been adjusted accordingly. The units in the new system might differ from the old ones [13].

V5 *Encoding*: Data values often have encoded meanings. The new system might have a different encoding scheme [12].

V6 *Inconsistent default values*: For a certain field, what is represented in one application as space, might be in another one 0 or -1 [2].

V7 *Null value semantics*: No distinction between non-existing and unknown values. This is a problem which becomes important when the new system does not accept non-existing data for a certain field.

V8 *Recording errors*: These occur regularly due to typing mistakes [15]. Recording errors might result in duplicate, erroneous or missing data.

...

It is worth noticing, that many of the mentioned problems are not unique to the re-engineering process, but also occur when heterogeneous databases have to be integrated [8], [20].

3 Example

To clarify some of the mentioned problems, we will use a simple example. We assume that our example application is used as a part of an information system of a university. The part we will focus on, is the application processing information about students. A flat file system is used to store the student information.

This application must now be replaced, for example because the administration decided to use a standard application with enhanced functionality or to use another hardware platform and a new database system.

In the old system, a student entity was represented as follows (we use a relational notation to represent the entities):

```
Student(Stud_Nr,Name,Adr_Street,Adr_Zip,Adr_Town,Fac_Nr,Fac_Name,
        Imm_Date,Exm_Date,Code)
```

A student has a unique student number, a name, one address, is related to a faculty and has an immatriculation and an exmatriculation date (in the form MM/DD/YY). The code field is composed of the year of birth, sex and an actual semester number.

The requirements for the new system are the following (the identifiers in parenthesis refer to the classification of Section 2):

- A student can have more than one address (e.g. home address, parents address, work address) (D3).
- The zipcode must be changed (a real-life situation in Germany 1993, where the whole zipcode-system changed from four to five digits. Moreover, the old numbering-system changed, so that all zipcode values had to be changed, too) (D5, V5).
- The students immatriculation and exmatriculation date must be enlarged to handle the century change appropriately (a frequently encountered problem of current applications). The field must therefore be enlarged to be able to hold the century (D5, V4).
- The complicated code field must be divided into different attributes to be able to access and modify this information more easily and more secure (D6, V5).
- The student relation should be normalized to avoid redundancies, duplicates should be removed (D3).

According to these requirements, the following steps are necessary:

- To support more than one address per student, the three address attributes must be removed and a new relation Address has to be created (D3, D5). Address consists of the student number, an address type (home, parent, work ...), street, zipcode and town.
- The code field attribute Code will be removed and the three attributes Sex, Act_Sem, Year_of_Birth added instead (D6). The values of these new attributes must be taken from the old Code field values (V5).
- The zipcode field must be changed to the desired format (D5) and the old values have to be modified according to the new zipcodes (V5).
- The two date fields must be enlarged (D3). The values of the date fields have to be modified to include the century (V4).

- The relation **Student** will be split into two relations, **Student** and **Faculty**. The faculty number (**Fac_Nr**) resides in the relation **Student** and represents a foreign key into the relation **Faculty** which consists of the faculty number and the faculty name. Duplicate entities in **Faculty** have to be removed (can be done automatically) (potentionally D4, V2).
- Similar entities which represent the same student must be removed (V1, V2, V8). The similarity between two entities might be decided according to the pair name / address. This process must be supported by a user which decides whether similar entities are duplicate entities or not and which one to keep [14].

All these steps lead to the new relations **Student**, **Faculty** and **Address** which are to be used by the new system:

```
Student(Stud_Nr,Name,Fac_Nr,Imm_Date,Exm_Date,Year_of_Birth,Sex,
        Act_Sem)
Faculty(Fac_Nr,Fac_Name)
Address(Stud_Nr,Adr_Type,Adr_Street,Adr_Zip,Adr_Town)
```

The example shows that even such a simple migration problem causes a lot of complicated data re-engineering tasks.

4   The Data Re-Engineering Process

It is a common principle to reduce the complexity of a task by splitting it into subtasks. It has also been usefully applied to the development of information systems. There is a broad range of well-known life-cycle-models (e.g. Waterfall, Spiral, Prototyping ...[4],[18]). A common characteristic of all these models is the distinction of different phases along the time-line. Analogous considerations led us to the decision to split the overall re-engineering process into phases, too. Our model distinguishes the following three ones:

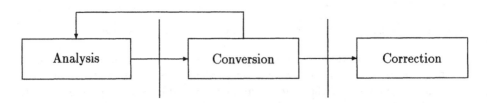

For the transition of data from an old system to a new one a migration path must be established. That requires information about the old as well as the new schema. There are often situations, where both of them are not defined precisely (e.g. because the documentation of the old one is lost or the requirements of the new one are not fully defined yet), so the old one must be reconstructed (reverse engineered), whereas the new one must be adapted during an *iterativ* process where information about the old system and the requirements of the new one must be brought into accordance. Moreover, invalid data should be corrected during an own correction step to improve data quality [14].

The three phases are interrelated and cannot always be performed in a strict sequential manner but every process depends on results of the other ones.

4.1 Analysis (Reverse Engineering)

The main purpose here is to sample and recognize information about data structures and semantics (e.g. consistency constraints) of the old system. Ideally, the result is the complete data description of the old system. All information recognised during this phase must be recorded in a repository for further processing [10].

4.2 Conversion

Once recognised, the schema and data values have to be adapted in accordance with the requirements of the new system. Usually, this conversion process will be iterative itself. There is no straight way from the old to the new schema. Often the new schema will be iteratively adapted, based on results of the analysis or even the correction. Besides the well-known modeling tasks performed during this forward-engineering phase, data values have to be possibly changed, too. The results of this task are the schema as well as the restructured data values of the new system.

4.3 Correction

After conversion, it must be assured, that the data is in accordance with the consistency constraints of the new system. Moreover, a data correction offers the opportunity to improve data quality, for example by eliminating wrong or duplicate data by validating them against reality [14].

After the completion of these three tasks, the data is ready to be used in the new system: the data re-engineering process is finished.

To a certain extent, any of these three tasks can be assisted by softwaretools. But it is important to notice that it is a strongly interactive process which needs a lot of human decisions. A fact that holds generally true for any reverse engineering task [25]. Our approach can be characterised as *semi-automatic*.

5   DART - a DAta Re-engineering Toolkit

The proposed three-phase model leads in a natural way to the architecture of
a supporting toolkit. For each of the three phases an extensible set of services[1]
for special purposes, controlled by a common interface controller and sharing a
common database and repository, is provided.

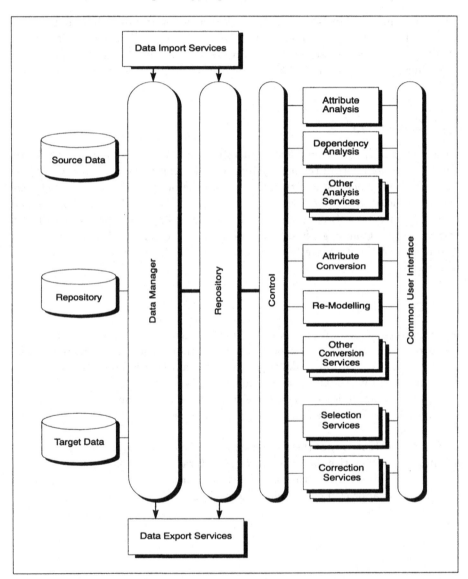

Fig. 1. DART - Architecture

---

[1] Instead of *tool* we use the notion *service* because in our architecture the different programs are based on a common control component and cannot be used independently.

5.1 Architectural Characteristics

The design of DART was guided by the following basic decisions:

– *Data model*: One of the main design decisions for DART was the restriction on "tabular" (structured) data. We chose the relational model [16] to store the data to be re-engineered. This decision was guided by the fact, that the relational model provides a sound theoretical basis, and a great number of systems and tools are available. Although this restricts the applicability of DART to data which can be transformed into relations, we are convinced that a broad range of information systems applications, especially older ones, fall into this category and relational interfaces to other popular systems (e.g. IMS) are available [29] (although we know, that such transformations can be a difficult and elaborate task as shown for example in [3]).

– *Extensibility*: We want to provide an extensible set of services. No single service can cover all the diverse needs of a data re-engineering process. A mechanism that allows the installation of special-purpose services is provided.

– *Data Import/Export Services*: The data re-engineering task should be separated from the problems of loading the data from the old system and dumping the converted data into the new system. Therefore we introduced a pre- and a postprocessing phase whose purpose is to interface DART with a broad range of systems.

– *Common User-Interface*: All services (including the installable ones) use the uniform user interface.

– *Central Repository*: All information is stored in a central repository and is available to all services by a centralized control component.

– *Experimental Character*: We suggest using data samples for experiments due to performance reasons and then applying the results of these experiments to the whole database. Based on these results, the user can then construct a migration plan.

– *Standardisation of basic operations*: Standard procedures for basic operations (e.g. parsing, scanning, browsing) for the practical process of data value re-engineering are provided. Therefore these basic operations do not have to be reimplemented, but can be customized for special needs.

We are using a commercially available database management system to store the metadata as well as as the data values and a 4GL environment for the implementation of the services.

5.2 Analysis - Phase

The data import services provide the analysis services with metadata information as well as with the according data values from the old system. The data import services might not be able to provide the metadata information or the information might be incomplete because old systems often do not use centralised metadata information (e.g data-dictionary). As a minimum, tablenames, attributenames and the data values in a string representation must be provided. The analysis services try to compute more information about the metadata using methods based on data values. It is quite clear that sometimes not the whole database can be used for computation due to efficiency reasons. Therefore the analysis services just use data value samples from the database to compute more information. The more accurate the samples are, the more precise are the results. The samples have to be choosen at random to have accurate results. Related work in the field of knowledge discovery showed the usefulnes of such an approach [36].

This phase is supported by two basic services, one for the analysis of the properties of a single relation, the other one for the analysis of dependencies and relationships [9]. Both services need interactive assistance.

Attribute Analysis. This tool is the basis of all other analysis activities. It provides information about basic data types and formats. The data import services might just have delivered the data values in a string representation, although the real representation is different (e.g. "123" is an integer and "2-2-93" is a date). Some of this information might also be delivered by human interaction by browsing the sample data. It is also possible to gain these informations from other sources (e.g. source-code analysis tools) [10]. With DART it is also possible to discover formats (e.g. 'mmddyy' or 'dd-mm-yyyy' for a date).

Dependency Analysis. Finding functional, multivalued and inclusion dependencies in large databases is an expensive operation. But at least for functional dependencies it is feasible for "narrow" data samples [9],[30],[31]. The results gained from data samples will probably not be exact, but can nevertheless be helpful as candidates which can then be confirmed or rejected by the user. The general problem of finding inclusion dependencies is NP-complete [31]. It can be reduced to $O(n^2 p \log p)$ (with p = number of rows and n = number of attributes) by considering only unary inclusion dependencies. The factor n^2 can be lowered further because there is no need to investigate attributes with different domains. Until now we do not consider multivalued dependencies because they are not crucial for normalization (3NF). Based on the knowledge about functional dependencies candiate keys can easily be found [34].

The information about the functional and inclusion dependencies as well as the knowledge about keys form the basis for later normalization in the conversion phase.

Installable Analysis-Services. The common interface allows the installation of further services. Examples are the computation of basic data-metrics or a service that helps discovering rules in data bases [19],[33].

5.3 Conversion - Phase

The meta data as well as the data values have to be converted according to the requirements of the new conceptual schema. The new schema is either well defined in terms of the new system or the new schema is interactively build from the old schema by the user.

This conversion phase is also supported by two basic services, one for the conversion of attributes and their according data values and the other one for re-modelling of the conceptual schema.

The whole conversion can firstly be prepared based on samples and then performed in a batch process on the whole database. The control component of DART provides a mechanism to build an "operations-plan" for the schedule of the needed conversion-services. This concept is well-known, especially for special purpose conversion problems [7].

Attribute Conversion. Attributes with coded semantics must be split into their basic parts. This implies creation of new attributes and deletion of old ones. The data values of the new attributes must be computed from the data values of the old attributes. Attribute domains might change as well. In that case, the according data values have to be adapted to the new domains.

Re-Modelling. This tool provides means to change the conceptual schema and to normalize the relations. It allows the establishment of new as well as the changing of old relationships.

5.4 Correction - Phase

Up to now, there are no specific correction services provided. But the same interface which enables the installation of specific analysis and conversion services can be used to install appropriate correction services. As we showed in [14] the correction task is highly interactive and needs almost always information about the real world. An easily implementable example might be the elimination of "similarities" (e.g. to reduce ambiguities). In such a case a selection tool could provide a set of entities with some common characteristics whereas in the correction task a user would then decide which of the selected entities to keep or to delete respectively. Appropriate algorithms to identify such similarities can be found in [11], [5] and [6]. Another important aspect that could be handled during this phase is the correction of spelling and typing errors [15].

6 Summary and Future Work

We presented a collection of regularly encountered problems during the data re-engineering process and proposed a 3-phase-model according to which the process can be performed. Except in very favourable situations, data re-engineering is a complex task that cannot be fully automated. We presented the architecture of an extensible toolkit. Our approach differs from other ones in not only covering the analysis and conversion phases but also in offering some solutions and ideas to the correction task.

A prototype is under current development. It is subject of further research to apply this prototype to real-life examples. A connection to existing software re-engineering tools has to be established to provide semantical information that cannot be reconstructed from the sample data. In our approach this information has to be provided interactively.

7 Acknowledgements

We would like to thank Christian Schucan for reviewing earlier drafts of this paper and providing detailed comments and constructive suggestions.

References

1. Chikofsky, E., Cross, J.: *Reverse Engineering and Design Recovery: A Taxonomy.* IEEE Software, January 1990.
2. Ricketts, J.A., DelMonaco, J.C., Weeks, M.W.: *Data Reengineering for Application Systems.* IEEE Conference On Software Maintenance, 1989.
3. Date, C.J.: *Why Is It So Difficult to Provide a Relational Interface to IMS?* Relational Database: Selected Writings. Addison Wesley, 1984.
4. Boehm, B.W.: *A Spiral Model of Software Development and Enhancement.* ACM Sigsoft, August 1986.
5. Wu, S., Manber, U.: *Fast Text Searching Allowing Errors.* Communications of the ACM, 10, 1992.
6. Baeza–Yates, R., Gonnet, G.H.: *A New Approach to Text Searching.* Communications of the ACM, 10, 1992.
7. Mamrak, S.: *Chameleon: A System for Solving the Data–Translation Problem.* IEEE Transactions on Software Engineering, 15, 1989.
8. Shet, A.: *So Far Schematically yet So Near Semantically.* IFIP DS-5 Conference on Semantics of Interoperable Database Systems. Elsevier Publishers, 1992.
9. Bitton, D., Millman, J.: *A Feasibility Study of Dependency Inference.* Proceedings of the Conference on Data Engineering, 1989.
10. Van Zuylen, H.J.: *The REDO Compendium.* John Wiley & Sons, 1993.
11. Hall, P.A.V., Dowling, G.R.: *Approximate String Matching.* ACM Computing Surveys, 12, 1980.
12. Ventrone, V., Heiler, S.: *Semantic Heterogeneity as a Result of Domain Evolution.* Sigmod Record, 20, 1991.
13. Chatterjee, A., Segev, A.: *Data Manipulation in Heterogenous Databases.* Sigmod Record, 20, 1991.
14. Aebi, D., Perrochon, L.: *Towards Improving Data Quality.* Proceedings of the CIS-MOD 93, Conference on Information Systems and Management of Data, 1993.
15. Kukich, K.: *Techniques for Automatically Correcting Words in Text.* ACM Computing Surveys, 24, 1992.
16. Codd, E.F.: *The Relational Model for Database Management.* Addison Wesley, 1990.

17. Silva, A.M., Melkanoff, M.A.: *A Method for Helping Discover the Dependencies.* Advances in Database Theory, 1981.
18. Pomberger, G., Bischofberger, W.: *Prototyping–Oriented Software Development.* Springer, 1991.
19. Parsaye, K., Chignell, M.: *Intelligent Database Tools and Applications.* John Wiley & Sons, 1993.
20. Navathe, S.B., Batini, C.: *A Comparative Analysis of Methodologies for Database Schema Integration.* ACM Computing Surveys, 1986.
21. Saltor, F.: *Suitability of Data Models as Canonical Models for Federated Databases.* Sigmod Record, 20, 1991.
22. Teorey, T.J.: *Database Modelling and Design–The Entity-Relationship Approach.* Morgan Kaufmann, 1990.
23. Hainaut, J.-L.: *Contribution to a Theory of Database Reverse Engineering.* Working Conference on Reverse Engineering. IEEE Computer Society Press, 1993.
24. Premerlani, W.J., Blaha, M.R.: *An Approach for Reverse Engineering of Relational Databases.* Working Conference on Reverse Engineering. IEEE Computer Society Press, 1993.
25. Chikofsky, E.J., Selfridge, P.G., Waters, R.C.: *Challenges to the Field of Reverse Engineering.* Working Conference on Reverse Engineering. IEEE Computer Society Press, 1993.
26. Aiken, P., Muntz, A.: *A Framework for Reverse Engineering DoD Legacy Information Systems.* Working Conference on Reverse Engineering. IEEE Computer Society Press, 1993.
27. Joris, M.: *PHENIX: Methods and Tools for Database Reverse Engineering.* Proceedings 5th International Conference on Software Engineering and Applications, 1992.
28. Sabanis, N., Stevenson, N.: *Tools and Techniques for Data Remodelling COBOL Applications.* Proceedings 5th International Conference on Software Engineering and Applications, 1992.
29. Paulley, G.N.: *Engineering an SQL Gateway to IMS.* Proceedings of the Workshop on Interoperability of Database Systems and Database Applications, 1993.
30. Mannila, H., Räihä, K.J.: *Dependency Inference.* Proceedings of the 13th VLDB Conference, Brighton 1987.
31. Mannila, H., Räihä, K.J. et al.: *Discovering Functional and Inclusion Dependencies in Relational Databases.* International Journal of Intelligent Systems, Vol 7, 1992.
32. Mannila, H., Räihä, K.J.: *Algorithms for Inferring Functional Dependencies from Relations.* Data & Knowledge Engineering 8, 1993.
33. Yasdi, R.: *Learning Classification Rules from Database in the Context of Knowledge Acquisition and Representation.* IEEE Transactions on Knowledge and Data Engineering, Vol 3, No 3, 1991.
34. Torgersen, S.: *Automatic Design of Relational Databases.* PhD Dissertation, Cornell University, 1989.
35. Kim, W., Seo, J.: *Classifying Schematic and Data Heterogeneity in Multidatabase Systems.* IEEE Computer, 1991.
36. Piatetsky-Shapiro, G., Frawley, W.J.: *Knowledge Discovery in Databases.* MIT Press, 1991.

Object View Broker:

A Mediation Service and Architecture to Provide Object-Oriented Views of Heterogeneous Databases

Jacques Durand, Murthy Ganti, Rick Salinas

U S WEST Technologies
4001 Discovery Drive, Boulder, CO 80303, USA
({jacques,ganti,rick}@advtech.uswest.com)

Abstract

We notice a data-modeling gap in current database business applications: the emerging data modeling paradigm for computation is object-oriented, while the incumbent data models for storage are mostly relational or hierarchical. The gap originates partly in the reengineering of applications and of databases, that do not proceed at the same pace. But it is also likely to be typical of heterogeneous systems in highly distributed software architectures. We propose a mediation service called Object View Broker, that provides object views of data stored in relational or other databases, to object-oriented applications. The Object View Broker manages these views in a multi-application, multi-databases environment, and provides customized services such as notification, caching and locking. We have implemented and used a version of Object View Broker for a service order distribution application at U S WEST.

1.0 Introduction

The automation of business processes is likely to rely on geographically distributed systems and to access heterogeneous data in heterogeneous environments. This integration is likely to occur in a bottom-up manner rather than in a top-down way: most of the components are already there, and they must satisfy a local strategy before addressing integration concerns. In an environment where multiple applications are accessing multiple, heterogeneous data sources, a mediation layer has been advocated [Bas88] [Wie92]. As data fetching becomes more complex in new networking environments, mediators relieve the applications from the burden of assuming this task as well as from data-source dependency.

Object-oriented technology is rapidly becoming the dominant application development paradigm. However, the storage of business data is still mostly relational, or hierarchical. This paper describes a mediation technology that provides a way to fill the data modeling gap in a distributed environment. The term "Object View Broker" (OVB) denotes a system that helps to create materialized object views from external, foreign data repositories. The system customizes these views for client applications, thus acting as an object server. Section 2 gives some insights on the U S WEST environment and requirements in terms of data access. Section 3 is a description of the Object View Broker architecture, its communication paradigm, its mapping technology and view management.

2.0 Context and Requirements

2.1 U S WEST Data Management Strategy

U S WEST is currently undertaking a reorganization of its data repositories. Data, as a corporate asset, is being organized into major databases that are relational. Each of these databases reflects a particular data area of the corporate business, and is called a CSDB (Corporate Subject DataBase). For example, there will be a CSDB for U S WEST products, another for U S WEST customers, etc. (The notion of customer alone is complex and requires a schema with more than 50 entities.) Access to these CSDBs will be mostly provided by a procedural interface that encapsulates predefined operations (create, update, delete) for each entity or group of entities. This interface also enforces data integrity and consistency. Applications will be allowed to directly access these CSDBs, but are also likely to maintain some local databases that may represent some pre-selection of CSDBs, in a "data staging" type of use. Finally, the transition will not occur in one phase and some legacy databases (e.g. hierarchical) will need to be integrated in the framework. Along with this data organization around local stores, CSDB stores and legacy stores, new data access schemes are being studied. They must support application specific needs for data access, data migration and interoperability, as well as data consistency maintenance procedures across these repositories.

2.2 Applications Requirements

- *Support for modeling mismatch.* New application development, as well as application re-engineering, will be predominantly object-oriented at U S WEST. Also, user interaction with data (ad hoc queries, browsing, data mining) will be driven by intermediate, user-centric semantic data models. Therefore, there is a clash between data models for computation and presentation (object-oriented, semantic) and the incumbent data models for storage (relational, hierarchical). Applications should be relieved from the burden of assuming this mismatch, when using these stores for object persistence.

- *Heterogeneity of data sources.* In this framework, applications will require access to heterogeneous sources of data (e.g. a local object-oriented database as transient store, CSDB as permanent store). The reasons that have led to a relational database technology for CSDBs are mostly conjectural: relational DBMSs have proved highly scalable in terms of volume of data and transaction throughput, and provide today the reliability required by critical business applications. In the future, the evolution of data servers (e.g. relational to object-oriented) is likely to generate another kind of ("temporal") heterogeneity. Applications should not have to cope with heterogeneous or changing data sources formats, and be assured of a good level of transparency with regard to its data sources.

- *Change management.* The CSDB schemas are likely to evolve. The impact of changes (database schema, procedural interface) on the applications should be reduced as much as possible.

- *Event management.* Several applications, as well as inter-database management procedures (consistency, updates, replicates) will be event-driven or event-dependent. The DBMS is not the right place to support such functions (which have more to do with the application logic). Instead, they should be supported by a middleware technology.

- *Interoperations services.* In large automated business processes, several applications may have to cooperate. This cooperation is usually related to "data events" (e.g. a new service order is recorded). It requires customized services that are associated to these data events, like notification to other applications, caching of data, blocking of other requests, etc.

An example of application that is currently in deployment at U S WEST is the re-engineering of Order Distribution Services (ODS). In a typical order handling system, multiple, usually automated, work centers collaborate in completing a work order. ODS aims at automating service orders flows with a framework that provides access to legacy systems and relational databases. At the core of ODS is an Object View Broker (OVB) architecture. Figure 1 depicts the architecture of the ODS framework.

The Object View Broker provides data communication and services to application systems, some of them are being re-engineered using object-oriented technology, others are new developments (C++ and CLOS). The OVB provides persistence to the object oriented data models of the new applications, using a relational data model for storage.

FIGURE 1. ODS general architecture

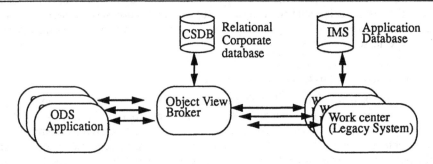

2.3 Requirements for Object View Broker

We have translated the application requirements into requirements for a middleware tech-. nology. Although object persistence functionality is a main requirement (r1) for the Object View Broker, it is just one of its objectives. Other required functions are: to manage materialized object views (r2) that may map in a complex way to pre-existing (non exclusively) relational databases (e.g. many to many class-table mappings), to provide services in a multi-client environment (r3) along with these object views (e.g. event-driven notifications to other applications, object locking, object caching). In addition, a flexible mediation technology raises other requirements for the Object View Broker: (r4) the peculiarities of the back-end database technology must be transparent to the application (e.g. the application code should not contain database DDL or DML code), and (r5) the Object View Broker code itself should be as independent as possible from client applications, as well as from database technology. This means that adding a new application or modifying the object model of an application should not require any downtime for the mediation system (e.g. no recompiling / relinking of its code). Similarly, substituting a database to another should also be handled at run-time. Finally, (r6) the Object View Broker must support interoperability between several data sources: one object view may actually map to several databases.

2.4 Related Work

Support for persistence. The requirements above call for a mediation function between object-oriented applications and relational databases. There are several available commercial products that provide a mapping functionality from object models to relational databases. Most of these tools are designed for supporting one major function: the persistence of application objects. The usual approach is to provide class templates generation with methods that directly handle the database interaction. In such tools, the input of the generator is an object model (e.g. OMT compliant) and a mapping specification. Major object-oriented database or knowledge-base vendors also provide a gateway to map relational databases. In both contexts, we have observed the following shortcomings of the mapping facility: (1) only straightforward (e.g. one class to one table) mappings are assumed, and (2) only standard SQL interfaces are supported (i.e. embedded SQL, as opposed to stored procedure interfaces).

Interfaces to databases. Some generic front-ends to databases aim at abstracting DBMS specific features. In the context of advanced user-interfaces, a commercial product like Open Books[1] aims at providing this transparency. One of the authors has also been involved in a multi-modal user interface for databases [DBC92]. Both approaches rely on an intermediate, user-centered data model. In a distributed programming environment, products like Uniface[2], ERNIE [Col91] provide a common, uniform interface to databases. The tools above are mostly focused on providing data source transparency and some database interoperability support, but do not integrate a capability that supports the mapping of application objects to other data models (they support at most the mapping of queries and methods, not of their result). They also do not provide interoperations services between applications.

Distributed Objects. The name "Object View Broker" does not relate to an Object *Request* Broker architecture (CORBA[3][OMG91]), the primary role of which is to provide a communication model for distributed object-oriented applications. We are not concerned here in the brokerage of requests (or method invocations) across distributed objects, but in creating, managing and serving object *views*, which involves some mapping technology and some support for DBMS-like functions on materialized object views. This is not supported by CORBA. Therefore, we rather see Object View Broker as being complementary to a CORBA layer by addressing the storage of objects on various data servers using adequate mapping technologies.

DOM (Distributed Object Management)[MHG92] is a framework that goes beyond inter-object communication, and addresses interoperability between applications, based on the object paradigm. Under this aspect, Object View Broker can be seen as a technology to implement a particular kind of DOM for managing databases as object resources. In particular, it provides the mapping support and view management to implement the Local

---

1. Open Books is a trademark from Open Books, Inc.
2. Uniface is a trademark from Uniface Corporation (US subsidiary).
3. The Common Object Request Broker Architecture is a standard issued by the Object Management Group.

Access Interface (LAI) of a DOM, which is absent from the Sybase LAI of the DOM prototype [Hor91]. Indeed, as explained later, OVB focuses on mapping the *result* of data server operations, not on wrapping the data server into an object model. A more detailed comparison of OVB with the DOM/LAI for Sybase is done in Section 3.4.1.

3.0 The Mediation Technology in Object View Broker

3.1 An Agent-Based Architecture

The Object View Broker is a technology that mediates between applications and data servers. On the client side, Object View Broker operates as an object server. On the data servers side, Object View Broker operates as a client. The components of Object View Broker are:

- *Client Object Broker* (COB). On the application side, client functions are implemented in form of a library that is linked with the application code. The library code (currently C++ or CLOS) is generated from an object model specification that complies with the OMT methodology, using a proprietary modeling tool. The object model may be shared by several client applications that use the same objects, or need to inherit from the same objects. Such a common model is called an object domain model. The COB classes encapsulate communication classes that handle interaction with the other agents of the Object View Broker.

- *Request Agent* (RA), on the data server side. A Request Agent is a client to databases servers. Each RA is representative of an application (i.e. of one COB instance) and handles communication with one or several database servers. The RA of an application is dynamically spawned when the application connects to the Object View Broker, and is shut down when the application disconnects. A pool of Request Agents that are clients to the same database server (each RA representing a transaction thread) exploits its multi-user capability. Each RA manages a request queue as well as data conversion functions (i.e. mapping to and from the storage data model). The communication COB/ RA may be synchronous or asynchronous, and the unit of communication on either way is the Request.

- *Event Manager* (EM). The COBs of different applications also communicate with an Event Manager agent. The Event Manager supports inter-application services based on events that are generated from two sources: the Requests sent by the COBs, and the responses produced by the Request Agents. An EM can store materialized object views as information associated to services that are required by the applications (e.g. caching).

FIGURE 2. Object View Broker basic architecture: the object mediation cluster

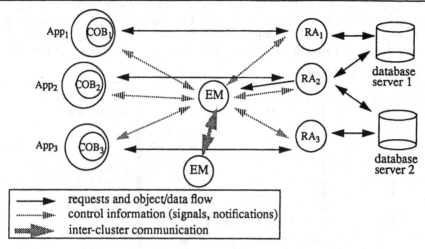

Figure 2 represents an overview of an Object View Broker architecture. The group of agents and applications that are connected to a same Event Manager is called an *object mediation cluster*. A mediation cluster gathers applications that are likely to share services and data on a frequent basis as well as inter-communication based on data events. Mediation clusters communicate between each other through their EM inter-connections (e.g. an application requires an object that is not "known" by its RA). Note that Request Agents are not shared by applications (although the RAs of a mediation cluster are all instances of a same program). This prevents a RA from becoming a bottleneck for dataflow. Concurrency management is then delegated to the database servers (although a RA supports some queuing, it is intended for a single transaction thread).

3.2 The Communication Model

3.2.1 Architecture

The communication between Object View Broker agents is based on a messaging paradigm. The notion of message is orthogonal to the underlying communication layer. In a first version of OVB, we used a proprietary communication layer library that provided high level abstractions for setting up client and server communication using the Unix socket protocols. Communication base classes were provided, which could be subclassed to suit specific client-server communication needs. This communication layer also provided monitoring services, message logging, and alarm services. Object View Broker can operate with any communication technology, provided that it offers the services above. The current version is using a commercial product (ezBRIDGE[4]) that provides the required flexibility in communication (connectionless) with adequate backlog and queuing capabilities.

The communication services, up to message management, are encapsulated by library classes, thus providing networking transparency to the application. For example, the base message class "IPC_Message" is subclassed in both COB and RA agents by some Mes-

---

4. ezBRIDGE is a trademark from Systems Strategies, Inc.

sage class, as is the base class "MessageAgent" that handles received messages on both sides. Figure 3 shows the functional partitioning of the classes in a COB library that implements a domain object model for a Service Order Distribution application. We use a proprietary object modeling tool (complying with the OMT methodology [Rum91]) for designing the domain model of the COB and for generating corresponding class templates.

FIGURE 3. COB Object Model

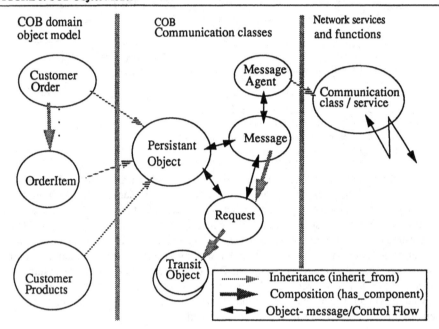

3.2.2 Transit Objects

In response to the Object View Broker requirements, we have developed an original mapping technology for the Object View Broker (detailed in Section 3.4). Data, as it flows between agents (COB/EM/RA) is structured in an intermediate form called Transit Objects (TO). From a networking perspective, the TO represents an intermediate data structure and format suitable for communication: a Request always contains application data in form of TOs. The TO is implemented as a unique object class, the code of which is independent from the application classes. Conversions methods (e.g. ASCII) required by the communication facility only need to be implemented in the TO class.

3.2.3 Messages and Requests

Messages. The OVB Message is the unit of communication in OVB. A Message is made of one or more Requests. Sending and receiving messages is handled by the Message class, which implements the high level layer of the messaging protocol used between OVB agents. The message class provides methods to convert between ASCII representation and internal representation.

Requests. In the high level Object View Broker communication protocol, a Request is always wrapped into a Message. On the server side, a Request is the elementary task to be handled by a Request Agent. A Request usually defines a database activity on a relational database. A Request may represent an operation over some attributes of an object, over an object or over several objects. However, a Request does not always have an object semantics: it may be related to some OVB specific service (e.g. dynamically set up a notification service for an application). A COB application may package many Requests into one Message in order to reduce communication overhead, and/or in order to define a single database transaction (see next Section). The answer to a Request is also a Request. Object data is represented in form of Transit Objects attached to the Request. Figure 4 illustrates the detail of the Request class.

FIGURE 4. The Request class

Request Data Members

Request_Number. An integer that will uniquely identify a Request within a message.

Request_Type. A value that identifies the type of Request (o.store, o.update, notification, service set-up, etc..)

Class_ID. The class identification (an integer associated to each class of the COB) of the main object that is concerned by the Request.

Query_String. A surrogate containing an identification of the service to be invoked (name, that will be associated by the RA to an existing database and to a predefined query or stored procedure).
If ad hoc querying is allowed, may contain the query text itself.

Input _TO. This is a Transit Object used as input by the Request.
In case of a "fetch" Request: contains the parameters required by the query to be invoked (e.g. a key attribute value for retrieving an object).
In case of a "store" Request: contains the object data to be stored or updated.

Output _TO. This is a Transit Object used as output by the Request. In case of a "fetch" Request: will contain the result of the invoked query (e.g. the data of an object). In case of "store" Request: contains some key information

Status. Contains the execution status of the Request (its transaction mode)

Request Functions Members

ASCII_Format. A method that creates an ascii representation of the Request object.

ASCII_Parse. A method that will construct the Request object from an ascii string.

Execute. A method that is invoked on the RA side to execute the specified query.

3.3 Transaction Management

Requests and Messages have a transaction semantics which is supported by the Object View Broker. However, transaction control can be given to the application (e.g. for long transactions). On the data servers side, a Request Agent represents a database client (transaction thread), thus relying on the DBMS concurrency control and transaction management. The Object View Broker does not directly support more complex transactions (e.g. distributed, nested transactions), but its architecture is open to external transaction support. For example, if a persistence operation on an application object requires access to two databases (i.e. a distributed transaction), the Request Agent for this application may deal with a transaction manager (e.g. Encina™, Tuxedo™) that advertises the correspond-

database services. The transaction semantics of Requests and Messages may vary as follows:

Case 1. Request transaction.

When a Request object is added to a Message object, it is not given the semantics of a transaction (by default, the Message is the transaction, e.g. when built by the persistence methods of a generated COB). However, the Request may be given a transaction semantics. This can be controlled by the application programmer if he/she directly manipulates Messages and Requests objects to build Messages. On the database side, a Request is associated with a query (e.g. a stored procedure call). In the ODS application, any kind of database access (create, read, update, delete) is supported by predefined stored procedures. Each of these procedures can execute in different modes: their transaction status is parameterized, and the stored procedure may commit or not.

Case 2. Message transaction.

The Message is the unit of data that the application sends and receives across the network. The Message is sent as a single communication unit and the application cannot take the control back between the execution of two of its Requests (unless the message is sent in asynchronous mode). Packaging several Requests into a Message is also a way to enforce the serialization of their execution (the ordering of Requests may not be guaranteed by the communication layer). When the Message is given a transaction semantics, each of its Requests is executed in *step-transaction* mode (i.e. is just a step in the transaction). The Message is said in *full-transaction* mode: it is responsible for committing the whole sequence at the end, or rolling back the sequence (or part of it).

Case 3. Multi-message transaction

In this mode of Message building, the Message will not commit after the last Request. Thus, the application can obtain Message results before the end of the transaction, and build the next Message based on these results. The risks of such transactions are: (1) deadlocks (e.g. it is no longer possible to foresee which resources will be required), and (2) the client application may hang while locking database resources and before sending the committing Message. Figure 5 summarizes the various transaction semantics of a Message.

FIGURE 5. Three transaction modes

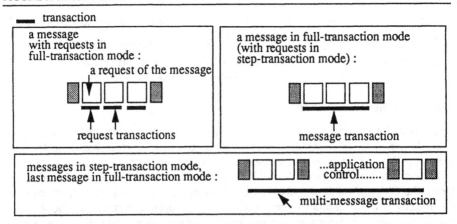

An application can handle communication at two levels. At the highest level of abstraction, objects methods encapsulate communication. For example, making a C++

Customer_Order object persistent is handled by the statement in Example 1, that builds and sends a Message with a (usually) single Request inside:

example 1.

```
Customer_Order *mycustomerorder; // declare a pointer

...

mycustomerorder->MakePersistent();// use persistence method
```

The application has also access to communication classes in order to control message building and sending. In the following example, the application groups two persistence operations into one message transaction (that corresponds to one database transaction):

example 2.

```
// create empty Message and empty Request objects
mymessage = new OVB_message(FULL_TRANS);
myrequest1 = new OVB_request();
myrequest2 = new OVB_request();
// store the order in a Request and put it in the Message
mycustomerorder->MakePersistent(mymessage, myrequest1);
// get related billing data
BillingDirective* bd = mycustomerorder->GetBillingData();
// store billing data in a Request and add it to the Message
if (bd) bd->MakePersistent(mymessage, myrequest2);
// now send the complete Message
mymessage->SendMessage();
```

3.4 The Mapping Facility

3.4.1 Mapping Strategy

One of the goals of Object View Broker is to provide transparency of data sources to each user application: the database technology should neither be visible from the application, nor impact its code. On the other hand, the Object View Broker needs to know enough of the semantics of the data it manipulates in order to perform associated services (e.g. caching, locking, notification require some information about key attributes). One solution could be for OVB to directly manipulate data in form of application objects. The agents of OVB would then work on a distributed base of application objects from end to end (e.g. relying on a CORBA layer). There are two drawbacks to this approach: (1) the independence of the Object View Broker from application object models is no longer possible (e.g. the Request Agent code must replicate the application object classes), and (2) some services may require some information that is lost or buried when data has been mapped to objects. For example, two objects o_1 and o_2, instances of two classes c_1 and c_2 in two different applications may map to the same data in the database. An Object View Broker service may rely on the ability to detect such an overlap, which may be hard to specify on the object classes themselves.

Partly because of the previous reasons, we have introduced an intermediate level of data modeling, called Transit Objects. A Transit Object (TO) structures the output or the input of a Request in a form that neither depends on the database modeling technology, nor is tied to the application object model. The object-relational mapping becomes a two-step process that is distributed between agents (COB and RA). The Transit Object format artic-ulates the two phases of the mapping. We consider Transit Objects as being *materialized semantic views* of the data as stored, while application objects are *materialized object views* of Transit Objects. From a software architecture viewpoint, a TO is implemented in form of a unique object class (e.g. C++) that is flexible enough to adapt to various map-pings (Section 3.4.2). Figure 6 illustrates the data mapping process.

FIGURE 6. Two-step mappings

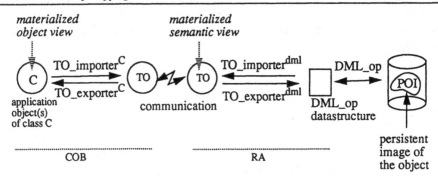

The application is only concerned with the mapping TO ↔ application object(s). TO_importers and TO_exporters that are application specific can be added as TO methods by subclassing the TO class. The mapping TO ↔ database relies on two processing capa-bilities: (1) the Data Manipulation Language of the data store, in form of database opera-tors called DML_op (e.g. stored procedure or SQL query), and (2) TO_importers and TO_exporters that are specific to the output of this type of DML_op (e.g. to map a TO from and to arrays of values that are parameters of stored procedures). Within the scope of access to a given database technology (e.g. relational + stored procedure interface), a sin-gle, generic mapping operator is sufficient (TO_importer^{dml} and TO_exporter^{dml} on Fig-ure 6). These mapping operators, as well as the TO constructors, are parameterized with a TO-structure (or TO-schema). TO customizing for some application object can then be dynamically accommodated, without altering the Object View Broker code.

This mapping strategy differs from the Local Application Interface of DOM [Hor91], as defined for Sybase. The DOM strategy is to encapsulate the DBMS (Sybase), its opera-tions (DML) as well as a particular database instance, in an object model. Note that this object model provides an object view of the relational database that is orthogonal to the applications object models (whereas in OVB, the design of Transit Objects provides a first level of views that can be customized for each applications). The Sybase LAI object model is intended to be operated through the DOM manipulation language and communication. The LAI provides a translator DOM queries→ SQL, while OVB does not provide such a translator (therefore, ad-hoc queries in OVB would have to be database DML dependent). OVB does not try to wrap the data server and its operations in an object manner, but is more focused on mapping the *result* of data server operations, into an object manner. There is some trade-off between the two approaches: interfacing the DML of the data server by an object DML provides flexibility in data manipulation on the application side, but is less efficient and safe than accessing data through an interface of predefined data-base procedures. The (object language / database DML) translation approach is suitable for light-weight applications such as user-interface systems (in fact, we implemented it in such a system [DCB92], where a semantic model and its DML are mapped to a relational database and SQL). However, in the ODS application, access to databases (CSDBs) is enforced through a stored procedure interface for efficiency and data integrity reasons.

3.4.2 Data Modeling of Transit Objects

From an Object View Broker perspective, a TO represents some intermediate, structured form of data that the Broker can manipulate and identify, yet doing so without knowing of the applications' object models nor of the database technology. From a data modeling viewpoint, TOs represent semantic, materialized views of the data as stored, that provide a semantically rich, uniform mapping base to applications. They are also appropriate for post-retrieval operations (horizontal or vertical compositions of TOs, splitting, projection, etc.). TOs do not model behaviors specific to application objects.

A TO data-structure has three layers: (1) a data layer called TO-data, (2) a schema layer called TO-schema that models the TO-data, and (3) a meta-model layer called TO-meta-model, that represents the constructs used in the TO-schema. The data-model of the TO is a semantic, functional data-model. Semantic modeling is known for its ability to map other data models [Huk87][LyVi87]. Combining functional and semantic modeling has been shown suitable for data-models integration in [ADK91][KKM93]. The functional model-ing paradigm also supports simple manipulations of complex objects [BBKV87] [Day87]. One salient feature of our semantic data-model is that meta-model layers are explicitly represented, using in turn semantic modeling constructs called DOT (or Data Object Type, for all kinds of data entities including complex relationships) and FOT (or Functional Object Type, for all kinds of binary relationships). These two constructs stand for the ulti-mate meta-meta-model for any TO and represent the only invariant in TOs, since the TO-schema and the TO-metamodel may vary from one TO to the other. A more detailed description of the data-model we use is found in [DBC92].

FIGURE 7. Example of TO data modeling

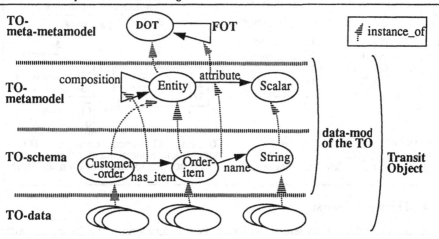

Figure 7 sketches a single Transit Object that models a customer_order database. Note that complex objects (e.g. with attributes or components) map to subgraphs in the TO-schema.

The notion of Transit Object corresponds to a semantic *database*, rather than to a single application object. This data modeling can accommodate transactions of various levels of granularity about application objects: a single TO can be used to map either a single attribute, or a composition hierarchy of objects, or a collection of such hierarchies. Depending on its communication needs, an application object can make use of several TO-schemas, that can be dynamically defined.

3.4.3 Implementation of a Transit Object

The TOs are instances of a unique class that is totally independent from any application model or from any database technology (implemented in C++ and in CLOS in the ODS application because different COBs are implemented using these two languages). However, the TO class may be subclassed by applications as well as by specific Request Agents in order to be extended with specific mapping methods. The TO is essentially implemented as a graph of lists of elementary types. Figure 8 compares the flat structure of the result of a relational join with its TO conversion. (The conversion requires a TO-schema, as explained in the next section.) We have done benchmarks on the cost of TO conversions. The cost of converting relational tuples into a TO datastructure is between 1/10 and 1/20 of a database transaction time.

In Figure 8, meta-level information (TO-schema) is added to the data part that results from the SQL query or stored procedure. The fields of the tuples resulting from the query (left hand side of the figure) are partitioned and re-arranged according to the TO-schema and its mapping directives. The sub-tuples produced by the TO conversion are organized in a graph (here a tree), that renders the structure of a customer order in our example (yet doing so without relying on program code that would depend on application classes).

FIGURE 8. Conversion of a relational result into a Transit Object

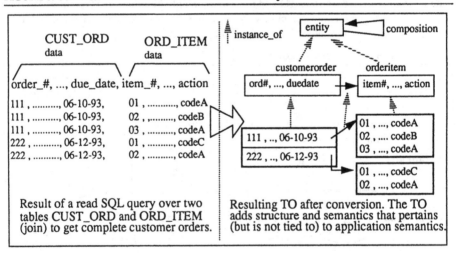

Result of a read SQL query over two tables CUST_ORD and ORD_ITEM (join) to get complete customer orders.	Resulting TO after conversion. The TO adds structure and semantics that pertains (but is not tied to) to application semantics.

3.4.4 Mapping a Request

A Request to fetch the persistent object image (POI) of an object (say a Customer_Order) will contain three major components: (1) the application Request name, (2) in the input_TO, some key information (called POIid), (3) in the output_TO, optionally, the TO-schema to be used to map the POI into a Transit Object. A default TO-schema is stored for each Request in the Request Agent. The RA maps the Request name to a pair <database, stored procedure call>, using a table called *CallMap* dictionary. It then maps the input-TO into input parameters for the stored procedure, using the appropriate TO-exporter. After execution, it maps the result into the output-TO, and sends back the Request. Figure 9 illustrates the processing of a fetch Request, by a Request Agent.

FIGURE 9. Request processing

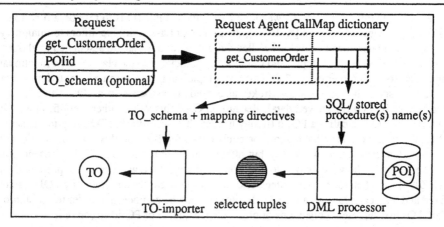

3.4.5 Change Management

The Object View Broker has been designed to minimize maintenance and evolution costs. Follows a list of situations that require some maintenance operation:

1. Modifications in the data resource. A schema change (e.g. de-normalization) (a) can often be made transparent by modifying the implementation of the database access interface (e.g. stored procedures). If not, the interface requires some modifications. These modifications may still be buffered by the mapping DML_operator/TO. If not (e.g. an attribute has been removed in a database entity), a TO-schema change in the associated Request is needed. In the last case only, the application mapping code needs some update. The OVB code does not need to be updated (TO-schemas can be modified at run-time in the CallMap tables of the Request Agents).

2. Substitution of one database to another. The corresponding entries of requests in the Request Agent table need to be modified, and a new request agent spawned to interact with the new data server. These changes can be handled at run-time, transparently to the application (depending on the communication tool, the application may have to be restarted).

3. Changes in the application object model. If a (mappable) class is created or modified, two situations may occur: (a) existing DML_operators can be reused (e.g. stored procedure). In that case, the application can either reuse the associated TO-schemas, or define its own in order to better suit the new objects. (b) new stored procedures need to be added (and new TO-schemas defined). The CallMap table of the Request Agent needs to be updated. In both cases, changes can be handled at run-time, without down time for agents and databases (stored procedures can be created on line).

3.4.6 View Semantics

Being defined as materialized views, Transit Objects have an "independent" view semantics [Day89]. The smallest area of data in the database that maps to a TO is called the Persistent Object Image (POI) of the TO. The POI can be viewed as the *base view* [HeZd90].

Consistency of TOs with the base data from which they are derived is not an issue as long as TOs are transient (it is the application responsibility to maintain consistency between its objects and the data store). However, some services require the temporary storage of TOs in the Event Manager (e.g. caching), or require to maintain a link between a TO and the base data (their POI) it maps to.

One way to maintain the link between the base data and the TO is to rely on a functional definition of view identity. In [AbBo91], the problem of assigning identifiers to imaginary objects (i.e. materialized views) is handled through functions that are associated to classes, e.g. oid = C(t) where t is a tuple, and C a function associated to the class. Such a functional approach solves problems like "do tuple1 and tuple2 map to the same object view?" For similar reasons, the Object View Broker also needs to associate to a TO a value that is function of its POI (or viewed data). Because in OVB this value rather identifies the POI and not the TO, we call it a POIid (it may happen that two different TOs map to the same POI, which means they have same or equivalent POIids). For this reason, we do not require TOs to have a view identity, but rather attach a POIid to them. Our representation of the POIid is however close to the notion of object view identity as presented in [HeZd90] for a heterogeneous framework. In this approach, the structure of a POIid is not fixed and may change from a view to the other. It may be composed in order to accommodate TOs that represent collections of objects. An example of POIid structure is:

```
<DBname, schemaname, tablename, <att1_name, att1_value>,
<att2_name, att2_value>, ...>
```

OVB does not handle the problem of updating keys that are used to define the POIid of an application object. A general update mechanism that also addresses the key attributes would require some update translation protocol, e.g. as defined in [BSKW91]. Although the Object View Broker does not currently provide view updates mechanism at TO level (i.e. TO as view), the notion of POIid which actually identifies the *base* of the view, can support such a function in the future. In particular, it can be used to detect side effects [UrCh92].

3.5 Event Management and Associated Services

Events are mostly associated with Requests. The Event Manager (EM) handles events of the form:

```
event_x = <time_stamp, application_id, class_id, request_info,
data_server_id, POIid>
```

Since there is an overhead cost in managing events, not all events are handled. Only events that match required services are actually posted and recorded on a blackboard. Event-based notification consists of sending messages to applications, depending on some events occurring in the EM. A notification service is described using rules of the following forms:

(1) $event_x \rightarrow action_y$

(2) $event_x$ & $event_y$ & .... $event_n \rightarrow action_y$

(3) $event_x$ & $event_y$ & .... $event_n \rightarrow event_z$

with actions being of the form:

```
<application_id, [class_id,] [object_id,] message_template>
```

where the message_template may contain slots for TOs, POIids, and parts of the triggering event.

Event management is used in ODS for implementing notification across applications, One application is creating Customer_Orders and stores them in the CSDB. Another application, the work flow manager, is reading these Customer_Orders to analyze them. A notification service has been attached to the creation of a new Customer_Order. Each time a new order is created and stored by the first application, the Event Manager of ODS notifies (sends a message to) the work flow manager.

Events are also used to implement some *soft* locking mechanism at object level. When the work flow manager works on a Customer_Order (e.g. modifies its status information), it prevents *some* work center application from accessing the Customer_Order, in order to avoid inappropriate reads. Other work center applications may be authorized to access it. This is a selective lock, that can be set up according to application specific semantics.

4.0 Summary and Conclusion

The Object View Broker provides the following services to object-oriented applications that require an access to non object-oriented data servers:

* *Mapping and data source transparency.* OVB isolates the applications from direct database access. It advertises database services through surrogates to the applications, and supports the mapping of requests to database operations. Transit Objects, as materialized semantic views, provide a semantically rich mapping base to applications, that does not depend on storage data models.

* *Event-driven services.* By using event-driven services that rely on Requests and object view semantics, OVB allows several applications of the same business area to coordinate their operations on object views.

* *Networking.* OVB agent architecture supports various distribution schemes and encapsulates communication services for applications objects. It also supports transactions of various data granularity, and provides data-source location transparency to applications.

The Object View Broker concept combines object views definition from various data models with the management of these views in a multi-user, client-server environment. It addresses the data heterogeneity issue and its management in distributed cooperative systems. We have proposed and implemented an original two-step mapping technology that can accommodate units of data of various sizes (attribute to collection of complex objects), by creating materialized semantic views (Transit Objects). Transit Objects isolate applications from data sources while providing the semantics required for middleware-level services.

References

[AbBo91] Abiteboul S., Bonner A. "Objects and Views". *Proc. of ACM-SIGMOD*, 1991.

[ADK91] Ahmed R., DeSmedt P., Kent W., Ketabchi M., Litwin W., Rafii A., Shan M.C., "Pegasus: A System of Seamless Integration of Heterogeneous Information Sources", *Compcon*, 1991.

[Bas88] Basu,A. "Knowledge Views in Multiuser Knowledge-Based Systems." *Proc.Fourth IEEE Int. Data Eng. Conf.JEEE*, CS Press, Los Alamos, Calif., pp.346-353,1988.

[BBKV87] Bancilhon F., Briggs T., Khoshafian S. and Valduriez P. "FAD, A Powerful and Simple Database Language", *Proc. of the 13th VLDB Conference*, September 1987, pp 97-105.

[BSKW91] Barsalou,T., Siambela,N., Keller,A.M., and Wiederhold,G., "Updating Relational Databases

[BSKW91] Barsalou,T., Siambela,N., Keller,A.M., and Wiederhold,G., "Updating Relational Databases through Object-Based Views". *Proc. of ACM-SIGMOD*, 1991.

[Col91] Collier G., Cohen,F., Salasoo,A., Pillalamarri, M., "CHEYENNE: A Large Object-Oriented System", *Proc. of BOOST'91, Bellcore Object-Oriented Systems Technology*, pp.37-47, 1991.

[Day87] Dayal U. et al. "Simplifying Complex Objects : The PROBE Approach to Modelling an Querying Them". *International Workshop on the Theory and Applications of Nested Relations and Complex Objects*, Darmstadt, West Germany, April 1987.

[Day89] Dayal U. "Queries and Views in an Object-Oriented Data Model". *2nd Int. Workshop on Database Programming Languages*, Oregon,1989.

[DBC92] Durand J., Brunner H., Cuthbertson R., Fogel S., McCandless T., Sparks R. and Sylvan L., "Data Model and Query Algebra for a Model-Based, Multi-Modal User Interface". *Proc. of the Int. Workshop on Interfaces to Databases Systems (IDS'92)*, R.Cooper, ed., Springer-Verlag, 1992, pp. 311-337.

[HeZd90] Heiler S., Zdonik S.., "Object Views: Extending the Vision". *proc. Data Engineering conf.*,1990.

[HuK87] Hull R., and King R. "Semantic Database Modeling: Survey, Application, and Research Issues". *In ACM Computing Surveys*, 1987, Vol. 19, Numb. 3, pp.208-211.

[Hor91] Hornick,M.F., "Integrating Heterogeneous, Autonomous, Distributed Applications using the DOM Prototype". anonymous FTP(ftp.gte.com, "pub/dom"), GTE Laboratories, Inc., Technical Report, 1991.

[KKM93] Keim D.A., Kriegel H.P., Miethsam A.. "Integration of Relational Databases in a Multidatabase System based on Schema Enrichment". *Proc. of RIDE-IMS'93*, IEEE Computer Society Press, , 1993.

[LyVi87] Lyngbaek P.,Vianu V. "Mapping a Semantic Database Model to the Relational Model", *Proceedings of ACM-SIGMOD* 1987, Vol. 16 n.3.

[MHG92] Manola,F., Heiler, S., Georgakopoulos,D., Hornick,M., Brodie,M., "Distributed Object Management", *International Journal of Intelligent and Cooperative Information Systems*, Vol.1, June 1992.

[OMG91] Object Management Group, "The Common Object Request Broker; Architecture and Specification", *OMG Document Number 91.12.1*, Draft 10 December 1991.

[Rum91] Rumbaugh J. & al. "Object-Oriented Modeling and Design", Prentice-Hall,Englewood Cliffs, New Jersey,1991.

[UrCh92] Urban, S., Chalmer, K., "An investigation of the view update problem for object-oriented views", *Proceedings of the 11th Int. Phoenix Conference on Computers and Communications*, 1992..

[Wie92] Wiederhold,G., "Mediators in the Architecture of Future Information Systems," *IEEE Computer*, Vol. 25, No 3, pp 38-49, 1992.

Enhancing Pre-existing Data Managers with Atomicity and Durability

Rajeev Rastogi[1] and Marie-Anne Neimat[2]

[1] AT&T Bell Laboratories, 600 Mountain Avenue,
Murray Hill, NJ 07974-0636
[2] Hewlett-Packard Laboratories, 1501 Page Mill Road,
Palo Alto, CA 94305

Abstract. Many of currently available managers of persistent data do not provide support for updates that are *atomic* and *durable*. Developing from scratch the requisite software for incorporating the atomicity and durability properties into each of these pre-existing data managers is a time-consuming and formidable task. It is hence desirable to design and build a general purpose recovery manager that can be easily interfaced with pre-existing data managers. In this paper, we consider four recovery manager architectures that are based on recovery algorithms proposed in the literature and recovery designs adopted in existing products. We evaluate the various architectures with respect to 1) the extent of the modifications they cause to the software of pre-existing data managers, and 2) the degree to which they affect the performance of the data managers. Finally, we relate the experience we had in integrating a spatial data manager with a general purpose recovery manager.

1 Introduction

If updates to persistent data are to preserve the integrity of data, it is essential that they be performed in the context of transactions that are both *atomic* and *durable* [GR91]. Atomicity ensures that transactions either execute completely or do not execute at all. Durability ensures that all the updates (to persistent data) made by committed transactions are permanent. In traditional database systems, the *recovery manager* (RM) component is typically responsible for ensuring the atomicity and durability of transactions. The RM, when updates are performed, is provided with redo and undo descriptions for the update, and appropriate locks are acquired to ensure that executions are *strict*[3] [BHG87, RKS93]. The RM logs the descriptions, and in case of transaction aborts, system crashes or media failures, directs database system components to redo/undo updates based on the redo/undo descriptions contained in log records.

Many of currently available managers of persistent data, or *data managers* (DMs), do not contain an RM component and thus do not support atomic and durable updates (e.g., spatial DMs for Geographic Information Systems, geometric modelers for CAD applications, text retrieval systems, etc.). It may be

---

[3] An execution is strict if updates performed by active transactions can be undone from their undo descriptions.

desirable to enhance these DMs with atomicity and durability, either as an afterthought or because they need to interoperate with other transactional DMs in the context of atomic and durable transactions. Yet developing from scratch the requisite software for incorporating the atomicity and durability properties into each of these pre-existing DMs is a time-consuming and formidable task. It is thus desirable to design and build a general purpose RM that 1) can be easily interfaced with pre-existing DMs and requires minimal changes to their software, and that 2) causes minimal degradation to the performance of the DMs.

In this paper, we present four RM architectures for the implementation of a general purpose RM (RM toolkit). We evaluate the architectures with respect to 1) the extent of the modifications that need to be made to the DMs, and 2) the degree to which they affect the performance of the DMs. Two of the RM architectures are based on ARIES — a state-of-the-art recovery algorithm proposed in [MHL+92]. We choose ARIES over other recovery algorithms proposed in the literature [BHG87, WHBM90, GR91, Lom92] because it is fairly simple, and it supports logging of *physiological* descriptions [GR91], that is, logical undo/redo descriptions of updates at the page level, as well as fine-granularity locking at the tuple level. The other two RM architectures are based on ARIES$^-$, a slight modification of ARIES, because RMs based on ARIES may not integrate smoothly with pre-existing DMs. The reason for this is that ARIES requires certain state information to be recorded in every data page. This enables redo descriptions to be applied selectively to pages during restart recovery, and is essential if physiological redo descriptions are to be supported. However, since most pre-existing data pages do not contain this state information, they need to be reformatted – a consequence of which is an increase in data page size, and thus an increase in the number of I/Os to stable storage. The proposed variant of ARIES, ARIES$^-$, does not require pages to store any state information, but it does have the subsequent disadvantage of not supporting the logging of physiological redo descriptions. We identify, for each of the proposed RM architectures, its interactions with components of the DM. Based on these interactions, we identify the modifications that need to be made to the various pre-existing components of the DM. Finally, we study, for the various RM architectures, the trade-off between the modifications they require to DM components and data pages, and the degree to which they cause the performance of the DMs to degrade.

2 Data Manager Architecture

In this section, we describe a fairly generic data manager (DM) architecture which models the architecture of a number of existing DMs. The spatial DM that we consider later in the paper has an architecture very similar to the one described in this section. In our architecture, a DM consists of three modules: the *application module* (AM), the *buffer management* (BM) module and the *I/O module*.

2.1 Application Module

The AM provides users with a high-level interface that enables them to specify operations (e.g., insert, delete, retrieve, update) on high-level data structures (e.g., tuples, relations, arrays, complex objects). The AM translates the high-level operations on high-level structures to low-level operations on low-level structures (e.g., writing bytes on persistent storage). The AM views persistent storage as a collection of data pages. Every data page contains one or more objects or records, and each record is stored in a low-level format as a sequence of bytes somewhere in the page. The AM is responsible for determining the mapping between the logical structures (e.g., tuples, arrays, etc.) and data pages.

2.2 Buffer Manager Module

To manipulate the data pages stored in persistent storage, the pages need to be read into the address space of the DM process. To this end, the DM process maintains, in its address space, a buffer consisting of buffer pages into which data pages are read from persistent storage. The BM module is responsible for mapping a subset of persistent storage into buffer pages in the address space of the DM process. The BM module has no knowledge of records or logical structures. Its interface provides the following functions that are invoked by the AM:

- **pinPage:** is invoked by the AM to request the BM module to pin a certain data page in the DM's buffer. In case the data page is not in the buffer, the BM locates an unpinned buffer page and reads the data page into the buffer page (the contents of the buffer page, if *dirty*, are written to secondary storage before the data page is read). The BM returns the address of the buffer page to the AM.
- **unPinPage:** is invoked by the AM once it has completed reading or updating a data page, to indicate that it no longer needs the page.

2.3 I/O Module

The I/O module is responsible for reading and writing pages into the BM's buffers. The I/O module provides the following functions to perform these tasks:

- **pageWrite:** takes as arguments a page number and a virtual memory address. It ensures that the page at the specified virtual memory address is written to stable storage.
- **pageRead:** takes as arguments a page number and a virtual memory address. It reads the contents of the page from stable storage into the specified memory address.

3 Recovery Manager Architectures

As stated earlier, a recovery manager (RM) is responsible for ensuring the atomicity and durability properties of transactions. In this section, we evaluate various RM architectures that are based on ARIES [MHL+92], and a subtle variant of ARIES, referred to as ARIES⁻. We begin by briefly reviewing ARIES, following which we describe ARIES⁻.

ARIES utilizes the popular technique of *logging* to guarantee the atomicity and durability of transactions. Every time a page is updated, a log record containing undo and redo descriptions of the update is appended to the end of a file, the log. The undo description for an update consists of information explicit enough to permit restoring the contents of the page to its original value before the update, should such an action be required. The redo description for an update contains enough detail to permit reapplying the update to the page should the page not migrate to persistent storage before a crash occurs.

ARIES supports the logging of physical as well as physiological redo and undo descriptions for updates. Physical descriptions typically consist of before and after values of all the bytes that were modified on a page as a result of the operation. Physiological descriptions, on the other hand, consist of high-level descriptions of the operation that caused the update to the page. Physical descriptions have the advantage of being *idempotent*, that is, the effect on the database is the same irrespective of the number of times the descriptions are used to redo/undo updates. On the other hand, physical descriptions consume a lot of space in the log. Furthermore, if a transaction's updates are to be undone using physical undo descriptions, the transaction must obtain page-level locks on updated pages; hence fine-grained concurrency control is hindered if logged undo descriptions are physical (note that the locks that a transaction must obtain are independent of the nature of redo descriptions logged). Physiological descriptions, on the other hand, are space efficient. Furthermore, in most instances, to undo a transaction's updates from physiological undo descriptions, the transaction is required to obtain only record-level locks. However, redos/undos performed using physiological descriptions may not be idempotent.

To be effective, logging is coupled with a policy of writing all the log records describing updates to a page to persistent storage *before* the page itself is written to persistent storage, referred to as *write-ahead-logging* (WAL). To enforce WAL, every log record has a unique *log sequence number* (LSN) associated with it, and LSNs of log records increase monotonically in the order in which log records are written. Stored on every page is a pageLSN, the LSN of the log record describing the most recent update to the page. To implement WAL, an updated page cannot be written to persistent storage before all log records with LSN less than or equal to its pageLSN are flushed to stable storage. To guarantee the durability of transactions, all log records describing updates performed by a transaction are written out to stable storage when the transaction is committed.

In case a transaction aborts, all its updates are undone using the undo descriptions stored in the log records. Furthermore, updates to pages during transaction undo processing are logged as during normal processing[4]. Since ARIES writes log records during undo processing, it does not require undo descriptions to be idempotent. Thus, ARIES supports the logging of physiological undo descriptions.

Restart recovery, in case of a system crash, is performed as follows. ARIES first determines redoLSN that has the following property: updates described by log records with LSN less than redoLSN have been written to secondary storage (a discussion on how *checkpoints* can be used to determine redoLSN can be found in [RN92a]). Next, all the page updates described by log records with LSN greater than or equal to redoLSN and that did not make it to secondary storage are redone sequentially (using the redo descriptions contained in the log records). Since with every data page, a pageLSN field is stored, it is possible to determine if the update described by a log record made it to secondary storage or not. An update to a page is redone only if the LSN of the log record describing the update is greater than the pageLSN stored on the page. This ensures that the same update is not applied to a page more than once, and thus redo descriptions do not need to be idempotent. Thus, ARIES supports the logging of physiological redo descriptions. No log records are written during the redo phase. Once the redo phase is completed, transactions that were active at the time of the crash are aborted, and their effects are undone as during transaction undo processing (the transactions active at the time of the crash can be determined by using information stored during checkpoints and then scanning the log. This is further discussed in [RN92a]).

In our analysis of RM architectures for pre-existing DMs, the use of a pageLSN by ARIES becomes an issue. Since we are considering coupling the RM with a pre-existing DM whose data pages may not contain pageLSNs, adding a pageLSN to each data page managed by the DM may be unrealistic if not impossible. As a result, we are compelled to consider a slight variation of ARIES that does not require pageLSNs, which we refer to as ARIES⁻. ARIES⁻ performs exactly the same actions as ARIES during normal operation and transaction undo processing. However, during the redo phase of restart recovery, it redoes, sequentially, *all* the updates described by log records with LSN greater than or equal to redoLSN. Thus, a consequence of eliminating pageLSNs is that an update to a page may be applied more than once. As a result, redo descriptions must be idempotent and ARIES⁻ only supports the logging of physical redo descriptions. However, since similar to ARIES, ARIES⁻ writes log records for updates performed during transaction undo processing and hence provides support for the logging of physiological undo descriptions as well as fine-granularity locking.

In subsequent sections, we evaluate four RM architectures: two of them, RM_1 and RM_3 are based on the ARIES⁻ algorithm, while RM_2 and RM_4 are based on ARIES.

---

[4] To prevent updates that have already been undone from being undone again in case of a system crash during undo processing, ARIES writes *compensation log records* (CLRs) as described in [MHL+92]. This is only an optimization, and is irrelevant to the interaction of an RM with other DM components.

3.1 Architecture RM$_1$

RM$_1$ is based on the ARIES$^-$ algorithm, and thus does not require a **pageLSN** to be associated with data pages. However, RM$_1$ requires redo descriptions for updates to be physical (undo descriptions for updates can, however, be physiological). To implement WAL, RM$_1$ maintains a data structure referred to as *updated page table* (UPT). The UPT contains an entry for each dirty data page in DM's buffer, updates to which are described by log records that may not have been written to stable storage. Stored with every entry in the UPT, is an **updateLSN**, which is the LSN of the log record describing the most recent update to the page. The functions provided by RM$_1$ are:

- **write_LogRecord:** appends to the log, a log record containing the descriptions of an update to a page. Arguments to the function include the page identifier of the updated data page, the *transaction identifier* (tid) of the transaction that performed the update, and the undo and redo descriptions for the update (the redo description, is restricted to be physical). If an entry for the updated page does not exist in the UPT, a new entry is inserted. Furthermore, **updateLSN** for the page in the UPT is set to the LSN of the log record written.
- **force_LSN:** forces to persistent storage all log records with LSN less than or equal to **updateLSN** for the data page whose identifier is passed as an argument, i.e., writes to secondary storage all log records describing updates to the page. The entry for the page in the UPT is deleted.
- **commit:** is invoked to commit the transaction whose tid is passed as an argument to **commit**. All log records describing updates performed by the transaction are forced to secondary storage and a commit log record for the transaction is written to stable storage.
- **abort:** To abort a transaction, RM$_1$ first determines the last log record describing an update performed by the transaction. It then undoes, in reverse order, all the page updates performed by the transaction. To undo the page update described by a log record, it invokes the **undo** routine in the AM and passes to it the page identifier and the undo description for the update (contained in the log record). Once all updates are undone, an abort log record for the transaction is written to the log.

During restart recovery, RM$_1$ first invokes the **redo** routine in the AM to redo *all* the updates described by log records with LSN greater than or equal to **redoLSN**. The AM's **redo** procedure is invoked with arguments that include the page identifier and the (physical) redo description that the AM provided to RM$_1$ when it updated the page. Once all the updates described by log records with LSN greater than or equal to **redoLSN** have been redone, RM$_1$ invokes **abort** (described earlier) for every transaction that was active at the time of the crash.

Integrating RM$_1$ with a pre-existing DM entails the following modifications to be made to DM components (see Fig. 1):

- **[mod 1]** The AM must invoke **commit/abort** to commit/abort transactions after it has unpinned all pages previously pinned by it. The AM is also

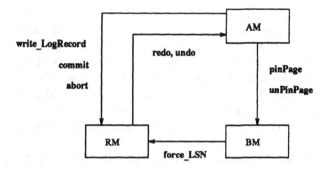

Fig. 1. Interaction of RM_1 with DM Components

responsible for obtaining appropriate locks for ensuring that executions are strict. The AM must hold onto these locks until the transaction completes.

- **[mod 2]** Before the AM invokes **unPinPage** in the BM module to unpin an updated page, it must invoke **write_LogRecord**.
- **[mod 3]** Before the BM's **pinPage** function writes a buffer page's contents to stable storage, it must invoke **force_LSN** with the identifier of the page contained in the buffer page as an argument. This is to implement WAL.
- **[mod 4]** The AM must provide functions **redo** and **undo** to redo and undo page updates, respectively, during restart recovery and transaction aborts. Arguments to both **redo** and **undo** include the page identifier of the data page requiring redo/undo and the redo/undo description for the update that were provided by the AM. **redo** pins the page in DM's buffer and updates the page using the redo description. No log records are written by **redo** when an update to a page is redone. **undo** uses the undo description to update one or more pages (the updated pages may be different from the page associated with the update to be undone). Also, the undo procedure requests RM_1 to write log records for pages that it updates as during normal processing. It does so by invoking **write_LogRecord** before it unpins an updated page.

3.2 Architecture RM_2

RM_2 is based on ARIES, and requires pre-existing data pages to be reformatted to permit the recording of a **pageLSN** in every page[5]. Storing the **pageLSN** in every page enables RM_2 to support the logging of physiological redo descriptions, in addition to physiological undo descriptions. RM_2 uses **pageLSNs** to implement WAL and thus does not need to maintain a UPT.

---

[5] **pageLSNs** are stored at the beginning as well as the end of a data page. A comparison of the two **pageLSNs** is used to determine if the page was written atomically (atomicity of page writes is essential if the logging of physiological redo descriptions is to be supported).

Compared to RM_1, the interface exported by RM_2 comprises additional functions to pin and unpin buffer pages. The reason is that AM functions are implemented based on certain rigid assumptions about data page sizes and data page formats, and have no knowledge of pageLSNs. This implies that pageLSNs must be hidden from the AM. Furthermore, the portion of a reformatted data page excluding the pageLSN information, which we refer to as the AM-visible page, must have the same size and format as that of a pre-existing data page. Thus, the size of a reformatted data page is greater than the size of a pre-existing data page.

If the AM were to invoke functions **pinPage** and **unPinPage** directly, it would be exposed to pageLSNs. This is not desirable as it would introduce substantial modifications to AM. Hence, RM_2 provides functions **rm_PinPage** and **rm_UnPinPage** that filter out the pageLSN information from data pages seen by the AM. Interactions between the AM and BM must now go through RM_2, which provides the following functions.

- **rm_PinPage:** pins a data page in DM's buffer by invoking **pinPage** in the BM module. It returns the address of the AM-visible page stored in DM's buffer. An argument to **rm_PinPage** is the page identifier of the data page to be pinned, which is passed as an argument to **pinPage**.
- **rm_UnPinPage:** unpins a data page previously pinned in DM's buffer by invoking **unPinPage** in the BM module. An argument to **rm_UnPinPage** is the page identifier of the data page to be unpinned, which is passed as an argument to **unPinPage**.
- **write_LogRecord:** appends to the log, a log record containing the descriptions of an update to a page. Arguments to the function include the page identifier of the updated data page, the tid of the transaction that performed the update, and the undo and redo descriptions for the update, and these are included in the log record that is written. Before returning, **write_LogRecord** sets the pageLSN field stored in the updated data page to the LSN of the log record just written. Note that both redo and undo descriptions for updates can be physiological.
- **force_LSN:** is invoked with the address of a buffer page in DM's buffer as an argument. **force_LSN** extracts the pageLSN for the contained data page from the header of the buffer page and forces all log records with LSN less than or equal to the pageLSN to secondary storage.
- **commit:** is identical to that of RM_1.
- **abort :** is identical to that of RM_1.

During restart recovery, RM_2 first redoes the updates described by every log record with LSN greater than or equal to redoLSN as follows. It first requests the BM to pin in DM's buffer, the data page with page identifier contained in the log record. It then determines if the LSN of the log record describing the update to the page is less than or equal to pageLSN for the page. If so, the update described by the log record has made it to secondary storage and the update need not be redone. Otherwise, RM_2 invokes the **redo** routine in the AM to redo the update with the following arguments: the redo description (contained in the log record) and the address of the AM-visible page pinned in DM's buffer. The **redo** routine redoes the update to the page using the redo description, following which, RM$_2$ sets **pageLSN** for the page to the LSN of the log record describing the update. Once all the updates described by log records with LSN greater than or equal to redoLSN are redone, RM$_2$ invokes **abort** for every transaction that was active at the time of the crash.

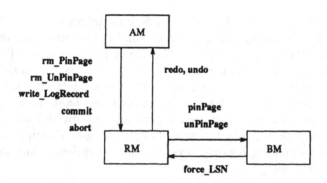

Fig. 2. Interaction of RM$_2$ with DM Components

Utilizing RM$_2$ to provide recovery support for pre-existing DMs requires certain modifications to be made to DM software (see Fig. 2). In addition to [mod 1] mentioned in the previous subsection, the following modifications need to be made to the DM components:

- [**mod 1**] The AM must invoke **rm_PinPage** and **rm_UnPinPage** instead of **pinPage** and **unPinPage**. Before the AM invokes **rm_UnPinPage** in the RM module to unpin an updated page, it invokes **write_LogRecord**.
- [**mod 2**] To implement WAL, the **pinPage** function in the BM module must be modified. Before the BM forces a buffer page to secondary storage, it must invoke **force_LSN** with the address of the buffer page as an argument.
- [**mod 3**] The AM must provide functions **redo** and **undo** to redo and undo page updates, respectively, during restart recovery and transaction aborts. Arguments to **redo** include the address of the AM-visible page pinned in DM's buffer, and the redo description for the update provided by the AM. **redo** updates the page in DM's buffer using the redo description. No log records are written by **redo** when an update to a page is redone. The **undo** routine provided by AM is identical to that described in [mod 4] in the previous subsection.
- [**mod 4**] Since pre-existing data pages managed by DM do not contain **pageLSNs**, they need to be reformatted to include with every page, a **pageLSN** field. This results in an increase in the size of data pages which could have

an adverse effect on system performance due to an increased number of I/Os to stable storage.

- [mod 5] Since reformatted data pages now contain an additional pageLSN field, the buffer page size in the BM component needs to be increased to accommodate data pages with pageLSNs.

3.3 Architectures RM_3, RM_4

To support checkpointing, the RM and BM must interact. This is described in [RN92a]. To shield the system integrator from the interaction between the RM and BM, an RM design adopted by Transarc's Encina product [Tra, RN92b] is to include the BM as part of the RM. In this section, we consider two RM architectures RM_3 and RM_4 that combine the BM module with RM_1 and RM_2, respectively. Both RM_3 and RM_4 maintain their own buffer in which their BM components pin and unpin pages when **pinPage** and **unPinPage** are invoked. RM_4 supports logging of physical as well as physiological descriptions, and RM_3 provides support for logging only physical redo descriptions, while undo descriptions can be physiological.

The functions **write_LogRecord**, **commit** and **abort** provided by RM_3 perform actions as described in Section 3.1. Furthermore, **rm_PinPage** and **rm_UnPinPage** respectively invoke the functions **pinPage** and **unPinPage**, that must now be provided by RM_3's BM component. Note that **pinPage** and **unPinPage** are not visible to the DM. RM_3 performs restart recovery as described in Section 3.1. RM_4 provides functions **rm_PinPage**, **rm_UnPinPage**, **write_LogRecord**, **commit** and **abort** that are implemented as described in Section 3.2. Specifically, the **rm_PinPage** and **rm_UnPinPage** only expose the AM-visible page to the AM, while the RM's BM component also stores the pageLSN with each page. RM_4 performs restart recovery similar to RM_2 except that during the redo phase, pages to which updates are redone are pinned in RM_4's buffer (and not DM's buffer). The RM component of RM_3/RM_4 also provides a function **force_LSN** that is invoked only by RM_3/RM_4's BM component to implement WAL as described in [mod 3] in Section 3.1 ([mod 2] in Section 3.2).

Both RM_3 and RM_4 replace the DM's buffer and BM (see Fig. 3), and require modifications [mod 1] in Section 3.1 and [mod 1] in Section 3.2 to be made to the AM. In addition, RM_3 requires modification [mod 4] in Section 3.1 to be supported by the AM, while modifications [mod 3] and [mod 4] in Section 3.2 need to be applied to the AM if RM_4 is used. Also, note that RM_3/RM_4's buffer page size must be at least as large as DM's buffer page size to ensure that an entire data page can be pinned in RM_3/RM_4's buffer.

Using RM_3/RM_4 has the disadvantage that the DM loses control over its buffer page replacement policy. Thus, if the BM component of RM_3/RM_4 follows a page replacement policy that is different from that followed by the DM's BM component, there could be a degradation in the performance of the system.

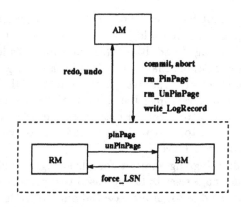

Fig. 3. Interactions of RM_3, RM_4 with the AM

4 A Comparison of the RM Architectures

	RM_1	RM_2	RM_3	RM_4
AM modifications	yes	yes	yes	yes
BM modifications	yes	yes	no	no
Retain control over buffer page replacement policy	yes	yes	no	no
Data reformatting, buffer page size modifications	no	yes	no	yes
Logging support for physiological redo descriptions	no	yes	no	yes

Fig. 4. A Comparison of the RM Architectures

In this section, we compare the various RM architectures based on the modifications that need to be made to the various DM components and various other characteristics that may adversely affect system performance (see Fig. 4).

An RM that provides support for logging physiological redo descriptions also requires a **pageLSN** field to be associated with each data page. Thus, there is a correlation between providing logging support for physiological redo descriptions, and data and buffer page size modifications. Similarly, an RM that includes a BM component replaces the DM's BM component, and thus eliminates BM modifications (to implement WAL and checkpoints), but it also causes the DM to lose control over its buffer page replacement policy. Thus, there is a correlation between the DM retaining control over its buffer page replacement policy and modifications made to the DM's BM component.

Since retaining control over the buffer page replacement policy is crucial for good performance, RM architectures RM_3 and RM_4 may be unsuitable for a number of environments. RM_1 and RM_2 are attractive recovery managers. Although BM modifications are required, the modifications are relatively minor and can be made without too much effort. On the positive side, RM_1 and RM_2 provide logging support for physiological undo descriptions, and thus support for fine-granularity locking. In addition, RM_2 also provides logging support for physiological redo descriptions that has two major advantages. First, it reduces the size of redo descriptions for updates, and thus, reduces the size of log records. Second, during restart recovery, pageLSN information can be utilized to prevent updates that have made it to secondary storage from being redone (note, however, that pages still need to be read from secondary storage and so there is no reduction in the number of I/Os).

However, providing logging support for physiological redo descriptions requires data and buffer page sizes to be increased to incorporate pageLSNs, which could hurt performance due to an increased number of I/Os. RM_1 does not require data pages to be reformatted, but supports the logging of only physical redo descriptions.

In a number of environments, logging physiological descriptions may be too complicated and it may be simpler and more feasible to log physical descriptions. For such environments, the increased complexity in terms of reformatting data pages and the performance issues that are associated with such a reformatting make RM_2 less attractive than RM_1. Even though RM_1 supports only physical descriptions, it still remains an attractive choice for a wide range of environments since physical descriptions can be made reasonably concise through the careful management of the internal structure of data pages.

5 A Case Study

In this section, we relate our experience in integrating a pre-existing spatial DM that provided no support for transactions, with a general purpose recovery manager. The spatial DM was used to store spatial objects representing streets and managed spatial data stored as points, lines, or regions. The general purpose recovery manager was the recovery module of the Encina Toolkit from Transarc Corporation.

As stated earlier, Encina's RM has an architecture that is very similar to architectures RM_3 and RM_4. The spatial DM had an architecture similar to the one described in Section 2 with the exception that it did not support an **unPinPage** function. Its **pinPage** function was called by update and read operations, and performed the following actions:

1. It first checked to see if the page was already in the buffer pool; if so, it returned the address of the buffer page to the caller.
2. In case the page was not in the buffer pool, it searched the buffer for a buffer page containing an unpinned page that was empty. If one was not found, it searched the buffer for a buffer page containing the least recently used (LRU) page. It then pinned the page and if the buffer page was not empty and was dirty, it requested the I/O module to write its contents to secondary storage. It then requested the I/O module to read the data page

into the buffer, unpinned the page, and returned the address of the buffer page containing the page to the caller.

Typical operations on a page were executed immediately after obtaining the pointer to the page in the buffer. This, coupled with the LRU buffer replacement policy, meant that no incorrect memory references were generated despite the lack of an **unPinPage** function, which effectively meant that pages were already unpinned by the **pinPage** function itself.

Integrating Encina's RM with the spatial DM as described in Section 3.3 would have meant replacing the spatial DM's BM component by Encina's RM's BM component. One of the difficulties in doing so was that the spatial DM had a buffer page size of 16KBytes while Encina's RM had a buffer page size of 4KBytes. The more serious problem was the lack of an **unPinPage** function in the spatial DM. Typically, calls to the RM to write log records are made once the AM completes all updates to the page and immediately before it makes the **unPinPage** function call. However, since we had not developed the application code for the spatial DM ourselves, and since its internals were familiar to us only at a very abstract level, the task of determining where to place calls to the RM to write log records and unpin pages became extremely difficult.

Thus, we decided to integrate Encina's RM at the I/O interface level of the spatial DM. That interface was well-defined and consisted of functions **pageWrite** and **pageRead**. We re-implemented the I/O interface functions using Encina's RM which in turn, makes calls to its own I/O component. We used Encina's RM in a mode that made it equivalent to RM_3, that is, where the **pageLSN** is not stored on data pages.

- **pageWrite:** first maps the spatial DM page to four consecutive RM pages (the spatial DM's page size is four times that of the RM's). For each RM page, it then does the following: (1) It pins the page in Encina's buffer by calling the RM's **rm_PinPage** function. (2) It compares the contents of the page in Encina's buffer pool with the portion of the page to be written and that resides in the spatial DM's buffer pool. It logs the before and after images of portions of the RM page that have been modified by invoking the RM's **write_LogRecord** function. (3) It overwrites the modified portions of the page in Encina's buffer pool with the corresponding portions of the page in the spatial DM's buffer. (4) Finally, it unpins the page by calling the RM's **rm_UnPinPage** function.
- **pageRead:** first maps the spatial DM page to four consecutive RM pages. For each RM page, it then does the following: (1) It pins the page in Encina's buffer by calling the RM's **rm_PinPage** function. (2) It copies the page from Encina's buffer to the appropriate location in the spatial DM's buffer. (3) It unpins the page by calling the RM's **rm_UnPinPage** function.

In addition to re-implementing the I/O interface functions, we also implemented **redo** and **undo** functions. The **redo** function is invoked by the RM at recovery time to redo the updates performed on an RM page. It is passed as arguments an RM page number and a redo description for the update provided to the RM when **write_LogRecord** was invoked. **redo** pins the page in Encina's buffer and copies portions of the page contained in the redo description onto appropriate portions of the page in RM's buffer. It does not write any log records. The **undo** is invoked by the RM when a transaction aborts or at recovery time. It is passed as arguments an RM page number and an undo description that had been provided to the **write_LogRecord** function. **undo** pins the page in Encina's buffer and copies portions of the page contained in the undo description onto appropriate portions of the page in RM's buffer. Before unpinning the page, it logs the before and after images of portions of the page that have been modified by invoking **write_LogRecord**.

Since redo and undo descriptions for updates are physical, before the spatial DM invokes **pinPage** to update a page, it obtains an exclusive lock on the page. Finally, the spatial DM application programs make calls to RM **commit/abort** commands to commit/abort a transaction.

Integrating the spatial DM with Encina's RM at the I/O interface level in the manner described above ensures the atomicity and durability of transactions because:

1. In the spatial DM, a buffer page updated by a transaction is written to stable storage (by invoking **pageWrite**) in the context of the transaction that updated the page.

2. In the spatial DM, when a transaction successfully completes execution (commits), all buffer pages updated by the tansaction are written to secondary storage.

3. In the spatial DM, when a transaction unsuccessfully completes execution (aborts), all buffer pages updated by the transaction are marked empty.

Point 1 ensures that log records describing updates performed by a transaction contain the tid of the transaction that performed the update. Since log records for updates to a page are written only when **pageWrite** is invoked, Point 2 ensures that log records describing updates to data pages made by a transaction are written to stable storage when the transaction commits. Finally, Point 3 ensures that all updates to data pages performed by a transaction and residing in the spatial DM's buffer are undone when the transaction aborts.

The approach that we have used to integrate Encina's RM with the spatial DM can be used to integrate Encina's RM with any DM that satisfies the above three points. Thus, even if a DM's architecture deviates from the generic DM architecture of Section 2, it may be possible to transform a non-transactional DM to a transactional one with relatively little effort. However, the approach does have a number of disadvantages. First, redo and undo descriptions for updates that are logged have to be physical. Second, copying must take place between the DM's buffer and the RM's buffer. Finally, the double buffering results in increased contention for main memory.

6 Conclusion

In this paper, we evaluated four RM architectures that can be used to provide recovery support for pre-existing DMs. Based on the interactions of the various RM architectures with DM components, we identified modifications that need to be made to pre-existing DMs. We discussed our own experience in integrating a pre-existing spatial DM with a general purpose recovery manager, and how the approach we took could be extended to arbitrary DMs. As a final note, it is worth pointing out that a single RM can easily support the four interfaces presented in this paper. The DM need only indicate the mode in which it intends to use the RM. Providing these choices is the ideal as it allows the system integrator to choose the best interface for a specific application.

References

[BHG87] P. A. Bernstein, V. Hadzilacos, and N. Goodman. *Concurrency Control and Recovery in Database Systems.* Addison-Wesley, Reading, MA, 1987.

[GR91] J. Gray and A. Reuter. *Transaction Processing: Concepts and Techniques.* Morgan Kaufmann, San Mateo, California, 1991.

[Lom92] D. Lomet. MLR: A recovery method for multi-level systems. In *Proceedings of ACM-SIGMOD 1992 International Conference on Management of Data, San Diego, California,* pages 185–194, 1992.

[MHL+92] C. Mohan, D. Haderle, B. Lindsay, H. Pirahesh, and P. Schwarz. ARIES: A transaction recovery method supporting fine-granularity locking and partial rollbacks using write-ahead logging. *ACM Transactions on Database Systems,* 17(1):94–162, March 1992.

[RKS93] R. Rastogi, H. F. Korth, and A. Silberschatz. Strict histories in object-based database systems. In *Proceedings of the Twelfth ACM SIGACT-SIGMOD-SIGART Symposium on Principles of Database Systems, Washington D.C.,* 1993.

[RN92a] R. Rastogi and M. A. Neimat. Enhancing pre-existing recovery managers with atomicity and durability. Technical Report 113880-940420-24, AT&T Bell Laboratories, 1992.

[RN92b] R. Rastogi and M. A. Neimat. On using the encina toolkit to provide recovery support for data managers. Technical Report HPL-DTD-92-21, Hewlett-Packard Laboratories, Palo Alto, 1992.

[Tra] Transarc Corporation. *Encina Toolkit Server Core: Programmer's Reference.*

[WHBM90] G. Weikum, C. Hasse, P. Broessler, and P. Muth. Multi-level recovery. In *Proceedings of the Nineth ACM SIGACT-SIGMOD-SIGART Symposium on Principles of Database Systems, Nashville,* pages 109–123, 1990.

A Personal and Portable Database Server :
the CQL Card

Pierre Paradinas[1&3] and Jean-Jacques Vandewalle[1&2]

[1] Rd2p, Recherche et Développement Dossier Portable, CHRU Calmette, rue du Pr. J. Leclerc, 59 037 Lille Cédex, France, tel. : (33) 20 44 60 44, fax : (33) 20 44 60 45, emails : pierre@rd2p.lifl.fr - jeanjac@rd2p.lifl.fr

[2] Université Laval, Dép. d'Informatique, Québec, Canada, G1K 7P4, tel. : (1) 418 656 2580, fax : (1) 418 656 2324, email : jeanjac@iad.ift.ulaval.ca

[3] Gemplus, B.P. 100, 13 881 Gémenos, France, tel. : (33) 42 32 50 30, fax : (33) 42 32 50 44, email : pierre@gemplus.fr

Abstract. Database applications and technologies are of central importance in many information systems a person may encounter. To obtain services, the end-users are required a smart card (plastic card containing a microcomputer), which is a device providing information about the user's identity and some related personal data. It can be updated and loaded with new data that will be used during further sessions. Moreover the data contained into the smart card can be used by other information systems, the data are carried away from a site to another. The individual mobility increases the need for a person to carry information about himself anywhere and at any time. For services providers, such as health professionals, it is essential to access to this information stored on several information systems. In many applicative areas, to provide different information systems linked and networked is a real challenge. Based on personal information about the bearer, the smart card is a key to access to different information systems and a mean to share and interchange data. The smart cards are evolving towards personal database functions. We briefly present the technology of smart cards, then we introduce a new approach : the CQL card (for Card Query Language). This card integrates the concepts of the Database Management Systems. Database engine is carried out by the card microcomputer, the card is a new database machine. It manages "users" entities which handle different "objects" according to their "privileges". CQL, a subset of SQL, is used to communicate with the card. Views enable sharing data among information systems. Access rights and privileges guarantee the data privacy. To ease the integration of this portable database we have implemented an ODBC driver enabling smart card connectivity with many applications and DBMS's. The smart card as a personal and mobile data server is a new support for databases, it involves new applications, such as health care cards or administrative document cards, and new ways of carrying and interchanging information.

Keywords. Personal Database, Smart Card, Database Interchange, SQL, ODBC.

1 The Database Card : a Personal and Portable Server

Considering the end user, information systems are becoming more and more important. They store a growing amount of personal information and they implement computing operations growing in complexity. Their importance in our life is obvious (in administrations, corporations, banking operations, shopping, travels, *etc.*). Some people take fright about the use of these information : may I know the data that an organization have on me? These data are they correct? How are they process? Are these data interchanged with other organizations? Is the data privacy guaranteed?... This paper addresses the problem of the interchange of data among different information systems. The key points we want to underline are :

- Data interchange is necessary. The end result of many computing processes depends on a good integration of information emerging from different information systems. For example, in medical information systems, such as in many other applications areas, patient data are physically and logically scattered into different information systems (public and private hospitals or clinics, general practitioners, pathology laboratories) and they may be required in order to make a diagnosis or a medical act. The privacy constraints of each system imply that it is very difficult to access to all information sources. It may exist a lot of information about the same person, but it is not physically gathered on the same spot or not reachable by all intervening parties [BP91]

- Each information system stores a lot of data about persons which are often similar (*e.g.* names, addresses, occupations, *etc.*) with many discrepancies. For example, in an information system, Mrs Smith is tagged as a medical student at the Laval University, whereas in another she is registered only as a student (because the speciality and the place are not relevant for that system). Databases are heterogeneous base on hardware (running on different computers), and also by their software (implementation, organization, human interface, command language). But they are also distinct by the kind of information they store, even if the information concerns the same person (or the same object)

- When you have to link information systems the above problems of heterogeneousness may become very difficult. The physical connection is not always possible due to the too important number of gateways between two sites, the communication difficulties and costs. The logical exchange of data may be shackled by different representations of them or different access languages [Bro93]. Finally, the data may be similar but not identical. In order to avoid data duplication or inconsistency of the end result, unification mechanisms have to be carried out. The unification concerns the data locations (in tables or files or others), the data types and also the data semantics (see the above example of the student Mrs Smith). Practical solutions are often based on a global view providing a general vision of all systems to be connected

- Information systems need to communicate and to interchange data for performing tasks and providing services based on multiple sources. Often it is not feasible because the information systems do not provide the mechanisms for exchanging or sharing their data. Moving Trans-European goods is an example of that problem : at each border, customs officers have to control the provenance of the lorry, its rights for crossing the border, its conformity to laws and regulations of the country, its route, the nature of goods, *etc.* The European Community has launched a project for computerizing these control operations [Inca92]. But the main problem in such a project is a political one. Politicians of each country oppose to interconnect their information systems. More than the very hard technical problem due to the number of countries and the heterogeneousness of their systems, they fear that confidentiality and security of their system may be jeopardized

In this paper we propose a way to overcome some of these obstacles. The solution consists on a portable equipment that contains the data to interchange. These data generally concern a person or an object (vehicle, good) characterized by a relatively small quantity of information, storable in a small device and carried where they are required. Such a device is likely a portable and personal database server. It should be sufficiently small to take place in a pocket, and should assume security controls and management operations on its data. It is a way to bypass the difficulties of connecting different information systems. The data travel with the person or the object, then they are available any time as soon as an information system needs them. Moreover, the information is timely available to a mobile computer, there is no time lag due to connection and communication with a remote database. An onboard system can directly access to the data stored in the portable device. Data are stored in a single device, they have a unique representation; problems for connecting the database, sending request and unifying different data semantics are reduced to the knowledge of the portable data organization. The security is reinforced by the portable device itself, designed for resisting to any physical attack and offering high level access controls

Smart card is a technological device solution for storing and managing personal data in a single chip microcomputer with CPU, program and data memories. The card chip is embedded into a plastic card. Thanks to its own stand-alone computing capabilities, its internal security logic and its memory capacities, the smart cards are used efficiently by many applications. For example, the electronic purse application use the card like cash flow. Money is made available through the card and may be cash in for any transaction where a card reader is available. Clubs use the smart card to hold member information, club privileges, payment records, *etc.* Smart cards are also used as subscriber card for Pan-European digital cellular radio telephone network, with pay telephones, by healthcare facilities, as security key to access buildings and computers, *etc.*

It is a portable device which protects itself and manages access controls on the data it contains. Therefore, it is applicable as a portable data carrier, it provides a technology for identification support and is able to authenticate any data exchange during transactions. But this is not sufficient. Because smart cards contain sensitive issuer's information and have to interact with many information systems, specific requirements should be implemented :

• The smart card should provide a way of sharing data among different information systems, and should maintain their privacy. A card users may only access to the card data for which he has rights. It is the question of sharing data and maintaining privacy

• Along its life cycle, the smart card structure should be able to interact with new users and new data. It is the question of card application flexibility

• Smart card has to be quickly and easily attached to different information systems whatever the computers, the operating systems and the applications. It is the question of smart card integration into the information systems

With these goals in mind, we propose a new smart card approach : the CQL card. In this card we have implemented and downsized the concepts of DBMS (Database Management System). A subset of SQL, CQL is used to communicate with the card and gain access to its data.

2   The CQL Card : A Technical Solution

The database card requires portability, intelligent functions, and confidential features. Smart cards offer these well-known features which have been successfully tested upon time. Smart cards are a convenient and highly secure medium for interaction with personal computer, communication devices, transactional terminals, and information systems in general. Nevertheless, smart cards still have difficulty in managing multiple application data interactions with other computer systems mainly traced down to their low level interface. In order to overcome these problems, a smart card based on database concepts, called CQL for Card Query Language has been developed with the following features.

2.1 Integrated Circuit Card (IC Card) and Portable Data file

The IC Card (usually called "smart card") results from the embedding of a single integrated circuit (a computer chip) into a plastic card (the size of a credit card) [Cri90]. The computer chip is programmed to perform specific functions such as updating and changing the information held on its memory. The key components of the chip architecture are as follows (*cf.* figure 1) :

• 8 bits microprocessor (*e.g.* 6805, 8051)
• input/output management module
• security block that assumes physical security and memory access controls
• ROM containing the operating system of the smart card (size from 2 to 16 KB)
• RAM used as a working memory by the microprocessor (size from 40 to 256 bytes)
• Non volatile memory like EEPROM (Electrically Erasable Programmable Read-Only Memory) used for storing the applicative data (size from 1 to 8 KB)

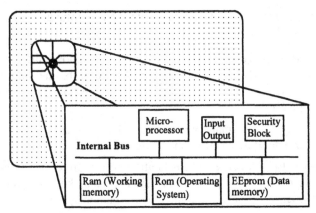

Fig. 1. Integrated circuit card architecture

Smart cards have to comply with the physical constraints defined by the ISO 7816 part 1 (physical characteristics) and part 2 (contact location) standards [Iso1] [Iso2]. The components of the chip have little dimensions, and the total chip area is about 25 mm^2; a larger chip might crack when the card is flexed. The main breakthrough we can expect is an increase in memory capacities (in the same dimensions), mainly with non volatile memory type Flash EEPROM (particular EEPROM memory that reduces the area of a memory cell by erasing a block of bytes rather than a single byte). Bigger memory capacities [Pat90] and new smart card microcontroller chips [Pey94] could be implemented for many applications, (for example student cards or patient cards) and could make possible the use of smart cards as multi-purpose portable and individual database servers.

Today, the operating systems for smart cards are generally based on file management systems. The privacy constraints for each card users imply that it is very difficult to access shared data stored in files. Many card users access to part of the data stored in the same file with different access right (read/write/update). But each access right enables accessing to all records of a file. If some particular records have to be protected they have to be stored in an another file. And so doing same data could be scattered in a multitude of file, resulting in difficulties for maintaining the information coherence. For solving this problem, we propose an operating system based on database concepts. We call a personal and portable database, a smart card used to gather information about the carrier in its database. Each information system may see the portable database as an adjunct source of data. By using DBMS mechanisms, each user, depending on its role, accesses to the data through specific views on the database. The authorized actions on the database are managed by the card. The location of the operating system (the database engine for us) inside the ROM memory of the card microcontroller is the one of the most important features of the smart card. Like that, the card insures its integrity (physical and logical protection of the card memories) and guarantees the consistency and the privacy of its data. By controlling internally the accesses to the data, and by carrying out the database engine inside, the operating system gives to a user only what he can get. It is a fundamental feature of all smart cards. The CQL card improves it by providing the notion of views on parts of data structure.

2.2 Overview of the CQL Card

The CQL card is the result of a research effort being done by RD2P [GG92] (Recherche et Développement Dossier Portable), the CNRS (Centre National de la Recherche Scientifique), the Medical and Scientific Universities of Lille and Gemplus corporation [Gem92].

The CQL card is the first smart card that uses DBMS concepts. This sophisticated operating system has been implemented thanks to the emergence of powerful card chips and by the use of a high level development system dedicated to smart cards. This development tool developed at RD2P named *C_Card* is described in [GP91]. It enables developing card ROM codes with the C language rather than specific machine languages. It generates a pseudo-code executed by an interpreter which is also loaded into the card ROM. The interpreter takes up less than 2 KB in the ROM. The CQL pseudo-code has been optimized in size and speed in order to be loaded into the remaining 8 KB of the ROM.

The database engine manages "users" which access to the database "objects" (tables, views and dictionaries) according to their "privileges". It is a relational database engine added to a secured users' management. The system manages all data and object structures. It uses its own tables for this purpose, in the same way as any other user. The system includes 3 tables :

- *table* * containing the description of tables, views and dictionaries
- *table* *A containing the description of users
- *table* *G containing the description of access rights (or privileges).

The applicative data and database structures are stored in the 8 KB of the card EEPROM. Data held in the card are accessed using CQL a high level Card Query Language [Par94] which is a subset of the standard SQL (Structured Query Language). The database engine carries out each CQL request as follows :

- receipt of a request
- syntactic analysis of the request
- user's access rights control
- execution of the request
- sending of a response

2.3 The CQL Language

The CQL language used to communicate with the card is described in the appendix. The bracketed numbers following in the text refer to the CQL commands described in this appendix. This subset of SQL has been chosen according to our needs of sharing data and maintaining privacy. The data are stored in tables. Views are logical and dynamic subsets of tables without data duplication. The owner of an object may grant privileges (select, insert, update or delete on table or view) to other users. Theses mechanisms enable sharing data and the card users' management guarantees the data privacy. It seems to us that it is a good solution for the specific problems of a portable data file. To resume, this subset enables us offering a consistent language to :

- manage the card users ([1] to [7])
- create database structures ([11] to [15])
- manipulate the database data ([18] to [25] and [29] to [34])
- grant and revoke privileges ([16] and [17])
- control the users' access rights ([3] and [8] to [10])
- and guarantee the database consistency ([26] to [28])

2.4 Users

The CQL card manages two types of users : the *Application Managers* (AM) and the *Standard Users* (SU), as well as two predefined users : the *Card Issuer* (CI) and the anonymous user called *PUBLIC*.

The Card Issuer and the user PUBLIC are predefined at the manufacturing level. They are unique and cannot be erased. The Card Issuer may create Application Managers and Standard Users. The Application Managers may create Standard Users. The user PUBLIC is the default user who does not have to present a password. The Standard Users and the user PUBLIC cannot create other users.

The users management is dynamic. The AM's and SU's can be created all along the card life cycle. The user's owner (the one who has created him) may delete him all along the card life cycle. There is no theoretical limit to the number of users. The card identifies a user by his name and his password, and monitors successive erroneous password presentations by a ratification counter. Once the ratification counter has reached its maximum value the user is locked and cannot anymore access to the database card.

2.5 Objects

The CQL card manages the following objects : tables, views and dictionaries. Objects may be created only by the Card Issuer and the Application Managers. The user who creates an object is the sole owner of this object with all the rights on it including the right to delete it. Nevertheless, at any time, he may grant to other users access privileges to any object he owns (*cf.* paragraph 2.6).

The basic object managed by the CQL card is the *table*. A table is defined by its name, a number of columns and a name for each column. Data are stored and accessed by rows. Only one type of data is authorized : varying length character strings. The CQL Data Manipulation Language (DML) is a compatible subset of the SQL DML. It allows to read (FETCH), add (INSERT), remove (DELETE) or modify (UPDATE) a row. By using a predicate clause (WHERE clause) the CQL card is able to process logical request on a table. The WHERE clause defines a condition for logically selecting a set of rows.

With smart cards using file structures the security granularity is the file, whereas with CQL the security can be expressed at data element level through relational *views*. A view is a select clause definition referring only to one table and recorded in the card. It defines a dynamic and logical selection of rows and columns onto a table. By using the mechanism of view the data of a table can be shared among several users without data duplication. Only the tables contain data, thus, in a view, it is only possible to manipulate data for reading and sometimes updating. Because the CQL card does not manage keys on tables, it is important to provide a column with unique values for avoiding trouble during an updating operation. By the mechanism of views an Application Manager can give to another user a specific "vision" to his data.

The *Dictionaries* provide general information on the database objects structure (tables, views and dictionaries) and on users privileges. The dictionaries are only accessible for reading. They store information that enables using a CQL card without pre-existent knowledge of the card database structure. By this feature which enables exploring the card database structure it is possible to design open systems.

2.6 Access Privileges

The creator of an object is the only owner of this object. They are the only one able to delete it and update it by reading, adding, deleting and updating data into it. The creator may decide at any time to grant one or more of these privileges to any other user. These privileges cannot be passed on to other users and can be revoked by the owner only. These characteristics allow the owner of a table to grant privileges concerning a table or a part of it, a view, and thereby to control the actions carried out on the data it contains. The owner of a table can define specific access conditions for each view he has created. Like that he can reliably control the accesses to the data stored in that table.

2.7 Security Mechanisms

Application security is guaranteed by the card through three mechanisms which perform access control by double authentication, implement a tracing function and insure the database integrity.

In addition to the administrative connection functions (presentation of the name and password), the card performs a function of *double authentication*. It provides the host system and the card with a guarantee concerning the identity of each other. This process is based on pseudo-random number generation and the secret key algorithm DES [GQU92].

The *Tracing* function is assumed by the card system upon recognition of the special identifier USER as the name of the last column of a table. In this case, for each updating operation onto a row of the table, the card system places the current user's name in the column USER. The table may thus be accessed by several users providing each of them verify the name of the latest one who has updated a particular row.

In many DBMS's there are mechanisms that assume the *database integrity i.e.* that assume transactions should leave the database in a consistent state. In the CQL card we have implemented the mechanism of one phase commit. The commit provides that all the modifications required since the beginning of the transaction are fully executed. The rollback is the command that restores the initial context before the beginning of the transaction. If the card is disconnected during a transaction, the next connection will be started by an automatic rollback.

3   Database Card Integration into the Information Systems

The database card can be seen as a link among many information systems which cannot or do not wish to communicate. It carries data of different systems offering interchanges of information and computing it in the same way. Therefore, the challenge for this database card is to be interoperable with many systems and to communicate with them under a uniform interface. Adopting a subset of SQL for its set of commands, the IC Card becomes accessible via a well-known language. However the problem of data-interchange among various databases and applications remains[Bro93]. In regards to this problem, a group of leaders in the database and systems industry, the SQL Access Group (SAG), has defined a Call Level Interface (CLI) which provide a common interface for accessing to heterogeneous databases. Based on this CLI, Microsoft proposes specifications of an API (Application Programming Interface) called ODBC (Open Database Connectivity) [Odbc92]. We have implemented an ODBC driver for the CQL card which enables using it with many vendor software and helping to solve the problem of the connectivity. This development has been evolved with the following guidelines :

- *Embrace Standard* : The CQL card complies with smart card standards ISO 7816 parts 1, 2 and 3 for physical characteristics, contacts location and transmission protocols. However the CQL card embraces DBMS standard for its set of commands, it uses a subset of SQL [Iso5], called CQL for data interchange

- *Top-Down Approach* : Considering the smart card ISO 7816 part 4 Draft standard on Inter-Industry Commands for Interchange [Iso4], using SQL as a smart card language may seem unusual. We claim that such language could ease the integration of smart cards into information systems. The use of computer standards rather than specific smart card standards favours the integration of smart cards and provides interoperability between smart cards and systems

- *Implement Middleware* : Formally, interoperability means the capacity for two components to exchange requests and responses based on a mutual understanding of messages [Bro93]. One way for providing a mutual understanding is to implement an intermediate software layer that encodes requests and responses into a uniform code. This intermediate software layer, often called *middleware*, has to be sufficiently generic in order to allow a wide range of applications to interact

The CQL ODBC driver enables using the CQL card through a wide range of market products. Like that, the use of the CQL card through these products simply requires a general knowledge of these products and of the smart cards which become very easy to use and represent real "plug and play" systems [PV94a]. An application using ODBC call level interface to access to data stored in databases is called an ODBC-enabled application. We can run an ODBC-enabled application with a CQL card via the CQL ODBC driver or with another data source via its corresponding driver. From CQL cards up to large databases the same code applies. Such interoperability enhances the integration of smart cards into information systems. It is particularly relevant for the portable data files area of application in which smart cards (*e.g.* health care cards) have to interchange data with a number of various systems (*e.g.* hospital information system, general practitioner PC, emergency portable computer).

3.1 ODBC Technology

ODBC addresses the heterogeneous database connectivity problem using the common interface approach (*cf.* figure 2).

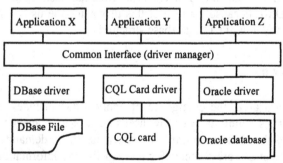

Fig. 2. Applications accessing heterogeneous data sources via a common interface approach

The ODBC interface allows applications to access data from a wide range of DBMS's. Each application uses the same code to communicate with many data sources through DBMS-specific drivers. Therefore these applications are independent of the DBMS's. A Driver Manager sits between applications and drivers providing a mutual understanding of the exchanged messages and a common interface for all applications.

The ODBC API functions are divided into three levels of implementation called respectively Core, Level 1 and Level 2. The first one is strictly an implementation of the CLI developed by the SAG which can be seen as the lowest-common-denominator. The second puts forward new functions for gaining information about the driver and the data source and for setting and retrieving the driver options. The latest allows ODBC to manage sophisticated databases capacities. An ODBC driver has to implement at least the functions of the Core and can process any part of the SQL grammar defined by ODBC. An application accesses a data source by function calls of one or more levels and submits SQL requests depending on the driver conformance. Application developers must decide whether to use the minimum level of functionality, or write the conditional code to test for extended functionalities. In either case, the Core level guarantees a working state.

3.2 Implementation of the CQL ODBC Driver

The CQL ODBC driver is a Windows Dynamic Link Library (DLL). To submit a SQL request to the CQL card and receive results, the driver calls the CQL DLL which sends the statements to the Card Reader Driver. This later routes the statements to the card and sends back the card responses.

The CQL ODBC driver carries out all Core and Level 1 functions and processes the SQL DML part - *i.e.* SELECT, INSERT, UPDATE and DELETE - defined by ODBC. The diver translates each SQL statement to the corresponding CQL statement. The SQL part that it is not supported by the CQL language (*e.g.* <ordered by> in a SELECT clause) is ignored although the statement is processed. The Level 1 of implementation has been reached using the dictionaries of the CQL Card which allow the driver to obtain information about the data source and the data source's system tables. The SQL grammar used by the driver has been limited to the DML because we restrict this driver for the use of structured cards and not for the creation of CQL database structures.

4 Conclusion

In the smart card area, the emergence of applications includes more and more intervening parties pointing out new needs. The file management techniques implemented in the first smart cards do not meet these demands. The database management systems were a technological gap for the information systems. The same gap is necessary for smart cards. We propose a smart card with a downsized DBMS. Each card user, depending on its role, has specific views and privileges onto the data stored in tables. The CQL card is a computer element that deals with information systems and it also must be integrated into these systems. For this reason we have implemented some standards of the DBMS's such as SQL and ODBC.

The CQL card as a database server can be connected to and used from multiple information systems, then the card is becoming an active link between these systems. The card is a device that offers solutions for the problem of interoperability between DBMS's that cannot or do not want cooperate. With the smart card, and thanks to its small size, each person may carry in his back pocket data about himself such as health diagnostics, access conditions to protected buildings, list of debit and credit transactions, etc. There is no question that the application area of smart cards will increase significantly. Thus, the design of information systems must deal with this new support of data. The challenge is to converge the two points of view; the first one concerning the global information system, and the second one the personal and mobile database server.

Acknowledgements

We gratefully acknowledge Georges Grimonprez and Edouard Gordons of RD2P and Gemplus for supporting our work and for their previous work on design and implementation of the CQL card. We would like also to thank Emmanuel Horckmans for his participation in the development of the CQL ODBC Driver without which this result would not have been possible. We are grateful to Andre Gamache (Laval University) for helpful suggestions and comments on earlier and final drafts of this paper.

References

[BP91]   R. Beuscart and P. Paradinas. *Smart Cards for Health Care, in* Telematics in Medicine, Elsevier Science Publishers B.V., North-Holland, 1991.

[Bro93]   M.L. Brodie. *The promise of distributed computing and the challenges of legacy information systems, in* IFIP Transactions A-25, Interoperable Database Systems (DS-5), Elsevier Science Publishers B.V., North-Holland, 1993.

[Cri90]   J. Mc Crindle. *Smart cards,* IFS Publications, Springer-Verlag, 1990.

[Gem92]   Gemplus. *CQL Card and Language Reference Manual,* Gemplus, 1992.

[GG92]   E. Gordons and G. Grimonprez. *A card as element of a distributed database,* IFIP WG 8.4 Workshop, P. Paradinas and G. White : The portable office. Microprocessor cards as elements of distributed offices, Ottawa, Canada, 1992.

[GP91]   G. Grimonprez, and P. Paradinas. *A new approach in code development : C_Card and Cossack, in* proceedings of CardTech'91, Washington D.C., U.S.A., 1991.

[GQU92]   L. Guillou, J-J. Quisquater, and M. Ugon. *The Smart Card : A standardised Security Device Dedicated to Public Cryptology,* Ed G. Simmons : Contemporary Cryptology, IEEE-Press, 1992.

[Inca92] European Nervous System (ENS). *The INCA project (Information network and card for the adapted management of European road transport)*, number E20003, EEC Documentation, 1992.

[Iso1] ISO/IEC 7816-1. *Identification cards - Integrated circuit(s) cards with contacts : Dimensions and locations of the contacts*, ISO, 1987.

[Iso2] ISO/IEC 7816-2. *Identification cards - Integrated circuit(s) cards with contacts : Physical characteristics*, ISO, 1988.

[Iso3] ISO/IEC 7816-3. *Identification cards - Integrated circuit(s) cards with contacts : Electronic signals and transmission protocols*, ISO, 1989.

[Iso4] ISO/IEC 7816-4. *Identification cards - Integrated circuit(s) cards with contacts : Interindustry commands for interchange (CD)*, ISO, 1992.

[Iso5] ISO/IEC 9075. *Information Technology - Database - SQL*, ISO, 1992.

[Odbc92] Microsoft Corporation. *Microsoft Open Database Connectivity Backgrounder*, Microsoft, october 1992.

[Par94] P. Paradinas. *The CQL Database Smart Card*, GMD, Smart Card Workshop, Darmstadt, Germany, February 1994.

[Pat90] M. Paterson. *"Memories are made of this..." ...a look at memory considerations for Smart Card applications*, Semiconductor engineering bulletin, Motorola Ltd, 1990.

[Pey94] P. Peyret. *RISC-Based, Next-Generation Smart Card Microcontroller Chips*, in proceedings of CardTech'94, Washington D.C., U.S.A., April 1994.

[PV94a] P. Paradinas and J.J. Vandewalle. *How to integrate Smart Cards in Standard Software without writing specific code?*, in proceedings of CardTech'94, Washington D.C., U.S.A., April 1994.

Appendix : The CQL Language

Administrative Command Class

[1] CREATE APPLICATION <application name> <ratification thresold> <password>; *to create an Application Manager*

[2] CREATE USER <user name> <ratification thresold> <password>; *to create a Standard User*

[3] PRESENT <user name> <password>; *to open a session with the card*

[4] CHANGE PASSWORD <previous password> <new password>; *to allow users to modify their password*

[5] UNLOCK <user name>; *to allow the owner of a user to unlock them when its ratification counter has reached the maximum*

[6] DELETE USER <user name>; *to delete an AM or a SU*

[7] STATUS; *to read the card serial number and the number of bytes used in the user memory*

[8] CREATE KEY <logical key name> <user name> <key value>; *to create or erase a key*

[9] AUTHENTICATE <user name> <logical key name> <host random value>; *to initialize a double authentication process*

[10] CHECK <user name> <encrypted password>; *to make an encrypted presentation of the password*

Structure Definition Command Class

[11] CREATE TABLE <table name> (<column name> [,<column name>,...]); *to create a Table*

[12] CREATE VIEW <view name> AS <select clause>; *to create a View*

[13] CREATE DICTIONARY <generic name of dictionaries>; *to create the tables, users and privileges Dictionnaries*

[14] DROP TABLE <table name>; *to drop a Table*

[15] DROP VIEW <view or dictionary name>; *to drop a View or a Dictionary*

[16] GRANT <list of privileges> ON <table, view or dictionary name> TO <user name>; *to grant a privilege on a object to a user*

[17] REVOKE <privilege> ON <table, view or dictionary name> TO <user name>; *to revoke a privilege granted on a object to a user*

Date Handling Command Class

[18] DECLARE CURSOR FOR <select clause>; *to create a cursor pointing onto a logical selection of rows*

[19] OPEN; *to position the cursor onto the first row which satisfies the logical selection*

[20] NEXT; *to position the cursor onto the next row which satisfies the logical selection*

[21] FETCH; *to prepare the data units pointed by the cursor to be sent back by the system after a READ RECORD command*

[22] FETCH_NEXT; *FETCH and NEXT command*

[23] INSERT INTO <table name> VALUES (<string> [,<string>,...]); *to insert a new row*

[24] ERASE ; *to delete the row pointed by the cursor*

[25] UPDATEC SET <column name> = <string> [,<column name> = <string>,...] ; *to update the row pointed by the cursor*

[26] BEGIN TRANSACTION; *to initialize a transaction*

[27] COMMIT; *to validate all transaction modifications*

[28] ROLLBACK; *to restore the initial state of memory prior to the beginnig of the transaction*

[29] READ RECORD <length requested>; *to read the data prepared by the FETCH and FETCH_NEXT commands*

Select Clause

[30] <select clause> ::= SELECT <column selection> FROM <table or view name> WHERE <where clause>;

[31] <column selection> ::= * | <column name> [,<column name>,...]

[32] <where clause> ::= <predicate> [AND <predicate> AND ...]

[33] <predicate> ::= <column name> <comparison operator> <string>

[34] <comparion operator> ::= < | <= | > | >= | = | <>

Intelligent Networks as a Data Intensive Application (INDIA)*

Rainer Gallersdörfer[1], Matthias Jarke[1], Karin Klabunde[2]

[1] RWTH Aachen, Informatik V, Ahornstr. 55, 52056 Aachen, Germany
{gallersd|jarke}@informatik.rwth-aachen.de
[2] Philips Research Laboratories Aachen, P.O. Box 1980, 52021 Aachen, Germany
klabunde@pfa.philips.de

Abstract. The Intelligent Network *(IN)* is an architectural concept that enables telematic services (freephone, virtual private network, televoting, etc.) to be rapidly deployed and effectively used in the telephone network. The INDIA project investigates database techniques for dealing with the severe data and service evolution management problems resulting from the IN concept. A concurrency management technique called Atomic Delayed Replication (ADR) is presented that takes advantage of the special application semantics of the Service Logic Programs that implement IN. It can address replicated concurrency control for both the service data and the service logic. ADR has been implemented on top of a commercial DBMS as part of an experimental IN environment.

1 Introduction

Given the enormous data management problems in telecommunications, the use of database technology seems a natural solution [19]. Nevertheless, telecommunications people have been highly critical of available database systems and have typically continued to develop their own special-purpose systems. Kerboul [18] discussed the main reasons for these difficulties along the three dimensions shown in Fig. 1:

Distribution is the essence of telecommunication networks and services, thus also for the supporting data. Data may be fragmented and replicated throughout the system [21]. Failures of nodes or links can not be ignored as the size of the networks may span nations and continents.

Consistency: The manipulation of data must keep them in a consistent state with regard to the application semantics. The transaction model is a well-understood concept for controlling the parallel execution of applications.

Performance: The introduction of new services only makes sense if they can be executed in real time with very many simultaneous users. This depends on the throughput for a single service and on the multiplexing capabilities of the service threads.

---

* This work was supported by Philips Research Laboratories Aachen.

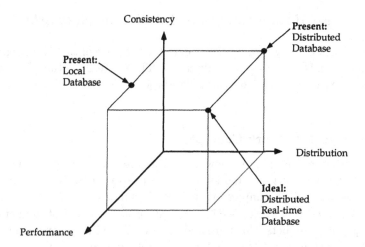

Fig. 1. Database trade-offs in telecommunications applications

From the viewpoint of telecommunication data management, present-day local databases offer reasonable performance and consistency, but obviously no distribution. Present distributed database techniques are good at distribution and consistency but much too slow. The *"ideal"*, a distributed, fully consistent real-time DBMS, seems out of reach.

To be taken seriously by the telecommunications community, database researchers must investigate trade-offs for the above dimensions which are suitable for particular application areas within telecommunications data management. In the INDIA project, we are studying this problem for the task of supporting Intelligent Network (IN) service management and evolution. IN has created a new market by making telephony much more flexible through new services such as virtual private networks, freephone, or televoting. It is obvious that the introduction of new services is cumbersome and expensive without appropriate database support since changes of (distributed) service logic and data will occur frequently.

In section 2 we start with a presentation of the general challenge of IN databases. The INDIA approach to the problem relies on a careful relaxation of the requirement of consistency to promote distribution (partitioning and replication) and performance. This implies specific guidelines for system architecture, database design, and concurrency control which are addressed by a new approach, called Atomic Delayed Replication (ADR). It is described in section 3 in conjunction with some currently existing solution attempts. The integration in the current INDIA prototype has shown significant improvements but also pointed out further challenges which are discussed in section 4. Section 5 summarizes our conclusions.

2 Database Requirements of Intelligent Networks

In this section, we first give a relatively detailed overview of the IN concept; readers familiar with IN may skip this subsection. The net result is that, for efficiency and reliability, we need a distributed database architecture with replication to support IN.

2.1 Intelligent Network Concept

New telematic services create a new market as they make telephony more flexible and convenient for users and step up business for operating companies and service providers [22]. Examples for such services include:

Virtual Private Network (VPN) is used for a small part of the network to set up short numbers which are assigned to phone lines. Participants in the VPN can call each other by dialling the short numbers. Number assignment in the VPN can be dynamically changed. Call billing may also be adapted in a very flexible manner.

Credit Card Calling allows call billing from any telephone using a credit card account. The credit card number and a personal identification number (PIN) must be provided before the connection to the other party will be established.

Freephone is a commonly known service that companies use for marketing. The caller is charged no money and routing to different company locations can be changed dynamically based on criterias such as network load or time.

Teleinfo can be seen as the opposite of Freephone. Additional fees are charged to pay the provider of the information.

Universal Personal Telecommunications (UPT) enables access to telecommunication services while allowing personal mobility. The user may be dynamically associated with a network address and is no longer tied to a particular access line or terminal.

Televoting is often used by television stations to obtain the opinion of watchers on some question. Many people call the same number and the main problem is counting the calls.

Based on demand, service providers constantly invent new and more sophisticated services. The usage and request for such services are expected to grow rapidly. One key to success in this business is support for the design and fast introduction of new services into telecommunications. The existing technology makes service creation and deployment time-consuming and costly as their functionality is programmed individually into the switching components of the current networks. The *Intelligent Network (IN)* is a novel architectural concept for telecommunication networks that enables network operators as well as independent service providers to swiftly introduce new services into networks. Furthermore, these services can be made flexible enough so that after deployment, service subscribers can directly tailor them to their requirements.

The International Telecommunication Union published a first set of recommendations on Intelligent Networks in March 1992 as a ITU-T (formerly CCITT) recommendation Q.12xy series [24].

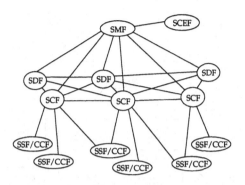

Fig. 2. Functional entities in the IN

The main idea behind the IN concept is the separation of switching functionality from service control. In order to achieve a high degree of flexibility, the service logic is realized by software modules called service logic programs *(SLPs)* that can be customized with subscriber-specific data. Storing them in a database is desirable as there may exist many SLPs which change frequently. Service data, and possible service logic programs, are stored in databases, called Service Data Functions (SDF).

The functional architecture of IN systems is shown in Fig. 2. Specific SLPs are designed in the Service Creation Environment Function (SCEF) using so-called Service Independent Building Blocks (SIBs) [1] – the abstract elements which typically also form the data model units of the SDF. The Service Management Function (SMF) is needed for downloading service logic programs and service data as well as for several other management activities such as billing and statistics.

An example SLP for the VPN is shown in Fig. 3. The entry nodes at the top of the graph specify when this service shall be invoked. In our example this VPN service is executed if anybody calls 01-600-123456 or if one of the three specified phone lines (ANI) in the right entry node is used. In terms of Fig. 2, this recognition of an IN call is done by the the Service Switching Function / Call Control Function (SSF/CCF). It sends a request to the Service Control Function (SCF), which is responsible for the selection of the service logic program and its execution.

In Fig. 3, the first executional statement is the input node which gathers the next dialed digits as the short number and branches. For every short number the desired charging and connection is specified in the branches. Here, so-called ANI lines are allowed to dial out in the # branch. The corresponding service data (here information about the mapping between short number and real target number) are provided by the Service Data Function (SDF).

An IN call may generally be indicated by initial digits 01, the indication for VPN is 600 in our example and the digits 123456 are the subscriber number. The subscriber is the person or company who buys the service from the service provider. For all these items (service, subscriber, person) we need to manage

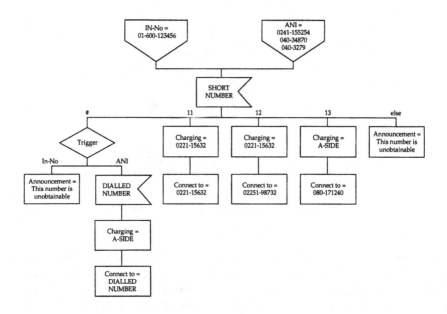

Fig. 3. A service logic program for Virtual Private Network

additional specific data, called variables. Examples are PINs for the person, mapping of short numbers to destination numbers for the subscriber of a VPN service or the usage counter for billing and statistics.

2.2 The IN as a Data-Intensive Application

The IN is a data intensive application in two ways: SLPs use a lot of distributed database information, but also themselves evolve as a distributed database. This observation led to the name of the INDIA project: Intelligent Networks as a Data Intensive Application.

As shown in Fig. 2 multiple entities of SSF/CCF, SCF and SDF can exist in an IN. An SSF/CCF communicates possibly with several SCFs. The SCFs can communicate with each other, and each SCF is able to access data from all SDFs which means that data can be distributed over several SDFs. Moreover, new services must be introduced, or existing services must be changed, while the system is running – schema evolution is essential for the IN.

As telecommunication systems are widely distributed [3] and highly parallel [8], the main problem for the database system is to provide consistent data for the service logic programs running at the same time, as well as for concurrent SLP maintenance operations. Fortunately, the SLP representation is sufficiently simple, and the individual services sufficiently independent of each other that the problem is not quite as bad as it might seem.

3 The ADR Approach

In 1991, Philips developed an IN prototype based on a centralized commercially available relational DBMS. The usage of a centralized DBMS avoids problems with concurrency control and persistency but rapidly leads to a bottleneck if you expect to handle thousands of calls concurrently. Scalability of the database by simply adding new resources is not possible. Integration into a company spanning world-wide telecommunication system can not be achieved.

3.1 Trade-offs for Choosing the DBMS Type

Data replication will be necessary to get performance because calls can be handled without remote access and the access is distributed over the system. Another advantage of replicated data is the increased availability.

As stated in the introduction, a major problem in such databases is the trade-off between distribution, consistency, and performance which is mainly influenced by the concurrency control policy. Summarizing our main observations on IN databases,

- we have to read and update distributed service data at the instance level as well as at the schema level (SLP definitions);
- interactivity, distribution, and reliability are of crucial importance to ensure service quality and avoid financial losses and image problems due to unavailability of a service;
- there are special properties such as the relative simplicity and mutual independence of SLPs and service invocations which can be exploited to reduce the need for global concurrency control.

The INDIA system addresses these problems and opportunities by flexible partitioning and replication of data. This is combined with the concurrency control technique called Atomic Delayed Replication (ADR) that significantly increases performance and distribution at the expense of using possibly outdated information. An additional requirement in the design of INDIA was that it can be based on standard database technology, in order to avoid the creation of new dinosaur software and to take advantage of advances in database technology (e.g., active databases).

To understand the trade-offs leading to the ADR approach, we briefly review the main approaches reported in the literature and available in commercial distributed DBMSs.

Figure 4 illustrates the basic problems. The three spiraled lines symbolize the history of three data objects A, B_{rep}, and B; B_{rep} is intended to be a replica of B. The dots symbolize groups of operations associated with transactions. Operation groups with equal subscript belong to the same transaction; they can have the right to read (first letter: R) or write (W); moreover, the difference between original copies and replicas is denoted by P (primary copy) and S (secondary copy).

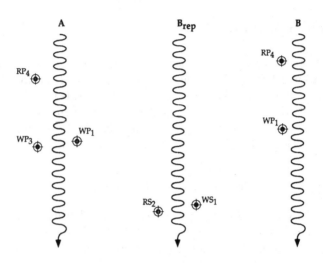

Fig. 4. Possible conflicts in replicated databases

The four transactions in the figure can be used to illustrate the different replication and concurrency control techniques. Firstly, it is obvious that transactions like T_1 and T_4 need global concurrency control with respect to A and B. If A and B reside on different sites, global distributed concurrency control is necessary. Special properties of IN make it almost always possible to avoid this by careful partitioning policies.

A second problem is the synchronization of the write operation WS_1 of T_1 on B_{rep}. Here, we can illustrate the distinction between the major replication techniques in the literature:

1. **Equivalent copies:** The secondary copies are always kept consistent with the primary copy (on which the original update was made) to the maximum possible degree. The correctness criterion is called *one-copy serializability* [6]. B_{rep} is updated in the same transactional context as B (and therefore also A). Generalized to the case of *all* secondary copies, we have the so-called ROWA (read-one write-all) policy. It has two main disadvantages: it does not work when even one node is down or the network is partitioned, and it makes write transactions very slow due to the need for global concurrency control. So-called quorum techniques in which at least a certain number of copies must be updated (but also more than one copy must usually be read to find the most recent one) try to avoid the problems but are often still too slow [11, 9, 13, 17, 20, 23]. Especially increasing the number of copies from *one* to *two* or *more* is very expensive as it introduces remote access for read operations - and thats what we want to avoid with replication! Therefore, commercial DBMS vendors (ORACLE, INGRES, SYBASE) give up full consistency, e.g. permitting certain lost updates in distributed processing situations [5, 25, 16], either optionally ("low-value transactions") or in a hardwired fashion. In the IN application, updates usually correspond to contractual relationships

with some customer and should therefore not be lost, at least not forever; the ADR approach therefore delays such updates but never loses them.

2. **Caching copies:** This approach avoids lost updates by distinguishing between one or more primary copies which run under full concurrency control, and secondary copies (caches) which are updated from the primary copy but allow normally only read access by other transactions. There are different update policies which we can illustrate using Fig. 4. An eager update would mean that WS_1 is synchronized with WP_1 and is therefore equivalent to the ROWA policy we criticized above. A lazy evaluation strategy would synchronize the update WS_1 with the first read transaction that notices that WP_1 has happened (cache is out-of-date), in our case RS_2. This makes the response time of read transactions quite unpredictable and should therefore also be avoided in the case of IN where these run under real-time conditions. A third possibility is regular updating of the cached copies (*taking a snapshot*) which gives up the requirement that secondary copies are completely up-to-date. In our example, RS_2 would read either the state before or after WS_1, depending on whether a new snapshot has been taken between WP_1 and RS_2. This improves performance at the cost of temporal consistency of the database, but it introduces the new problem of when to update the snapshots and does not take advantage of different network loads at different times.

3.2 Atomic Delayed Replication

ADR combines the caching copy approach with the idea of detached sub-transactions proposed in the HiPAC project as a possible execution model in active databases [7], and with intensive logical partitioning to reduce localize concurrency conflicts. Only this threefold combination makes the ADR approach feasible for IN.

In ADR, WS_1 of figure 4 is started as a separate so-called reproduction transaction from WP_1 and is executed atomically but possibly delayed. Read transactions on secondary copies (like RS_2) are given preference over reproduction transactions. The net effect is that neither (primary) write nor (secondary) read transactions are held up unduly, and that reproduction transactions are executed "as eager as possible", i.e., immediately if there are no competing read transactions and delayed if there is heavy reading of the old version. In other words, it takes advantage of low-load situations and therefore contributes to load balancing. There are some implied requirements for techniques to make sure that reproduction techniques get eventually executed but their detailed discussion is beyond the scope of this paper.

Returning a last time to Fig. 4, we can summarize the ADR approach as follows:

- Updates are propagated from primary (WP_1) to secondary copies (WS_1) through detached reproduction transactions.
- Writes (WS_1) and reads (RS_2) on secondary copies are synchronized by the concurrency control protocol of the local databases, with a preference for the reads.

– Multi-object reads (RP_4 on A and B) and multi-object writes (WP_1 on A and B) across the network are largely avoided by suitable object groupings (called partitions); where necessary, they are synchronized under the global distributed concurrency protocol of a commercial distributed DBMS.

Together with the special properties of IN applications, the ADR approach has a number of consequences which have been addressed in the design of the INDIA environment:

1. The database is organized in a large number of small clusters or *partitions* employing mixed fragmentation [4]. The partitions form the unit of replication, and structure the transactions into steps depending on the kind of operations working on partitions. The definition of these partitions is intended to ensure maximum locality of transactions; conversely, the partitions are derived from usage patterns in transactions.

2. For every partition the database administrator *(DBA)* defines *one* database server and therefore the local database containing the primary copy. Additionally, he may define other local databases containing replications of a partition, called the secondary copies. The division in primary and secondary copies generates two levels of consistency within the global database. If data of a partition represents the state of the related part of the real world, then we say it is *internally consistent*. If the data of all partitions together represent a valid state of the whole represented real world, then we call it *externally consistent*. Transactions can choose the appropriate level. If for some operations of a transaction the partition-internal consistency is satisfactory, then they can be executed with low concurrency control overhead. To be more concrete we ensures that:

   (a) All data contained in all primary copies are partition-external consistent and up to date.

   (b) Data of one secondary copy are internal-consistent but possibly not up to date.

   As a consequence, there is no global consistency across different (secondary) partitions even in the local databases.

3. The above-mentioned choice cannot be completely transparent to the IN transaction programmer. Firstly, the distributed database system operates at the level of location transparency [4]. That is, the transaction programmer must identify the partitions he wishes to work on. Secondly, he must divide the transaction program into at most *one* write step (for all write operations plus read operations requiring external consistency) to be executed on primary copies and *zero* or *more* read steps (which can usually be executed on secondary copies). Every read step is executed on a copy as a local transaction on the local database. There is no need for distributed concurrency control or distributed atomic commitment. The same is sufficient for a write step accessing only *one* partition. A write step accessing several partitions is executed as a global transaction on the involved primary copies with distributed concurrency control and distributed atomic commit *(two-phase commit)*. Updates on secondary copies are performed *asynchronously*

after the updates of the write step occur on the primary copy. Propagation is done by triggering a so-called *decoupled reproduction transaction* (cf. the idea of detached mode in [7]) under local concurrency control in the database containing the secondary copy. This reduces concurrency control and atomic commitment when secondary copies are used as there are no mechanisms of replicated distributed databases involved. It follows that data of secondary copies can be accessed at the full speed of the local database.

4 The INDIA Environment

The ADR approach implies a specialization of the IN architecture (Fig. 2) which has been implemented experimentally in the INDIA prototype based on distributed databases. In this section we describe the implementation and our experiences.

4.1 Implementation of the INDIA Environment

As shown in Fig. 5. Each of several *service control points (SCP)* has its own

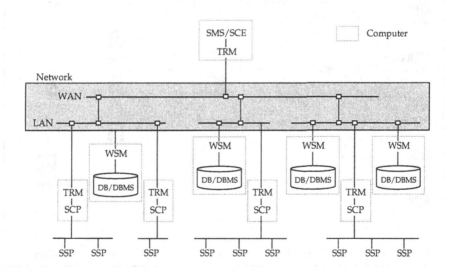

Fig. 5. The INDIA architecture

database (DB) managed by a local DBMS. All these local databases together form the distributed database. An SCP manages lots of *service switching points (SSP)* that signal the start of a special IN service by a dedicated number prefix or through a trigger attached to some phone. The SCP accesses the database through the module *transaction routing manager (TRM)* which tries to fulfill the request using the local database. The request is forwarded to another database holding the desired partition if the contents of the local database is not sufficient. Access to the databases is managed by the module *write step manager (WSM)* that is also responsible for the propagation of data modifications. The *service management system (SMS)* and the *service creation environment (SCE)* via the SMS must also access the databases through the module TRM.

The ADR approach was first realized separately using SYBASE relational databases as local database servers and communicating processes (TCP/IP) to achieve asynchronous propagation. The global concurrency control throughout the primary copies was implemented using the *open two-phase commit* protocol from SYBASE. The integration into the IN prototype followed after the evaluation of the first implementation. In Fig. 6 a snapshot of the running system is shown by a screendump of the connection monitoring tool.

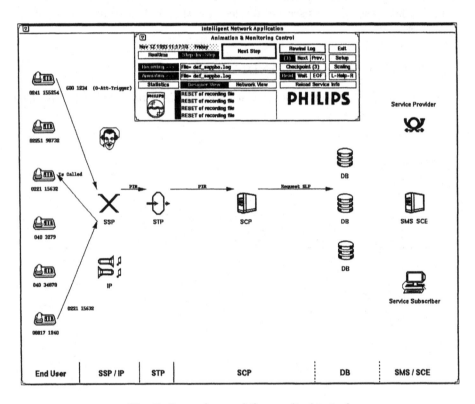

Fig. 6. Screendump of the monitoring tool

4.2 Experiences and Extensions

The ADR approach has some obvious theoretical properties concerning scalability. Applications mostly concerned with read access use local concurrency control in ADR. Here, the throughput of the whole system grows linearly with the number of database servers if the load is distributed evenly; the system scales up very well. The cost of update operations for each database server remains the same if partitions are replicated. The execution of a single transaction is slowed down by a constant factor caused by the realization of the ADR mechanism.

In applications where the frequency of read and write operations is evenly distributed, one may not want to replicate some partitions. The expense for update propagation seems unnecessary if reads of this updates do not happen very often. There is still an advantage to distribute the load by fragmentation without replication by placing the primary copies onto different database servers. Scalability may become limited in this case by network bandwidth due to necessary remote reads of the primary copies.

In applications mostly concerned with update operations, replication is not good under performance aspects but may still be needed for reliability. The achieveable scalability is similar to the second class. Scalability can be increased if the semantics of data can be used, especially if the semantics allows replication of the data element. An important example is the counter semantic which appears in many IN applications.

Since services are largely independent of each other, they can be optimized separately. As we are not aware of a benchmark of IN applications, our evaluation strategy has been to look at the characteristics of existing IN applications. We mention three of the examples given in Sect. 2.

Virtual Private Network is typical for a service concerned mostly with read access. Normally changing number assignment in a network happens not very frequently compared to their usage ratio. Similar arguments apply for Credit Card Calling, Free Phone and Teleinfo. **Universal Personal Telecommunications** is a service with a mixed read/write distribution. It depends on the mobility of the subscriber. More updates than reads will arise if the person is traveling a lot and therefore changing the location information often but the person seldom receives calls. Mobile communications is an extreme example which we do not deal with here ([15, 2]). **Televoting** is a typical member of the write class but its semantics allows distribution due to commutativity.

In the INDIA implementation, the usage of a commercial DBMS avoids unnecessary re-implementations of local concurrency control, recovery and optimization techniques. This leads to relatively small code size where much of the service functionality is managed in the database representation of the SLPs. On the negative side, the strict separation of modules forced by using external software causes communication overhead. More sophisticated trigger concepts from active databases [7, 14] will make the WSM module unnecessary. This allows the integration of the ADR mechanism into the DBMS. Another problem is the aging of secondary copies, especially if network failures are not detected. Method to specify a t-bound [10] making sure that data is not older than a specified time t are an important extension to ADR. Multiple primary copies are desirable for the distribution of write operations. This would eliminate the *hot-spot* [12] property of write operations. Fortunatly this can be already done for the semantics of some data element like e.g., a counter.

5 Conclusions

In this paper, we have presented a specific trade-off between the goals of distribution, performance, and consistency in Intelligent Networks. ADR combines three well understood concepts to achieve a suitable trade-off between high distribution, efficiency, and consistency: **fragmentation and replication** of distributed databases to reduce the amount of information which must be handled by the concurrency control mechanisms; **asynchronous update propagation** shortening the response time and increasing the availability. **detached actions in active database systems** to implement this extension on top of existing technology.

ADR satisfies many of the special requirements of IN. It has the advantage that it can outsource the local, even the traditional distributed database management tasks to commercial DBMSs, thus also participating in their advances – for example, in the direction of active databases. ADR also exploits some special IN features such as the strong partitioning of database objects, the relative simplicity and independence of services (important for length of transactions and for schema changes), and the commutativity of many typical operations.

As the discussion showed, the practical experience with the prototype has been very encouraging on typical IN service applications but we still have to cover a lot of other examples and make measurements with service-mix benchmarks (which, to our knowledge, currently do not exist and therefore have to be designed as well). Even the existing experiences have pointed out a number of areas in which further research is needed, and other telecommunications software database applications may pose other trade-offs which would lead to totally different solutions. We were surprised to see how little has been published on this important application domain and think that database technology has much more to offer once it gets a bit closer to the domain.

References

1. S. Abramowski, M. Elixmann, H. Gappisch, U. Heister, U. Heuter, K. Klabunde. A Service Creation Environment for Intelligent Networks. In C. Petitpierre and W. Schlegel, editors, *Proc. of the 1992 Int. Zürich Seminar on Digital Communications*, ETH Zürich, Switzerland, March 1992. IEEE Catalog No. 92TH0439-0.
2. Daniel Barbara and Hector Garcia-Molina. Replicated Data Management in Mobile Environments: Anything New Under the Sun? In *IFIP Conf. on Applications in Parallel and Distributed Computing*, Caracas, Venezuela, April 1994.
3. Olivier Boulot, Gilles Bregant, and Christian Vernhes. Long-Term IN Architecture Applied to UPT. In *The Fourth Telecommunications Information Networking Architecture Workshop*, volume II, L'Aquila, Italy, September 1993.
4. Stefano Ceri and Giuseppe Pelagatti. *Distributed Databases: Principles and Systems*. McGraw-Hill, 1984.
5. Malcolm Colton. Replicated Data in a Distributed Environment. In *Second Int. Conf. on Parallel and Distributed Information Systems*, San Diego, January 1993.
6. Susan B. Davidson, Hector Garcia-Molina, and Dale Skeen. Consistency in Partitioned Networks. *ACM Computing Surveys*, 17(3), September 1985.

7. U. Dayal, B. Blaustein, A. Buchmann, U. Chakravarthy, M. Hsu, R. Ledin, D. McCarthy, A. Rosenthal, S. Sarin, M. J. Carey, M. Livny, and R. Jauhari. The HiPAC project: Combining active databases and timing constraints. In *Proc. ACM-SIGMOD Int. Conf. on Management of Data*, March 1988.

8. M. Driouche et al. Sabrina-RT, a distributed DBMS for Telecommunications. In *Advances in Database Technology - EDBT88*, 1988.

9. A. El Abbadi and S. Toueg. Availability in Partitioned Replicated Databases. In *Proc. ACM-SIGMOD Int. Conf. on Management of Data*, Washington, 1986.

10. H. Garcia-Molina. Read-Only Transactions in a Distributed Database. *ACM Transactions on Database Systems*, 7(2), June 1982.

11. G.K. Gifford. Weighted Voting for Replicated Data. In *Proc. Seventh ACM Symposium on Operating System Principles*, December 1979.

12. T. Härder. Handling hot spot data in DB-sharing systems. *Information Systems*, 13(2), 1988.

13. M. Herlihy. Dynamic Quorum adjustment for Partitioned Data. *ACM Transactions on Database Systems*, 12(2), June 1987.

14. Meichun Hsu, Rivka Ladin, and Dennis R. McCarthy. An Execution Model for Active Data Base Management Systems. In *Proc. Third Int. Conf. on Data and Knowledge Bases*, Jerusalem, Israel, June 1988.

15. T. Imielinski and B.R. Badrinath. Querying in Highly Mobile Distributed Environments. In *Proc. 18th Int. Conf. on Very Large Data Bases*, 1992.

16. INGRES Replicator. Press information (in german), Ingres GmbH, May 1993.

17. S. Jajodia and D. Mutchler. Enhancements to the Voting Algorithm. In *Proc. 13th Int. Conf. on Very Large Databases*, Brighton, September 1987.

18. R. Kerboul, J.M. Pageot, and V. Robin. Database requirements for Intelligent Networks: How to customize mechanisms to implement policies. In *The Fourth Telecommunications Information Networking Architecture Workshop*, 1993.

19. O. Kiyoshi, A. Mikio, and F. Hiroshi. Data Management of Telecommunication Networks. In *Proc. ACM-SIGMOD Int. Conf. on Management of Data*, 1988.

20. N. Krishnakumar and A.J. Bernstein. High Throughput Escrow Algorithms for Replicated Databases. In *Proc. 18th Int. Conf. on Very Large Databases*, 1992.

21. A. Payne. Designing the databases of the intelligent network. In *Eighth Int. Conf. on Software Engineering for Telecommunication Systems and Services*, 1992.

22. Thomas J. Plevyak, editor. *Marching Toward the Global Intelligent Network*. IEEE Communications Magazine, Special Issue, March 1993.

23. C. Pu and A. Leff. Replica Control in Distributed Systems: An Asynchronous Approach. In *Proc. ACM-SIGMOD Int. Conf. on Management of Data*, 1991.

24. ITU-T Recommendations Q.12xy. *Intelligent Networks, final version, WP 11/4*. Geneva, March 1992.

25. SYBASE Replication Server. Technical report, SYBASE Inc., May 1993.

Springer-Verlag
and the Environment

$\mathbf{W}$e at Springer-Verlag firmly believe that an international science publisher has a special obligation to the environment, and our corporate policies consistently reflect this conviction.

$\mathbf{W}$e also expect our business partners – paper mills, printers, packaging manufacturers, etc. – to commit themselves to using environmentally friendly materials and production processes.

$\mathbf{T}$he paper in this book is made from low- or no-chlorine pulp and is acid free, in conformance with international standards for paper permanency.

Lecture Notes in Computer Science

For information about Vols. 1–739
please contact your bookseller or Springer-Verlag